DAVID R. ROSS, with his Scottish sense of the ridiculous, coupled with a bit of Celtic irony, wrote as part of the author profile for his *On the Trail of William Wallace* book:

> 'He was born near Glasgow at a very young age, and can trace his family tree back to at least the 1950s.'

This, of course, was meant to be a joke, and an antidote to all the books he has read where the authors tell of their own personal family trees, and how they can trace their own history back to the Norman Conquest of England.

Alas, he has been dismayed at the several communications he has received saying that surely all of us were born at a very young age. Even worse were the instructions on how one could use birth certificates to trace one's ancestry, and that to go further back than the 1950s is a reasonably easy process.

He would like to state that he was indeed born at a very young age, and that as he has no idea of his grandfather's name, he cannot trace his family tree back very far. Being Scottish, he would have no objection to someone else paying for the research required to find his lineage, but he already knows it probably is a long list of sheep stealers, caterans and vagabonds.

He would like to think that some of his blood was at Bannockburn and Stirling Bridge, albeit in a lowly position.

He in fact stated in his book *A Passion for Scotland* that he would have liked to have stood in the front line at Bannockburn, although the timing of his Scottishness was a bit out. He was most tickled when that book was reviewed in the *Scots Magazine*, and the reviewer made mention of this statement, adding that he himself would have been happy to have settled for the televised highlights!

He would also like to point out that if a particular book is not written by 'David R. Ross', then it is not him, as there are several writers by that name without the middle initial. He hopes that he has many years left yet to roar about his beloved Scotland on his motorcycle, discovering the sites where the ancestors of his people made their marks.

We, as Scots, only have the lease of this land for a lifetime each, and as there are only five million of us, Ross regards himself as a very lucky man indeed.

This book is not meant as a be-all-and-end-all guide to Scotland. It is just a tour round some of the places Ross has had fun discovering, and he very much hopes that you have fun touring round this most ancient of realms too.

Desire Lines
A Scottish Odyssey

DAVID R. ROSS

Luath Press Limited
EDINBURGH
www.luath.co.uk

First published 2004

The paper used in this book is recyclable. It is made
from low-chlorine pulps produced in a low-energy,
low-emission manner from renewable forests.

Printed and bound by
Bell & Bain Ltd, Glasgow

Maps by Jim Lewis

Typset in 9.5 Sabon by S. Crozier, Nantes

Contents

1   Where Black and White Merge and Become Grey   1

THE JOURNEY BEGINS AT SOUTHWAITE SERVICES ON THE M6. THE ROUTE GOES TO CARLISLE, TO BRAMPTON, AND LANERCOST, AND THEN FOLLOWS HADRIAN'S WALL. NORTHWARDS TO BELLINGHAM, OTTERBURN, THEN UP REDESDALE TO CARTER BAR ON THE BORDER.

2   Scotland at Last   19

BEGINNING AT CARTER BAR, THE ROUTE FOLLOWS THE A6088 TOWARDS HAWICK. THERE IS A LITTLE DEVIATION EAST ON THE A698 TO HORNSHOLE, THEN INTO HAWICK. ONWARDS TO SELKIRK, ABBOTSFORD, MELROSE, SCOTT'S VIEW, DRYBURGH, KELSO AND COLDSTREAM.

3   Abroad Again   45

BEGINNING AT THE TWEED AT COLDSTREAM THE ROUTE EXPLORES CORNHILL, TWIZEL AND NORHAM. THERE IS THEN A SMALL DEVIATION ACROSS THE TWEED TO LADYKIRK IN SCOTLAND, BEFORE CONTINUING TO BERWICK UPON TWEED, AND ON TO THE BORDER AT LAMBERTON.

4   Cliffs and Castles   57

FROM LAMBERTON THE ROUTE GOES THROUGH BURNMOUTH, EYEMOUTH TO COLDINGHAM. THEN THERE IS A SMALL DEVIATION OUT TO ST ABBS HEAD BEFORE MOVING ON THROUGH COCKBURNSPATH, DUNBAR, WHITEKIRK, TANTALLON, NORTH BERWICK, DIRLETON, ATHELSTANEFORD, PRESTONPANS AND MUSSELBURGH.

5   Edinburgh   81

ON FOOT, THIS CHAPTER EXPLORES EDINBURGH CITY CENTRE, STARTING AT THE CASTLE AND GOING DOWN THE ROYAL MILE TO HOLYROOD. THERE IS A DEVIATION TO GREYFRIARS CHURCH AND THE MUSEUM OF SCOTLAND DOWN GEORGE IV BRIDGE.

6   The Forth Valley   99

FIRST EXPLORING ROSLIN, THE ROUTE THEN TAKES THE EDINBURGH BY-PASS TO THE M8 AND THEN ONTO NEWBRIDGE, KIRKLISTON, SOUTH QUEENSFERRY, HOPETOUN HOUSE, BINNS, BLACKNESS, LINLITHGOW, CAIRNPAPPLE HILL, TORPHICHEN, AND FINISHES AT THE BRIDGE OVER THE RIVER AVON ON THE A801.

Acknowledgements

TO MY DAUGHTER Kimberley, who is my very reason for being, and although at 16 she can be a scunner at times, she is not nearly as bad as I can remember being at that age.

Linda Donnelly, thanks for your evenings spent typing sense into my scrawlings.

To all those mentioned in this script, people who have told me the odd historic tale in passing, and the close friends and patriots who help me on a regular basis, especially Brendan and Anna who allow me to sleep at their place on my excursions into the north.

Lynn for her unfailing support and ability to push me to expat Scots in North America, all at the Society of William Wallace, and to all those seekers of Scotland's freedom, no matter their organisation, and also those individuals who believe in their hearts and minds in this little scrap of mountain and moorland.

But most of all I humbly dedicate this book to the late Bob McCutcheon, historian of Stirling, who helped me in my early quests, and to whom, due to my own shortcomings, I never got to say cheerio.

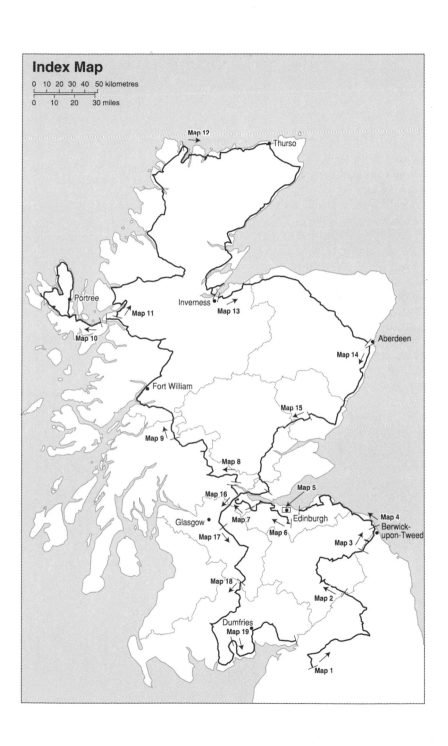

Index Map

0 10 20 30 40 50 kilometres

0 10 20 30 miles

Map 12

Thurso

Portree

Map 11

Inverness

Map 13

Map 10

Aberdeen

Map 14

Fort William

Map 15

Map 9

Map 8

Map 5

Map 16

Glasgow

Map 7

Edinburgh

Map 4

Berwick-upon-Tweed

Map 17

Map 6

Map 3

Map 18

Map 2

Dumfries

Map 19

Map 1

Preface

I WENT TO PICK up my friend Ross from his work in Airdrie. He was waiting for me as I pulled up in the car. There was a girl with him who he worked beside. Her name was Gail. The three of us went for a drink, and I asked Gail what she had done before her current employment. She told me she had been at art school, but hadn't finished the course. She told me about a project she had done entitled 'Desire Lines'. 'What's a desire line?', I asked, as it was a term I was not familiar with. She explained. 'You know how planners build pathways across grassy areas or other stretches of ground? And how they tend to build these walkways with right angles? Well, you know how you always see a path worn across the grass because people have taken the shorter route – the route they wish to take rather than the one the planners have laid out for them? That is a desire line. It is the people's desire to take that line rather than the one that has been laid out for them.'

That is what this book is.

A collection of my desire lines. A route put together to give you a picture of my Scotland, and how I perceive it.

Introduction

THIS BOOK IS A tour round the Scotland I love. There is not really a rhyme or reason to the route. When I came to each junction, I thought about what was in either direction, and followed my nose. It could be a difficult decision, as there was so much that I could take you to see in either direction. As I travelled on, it all really started to write itself.

I know that many folk hate to see road numbers written out, but I could not think of a better way to give you directions, and it is generally these road-designation numbers that are written on each sign you come to, so it made sense.

I just hope some of this is inspiring enough to get you to go and see for yourself. At the end of the day, I'm just an ordinary Scot who has a deep love for my country, its landscape, its history, and for the future of its people.

Caledonia has been everything I've ever had. And I may occasionally be lucky enough to wander the planet a little, and see other lands and cultures. But when I return and cross the border, that little sign does not say 'Welcome to Scotland' to me. It just says 'home'.

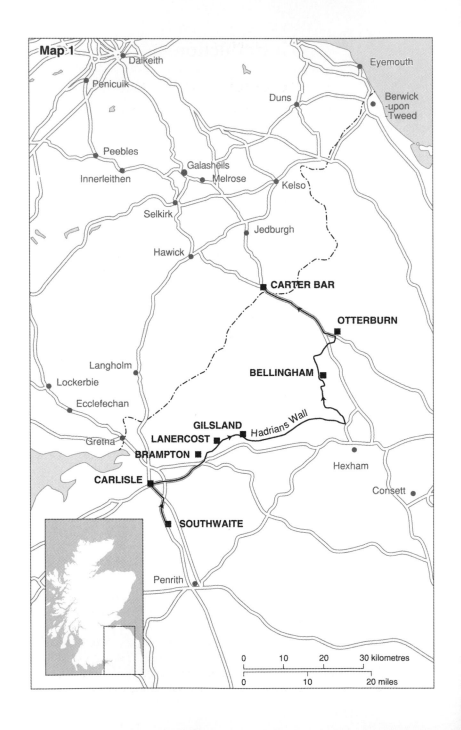

Map 1

Dalkeith
Eyemouth
Penicuik
Duns
Berwick-upon-Tweed
Peebles
Galashiels
Innerleithen
Melrose
Kelso
Selkirk
Jedburgh
Hawick
CARTER BAR
OTTERBURN
Langholm
BELLINGHAM
Lockerbie
Ecclefechan
GILSLAND
Gretna
LANERCOST
Hadrians Wall
BRAMPTON
CARLISLE
Hexham
Consett
SOUTHWAITE
Penrith

0   10   20   30 kilometres
0   10   20 miles

CHAPTER ONE

Where Black and White
Merge and Become Grey

I'M STARTING THIS book about my Scotland in the north of England.

That may seem strange. But so much of Scotland's history is written across the northern shires of her southern neighbour that I hope that this chapter will make some sense as it unfolds.

Where do I start this journey? All journeys have a beginning, and I have mulled this over and decided to place my starting point at Southwaite Service station on the M6. It stands some 15 miles south of the Scottish border in that great northern shire of England, Cumbria.

It is a handy reference point. Most visitors to Scotland approach by the M6. But it is a little more than this. Many times when accompanying friends driving south, they have said 'We'll push on to Southwaite before we stop for petrol', or breakfast, or whatever. This is because it is 'over the border'. A psychological barrier has been crossed. So it would seem as good a place as any to start – the Southwaite Services northbound. The last services in England – and we pull out on to the M6, heading towards Scotland – but not across the border just yet. There is much of Scotland's story written in this area, etched onto the landscape, and I want to visit it first, and for you to come with me. It is only a few minutes to Carlisle. 'The Border City', state the guide books.

Let's drive into Carlisle, but let's look at the place from a Scottish perspective. Carlisle is an ancient town, and of course the fact that it stands so close to the border with Scotland means that much of the history of the two countries has been intertwined there.

The ancient town was based around its two main edifices, the castle and the cathedral. They were originally both constructed in the same era – the late 1000s. The core of the castle as it stands today is the original Norman keep. The Normans introduced the art of building mighty castles in stone into England after their conquest of that country in 1066. This original keep stands tall, overlooking the later additions and curtain walls, all standing on a defensive bank above the River Eden. The castle has a grim aspect,

a reminder of lordly power, and retains even in today a certain air of malevolence. This has not the kindly aspect of a German *Schloss* or proud Scots
tower house. Perhaps I have a bias, as I know that it has proved to be a
structure where many of my countrymen have entered, never to leave. The
more I look at it, the more it seems to compound that feeling of grimness
that seems to emanate from the red stone itself.

William Wallace, one of Scotland's great heroes, was here during the
invasion of England in the winter of 1297–8, after his stunning victory over
the forces of that country at Stirling Bridge the previous September.

The castle was far too hard a nut for the Scots to crack, Scotland being a
comparatively poor country, and unable to find the resources needed to
build and transport the mighty siege engines required to reduce such a massive structure.

The Scots under Wallace did gather at the walls here, and demanded the
surrender of the fortress, but I'm sure the English garrison realised what
empty threats these were, and chose to ignore them, safe behind their massive walls. This was not Wallace's only visit to Carlisle, as after his shameful
betrayal and capture near Glasgow in 1305, he was brought by back roads
to the border and handed over to English lords here, then taken onwards to
Smithfield in London for his hideous execution. This took away one of our
great freedom fighters who had defended us from the yoke of English rule.
But it also gave us a martyr who gave all he had for Scotland. Wallace has
been adored by the Scots ever since. Hollywood realised the figurehead that
Wallace was when it released the movie *Braveheart* in 1995, a version of the
struggle of Wallace's life – and his dream of bringing freedom to his people.
It brought William Wallace to a worldwide audience, and that audience, no
matter their culture or creed, could identify with the essential right we have
to decide the destiny for our own people.

After Wallace's murder for a crime he was not guilty of committing – that
of treason – his mantle was donned just a few months later by Robert the
Bruce, the hero-king of Scots.

King Robert suffered many setbacks early in his reign (1306–29), having
not only to fight the English, but to combat many Scots who put the good
of England before that of their own nation. Two of his brothers, Thomas
and Alexander, effected a landing in southwest Scotland, at Loch Ryan in
Galloway, having sailed with a body of men from Kintyre and Ireland. This
landing met with complete disaster: the Bruce brothers and others were
captured, Alexander badly wounded, and taken to the castle at Carlisle.
They had been betrayed by Scots sympathetic to the cause of England. On
the orders of King Edward 1 of England, nicknamed 'Longshanks', these
captives were hanged and beheaded. The heads of the Irish sub-king,
Malcolm MacQuillan, Sir Reginald Crawford and Alexander Bruce were

fixed to the three gates of Carlisle. Thomas Bruce's head was affixed to the top of the castle keep.

I often glance at the ramparts of the castle and think of poor Thomas. I seem to be unusual in this respect. I suppose most people drive by the castle without even a glance or a thought of its history.

Alexander Bruce was a scholar at Cambridge – in fact, he was regarded as the best of his time – and his horrific death was regretted by many who had known him from his days spent there.

Edward Longshanks is a name abhorred in Scotland. He was a potent and warlike king, and the armies of England were extremely powerful in those days – indeed, they were probably the best-trained in Christendom. Unfortunately for Scotland, Longshanks was determined to expand his borders, and he coveted the realm that bordered his to the north. Tens of thousands of Scots died trying to thwart his ambitions.

He died close to Carlisle, after spending a few days here. He had had a seizure – he was in his late sixties, a great age for these days, but news of the continued gains of King Robert the Bruce reached him, and he rose from his sickbed to wage war once again against Scotland. He donated the litter in which he had been carried to Carlisle to the cathedral, and marched his army a little northwest to the village of Burgh by Sands in order to cross the Solway Firth at low tide and land on Scottish soil. But it was not to be. A little north of the village he suffered a stroke and realised his end was near. Legend states that he ordered his son, later Edward II, to place his body into a pot of water, where it could be boiled till the flesh fell from the bones. These bones were to be carried onwards into Scotland till that nation was entirely crushed. The flesh could be discarded. Longshanks' son was somewhat different in temperament to his father. He had his father's brain and entrails removed, his body embalmed and sent south to Westminster Abbey where it still lies, in the chapel of Edward the Confessor. I make a point of going to visit him every time I am in London – just to remind him we are still around. I like to lean over his sarcophagus, face close to his on the other side of the cold stone, and tell him 'still here Eddie!'

The brain and entrails – the brain that killed Wallace, the brain that started all the animosity between my nation and his – were taken to the abbey of Holm Cultram, in the village of Abbeytown, some 18 miles west-southwest of Carlisle, and there interred. Strangely enough, the father of King Robert the Bruce is also buried at Holm Cultram, and his gravestone is on show, standing upright in the porch of the abbey. It is typical of graveslabs of that time, having an intricate floral work carved into the stone, which I believe represents the tree of life.

A pillar out on the grassland of the southern edges of the Solway, just north of Burgh by Sands marks where Edward Longshanks breathed his last. I have stood there many times, and in all sorts of weather, looking out

over the water to the hills of Scotland, the same view that he saw as he
moved on to hell. It is a place for contemplation. He tried so hard to enslave
my people, and although he often rode over the face of my country, he
never ruled us. I curse him as I take a last look at his memorial, and turn on
my heel to climb back on my motor cycle parked a few hundred metres
south at the road end.

Perhaps he and I will meet in the afterlife? It takes away any fear I have of
death, as I look forward to having a square go with him, as we say in
Scotland – stripped to the waist and no nipping!

Perhaps this is the place to remark on how Burgh by Sands should be pronounced. I mentioned Burgh by Sands once at a talk I was doing about the
Scottish Wars of Independence, and said it just as you see it written. A
member of the audience, who originated from the area of Carlisle, informed
me that it was actually pronounced 'Bruffby Sands'.

Well, there you go!

I can imagine the news of Edward Longshanks' death spreading out
across Scotland, and the sighs of relief this news would have produced, not
least from King Robert.

⁎   ⁎   ⁎   ⁎   ⁎

Carlisle Cathedral, where Longshanks donated his litter, is a jewel of a
building. It has always been a place to fascinate and intrigue, although it
has not been a place of happiness for many Scots, it having been used as
prison at times, building of worship notwithstanding.

There is original wood panelling inside, all hand-painted with biblical
tales, which has withstood all that the centuries have thrown at it. Some of
the woodwork is magnificent. My favourite touch in the building is the face
of the Virgin Mary in the ceiling. It looks as if she is staring through a hole
in the roof, looking directly down on the congregation. Put there by some
mason to cow them into terror of the afterlife, no doubt.

Once on a visit to the cathedral, a member of staff told me a story.
Whether it is true, I have no way of knowing, but it sounded feasible
enough, and it was a good yarn too. When the railway came to Carlisle in
the 1800s, it had been decided to build the tracks passing right by the cathedral. One of the local dignitaries took exception to this – quite rightly so –
and did all in his power to have the line moved elsewhere. The line was
moved, thereby saving this ancient edifice from having the indignity of railway tracks running by it. But it turned out that the track was routed close
by the aforementioned dignitary's house. In revenge, the railway companies, who had had to spend extra money re-routing the line, instructed their
drivers to blow their whistles every time they passed his property, day or
night, thereby ensuring he got no respite and was rudely awakened whenever possible. This of course was the best part of 200 years ago – but today

drivers still sound their horn when passing the spot. Asked why they did this, they replied that when they became drivers, other drivers told them to sound their horn at that spot – but they had no idea why!

The cathedral held prisoners who had been captured in the 1745 rising led by Prince Charles Edward Stuart – or as he is better known, Bonnie Prince Charlie. Charlie was of the direct line of Stuart (or Stewart) kings of Scotland, but their throne had been usurped by the Germanic House of Hanover, who had ousted them from the 'British' throne. Charlie landed in Scotland, gathering the Highland Clans to his standard, and had marched as far south as Derby, deep into England. But circumstances stopped him pushing on to London. On the army's retreat, many wounded and unfit men were left behind at Carlisle. When the Hanoverian forces under William Duke of Cumberland captured the city, these poor souls were kept in the cathedral and the castle, before being executed in the most horrific manner, being hung, drawn and quartered. This was the English idea of punishment for treason. It involves being hanged, but taken down while conscious. Then the victim's stomach is cut open, and his intestines drawn out while he is still alive. Then the butchery is completed with the body being quartered, or cut to pieces. It seems to be derived from the idea of the dead arising on Judgement Day – so the English were determined that any-one who opposed them would have no body to face the risen lord, so would be damned forever.

It is from these executions that the famous ballad *Loch Lomond* takes its lyrics, where a condemned man said to his sweetheart:

You take the high road
And I'll take the low road
But I'll be in Scotland afore ye,

meaning that his spirit would fly to his beloved hills of home. Another reminder of the times of Charlie exists in the Marks and Spencer store in the centre of town. This building stands on the site of what was his head-quarters in Carlisle, and it has an inscription on its frontage to announce this fact. Unfortunately William Duke of Cumberland also stayed within this building, and his name is etched in the stonework at the other end of the building.

Mary, Queen of Scots, was another visitor to the cathedral. She had fled to England seeking sanctuary from some of the lords of Scotland, after her defeat at the Battle of Langside at Glasgow. The English saw her as a threat to the reign of their Elizabeth I, and during the early days of her long captiv-ity she was held within the castle, but allowed to worship at the cathedral.

Mary, who lived in the sixteenth century, is probably the most famous Scotswoman ever – on a worldwide basis. Her life story has always intrigued, and she has been the subject of many books and films. Her tragic life came to an end at Fotheringhay Castle, now gone, where she was beheaded. She was buried first at Peterborough Cathedral, but was later moved to Westminster Abbey. I don't know if I would relish sharing a building for eternity with Longshanks!

Before we leave Carlisle, we should bring an account of the Border reivers into the equation. The reivers were the warlike clans that lived, as their name suggests, in the border country of Scotland and England – Elliots, Armstrongs, Johnstones, Scotts and Maxwells. There was no-one who was really too sure of the line of the actual border, and the borderland north and east of Carlisle became known as the 'Debatable Land'. These reivers liked nothing better than to raid over the border into England, or vice versa, to do a bit of cattle rustling.

Families had inter-married on both sides of the border, and allegiances were forged which transcended the allegiance owed to the kings of Scotland and England, and the perfect example of this is the story of Kinmont Willie.

Kinmont Willie, or more properly, William Armstrong of Kinmont, was the laird of a small border estate at Morton Rig. He had incurred the wrath of the English Warden of the West March, Lord Scrope. Let me explain. To try and keep the peace, the monarchs of both Scotland and England had appointed wardens of their respective border areas, one for each of the east, middle and west marches, or areas where the borders march against each other, so there were six in all, three Scots, three English. Lord Scrope became increasingly tired of the incursions Kinmont Willie made into Cumberland and Northumberland in northern England, stealing cattle and gear, through the 1580s and on into the 1590s. In one audacious raid, he was identified as the leader of a thousand Scots border horsemen who raided into English Tynedale and drove off over a thousand head of cattle!

One day Kinmont Willie was riding down the banks of the Liddel Water, when he was spotted by two hundred English horsemen, who then chased him for three or four miles before he was taken prisoner. He was promptly carried to the castle at Carlisle, locked in a dungeon and clamped in irons. It was the night of 17 March 1596.

When word of Kinmont's capture was brought to Lord Scrope's opposite number on the Scottish side, Walter Scott of Buccleuch (pronounced Buck-loo), an ancestor of the famous Scottish writer, Sir Walter Scott, he was outraged. In the words of the old border ballad about Kinmont Willie:

And have they e'en taken him, Kinmont Willie,
Without either dread or fear?
And forgotten that the bold Buccleuch
Can back a steed or shake a spear?

It took about a month for Buccleuch to make his move. At a horse race at Langholm on 12 April, arrangements were made to rectify the situation. In the dark of that night, the 13th, horsemen gathered at Kinmont Willie's tower of Morton Rig, some 80 in all. They included Armstrongs, including Kinmont's seven sons, Buccleuch's own Scotts, and Elliots from Liddesdale. They set off in the dark to cover the miles to Carlisle Castle. The utter darkness in the border hills and mosses of that April night would not have proved to be a great drawback to these riders. It was said that these reivers could sit a horse before they could walk, and could sense their way through the darkness of the Debatable Land.

The Scots carried ladders with them, but looking at the strength of the castle at Carlisle, it is obvious that there was help within these ominous walls. As said, inter-marriage and alliances gave people a foothold on either side of the border. Kinmont Willie obviously had friends and admirers in the castle garrison – or maybe they were bribed to turn a blind eye or give information. Certainly, Buccleuch knew exactly where Kinmont was within this mighty keep, and he was bodily lifted by a sturdy reiver by the name of Red Rowan, and carried outside, still chained and shackled.

Scrope's later report stated that the guard was 'on sleep or gotten under some covert to defend themselves from the violence of the weather'. The Scots rode hurriedly for the Scots border at the River Esk, and on to a blacksmith's cottage between Longtown and Langholm, where the smith was roused to break off the chains.

Legend tells us how the smith's daughter, then only a child, recalled this incident in later life. She continued that she 'saw in the grey of the morning, more gentlemen that she had ever seen before in one place, all on horseback, in armour, and dripping wet – and that Kinmont Willie, who sat woman fashion behind one of them, was the biggest carle (rogue) she ever saw – and that there was much merriment in the company.'

And with no little wonder. One look at the keep of the castle of Carlisle gives one a good grounding of the difficulties inherent in springing a prisoner from within. So many Scots entered this place, never to come out alive, that it was obviously inside help that enabled Kinmont Willie to make his escape back to Scotland. Prisoners have carved their names into the stonework of the walls, and these remain in mute testament to the poor souls incarcerated here.

The castle today has an exhibition inside to tell the story of some of the Jacobite prisoners captured fighting for Bonnie Prince Charlie, but a visit should be made to the city's Tullie House Museum, which tells much of the history of Carlisle through the ages, displaying artefacts from the Roman occupation, Hadrian's Wall running just a little north of Carlisle itself, and exhibits taking us right through all the conflict with Scotland that this frontier settlement faced down the centuries.

＊　　＊　　＊　　＊　　＊

Driving east from Carlisle, we head towards the little town of Brampton, heading east on the A69, crossing the M6 as we go. The M6 of course leads north to Scotland itself, but there is much to see in this border country yet that has a Scottish slant to it – so Scotland itself can wait while we explore. The M6 comes to an abrupt halt at Carlisle, and the last ten miles to the border goes on a downgrade to a dual carriageway – a stretch of road the Scots refer to as the 'Carlisle Corridor'. The M74 coming south from Scotland stops at the border, as there was only the jurisdiction available on the Scots side, of course, to take it that far. The English obviously feel that their motorway reaches their northernmost city, so why extend it north to the Scots border?

This pigheadedness alone should be enough to make your average Scot question the pros and cons of the Union with England. Not that I would be happy with Union for gain. Bruce was described once by an Englishman as 'a Scot born in Scotland' – and that is what I am, and all I require. There is no attraction in my people being part of a conglomerate that treats them with disdain, there is no attraction because I am a Scot and that is the crux of any debate about Unionism for me. Why? I am Scottish. That's it. No more debate than that.

Brampton is a lovely wee market town. I remember when all the east–west traffic passed through it, but the town has now been by-passed, bringing it an air of tranquility.

I remember being in the centre of the town when there was two minutes' silence held for the terrorist bombing of the World Trade Centre, and all the town went silent, everyone standing stock still on the pavements. I had just come out of a baker's, clutching a pint of milk and a bag of various bits and pieces for lunch. Like most bikers, I am happy to scan the passing shops for a baker's when hunger sets in, and like to buy a pie of sorts or a sandwich (scone and butter an added delight if available) along with the ubiquitous pint of milk, then I sit down by my bike to consume the lot, taking in my surroundings while doing so.

Brampton has its core laid out around its old market square, and markets still take place regularly. The little street which runs north from the market square in the centre of town is High Cross Street. There is a shoe shop on the right, a little white building dating from 1603 – the year that James VI of Scotland inherited the throne of England. It bears a plaque, telling of an event in this building's history, which took place in 1745. Bonnie Prince Charlie stayed here; half of his army camped or lodged in the vicinity while the other half besieged Carlisle. They were successful in taking Carlisle, of course, and word was brought to Charles here, whereupon he set off to ride in triumph into the city.

As word came to Charles, he must have thought that all his endeavours were coming to fruition. A successful landing in Scotland, followed by the rising of the clans, marching south into Edinburgh, Scotland's capital, then the fall of this northern English city. It would seem that all was going his way at this stage, and his heart must have been full at the prospect of regaining the throne of his ancestors. It was not to be, however; all the hopes and dreams were smashed forever on the battlefield of Culloden in 1746.

There is a monument, a relic of the darker side of the '45, as it is known in Scotland, in Brampton. If you take Gelt Road, running south from the town centre, then turn right on to Capon Tree Road, in a little cul-de-sac at this road's end is the site of the original 'Capon Tree' from which this road takes its name. A stone marks the site of the Capon Tree, standing among trees that, on my last visit, were dripping with rain. As I stood reading the inscription on the stone, rain started to drip from me too, but it brought a certain poignancy to the scene.

'This Stone is placed to mark the site of the ancient Capon Tree under whose shade the judges of assize rested and upon whose branches were executed October XXI MDCCXLVI for adherence to the cause of the Royal Line of Stewart. Colonel James Innes, Captain Patrick Lindesay, Ronald MacDonald, Thomas Park, Peter Taylor, Michael Delard. These six men were executed here for supporting Charles's cause.'

These poor souls breathed their last here, for their loyalty to the Royal House of Scotland. If it were not for the rain, I would have been able to see Scotland, only a dozen miles to the north, its hills visible from here on a reasonably clear day. To me, it seems a hellish end to die within sight of Scotland, but without being on the soil of home. I saluted these men as I dripped my way back to the bike to continue my journey.

Making one's way back down to the town centre, and passing the shoe shop that was Charles' headquarters, at the junction at the main road, we turn right and on the edge of town you will spot the signposts pointing the way down a side road to your left that leads to Lanercost Priory. The priory sits in a vale of the River Irthing, and it is a place I have much affection for. I love the old bridge over the river as you approach the Priory, built in 1722, superseded by a later structure from the 1960s, but it is nice to pull in and walk over the old bridge.

There is a little sign as you drive through the old archway into the priory grounds, that bears a sign requesting motorists to retract car aerials as the cattle will chew them. Signs like this always bring a smile to my face.

Although much of Lanercost is in ruins, part is still roofed and used for services. You are allowed access to the part of the church that is still used, and you pay a small fee to explore the rest of the ruins. There are some interesting old tombs in the body of the ruins of the Dacre and De Vaux families, and the nearby graveyard is worth a wander. It may sound a bit macabre, but history of course entails dealing with people who have passed on, so I always enjoy roaming old tombs, churches and graveyards, just to read inscriptions and learn the story of some of the people interred there.

Before you enter the door of the priory, turn and look at the old manor house that stands on your right, with its lead latticed windows. This building, still in use, is known as the 'guest house'. It was constructed as a headquarters for Edward I, Longshanks, near the end of his reign. He based himself at Lanercost to direct the sphere of operations in his war against Scotland, so England was actually ruled from here at one point in its history.

Wallace was here during his invasion of England in the winter of 1297–8. The monks at Lanercost, like many groups of monks all over Europe at that time, were the news gatherers of their day, and they wrote chronicles containing all the snippets of information that come to them. The *Lanercost Chronicle* has survived, and it gives us much information about the Wars of Independence that Scotland fought against English overlordship in the late thirteenth and through much of the fourteenth century. Due to Lanercost's proximity to the border with Scotland, it is an invaluable guide to these times. A copy of the script, translated into modern language, is available at Carlisle Library, and many extracts from the chronicle are copied into modern academic history books.

The English monks of course abhorred Wallace's lowborn status, and did not see him as a worthy adversary to their mighty king Edward. As Wallace's men ransacked their way through the northern shires of England during their invasion, and visited the priory itself, the monks recorded it – and vented their spleen against William Wallace himself.

The chronicle is, as you can imagine, very biased towards the English point of view, with vitriol directed against the Scots wherever possible. I have no idea where the original chronicle is now – probably kept at some institution in England's south – but I would love to see it.

Lanercost benefited hugely from the wars with Scotland, becoming a wealthy place with the riches looted from Scotland's border abbeys, but its attraction is the people who have walked these flagstones and looked at that roofline before me. Wallace, Scotland's great enemy Edward Longshanks, and our own hero-king, Robert the Bruce, who stayed here during one of his incursions into northern England. As I approach Lanercost, I can see it sitting in its green vale, just as they did.

Robert the Bruce was the only king Scotland ever had who managed to gain military superiority over the English on a sustained scale. He eventually wrested control over all the north of England, the cry 'the Scots are coming' creating terror all the way to Preston in the west and the Humber estuary in the east. Bruce was well aware that enforced control of another nation was a hateful thing, but it was the only avenue open to him to try and gain complete recognition from England of Scotland's status as a country free from overlordship. He succeeded in this quest only a year before his death in 1329, the English commissioners signing the document known as the Treaty of Edinburgh in 1328 recognising this fact. But his life's work had been completed.

His was an extraordinary life. As a teenager, I began to learn his story, and the more I delved into his character, the more impressed and personally humbled I became. He fought incredible odds – and he prevailed. What a man! He had luck on his side too, as he had a band of captains, each a hero in himself. The good Sir James of Douglas, Thomas Randolph, later to be regent of Scotland in Bruce's son David II's minority, King Robert's brother Edward, Walter Stewart, Neil Campbell, Hugh Ross, and many others. He also had the backing of the church in Scotland, a highly influential body at this time, who were firmly behind the fight for Scotland's liberation.

It inspires me to be able to visit places that he knew well – the fact that Lanercost's glory has come from much Scottish deprivation notwithstanding.

Leaving Lanercost, you turn right out of the gate and continue on the road that you were on. The road climbs, and after a mile or two you will notice that there are undulations at the roadside, which run parallel with your route. These are the first traces of Hadrian's Wall – the northwest boundary of the Roman Empire. Bits of stonework start to appear, and then you can make out the few courses of masonry that remain of defensive towers.

The Romans arrived at the borders of what we now know as Scotland around the end of the first century AD. There were various battles between the legions and the local tribes, but the Romans prevailed and built some forts deep in Scottish (the Romans called what we know as Scotland 'Caledonia') territory. The Caledonian tribes overran these forts and one of the crack legions was brought forward to deal with these 'rebels'. The Ninth Legion, a Hispanic legion, was sent north, but never returned, their fate silently lost in an unrecorded massacre.

The Emperor Hadrian decided that Caledonia was not worth the loss of another legion, and built his great wall – 70 miles from sea to sea.

You are now high above the north side of the River Irthing, which flows down by Lanercost, and the countryside to the south is laid out before you. Tantalising glimpses show hills in the distance to the north – Scotland. There always seems to have been a change here. A change of character, of attitude. The Romans knew that the tribes to the north of this line were different in temperament to those to the south.

The Romans did push into Caledonia, of course, building the Antonine Wall further north, but it was only for a short duration and the Roman influence never created the impact it made further south.

The further you drive away from the main centres of civilisation, like the Carlisle, area, the more you come across relatively unscathed stretches of wall, due simply to the fact that the wall has proved to be a convenient quarry for the best part of two millennia, and the remoter bits were left alone.

As I drive along its length on the bike, and watch how the wall undulates over the terrain, I often wonder what the guards on patrol thought as they gazed to the north, here on the edge of their vast empire. Most probably 'What the hell am I doing here? It's bloody freezing, and it looks like rain again', in Latin, of course.

I look at the work involved in building this wall, and marvel at it. The dressed stone, the forts, the military supply roads. I often wonder what the men who laboured so hard on this would make of it if they could see it now. Stretches depleted of its stone, stretches gone completely. All those millions of man-hours – and for what? It lies abandoned, although its builders probably thought it would last a thousand years in its full working order. They would probably think, 'I worked my fingers to the bone, and it lies forlorn, nothing much more than a tourist attraction.' Seems such a waste somehow.

It has been pointed out to me that I have spent a fair proportion of my life working out in gyms, and at the end of the day, for what? Hmmm. There is a moral there. Not sure what it is, but it's there somewhere.

* * * * *

Follow this road from Lanercost on, passing vestiges of wall and military way (the Roman marching and supply route) till the remains of the camp of Birdoswald is reached. There is a small museum here, basic in its outlook, but east of here the wall stretches away into the distance, much more impressive than hitherto. The outline of the camp here is quite well-defined, but I recommend walking to the rear of the camp and looking at the stupendous drop down to the river, the same River Irthing that flows by Lanercost, and the view to the countryside beyond.

Back on the road, which takes a right angle north here, you soon strike the junction with the B6318, where you turn right, and a kilometre or two takes you to Gilsland. The wall runs right though this village. Last time I was here, I watched the kids playing in the grounds of the little primary school, the wall once running right through these grounds. Where once Roman Legionnaires patrolled, children now played their games. In a little village like this, I suppose they have grown in such close proximity to this vast throwback to the past that it is part of everyday life.

Taking the road on towards Greenhead, we cross into the other great northern shire of England, Northumberland. From Greenhead we continue hard east on the B6318, and one of my favourite motorcycling stretches. We are a little south of the wall the whole way here, on a road with some fabulous straights, and at certain times of the year, very little traffic. Some tiny hamlets with great names too – Once Brewed and Twice Brewed are classic examples.

I remember the first time I was on this stretch, I was accompanying a friend driving a van, and I was in the passenger seat reading a book. There are some amazing hidden dips on these straight stretches, and my friend, knowing I wasn't watching the road ahead, hit one of these dips at quite a turn of speed. He managed to get my head to crash off the roof. It was quite a feat considering it was a big van!

The wall here too is at its finest, not just because we are far from centres of population to quarry it, but also because there are some quite dramatic cliffs and gullies, and the wall roller-coasters over these, almost like the exotic stretches of the Great Wall of China seen in tourist magazines. There are the remains of Housesteads Fort, a large camp, and further east, near the end of this brilliant stretch of driving road, is a temple dedicated to the Roman God, Mithras.

I have seen this undulating stretch of wall in films – most notably in *Robin Hood, Prince of Thieves*, where the star, Kevin Costner lands at Dover, and by nightfall he is at the other end of England!

At this road's end you meet a roundabout, and the B6320 branches off here to the north, signposted for Bellingham and Otterburn.

There are other routes north, a little further on, that all meet before the border with Scotland, but the reason I have chosen the B6320 is because it follows the valley of the River North Tyne, an ancient route used by raiders in both direction in past times. The River North Tyne, further downstream, unites with the South Tyne to form the famous river that flows through Newcastle upon Tyne, and for the academically challenged, it is so-called because there was once a new castle built here which stood above the River Tyne. The castle, if you are ever in Newcastle, is well worth a visit, the panorama over city and river from the roof a must-see, and there is a surprising amount of Scottish weaponry on display.

After his dismembering, one quarter of William Wallace was displayed at Newcastle to dishonour him, somewhere in the vicinity of the castle.

It always amazes me the number of people who say to me 'Is there a castle in Newcastle?' It stands prominent near the famous bridges, on a crag on the north bank of the Tyne.

But, let's get back to the B6320. This road skirts the famous Kielder Forest and Northumberland National Park, and although just over the border, and a playground for many of the inhabitants of Newcastle, it is an area unknown to most Scots.

The road meanders between rolling fields, and there are stretches where it is tree-lined, then you come into the village of Bellingham, which has several old hotels and inns squeezed into it. It would make a good base to explore the vast areas of woodland comprising the Kielder Forest. Bellingham, incidentally, is pronounced 'Belling Jam'. There is nothing

worse than saying the name of a place incorrectly in front of locals, and I
have done it times without number!

After Bellingham, the last few miles of the B6320 pulls up on to bleak
moorland, the lonely haunt of sheep, and again a great motor-cycling
stretch. I've been lucky here several times, it has always threatened to rain,
but never has, and moorland like this seems to transform itself into a
primeval wilderness with a mild hint of threat in rainy weather.

Civilisation looms in the shape of the A68, quite a major road, but at the
crossroads we go straight across, and it is only a few minutes drive before
we come down into the village of Otterburn.

The first building we encounter is Otterburn Mill, which has a display of
some of its ancient working machinery still in situ.

The main attraction of Otterburn for me is the famous battle fought here
in 1388.

After Otterburn Mill, we come to the A696 and we turn left here, heading
ever further north now. Just outside the village there is a stand of trees to
the right of the road, and you can turn in and park among them. There are
information boards, and a memorial to the battle.

There is a little debate to the actual site of conflict, but traditionally this is
the spot.

It all started at Souden (sometimes Southdean) Church, the ruins of
which are at the side of the A6088, north of here, between Carter Bar and
Hawick. The Scots army gathered in the vicinity of this old church, in their
many thousands, under the Lord of Douglas, prior to their invasion of
northern England. The Scots did not seek this invasion as an aggressor. The
English had overrun much of Teviotdale, and the Scots had done their best
to eject them from home soil. Richard II of England then invaded Scotland
in August 1385 and burnt the abbeys of Dryburgh and Melrose. Three
years later, the Scots decided to seek revenge.

Outside the walls of Newcastle, the Scots managed to capture the banner
of Henry Percy, Earl of Northumberland, better known as 'Hotspur'.
Capture of one's banner, or colours, was regarded as a huge loss of face,
and Douglas had it proclaimed that the Scots would not cross the border
for three days, thereby giving Hotspur the chance to recapture his banner
and redeem his honour. Hotspur was able to field many thousands of men,
and quickly gathered a powerful army and set off in hot pursuit.

There was no love lost between English Hotspur and the Scots Douglas.
Both were the heads of the most powerful families on their respective sides
of the border, both had been involved in raids against the other's properties,
and traditionally there had been great rivalry between their houses for
many years.

On their return journey towards Scotland on 19 August 1388, the Scots
army camped at Otterburn. Some urged that they should push on, but

Douglas (grand-nephew of Robert the Bruce's great captain) said that Hotspur should be give the chance to redeem his banner and his honour. They settled for the night at the remains of an old Roman camp, and were shocked as Hotspur appeared as dusk fell, his men charging straight into the attack, so eager was he for revenge.

Jean Froissart was a European chronicler of this time, and a great one for reporting battles. Of Otterburn he wrote, 'Of all the battles and encounterings that I have made mention of here before in all this history, great or small, this battle that I treat of now, was one of the sorest and best fought, without cowards or faint hearts.'

Somewhere on the field in the early part of the battle, Douglas was sorely wounded, legend stating that this act was treasonably done, the lethal blow being struck by Douglas' own armourer – who of course would know where there was a chink in the armour allowing him to stab his master with a dirk.

Douglas, realising that his wound would prove fatal, asked his men to help him hide his distress from the rest of his army, and to secrete his person in some nearby bushes. Here he died, his absence not noticed in the fast-approaching darkness, and the Scots fought their foes on into the night.

As Froissart stated, no cowardice was shown, and as men fought and slew, slipping on the gore soaked moorland, the moon rose. A full moon, which shone down on a state of madness on the moors by Otterburn. Two armies locked in a fight to the death.

In the midst of this, Sir Hugh Montgomery, a knight from Eaglesham in Renfrewshire, entered into combat with none other than Hotspur himself.

Sir Hugh must have been a fighter of some ability, as he disarmed Hotspur and forced him to yield. Hotspur, being a man of chivalry, asked that he yield his person to none other than Douglas. He was taken to the bushes where Douglas' body was hidden, and asked to yield there. The English started to lose heart as word spread that their leader had been captured, and their formerly closely ordered ranks began to disintegrate. The Scots took advantage of this and the slaughter became great. It was said that when the battle was over, the English dead amounted to over 1,800, whereas the Scots had only 100 dead.

This battle of Otterburn seems to be better known south of the border as 'Chevy Chase' due to Hostpur's chase of the Scots towards the Cheviot Hills.

Douglas' body was taken north and buried in Melrose Abbey, tradition stating that he lies under the Monks' Choir, beneath the 'Douglas Window'.

Many of the English dead were buried at the little church of Elsdon, a little east of Otterburn Village.

Sir Hugh Montgomery returned triumphantly to Scotland with his captive, and Hotspur's ransom gave him the wherewithal to build himself a fine new castle, Polnoon, the last vestiges of which stand above the River Cart near Eaglesham.

Otterburn has gone down in history in Scotland as the battle where the dead man won the fight.

*   *   *   *   *

Turning north again on the A696, we hit the junction with the A68 which we crossed earlier on the way to Otterburn. The road is now the A68, although at the junction the A696 takes precedence. We are following the course of the River Rede here, back towards its source, driving through the little hamlets of Horsley and Rochester, an area much used by the military for training exercises.

The countryside becomes wilder now, and more desolate, then the expanse of Catscleugh Reservoir appears on your left. From here runs the Rede, and this area was anciently 'Redesdale', a route of raiding armies in both directions. Driving such routes on the bike, I always try to cast my mind back and imagine these huge armies, men, horses and baggage trains, using these ancient roads, now superseded by modern tarmac, but these men were able to gaze up to the hilltops, and see their outlines as I see them today.

The road climbs upwards, on to steep moor-clad heights, outliers of the Cheviot range of hills. Then, as you approach the lofty summit, a monolith, a huge standing stone, appears, followed by another on the opposite side of the road. They are reminiscent of the huge dolmen of Stonehenge – and each has a word etched into its face.

'Scotland'.

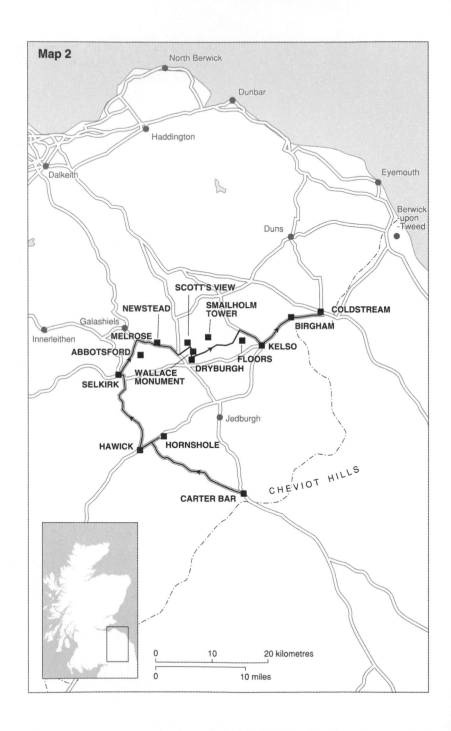

CHAPTER TWO

Scotland at Last

BEGINNING AT CARTER BAR, THE ROUTE FOLLOWS THE A6088 TOWARDS HAWICK. THERE IS A LITTLE DEVIATION EAST ON THE A698 TO HORNSHOLE, THEN INTO HAWICK. ONWARDS TO SELKIRK, ABBOTSFORD, MELROSE, SCOTT'S VIEW, DRYBURGH, KELSO AND COLD-STREAM.

IF YOU ARE GOING to drive in to Scotland, Carter Bar is the way I would recommend. That is one of the reasons I brought you across from Carlisle. From Carter Bar the view over southern Scotland is like a film set. Unreal. Is jaw-dropping too strong a term? It certainly has the ability to drop mine. Coming up onto the bleak shoulder of the Cheviots after the emptiness of Redesdale, it seems inconceivable that Scotland would suddenly be laid out like a dreamland, all rolling farmland and fertility.

I hope that if you drive from the south up to Carter Bar, the weather smiles upon you. Not necessarily warmth – not much chance of that in Scotland, but a clarity that gives a clear view to take in the magical scene.

I always park the bike up in the car park and just drink it all in.

Ruberslaw and the Eildon Hills prominent, and a hundred, nay, a thousand places that ring through the pages of Scotland's history. The Borders.

I think Carter Bar is such a shock to the senses because it is inherent in one's mind that Scotland is bleak and mountainous compared to milder England. Carter Bar dispels that. Scotland looks kind and welcoming, a myriad of greens in the woodland, the fields and the hedgerows.

If I had been away from Scotland for years in some enforced absence – and it would have to be enforced – I would want to come back by arriving at Carter Bar.

I would park and stand by the monolith that proclaims 'Scotland' and I would look at that view and think how lucky I was. And that I was even luckier in the fact that I was not there as a tourist, but as a man who can look upon that vista and think 'home'.

Scotland. Mine. Not in ownership of course, none of us get that privilege, but I get a little lease of her for a lifetime. I get all that scenery, all that history. And I get to motor-cycle over it all. Some of us are truly blessed.

Up here on Carter Bar itself, took place part of the tapestry of the history of the land laid before you – 'The Raid of the Redeswire'. I spoke about the Wardens of the Marches in the last chapter, explaining how there were three

English and three Scots wardens appointed to keep the peace in this area in the turbulent times of the centuries after Scotland's War of Independence.

On 7 July 1575, the English Warden of the Middle March, Sir John Forster, backed by many followers from the Tynedale area especially, met with John Carmichael, Keeper of Scotland's Liddesdale, and his men, deputising for the indisposed Scots Warden of the Middle March, William Kerr of Ferniehurst.

Forster was a rogue, and is well-documented as such, whereas Carmichael was a straightforward and honest man, and always played fair in his dealings with the English.

The Wardens would meet on a yearly basis to settle any differences that had arisen over the past twelve months. Wrongdoers would be handed over where necessary for justice for crimes committed over their respective borders. These meetings took place at the Redeswire, just by the road crossing at Carter Bar.

The Scots 'filed a bill' demanding the person of one Robson of Fawstone, a Tynedale man, who had committed various offences against Scots' property. Forster refused to hand him over, but promised to produce him at the next meeting. Carmichael refused to proceed as he felt Forster was not playing fair. One Englishman writing to Elizabeth 1 of England regarding Forster's behaviour stated 'The felonies etc. overlooked by Sir John Forster while warden, and the injustices and best gentlemen, would fill a large book' – so it seems Carmichael had grounds for his suspicions. Carmichael aired his feelings, and Forster retorted by saying that Carmichael was not even a warden, but a deputy, whereas he, Forster, was full Warden of the March. The exchange grew more heated as aspersions were aired regarding each other's families, and you can be sure the Borderers nearby were not slow in goading each other either.

Suddenly the shout went up from the English ranks 'To it, Tynedale!', and they let loose with a flight of arrows which killed several in the Scots ranks. The English drew their weapons and surged forward, one historian stating 'from words they fell to strokes'. The Scots fell back under this onslaught, completely unprepared as they were for this sudden turn of violence. Things were looking grim, and a massacre was on the cards, but all of a sudden a new cry filled the air, resonating from the heather-covered braes. 'Jetharts here, Jetharts here!'

A contingent of horsemen from Jedburgh (the local name for the place is Jethart) had arrived late for the meeting, and at a distance, seeing the English attack, urged their horses into a gallop, as the riders got ready to wield their fearsome Jethart staves, a favoured local weapon comprising an axe head and spike on the end of a long wooden pole.

Smashing into the English ranks, they killed 24 of them, including the deputy warden, Sir George Heron. Many were taken captive, including

Forster himself. They were taken to Edinburgh where an embarrassed Regent, the Earl of Morton, decided it was prudent to release them and let them return home. Elizabeth 1 of England's envoy at Edinburgh wrote that 'peace or war hangs now by a twine thread'.

In a whitewashing exercise, the incident was officially called the 'accident' at the Redeswire.

John Forster became a target of the Scots after this 'accident', and there is a record of 30 of them surprising him at Bamburgh Castle in Northumberland with intent to slay him, but his wife managed to put the bedroom door-bar into place, and they were unable to lay hands on him. He eventually died in his bed in 1602, reputed to be 101 years of age.

Carmichael, an efficient man, eventually became Warden of Scotland's West March, and was killed by a bullet shot from the gun of one of that notorious clan of Borderers, the Armstrongs, in 1600.

A stone marks the site of this 'accident' at the Redeswire, and it stands just a little to the east of Carter Bar. I had never seen the stone, so parked the bike up alongside a dozen or so others on my last visit, to go and find it. There were various bikers sitting about, smoking cigarettes, and they nodded to me as I rested my current steed, a Honda Pan European, an 1100cc tourer, on its side stand.

I crossed the road, climbed over the gate, and set off on the slight uphill rise of the ridge to the east. The ground is quite boggy, and as I was weighed down by heavy boots and leather, I got sucked into the soggy going underfoot. A few hundred metres into this and I glanced back to the road. I could see the bikers gathered were now sitting in a row, appearing to take quite an interest in my ploughtering about. 'They're watching me to see what I'm up to', I thought. For perhaps fifteen minutes I walked up and down, searching for the elusive stone. It's pretty bare moorland, a stone should not have been too difficult to locate, but I have found that when I am looking for sites which I would have thought straightforward, I am often searching for quite a while before my objective is finally reached – and I've often been within a few metres of it several times beforehand!

I turned and looked down at the road. The row of bikers was still watching with keen interest. I cut my losses and walked back down to where I parked. I climbed over the gate and crossed the road. 'Any of you guys local?' I enquired of the bikers. 'Jethart', one announced. 'Do you know where the Redeswire stone is?', I asked. 'You were pretty close a couple of times', he replied, 'and we waited to see if you would find it'.

'Great', I replied sarcastically, 'So where is it exactly?'

'About two hundred metres up, but over the dip slightly on the Scottish side of the Border', he replied. Then they all started to climb on their bikes as I re-crossed the road and climbed the gate again.

'You can't miss it!' one shouted, helpfully, as they rode away, pissing themselves laughing.

'Bastards!', I thought, laughing at them – and at myself too.

But at least the directions were spot-on. It was over the dip, slightly on the Scottish side, so I had missed it first time.

You see, many of the Border towns of Scotland celebrate their own 'Common Riding' events every year, events usually centred around an event in the town's history, and in these parts that history is usually centred around the constant warring with the English. The town of Jedburgh, as part of their 'Common Riding' events, ride on their horses up to this high ridge overlooking England to the south, and they celebrate their town's involvement at the Redeswire in 1575.

Some of those bikers had probably ridden horses up to this spot in memory of their forefathers, and would have been proud to do so. The term 'Common Riding' comes from the horsemen and women riding the boundaries of the common lands of the town to check for English invaders – a practice followed to this day – and for the far distant future, so much of their culture locked into these events, that I can never see it dying out. As long as people are proud to be Scots Borderers, the Common Ridings will take place.

The stone bears the date 1575, and on one side proclaims 'Jetharts here!' and on the other, 'To it Tynedale!'. It has a rusted iron railing surrounding it, and if it is dry enough to sit down, it is worth doing so for two reasons: first, the view, and second, to take stock of the events that took place here in 1575.

This is the crux. I love to be able to visit the sites of the events of Scotland's history and cast my mind back, hearing the gallop of hooves and the cries of 'Jetharts here!'.

Back on the bike and onwards into Scotland, the A68 dropping down into the idyllic view seen from this high ridge on the Cheviots. Not too far though, and the road forks, the left branch leading towards Hawick in the form of the A6088, and this road we take, dropping in altitude constantly. Keep you eyes peeled though, as on your left, by the side of the road, the scant ruins of Souden Kirk appear. The name is actually an abbreviation of 'Southdean', but it seem to have been known as Souden from its inception, even the continental chronicle of Jean Froissart calling it 'Zedon' church.

This little church, consisting of not much more than low walls now, was where Douglas mustered his army in 1388, before his invasion of England, culminating in the Battle of Otterburn.

Such a quiet little spot today. Strange that it once echoed with the gathering of many thousands of armed men and horses. They must have filled all the surrounding fields and hillsides. A hive of activity.

Carrying on driving the A6088, you pass under Bonchester Hill, close to the right of the road, 323 metres in height. It is a beautiful, green, round-shouldered hill. It has traces of ancient fortifications, and legend states that its name comes from *bona castra* – a good camp – in the language of the Romans. A little further on we hit the hamlet of Bonchester Bridge, a settlement that takes its name from the bridge over the Rule Water here.

Another few miles and we come to the junction of the A698, and turning left takes us into the outskirts of Hawick, but before driving into Hawick, it is worth turning right and following the road for a mile or so, the River Teviot on your left, till you come to a little road branching off to the left, steeply downhill, to cross an old narrow bridge over the Teviot. There is no sign for this road, but there is a notice warning that the bridge is weak. Between the A698 and the bridge there stands a tall pillar-like monument, carrying the inscription '1514 – Lest We Forget'.

This monument marks the Hornshole, and is the scene of an extraordinary event.

Scotland had suffered a crushing military defeat at the Battle of Flodden in 1513, only a year before. Many thousands of Scots fell, and few families did not lose a son, a brother or a father in the carnage – but the Borders of Scotland suffered terribly: very few able-bodied men between 16 and 60 survived to return to their families. The country lay open to the deprivations of English raiders, and in 1514 a large party of southron marauders wreaked havoc in the Hawick area. Sated with rapine and plunder, the English camped in the vicinity of this monument at the Hornshole, and with the lack of opposition left in Scotland, they did not bother to post sentries to guard the camp.

The residents of Hawick had, of course, taken to the surrounding hills at the approach of this English raid, but the martial spirit of their dead fathers was inherent in many of the youths of this district, and as night fell they began to gather …

The English, sleeping, and the majority the worse for drink, never knew what hit them. The lads of Hawick had gathered what horseflesh they could find, and charged the camp in the dead of night, crying 'Teribus!', their ancient war cry, stampeding cattle before them. Most of the sleeping English never got the chance to rise, never mind draw steel, before they were crushed underneath galloping hooves, and those who managed to stagger to their feet were cut down by swords wielded in the hands of boys, the eldest perhaps only fifteen.

The kids of Hawick took the revenge for the slaughter of their fathers the year before. They managed, somewhere in the middle of the carnage they created, to grasp the battle standard of their foes, and the children of Hawick rode back into town, their foes vanquished, their leader carrying the captured banner aloft in triumph.

It is a delight to take a look over the bridge that spans the Teviot here and watch the deep water run between the cliff-like banks. I've always had a penchant for jumping from heights into water, and have done so at many impressive parts of Scotland, and the drop into the Teviot here has its attractions! But enough of my foibles.

Retracing our route back along the A698 into Hawick, we eventually hit the town centre. Hawick is a bustling busy town, bigger than people generally imagine, and it sits in a dip of the valley of the River Teviot, surrounded by high ground, and it is a large place to have no real major road run to it, but to its inhabitants it is 'Queen of a' the Borders'.

As you drive down through the town's High Street, the focal point is the statue in the middle of the road. It is a statue of a youth astride a horse, a youth holding aloft a captured English banner, an expression of extreme joy on his face. It is a statue that sent shivers down my spine the first time I saw it and realised just what it meant and what it stood for.

And I have never looked at it since and not been filled with emotion. Patriotism. Pride. Sorrow. Joy.

There is a word carved into the plinth: 'Teribus'.

There is a song which is sung in Hawick, at the town's Common Riding. As previously stated, Jedburgh has the Raid of the Redeswire as the central theme of its Common Riding. In Hawick it's the Hornshole and how the town's youth – its 'callants', routed an English raiding party. And the song of Hawick runs:

Scotia felt thine ire, O Odin!
On the bloody field of Flodden,
There their fathers fell with honour,
Round their king and country's banner.

Teribus, ye Teri Odin!
Sons of heroes slain at Flodden,
Imitating Border bowmen,
Aye defend your rights and common.

The first line of the chorus comes from an ancient tongue – Cymric, or Old Welsh – and translates as 'May Thor have us, both Thor and Odin'. The verses of the complete song were written around 1800. The song describes how the 'callants' of Hawick defeated the English, and finishes with the verses :

Hawick shall triumph 'mid destruction'
Was a druid's dark prediction.
Strange the issues that unrolled it,
Cent'ries after he foretold it.

Peace be thy portion, Hawick, for ever!
Thine arts, thy commerce flourish ever!
Down to latest ages send it –
Hawick was ever independent.

The great martial spirit of Scotland is safe in the memories of its sons and daughters, and it is apparent in the blood that runs through the veins of the Borderers of Scotland. The ordinary folk that I pass on Hawick's High Street are the direct descendants of those who fell at Flodden. Of those who were present at the Hornshole, and are filled with the bloodline of so many who were in the front line against the vicious incursions of England. It is no wonder that that pride is manifest today.

Too often, Scotland's history is depicted as 'Highland' in dress and culture – but the Borderers bore the brunt of keeping Scotland free, and the Hornshole is a little part of her story that should be more widely known.

The statue of the youth astride the horse was created by William Beattie, who was a native of Hawick. It was unveiled on 4 June 1914.

Perhaps it is because William was a native of Hawick that he managed to capture so much passion in a statue. The horse, with its head lowered, looking spent and tired in comparison to its rider, is to me absolute genius.

William Beattie was born in 1886 and was killed in France in 1918, during the First World War, where he had reached the rank of major. But his spirit lives on in his work, his statue in Hawick an inspiration to every Scot.

A good way to look over Hawick is to climb the Mote Hill and look out as some of the earlier inhabitants of the town did, gazing out from the top of their artificial 'knowe'. At the southern end of the High Street, the road crosses the Slitrig Water, shortly before it joins the River Teviot, then if you take the first street on the left and follow it up its long steep hill, the Mote Hill is about half way up on your left. It is about 30 feet high, and some 300 feet in circumference, and has a staircase running up one side to facilitate access to the top. The original castle of Hawick stood here. The manmade mound constructed for defensive purposes, and the original fortification was owned by the Lovel family, and it was created in the 1000s.

There is a good view over the town from this spot, looking down on the High Street and out over the surrounding hills. The little wooden bench on top is a nice touch, and I bet many young courting couples have sat upon it of an evening, looking out at this view.

If I was a young 'callant' in Hawick, I would certainly have taken a young lady up to the top of the 'Mote' to admire this vista, among other things, and would probably have bored her to death telling her of the history of our surroundings.

On the opposite side of the Teviot from the Mote Hill stands Wilton Lodge Park. Here stands the town's museum, war memorial and an interesting monument to Jimmy Guthrie, with a statue of the man atop a tall plinth. Jimmy Guthrie was a well-known racing motorcyclist, who was killed in a crash in Germany in 1937.

Having been a motorcycle rider since I was old enough to be one, I have nothing but admiration for men who have that sort of ability – to elbow other riders out the way at 180 mph! I generally find that there are two expressions involved in riding a bike at a great rate of knots. One is Wahoo! The other is Shit! Shit! Shit! As you watch a dull object grow much larger through your visor.

Joking aside, it takes a lot of guts and a huge lack of fear to be a motorcycle racer – and Scotland has produced many. We also seem to produce more than our fair share of motor-racing and motor-rally champions too.

We are going to leave Hawick and head a little north to Selkirk, driving along the A7. It is well signposted from Hawick town centre.

As Hawick sits on the valley floor of the Teviot, the road climbs steeply as you leave the town. As we reach the top of the gradient, where Roxburghshire meets Selkirkshire, there is an astonishing view behind (weather permitting) looking over the valley of the Teviot to the Cheviot Hills beyond. Panoramic it certainly is. That line of hills is like a backdrop to Scotland, knowing that the far side of those hills means 'England', but we push on deeper into Scotland, heading towards the large transmitter which stands to our right as we grow closer to Selkirk.

If we head right into the centre of Selkirk, we come to the little square with its mercat cross. This cross figures prominently in the Common Riding festival which is held here, with a flag-waving ceremony taking place. You see, Selkirk sent all its able-bodied men to Flodden's fateful field in 1513, 80 of them in total, and only one returned. He was reputed to be the town clerk, a man by the name of Walter Brydon – a good Borders surname, that – and I have heard other Borders townsfolk comment 'Aye, trust a Selkirk lawyer to survive!'

The memory of Flodden is strong in these parts.

There was no shame in this returning of only one man, as he came back clutching a captured English banner. He walked as far as the town square where he cast down his flag, in mute testament to the fact that he was the only person who would return. The flag that he carried is preserved in the town's little museum.

So, in recognition of Walter, every year the chosen standard bearer 'casts the colours' in the square, a flag-waving and weaving ceremony that requires all the strength that one's wrists can muster!

As Hawick has its 'Teribus' song, So Selkirk has its own ditty:

Up wi' the souters of Selkirk
And down wi' the Earl of Home!

And up wi a' the braw lads
That sew the single-soled shoon!

This is said to be a reference to Flodden and the fact that Lord Home was the only survivor of any note. Selkirk was in its earlier days a great place for shoemaking, the Scots word for this trade being a 'Souter'. In fact, the trade was once so prevalent in Selkirk that the town provided more than half of the 6,000 pairs demanded from the magistrates of Edinburgh by the Jacobite army of Bonnie Prince Charlie in 1745.

The words 'single-soled shoon' refer to the fact that the souters made a leather shoe with only a basic leather sole added, the purchaser being expected to add an extra thicker sole to their own needs. There is another fabulous statue referring to Flodden in Selkirk. It is a monument to the lone flag bearer, a Borderer armed in steel jack and helmet, and on the plinth is inscribed 'O Flodden Field'. Flodden may have caused so much grief in this area in its time, but that sorrow has caused some fabulous sculptures to be created in its memory. The statue here was unveiled in 1913 – the four-hundredth anniversary of the battle. Selkirk also boasts a statue of the writer, Sir Walter Scott, who was sheriff of Selkirkshire at one time, and it stands seven and a half feet on a pedestal 20 feet high. It was sculpted by Handyside Richie, who was also responsible for the statue of Scotland's great hero, Sir William Wallace, which stands at the front of the Athenaeum building in Stirling.

Another monument, by Andrew Currie, was erected in the High Street in 1859 in memory of Mungo Park (1771–1805). Mungo was an explorer, born at Fowlshiels on the Yarrow Water, not too far from Selkirk itself. The remains of his birthplace stand at the roadside (the A708) near the ruins of stark Newark Castle. Mungo made two expeditions to try to find the source of the River Niger, being tragically killed on the second trip.

What surprises me is how late in life I first heard the name of Mungo Park. A friend lent me a book about him when I was in my late twenties, and reading it, I was surprised that I had never heard his name mentioned at school.

Just off the square, down a little lane, stands the museum. It has some interesting artefacts. The Brydon sword, a relic of Flodden, always gets my attention. On my last visit there was a life-size figure of a knight in armour, a representation of Sir Aymer de Valance. Very nice – but why an English knight who was an aggressor to Scotland, a henchman of the hated Edward Longshanks? Scotland has its heroes who operated in this part of the country to try and foil the ravages of people like de Valance: the Good Sir James Douglas for example. Wouldn't he be a better example?

The far end of the lane opens out by the ruins of the Kirk of the Forest. Selkirk was once the main town of the huge Ettrick Forest. The forest still exists in segments of course, but in earlier times it covered a huge area of the surrounding country. Felling for cultivation, and sheep preventing new growth, has decimated much of it. It figured hugely during the Wars of Independence, giving shelter to the aforementioned Good Sir James, along with our great heroes, Wallace and Bruce. In fact, older documents refer to it simply as 'the Forest', so famed was it. Even Longshanks did not send his troops into its fastnesses, the Scots within would have cut them to ribbons, it offering much scope for easy ambush.

So, the Kirk of the Forest took its name from its location, but the kirk is famed as the site where William Wallace became 'Sir' William, when he was created Guardian of Scotland after returning from his invasion of northern England during late 1297. Only the walls remain of the kirk, but a metal plaque at the doorway announces its Wallace connection, and that the church is also the last resting place of the maternal ancestors of Franklin D Roosevelt.

There has always been debate regarding the identity of who actually knighted Wallace. The chronicles state that it was one of the leading men of Scotland, but they give no other detail.

The late Nigel Tranter, acclaimed novelist and writer, put forward the theory that the future King of Scots, Robert the Bruce, knighted Wallace. In theory, any knight could create another, but generally only royalty or the leading magnates did so.

Tranter looked at the earls of Scotland living at the time of Wallace's knighthood. Some were only minors. Some lived too far away to be likely candidates, and some were too infirm or elderly to be campaigning or to have travelled to Ettrick Forest. Bruce, by this process of elimination, seems to be the most likely candidate, but the truth is that unless new documentation comes to light, we will never know.

Certainly before the creating of Guardian at the Kirk of the Forest, Wallace is simply 'William'. After this date he is always referred to as 'Sir William'.

You can stand in the ruins of this little kirk and imagine Wallace on bended knee as the sword was lowered to touch each shoulder, his head bowed, and no doubt praying that he would be able to do his utmost for Scotland.

Selkirk itself stands high above the Ettrick Water, and if you drive down to and cross the river, the haughland to the west is the site of the Battle of Philiphaugh, fought in 1645. Haugh is of course the Scots for the flatlands stretching out from the edge of a river.

Philiphaugh was fought between the Covenant forces under the command of General Leslie, and the royalists under the command of James Graham, the Marquis of Montrose, a man usually referred to as simply 'Montrose' by most Scots.

Montrose had actually originally been a member of the Covenanting forces, a movement that had risen to push for religious freedom in Scotland, but it soon became corrupt, and when it turned against the ruling house of Scotland, the Stewart dynasty, Montrose felt that he could no longer support it.

The Covenant forces took their name from the 'Solemn League and Covenant', a document drawn up to state their grievances. Montrose had led the royalist forces of Scotland to a series of stunning victories, even when vastly outnumbered, over the last year, but Philiphaugh was to prove his undoing.

He had been betrayed to the forces of the Covenant by the Earl of Traquair, who had told of his whereabouts – and his lack of numbers. You see, Montrose had only 600 fighting men, and Leslie commanded 6,000, so Philiphaugh was a rout and no real battle. But it was not the fight itself that was to be so shocking.

The Covenanting ministers of the Kirk who marched with the forces of Leslie demanded revenge, and in the aftermath of the battle they ensured that all the wounded were slain out of hand. But there was worse. The prisoners were slain, then so were all the women and children who had been with Montrose's army – all in the name of God.

Christianity is supposed to be a religion of forgiveness, but the ministers who perpetrated the sins after Philiphaugh, on some 500 non-combatants, stained not only the history books of Scotland, but the credo of their own beliefs.

Back to the centre of Selkirk, and we take the A7, running north from the square, continuing down by the baronial County Buildings and we eventually come out of town and on to the banks of the Ettrick Water. After a mile or two we come to a bridge, and as we cross we are at the junction of the Ettrick and the famous River Tweed, one of the great rivers of Scotland, and famed for the part it plays in the story of the Border country. Following the north bank of the Tweed for another couple of miles, we come to a large roundabout, just west of Galashiels.

Gala, as it is commonly known, is a bustling little town, and the jewel in its crown is its statue of a mounted 'Border Reiver' which serves as its war memorial. But here we are turning east on the A6091, where we re-cross the Tweed, looking towards the triple tops of the Eildon Hills. At the next roundabout, you will see that the way to Abbotsford is signposted, and we turn to visit the home of Sir Walter Scott, still owned by his family, and it is a shrine today to the memory of the man.

I have to admit that I have tried to read Scott, but I find him very 'wordy' and he seems very dated to me in his attitude. I am also a bit suspicious about where Scott stood in the scheme of things where Scotland was concerned. He seems to me to have been happy to promote the ideals of Unionism with England. But no matter – no-one can deny that Sir Walter Scott gave Scotland back her history. He made it fashionable to be Scottish and happily promoted all things Scottish at the same time. He is more than a little responsible for the whole tartan and heather image too, but I suppose if I look at the man in retrospect, he did much for his country at a time when many saw her only as 'North Britain', and for that I should be at the very least a little grateful.

Abbotsford House was built between 1817 and 1824, and Scott himself died here in 1832. It contains many historical Scottish relics too. Scott was a great collector, and for anyone like myself who adores the history of Scotland, some of these should not be missed.

There is a crucifix that was once held by Mary, Queen of Scots. There are copies of candlesticks that once belonged to Robert the Bruce. They are strangely modern in aspect. There are little quaichs (drinking cups) made from the wood of some major historic sites. One of my personal favourites is the sword and dirk of Rob Roy MacGregor. The sword is a fine basket-hilted sword, with the name Andrea Farrara etched into the blade. This name is a story all in itself.

Andrea Farrara was a famous swordmaker – Italian, I believe – who happened to get a noblewoman pregnant in his homeland and had to flee. He landed in Scotland, and when this was brought to the king's attention, Farrara was given sanctuary, under the condition that he would continue to make fine swords. So, Farrara swords became extremely sought after, and for centuries after it seems nearly every swordmaker in Scotland etched 'Andrea Farrara' onto their blades, both as a sign of quality and obviously in the hope that people would think they had an original blade. So much so that half the swords in our museums have Farrara etched into their blades! Whether the Rob Roy sword is an original Farrara, I do not know, but it is certainly a very impressive 'basket-hilter'.

I was with a friend at Abbotsford once, actually helping to move some of the artefacts, and I gave him a nick with Rob Roy's dirk – just enough to make a slight cut. 'What was that for?' he exclaimed (I've taken out the swearing). I replied that he had been cut by the dirk of none other than Rob Roy MacGregor, and he should be proud. And he did boast about it in the pub that night!

Rob Roy's dirk looks very much like many modern ones, having the black carven handle, and cairngorm stone set in the base of the hilt. The only difference is the fact that the blade is more like a Bowie knife, rather than the pointed type that is more prevalent nowadays.

There are many other weapons on display at Abbotsford; in fact, the place is crammed with artefacts, and it has always been a delight for me.

The house has pleasant gardens, and looks out onto the River Tweed. Although the name 'Tweed' is famous worldwide as a durable fabric – even the lining of my current bike jacket is Harris Tweed – the name has nothing to do with the river. The fabric is actually called 'Twill' and it was a spelling mistake where Tweed was inserted for Twill on a form that caused the change to take place. Strangely, when Scott purchased the land here to build the house, it was known as 'Clarty Hole', and as 'clarty' is the Scots for filthy or dirty, he promptly changed it to Abbotsford, in deference to nearby Melrose Abbey, or at least, the abbots thereof. Clarty Hole now seems a strange name for such a beautiful little spot, but perhaps Sir Walter made some great changes.

Leaving Abbotsford and turning left to reach the roundabout on the A6091 again, we continue east towards yet another roundabout, and we take the turnoff for Melrose. The beautiful little town of Melrose sits snugly between the Tweed on the north and the heights of the Eildon Hills to its south.

The Eildons are a much loved feature of the Borderland. Prominent in crossing Carter Bar, and clearly visible from much of the eastern Border country, they are an enduring symbol of this landscape, loved by many, and not just of this age. The earliest peoples to settle here recognised them for their defensive capabilities, the Romans came and they called them Trimontium, from the triple peaks whose outline is so easily recognisable from great distances. They attain 1,385, 1,327 and 1,216 feet respectively. The centre hill is the highest and is a fabulous viewpoint. The easternmost has the remains of a huge fortification on its summit, enclosing the whole hilltop.

These hills must have been a welcome sight to returning Scots over many centuries. From tribal days to the days of the early kings, aye, even to Wallace and Bruce returning from incursions into England, just as they must have brought a tear to the eye of soldiers returning in eras of more modern warfare.

Even though my blood does not stem from the Borders of Scotland, espying these hills as I drive always brings a little smile of recognition, as my brain registers the Eildons. They seem to embody the very spirit of the Borderland. Upright. Timeless.

Certain areas all over the planet have a natural feature in their landscapes that people can interconnect with the culture there. Like Table Mountain in South Africa, Ayers Rock in Australia, or Mount Rushmore in the USA (although man has helped nature there somewhat!) the Eildons have that same certain something. They speak of the Borders.

Melrose is a lovely wee place, clustered around the ruins of its once proud abbey. Ruined, but it still casts a watchful eye over its surroundings. It is a delightful ruin though, the red of its stonework pleasing to the eye. The abbey was founded by King David I of Scots in 1136. David I was the son of Queen Margaret and King Malcolm Canmore of Scots – his mother was later canonised and may be better known as Saint Margaret. He seemed to inherit her religious zeal, and he was responsible for the founding of many of Scotland's religious buildings.

King Alexander II was buried at Melrose, even though he died on the island of Kerrera off Oban on the opposite side of Scotland. He was buried by the High Altar, but nothing marks the spot. It would be nice if a small plaque proclaimed this fact. Very few of the monarchs of Scotland have last resting places which are marked in any way.

Melrose Abbey was sacked and burnt repeatedly by English invaders, most notably in 1322, 1385 and 1545. Obviously they would desecrate and smash all the ornate tombs within, but a little sign stating 'Near this spot lies Alexander II – King of Scots' would be fitting. It's not that I'm heavily into the whole royalty thing, but the history of our small land is what we all have that binds us together, and we should acknowledge all that has gone before, and ignoring a king's grave is denying a huge chunk of our past. We need to nurture our history. It will make us stronger.

In my book *A Passion for Scotland* there is a particular line. I just wrote it, I didn't give it a special significance, but it was pointed out to me by several people, especially Duncan Fenton, my vice-convener at the Society of William Wallace. I wrote 'I have never met anyone who has learned her (Scotland's) story and thought less of her future'. And that is the way it is. Everyone I have ever met who has learnt of Scotland's past cares deeply about where she is going. And that going is the obliteration of serfdom. A real nation again. It is there. Let us grasp it together.

There are some interesting statues still adorning Melrose Abbey, statues which have survived English deprivations, and the stupidity of the Reformation in Scotland, where the Scots themselves smashed anything ornate, because in their narrow minds it smacked of Popery. Funny thing, religion.

There is a carving of a pig playing the bagpipes, which I have always really liked. If this carving is as old as the abbey itself, it makes me wonder how long the pipes have been played in Scotland. Perhaps they were old in Wallace's day. Perhaps they skirled at Stirling Bridge. No wonder many of the English hate the sound. Bit of race memory from a thousand battles!

The most interesting relic contained at Melrose Abbey, an artefact which should make it a place of pilgrimage all by itself, is the heart of Robert the Bruce, King of Scots. On his deathbed, Bruce told his lords how, as a young knight, he had made a vow that if he managed to free Scotland from the yoke of the English, and make Scotland strong and free, he would lead an army of Scots on crusade against the occupiers of the Holy Land.

Bruce managed to free his country, but when the English recognised Scotland as a separate entity, Bruce was a sick man and only a year away from death, worn out by a life spent in Scotland's service. But on his deathbed the vow he had taken as a young knight hung heavy on his conscience.

There was a way that he could try to fulfil his vow, even though his body was failing. It was decreed that James Douglas, the Black Douglas, the Good Sir James, would lead the Scots on this crusade, and Bruce's heart would accompany them. When Bruce expired, his breastbone was sawn through, and his brave heart was removed and placed in a casket. The Scots under Douglas set sail for sunnier climes.

Reaching southern Spain, they found that King Alfonso was having difficulty with the Moorish forces that were occupying part of his country. The Scots decided to help. It was, after all, a fight against the forces arrayed against Christendom. In a battle at the Castle of the Stars, or el Castillo de las Estrellas, the Scots were surrounded by the Moorish forces, and the bold Douglas was cut down. His body was found though, and it was brought back to the little village of Douglas in Lanarkshire. Bruce's heart in its casket was brought here to Melrose, and buried with honour – the rest of his body having been interred at Dunfermline.

A letter has survived – Bruce's deathbed letter – which states that he wished his heart to return to Melrose after the adventures he knew it must have. The heart rested undisturbed for many centuries, but was dug up in the early 1900s, then reburied. Then it was exhumed again near the end of that century, and this time a lot of scientific research was carried out. I was at the ceremony of reburial, the heart, of course, brought back to Melrose. Today it lies, in a new casket, kept within a concrete box, and buried beneath a round plaque. This plaque bears some words of John Barbour's.

Barbour was Archdeacon of Aberdeen, and composed an epic poem of the times of Bruce in the 1370s. Translations of this are available in book form, and even today it is a fabulous read. Barbour was a good gatherer or the stories of Bruce, and was able to collect eye-witness accounts to include in his work. Every Scot should at least know of it, even if they never get round to actually reading it!

The plaque reads:

'A noble heart may have no ease if freedom fails'.

Do I really need to point out how true and pertinent this is, not only to the Scotland of the fourteenth century, but to modern Scotland?

After taking in the various artefacts to be seen within the abbey precincts, including various Roman findings, leave the abbey, drive to ones right, north towards the Tweed, and follow the road round its tight dogs

leg bend left, and carry on towards the village of Newstead, with its site of
a large Roman camp. Newstead is a pretty wee place and worth a look. You
eventually meet up again with the main route you were on prior to entering
Melrose. Turning left, it is only a few hundred metres to a large roundabout, where you take the first exit left, signposted Edinburgh. Here you
cross the Tweed on a modern bridge, but a glance upstream shows you the
older single track bridge, then the high old railway bridge, testament to the
earlier means of transport on this ancient route. Just after this river crossing, there is a junction to your right, signposted 'Scott's View'. Taking this
junction, you can, if you wish, park hereabouts and wander over the old
bridge over the Tweed just mentioned. There is some interesting poetry
carved into blocks at the old bridge's far side. We drive on through
Leaderfoot, which, as its name suggests, stands at the confluence of the
Leader Water and the River Tweed, but it is today more just a name than
any real habitation. Once through Leaderfoot, the road gradually rises till it
is high above the River Tweed. There is a viewpoint and lay-by on your
right. This is the famous 'Scott's View', a vista loved by Sir Walter Scott. It
is very impressive, this view over the Eildon Hills and surrounding countryside. Scott loved it so much that he would always pause his horse here, and
spend a few minutes drinking it all in. You too can stand here and admire it
just as he did. And there is much to admire. I can understand why he loved
this vista so much. I don't think I have ever gone by on the bike and been
able to resist stopping to look out at all that glory. The view over the
Eildons is superb, the eye drawn to them, upwards from the river far below.

The story goes that when Scott's funeral cortege came this way to take
him over the hill to Dryburgh and his last resting place, his favourite horse
pulled the hearse. When the horse reached this spot, it paused for a minute
or two before trotting on, just as it had done for its master in life.

A little further on and we pass through Bemersyde with its old house,
owned by the Haig family. A famous prophet once lived in these parts,
Thomas the Rhymer by name. He came from the little village a few miles up
the Leader Water, and his proper title was Thomas Learmonth of
Ercildoune, the old name for the modern village of Earlston. He was born
about 1225, and died around 1307. Thomas is reputed to have been taken
to Elfland by the Queen of the Faeries, disappearing into the Eildons, and
reappearing seven years later with the ability to prophesy. One of his
rhymes ran like this:

Tide, tide, whatever betide,
Haig will be Haig of Bemersyde.

And several hundred years on this is still very much the case. After the First
World War, the estate was presented in perpetuity to Earl Haig in gratitude

for military services. The house stands over to your right, and can be seen from the road, extending out from its original old tower-house. Just a few hundred yards further south, there is an inshot to your right with several parking places. A track leads off, and it is well worth walking the quarter mile or so to see the impressive statue of Sir William Wallace high above the Tweed. I have taken many friends to this spot over the years, and they are always taken aback at the sheer physical size of this monument. This very middle-aged looking Wallace holding his mighty sword was actually the first Wallace monument raised in Scotland. It was commissioned by the Earl of Buchan and it was unveiled in 1814. Being created of sandstone, it had deteriorated badly over the years, but it was restored in the early 1990s. If I climb up on the plinth, I can actually stand between his feet, and my head only reaches to knee height – and I'm six feet five inches.

There is a great view out from here, high on Bemersyde Hill. In front of the statue there is a separate little spine of rock, and it has set upon it an inscribed urn. There is a small box on a pole too, in which visitors can leave notes, so if you want to, remember to take a paper and pen with you.

The statue of Wallace was built here, high above the Tweed, to depict him 'frowning towards England'. So many statues of Wallace depict him as being older than he was in reality. It is as if their builders wanted to make Wallace older to make him look more 'life experienced' in some way. In fact, Wallace is depicted in so many different ways, and in so many different styles and eras of dress in the various statues around Scotland, it is a subject that has intrigued me all by itself.

The thing that I like about this particular Wallace statue is that it may be colossal, but it also has, somehow, a feeling of fun about it, which does not detract from or demean Wallace in any way. It has no brooding malevolence about it.

Retracing your steps to the parking place, and then carrying on along the main road, you go steeply downhill to a junction, and turning right down this dead-end road brings you through Dryburgh to the ruins of Dryburgh Abbey.

The ruins are situated in a loop of the River Tweed, and it is a place of great beauty. Many come here to visit St Mary's Aisle within the abbey ruins, as it is the burial place of Sir Walter Scott and members of his family, JG Lockhart, Scott's biographer, Field Marshal Earl Haig, and also of the Earl of Buchan, responsible for the Wallace statue on the hill above.

When I was here last, an old man approached, and stood alongside me looking at all those impressive tombs, leaning on a well-used walking stick. He turned to me and said, 'I love looking at this lot, son – it makes me feel that young!' before he shuffled off. Brilliant – what an outlook on life!

The abbey was founded in 1150, but like so many architectural beauties in the borders of Scotland, it became a magnet for the deprivations of successive English invaders, and it was particularly badly damaged in 1322, 1385 and 1544. The ruins were presented to the nation by Lord Glenconner in 1918. The west front with its thirteenth-century portal, and parts of the nave, transepts and Chapter House still stand, and show building work dating from the 1100s to the 1400s. Part of the cloisters remain, as does the refectory with its rose window, and there is a large fireplace in the 'calefactory'. I read the word 'calefactory' in a guidebook, and had no idea what it meant, so I pulled a dictionary off the shelf to look it up. The word was not in the dictionary I have, but it just means the 'warming room' – a place where the monks could have a heat at the fire! The word *calorie* has the same root.

As the other border abbeys, Jedburgh, Melrose and Kelso, are all situated within towns, Dryburgh has a serenity all its own. The trees in the grounds, collected from all over the world are very impressive. The local bird life certainly loves them! I sat and watched a family of treecreepers perform acrobatics on the underside of the branches.

There is a pillar that has a carving of James I on one side and James II on the other. There are very few memorials in stone to the Stewart dynasty of Scotland, so that these are a welcome find. It is bizarre when we think of all the towns and cities of Scotland and realise that there is basically nothing to the memory of this most famous dynasty of Scots history standing anywhere.

Dryburgh, as said, has a serenity about it. It is a very beautiful and impressive site, and I so wish it had withstood the ravages of time and invasion to be a lasting memorial to the genius of the masons of Scotland's medieval period.

Leaving Dryburgh, we drive back up to the junction coming down from the Wallace statue, only this time we carry on eastwards, and after a mile or so and a dog-leg bend we come to the T-junction where this road meets the B6404, and here we turn east (left), heading towards Kelso.

Carrying on along this road, you will notice an edifice, standing on a raised piece of ground, over to your left. This is Smailholm Tower. Access is gained by taking the first left after you actually pass the tower, then taking another left once you come to a little plantation.

The tower was probably built by David Pringle, laird here from 1495 to 1535. This wee castle saw much action, having been attacked by the English in 1543, 1544 and 1546, when the garrison of Wark Castle in England's Northumbria made off with four prisoners and sixty cattle. Obviously they must have had a bit of a bee in their bonnets where Smailholm was concerned. On a better note, Sir Andrew Ker managed to defend the castle against a party of English musketeers in 1640. Around this time the Scott family inherited the place through marriage. The castle was handed over to state ownership in 1950. It is open to the public, and the farm underneath was where Sir Walter Scott was raised. You walk up its grassy knoll to reach the tower, and a look over its little crag shows you what an obvious defensive site this is. It is a perfect photo opportunity too, the castle standing proud above its little lochan. You visit each floor in turn by the towers' spiral staircase, till you reach the top floor where there is a door at either side that takes you out onto the towers' battlements. There are pleasant views out in every direction from the castle.

Back to the B6404, and we turn left again, and continue towards Kelso. After a mile or two we reach the junction with the B6397, where we turn right, then after a few miles we reach a major road in the shape of the A6098 and the final short run into Kelso itself. The angle between the B6397 and the A6089 at the junction at which you have just turned right, forms part of the boundary of the policies of Floors Castle and the walls you see stretching out in either direction are the bounds of the property. The cost of building such a wall must have been astronomical. All those blocks – millions of them, all shaped by the work of masons! Floors is a mightily impressive building, open to the public at certain times. It was designed in 1718 by Vanburgh, with alterations by Playfair. It is a picture of stately elegance, often used as a set for filming purposes, and posed as 'Greystoke' in the Tarzan film with Christopher Lambert in the leading role.

There are really fancy gates connecting the grounds of the house with Kelso itself, leading into Roxburgh Street. They were erected in 1929, and have wrought iron work overlaid with gold leaf. Locally – not very surprising really – they are known as 'The Golden Gates'.

A holly tree in the grounds is said to mark the spot where James II of Scots died. The English had taken Roxburgh Castle (nothing unusual then) and the Scots laid siege to it, setting up their cannon in the grounds of what is now Floors. King James was determined to try out some of this new-fangled artillery, but unfortunately the cannon burst as it fired, killing him instantly. He was taken to Holyrood Abbey for burial, and it was left to his queen, doughty fighter that she was, to complete the job of bringing the castle securely back into Scottish control. We will come back to Roxburgh Castle shortly.

Kelso is a delightful town, with a finely laid-out square or market place. It is a town steeped in history. Mary, Queen of Scots visited it. In 1745 Bonnie Prince Charlie's army came through on their march south to Derby. In fact, legend states that Charlie's horse shed a shoe on the way, and there is a horseshoe mark in Roxburgh Street, in the middle of the road, supposedly showing the spot.

Heading towards the River Tweed, which runs to the south of the town, the ruins of Kelso Abbey stand to our left. It was founded on 3 May 1128 by King David 1 of Scotland, the man responsible for so many of the fine abbeys of Scotland. It was said that it was the most magnificent of the Borders abbeys in its day, but sadly all that really remains is one large tower. The English again. On 20 June 1523 they demolished the vaults of the abbey and its church of St Mary, fired all the cells and dormitories, and unroofed every single part of the building. As you can imagine, it never really recovered from this, although parts were in use after this date. After his father was killed by the exploding cannon, Prince James was crowned James III of Scotland within these walls, but the abbey has also seen a royal burial in its history. Henry – heir apparent to the throne of Scotland, and son of the founder, David 1, died in Roxburgh Castle and was buried within the abbey.

James VIII, the man history books refer to as the 'Old Pretender' was proclaimed King of Scots at the cross of Kelso in 1715, amid cries of 'No Union!'

I find it quite derogatory that he is called a 'Pretender' to the throne, when he was in fact rightful heir to the crown of Scotland, but religion got in the way somewhere, and the crown was given to an alien race. Pretender? I think we should kick that in to touch. How can a direct descendent of the line of Kings of Scots since the dawn of time be ousted by Germanic stock and then called Pretender? Propaganda plays its part.

The bridge across the River Tweed down past the abbey was built by Rennie between 1800 and 1803 at a cost of £17,802. It served as a model for his later Waterloo Bridge in London, now demolished, but two lamp-posts from the London bridge grace this Kelso one. This bridge replaced an earlier one washed away in a flood in 1797.

Just a little upstream the two mighty border rivers of Tweed and Teviot co-join, and the name of Tweed prevails for the rest of its journey to the sea. If we turn right at the end of Rennie's bridge and follow this road, cross-ing the Teviot bridge on the way, a short distance takes us to the ruins of the once mighty Roxburgh Castle. Floors Castle looks very impressive to the north. The castle sits between the two rivers – Tweed to the north, Teviot to the south. This was, at one time, not just a fortification but a bustling metropolis, and one of the four original burghs of Scotland (The others were Edinburgh, Berwick and Stirling). King Alexander III was born here in 1241, and it saw much action during the Wars of Independence, the Good Sir James Douglas taking it back from the English by disguising his men as straying cattle in the dusk to get close to its walls, before launching an ambuscade.

Roxburgh seemed to be a magnet for English aggression, and there seemed to be a constant wrangling, with England taking the castle, and the Scots trying to recapture it.

It is strange that this former town and castle is deserted today; all that serves to show its former glory are a few fragments of masonry. Even stranger is the fact that there is another village by the name of Roxburgh, still thriving, two miles away to the south west.

I have always liked Roxburgh though: its situation between the two rivers, and just the fact that so much of Scotland's story has been played out here. It is almost eerie to wander its grass-grown ruins and think of the thousands of people who have come and gone here, mere shadows left of its glorious past.

It can be difficult to park at, however, but there is a lay-by at its far end.

We now re-trace our route back to the centre of Kelso, and we take the A698 the nine miles or so to Coldstream, following the Tweed for much of the way.

We pass through the village of Birgham, a quiet sleepy little place, but it too has its fair share of an eventful past. King William the First of Scotland, known as the Lion, and several of his nobles and prelates, met with an ecclesiastical envoy from Henry II of England here in 1188, to refute the alleged supremacy of the English church over the affairs of the Scottish church. There was a convention of the Scottish Estates here in 1289, to discuss the proposed marriage between Margaret, granddaughter of the late Alexander III of Scotland and Prince Edward of England, the same Edward who, as King of England, suffered ignominious defeat at Bannockburn 25 years later. Unfortunately, poor Margaret, better known as 'the Maid of Norway', died when she reached Orkney, on the way to start her reign of Scotland, and this paved the way for Edward I of England – Longshanks – to claim overlordship of Scotland, and start the wheels in motion that led to the Wars of Independence.

But this little village is best known for the Treaty of Birgham, drawn up in 1290 to establish the details of Scotland's independence in the face of aggression from English Edward. It stated that the 'Scottish Kingdom should be separate, apart and free in itself without subjection to the English Kingdom'. Would that the spirit of the men responsible for the drafting of this document were here today.

As we come level with Birgham, the Tweed becomes the border with England, so it is that country that you see on the other side of the river from here on eastwards.

A little further and we come to the junction with the A697, the main route north to Edinburgh from this part of the borders – famed for its plethora of police speed cameras – but we turn right to drive the mile or two into

Coldstream. On the outskirts of this small but widely known place, we pass
the entrance to 'The Hirsel', the private residence of Lord Home, although
there is access to the grounds. Lord Home is pronounced 'Hume', and he is
a descendent of the famous Good Sir James Douglas, mentioned elsewhere
in this work. He has in his possession the sword gifted to the Douglas by
Robert the Bruce, when Bruce was on his deathbed and was commissioning
Douglas to take his heart on crusade after his death. Why is Home pronounced Hume, I hear you cry? I believe the name has stuck simply because
when Borderers say 'I am off home', they tend to pronounce it 'hyim', and
hearing this, foreigners have thought it 'Hume'!

I have fond, fond memories of Coldstream. The first really big speech I
ever did was at the invitation of Harry Brydon of Coldstream, who asked
me to 'do' the Flodden Oration, commemorating the battle of 1513, back
in 1995. I was back here in 1996 to watch the Stone of Destiny return to
Scotland. As I stood among the trees above the bridge, waiting for the Stone
to appear, I remember spotting the plaque halfway across the bridge, right
on the border with England in midstream. I turned to some of the locals
and asked what event the plaque was for. I was informed that it commemorated Robert Burns, the famed Scottish poet, and that he visited
Coldstream, and crossed the very bridge in front of us that the Stone of
Destiny was about to cross, albeit in the opposite direction. As stated, the
plaque was right on the English border, so I enquired what the wording
on it was. 'That's far enough!' replied the locals in unison. Brilliant.
Unfortunately, it actually records that, on 7 May 1787, Robert Burns first
visited England by this route.

A tall fluted column near the bridge commemorates Charles Marjoribanks, a former MP for Berwick. It is 70 feet high, and it was erected in
1834. The original statue on top was created by Handyside Ritchie, who
has already been mentioned with regard to Selkirk, but this statue was shattered by lightening in 1873, and replaced by another, four tons in weight,
by the Border sculptor, Mr Currie of Darnick. Four tons? I always marvel at
how that was done in the days before modern cranes. These boys certainly
understood how to use ropes, blocks and tackles!

There was at one time a Cistercian priory in Coldstream, founded in
1143 by the Earl of March. It stood a little eastward of the market square,
and in 1834 many bones and a stone coffin were dug up. Legend states that
the prioress here brought back many of the bodies of the foremost that fell
at nearby Flodden, to at least have them decently buried in Scottish soil, but
not a trace of this edifice now remains.

A glance at an Ordnance Survey map will show that a mile or two north
of Coldstream stands a farm by the name of Skaithmuir. A little-known battle took place in this vicinity on St Valentine's Day, 1316. The Scots had

been besieging Berwick upon Tweed, trying to wrest it from English hands to consolidate their hold on their nation after Bannockburn two years before. The English were starving, due to the Scots' blockade of Berwick, and 80 Gascon knights among the town's garrison decided to go out foraging. They went up Tweeddale, rounding up cattle, when word was brought to the Good Sir James Douglas of their actions. He quickly rounded up a small force and set off in pursuit. He confronted them here at Skaithmuir (pronounced Skay-muir locally) and set his men up at the little ford. When the Gascons saw that he had only around forty men they immediately attacked. Douglas slew the enemy leader, and his men fought like demons. Although they faced twice the odds, the Scots prevailed. Douglas said later it was the hardest fight he had ever been in – and for Douglas to have said that, it must have been a hard fight indeed!

There is no marker relating to this action, but it is surely a tale worth the telling.

Coldstream is probably best known for the Coldstream Guards, a regiment formed by General Monk in 1650. There is a plaque on a house in Market Square stating:

Head Quarters of Coldstream Guards
1650
Rebuilt 1865

Coldstream built itself up over the centuries by its proximity to the ford over the Tweed here. It is the first real major fording place upstream from Berwick.

I have often walked down to the riverside here, at the grassy stretch between river and town, and looked over the river, not exceedingly broad here, to England. It was at this spot that the Wars of Independence began, as this is where Edward Longshanks brought his army, 'the mightiest in Christendom', over the ford to ravage and subdue poor Scotland in 1296. Many armies of invasion, something like 80 in total, have crossed these fords to try and subjugate Scotland since. It always makes me stop and think as I gaze over the rippling water, and raise my eyes to the far bank. It is as if I can see those many armed and armoured riders, plunging their horses down into the water and splashing across. But we have survived all that they could throw at us.

There is a great raised walk from here, rising high above the river to the Marjoribanks monument, but as it has no parapet, it is not for the faint-hearted.

As we head towards the aforementioned bridge over the Tweed, where the main road takes its dog-legged bend, there is an old Toll House. Marriages were performed here for eloping couples from England, Gretna

Green-style, up until 1856. We turn on to the bridge, designed by Smeaton and opened in 1766, and once more cross back over the border into England. There is a lot of the story of Scotland that has taken place on the foreign soil of the other side.

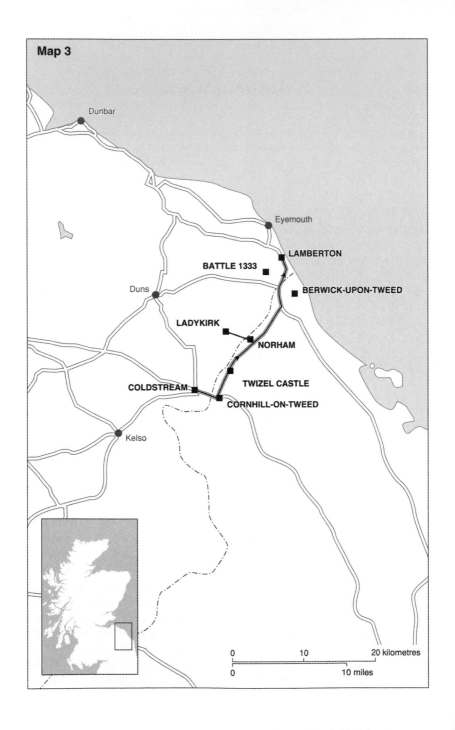

Map 3

Dunbar

Eyemouth

LAMBERTON

BATTLE 1333

Duns

BERWICK-UPON-TWEED

LADYKIRK

NORHAM

COLDSTREAM

TWIZEL CASTLE

CORNHILL-ON-TWEED

Kelso

| 0 | 10 | 20 kilometres |

| 0 | 10 miles |

CHAPTER THREE

Abroad Again

BEGINNING AT THE TWEED AT COLDSTREAM THE ROUTE EXPLORES CORNHILL, TWIZEL AND NORHAM. THERE IS THEN A SMALL DEVIATION ACROSS THE TWEED TO LADYKIRK IN SCOTLAND, BEFORE CONTINUING TO BERWICK UPON TWEED, AND ON TO THE BORDER AT LAMBERTON.

CROSSING BACK OVER the Tweed into England at Coldstream is a bitter-sweet experience. There are places just over the Border here that have had a huge impact on today's Scotland, and I love to visit anywhere that has a Scottish connection, but much of what has taken place in this northern corner of England has not been for Scotland's good.

After a few hundred yards' drive into England we come to the village of Cornhill-on-Tweed. It is distinctly English in feel and architecture, even though it lies so close to Scotland. I've just thought about that last statement. I could never imagine writing that the opposite way round. 'It looks Scottish even though it lies so close to England'. Sometimes I let my Scottish bias run away with me.

In the centre of the village there is a roundabout, and we take the A697 south, signposted 'Morpeth'. We are in rolling green fields here, the Cheviots to the southwest, but there is a ridge that sits closer, with a farm-house on its top. This is Branxton Hill. Many thousands of Scots marched over that high ridge, by the site of the later farm-house, to their deaths..

After a couple of miles a small signpost points the way down a small farm road to the right – 'Flodden Field'. This little road comes into the tiny village of Branxton. A hard right in the village takes us round to the village church. Park here and take a look up towards that farm on the ridge above. The Scots came down that slope, down towards the English army in the dip below, on 9 September 1513. They were cut to ribbons. The defeat here at Flodden Field had a traumatic effect on Scotland as a whole, but was probably most keenly felt here in the Border country, Scotland's 'buffer zone'.

There were two main reasons for the presence of the army of Scotland in northern England. The first was due to the 'Auld Alliance', the second was England's claim that they were overlords of Scotland. These reasons should be explained for the layman. As France lies to the south of England and Scotland to the north, a treaty of mutual aid had been decided upon by both France and Scotland, that if England tried to invade either country, the other member of this alliance would begin aggression against England. It was a way of trying to counter England's constant desire to force rule on its neighbouring countries. It is called the 'Auld Alliance' in Scotland as it was first signed back in 1295 in an attempt to counter the aggressive inroads upon Scotland by Edward 1 of England during the reign of John Balliol. (Whenever I mention Longshanks in this book, I would appreciate it if you would boo and hiss loudly – even if you are on the train!).

Anyway, Henry VIII of England – he of the six wives – was invading France, and the Queen of France sent James IV of Scotland a gold and turquoise ring with a plea for James to advance into England, thereby fulfilling Scotland's side of the Auld Alliance. On top of this, various English monarchs over the centuries had claimed 'overlordship' of Scotland, stating that Scotland was some sort of 'sub-nation' of England.

Robert the Bruce had forced the English to stop this claim in 1328, when they signed the Treaty of Edinburgh recognising Scotland's complete and utter independence, as is only right and proper.

But Henry VIII went back to trying to claim this overlordship, his government in fact stating that James IV was 'very homager and obediencer of right to your Highness'.

James IV was a much-loved king, very much regarded as Scotland's 'Renaissance Prince' and he gathered his army on Edinburgh's Burghmuir and marched them south. This army, once across the border, deployed on Flodden Hill, from which the battle takes its name, but when the English army under the Earl of Surrey approached and circumnavigated the Scots to the north, crossing the River Till to the east by Twizel Bridge, thereby cutting off their retreat, the Scots moved to the ridge of Branxton Hill, which towers above you now.

James IV was a chivalrous man, and marched the Scots over the brow of Branxton, giving up their strong position, to fight the English on the more level ground below. The Scots expected to fight in the Swiss style, the Swiss at this time having a very advanced grasp of military strategy. But the weaponry was wrong. And the terrain was wrong.

The Scots were armed with long spears, hoping their impenetrable hedgehog of points would have them advancing right over the English army below. It had been very rainy that September, and they struggled to keep their feet and formation down that escarpment. One man falling would have been enough to cause several of his fellows to trip and slide, and carrying long spears meant that the Scots depended on a united front.

They hit the English front ranks in disarray, and the English were armed with a weapon known as the 'bill' – a six-foot spear with an axehead and a hook projecting just below the tip. With these they were able to pull down the Scots' long spears, or cut the points from them. They began to scythe their way through the Scots ranks – and the Scots fell like corn.

Many Scots threw down their long spears and drew their swords. But where the spears had proved too long to be effective, their swords were out-reached by the bill and they were slashed and cut where they stood. Nightfall gave some Scots the chance to escape the carnage, but the losses had been terrible.

Somewhere in the middle of this, King James IV of Scots fell, pierced by many arrows and one hand hanging by a strip of flesh. He was surrounded by a pile of the cream of Scotland's chivalry, and countless thousands of the common men of Scotland, who had been surrounded and fought till the fatal blow came. James's body was found the following morning and car-ried into the little church at the north end of the field. And here you turn, and walk the few yards into little Branxton church. Some of the building is the original where James's body was carried, but later work has been sym-pathetic and it has the feel of the centuries about it. Exiting the church, I find my eyes are constantly drawn to that ridge above. I can see my coun-trymen marching in phalanx over that edge, and they looked directly towards Scotland as they did so, only a few miles to the north.

The Eildons, that indomitable symbol of the borders, are visible to the northwest. I try to envisage their emotions as the Scots surged forward, over the edge with their enemies arrayed below.

Dying in sight of Scotland, but not upon its soil.

The dead were buried in mass graves. One stands to the west of Branxton Church here, and another is to the west of the battle's memorial. To reach this memorial continue a little further along the road you are on. A car park appears on your left, with a pathway beyond that, which takes you up to the cross that marks the battle. There are information boards here, and you are looking over the main area of conflict.

The aforementioned grave pits are visible in aerial photographs. A whole generation of Scots manhood, here for eternity. Flodden has a feeling to it. Apart from the effects of farming, the landscape looks very much as it did on the day. I can't explain it, but it has that certain something where you can feel that dramatic events took place here.

If you return into the village from the monument, then take the little farm road off to your right, just past the phone-box, which leads up towards the edge of Branxton Hill, you will find that just before the real climb up to the summit, there is a slight dip where a little stream runs. Here on your right was where the greatest carnage of the battle occurred. Here is where James IV of Scotland died, within a spear length of the English Earl of Surrey.

Surrey was granted the title 'Duke of Norfolk' for his victory. His coat of arms includes a Lion Rampant, sawn off at the waist, an arrow piercing its mouth. This is how James IV died, an archer at Surrey's shoulder letting fly into James's yelling mouth as he tried to take out the enemy commander as a last-gasp effort.

This is a huge insult to my people. No Scots family has a coat of arms that insults England in such a way. There is no chivalry in such a gesture.

James' remains were embalmed and taken south. All we know of him now is that his head is buried under the building which stands at 2–12 Gresham Street in London – the former site of St Michael's Church of Wood Street, demolished in the very early 1900s.

I covered some of this in my book *A Passion for Scotland*. The ring sent to him by the Queen of France, along with the weaponry that James bore, is now within the College of Arms in Queen Victoria Street in London, the headquarters of English heraldry.

If you want to read about Flodden in depth, the best I can recommend is Niall Barr's *Flodden 1513*. It lays it all down in an academic, but readable, style.

I'm afraid you are going to have to retrace your route here, the few miles back to the roundabout at Cornhill-on-Tweed, to continue our journey. At this roundabout, you are turning right, eastwards, on the A698.

Just after you pass the Tillmouth Castle Hotel entrance on a tight left-hand bend, the road dips to the modern bridge over the River Till. Just after the bridge there is an in-shot to your left with enough space for several vehicles. Pull in here, and you will see that next to the modern bridge you have just crossed, just a few feet downstream is the old bridge over the Till, known as Twizel Bridge. This is the actual bridge that the English under Surrey crossed to circle round to the north of the Scots at Flodden. Have a walk across. It is not very wide. A couple of horses abreast, or a cannon, is as much as it will take at a time. Surrey crossed here with the full force of his army.

If only James's chivalric nature would have let him contest the crossing of this bridge down in the dip, the Scots would have won the day. His commanders beseeched James to let them do so, but he would not give his Royal command.

The rest we know, so I find it quite thought-provoking to walk westwards over this arch of stonework over the River Till, as that full army did in 1513, and think of chances wasted, and a generation of Scotland's finest gone.

Through the old gate-posts where you have parked, a path follows the river, and another strikes directly uphill. The uphill path leads to Twizel Castle, standing high on a wooded crag, towering above the river. Alternatively, if you are lazy and want to get 'your feet less dirty', as we say in Scotland, you can drive on a little, take the next left, and it will take you up to within a field's length of the castle. A castle has stood here since ancient times, in this very defensible position in the angle of the Rivers Till and Tweed, to protect England from marauding Scots.

There is a little wooden sign on the outside wall of these ruins stating 'Twizel Castle 1312'. But although there is some ancient stonework inherent, it seems that this impressive pile is mostly a folly dating from the late 1700s or early 1800s, built by later owners of the land, and apparently owned today by the nearby aforementioned Tillmouth Castle Hotel.

It is worth a look though. Wish I had that sort of money to spend on a house – never mind a sham castle!

Back on the A698, continuing eastwards, another few miles and you will see a road leading off left, signposted Norham. Take this road down to the village itself. But before we take a look at Norham, if you take a left in the village, taking the road signposted Swinton, there is a bridge over the Tweed here that takes us over again into Scotland. Sorry to be a bit complex, but it's worth it, trust me.

The bridge you cross was built in the late 1800s, replacing a wooden one built on stone piers in 1839. Before that, it was just a case of wading or riding across and hoping for the best. Many famous names from history have done just that. Malcolm IV, Robert the Bruce, William the Conqueror, Edward Longshanks (hiss!), John Knox, Oliver Cromwell, Sir Walter Scott and Sir Robert Carey, who, on the death of Elizabeth I of England, rushed north to tell James VI of Scotland that he was now ruler of England too.

Certainly something to think about as you look over the river here. I don't suppose that high bank that skirts the Scots side has changed much since Robert the Bruce took a soaking here.

Driving uphill at the far side, you come to a crossroads, a stone well in the form of a fountain, erected for Queen Victoria's fiftieth year on the throne (sigh!) standing on your right, and right is the direction we turn, to reach Ladykirk Church.

The ford in the river below is the reason for the existence of this church. James IV of Scotland, he who was slain at Flodden in 1513, crossed the river here in 1496 and 1497, and on one of those occasions he was swept away and almost drowned. He vowed to build a church dedicated to the Blessed Virgin of the Steill who had ensured his survival (a steill is a pool where salmon nets are placed) and that this church would be safe from fire and flood. So this stone church was constructed to be impervious to fire. The stone roof is amazing.

The fact that Norham Castle is visible from here, and it being the principal English castle of the borderland, and that this is a church whose fabric would be impervious to burning, of course had nothing to do with it!

The name has been shortened to Ladykirk, and other than the amazing fabric of this ancient building, it has some interesting bits and pieces inside. There is a bust of James IV and his three children by Handyside Ritchie, a sculptor mentioned elsewhere in this book, and there is an ancient chest, known as a 'mort chest', which came from St Nicholas' Church in Liverpool. It is covered in carvings.

From here we re-cross the bridge into England and Norham. Take a look at the old church here – St Cuthbert's. It was built at the same time as Norham Castle, which dominates the village, the castle sitting on a high bank to the east. It was the same architect that was responsible for both, and both were begun around 1165. The church sits between the village and the Tweed.

It was, I am ashamed to say, within this church that John Balliol (King Of Scots 1292–6) did homage to Edward Longshanks of England. Although Robert the Bruce managed to overturn all these claims of England's in the stipulations of the Treaty of Edinburgh in 1328, the church here is not slow in mentioning Balliol's shameful oath-taking. Robert the Bruce actually used this church as a base during his siege of Norham Castle in the 1320s. It was during this siege that England suddenly had enough of Scottish inroads, and capitulated, recognising Scotland's right to freedom. Doesn't mention that in the church's literature though!

There is an interesting knight's tomb within the church which dates from around 1300. The effigy was actually found when the old mud floor of the church was cleared out, and it was placed in the wall niche that was presumably its original position.

The village of Norham has an ancient feel to it, and the lines of the current buildings obviously follow the lie of the medieval version. On the village green stands an old market cross, strangely shaped, and the stone of it worn by weather and age.

This takes us on to the castle itself. Although ruined, Norham Castle still looks strong and impressive. Its massive square keep is guarded by a ravine on one side and a moat on its others. It must have looked very daunting when it was at the height of its power. It was of course built to cow this part of the border, and it was built here frowning across to Scotland as a symbol of England's might.

Norham Castle's real Scottish connection comes from the fact that the first great War of Independence both started and finished here. Edward Longshanks made it his headquarters in 1291,when he came north to pick John Balliol as Scotland's king, tricking the people of Scotland into accepting his terms. Robert the Bruce was besieging the place when the English gave in to his demands for Scotland's right. Bruce had annexed northern England as far south as the Humber in the east and Preston in the west, and Norham was one of the few fortresses that managed to hold out against the inroads of the Scots. This shows the strength of the place. It should be stated that Bruce and his men knew what a hateful odious thing it was for one country to have a hold over another, and incursions south were only done to try and bring England to the negotiation table to recognise Scotland as a nation state. It was never the intention to conquer and consolidate.

Strange as it may seem, Norham was controlled by the Bishops of Durham, and although it was damaged several times by Scots cannon, the Reformation is what hastened its end, the church control of this fortress slipping away in 1559 and it was left to moulder to the present ruin.

Much of Scotland's misfortunes at the time of Wallace and Bruce, were planned at Norham. It is this which holds a strange attraction for me when wandering the place. Longshanks plotting to make Scotland the northern extension of his domain. As he sat at table here making his plans, he was probably unable to foresee that Scotland would prevail in the end.

Onwards, and we carry on eastward past the castle till we again reach the A698, and we turn left, heading for Berwick-upon-Tweed, and the east coast.

There is much suburban sprawl at this side of Berwick, industrial estates and such like, so when we cross the course of the A1, the great north-south route, at a roundabout, we just follow the signs for Berwick Town Centre, and we enter Berwick proper by crossing the road bridge over the Tweed. The river has widened considerably here, ready to discharge into the saltwater of the North Sea. Berwick is supposedly an English town today, a strange deviation of the border swinging northwards round the town, but Berwick will always shout Scotland to me. It looks Scottish. It's on the Scots side of the Tweed. It stands on its hillside looking over that southern vista that is England, and as I cross that river into the town, I know when I reach the northern bank I am in Scotland.

Scotland has a 'feel'. Berwick is Scottish.

The late great Nigel Tranter wrote of Berwick: 'During the war years, how often I watched homing servicemen rise from their train-seats, to peer forward at approaching Berwick-on-Tweed, and blink – that is, when I was clear-eyed enough to observe them'.

He knew. They knew. I know. It just is.

Berwick is a walled town, and a walk along the Elizabethan walls is probably the best way to take it all in. And you will not fail to notice that the strongest of these defences face north – towards Scotland. There are other older walls in Berwick too, built by Longshanks after he committed the worst atrocity ever seen in the island that contains Scotland, England and Wales. At the very top of the town stands the railway station, and the platforms stand right in the core of the medieval castle. The Victorian era was not a great one for conservation, and much of the castle was swept away to make room for the tracks to go through. As you cross the station footbridge and descend to the far side, you will see a large sign hanging from the roof announcing that this was the site of the castle's great hall, and it was here that Edward Longshanks chose John Balliol to be King of Scots. Across from this side of the station stands what remains of the castle, with the original stone walls running right down to the Tweed.

John Balliol became King of Scots in 1292. But Longshanks started to browbeat him, and demanded that the army of Scotland should go and fight in England's continental wars. In reply to this affront, the Scots entered into an alliance with France – the Auld Alliance.

Edward of England decided that the Scots should be taught a lesson. He brought the army of England north. It should be remembered that at this time, the army of England was regarded as being the most efficient fighting machine in Christendom: veteran troops with experience ranging from the Crusades to continental wars.

Edward Longshanks brought this force over the fords at Coldstream, then marched it downstream to Berwick. The Dragon Banner was unfurled. This meant that no mercy would be shown.

His seasoned troops smashed through the flimsy earthworks at the first assault.

Killing commenced.

Berwick was at this time the largest town in Scotland. Glasgow and Edinburgh were mere hamlets in comparison. Berwick was the home to probably something like 18,000 souls. It did huge trade with continental Europe in sheepskins and Celtic art amongst other produce, and it is said that in a single year, exports at Berwick could amass as much wealth as a third of the ports of England combined. Covetous eyes of Englishmen often turned north in the direction of Berwick, and England's kings were not the hindmost in this.

The slaughter of the inhabitants continued unabated for three days. It is reckoned some 15,000 died. Men, women and children. On the third day it was reported that Longshanks saw one of his men cut a woman's throat while she was actually giving birth. Apparently this was too much even for that Crusade-hardened individual, and the slaughter came to a stuttering halt.

The castle held out a little longer before surrendering on terms offered – terms which Longshanks promptly ignored. The castle's governor, Sir William Douglas, was led south in chains. His son grew and never forgot, and for years the Good Sir James, the Black Douglas, would take a terrible revenge on the northern shires of England.

It was after this terrible slaughter and a triumphal march through Scotland that Longshanks had the nobility come to Berwick to sign a document under duress, swearing fealty to him. This document has ever since been known as the 'Ragman's Roll' due to the state of the downtrodden Scots who were forced to sign it. It is from this document we get the word 'rigmarole', meaning something time-consuming and worthless. The fact that the streets of Berwick were full of stinking corpses was to paint an indelible picture on the minds of the attending Scots of what defiance to England entailed.

So worked the mind of Edward Longshanks.

He had Berwick resettled with many English incomers, along the same lines as Hitler's policy of *lebensraum*, or living space, whereby the indigenous population was turfed off their land for foreign incomers.

Berwick was to be recaptured by the Scots, and it changed hands several times before England managed to hold it fast in 1482 during the reign of Richard Crookback.

The population of Berwick today is around the 12,000 mark, so the place has never really recovered from the works of Edward Longshanks more than seven centuries ago.

A lady, Wendy Wood by name, was very active promoting complete separation from England during the mid 1900s. One of her ploys comprised uprooting the 'England' sign from its position a few miles north of Berwick and having it re-sited midway across the bridge over the Tweed. It did not remain there long, but she made her point. It is a pity Wendy did not live long enough to see Scotland start to take its first faltering steps toward self-respect with a form of parliament being put in place.

It sickens me to see Berwick as an English town today though. It just means that Longshanks' plans came to fruition. I don't want him to have that satisfaction, even in death.

Three bridges span the River Tweed, in the centre of Berwick. Highest is the Royal Border Bridge, carrying the railway south from the castle site, next is the 1928 bridge built to carry what was at that time known as the 'Great North Road', and furthest downstream is the 'James VI' bridge. It is so-called because when James VI inherited the throne of England on the death of Elizabeth I, he crossed the shoogly old wooden bridge here on his journey south. It so terrified him that he instructed that a new bridge should be built, and this bridge is the result. It is a beautiful bit of engineering, comprising 15 sturdy arches, and it is no less than 1,164 feet in length. You can still drive across it, and it would be a great way to enter Scotland, but you can now only drive across it in a southerly direction.

There is much worth seeing in Berwick. For example, the Town Hall, which stands in the centre of the town's main street, Mary Gate, and the old barracks designed by Vanbrugh.

In the northeast of the old town, hard against the walling, there is a broad dead-end street, almost a square, named Wallace Green. It is believed that this is where one of Sir William Wallace's limbs was displayed in Berwick after his shameful murder in London. There is a church called St Andrew's in this street, and many places with a Wallace connection have a St Andrew's church. St Andrew is, of course, the Patron Saint of Scotland. For example, the Wallace family were said to have originated in the Welsh Marches of England in a little town called Ness, and the name Wallace is simply old Scots for a Welshman.

Several generations of Scottish birth on, William was born, but I was surprised to find that the tiny ancient church in Ness is called St Andrew's. An omen for the future of the Wallaces perhaps? Many is the time I have parked the bike up for a while in Wallace Green and cast my mind back to the time when a cart came from the south, carrying a grisly memento, ready for it to be nailed up in an attempt to humiliate the memory of Scotland's great hero. But it will take much more than the smallmindedness of Edward Longshanks to debase the memory in Scots minds of William Wallace.

Berwick's importance in Scotland's history can perhaps be emphasised by remembering it was one of the original four burghs. The other three were Roxburgh, Stirling and Perth.

I have noticed that the Saltire is often displayed in Berwick, and Scottish insignia is much in evidence. The underlying mentality seems to be Scottish too. Hopefully the day will come when we welcome Berwick back into the fold. Scotland's southeasternmost town.

Driving through the Scotch Gate in the walls, and up past the railway station with its castle ruins, the road forks. The right-hand road is signposted Edinburgh, the left Duns. Take the Duns road and drive through the suburbs of the town, and eventually the A1, north–south route is reached. Go directly across here, and you will see signs pointing the way to Halidon Hill. As you turn right up the hillside, there is an in-shot in to your left where there is a car park and an information board.

There is a superb view over the town of Berwick from here, with the sea stretching beyond. The coastline of northeast England stretches to infinity. It is a pity that such a nice view is marred by the fact that a Scots army took a heavy defeat on this spot in 1333.

It was a defeat caused by stupidity, and a lack of understanding of the lessons taught by the late King Robert Bruce, who had died only four years before. Bruce would never risk a single Scot's life and, with the English numbering ten in population for every one Scot, knew the folly of open confrontation unless the ground itself was capable of being an ally.

Although England had signed various peace treaties recognising Scotland's sovereignty, again they sent an army north to assail Berwick. Such a rich picking just across the border seemed to be too much for them to bear. As they began to besiege the town, the Scots, under their new regent, Archie Douglas, younger brother of the Good Sir James, raided into England in the hope that the English would lift their siege, to return to protect their homeland. But the English hardened their hearts and continued with the job in hand. The Scots turned north again, and the English army deployed atop this Halidon Hill, where you now stand.

For some unbelievable reason the Scots made a frontal assault up the hillside directly up the slope where this car park is today. The English had become masters of the longbow, six feet of yew firing yard-long shafts tipped with steel. The shafts began to fill the sky as the Scots marched stolidly up this hillside, a forest of spears, emulating Bruce at Bannockburn, but Bruce had destroyed the threat from the English arrow first. The hail of shafts grew stronger, and it was said the Scots turned their faces away as if they were marching into a storm of sleet.

The schiltroms (the name for a hedgehog-like body of spearmen) began to deteriorate under this hammering, the lines buckling before they could even make contact with their foes. The carnage became terrible, the schiltroms suddenly collapsed, and the English heavy cavalry charged, the Scots unable to form a cohesive defence. Douglas was mortally wounded. Six earls of Scotland died, along with 70 barons, 500 knights and squires, and countless numbers of nameless spearmen. It was said that there were only twelve English archers and two horsemen killed.

Oh Scotland. Why did you not attack them piecemeal around Berwick's walls? England has always been the larger and richer country, and the chivalrous way of the open battlefield confrontation was always going to be a useless option for Scots, no matter how valorous.

The English took Berwick, and it would be years before Scotland won it back. The knowledge of Halidon Hill tempers the view here out over the surrounding country, and can dim the fair prospect laid out before you. From here I climb back aboard my bike, the engine fires up, and I continue up and over the hilltop, the road curving right, dropping to join the A1, where you turn left to the north. A few hundred yards east as you drive north, the cliffs drop away and the expanse of the North Sea dominates. A mile or two further north on this main road, a lay-by appears on your left, at an area known as Lamberton Toll. There is a sign here, feeling a few miles out of place to my senses. Again, it has one word upon it.

'Scotland'.

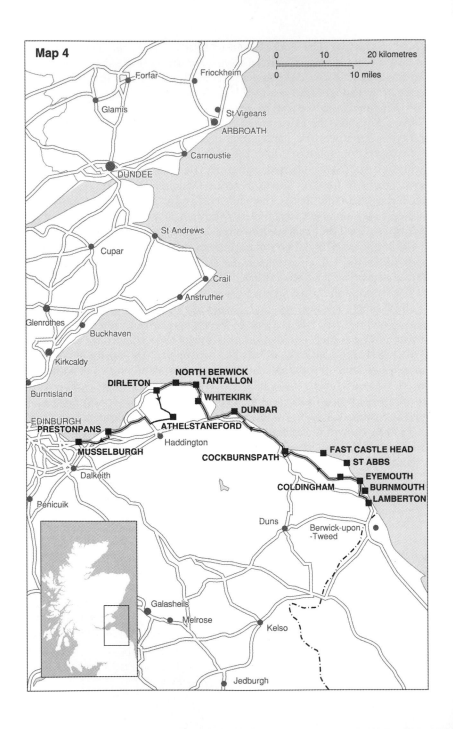

Map 4

| 0 | 10 | 20 kilometres |
| 0 | | 10 miles |

Forfar
Friockheim
Glamis
St Vigeans
ARBROATH
Carnoustie
DUNDEE
St Andrews
Cupar
Crail
Anstruther
Glenrothes
Buckhaven
Kirkcaldy
Burntisland
NORTH BERWICK
DIRLETON **TANTALLON**
WHITEKIRK
DUNBAR
EDINBURGH
PRESTONPANS **ATHELSTANEFORD**
Haddington
MUSSELBURGH
COCKBURNSPATH **FAST CASTLE HEAD**
Dalkeith **ST ABBS**
EYEMOUTH
Penicuik **BURNMOUTH**
COLDINGHAM **LAMBERTON**
Duns
Berwick-upon-
-Tweed
Galasheils
Melrose
Kelso
Jedburgh

CHAPTER FOUR

Cliffs and Castles

FROM LAMBERTON THE ROUTE GOES THROUGH BURNMOUTH, EYEMOUTH TO COLDING-
HAM. THEN THERE IS A SMALL DEVIATION OUT TO ST ABBS HEAD BEFORE MOVING ON
THROUGH COCKBURNSPATH, DUNBAR, WHITEKIRK, TANTALLON, NORTH BERWICK,
DIRLETON, ATHELSTANEFORD, PRESTONPANS AND MUSSELBURGH.

UP NORTH ALONG the A1 then. The North Sea off to your right, road and railway squeezed in along the cliff tops. I have always liked roads that run along cliff tops. Even as a very small child I can remember the attraction, and I still find myself constantly glancing over, thereby being a danger to every other road user. More of a danger to myself I suppose. As a motorcyclist I'm definitely going to come off (literally) second-best.

There is some astonishing scenery in southeast Scotland, with a magnificence and rawness of nature that I suppose most Scots don't realise exists. The best way to see it is to watch for the junction ahead that is marked 'Burnmouth and coastal route'. Taking this right turn will reveal some of this scenery to you.

Burnmouth is a delightful little fishing village standing at the foot of sandstone cliffs. It has been in existence a long time, this little place, as there were two treaties signed here between Scotland and England – the first in 1384, the second in 1497. Strange to imagine the representatives from each nation arguing their viewpoints here. Wonder if they went for a drink together afterwards – or did they keep to their own respective camps? The quality of the alcohol available would probably have been very good though, as the cliff-girt seaboard of this part of Scotland has always been famous for its smuggling.

We continue on along this coastal route, the A1107, and it is not long till we reach Eyemouth. This coastline has few places capable of building a reasonable sized port due to the cliffs, but here the Eye Water enters the North Sea, giving the town its name, and breaching the buttressed coast, allowing this settlement to spring up.

When you hit the roundabout on the outskirts of town, turn to follow the winding road through the ship berths of the harbour towards the sea. Once through the spread of modern housing, we reach the old town of Eyemouth, all climbing streets and twisty alleyways. It is quite a big wee place – if you get my drift! Looking across the harbour there is a very prominent house on the far bank of the Eye Water, a squat grey mansion by the name of Gunsgreen House. It was built by a member of the Home family – already mentioned as notable land owners in the border area. It is a strange situation for a palatial residence, built directly above the bustle of the harbour, with a steeply dropping frontage to the water. Obviously the laird wished to keep an eye on the comings and goings of the port below! I can imagine that when this house was built, there must have been many mutterings in the village, and much umbrage taken at this intrusion into people's personal concerns, but I suppose over the years Gunsgreen House has become part of Eyemouth's identity, and certainly when I picture Eyemouth, the harbour with Gunsgreen standing in the background springs to my mind. Perhaps the Home laird, knowing the amount of smuggling that went on in this area, wanted to stamp it out – or perhaps he wanted his fair share of the trade!

There is a headland to the north of the town, known as the 'Fort', where you can still discern a series of grassy mounds. These were actually built by the English in 1547, to guard the town's use as a supply depot for yet another attempted invasion of Scotland. This invasion culminated in the Battle of Pinkie, which we will deal with later. Oliver Cromwell also strengthened these fortifications whilst trying to bring Scotland under his control. Cromwell and his Parliamentarians had toppled the monarchy in England, culminating in the execution of Charles I. He wished to bring Scotland in on this design too, but the Scots were not so enamoured at having a Stewart king executed, even though this one was London-based. He was of the old royal line of Scotland and opposition was strong. Cromwell is not remembered with much gusto north of the border.

As Berwick was under English control by this time, Eyemouth was the first 'Scottish' port heading north up the east coast, and we can see how their attention jumped a little further north once Berwick was taken, encroaching further into Scots' territory. While up here at the Fort, this may be the best time to appraise you of a terrible episode in Eyemouth's past.

While the local fishing fleets were out at sea on 14 October 1881, a terrible storm hit. The vessels tried to reach the harbour, below you here at Eyemouth, and safety from the mountainous seas. The storm broke masts and tore down rigging. Many boats capsized, and more still were driven onto the cruel, jagged rocks, dangerous even on the calmest of days, which are scattered along this seaboard.

One hundred and ninety-one men were drowned. One hundred and twenty-nine of these lived in Eyemouth itself. One hundred and seven of these men were married and left that many widows, and three hundred and fifty-one children under the age of 15 were left fatherless. All those men lost from a town whose whole parish only contained 2,800 souls. For weeks afterwards families searched this savage coastline looking for the broken bodies of their menfolk. A memorial stands in the town to their memory.

Back out to the A1107, and it is only three miles to Coldingham, a place of no little importance since recorded history began. Coldingham sits in a little dip and you are basically in the place before you realise it, if you see what I mean. There are some brilliant old dwellings here, built long before the ideals of modern planning, and the place is much the better for it. At the northern side of the village is an area called the Boggan, which has some of the most picturesque older houses.

You will notice that the houses in the east coast of Scotland bear a feature that you do not see elsewhere in the kingdom: red pan-tiled roofs. Pan tiles are heavy, shaped slates, quite unlike the grey slate you see on roofs elsewhere in Scotland. These red roofs are a very attractive feature, and are due to this area of Scotland's proximity to the Low Countries. For many centuries, ships sailed from this coast, and from the Forth and Tay estuaries, carrying goods made in Scotland, and great loads of wool and sheepskins too, to the ports of Holland etc. To ensure a safer journey home, the ships' captains would buy a load of these red pan-tiles to give the ship a bit of ballast, as they were cheap and plentiful, and did the job. Back in Scotland they would sell them off. Hence the red roofs in these parts of Scotland.

The reason for Coldingham's fame is its priory. Sadly, only vestiges remain of its former glory. It was founded in 1098 by King Edgar of Scotland, son of Malcolm Canmore and St Margaret. Alas, Edgar became king with aid from William Rufus of England, son of the William the Conqueror of 1066 fame, and he fought beneath the banner of St Cuthbert. So, while the priory was sited in Scotland and often endowed by Scottish kings and nobles, the English appropriated a great part of its extensive revenues. In 1509 it was finally wrested from English control and placed under the care of Dunfermline Abbey. Unfortunately, it was badly damaged at the Reformation in Scotland in the 1560s, and it was further damaged by Cromwell in one of his further incursions into Scotland. The old choir of the place was patched up in 1855 for use as the local parish church, and this is the pretty mundane building that graces the site today. There are things worth looking out for however. A strange wall crosses the churchyard, constructed from medieval grave slabs of either churchmen or knights, and probably both. These old slabs used to lie flat over burial places, but they have been erected upright to create this wall, which also contains some old gravestones with skull and crossbones inscribed upon them, and it has some old piscinas too. Piscinas are carven stone bowls for holding water to cleanse the hands, or holy water for services. It comes from the Latin, same root as Pisces – as in fish, as in water.

(For those in the know I don't mean to be insulting by pointing this out, but too many times I see words used when I am reading and I don't know what they mean, or writers will leave a passage as it is written in Latin or

French, assuming the readers can understand, and in my case this generally means having to look up a translation, so I'm saving you the trouble)

The rest of the priory ruins have been tidied up and landscaped, and the old well still exists too, covered by an iron grating. The priory is right in the centre of the village at a tight bend in the road. It is signposted, so it should be easy to find.

If you carry on down the road that forks at the priory, the B6438, it takes you down to St Abbs, about a mile distant. St Abbs is a tiny wee place, a few interesting hotels and guest houses, with its church on a little hilltop slightly inland.

Although Coldingham has its ancient priory, there was an even older establishment hereabouts from which St Abbs takes its name. St Abba or, sometimes, Ebba was a daughter of an early king of Northumberland, and she founded a monastery here where she resided till her death on 25 August 683. It is said that St Cuthbert himself came north from Durham to visit her in 661, when he walked into the sea till it reached his neck and stood there in prayer. Legend states that the seals swam in to nestle at his sides. 'Chilly' is the word that springs to my mind. The vikings later came to sack and pillage these coasts and as they approached St Abbs in their fearsome longships, which for years were the scourge of Scotland's coasts, the nuns here, to preserve their honour, cut off their noses and lips so that the Northmen would not find them attractive. This too of course is legend, but the thought of it still disturbs me, even more so that the story may be true, and their belief may have given these women the strength to commit such acts upon themselves.

Driving uphill out of St Abbs, back towards Coldingham, there is a little road branching off to your right just where the road takes a dog-leg bend left. There is an office here for the local nature reserve, but the road continues on towards St Abbs Head, the most impressive knuckle of cliffs in all this savage seaboard. It is a very narrow single track road – in fact it is really only the supply road for the lighthouse that stands on the cliffs, so please, if you drive along it, show consideration in your driving and your choice of parking place too. To give you an idea of what's needed, I fell off my bike the last time I drove this road. A stupid lack of concentration, coupled with the astonishing scenery, and I touched the grass verge and the bike slipped down the banking. My physical strength coupled with the Honda Motorcycle Company's excellent idea of fitting protruding crash bars on the machine I drive left both me and my machine without a scratch, but you are warned as to gradients and blind corners for the next few miles.

The road climbs, only to drop again to Mire Loch, and the road twists round its head, bringing the panorama of Pettico Wick into view, far below. The loch is far above sea level, yet only a few hundred yards from the sea.

Although desolate looking now, these are the remains of seven ancient settlements in this area, so it was populated once.

From the loch's head you are looking north up the jagged coast, buttresses of cliff stretching miles into the distance.

The road rises again steeply and up onto the edge of St Abbs Head itself.
You can park here next to the entrance of the lighthouse precincts. The
lighthouse was built in 1861 and shows a flashing light every ten seconds
which is visible for 21 miles. Walk to the edge first, but please do me a
favour and don't fall over. In fact, do yourself a favour and don't fall over. It
is quite a drop – the sea wild even on the calmest days, and fangs of rock
far, far below. Wreckers used to work this coast, luring ships to their doom.
Standing here will make you understand why.

When storms whip along this coast the spray from the breaking waves
flies far inland. I don't think I would like to have a peer over these cliffs in
gale force winds; it's a slow lean forward when it's sunny and calm! This sea
and landscape are exactly what I meant when I spoke of the *rawness* of
nature unexpected in this area.

Something like 60,000 pairs of sea birds nest on the cliffs at St Abbs, and
this is why it is a protected area. Even when it is not the breeding season the
cliffs are splashed white with guano (bird shit to the layman). Just behind
the entrance to the lighthouse there is a summit that stands a little higher
than the rest, Harelaw by name. It is worth walking the extra feet to the top
where there is an indicator to go with the stupendous view, so that you
know what the various landmarks are. Some five miles to the north it is
possible to pick out the fang of masonry right on the cliff edge: the remnant
of Fast Castle, which we will reach in due course.

We have to drive carefully back the few miles to Coldingham, and follow
the A1107 onwards. We drive across Coldingham Moor, a tract of almost
6,000 acres, which was a mossy waterlogged waste in the 1700s, but has
been drained and reclaimed and brought under the plough.

At the far side of Coldingham Moor, a little unclassified road strikes off
right, leading past a transmitter mast down to Dowlaw Farm. At the road
end a path leads on to Fast Castle, below the cliffs but still perched high
above the sea. Some of the cliffs and crags here have resounding, evocative
names. Meikle Poo Craig. Black Bull. The Little Rooks. Wheat Stack.
Souter. Brander. Mawcarr Stells. All with histories of their own.

Fast Castle is merely a couple of spikes of masonry now, and is only
worth the visit for those interested in the place as an entity, or for the view.
Fast Castle is first mentioned in our history in 1333, just after the reign of
the mighty King Robert Bruce, who died in 1329. It changed hands many
times, sometimes to the English, but often between various Scottish families. It later fell into ruin, and was said to have been further badly damaged
when struck by lightning in 1871.

Sir Walter Scott wrote of Fast 'Imagination can scarce form a scene more striking, yet more appalling, than this rugged and ruinous stronghold, situated on an abrupt and inaccessible precipice, overhanging the raging ocean...'

Nigel Tranter stated 'Whoever built a castle here was undoubtedly of a strange and stormy mind.' James VI of Scotland, and later James I of England when he inherited that throne, once sailed below and stated 'The man who built it must have been a knave at heart!'

Strangely, his ancestor, James IV, who was slain at Flodden, had Princess Margaret Tudor, sister of Henry the Eighth of England, lodged here when she came north for her marriage to the Scots King. As she was only 14 and used to the gardened manors of the south of England, she must have been daunted by this strange, eyrie-like place, high above the crashing waves.

For a while Fast was the domain of the Logans of Restalrig. One of this number, Robert Logan, dwelt here during the time of James VI, and kept this part of the border in constant ferment with his catalogue of assault, murder, theft and rebellion. His is a strange and murky character, and he seemed to get away with a lot of this because he could lock his doors at Fast and ignore the laws of the land.

In 1594 Logan entered into a curious pact with John Napier, a world-famous academic, Laird of Merchiston in Edinburgh and inventor of logarithms. This compact was devised so that Napier could assist Logan in detecting treasure that was supposedly hidden somewhere within Fast.

It is a bizarre episode, with Napier being asked to 'search and seek out, and be all craft and ingenuity' to help detect this mysterious treasure. Even a jet-black cockerel was sacrificed, and as happens on a regular basis in these things, a curse was thrown in for good measure (á la Tutankhamen's tomb). This treasure hunt continued in recent times with a diviner using his skills to detect this still-undetected mysterious treasure, publishing a book on the subject, then dying suddenly.

See Fast? See mysteries?

Robert Logan's downfall came in another mystery: the Gowrie Conspiracy, a supposed murder plot to assassinate James VI, most of the detail of this plot supplied by the king himself, at Gowrie Castle. Gowrie stood in Perth, and we will visit its site in due course on our travels when we reach Perth. Logan hired a lawyer from Eyemouth, one George Sprott, to defend him. Sprott was eventually hanged as James VI did not like to be crossed. Logan died in his bed. It was as if King James just could not pile up enough evidence to nail Logan, and so hanged his poor lawyer instead.

So it's back to the A1107, and onwards. As we come towards the junction with the main route north, the A1, which we left at the Burnmouth turn-off, the road twists and turns, then crosses a pretty ordinary looking bridge. But a completely different vista is exposed if you can pull in and park and walk onto the bridge to peer over the side. The drop to the stream that runs below is quite staggering, and is partly hidden by the surrounding foliage in the summer months, so it is only when you walk out onto the bridge to look over that it becomes apparent. This is Pease Dean, the stream running out to Pease Bay, a popular beach. Pease Bridge was built in 1786, although it has been altered since, and at that time it was claimed to be the highest bridge in the world!

Before the bridge was built, the old track went down and up in a series of zig-zags. The only way for an English army of invasion, using this east coast route, to advance northwards, was to use this path crossing Pease Dean. Therefore it was often used to hold up advancing invaders. The Lammermuir Hills start to rise at the other side of this ravine, and that is difficult ground to take that many men over, so this was the preferred way for an army to march, the difficulty notwithstanding.

Cromwell passed this way in 1650, and he later reported to his parliament that this was a place 'where one man to hinder was better than twelve to make way'. It is a pity that the Scots did not make more of Pease Dean's uses, especially where Cromwell was concerned. The bridge, which crosses at the line of the old track, is 300 feet in length, 15 in breadth and 127 feet above the burn (we call streams 'burns' in Scotland) and it was long regarded as one of the most wonderful structures in Scotland.

As you turn right to head northwards towards Edinburgh on the A1, you at once cross another ravine which contains the Heriot Water. There is a viaduct here to carry the road, which again is not immediately apparent, but you will notice on your right there is a ruined tower on the edge of the ravine. Scotland is dotted with many of these fortified tower-houses, similar to Smailholm, visited earlier. Some are lived in, some are derelict, and some are ruined like this one.

There was actually trouble here when there was an argument of ownership between the Douglases and the Homes, till the Douglases turned up with 3,000 of their followers to press their case. This was in 1546. It is guessed that the tower was constructed sometime during the reign of James IV of Scotland, that is, sometime between 1488 and 1513.

We pass the village of Cockburnspath itself. In the village is an old thistle-crowned Mercat Cross, which is early seventeenth-century. The church in the village is partly fourteenth-century, and this church has a curious round tower. But we push on up the A1, and at time of writing there is sorely needed upgrading work being carried out on this route, so perhaps your journey will be quicker and less interrupted than mine, temporary traffic lights causing much delay. I'm lucky that I can generally meander past waiting queues on the bike, and be first to get away as the lights change. It can be cold and wet on the bike on long motorway journeys, but on any other type of road I would seldom be in or on any other kind of vehicle.

Another few miles, following the coast northwest, passing the bulk of
Torness Power Station en route, we come to the sign posts pointing the way
to Dunbar. As we fork off the A1 onto the A1087 which takes us through
the suburb of Broxburn towards the town centre, you may wish to pull up
and look at the height of Doon Hill, on your left and slightly behind. It is
large, over 500 feet high, and is cliff-like in aspect. A glance at the
Ordnance Survey map will show the crossed swords symbol, signifying
battle-sites, two of which are marked under the sea-facing front of this
hill. One is marked with the date 1296, the other 1650. Both are dark dates
in Scotland's history. And even worse, they marked acts of complete and
utter folly.

After Edward Longshanks of England crossed the fords at Coldstream
and sacked Berwick on Tweed in 1296, his army moved up the east coast,
very much as you have done, and laid siege to the castle of Dunbar. The
Scottish feudal host gathered at their traditional meeting place at
Caddonlea, where the Caddon flows into the Tweed, far upstream, then
they cut across country to confront the invader here. The Scots army
appeared on the top of Doon Hill, and a glance up will show you how unassailable they would have been up there.

The English forces, deployed around Dunbar, amassed and marched forward to confront the Scots. For some inexplicable reason, the Scots came
down from their height, giving up all the superiority they possessed. It was
reported that as the English army crossed the valley of the Spott Burn, the
Scots thought that they were breaking up and so attacked, but of course an
army with the experience that the English had at this time were not to be
caught so easily and re-ranked in good order to break the Scots' charge.
The nobility of Scotland was scattered, with many captured, and the ordinary foot soldiers were cut to pieces.

One of the nobility caught was a young knight called Andrew Murray,
who was taken to Chester and imprisoned there, but he was to escape and
co-command the Scots with William Wallace at Stirling Bridge the following year, 1297. In fact, it is possible that Wallace himself fought at Dunbar,
as he was soon to come to prominence in our history books.

King John Balliol fled north, only to be captured later.

I have never been able to understand how such a serious error of judgement could be made, giving up the hilltop and coming down to that
carnage. Even more staggering is the fact that it did not just happen once in
the same spot, but twice. This is why that second symbol is on the maps,
dated 1650.

Cromwell this time. Longshanks the first. Two of Scotland's great
unfriends. Cromwell's army was besieging Dunbar, and the Scots again
appeared on the height of Doon Hill. Again they gave up the advantage of
ground and came down to be cut to pieces. An unlearning process.

There is a monument to the second Battle of Dunbar in 1650, sited near your current location. It bears some words of Thomas Carlyle. 'Here took place the brunt of the essential agony of the Battle of Dunbar'. I know, I think it's a terrible inscription too. This battle was fought just at the west side of the modern A1 here, by the farm of Little Pinkerton. The 1296 battle was a mile further west where you cross the Spott Burn just before you enter the village of Spott itself.

Robert the Bruce did his best to instil in Scots the importance of prudence. You see, there have always been ten Englishmen for every Scot. There are roughly five million Scots to 50 million English. Even at the time of Bruce and Wallace the ratio was the same, 500,000 Scots to five million English. This advantage in numerical superiority, coupled with England's greater monetary wealth, was always going to weigh heavily in that country's favour during its constant aggressive inroads.

Bruce devised ways of dealing with this, and it was summed up in the rhyme *Good King Robert's Testament*

> On foot should be all Scottish war
> Let hill and marsh their foes debar
> And woods as walls prove such an arm
> That enemies do them no harm
> In hidden spots keep every store
> And burn the plainlands them before
> So when they find the land laid waste
> Needs must they pass away in haste.
> Harried by cunning raids at night
> And threatening sounds from every height
> Then, as they leave with great array
> Smite with sword and chase away
> This is the counsel and intent
> Of Good King Robert's testament

If only the later generation of Scots learned from their ancestors. We need to do this in future. Else our nation will always be serfs.

As it says on the memorial marking Bruce's heart at Melrose:

A noble heart may have no ease if freedom fails.

Carrying on the A1087 into Dunbar town centre, on our left stands the parish church. It was built in 1819–21, and replaced an earlier church founded in 1342. It has a steeple 108 feet high which serves as a landmark for mariners. Inside this church is an impressive tomb, still standing from the earlier building. This superb monument was erected to the memory of George Home, Earl of Dunbar, who died at Whitehall in London on 29 January 1611. He was a great favourite of King James VI of Scotland and I of England, and he held the office of High Treasurer in Scotland and Chancellor of the Exchequer in England.

He was embalmed, his body placed in a lead coffin, and he was sent to Dunbar 'where his executors erected a very noble and magnificent monument of various coloured marble, with a statue as large as life'. The monument is 12 feet broad and 26 feet high. The Earl is represented, kneeling on a cushion, praying, with a Bible open before him. He is clad in armour, seen under his knight's robes. Two knights act as his supporters, and above are the two female figures of Justice and Wisdom, and above again, the figure of Fame sounds her trumpet and Peace holds her olive branch. At the base of the monument is the vault which holds the aforementioned leaden coffin.

Continuing, we carry on into Dunbar's High Street. Halfway down on the right is the old Town House and Market Cross. The Town House is a quaint building, with an unusual six-sided tower, dating from 1620. In front of it is a statue in commemoration of John Muir, who died in 1914. John is regarded as being the father of conservation, and his beliefs in keeping tracts of countryside in their natural state led to our modern ideas of National Parks. He had a huge influence in the way that the United States approach their conservation. He was born in Dunbar's High Street in 1838, house number 126–8, and this property is now a museum, telling the story of his early life, and the value of his legacy for future generations.

Carry on down to the harbour, down at the sea front. At the far end of the harbour lie the now scant remains of the fortalice from which Dunbar takes its name. The word *Dun*, so often found in Scotland, eg Dunfermline, Dunbarton, Dundee, means a fortification, and in Dunbar's case it comes from the Gaelic *dun-barr*, or fort on the point. These few crumbling walls of rubble, the original facings plundered long ago for building materials, mark the spot where some of the deciding moments of Scotland's history took place. Sadly, even in the time scale since I visited Dunbar for the first time, the remains have deteriorated.

Dunbar was an astonishing place in its heyday. The castle was built on several rock stacks, connected by bridges covered by masonry. When I first came here, one of these bridges connecting two different segments still spanned the gap, but has sadly now fallen. The stonework lies in sections on the shingle below, but you can see where it has fallen from, and this will give you the general idea. You can walk up on to the stack above the harbour, but there is nothing much to see now, except fragments of ancient masonry, home now to nesting seabirds. There is a sheer drop down to the channel that forms the harbour entrance at the far side of these ruins, and I've always wanted to take the plunge over and into the water. Anybody actually looking at the drop would probably think it was madness, but it has been a hobby of mine over the years – after ensuring the water is deep enough and free of obstructions, of course!

I often meet people who don't like peering over sheer drops as they say they get the feeling they want to jump. I get that too, but in my case there is sensibly deep water below, not just the ground to break my fall.

Dunbar marks the very edge of the Firth of Forth, and from here when it is clear, you can see the opposite side of the river's mouth at Fife, many miles to the north. The castle's foundation is lost in the mists of time; we can simply say that it is a place of hoary antiquity. It was at Dunbar that True Thomas of Ercildoune – Thomas the Rhymer – made a prophecy on 11 March 1286 that ran according to the chronicles:

> Alas for tomorrow, a day of calamity, and misery!
> Before the twelfth hour shall be heard a blast so vehement as shall exceed those of every former period – a blast that shall strike the nations with amazement – shall humble what is proud, and what is fierce shall level with the ground. The sorest wind and tempest that ever was heard in Scotland!

As the next day, the 12th, was calm, the occupants of the castle were non-plussed at the dire warnings the Rhymer had given, but just before noon a rider spurred up to the castle to inform that King Alexander III of Scotland was dead. His body had been found lying at the bottom of the cliffs at Kinghorn, on the far side of the Firth, his neck broken. This was to result in the biggest calamity in Scotland's story, the death of the king paving the way for the aggression of Edward Longshanks and the Wars of Independence with England. Many bloody years of fighting would follow.

During these wars, the Earl Patrick of Dunbar often traitorously took the side of England, though after Scotland's crucial victory over England at Bannockburn in 1314, he joined the Scottish camp, obviously trying to keep his position by jumping to whatever side seemed to be gaining the upper hand. According to the minstrel Blind Harry, Wallace had given his father, the Eighth Earl of Dunbar, a hard time, he just managing to escape from Wallace's ire and vengeance for being lax in his patriotism. It is a pity that Earl Patrick did not change his allegiance a little earlier.

When it was obvious that the day was lost at the Battle of Bannockburn in 1314, and Edward II, King of England and son of Longshanks, decided it was time to run away, he did so with 600 knights packed around him in phalanx. Robert the Bruce knew that the capture of the King of England would buy Scotland its freedom from any of England's claims of overlord-ship, plus there would be a healthy ransom thrown in for good measure. So he sent the Douglas, the Good Sir James, after Edward of England with only 80 horsemen. The English knights were so demoralised, and so afraid of Douglas, that they dared not halt.

Bruce knew that although the battle had been won, there were still many thousands of Englishmen in the vicinity unbloodied, and so he could not spare the Douglas more than the valiant 80. Barbour, in his epic poem *The Bruce*, written in 1370, tells us that the English were not even able to stop to do the toilet, so sorely were they pressed by Douglas's men. They must have just peed their saddles and armour.

Anyway, the English reached Dunbar and the traitor earl allowed them entry into the castle and safety. Edward was able to take a ship south to Bamburgh Castle and English soil. At this point the earl came over to the Scottish side. If only he had handed Edward over to Scottish hands, or announced his 'Scottishness' earlier, he could have saved many thousands of lives of his countrymen, women and children.

This has always been the problem with Scotland. I'm a Scot and I know what we can be like. If we always put Scotland first, we would all live better, more comfortable lives, with dignity and a sense of duty to our fellows, but this strange part of the Scots psyche that is willing to be persuaded by Englishness has always been there – right through every era of our history. And I for one cannot understand it. I don't have a problem with the English. But I am a Scot, and I want other Scots to get a grip of themselves and realise that their nation is a result of what they feel, and how they perceive that nation to be.

There are brighter moments in the history of Dunbar Castle, though. The English again assailed the place in 1339. But the castle, and Scotland, had a worthy commander. Her name – yes, *her* – was Black Agnes. King Robert the Bruce's two great captains were the aforementioned Douglas, and the other, a great companion of Douglas too, was Thomas Randolph, the Earl of Moray (pronounced Murray) and Black Agnes was Thomas Randolph's daughter. She was the daughter of a hero and had inherited his qualities. She was a true Scot and knew where her loyalties lay. Her men called her Black Agnes because she was olive-skinned and dark-haired.

The huge English host under the Earls of Arundel and Salisbury used siege engines to hurl huge stones to try and lay low the walls of the fortress. Agnes walked the battlements, and when the stones struck she, or one of her ladies, would wipe the walls with a white handkerchief in scorn:

With a towel, a damiselle
Arrayed jollily and well,
Wippit the wall, that they micht see,
To gere them mair annoyed be
(*Wynton's Chronicle*)

The Earl of Salisbury, at vast expense and labour, had caused a war machine known as a 'sow' to be constructed. As this machine was rolled close in to the castle walls to allow its destructive work to begin, Agnes ordered her men to drop a large fragment of rock from the battlements on top of the sow in order to smash its timbers. This was done, and as the surviving Englishmen scrambled out from the debris, Agnes jeered to Salisbury that, 'his sow had farrowed!' Salisbury had later to explain his inability to take Dunbar to Edward III of England, and the chroniclers reported that he wailed 'Came I early, Came I late, I found Agnes at the gate!'

I often hear from women that have heard the story of James Douglas and his various exploits, and this coupled with his unswerving loyalty to his country, seems to have them always saying that they would like to have met him. I know it's because Douglas, seven centuries on, still has the ability to make female hearts flutter, and when you know his story, it's more than understandable. I suppose I have my own version in Black Agnes. It strikes me that I would like to have met Agnes. My kind of Scotswoman!

The English burnt the town of Dunbar in 1544, and rather than being seen to paint them in as black a light as possible, I will give an extract from their own report. I have modernised the language a little:

> We burnt a fine town ... called Haddington, with a great nunnery and a house of friars. The next night we encamped beside Dunbar. That night they looked for us to burn the town, but we put this off 'til the morning at the dislodging of our camp, the burning being done by 500 of our soldiers backed by 500 horsemen. And the reason we did this in the morning was because the townsfolk watched us all night, and seeing us strike camp and seemingly depart, thought themselves safe and had newly gone to bed. They were asleep when our men closed in, so with fire, men, women and children were suffocated and burnt.

Mary, Queen of Scots, whose tragic story has been brought to a world stage through books and film, visited Dunbar Castle three times during her career. Much of the castle was demolished by the orders of the then Regent of Scotland, Mary's enemy, in 1567. Time has not helped its condition, nor has its use as a handy quarry been in its best interests, and the building of the modern harbour has also hastened its destruction, but the people who have visited Dunbar and the events that have taken place here, still hold a magic that I, for one, can certainly perceive, its ruined state notwithstanding.

The harbour below was the place that the Redcoat troops were landed before the fateful Battle of Prestonpans in 1745, which is an event we shall come to shortly.

Back up to the High Street, and then continue westwards along the A1087, driving through Belhaven, now really a suburb of Dunbar. Belhaven is famous for its brewery, which makes traditional Scottish beers, sold all over Scotland.

We again connect with the A1 at a roundabout on the edge of town, and again we drive towards Edinburgh. After a minute or two we see the junction to the right, where the A198 runs to North Berwick. Turn onto this road, and notice the tall standing stone in the field to your right. There are many like this in this area, the whys and wherefores lost to our knowledge, but it is still great that they have survived so long. All it is is a lump of rock stuck longways into the ground. I don't know what it is, though, that attracts me to them so much. I always notice them, my brain always registers their presence, a sort of 'Aw, there's a standing stone there' goes through my mind as I pass them on my bike. Is there a magic to it? Is it the ages that it has stood there? Or is it a nod to my distant ancestors, and the fact that they once had the tenancy of Scotland, long before my time, and I can look upon this monument of theirs and acknowledge them?

On along the A198 then, nice and straight and picturesque, through the scatter of dwellings that is Tyninghame, and another two miles and we come to the little village of Whitekirk at its bend in the road.

Whitekirk has quite a story to tell. The name comes from the village church, which was painted white at some time in the past, in its long and ancient story. It is reckoned that there has been a church on this site for 1,500 years! The Christian faith was brought to East Lothian, as this area of Scotland is called, in the late sixth century by St Baldred, a Celtic monk based at Lindisfarne, and a follower of St Columba. Columba is a big name in Scottish history, being not only a Christian missionary, but a larger-than-life figure who stamped his personality across Scotland's landscape. Columba was active in Scotland from AD 563, following in the footsteps of St Ninian, our first missionary, in AD 400.

Anyway, I digress again. The church here was probably founded in Baldred's time. A rocky area of the coast nearby is actually known as St Baldred's Cradle. There was a well near the church renowned for its healing powers, but drainage of the countryside meant that the well had dried up by about 1800; to give an idea of the importance and popularity of this well, in 1413 no fewer than 15,653 pilgrims visited it!

In 1356 the English King Edward III invaded this part of Scotland, and Whitekirk was plundered. His ships had berthed on the coast nearby, and his soldiers made for this place of pilgrimage. There was an image of the Blessed Virgin inside the church, and she was adorned with jewellery left by the pilgrims. One of the English rudely plucked a gold ring from the Virgin's image, and at that moment a crucifix fell from above and dashed his brains across the floor. The chronicles tell us that when the robbers returned to their ships at the mouth of the River Tyne nearby, a vehement storm arose and wrecked their craft. This story gained widespread fame, and was talked of over Europe. There are two versions of where the story goes from there. One version tells us that a young Italian nobleman named Aeneas Silvus Piccolomini heard this story and wished to visit the church where this miracle had taken place, and when he landed in Scotland in midwinter, he decided to walk barefoot the ten miles to Whitekirk to show his devotion. The other, more believable, version tells how Aeneas was sent as an envoy to King James I of Scotland, but the English king would not give him safe conduct to pass through his realm. So he sailed to Scotland in 1435, and off the coast his ship got into difficulties. He vowed that if he could survive this ordeal he would offer thanks at the nearest church dedicated to Our Lady. When shipwrecked, Aeneas survived, and so he walked the ten miles to the church in gratitude. I don't think that the chronic rheumatism that he reportedly developed whilst undertaking this feat, that lasted till the end of his days, would have been so gratefully received! Aeneas later became Pope Pius II, so this is one church which can at least claim a visit from Il Papa!

I have been lucky during my visits to find the church unlocked, so I hope you are lucky enough to gain entry yourselves. The church was badly damaged by fire in 1914, members of the Suffragette Movement, striving for the right of women to vote, being held responsible. Repairs were carried out. The interior still retains its early stone roof, and you can easily sense the age of the place. Just to the right of the front door you will notice a very large slab. This was moved from the chancel of the church some two centuries ago and originally had a life-size figure of a churchman inscribed upon it, but weather has erased it. Take a walk around to the back of the church and notice the old building on the rise behind. This is a tithe-barn, built to house pilgrims and store grain. Surviving tithe-barns are very rare in Scotland. Part of it seems to be the remains of a fortified tower built in the times of James V of Scotland in 1537, and later extended. Round about are earlier remains, mentioned in old documents as accommodation for pilgrims. I used to drive past here in earlier years and look at this old tithe-barn lying empty, but roofed and in a tolerable state of repair, and think about what a brilliant house it would make. This has been done in the last few years, and at the very least it means this building will be saved for foreseeable future. Wish it were mine – but if wishes were money, I would be a millionaire!

Before we leave Whitekirk, I should point out that the odious Cromwell used the church here as a stable for his horses, and barracks for his men, during the siege of Tantallon in 1651. And it is Tantallon Castle we travel to next. It's just a case of continuing along the A198 to North Berwick, the road that you are already on, for another 2.5 miles. The castle will start to appear to your front right, then you will see the turnoff signposted. It is an amazing place – entirely different from every other castle in Scotland. It appears to be just one long wall with towers and a gatehouse, and that is exactly what it is. It is only as you get closer that you realise that that wall cuts off a promontory, jutting out into the sea, with no real need for other defences, the sheer drops to the sea all around the only other defence needed. But there is no mistaking the lordly power of this edifice; it was built to impress and it serves that purpose admirably. What date the first fortification was built here is unknown, and the castle first comes into our history books when the Douglas family took control of it in 1371. The badge of the Douglas family is the heart of King Robert the Bruce, carried on crusade by the Good Sir James, surmounted by three stars, and it is that emblem of the bloody heart that crumbles on the stone shield above the entrance. You will notice that most of the castles in Scotland have the coat of arms of the owners above the doorway. Some only have the rectangular space where the stone bearing this emblem has been purloined, but it is a common feature.

There was a notable siege here in September 1528, when the Earl of Angus defied the then King of Scots, James V, and that monarch turned up in person to oversee the assault, bringing many cannon with him, two in particular from Dunbar Castle, which we have already visited. These cannon gloried in the titles of 'Thrawn Mouth'd Meg and her Marrow'. King James did all in his power to take the place, but spent months at the task in vain, eventually retiring, the castle still in the Earl's hands. The king only gained control when the earl fled to England. Mary, Queen of Scots, made a visit to Tantallon in 1566.

The Scots used the castle for defiance of Cromwell. A party of horsemen based here caused havoc with Cromwell's supply lines, and in 1651 he sent 2,000 men with many cannon against it. There was a constant bombardment for 12 days before Cromwell managed to make a breach in the northwest tower, and overwhelm the 80 or so inside. The footings and earthworks to site Cromwell's cannon can still be discerned in front of the castle. After 1670 the castle was abandoned and left to decay. The interior is a maze of broken staircases, ruined chambers and deep, dismal, subterranean dungeons. Much of the fabric is hollowed like a honeycomb, due to the influence of the climate over the centuries on the ancient stonework.

Just off the coast here is the Bass Rock, a stupendous rocky islet that you cannot miss! It rises 313 feet out of the sea, one and a quarter miles off shore. It has served as a prison in its time. St Baldred, mentioned elsewhere in this chapter, died here in AD 756. The fortifications which once stood here were demolished in 1701, but there are still scant remains. The Bass is notoriously difficult to land on, even in the finest weather, and it is home to one of the biggest colonies of gannets on the planet. It's spectacular to watch these birds dive from great heights, wings folded in to make them seem like missiles, as they catch fish. They are even able to judge the refraction caused by the water, and spear their catches with their beaks first time. What looks like snow on the rock is actually guano, such are the numbers who nest here.

Back out the access road, back onto the A198 and onwards another couple of miles, and we hit the outskirts of North Berwick. The most striking thing that hits you first about the place is North Berwick Law, law being the old word for a hill, and hill it very much is. The countryside around here is relatively flat, and the Law stands abrupt above it all, and it is a landmark which is discernible from many miles away, and recognisable from many miles away. It stands 613 feet high. You will notice that there are structures on the summit. One is the remains of a watchtower, like a little ruined house that dates from the time when there was war in Europe with Napoleon, and on the very top is an archway, made from the jawbones of a whale – I wonder whose idea that was!

Picture the scene, the body of a whale is washed up, and somebody thinks 'I think we should keep the bones of that whale's jaw, and carry them up the Law, and stand them upright like an arch', and the various listeners replying, 'What a great idea – let's do it!'

Actually, there are several instances I can think of offhand where I have seen whalebones used to construct an arch in Scotland. Not much else you can do with them, I suppose. There is a path running to the top of the hill, with parking places, just beside the B1347 that runs south from the centre of North Berwick. There is a fine view from the top, looking over the Lammermuir Hills to the south, to Edinburgh's Arthur's Seat in the west, and over to the Lomond Hills in Fife, on the other side of the Firth of Forth.

If we follow the A198 into the town centre until we reach Quality Street, this road will take us down towards the harbour area. Here is the Seabird Centre, a visitor attraction that also has a café and a large gift shop, but you will notice a red granite Celtic cross standing by the road. It commemorates a tragic incident that took place. Its inscription reads: 'Erected by public subscription in memory of Catherine Watson of Glasgow, aged 19, who was drowned in the East Bay 27ᵗʰ July 1889, while rescuing a drowning boy. The child was saved, the brave girl was taken.'

Right behind this monument are the scant remains of the Auld Kirk. It originally stood in a sandy islet, with arches connecting it to the mainland, but the various extensions to the harbour area have now ensured that it is firmly attached to the shore. This church gained notoriety in the witch trials of 1591 in Scotland. King James VI had sailed to bring his new queen, Anne of Denmark , back to Scotland. James VI (later also James I of England) was a bizarre individual, seeing the work of Satan, intrigues and plots in every situation. But he had a clever mind too, and this strange balance of character that he had led him to be nicknamed 'The Wisest Fool in Christendom'. As his ship sailed towards the Firth of Forth, a storm blew up which James claimed was the work of witches. Witnesses were found who testified that 94 witches and six wizards had danced in the churchyard here, to one Gelie Duncan playing the Jew's harp (I believe this little metal mouth instrument is called a jaw harp elsewhere in the world). At the trial it was stated that 'The Devil started up himself in the pulpit, like ane meikle [big] black man, and callit every man by name, and every ane anwerit "Here, Master". On his command they openit up the graves, twa within, and ane without the kirk, and took off the joints of their fingers, taes, and knees, and partit them amang them.'

It was believed that these people were responsible for casting up the storm that had so terrified King James. James was a great one for witch trials, and burnings too, and many unfortunate women met terrible ends, in the most hideous agonies, due to his interest in sorcery. It is strange that it is this man who is responsible for the Bible as we know it today, as you will notice that most fly leaves state 'King James Version' on them. Yes, the very same James VI of Scots responsible for witch burnings, translated the Bible from the original Latin scriptures. Even the Mormon Bible is the 'King James Version'. It often brings a smile to my face to think of this. So, you can stand in these scant church ruins and remember that 'the Devil started up himself in the pulpit.' I've always had a penchant for visiting sites where the great heroes of Scottish history, and even the downright bad, have stood, but this is one that stands out on its own.

North Berwick was once a very popular bathing resort before Scots discovered package holidays, and – shock! – warmer sea water abroad. But it is still famous as a golfing centre and has its attractions for me in the narrow streets of the old town, almost a throwback to the glory days when it was a popular holiday destination. The A198 runs through the town and carries on to the west in the direction of Edinburgh, and we follow it too.

A mile or two of countryside and we approach Dirleton. A road branches off to the right, runs through the village, and then re-joins the main route that we are on. Take this right turn, and passing a few houses, we come to the grassy area that is the village green. It is an idyllic little scene, and looks entirely peaceful, but turn and look to your left and you will see this sleepy place has had its fair share of a troubled past, as the ruins of once-mighty Dirleton Castle rise through the trees and shrubs in testament of this.

The castle was built in the mid-1200s by the de Vaux family, in the reign of Alexander II. It suffered a ferocious siege during Longshanks' re-invasion of Scotland in 1298, in revenge for Wallace's victory at the Battle of Stirling Bridge the year before.

Edward Longshanks' army had pushed on to Kirkliston on the other side of Edinburgh, and he left Bishop Anthony Beck of Durham (although a churchman, he was also a man of violence, as he proved on many occasions where Scots were concerned) to take Dirleton. Beck found Dirleton too tough a nut to crack, and he sent Sir John Fitz Marmaduke to Longshanks for fresh instructions. Longshanks told him 'You are a bloodythirsty man. I have often had to rebuke you for being too cruel. But now be off, use all your cruelty, and instead of rebuking you I shall praise you.' For someone of the King of England's calibre to make such a statement to Fitz Marmaduke, then this Fitz Marmaduke must have been a nasty piece of work indeed. What did Scotland ever do to deserve such treatment? Sadly, Beck managed to take Dirleton, and I feel sorry for its garrison, left to the devices of those bloodthirsty Englishmen.

Its present ruinous state is due in great measure to Cromwell – nothing funny about the fact that Cromwell and Longshanks often seem to go hand-in-hand when it comes to the black spots in Scotland's history. His cannon caused much of the present damage in 1650 when he also hung the castle's captain and some of his followers for good measure. All this aside, the castle is a pleasant place to visit, and there are some lovely landscaped grounds now surrounding its ancient stonework.

Carry on through the village till you again come to the A198. But as you turn right onto this road, you are immediately taking the first left. It is almost a staggered crossroads, only a few yards until the turnoff, signposted Drem. This road, the B1345, arrives at Drem after two and a half miles. You will notice that there is a prominent whaleback-shaped hill to the southeast (you are heading south here).

This is Traprain Law. It stands out against the backdrop of the Lammermuir Hills. This hill has remains of an early settlement on its summit. In fact, a hoard of Roman silver was found on this hill in 1919. Now known as the Traprain Hoard, it is on show at the Museum of Scotland in Edinburgh. This hill, like North Berwick Law, is a very noticeable landmark, and it has probably already been noticed on the meanderings I have taken you on. It is only fair that I told you what it was! It is 724 feet high, by the way. It scunners me that there is a quarry eating away at Traprain. Why? This is a historic site, and I'm surprised that this is allowed to take place.

Back to Drem. Now pay attention. Follow the main road through the village, and just as you pass the railway station there is a small road off to your left, signposted Athelstaneford. You cross the railway tracks, and this is a small road with some tight twists and turns to begin with. Two miles on you come to a junction with a slightly larger road, the B1343, where we turn right into Athelstaneford itself. It is a village of low cottages. Picturesque. Not very large. But it may well be one of the most important sites in Scottish history, because tradition states that Athelstaneford is where the Saltire, the beloved blue and white flag of Scotland, was born.

It is said to have happened like this. There was an army of Picts, under their king Angus, and Scots, being pursued through East Lothian here by a much larger army of Angles from the kingdom of Northumbria. Among the Picts and Scots was one Kenneth MacAlpine, who would unite both these tribes under the name of Scots in the next few years. The Picts and Scots knew they were heavily outnumbered, and the chances were that they would be annihilated in the forthcoming fight. But rather than flee and be cut to ribbons, they decided to make a stand and die like men, fighting with swords in hand. Fearing the forthcoming battle against such heavy odds, they prayed for deliverance, and to their amazement, a huge white cross appeared against the blue of the summer sky. It was the diagonal cross on which St Andrew had been crucified. The Saltire. It was a sign that God was on their side, and the Picts and Scots vowed that if victory was theirs, St Andrew would become their patron saint. The Northumbrians attacked, led by their commander, Athelstane. Heartened by the appearance of the omen in the sky, the Picts and Scots fought like men possessed, and the enemy began to fall back with much slaughter. It became a rout, and Athelstane was slain, it is said, at a ford, most probably on the Peffer Burn to the east. This is where the name of the village originated – Athelstaneford. The battle is traditionally supposed to have taken place in AD 832, though much about the event is historically uncertain.

So, from this date, the flag of the people who were very shortly all to be known under the moniker 'Scots', has been a picture of the event which took place here. The white cross against the blue of the summer sky. And for almost 1,200 years, it has gone wherever Scots have gone in the world. Not just a design on a piece of material, but a record of an event from our past, which we can all identify with, and all have a part in. Often I see examples of a dark blue hue, which is wrong, but I would rather see a wrongly shaded blue Saltire than no Saltire at all!

After the Union of the Crowns with England in 1603, James VI of Scotland and I of England tried to stamp this Union by combining the flags of Scotland and the red St George's cross of England in one unit, the Union Flag, sometimes erroneously referred to as the 'Union Jack'. This flag is actually a royal flag and has no precedent in law. But I am glad to say that its presence is diminishing, and the people of both Scotland and England are returning to their own respective flags.

To me and many of my fellow Scots, the Union Flag is a flag of oppression, and we don't just mean in Scotland. Too often it has been used in the domination of other countries, and I would rather see my people fly their own blue and white emblem, a flag that can be flown proudly anywhere on the planet without upsetting anyone.

You will notice that the Saltire flies proudly outside the little school in Athelstaneford, and I wish more schools in Scotland would follow this example, instilling a pride of place and nationhood in our youth. But the place to visit in Athelstaneford is the church on the right of the main street running through the village.

Facing the church, you will notice there is a stone memorial over to the far right in the churchyard. This inscribed stone shows the two armies, with the Saltire spreading across the sky in the background, and there is of course a flagpole flying a Saltire alongside. The earliest church here is mentioned as being built in 1178, and the current edifice dates from 1868.

The church is usually open during daylight hours, but what the visitor really wants to have a look at is round behind the church's left hand side. Here stands an old doocot (what we Scots call a dovecot, cot I suppose being short for cottage, a place where pigeons were kept for food in medieval times. There are quite a lot of these still standing, many close to castles). This particular example dates from the later 1500s. I remember being here in the early 1990s and I stuck my head through the door to absolute mayhem inside, as the place was crammed with pigeons, still living there even though the place had fallen into disuse from its original function hundreds of years before. But it is today a wee audiovisual centre. When you shut the door the audiovisual display starts and the Saltire is projected onto the roof, and a narrator tells the story. It is great that this ancient wee place has been saved and restored for this purpose. The only sad thing is that the £90,000 needed to do this was raised by public subscription. It seems that the people care, but it is shocking that Scotland the nation seems to be unable to celebrate the birthplace of her flag by using money donated by a Scottish government.

Outside the doocot is a plaque, giving a view over the surrounding fields where my ancestors adopted the symbol of my nation. I wonder if they would be surprised that it still lifts the hearts of true Scotsmen and women in the twenty-first century? Athelstaneford should be a place of pilgrimage for every Scot.

We continue westward on the B1343, a rocky ridge south of us on our left. You will see there are some low ruins on this ridge, the remains of Barnes Castle. Well, remains is not really the right word, as it is really only the basement of a house that was never completed, a house begun by Sir John Seton, Treasurer for King James VI. He died in 1594 and building work ceased. As it is only the vaulted basements that stand, it is known locally as the 'vaults'.

A mile further, after a tight bend at a little ridge over a burn, there are the ruins of another castle among farm buildings. This is Garleton, built in the late 1500s by Sir John Seton of Garleton. Only the east and north walls remain with a round corner tower. Cross straight over a junction here, still following the ridge. On the end of this ridge there is a tall chimney-like structure, and this is a monument to the fourth Earl of Hopetown. If you wish, you can park and walk up the path to the summit and view this monument.

Just after this monument you come to the junction with the A6137, and here you turn right, towards the north. A mile and a half further and you come to a roundabout, and here you turn left on to the B1377, and we head the few miles to Prestonpans. We drive through the village of Spittal, and just after you will notice the tower of Redhouse Castle. It was built around 1600 by James VI's 'Keeper of the Signet'.

At Longniddry we join a more major route, but we continue straight on, still heading for Prestonpans. Two miles more and we hit a roundabout on the edge of Prestonpans itself, and we drive straight through. Just after this roundabout you will notice a squat large cairn on your right. All it has carved upon it is '1745'

Cairns are the traditional way of marking events or occasions in Scotland. In a country with much stone, it was obviously the sensible thing to do. Stones would be piled up to create a marker of sorts. Originally they would just be piled up, but in later years dressed stone was used, or at least cement was used to construct something more permanent out of the local stone. This particular cairn marks the Battle of Prestonpans, and obviously the date was 1745. The '45 is what it is generally called in Scotland: the time when Bonnie Prince Charlie, the heir to the deposed House of Stewart, made a landing in the Hebrides of Scotland, raised an army of loyal high-landers, and marched south to try to depose the usurpers of his throne, the House of Hanover, royals of Germanic stock. The Stewarts had been ousted from their throne in England, although they represented both Scotland and England – for mostly religious reasons, but it was a narrow margin, with only one vote in it.

Many Scots still had strong feelings for the House of Stewart, and felt no affinity for the Germans currently on the throne in London. They were ready to march south to prove this point, and Charles' appearance in Scotland was the catalyst needed. The first battle that Charles's army fought was here at Prestonpans, where the sides were evenly matched, both having in the region of 2,500 fighting men.

Now, the important thing about Charles's army was that it was comprised of ordinary men. They were crofters and farmers and the like, but they came to fight as the idea of 'man-rent' was still strong in Scotland. What this means is that part and parcel of the men being allowed to farm the land was that they should also be ready to fight for their lairds if need be too. It is the basics of how the clan system worked. On the other hand, the Redcoat gov-ernment army which they faced were regular soldiers, trained and uniformed and used to war. This army comprised the men landed at Dunbar, mentioned earlier, and other troops who were based at Edinburgh and had prudently retired when Charles's army reached the capital.

The Redcoats had taken up a strong position, their flanks protected by a bog, now drained. But as a large proportion of Charles's army were Highlanders, this bog did not prove any great obstacle, and they crossed it under cover of darkness. At first light, one of the Redcoats realised what had happened, as he saw the line of tartan form up. A cannon was fired, the ball smashing the legs of one of Clan Cameron, and Charles's army immediately launched into a full charge, all flying tartan and flashing steel in hand.

The trained soldiers of the Redcoats suddenly decided that they would rather be elsewhere. The charge of Charles's army, the feared 'Highland Charge' – no tactics, just brute force and violence, cut the opposition to pieces, and it was all over in two or three minutes. Out of the 2,500 trained soldiers, only 600 escaped. 500 were killed outright, and 1,400 were taken prisoner or surrendered. Nine hundred of these had terrible cut wounds, caused by the sweeping basket-hilted broadswords, claymores, and Lochaber axes of Charles's army.

Charles's untrained crofters and farmers lost only between 30 and 40 souls. Eye witnesses reported that the field of battle was strewn with body parts, even facial features like noses and lips lay on the grass, the ferocity of the bloodlust of the Highland Charge doing its terrible worst.

Basket-hilted broadswords are the type you commonly associate with Highlanders, with an ornate basket to protect the hand. Claymores are large, two-handed swords with down-sloping crossmembers, the correct term being quillions, and trefoils or quatrefoils on the ends – little circular shaped rings in a pattern, either three or four as the name suggests. Lochaber axes are wicked curving blades on a long pole, a slashing weapon, the name coming from an area of the Highlands.

One of the leaders of the Redcoats was a certain Colonel Gardiner, and he was unfortunate enough to be slain in his own garden! He had moved into a property at Prestonpans, and he was killed by a slash from one of the aforementioned Lochaber axes. The axe itself has survived and is kept within the White Tower, the oldest part of the Tower of London, where it is on show.

If you turn into the road on your left at the cairn, you go into an industrial area. You can't help but notice a big pyramid-shaped hill. Don't exactly know why it was built, but there are paths to the top and information boards up there giving you the story of the battle. It's probably a big storage tank or similar. It overlooks the whole battlefield, so it is a perfect viewpoint. Perhaps a reservoir?

Back to the cairn, and turn left back onto the route we were following westwards. Just a little further on is the railway station. Pull in to the car park here, and cross the bridge over the lines. As you exit the station at the opposite side, there is a gap in the wall. Follow the path through this gap, running parallel with the railway tracks, and you will find a monument to the memory of Colonel Gardiner, created in 1853 by an Edinburgh sculptor named Archibald Ritchie. Immediately south of this monument is Gardiner's house, Bankton, where he was slain. It is an orangey-coloured house, very grandiose. Gardiner himself was buried in the churchyard of nearby

Tranent, but there is no marker on his grave. Bankton is a private residence, but the monument affords a good view. When I was a teenager, I can remember this house being a burnt-out ruin, so the restoration is remarkable.

Within walking distance of the railway station car park there are three very interesting buildings, just a little further down the street and in to your right will take you into their vicinity.

On the left side of the street here is Northfield House, a commodious building of the late 1500s. It does have a doorway with an inscription above dated 1611, but this refers to later alterations. It is a private house, occupied and in good order, with quite a high wall blocking its lower storey from the street, but it is such an attractive building with little pepper-pot turrets at each corner, so it is worth a cursory glance at least.

At the junction immediately across the road there is a house built just a few years after Northfield, Hamilton House. This house belonged to the family of the same name, and is happily under the care of the National Trust of Scotland, so its future is secure.

Just past Hamilton House you can turn in to an area of parkland, and here stands the old Preston Tower, a fortified building dating from the 1400s. It is a lofty building, rising over 60 feet high. Two extra floors were added in the 1600s, strangely being added on top, rather than the usual type of extension which is added like a wing.

This place has seen some action, being burnt during an invasion by England in 1544. It was repaired only to be burnt by Cromwell in 1650. Restored again, there was an accidental fire in 1684, when the building was finally abandoned. A doocot nearby which served the tower was built in the 1600s. Nearby is also the Preston Market Cross, built in the 1600s and regarded as one of the finest in Scotland.

Often I get mail from people who have read one or other of my books, and they will tell me how they looked for such-and-such a spot, but couldn't find it. My advice is always the same – *ask*. That's how I manage to find sites in the first place. There is nothing to beat local knowledge, and people are generally very helpful. I don't understand why people will drive miles to look at a site, then return without seeing it. Just ask a passer-by.

You will have noticed that the surrounding country is getting more and more built-up, and more industrialised, far more so than anything we have passed through so far. Edinburgh, Scotland's capital, looms. We are into commuter belt here, and close to the city's suburban sprawl. But perhaps I should explain why Prestonpans is named thus before we leave this vicinity. In times past there were huge 'pans' in this area, down at the seafront. These would be filled with salt-water, then fires were lit underneath to boil off the water, leaving the salt, which was in demand for seasoning, as salt always has been. Originally called Preston, the name Prestonpans gradually took over. The salt-pans have long gone, but the name remains.

Back to your vehicle then, and drive westwards again from the station, following the road you are on, now named the B1361. Another mile takes you to a roundabout, go straight through and we pass through Wallyford.

Another mile and we come to a junction connecting us to the A1. We turn onto this major route, westwards to Edinburgh.

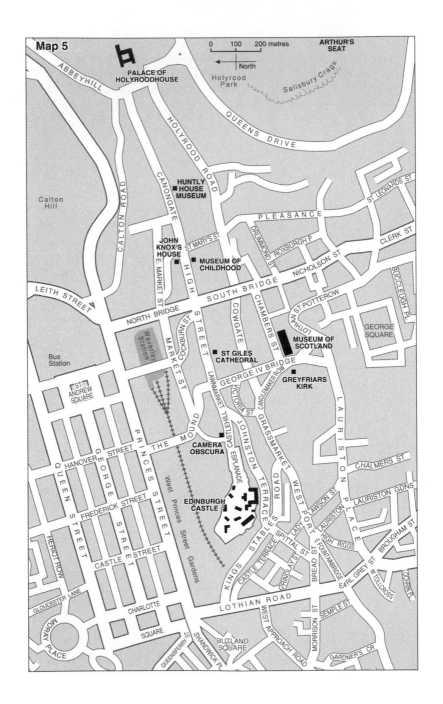

Map 5

PALACE OF
HOLYROODHOUSE

ARTHUR'S
SEAT

0   100   200 metres

North

Holyrood
Park

Salisbury Crags

ABBEYHILL

Calton
Hill

HOLYROOD ROAD

CANONGATE

CALTON ROAD

QUEENS DRIVE

HUNTLY
HOUSE
MUSEUM

ST MARY'S ST

PLEASANCE

ST LEONARDS ST

JOHN
KNOX'S
HOUSE

MUSEUM OF
CHILDHOOD

DRUMMOND ST

ROXBURGH P

NICHOLSON ST

CLERK ST

BUCCLEUGH PL

LEITH STREET

E MARKET ST

HIGH STREET

SOUTH BRIDGE

COWGATE

CHAMBERS ST

POTTEROW

GEORGE
SQUARE

NORTH BRIDGE

MARKET ST

COCKBURN ST

Waverley
Station

CHAMBERS ST

MUSEUM OF
SCOTLAND

LOTHIAN ST

Bus
Station

ST GILES
CATHEDRAL

GEORGE IV BRIDGE

LAWNMARKET

CANDLEMAKER ROW

GREYFRIARS
KIRK

ST
ANDREW
SQUARE

VICTORIA ST

GRASSMARKET

LAURISTON PLACE

CHALMERS ST

HANOVER STREET

GEORGE STREET

PRINCES STREET

THE MOUND

CAMERA
OBSCURA

JOHNSTON TERRACE

WEST PORT

LAURISTON GDNS

QUEEN STREET

FREDERICK STREET

West Princes Street Gardens

EDINBURGH
CASTLE

ESPLANADE

KINGS STABLES RD

LAWSON ST

LAURISTON ST

HIGH RIGGS

BROUGHAM ST

HERIOT ROW

CASTLE STREET

CASTLE TERRACE

SPITTAL ST

LADY LAWSON ST

BREAD ST

E FOUNTAINBRIDGE

EARL GREY ST

W TOLLCROSS

LOCHRIN PL

GLOUCESTER LANE

CHARLOTTE

SQUARE

LOTHIAN ROAD

MORRISON ST

SEMPLE ST

MORAY PLACE

QUEENSFERRY ST

SHANDWICK PL

RUTLAND
SQUARE

WEST APPROACH ROAD

GARDNER'S CR

CHAPTER FIVE

Edinburgh

CITIES ARE CITIES are cities, if you get my drift. All cities in this day and age share the same amenities and services. They have hotels and restaurants and shops galore. Edinburgh can be stunningly beautiful, vistas within the environs of its centre can be breathtaking. But it has its uglier side too in some of its sprawl, again like every other city. As you can perhaps imagine, I will be concentrating on some of the places in the city that contain chapters of Scotland's story. All roads lead to the city centre, and that spectacular vista to the castle from Princes Street, and it is from the castle, high on its rock in the very heart of the town, that we take our bearings – it is only right that that is the place to begin.

Edinburgh Castle is the most popular tourist attraction in Scotland, and Edinburgh is not only the capital of Scotland, but also the 'tourist' capital, although Glasgow is much larger and has many attractions of its own. Most of the 'touristy' sites in Edinburgh are within walking distance of each other if you are reasonably fit. North American visitors especially must be surprised at the compactness of Scotland's towns and cities, and everything can really be walked to from everywhere else, a mile or so being the furthest you have to walk to get anywhere. The parking problems are the same in Edinburgh as anywhere else, so you are best to stick you vehicle in a car park and walk for the rest of the day. This is where a motorcycle comes into its own, especially if you have panniers where you can pack away your helmet and gloves to avoid being encumbered.

So, we'll start at the castle. You pay a fee to enter, but this is reasonable when you could spend a day within its walls and not see everything. As you cross the drawbridge to enter, you will see the main doorway is flanked by statues of Wallace and Bruce. It was this statue of Wallace which was responsible for the motion picture *Braveheart*.

Randall Wallace, the screenwriter of the film, is from the United States, and had never heard of William Wallace. As he entered the castle on a visit to Scotland, he noticed this statue, and the name 'Wallace' inscribed nearby. Having the same surname, but never having heard of the great patriot, he asked one of the staff at the castle who this Wallace was. 'That, Sir,' came

the reply, 'is our greatest hero!' Intrigued, Randall started to read all he
could about this famous Wallace when he returned to the States. Eventually,
he discovered the work of Blind Harry, Wallace's biographer in the 1400s,
and *Braveheart* was the result.

The film educated a new generation of Scots about Wallace, but it also
brought his name to a world stage, and as people everywhere identify with
the basic right to fight for your nation's freedom against an aggressor, his
single-minded devotion to his native soil brought him many new admirers.
Strangely, Edinburgh Castle is probably the greatest citadel in the land, but
it does not have many historical connections with either Wallace or Bruce,
although Bruce's nephew, Thomas Randolph, the Earl of Moray, took
Edinburgh back into Scots hands during Bruce's campaign.

It is quite a story too. Randolph made contact with a Scots member of the
garrison who would climb down the Castle Rock to visit a sweetheart in the
town. Randolph took a hand-picked squad up this perilous ascent, but as
they neared the base of the walls, one of the English guards decided to play
a trick on a friend. He tossed a stone over the walls which bounced into the
abyss below, crying, 'Away, I can see you!' The Scots, in their exposed position, crushed themselves into the rock face. I can imagine them there, breath
caught, eyes shut and hearts pounding, waiting to be picked off by archers or
even stones dropped from above, but the guard moved off, laughing to a
companion. Randolph's men used rope ladders to quickly scale the walls,
and heavy hand-to-hand fighting took place, but the upper hand fell to the
Scots and the castle was back in the hands of its rightful owners.

It is the Castle Rock itself that is probably the most impressive aspect of
Edinburgh Castle, and it is of course the reason the castle exists at all. It is a
remnant of an extinct volcano, and you will see the evidence of volcanic
activity all over Edinburgh. Although that is not the first thing which
springs to the mind of visitors, it shapes every vista in the city.

The Castle Rock is such an obvious defensive site, that the date of the
first fortifications on it are lost in the mists of time – and under centuries of
later building work too, and though the city is laid out like a map from the
viewpoint of the castle battlements, the view north to Fife and the Lomond
Hills, and south to the Pentland Hills which enclose the city in that quarter,
are as they were to the eyes of the earliest settlers.

I have my favourite attractions in the castle, and one of these is the one
o'clock gun. Every day other than a Sunday, a field gun is fired from the
battlements at exactly one o'clock. The gentleman responsible for this operation is one 'Tam the Gun', and the report echoes across the city. Most of
the inhabitants are so used to it that they don't even notice it, but it still
makes me glance at my watch to check the time. I can remember standing
watching the gun being fired when I was a small boy, and I seem to have
been present at a firing every year or two ever since. I always forget just

how loud it is, and each time I take great delight in watching the assembled watchers jump in fright.

Talking of guns, no one should miss Mons Meg – a stupendous bit of artillery. She is a huge medieval cannon, and saw much action around Scotland. The mind cannot envisage how difficult it must have been to drag that monster over mud tracks, and the cannonballs themselves are huge. I have no idea how they even raised them to put them into Meg's mighty mouth. Mons Meg is now kept in one of the old storerooms of the castle, and to my mind she is one of the enduring symbols of Scotland, and would it be too much to say I actually love that big cannon?

She sings 'Scotland' to me.

Again I remember her from my boyhood visits to the castle.

It is thought that she was named after her creator's wife, Meg, who resided in the village of Mollance, Mollance Meg being shortened to Mons Meg in familiarity. There are those who like to argue that she was cast in Mons in mainland Europe, but I prefer to think of the master of ordnance that created her being Scottish and having a smirk to himself while naming her after his wife.

Anyway, go and see her and marvel. Stick you head up her barrel if you are brave enough. You will see there is a crack in her metal, and it was that which put her into retirement, as further use would have perhaps burst her. King James II was killed by an exploding cannon at the siege of Roxburgh Castle, and I doubt anyone who saw that would wish to be put in a similar position.

The oldest building in Edinburgh stands within the castle. It is the tiny St Margaret's chapel built onto the highest part of the living rock. Margaret was born in Hungary, but was of the blood royal of England, being a granddaughter of the English king Edmund Ironside. The Norman Conquest in England caused much trouble with much of the ruling class already installed there, and Margaret and some of her family fled to Scotland. Malcolm Canmore was at this time King of Scots. He saw Margaret and married her, falling head over heels in love-at-first-sight. Margaret introduced the doctrine of the Catholic Church, ousting the traditional Celtic Church that had done okay so far thank you very much. So Margaret had her little chapel built on the highest point of the castle rock, probably just after her arrival in Scotland in 1070, and it has managed to survive all that the ages have thrown at it since. It is a tiny, austere little place, less than 30 feet long. Its tiny windows are filled with stained glass with religious images – bar one, which has Sir William Wallace as its theme, showing how deep the man's memory is embedded in the heart of the nation. Funny wee place to stand in, Margaret's chapel. She prayed here almost 1,000 years ago, and this is a building familiar to many of the great figures of Scotland's history since that time.

There are always fresh flowers within the chapel. These are changed every week, and the woman picked to carry out this task is always named Margaret. I don't mean it's the same Margaret who's picked every time – it's different women who just all happen to be called Margaret!

My mother had me very late in life, and she was twenty-one or two when World War Two broke out. She used to take me to the castle and she would go to the Scottish National War Memorial, a building on the north side of a part of the castle called Palace Yard, where she would flick through the Books of Remembrance and point out the names of many relatives who had been killed in either 1914–18 or 1939–45.

My mother died when I was relatively young, and I wish I had paid more attention to what I was shown on these visits, as it is all lost to me now. I remember vividly though, the sculpture that is the centrepiece of this memorial. An angel, looking down from the ceiling, and I used to look up at that figure with awe, and still do. The power to create which some people have within them, to envisage such a work as that, is extraordinary. I defy anyone to look upon it and not be moved. It has been said to me on many occasions that once the generation that remembers World War Two has gone, then Scotland will be able to find herself. That may be true. I can understand that people remember how we stood with England to counteract the threat of tyranny, but Scotland is a nation. Not just the northern extension of England. I mean no disrespect – too many of my own family have died in wars for that. But I want the people of Scotland – Scotland! – to decide when we fight and what we fight for. I don't want to be told from the capital of a foreign country. And too many times in my own lifetime I have heard the word 'we' on the 'British' news.

What do you mean by 'we'?

Let my people make their own decisions regarding their own destiny.

Strangely, since I wrote that last paragraph, Scots have been fighting in Iraq. I don't really know why. Never met an Iraqi in my life to my knowledge, and even if I have, they have never done me any harm, yet my countrymen are at war with them. I do not want the warmongering of a London government forced on my people again. And that includes my family.

At the opposite side of Palace Yard is the old Palace, built between the 1400s and the 1600s. Here are kept the crown jewels, which we call 'The Honours of Scotland'. I believe they are the oldest crown jewels in the world – certainly they are older than their English counterparts. They have been joined by the fabled Stone of Destiny in recent years – it having been returned after a 700 year absence.

There has been much debate on whether it is the original stone, and conspiracy theories abound – enough to fill a book, but it is certainly the stone that was firmly ensconced in the Coronation Chair in Westminster Abbey.

In fact, as I write this, I am just a couple of weeks back from a trip to London. As usual, I visited Westminster Abbey, and was rather taken aback to find a sign resting against the aforementioned chair. It said:

The Stone of Scone [the English tend to call it that as that was where they stole it from!] brought here by Edward I to show the union he created between Scotland and England in 1296 …

Brought! – it didn't mention anything about the 15,000 men, women and children he slaughtered at the Sack of Berwick. He created no union. He invaded and violated and tried to annex a separate kingdom. There is no honour in that. The bloody Wars of Independence followed, to ensure Scotland again became a separate entity.

But, back to the Honours. They have had a colourful career all of their own, having been smuggled away from prying southern hands in their time, and they were locked in a chest and forgotten after the Union of 1603. It was the writer Sir Walter Scott who 'rediscovered' them, and they have been on show in the castle ever since. It is said that the Crown of Scotland contains the gold from the crown worn by the mighty Bruce.

Adjoining is the Old Parliament or Banqueting Hall, now mostly an armoury, but still impressive nonetheless. Next to this is a suite of rooms known as Queen Mary's apartments, used by Mary, Queen of Scots herself. There is a little bedroom among these where she gave birth to James VI – later to be James I of England, and this little room has a window that looks out to a long drop over the Castle Rock itself. The city has grown somewhat since Mary herself looked out of this little window.

The castle has many other attractions, dungeons, museums dedicated to the military services, etc, – but what I have mentioned above are my favourites.

If we leave the castle and cross the esplanade, where the world famous Edinburgh Military Tattoo takes place, we carry on down onto the Castlehill, the name of the street which begins the 'Royal Mile'.

The Royal Mile is what Scots call the stretch of road which runs the approximate mile from Edinburgh Castle down to Holyrood Palace. They call it that because the royals used to walk or ride that mile or so between the royal palace and the royal castle. You might also be intrigued to know that as you walk downhill all the way to Holyrood Palace, you are actually walking on an old lava flow. You see, the Castle Rock is the core of an old volcano, as I've already mentioned, and the Royal Mile runs on the spine of the hardened lava that ran out from it. Good, eh?

So, down the little narrow stretch of the Castlehill, and past the roundabout, where the road becomes the Lawnmarket. Notice on your left a smashing old building named Gladstone's Land. Tenement houses in Scotland are sometimes called 'lands'. This is a fine old six-storeyed house, and its name comes from Thomas Gladstone, who was an Edinburgh burgess who built the place in 1620. It retains its arcaded front which many of the buildings in the Royal Mile originally had. The National Trust for Scotland looks after it now.

A few yards further on and we come to an intersection. It's a wide road called George IV Bridge, because it's a sort of bridge, and at one time our town planners liked to lick the rear ends of 'British' royals, and name things after them. If we turn right here and walk on, we cross over the Cowgate far below – so George IV Bridge lives up to its 'Bridge' bit. We come to the junction with Chambers Street and here stands the Museum of Scotland. It contains relics from every era, from the earliest traces of man's arrival, to the industrial age. My very favourite object? That's a difficult one. I have a soft spot for 'the Maiden', the original guillotine which was used for public executions in Edinburgh. I can stand and gaze at it, and think how it must have felt to know you had to put your head in there and listen to the thin screech as the blade came down ...

The best line regarding this object was one victim who, whilst about to put his head on the spot, said to the crowd, 'Tis the sweetest maiden I have ever kissed!'

I like the Lewis chessmen too. These were old medieval chess pieces found on the island of Lewis. But perhaps they are a bit Viking influenced. Best of all for me is the Breacbannach. It's a silver gilt box shaped like a little house, which once held a relic of a saint. Some say St Andrew, some say St Columba. This box was carried before the Scots at the decisive Battle of Bannockburn in 1314. When it was held aloft the Scots dropped to their knees in deference.

The English king, Edward II, cried 'Look, those Scots are begging for mercy!' But he was wrong. Very wrong. And as those Scots arose, they knew that they would win or die that day. They knew that it was the day, the hour. Scotland as an entity depended on those Scots, my forebears, who fought that day. And they looked at that little box held aloft, and they muttered whatever words they needed to give them backbone, to give them the spirit to be willing to risk all for the future generations unborn and to come in Scotland.

As for me, I'm grateful. And I can come to this museum and see that little box shaped like a house and covered in Celtic carvings, and I look upon it as they did on that day, seven centuries ago, and I feel the link. I don't imagine that they could envisage me looking upon it after all this time. But I can see them in my mind's eye, and I understand. That little box is one of the most important artefacts of Scotland. And it is my very favourite in the museum.

Just across from Chambers Street, on the opposite side of George IV Bridge, is a small street running downhill, called Candlemaker Row. At the top there is a gate, an entrance which takes you into the churchyard of

Greyfriars Church. Just outside this gate there is a pillar-shaped fountain with a little dog on top – Greyfriars Bobby. Bobby was a terrier who, when his master died and was buried in Greyfriars Churchyard, stood watch over his grave from 1858 until 1872. And he died there after those 14 years of loyalty, a much loved and famous figure.

When Bobby died, he was buried in Greyfriars alongside his master. His story was even made into a Disney film, shot on location here in Edinburgh. As you enter the graveyard Bobby's grave is in front of you, his master is a little downhill to the right. The church itself was built in 1612, although restoration work in 1936 does not make it look that old.

There are some interesting old graves in the graveyard, and one or two famous personages from history are here, Regent Morton, who, as his name suggests, was a regent of Scotland, and Captain Porteous, who incurred the displeasure of the citizens and they lynched him, even though he was captain of the town guard. This act was the culmination of trouble in the city which has gone into our history books under the title of the 'Porteous Riots'.

At the back of the graveyard at the left-hand side is a long narrow extension, with little walled lairs lining it. This is the part of the cemetery known as the 'Covenanters' Prison'. Those with an interest in the occult claim that this is one of the most haunted places in all of Scotland.

It all started in 1638, when Scots began to demand religious freedom, and a plea for this was drawn up in a document named 'The Solemn League and Covenant', which people queued to sign as it lay on a tombstone in the graveyard. One of the first signatories was James Graham, the Marquis of Montrose, known to most Scots simply as Montrose, one of the greatest soldiers Scotland has ever produced. But the aims of the Covenant changed, and this drove Montrose to switch sides and fight against his former allies. He was eventually captured and executed in Edinburgh. A sword which was carried at this execution is kept within Greyfriars. The Covenanters, as the signatories were called, continued in one form or another, and were heavily defeated at the Battle of Bothwell Bridge on the River Clyde in 1679. They were marched here and kept in confinement, and that is how the name 'Covenanters' Prison' came into being.

These poor wretches were kept crammed into this small space, some 1,200 of them, for five months, with no shelter from the elements, and it would seem the only food and water they received was from the hands of sympathetic townsfolk. They are remembered by the Martyrs' Memorial. It is an eerie place, this corner of the churchyard. It is as if those that have gone before have left some trace, some shade of themselves. Cemeteries can be strange places at the best of times, but this one has a feel all of its own. There is an unusual view of Edinburgh Castle from the main graveyard, too.

The old wall that runs through the graveyard is part of the old city wall.

Leaving Greyfriars, you will notice that just a little down the gradient that is Candlemaker Row, there is a pub called Greyfriars Bobby. I remember being in this pub half a lifetime ago and noticing that Walt Disney had signed the wall, having been here during the making of the film that shares the pub's name. I've been in since, but failed to notice the signature, and hope it has not been wallpapered over in the interim.

So, back to the Royal Mile, retracing your footsteps. When we reach it, we turn right, downhill, this stretch bearing the name High Street. On the right hand side, side onto the street, stands the High Kirk of Edinburgh, St Giles. You will notice that there is a heart shape laid into the cobbles here as you approach the church, and this is referred to as 'The Heart of Midlothian', Lothian being the area of Scotland in which Edinburgh stands. Here stood the old town tolbooth, long demolished.

St Giles was largely built in the 1300 and 1400s. The tower dates from 1495 and is surmounted by its famous 'crown' steeple. There has been a church on this site since before AD 845. This early church was replaced in the early 1100s in the reign of Alexander I, and stood at the northwestern corner of the present, larger building. Unfortunately, the English invaded in 1385, and Richard II of England burnt Edinburgh, and the church here along with it. There are three octagonal pillars on each side of the west end of the choir, and these may be a remnant of this earlier church, used in the later building work. Originally, the supposed arm-bone of St Giles was kept within the church as its most venerated relic, but it disappeared in 1560. But in Autumn 2002, while work was being done on the interior walls, an arm bone was found hidden in a cavity. Could it be that it was hidden to keep it from the ravages of the Reformers? Carbon dating will at least give a clue to as to the antiquity of this object.

The church was once filled with previous relics, but these were destroyed at the onset of the Reformation in Scotland, the time when people began to throw off Catholicism and embrace the wave of Protestantism that was sweeping across northern Europe in 1556.

John Knox, the man very much responsible for these changes in Scotland, became the minister here in 1559, and he is in fact buried under the car park at the southern side of the church! The church is open during the day and is a great tourist attraction. At the time of Charles I it was elevated to the status of cathedral, but this only lasted a few years. Strangely this name has stuck though, and many people refer to it as St Giles' Cathedral still – I have even referred to it under that name myself on occasion.

In 1637, there was a famous incident when one of the congregation, Jenny Geddes, threw her stool at the Dean, crying 'Ye'll no read the mass in my lug!', which sparked huge religious revolt and unrest over Scotland. This was because Charles I in far away London, tried to impose Anglican Church practices on Scotland, but to the people here it smacked of 'Popery', and there was much outcry. It was this that led to the signing of the Covenant in Greyfriars churchyard. The ensuing bloodshed lasted many years. Charles I was eventually to be beheaded in London's Whitehall, and Cromwell came to power, and used that power to try to subjugate Scotland.

Montrose was eventually captured and brought to Edinburgh, and he was executed and dismembered outside St Giles in the Royal Mile, but at the Restoration, when Charles II became king, and the power of Cromwell's 'parliamentarians' had been broken, as much of Montrose's remains that could be found were gathered up and buried in St Giles' Chepman Aisle. This aisle stands over by the church organ, on the south side of the church, and no visitor should miss seeing Montrose's tomb. It is beautifully carved, showing Montrose in repose, and is arguably the finest tomb in Scotland. Every May the Graham family visit the tomb of their illustrious ancestor, where Forget-me-nots are scattered over it. Don't miss the Thistle Chapel at the church's south east corner, built for the Knights of the Thistle, a Scottish chivalric order. It contains some of the finest wood carving I have ever seen.

Out of the door of St Giles, and back on to the High Street of the Royal Mile. Notice the Mercat Cross on the right-hand side of the street, just after St Giles. The Mercat Cross was first mentioned in records in the year 1447, and the present one is the third to stand on the site. It has been moved a few yards over the centuries. The shaft on the top, which bears the Unicorn representing Scotland, is original, having been saved when the earlier versions were destroyed. This Cross represents the centre of public life of the nation. From here kings were proclaimed. Public executions were performed (including that of Montrose), prisoners were chained to the pillory, traitors outlawed, and bankrupts exposed to the derision of the mob.

Walking on downhill, we cross North Bridge and South Bridge, streets branching off north and south, and you will see that the Royal Mile narrows in front of you, due to an old house that juts out into the left-hand side of the street. Everybody knows this quaint old building as John Knox's house, and it is a fine example of the more ancient houses of Edinburgh, curiously gabled and picturesque. But did Knox ever actually live here? It is possible that he did dwell here from 1569 until his death in 1572, but this is merely conjecture. The house was built by the goldsmith to Mary, Queen of Scots, and contains old wooden galleries. On a lintel of the ground floor is the inscription 'Love God above all, and your neighbour as yourself' in old Scots.

I do have a problem with Knox, but not because of religious change. The church had grown corrupt and a good shake up was required. In saying that, I cannot go the 'thou shalt not' hypocrisy. When religion came to Scotland, it was a religion of peace and compassion, which praised personal ability. This was replaced by a stern hard Calvinism that replaced compas-

sion. Why one man should have the power to preach his form of righteous-
ness on others is beyond me. Every life form in the universe knows
inherently the difference between right and wrong. It's just that with people,
some of them are not troubled too much by conscience, and can commit
crime that harms another, through personal injury or theft or similar. We
have the police to deal with that. But to dictate morals? We all need moral-
ity, but what gives Knox the right to tell a nation what is wrong and right?
But my real problem with Knox, and many of the other reformers, was the
destruction of what they termed idolatry. Shake up the church, yes. Smash
everything artistic, no. Statues, tombs, paintings, even relics were
destroyed. Such a waste. Wouldn't it be fantastic if our churches were as
ornate as originally intended, and all that early medieval artistry was in
place, and wouldn't it be fantastic if the tombs of our monarchs still
existed? There is not a single tomb of a king or queen in Scotland which is
original. Some have a later marker showing the spot, but this is very few of
the impressive numerical total. Most were destroyed at the Reformation.
How the hell does a tomb smack of idolatry? Badness is the term I would
use for this.

On a lighter note, on the opposite side of the street is the Museum of
Childhood. It's been a while since I visited it, but as a kid I loved it. It has
toys from different eras, including clothes and books.

Just after John Knox's house, there is a junction where Jeffrey Street and
St Mary's Street reach the Royal Mile. You will notice that there are metal
plates sunk into the road surface here, and these show where the Flodden
Wall once stood. It was so called as the city wall was in a patchy state of
repair, and when the shock news of the terrible defeat at Flodden reached
Edinburgh, the citizens did their best to put it in some sort of defensive
order. There was a gate in the wall here too, known as the Netherbow Port.
There is a pub on your right called the World's End, which I suppose it was,
to the citizens of old Edinburgh.

After we cross this junction, this part of the Royal Mile is known as the
Canongate. Gate in Canongate will be from 'Gait', as in walking, and nothing to do with a gate, as in doorway. Canon of course is a religious term,
and will stem from the fact that Holyrood Abbey sits at the bottom end of
the Royal Mile.

On this stage there are two interesting old buildings, one on the left, one
on the right. On the left is the Canongate Tolbooth, a fascinating old building dating from 1591, with a large projecting clock. It was formerly a
prison and a courthouse. It is now open to the public as a museum. Just
across the road is Huntly House, dating from 1570, the name coming from
the fact that it was built as a town house for the Marquis of Huntly. It has a
unique timbered front. It contains a collection of relics from Edinburgh's
past. I think what surprised me most was that there are photographs of

Greyfriars Bobby inside. I never knew there were photos of him in existence. I keep forgetting that photography has been with us quite a long time. They have his collar too! As Bobby was a stray, and lived in Greyfriars churchyard, there was a problem as he never had a licensed collar, which meant that he could be a victim of the dog-catcher and be put down. The Lord Provost of Edinburgh stepped in and paid for a collar out of his own pocket, and it is in the case alongside his photographs. I liked it, anyroad. Are there any other Disney films where you can see a photograph of the star?

On down the Canongate, and we pass the new building work for the Scottish Parliament. As a Scot, can I just say, ridiculous site, ridiculous building, ridiculous money. And that is from someone who has spent his whole life wishing for a Scottish Parliament to become a reality. It should have been on a site that people could look up to – the top of Calton Hill being a possibility. The many hundreds of millions of pounds it is projected to cost could be better spent – after all, there are only five million of us. I feel that a foreign architect was not the correct choice either. As it will exist for many centuries, it would have been better if it could have been a Scot who designed it to inspire future generations. It would have been a lot better to have kept the architect's fee in Scotland too (said like a true Scot)! We have had some fabulous designers and architects in Scotland over the centuries. Have they all disappeared? Hmm. We have had people like Wallace and Bruce putting freedom to the top of the agenda, but politicians of that calibre seem to be pretty thin on the ground in this day and age. Quid pro quo.

At the end of the Royal Mile stands Holyrood, or to give it its Sunday name, the Palace of Holyroodhouse. The name should be explained first. David I of Scotland left the castle with his retinue to go hunting. He was in the area where Holyrood now stands, but at that time it was an area of marsh and forest. King David became separated from his companions, then became unhorsed by an attack from a stag. As the stag came in to gore the king, he held out a rood – the old Scots for cross, and the stag ran off into the undergrowth. David, who was a great church builder anyway, founded the abbey here in gratitude, with building commencing in 1128.

Its badge, which is a stag's head with a cross between its antlers, is also the badge of Edinburgh's Canongate, and it appears on buildings of the city. David I was the son of Malcolm Canmore and his queen, later to be canonised and known widely as St Margaret. Margaret had in her possession what was believed to be a piece of the True Cross on which Christ was crucified, which the Scots named the Holy Rood. This piece of the cross in its cross-shaped ornamental case, was kept in the abbey here, and it may have been the same which David I held to drive off the stag.

Certainly, the Holy Rood was once a great talisman of Scotland, along with the Stone of Destiny. The Holy Rood was taken to England by

Longshanks, returned to Scotland at the end of Robert the Bruce's reign, then taken into battle against England by Bruce's son David II. It was captured by the English at Neville's Cross in 1346. The Holy Rood of Scotland was put on display at Durham Cathedral, but it disappeared at the Reformation. Its whereabouts are unknown, but if you do know where it is, could you let Scotland know? Thanks, we would appreciate it!

Many guests and visitors began to stay at the abbey, and it had quite extensive outbuildings for this purpose. Eventually in the reign of James IV (1488–1513) work was begun on the palace block, the bulk of work taking place during the reign of James V. The opposite wing, identical to the earlier one, was built between 1670 and 1679. The Palace became the premier royal residence of Scotland. It has seen some major incidents in its time. The one that springs to mind for most Scots is the murder of Rizzio.

Rizzio was Mary, Queen of Scots' personal secretary. He was of Italian stock, a fine musician and clever at languages, but had a brusque manner which upset many of the Scottish lords. Eventually, Mary's husband, Lord Darnley, was led to believe that there was an affair between Rizzio and the Queen. A plot was hatched, and when Mary was at supper with Rizzio and a few of her ladies, the lords, Darnley included, burst in and stabbed Rizzio more than 50 times.

Bonnie Prince Charlie resided at Holyrood, his ancestral home, while he was in Edinburgh.

You can pay and tour some of the historic apartments of Holyrood Palace. I don't have a huge interest in the goings-on of our recent 'British' royals, but the tour is fabulous, allowing access to the Great Picture Gallery, hung with portraits of Scottish kings painted by the Flemish artist De Witt between 1684–6. He used only a few people to pose for the subjects of these portraits, so these 'Kings' have a remarkably similar look about them.

Bonnie Prince Charlie held receptions and balls in this gallery, when his star was at its height, and the dreadful Battle of Culloden and its consequences were far over the horizon of the future. You can see the bed Charlie slept in, various reception rooms and rooms with royal connections, but best of all, I think, are Mary, Queen of Scots' rooms.

Mary's bedroom is exactly as it was, having been left alone when refurbishing work has been carried out at the Palace. Next to her bedroom there is an apartment with some fabulous artefacts, including items of Mary's jewellery, and a sword worn by the Bonnie Prince. The floor has dark patches, claimed to be the bloodstains of the murdered Rizzio, but it is believed that these stains were the deliberate act of guides in the 1800s, as tourists of that time wanted to see blood, so the bloodstains were conveniently provided!

After the tour of the Palace rooms, you are allowed some access to the grounds, which allow you to look at the ruins of the abbey founded by

David I, and it is this abbey, nothing more now than a shell, that enthrals and intrigues me most out of all that stands in this historic vicinity. This rickle of stones, once magnificent, saw the royal marriages of James II and James III, Mary, Queen of Scots to Darnley, the presentation to James IV of the Sword of State, sent from the Pope and now part of the Honours of Scotland kept at the Castle, and the coronation of Charles I. You probably will not be too surprised to find that the English burnt the place in 1544 and 1547. We do not have a record of burning English religious establishments, so I don't really know why they had to behave like barbarians when they continually raided over the border. When Windsor Castle in England was damaged by fire recently, taxpayers' money was used to repair the damage. Perhaps the English would like to finance the rebuilding of Holyrood Abbey? And perhaps the money could be found to reconstruct all the great border abbeys too?

Cromwell was good enough to set light to the place too.

Royalty were laid to rest here. David II is here, James II was buried here after being killed by the exploding cannon at Roxburgh, James V and both his queens are here, and Lord Darnley is too. The roof collapsed in 1768, and the church lay in ruins for many years, but there is a royal sepulchre at the back of the ruins in the south-east corner, where as much of the royal remains that could be rescued are interred. There is some more detail of this in my book *A Passion for Scotland*.

Before we leave Holyrood's precincts, please notice the quaint little building on the edge of the grounds, known as 'Queen Mary's Bath House'. This ancient building was originally a lodge or pavilion, and tradition tells us that Rizzio's murderers escaped through this building. When restoration work was carried out, a richly inlaid dagger was found in the rafters and it may have been that one of the murderers threw it there during his escape.

Behind Holyrood rises the steep cliffs of Salisbury Crags, the lower slopes of the 822-feet-high Arthur's Seat. Because of the way it suddenly towers out of the cityscape, seasoned mountaineers have guessed its height to be around 2,000 ft! No visit to Edinburgh would be complete without a walk to its summit, so if you are fit enough, and want to see a view and a half, make the effort! There is a fairly easy route. If you can drive to the vicinity of Holyrood, turn right at the frontage onto Queen's Drive, which circles the hill, turn left and drive along under the ruins of St Anthony's Chapel on the hill above. After the little loch, turn right and up the hill. At the very back of the hill there is another loch, with parking places, and here you are a good percentage of the way up towards the summit already, so follow the obvious path to the summit cairn. Edinburgh is laid out like a map below. Arthur's Seat is of course a result of all the volcanic activity that has taken place in this area, and the various undulations caused by this are clear from the summit. If you are not fit enough to climb to the top of Arthur's Seat, you could drive to the top of Calton Hill with its monuments, at the opposite side of Holyrood. It gives a picture-postcard view of Edinburgh.

As said, cities are cities are cities, and Edinburgh has much to offer. Many museums and galleries are spread over the city, and what is known as the 'New Town' has its attractions too, but to do it all justice would take many books to cover each and every aspect. I just wanted to slip in a few favourites in a short walk.

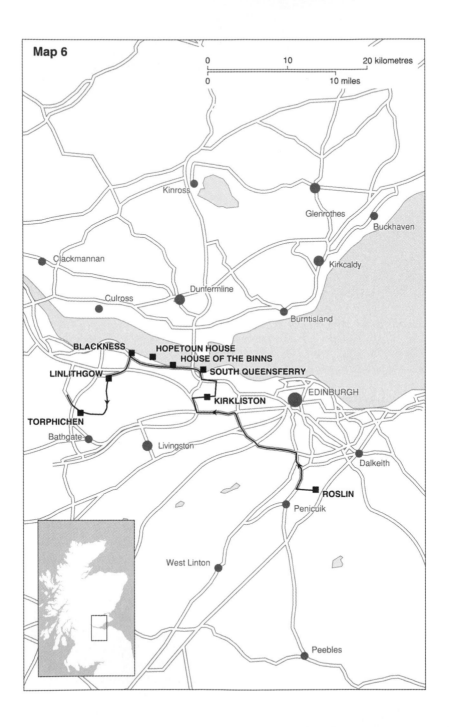

Map 6

0   10   20 kilometres
0   10 miles

Kinross

Glenrothes

Buckhaven

Clackmannan

Kirkcaldy

Culross

Dunfermline

Burntisland

BLACKNESS   **HOPETOUN HOUSE**
                       HOUSE OF THE BINNS
LINLITHGOW   **SOUTH QUEENSFERRY**

                       KIRKLISTON   EDINBURGH

TORPHICHEN

Bathgate   Livingston   Dalkeith

                                            ROSLIN

                                            Penicuik

West Linton

Peebles

CHAPTER SIX

The Forth Valley

FIRST EXPLORING ROSLIN, THE ROUTE THEN TAKES THE EDINBURGH BY-PASS TO THE M8 AND THEN ONTO NEWBRIDGE, KIRKLISTON, SOUTH QUEENSFERRY, HOPETOUN HOUSE, BINNS, BLACKNESS, LINLITHGOW, CAIRNPAPPLE HILL, TORPHICHEN, AND FINISHES AT THE BRIDGE OVER THE RIVER AVON ON THE A801.

FROM EDINBURGH, any road south will take you to the City Bypass, the road which rings around the southern environs, connecting the motorway networks. I really, really swithered about whether to include Roslin Chapel in this section, and I was going to head due west from the city and pass on it, but here goes.

The reason I have a problem with this spectacular little building is because of the number of claims surrounding the place, almost all of them arrant nonsense. I get loads of letters and emails from North America. Something like half of them mention Roslin. Tales of the Holy Grail hidden there, Jesus' head buried under a pillar, and Templar secrets, are just the tip of the iceberg. There are several books on all this. Not a shred of evidence, of course, but Americans don't know this, and think if it's written down then there must be some semblance of reality and truth in it all. If I hear one more person telling me how Bannockburn was won because the Templars …. Listen. There is no basis for this. There is not a single mention of it in our records or historical sources. And yes, it is convenient to say that because the Knights Templar were suppressed by the Pope that this could not be mentioned in chronicles. So all you claimants, please stop issuing books with conjecture stated as reality. We don't need our history to be blurred. We need the facts. And instead of all these claims, just show us the evidence. For example, these publications often show photos of medieval graves with a sword inscribed, and the caption saying 'graves of Knights Templars'. Every medieval church in Scotland usually has a few of these, they are the norm, and not Templar-related.

Right. Now I've got that off my chest, let's get to Roslin. The A701 heading south out of the city to Penicuik heads directly towards Roslin. This and its famous chapel are signposted. Other than that, you can drive for the bypass, then follow the Edinburgh bypass until you reach the appropriate junction where the A701 goes underneath. Roslin Chapel, on the north edge of Roslin Glen where the River North Esk runs, has the most richly, ornately carved interior of any church in Scotland. Every arch, every pillar boss, every roof rib, is encrusted in carvings. Foliage, faces, animals and human figures are everywhere. It has all been covered in a white plaster wash in modern times, but it would have originally been in full colour, which must have been a veritable blow to the senses on entry indeed!

William Sinclair, the third Earl of Orkney, commissioned work to begin here in the 1440s, replacing an earlier church. The structure was originally meant to be 55 metres long, but the building only measures 21 metres long internally, so it never came near the size originally intended. In fact, only the choir of the church was completed, but this does not detract from the complexity of decoration inside. At the east end of the church is a large sacristy below ground level. Monuments inside include a fifteenth-century incised slab of a knight's tomb, the tomb of George, Earl of Caithness, who died in 1582, and there is a coffin lid, most likely from the 1200s, that for some reason has been later inscribed with the name William de Sinclair. There is an interesting carving in the chapel ceiling of what is reputed to be the death mask of King Robert the Bruce, and I wrote some detail concerning this in my book *A Passion for Scotland*.

Roslin's most famous feature is probably the 'Apprentice Pillar', which has a story centred around it. The pillar itself has four strands of foliage starting at each of the corners of the base, and they spiral round the column to the top. The base has winged serpents, necks intertwined, biting their own tails. The story goes that the earl wished the pillar to be carved like one he had seen in continental Europe. The master mason just could not cope with the complexity of the design, so the earl sent him to view the original. While he was away, his apprentice mason decided to try and execute the design on his own, the pillar as we see it today being the result. When the master mason returned, he was so furious and jealous that he lifted a mason's mallet and struck the apprentice a blow which killed him.

This is said to be a modern legend, and is a universal folk tale told of several locations, but what is interesting is that the Primate of Scotland, the Archbishop of St Andrews, refused to consecrate the building until an act of atonement was made, because of the blood that had been shed in the building. High at the west end of the chapel are three carved heads, said to represent the mason, the apprentice and his weeping mother.

No matter what, Roslin is a place to visit and marvel at – just try and ignore the mostly fabulous claims that surround the place! To be honest, I often think of the masons having fun carrying out the work (unless you were the aforementioned apprentice!) and laughing, trying to outdo each other. It's just in this day that people become all po-faced about it. If there were 'hidden meanings', why didn't they just carve the story in stone? Like the pig playing the bagpipes at Melrose Abbey, there has been fun involved too. It amazes me though, that they could work in the relative darkness of these places, candlelight being their only source of illumination other than the little daylight that filtered in. Roslin is very Scottish, however, and although austerity is usually what we associate with religious buildings here, it still has that 'Scottish' feel to it.

To the right of the churchyard is the old inn, sadly neglected. It dates from 1662, and has had many famous visitors, including Boswell and Johnson, Burns, Scott, the Wordsworths, and the Prince of Wales, the future Edward VII. A little further on, a path cuts downhill to a more recent grave-yard. A few yards down, if you take the path off to the left, this will lead you on to Roslin Castle. Brilliant. That's how I describe it. What a site! I absolutely love it. The path crosses a drawbridge-like gap to give access to the spur of rock on which the castle stands, and the drop is great enough on either side to be memorable good fun!

There are remains of older work, fragments and fangs of masonry among later buildings, the original castle having been destroyed during an English invasion under the Earl of Hereford in 1544. Now that shouldn't come as a shock!

The later buildings on the site date from the 1500s and 1600s. It is a pri-vate residence, so please be unobtrusive. There was a battle fought in this area in the days of Wallace, the Scots led by the Red Comyn and Sir Simon Fraser. There is an abiding legend that Wallace was actually present at this battle in 1303, having just returned from his missions abroad. Certainly there is a 'Wallace's Cave' in this area. It is marked on Ordnance Survey maps.

Back to the Edinburgh City Bypass then, where we turn towards the west, signposted to Glasgow, the Forth Road Bridge and Edinburgh Airport. It can be a terribly busy stretch, this, at rush hour, so do try to avoid it at that time. I do love the view up to the Pentland Hills on this stretch of road, the artificial ski slope on the easternmost of the Pentlands, Caerketton Hill, being very prominent. Some have claimed that Pentland is just a corruption of 'Pictland', a throwback to our earlier ancestors. The same source is claimed for the Pentland Firth, an arm of the sea much further north. Another four or five miles on, and keep your eyes peeled for the M8 turnoff, heading for Glasgow and the west. Take this slip. Once on the M8, it is a few miles to the first turn-off, which is signposted to the Forth Road Bridge. We take this downhill, where there is a slip road off to the left to Newbridge and its large roundabout.

I know this all sounds complicated, and I wish I could make it simpler, but they are all well-marked routes, the distances are not great, and it should be straightforward once you are on the move.

Once you come up to the roundabout, take the second exit on your left, the A89 signposted Broxburn. Our destination is actually right alongside this roundabout, and we can see it from here, but as said, take the A89, then take first left at the lights, then left again into the dead end street which leads back towards the roundabout, and park at the road end. There is an opening in the bushes and the path leads us to a prehistoric monument, its full name being the Huly Hill Round Cairn and Standing Stones. There is a modern wall built around the Huly Hill itself, but it's about 30 metres across and three metres high. Surrounding it there has originally been a large stone circle, about 100 metres in diameter, but only three stones remain. The rest have probably been removed over the centuries for building work, walls, lintels etc, and there have been many intervening centuries since this was first built, because it's 3,500 years old.

I've stood on the middle of the mound and tried to envisage things as they were. It's bizarre to try and perceive how its builders would feel to see it today. The motorway network is only yards away. The runway for Edinburgh Airport is at the other side of Newbridge Roundabout. Jets come in to land, only a few hundred feet above, undercarriages already down, and engines thundering.

There are many sites as old as this in Scotland, but I felt Huly Hill was a prime example to show the contradictions of the millennia that have passed. Also I am surprised at the amount of acquaintances that know Newbridge Roundabout well, and have been equally surprised when I have mentioned the hill and stones alongside, having never noticed them. The central round cairn was opened in 1830, and a bronze sword was found within.

There is another standing stone, known as the Lochend Stone, almost three metres high, in the industrial estate on the other, eastern side of the roundabout, about 350 yards away. It is just inside the perimeter fence of the factories on the southern side of the road. There may be no connection, but the chances are it is an outlier and was part of a large conglomeration on this site. I get a feeling from these places, something of the ages, tangible in the air, and this monument so close to the suburban sprawl of Scotland's capital has a feel all its own, only heightened by the traffic thundering past.

This is where things get difficult. I have real trouble now deciding what route to take. There is so much to the west of here, all in a narrow strip south of the First of Forth, but I'll try and compromise by meandering from the water's edge inland here and there.

So, back to the traffic lights just round the corner, and left again back onto the A89 westwards. We cross the River Almond, then there is another set of traffic lights. The road off to the right is the B800, signposted Kirkliston. Just as I turned into the straight stretch here, a funny rattling came from the front wheel. Not sure if something had got stuck in my mudguard and freed itself, but I was worried a wheel bearing was giving up the ghost.

We follow the river, travelling under the M9 Edinburgh/Stirling motorway, and from the lights it's only a mile or so to Kirkliston.

Kirkliston takes its name from its old church, which stands on the left-hand side of the road in the centre of the village. There is an interesting old square between the road and the church. The nave and tower are very old, built between 1190–1210, but the church has, of course, undergone alterations. The north transept was added in 1883. The church is not generally open, but you can walk right round it and admire the architecture.

Looking out over the surrounding landscape, it is difficult to imagine a huge medieval army camped hereabouts, tents pitched, banners and pennons flying. But this was the case. Two days before the fateful Battle of Falkirk in July 1298, where the Scots under the command of Sir William Wallace were defeated with much slaughter, the English under Longshanks were camped in this vicinity. Wallace had operated a scorched-earth policy, and the English were starving, unable to find cattle or grain. Some transport ships managed to dock at Leith, the port of Edinburgh, but they contained only wine. Making a rare mistake, Edward Longshanks had this rationed out to his troops. Drunk, his Welsh footmen killed some English priests and had to be charged by heavy cavalry. Eighty Welshmen were killed. There was real animosity, with a stand-off between the two nationalities. Well, when you sup with the devil ….

When informed that the Welsh were threatening to join forces with the Scots, Longshanks retorted, 'What does it matter? Let them join the Scots, then I will defeat them all in one go'. Wallace had done his job well, creating dissent and hunger amongst the invaders. But things were to change here at Kirkliston. Two Scottish traitors asked for audience with Longshanks, the Earls of Angus and Dunbar. They informed the King of England that the Scots were at Falkirk, only 18 miles to the east. This heartened the English, they could bring their foes to battle and do the job they had marched so far to do. They pushed on to Linlithgow and camped there the following night, July 22, then brought the Scots to battle on the following day.

Perhaps 10,000 Scots died at Falkirk, thanks to two traitors. How can men live with themselves, having betrayed their own flesh and blood? They must have known beforehand what the consequences of their actions would be. They put England before their own. I hope Edward Longshanks was so grateful he gave them land and riches to outweigh the amount of blood they shed, orphans they left, and a land cowed under the boot of the invader. The battle might have taken place elsewhere, but the outcome was decided within sight of the church here at Kirkliston.

Follow the B800 directly through the village, under the railway bridge at the far end, and on to the roundabout, where we carry straight on through, on to the A8000, signposted for the Forth Road Bridge. This road is a bottleneck at busy times, but upgrading is underway. We follow it for less than two miles though, the Forth Road Bridge beginning to come into sight, when we come to another roundabout where we turn right, and into the town of South Queensferry. It's a steep downhill road into the town centre, going over the valley edge, and at the bottom of the hill we take the right turn into the main street, which follows the shore eastwards.

Just as you turn in here you will notice on your left at this junction there is an attractive example of a mid-seventeenth century laird's house. This is Plewlands House. Although it is a strong looking place, it has no defensive features as such, as it was built at a time when things were a little more settled in Scotland, and the style of architecture was changing to suit. In the mid-1900s there were plans to demolish this building, but the ensuing outcry meant that it was given over to the care of the National Trust for Scotland, so its future is assured.

Into the cobbled main street, and there is an interesting plaque and well commemorating the town's first piped water supply, and a little further along, also on our right, is a building known as Black Castle. It is painted black of course, bears the date 1626, and it would originally be the town lodging of some Lothian laird, but is today private housing. On our right, the south side of the street, there is a second, raised thoroughfare, an old feature that I really like, with its own row of shops and houses above the main street's own.

On the left here is the building containing the town's museum, containing some interesting data on the famous Forth Road and Rail Bridges, and information on the 'Burry Man'. South Queensferry has its local fair every year, and the highlight is this phenomenon. A local man is chosen every year – a great honour – and is dressed and covered in burrs, spiky seeds, whereupon he tours the town. It is a long day, especially so dressed, and it takes great stamina to endure the day's itinerary. There is a mock-up of the 'Burry Man' in the museum. The reason for the appearance of this curious character is unknown, but it is thought that in the old days when times were hard, in a poor fishing season for instance, the Burry Man was a scapegoat who was led through the town then expelled in the hope of removing bad luck. It's great through, that in the twenty-first century the old traditions are not allowed to fade, and every August the Burry Man does his best to raise money for charity.

Another few yards, a last twist of the cobbled street, and we are on to a stretch of open promenade giving a panoramic view of the famous bridges.

The Railway Bridge is world famous and rightly so. It is a monument to the glory days of Scottish engineering, and seems massive in comparison to modern bridges of similar length. It contains 50,000 tons of steel girders, has a length of just over 2,765 yards. Fifty men died in the building of it and there were 500 injuries. Looking at it, it is best to wait until a train crosses it, as it is then that you have something to give you an idea of scale, to let you see the immensity of this structure. It was built between 1883–90, and the painting of the steelwork is a constant task. It takes three years to paint the bridge, and when the crew are finished, they go to the opposite end and start again. This has gone into folklore in Scotland, people referring to seemingly endless or repetitive tasks as being 'like painting the Forth Bridge'. The bridge uses Inchgarvie Island out in the Firth as support, and this island carried a fifteenth-century fortification whose garrison held out against Cromwell in 1650. What is probably a shock to most people seeing this bridge for the first time is that it is red. The paint to seal the metal is what we in Scotland, at least in my experience, call 'red lead', so we have a big red bridge here.

In comparison, the Forth Road Bridge looks svelte and slim and ladylike. 2,415 yards long, its towers rise to 512 feet, and as well as the road, there are wide footpaths-cum-cycle tracks at either side. It is good fun to walk over it. It amazes me that more people don't do this. When I mention to people that I have driven to the Forth Road Bridge, walked over one side, gone through the wee underpass at the opposite end, and walked back on the other side, they always seem surprised. You are guaranteed a spectacular view, and big boats going underneath are a bonus. It took six years to build this bridge, and it was opened in 1964.

There are many bigger, longer bridges in the world, but I think what makes this view so special is the comparison between the two, the Road Bridge a suspension bridge, the Rail a cantilever, and how engineering changed in the 74 years between the two structures.

Right up to the opening of the Road Bridge, a ferry plied its way between South Queensferry here, and North Queensferry, its smaller neighbour on the opposite shore of the Firth. This is a story at the core of Scotland's history, and a well known one too. Malcolm Canmore's queen, the later-canonised St Margaret, in her determined (and successful) efforts to Romanize the church in Scotland, personally instituted the ferry service here. It was for visitors and pilgrims to the great new abbey at Dunfermline, not too far from the northern side. North and South Queensferries grew and prospered, the names, of course, a result of the Queen's ferries here, and the pier just west of the railway bridge is the site from where the original ferries embarked. You will notice there is an old inn, the Hawes Inn, facing this pier, and this building, dating partly from the 1600s, has historic literary connections. It is associated with Sir Walter Scott's *The Antiquary*, and it is said that Robert Louis Stevenson began writing the world-famous, and much-filmed *Kidnapped* in room 13. The first time I visited the Hawes Inn was with a motorcycle club on a ride-out. I thought it was great. You could park out front, take your beer outside, and look at that tremendous view.

Ferries still sail from the pier opposite too, in the summer months at least. They take visitors to the little islands out in the Firth – Inches, we call them in Scotland.

There is a great wee sail out to Inchcolm with its well-preserved ruined abbey, if that is not too much of a contradiction in terms. A famous old history of Scotland was written at this abbey in the 1440s. It is called the *Scotichronicon*, and its author was Walter Bower, the abbot of Inchcolm. I have read and used Walter's work for reference so many times – in fact I just took a book of his off my shelf to glance over while writing this, and I wonder if he could imagine me reading his work almost six centuries on. He was a bit of a wit was Walter, as when he finished working on the *Scotichronicon* after many, many years, he wrote at the end of it 'Christ! He is not a Scot who is not pleased with this book!' Isn't that great? Walter was a patriot, and reading his personal viewpoints regarding Scotland, he makes quotes that I identify with immediately, how he was unable to understand why some Scots don't put Scotland first for example. You make me realise that the centuries mean nothing, Walter. We are all Scots with our own little eras of tenancy of the land. Pride and freedom meant as much to you as they do to me.

Take a last look at that epic view of a bridge to the left and a bridge to the right, then drive back through the town to where you originally turned in to the main street at Plewlands House. Only this time we do not go back up the hill, but turn right and continue through the town westwards. A few yards on, to your right, is South Queensferry's old St Mary's church. It was built in the 1400s to serve a Carmelite Friary, now long gone, and it served as the parish church from the 1560s till 1633. The place was restored from ruin in the 1890s.

The choir contains memorials to the Dundas family, with an interesting slab to George who died in 1600, and his wife Catherine. We continue just a little along this road, the B924, under the Forth Road Bridge, where we come to signs pointing the way to Hopetoun House, one of the greatest of Scotland's stately homes.

The Hope family came to West Lothian in 1657 to expand their silver and lead mining interests here. The improvement in agriculture at this time, which they utilised on their already large estates, coupled with the wealth they made from mining, allowed them to build their palatial mansion. You follow this narrow road for two or three miles, going through housing then into the estates' wooded policies, then suddenly the house comes into view.

It is splendid, the main house in the centre, facing east, with curved arcaded wings and two storey end pavilions, surmounted by cupolas. This huge semi-circular frontage measures 520 feet across. The absolute wealth involved hits home at once! It was commenced in 1696 by the noted architect, Sir William Bruce, and although it is regarded as his masterpiece, he died before it was finished. It was completed by William Adam, and his son Robert, Robert Adam being famous for his designs on a world stage. The building is rich in treasures, and includes a museum. There are all the usual features, decorative work, panelling, and some great works of art. It is open to the public from May until the end of September, and as you can imagine, it is a popular venue. The grounds too are extensive, and part of this property was once a power base of the Black Douglas family in medieval times.

Leaving Hopetoun House makes things a little tricky. You may be exiting by a different gate, but no matter which way you do it, you should end up on the A904, quite a major route. If you can go back to South Queensferry, and your original approach to Hopetoun, it is a case of turning right, uphill, and you will shortly reach the A904, where you turn right, westwards. A mile or two along the A904, you come to the village of Newton, a little further and you come to Woodend, where you will see a little sign pointing towards the direction of Abercorn Church where you turn right, down the edge of Hopetoun Wood, on an unclassified road. At the T-junction at the hamlet of Parkhead a half-mile on, turn left, and this takes us round the edge of the Hopetoun Estate to Abercorn. Just look for the signs that lead you to the little church, parking at a dead-end among the cluster of houses that were once buildings connected with Hopetoun House and its day-to-day running.

Abercorn Church is on an ancient site, mention of it going back to AD 685, but the church we see today was built in the 1100s and was reconstructed in 1579. There are later burial aisles added to its south side. As you enter the churchyard, there is a little building on your right which serves as a museum, and it has the remains of a very tall Celtic cross, and some hogsback tombstones inside. Hogsback tombstones are like upturned longship hulls, ornately carved, and are associated with viking burials.

There are many tombstones from the 1600s and 1700s in the graveyard, and a short wander will reveal some interesting inscriptions, many of them estate workers from Hopetoun. Notice the blocked up original doorway from the 1100s on the outside. The church is generally unlocked and a rove around the interior will reveal the elaborate loft created for the Hope family, which gives the impression that the Hopes have to be worshipped within rather than their makers! Nigel Tranter, late lamented Scottish author, pointed out that there is a sad stone within the church on the chancel floor. This is now a little used area through a door, and lying at the eastern end of the building. It bears a shield with only the initials I.M. on its right-hand side, representing a wife, but the husband's initials were never added to their place on the left, as the Reformation took place in Scotland between their respective deaths. Burials within churches were forbidden from then on, and so he was interred outside. It's a shame that they cannot lie together for eternity as intended.

Abercorn was a powerbase of the Black Douglas family, but all that remains of their castle is a slight grassy mound.

Out from the parking place by the church, and we turn right and continue roughly westwards on the little road we were on. There is woodland on the right, and in the winter months when there is little foliage, you will notice the old tower house that is Midhope Castle. It was most likely built in 1582, as this date appears on a carved stone. It was built by one Alexander Drummond, but eventually came under the control of the Hopes of Hopetoun House, the name of this old castle, Midhope, being purely coincidence. Continue on along this road, and as it begins to swing south, it again rejoins the A904, with a little school standing to your right at the junction.

We turn right, and another mile or two of the A904, and you will see signs pointing to 'The Binns'. This is the home of the Dalyell family (pronounced Dee-yell). Although there are mentions of this estate as early as 1335, the Dalyell family moved here in 1612. There is an old tower on Binns Hill, just to the east of the house, a notable landmark. You turn right into the grounds, the house open to the public daily mid June until mid-September, and although the Dalyell family still live here, the house is under the care of the National Trust for Scotland. The son of the purchaser of this estate was a notable soldier, but not always for Scotland's good. He went by the name of General Tam Dalyell. His generalship was won fighting for the Czar in Muscovy, where, it is said, he had learnt to roast prisoners, and he threatened to spit and roast Scots likewise, when he returned. He savagely dealt with Covenanters, and he is particularly remembered for his slaughter of them at Rullion Green in the Pentland Hills.

General Tam caught a tired force of 1,000 Covenanters in the hills, and let loose a force of 3,000 government troops on them. The ones who died were probably the lucky ones, as the rest were hung, 35 of them before their own houses as a warning, and others were shipped as slaves to the Caribbean. Strangely, in his elder years he busied himself with rare and curious plants, and laid out the gardens. He also raised the Scots Greys regiment at the Binns in 1681. This regiment existed until 1971, when they were disbanded where they were raised, here at the Binns, and amalgamated into the Royal Scots Dragoon Guards.

It is a strange thing, but most of the more famous Scottish regiments, the Black Watch, for example, were actually raised to keep other Scots down. But as the years have passed, these regiments have evolved traditions and a history of their own, and I can remember the outcry that there has been when some of them were told they had passed their sell-by date and were to be disbanded. I have never really understood this as these Scottish regiments were raised by the powers that be in England, and never usually for the benefit of their fellow Scots.

The current owner of the Binns is well-known in Scotland, a noted politician, and another Tam Dalyell, who for his entire career was a determined fighter against Scotland taking any form of autonomy.

Internally, the house has some very fine plasterwork, some curious old furniture and a collection of family and royal portraits, one or two said to have been saved from Linlithgow Palace, which we will visit shortly.

As we come back out of the driveway of the Binns, back to the A904, and turn right, we immediately turn right again, onto the B9109, following the signs a mile and a half to Blackness Castle. The road is a dead end, but the castle is one of the most unusual in Scotland, and stands on a spit of land projecting out into the Firth of Forth, and is well worth seeing.

It was built in the 1440s by Sir George Crighton. In 1453 he handed Blackness over to royal care, describing the castle as an 'unsinkable ship', which it basically is. It is bow shaped at the front, stern shaped at the rear, and even the internal towers give it a ship-like appearance, with the central block looking like a mainmast.

Sir George's dispossessed son James Crighton captured the castle, so King James II of Scotland was forced to besiege and capture the place, and it was responsible to the Crown from then on. It was long used as a prison, and was garrisoned right up until the 1870s. It then became an ordnance depot and store, housing shells for cannonry etc. Although open to the public, it is mostly bare walls within, but its unusual shape makes it interesting, and the views up and down the Firth of Forth are well worth seeing too. Blackness Bay on its west was once a busy shipping haven, and on my visit there was powerboat racing going on. It was interesting to watch this in the knowledge that an English fleet burnt ten Scots vessels here in 1548.

From Blackness we have to re-trace our route a little, but follow the B903 directly back, with no deviations, until you reach the T-junction with the A904. Turn left towards Linlithgow, and keep straight on to Linlithgow when the road becomes the A803.

As we touch the outskirts of Linlithgow, there is a farm on our left-hand side. This is Burghmuir Farm, so called because it is built on the land that was the old Burgh Muir of Linlithgow – land owned by the town. It was here that Edward Longshanks' English army camped on the eve of the disastrous Battle of Falkirk in July 1298. You will notice that rising behind the town there is a large whaleback hill. This is Cockleroy Hill, and legend states that William Wallace lay atop this hill waiting and watching, assessing and hoping.

On, and we go straight through the roundabout at the end of the town's High Street. You are probably best to park here, and walk on to see the rest of Linlithgow, as it is not a large place. Just after the roundabout on your left is an old stone well, St Michael's Well, dating from 1720. It is inscribed 'St Michael is kind to strangers'. Linlithgow has many wells and fountains, and St Michael is the patron saint of the place, so that at least explains why this well is so named.

Incidentally, you may notice the town's coat of arms displayed on buildings, or you may notice it carved on stone on old edifices, and it features a
dog, the dog in question being a black bitch. 'Black Bitch' is the nickname
for an inhabitant of Linlithgow, and I remember chairing a meeting of the
Society of William Wallace once where a dark-haired girl turned up. Seeing
that she came from Linlithgow, I said to her 'I see you're a black bitch
then?' – to sharp intakes of breath from the assembly. I think they were
even more confused when she smiled and replied in the affirmative!

Just by the well there is a little plaque, six or seven feet up on the corner
of a building, stating that this spot was the site of the location of Scotland's
first petrol pump, set up in 1919, and selling Spratts petrol!

Cross the road, and a little further along on your right is the town square,
the Information Centre behind, and a peculiar old fountain in the centre.
This is the Old Cross Well, built in 1807 to replace an earlier one that was
destroyed by Cromwell in 1659. It is unusual in having 13 jets, with some
amusing carved figures, including musicians. You will notice the Black
Bitch carved here.

I think it is great when towns keep their own unique identities like this,
and down the generations the populace have been happy to be Black
Bitches and have identified with St Michael. I'm not a great one for the narrow mindedness of political correctness, taking away old names as they
sound a bit 'iffy' to modern sensibilities, and for everyone thinking in the
same narrow spectrum. *Vive la difference*, that's what I say!

Take the cobbled lane up the side of the Information Centre, that rises
uphill towards the gatehouse which is the entrance to the precincts of
Linlithgow Palace and St Michael's Church. On your right going up this
lane is a series of plaques 'showing the Royal Line from Mary, Queen of
Scots to our current monarch'. What a pile of nonsense! There must have
been someone in the town responsible for this outrage, some arch-unionist,
to have got away with this. It misses out James VII for a start, and it actually
concentrates on a Hanoverian descent, the same Hanoverian regime that
was responsible for the destruction of Linlithgow Palace, as today it is nothing more than a shell. This isn't just me, by the way, many people have said
to me over the years, 'have you seen that bloody wall in Linlithgow....'

So walk quickly past this wall, keeping your eyes averted, and concen-
trate on the gatehouse in front. It was erected by James V and bears carved
panels with the badges of the four orders of knighthood which he held, the
Garter, the Thistle, St Michael and the Golden Fleece.

Once through this gate, the church of St Michael is directly on your right.
It is open to the public most of the year. You will notice the strange top to
the steeple. It looks metallic, is made of timber clad in aluminium, and it
represents Christ's crown of thorns. It has its critics, but I remember going
through Linlithgow on a train when I was eight or nine, and I noticed this

strange top to the steeple, the sun glinting on it, and it intrigued me at that age, and I've always remembered it. The original steeple looked like the crown atop St Giles in Edinburgh, but it became unsafe and was removed in 1821. It took until 1964 to replace it, but at least in those intervening years there was constant thought as to how the old crown could be replaced. There has been a church on this site since earliest times, but work began on the current building after 1424, but many older stones from earlier buildings were used. Funny, but it is important to me, that information that older stones were used. I once heard the line, although I'm not sure of its source, (maybe MacDairmid?) 'You see ruined buildings, but funnily enough, you never see ruined stones'. True. The stone itself could be a billion years old, but we worry about the antiquity of the structures themselves.

I hope you can gain access to the church, where guidebooks are on hand to explain everything about the history and fabric of the place. My particular favourite here is St Katherine's Aisle, a small projection on the southern side of the church. It was here that King James IV was praying before the forthcoming conflict with England that was to end so disastrously on Flodden field in 1513. A ghostly figure appeared, finger outstretched toward the King, warning him not to undertake his campaign. This harbinger of doom is mentioned in many of our history books, but the modern view is that this 'ghost' was probably arranged by King James IV's wife, Margaret Tudor, sister of the King of England, to try and avert the strife between the two nations.

There is a nice plaque on the wall of this aisle to 'Anselm Adornes, merchant, diplomat and friend of Scotland'. Information in the church tells that his heart was taken to Bruges where it still lies beneath the high altar of the Jerusalemkirke, whereas the rest of his body is here in St Michael's. I wish I knew more about the man, but that is the beauty of my quests: they are never-ending and new roads in history constantly open up to me, just as they do in motorcycling.

Up in the tower of the church are three bells, the largest almost a yard across, and it bears the inscription, 'The town of Linlithgow made me – I am called Blessed Mary – in the time of our august Lord James the Fourth, in the year 1490'. So the bell that King James IV heard then still tolls out across the town, the same bell that would have announced the disaster that was Flodden, that tolled the news of the birth of Mary, Queen of Scots in the palace nearby, is a direct link across the centuries from that time until now, and may Blessed Mary ring across many more centuries, and see Scotland one day be the free nation she once knew.

There are two other bells in the tower, one slightly smaller than Mary, by the name of St Michael Archangel, and the smallest bell is called Meg Duncan, and Meg has knelled her presence across the town since 1718.

I like it when objects are given names like this, like Mons Meg, our Edinburgh cannon. It gives them a Scottishness, a familiarity. Many people have come and gone over the centuries in Linlithgow, but there is a common thread.

Outside again, and it is only a few steps to the Palace. Huge, gaunt, stark. A colourless place which was once full of colour. It is worth walking around the outside of it first, before exploring its many chambers and corridors from within. You will see that it stands on a promontory, jutting out into Linlithgow Loch. It does not seem like a particularly defensive site if approached from the High Street, but up here things take on a different aspect. The first fortifications here were most likely from Roman times, and it would seem to have been used for a similar purpose ever since. Edward Longshanks built a 'peel' here, a palisaded stronghold 'meikle and stark', but it was captured by the Scots at the time of King Robert the Bruce, when a local, William Binnie, jammed a haycart into the entrance, allowing the Scots to attack and overwhelm the garrison. Grateful King Robert granted Binnie a gift of land, and a few miles from the town there are still farms bearing his name, like West Binny and Binny House.

The stonework we see today dates from the early to mid-1400s. The loch below is full of aquatic birds, ducks, swans, coots etc, and if you walk down to the west to where the town comes close to the water, literally hundreds will come close looking for titbits. I like the eastern side of the Palace myself, with its great doorway, the slots for the drawbridge and the holes for the portcullis chains still visible. In the inner side of this doorway, you will notice that there are niches for statues. There was one of the Pope to symbolise the church, a knight to indicate the gentry, and a labouring man to represent to commons, and each had a scroll above their heads with words of wisdom etched upon them. Unfortunately, these are all long gone.

You pay a fee to enter the Palace, and entrance takes you directly into the central courtyard, which contains a large carven stone fountain from the 1500s. It is currently undergoing restoration. James V of Scotland was born here, as was Mary, Queen of Scots, and the room is on the west side at first floor level. As Mary was born, her father, the aforementioned James V, lay dying at Falkland Palace. The Great Hall is still impressive, but I particularly like Queen Margaret's Bower, a little room high, high on a turret, where the Queen kept vigil while James IV fought at Flodden. There is an impressive airy view from here over the Palace, the loch, the town and the surrounding countryside.

Bonnie Prince Charlie stayed here in 1745, when the central fountain ran with wine. But why is the place a shell today? In 1746, Redcoat troops were stationed here, and the place 'accidentally caught fire'. They marched away from it, no effort was made to try to control the flames, and no finger of blame was ever pointed. This place was, after all, a Royal Palace of the

Stewart Dynasty, and these Redcoats represented the usurping Hanoverian Dynasty, so it would not take much prompting to destroy this edifice.

Unfortunately it contained a lot of what was important to the history of a nation – Scotland, and every Scot since has been a little poorer in their heritage due to this act of vandalism. It is interesting to note that in 1891, the Town council petitioned Parliament with the notion that the Palace could perhaps be refurbished and put into use as a museum of Scottish antiquities. This, of course, never came to fruition, but it was an interesting concept.

As we pass back through the James v gatehouse to return downhill to the town, it is worth turning left and through the gate to have a quick look in the cemetery of the church. There are many niches in the walls of the building itself to contain statuary, all now gone, bar one. This is the statue of St Michael which is on the corner facing the gate. Strange that this has prevailed, so that every visitor to the church over the years sees that one survivor. I would like to think fate was involved here, St Michael being so special to Linlithgow, and that perhaps at the Reformation the locals refused to destroy his image. But it has been pointed out that the statue is built into the fabric of the stonework and perhaps it could not be done away with.

Also in the graveyard, lying alongside the church, is the remains of the huge metal cage which was hired out to families as a 'mortsafe' to be placed over a recent grave, to deter the grave robbers from 'resurrecting' the body and selling it to the anatomy lecturers in Edinburgh.

Back out to the square with the Old Cross Well, and cross the road to the County Buildings. There is a large copper plaque set into the wall which records the famous shooting of the Earl of Moray, Regent of Scotland, near this spot in 1570. He was shot by Hamilton of Bothwellhaugh, legend saying it was in revenge for the rape of Hamilton's wife though it was more likely politically motivated, the shot coming from a window overlooking the street. The bullet passed through Moray's body between waist and thigh, and 'retained enough impetus to kill a horse near the regent's side'. He was carried to the Palace, but died a few hours later. The plaque was designed by Sir Noel Paton, a favourite painter of mine, whose name will appear further on in this book, and it was executed by a Mrs DO Hill. It was unveiled in 1875. The gun which fired the fateful shot was preserved for many years in Hamilton Palace, but as that Palace is long demolished, I have no idea of the whereabouts of the gun now.

It is worth taking a stroll further west along the High Street, just to look at the architecture. There are unsightly modern blocks of flats on the north side of the road, between High Street and the loch. Many old buildings of character were swept away to build these, but I hope we have learnt from the many mistakes made in Scotland in the 1960s and '70s. Some of the older buildings on the south side of the street are great, though. At the very end of the south side there is a fine example of a country laird's mansion, West Port House, a Hamilton property dating from 1600, but containing even earlier works. On the opposite side of the road here is the pub, The Black Bitch, and I want you to bear it in mind as you need it for the next set of directions.

Returning to your vehicle, drive along towards the Black Bitch, where nearly opposite a road goes off to your left (south). It is signposted 'Beecraigs Country Park'. Follow this, under the railway bridge, then cross the Union Canal, the old canal which links Edinburgh to Falkirk, continuing straight uphill, towards the bulk of Cockleroy Hill, slightly right. Continue on this road, ignoring side routes, and you will eventually come into thick woodland just east of Cockleroy.

There is a parking place in the woodland on your right, and a path leads through the trees for a few hundred yards, coming to a stile which takes you onto a flank of Cockleroy, and it is a short stiff pull to the top. You will need to have a degree of fitness, and decent footwear too, but for that little burst of stiff ascent there is a magnificent prospect over the Forth Valley, the Forth Bridges, visited earlier, visible to the east, the river snaking to its source in the Highlands to the west, and the petro-chemical complex of Grangemouth down below on the riverside. There are two summits, a gentle slope between them, and the dip between is known as 'Wallace's Cradle'. Legend tells us that this was where Wallace the Patriot watched the English approach, and observed them camping for the night on the town's Burghmuir. Linlithgow is laid out below, its loch, its palace and St Michael's Church all prominent. I look at this view through Wallace's eyes, managing to erase modern developments from the scene, and seeing the landscape, the outline of the hills, the waters of the Forth, as he did. I feel the connection.

Back to the car (or bike, if you are lucky – especially with the weather!) and continue on. A mile or so and there is a little turn-in on your left. This is the place of remembrance for those Scots who died in the Korean War, 1950–3. There is a little wood and glass building with plaques remembering the names of the dead, and a visitors' book. Trees have been planted, surrounding this site, only tiny saplings just now, but they will blossom and grow. I hope this place will be allowed to blossom and grow too, as it is left open to the public on trust.

You might be interested in continuing up the path that leads up the hillside beyond too. This leads to an old 'Sanctuary Stone' after about a third of a mile. There is a drystone wall right on the top of the hill and the stone is built into it. It is large and square, and bears a double-barred cross etched into both sides. There are several of these stones in this area, marking the area where people could claim sanctuary in connection with the nearby Torphichen Preceptory. We are going there very shortly, so all will be explained. At the next junction, there are signposts to Cairnpapple Hill.

The roads here are all minor roads with some blind bends, so please drive with care. It is not too far a drive to the lay-by which allows access to Cairnpapple, less than a mile.

Stairs lead the rest of the way to the top of the hill, and from the lay-by to the summit is only a few hundred yards, the road having reached most of the way up its 1016 feet.

Cairnpapple's summit is an ancient burial site, but it is much more than that. You can see why our ancient ancestors chose this spot for ritual and burials. Visiting it on a crisp winter's day, I could see the peaks of the Isle of Arran to the west, North Berwick Law away to the south east, and I named many snow-capped Highland peaks away to the north and north-west. The Ben Lawers group, the Tarmachans, Ben More and Stobinian, Ben Lui away north above Tyndrum, and one at the very distance of the curvature of the Earth which I finally realised was Ben Cruachan, away by Oban, at least 100 miles away. There can be very few places in Scotland where you are given such a magnificent prospect for so little effort. As there is a custodian present here in the summer months, based in the tin hut which looks like a relic from World War Two, he must relish being able to look at that view, watching it change day by day.

The burials on the summit of Cairnpapple go through five main phases. The earliest remains date back to 2800 BC! Then there are later rock-cut graves for crouched burials and the sockets for a circle of standing stones. There are still the remains of deep ditches surrounding the site too.

Later there has been a huge burial cairn comprising millions of stones to cover what were obviously the last resting places of some very important people, and although much of this has disappeared over the centuries, most probably as an easy source of building material, a reconstructed cairn has been built to protect the surviving graves. In the summer months, the custodian will open the metal hatch on top of this modern cairn and allow you to go inside, but don't feel this is a place that should only be visited in the summer. Standing atop this cairn with that magnificent prospect laid out in front of you gives the effect that you are on a flying carpet. Five thousand years ago this hilltop was a hive of activity. Today you are likely to have it to yourself – apart from the ghosts of all the intervening generations!

Looking directly east from here you will notice a whaleback of rock a few miles to the east. This is Binny Crag, its name coming from the William Binnie or Binny, who freed Linlithgow Peel from English control. It is best approached from the little farm road that passes its southern side. A haul to the top up its slope reveals a sheer drop on its western side, very impressive, and obviously all of volcanic activity in origin. Cockleroy, Cairnpapple and Binnie Crag, all within sight of each other, are a great day out for the reasonably fit. Cockleroy with its Wallace connections, Cairnpapple with its ancient graves, and Binny Crag with its connections with the times of

Robert the Bruce, giving a historic slant to a bit of exercise and great views.

The only black spot in a visit to Cairnpapple is the large communications mast built overlooking the cairn. It just seems unbelievable, like putting a phone mast on top of one of the pyramids. I know it is a perfect spot for such an eyesore, but ethically? I've taken many people to Cairnpapple over the years, and every one has commented on that bloody big mast.

Back down the stairs to the lay-by on the road then. Re-trace your route down to the T-junction and the road you came along from Linlithgow. Go straight by the Linlithgow road, carrying straight on. A little ahead the road forks away from you in a Y shape – take the right-hand road, and we head towards Torphichen. There are no signposts on these stretches, unfortunately. We soon reach some of the modern housing which has been built in recent years, all on the right side of the road, and we go downhill into this ancient village, and as we hit the village proper, we come to a junction where we take a right turn.

Torphichen is Gaelic for the Raven's Rock, and the village nestles on the edge of the hilly country we have just passed through. Torphichen is not a big place, and in the centre of the village you will see the sign for 'Torphichen Preceptory', which stands just off to our right. I remember looking up the word preceptory in a dictionary. Apparently it's a 'subordinate community or estate of knights of a religious or holy order'. So there we go.

The knights here were the Knights Hospitallers or the Knights of St John of Jerusalem. They were formed at the time of the Crusades, and had healing knowledge. It is reported that Edward Longshanks received treatment here for broken ribs while he was in Scotland, after being trampled by his horse. Hope it was a Scottish horse. Anyway, this building is mentioned in our records in 1168, and although only part of the main body survives, they are impressive in the fact that they look like church buildings, but are also very defensive looking in aspect. A church dating from 1756 has been built on part of the site, using foundations of an original building. Although the preceptory lies empty, it is roofed, and I can remember one or two interesting carvings on the stonework inside.

Sir William Wallace was here too, after the decisive battle of Stirling Bridge in September 1297. We know this as he wrote a letter, dated and marked 'Torphichen', which was sent to one of his captains, Alexander Scrymgeour, who had been left besieging the castle at Dundee. Scrymgeour was made hereditary standard bearer of the battle army of Scotland, a post given the royal seal of approval by King Robert Bruce a few years later, and I am proud to say that Scrymgeour is still the holder of this title today.

Within the preceptory churchyard stands a cross-inscribed stone, which is believed to mark the centre of the privileged sanctuary ground. It also has prehistoric cup marks upon it, so this stone has probably quite a story to tell! The outlying sanctuary stone on the hilltop by the Korean War Memorial is an outlier of this central stone. There are several that have survived, markers spread out in a circle, a mile or so distant, which marked where malefactors could claim the ancient rite of sanctuary to protect them from their pursuers.

In the village, not far from the preceptory, is the Torphichen Inn, a hostelry which bears a red cross and the name of Hugo de Payens on its frontage. I'm a little bemused by this, as that cross and Hugo himself are associated with a different order of Knights called the Knights Templar. The Templars have no connection with Torphichen and the Knights of St John, other than being similar orders from the same era, but so much myth has been written, with much bending of the truth, that the whole has been blurred in consequence. When the Templars were suppressed in 1312, however, the Knights of St John did inherit all the properties which the Templars owned in Scotland, but Torphichen was never under Templar control. You may be interested to know that the St John's Ambulance Brigade and several other organisations take their name from the Knights Hospitallers.

Back to the road end from the preceptory then, and we turn right and continue to follow the road we were on, now marked on maps as the B792. Follow this road on for a mile till you reach its junction with the A706, a more major route. Turn left here, and after a few yards there is a junction off to the right marked 'Falkirk'. This takes us steeply downhill through trees to join the A801 just before it crosses the bridge over the River Avon (the Gaelic word for river is *abhainn*, and as 'bh' is pronounced v, you will see the source. There are many rivers in Scotland called Avon, or even Almond and other similar names, all originating from this Gaelic root).

Upstream from here a mile, on this bank, there is another 'Wallace's Cave', legend stating that Wallace was here after the battle of Falkirk

I remember the scene in the film *Braveheart* where the Scots were licking their wounds, sitting on a riverbank after the Battle of Falkirk, and I was struck by how much it resembled the area round this cave, the Avon running close by. The cave is marked on Ordnance Survey maps, and is signposted from the B8047 a mile south of here, but it can be tricky to take the right route in the heavily wooded terrain. But at the moment, we cross the Avon on the old bridge here, and we leave that part of Scotland called Lothian and enter what is known as the cockpit of Scotland, a name that resounds through our history – Stirlingshire.

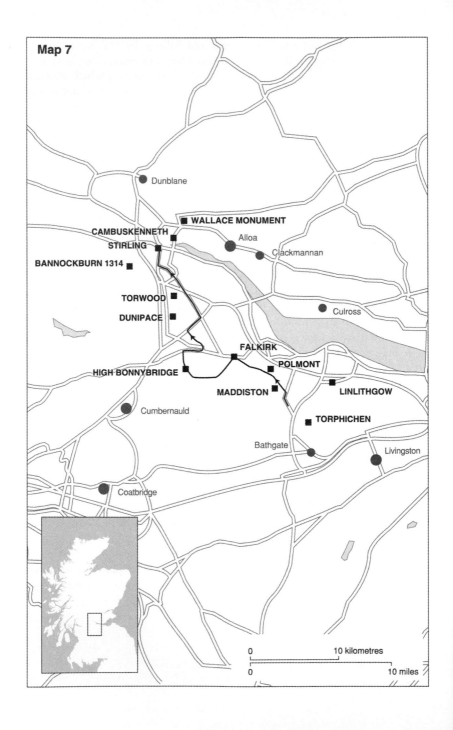

Map 7

Dunblane

■ WALLACE MONUMENT

CAMBUSKENNETH
STIRLING ■
Alloa
Clackmannan

BANNOCKBURN 1314 ■

TORWOOD ■

DUNIPACE ■

Culross

FALKIRK
POLMONT

HIGH BONNYBRIDGE ■

MADDISTON
LINLITHGOW

Cumbernauld
TORPHICHEN ■

Bathgate
Livingston

Coatbridge

0   10 kilometres

0   10 miles

CHAPTER SEVEN

The Heartland

BEGINNING AT MADDISTON, WE GO TO POLMONT, FALKIRK, BONNYBRIDGE, LARBERT, TOR-WOOD, TO THE ROUNDABOUT ABOVE THE M9 AT STIRLING SERVICES, BEFORE GOING DOWN TO BANNOCKBURN, ST NINIANS, STIRLING, CAMBUSKENNETH, AND THE WALLACE MONUMENT.

SO, CROSSING THE River Avon takes us into Stirlingshire. Stirling, the county town, is known as the cockpit, or driving seat, of Scotland since it has been said that to hold the mighty castle there is to control or pilot the whole country. And this country has seen more than its fair share of action when it comes to battles and battlefields, topography being the cause, and I hope that will become apparent as we continue.

We climb up out of the gut of the gorge of the Avon on to flatter ground, rolling farmland, much of it moorland in the not-too-distant past. You will notice signs pointing to Candie. Sometimes you come across such unusual wee place-names in Scotland, and I'd like to know the origin of this particular one, but we carry on along this main road regardless.

After another mile or so, the A801 eventually reaches a large roundabout at Bowhouse. Take the second exit marked Maddiston B805. I hope you get a clear day. There is a view across the Firth of Forth here to the Ochil Hills, standing proud, rising high like a wall out of the flat plains of Fife, a throwback to huge upheaval when the Earth was younger and still taking shape. I love the views of the Ochils from the south: such an impressive sight, and just as my ancestors would have seen them. As I write this, I was lucky enough to see them with their tops covered in what looked like icing sugar, the first smattering of winter snow. The highest of the Ochils is Ben Cleuch at 2,363 feet. It might not sound like much to folk from mountainous nations, but when you see them from near sea level, and with the almost wall-like qualities the Ochils have, 2,363 feet is pretty impressive!

We drive on through Maddiston, and on to the next community, Rumford. This is a different Scotland we are entering. A Scotland with an industrial past – not the Scotland of the tourist brochures. It might not be the prettiest side of the country, but this area has a history, which predates the Industrial Revolution. It was, I believe, this route through Rumford which Edward Longshanks and his mighty English army took before the fateful Battle of Falkirk in 1298. Keep driving and you will see why. Look out for a road that branches off at a right angle to your left (does that make sense?), called Sunnyside Road. It's just after a tricky junction. Keep your eyes peeled for it please – I don't want you seeing Sunnyside Road as you come level with it and some hard braking results in one of those damn collisions that raise your insurance premiums. Anyway, Sunnyside Road goes out into farmland, with an old wall on your right. Follow it uphill another mile, and you hit a nice wee village called Wallacestone. A white pillar made of concrete, about ten to twelve feet high appears in some open ground on your right, and just after that there is an entrance where you can drive in and up towards the pillar. Park here and realise you are on the edge of an escarpment that overlooks the Forth Valley, and just marvel at the view. (Again, this is bloody Scotland, and I have been here very many times to look out at rainy misty nothingness, but if you get a clear view, it is amazing).

The southern edge of the Highlands lies off to the northwest; the Forth plain with its teeming industry at Grangemouth lies below. The Forth Bridges are visible over the shoulder of ground to your left. Over to your northwest Stirling Castle stands atop its rock some 18 miles away. The Great Hall at the castle has recently been refurbished and is a funny creamy yellow colour which the powers-that-be call 'golden', but it at least makes it stand out even at this distance.

So, why Wallacestone, why this pillar? Below you on the left lies Callendar Wood. You can see some of the tower blocks of flats of Falkirk peeping over the tops of the trees. The tree line of Callendar Wood has not changed at this side too drastically over the centuries. There is an old estate wall for Callendar House, an old fortified house that stands within this woodland. The wall is very old, not as old as Wallace's time, but it has stood in one form or another for hundreds of years. English accounts for the battle of Falkirk in 1298 say that when they approached the Scots, they were on 'this' side of Falkirk, i.e. the side facing Linlithgow, where the English had camped (remember Burghmuir?) and they had woodland at their back, and water before them. The accounts also tell us that the Scots faced south. So, the spot directly in front of Callendar Wood fits the site perfectly for the battle. There is water down in the gut before you in the shape of the Westquarter Burn and the Hallglen Burn. In fact they merge in front of this woodland, directly under the aptly named Woodend Farm, and I believe this farm is the site of the deployment of the Scots army at the Battle of Falkirk. This farm is visible from Wallacestone at time of writing, but just above nearer trees, more recently planted, so it may not be visible in the future.

Wallace knew that the English were approaching from Linlithgow, and left his spearmen, massed in great groups called schiltroms, to head for higher ground to see if the enemy was in sight. He and several of his captains came to this very spot. Well – it's obvious, isn't it? Just look at the view!

Wallace, of course, had to keep within a reasonable distance of contact with his army. Legend tells us he stood on a boulder here for a better view. The English reports tell us that they spotted a group of Scots on a hilltop, and some knights galloped forward to try to bring them to combat, but that the Scots disappeared downhill and off into the mist down in the dip towards Callendar Wood. This would probably have been Wallace, hastening back to his army.

So, this is how this village of Wallacestone gained its name, from the stone which the generations onwards from 1298 pointed out as being the very one where Wallace, the great Scottish patriot, actually stood to watch for the approach of the English. Alas, the stone is long gone, chipped away by succeeding souvenir hunters over the years. The present white-painted concrete pillar was erected in 1810. The stone stood just a little to the west. It's good that the spot has been commemorated.

I love to hear the wee stories that spring up around sites like this. One that I heard about this spot was that when asked, some of the local kids said that Wallace had actually run up the hill here, carrying this pillar, and he rammed it into the ground to climb up onto it, 'tae watch for the English'! A brilliant mix of truth and childish invention, and it lets you see what a superman Wallace is in the imagination of Scots, as that pillar must weigh at least a bloody ton! I'd have trouble running uphill with that myself, I must admit!

There was a brilliant spelling mistake on the inscription on the pillar which was rectified a couple of years ago. The word *Scottish* looked as if it had originally been inscribed *Scotish*, then it appears that someone must have pointed this out to the sculptor, who then tried to rectify it by adding an extra stem on either side of the original stem of the 't'. So now we had what looked like 'Scotttish'. It has been patched up now to look right, but I liked the error and wondered at the tale behind it. You can still see what I mean if you look closely.

Take a last look at that incredible vista and then return to Sunnyside Road and follow it back downhill to the B805, where you turn left to follow your original route. This is a consistently built-up area, with no distinct boundaries, and for the next mile we drive through Polmont, first, then into Redding. Drive straight on through any roundabouts encountered. We cross the Union Canal, then a railway line, and we immediately come to a roundabout. Pull in and park here, so that you can take a look at the little monument standing on a piece of open ground to your right. It is of black polished granite, and bears the inscription:

Erected to the memory of the 40 men who lost their lives in the disaster at Redding Colliery, Tuesday 25th September 1923

Then underneath is added:

5 were rescued after 10 days entombed.

I can't imagine the horror of being entombed far underground, after a disaster like that, for ten whole days. Did their rescuers come upon them
suddenly? Did they not know that they would survive? Walk around the
monument and have a look at the reverse side too, from the other side of
the bushes. Most people probably don't do this. The reverse side says:

The Sir William Wallace Grand Lodge of Scotland Free Colliers erected
this memorial, 27 September 1980. Enhanced 21 September 2002.

I remember that day well.

In my capacity as a 'motorcycling historian', I had met up that morning
with two guys from a Californian motorcycling television show, to take
them round some Wallace sites in central Scotland. One of them gloried in
the name Graham William Wallace! They were driving Indian 1800cc
straight-four-engine motorcycles (tons of grunt, but not great on corners –
and we have plenty of corners in Scotland (I'm not saying I'd say no to one
though!). I was on my trusty Honda Pan-European. I took them to
Wallacestone, and was just telling the story when I heard strains of *Scots
Wha Hae wi' Wallace bled* in the distance. It turned out that the re-dedica-
tion ceremony was taking place at the monument. My companions snapped
away, delighted with such a great photo opportunity.

They noticed that as the miners marched they linked pinkies. I believe this
was the procedure used if there was an accident down in the mines, like ele-
phants walking trunks-to-tails. They could walk in line, but still had hands
free to save themselves if there was a trip in the darkness or similar. Sir
William Wallace was a popular figure in the imagination during the miners'
fight for better working conditions. His fight for the essential and basic
freedoms for Scots men and women is not confined to the battlefield in the
psyche of the Scots.

Onwards again, continuing on the B805, downhill constantly, drawing
closer to Falkirk. You reach a roundabout, Falkirk marked straight ahead,
and the road off to the left is marked Hallglen. If you wish, deviate a little
here, and take this road. It is only a half mile or so to Woodend Farm, the
place where, I believe, the Scots stood at the Battle of Falkirk in 1298. It is
difficult to park on this main road, adjacent to the farm, although when it is
quiet I have put the car half on the pavement. The bike does not cause me
such problems. A hundred or two yards on there is a road which branches
off on the left, entering a housing estate, called Glenburn Road, so you can
park there and it is only a short walk back.

On the main road below the farm a bridle path goes off due south, and a
few yards down you will come to the junction of the Westquarter and
Hallglen Burns. These, before modern landscaping and drainage, would

have formed a boggy marsh at their junction, and English accounts tell us that when their heavy cavalry charged, the riders hit a wet area which they could not cross and had to wheel east and west to circumnavigate. This fits. The Scots' schiltroms, or massed groups of spearmen, would have stood where the farm is now. The road you have just driven has changed the gradient of the escarpment, but it was a reasonable site for Wallace to have chosen at short notice, the woodland directly behind being convenient for melting into if the outcome of the fight started to go the wrong way. The trees would provide a reasonable escape from heavy cavalry and cover to shield fleeing men from arrows. And it was the bow that won Falkirk. The heavy cavalry could not pierce the groups of spearmen, but massed archery could – and Longshanks had 12,000 archers at Falkirk. The Scots were sitting targets. The English only had to get their trajectory right and fire into the mass. The Scots fell in their thousands under the incessant hail.

For the next two centuries the English longbow would prevail on the battlefields of France – and Scotland on occasion – but Falkirk was the first incident where the power of the cloth-yard shaft would show its capabilities, and it would devastate armies again and again, until gunpowder made it obsolete.

I sit here on occasion, looking across the burns, and I glance over and up to Woodend and see my ancestors striving to hold off the constant charges of cavalry. I can see Wallace in the midst of his men, shouting to be heard above the din, the crash and clash of battle, the neighing of horses and the screams of men. He shouts to urge them on. Not to waver. 'We fight for Scotland! SCOTLAND!'

And I can see him when the fight was over and lost and ten thousand bodies lie bloody on that rise, yet he lives on, he has escaped to safety. The tears run as he knows the cost his fellow countrymen have paid endeavouring to withstand England's enforced serfdom. How can a man deal with such pain? These men came to fight for their freedom and died under his command. The guilt he felt must have been terrible and his conscience taken its toll. I know how it must have felt though, because I would have stood shoulder to shoulder with my fellows.

Some things are worth fighting, and dying, for.

Retrace your steps, and head back down to the roundabout at which you turned left to Hallglen earlier. Take the next exit on the left to Falkirk, and a few yards on there is another roundabout, where again you take the first exit left, signposted Falkirk and Callendar House.

You have just left the northern outpost of the Roman Empire!

As you drive along this stretch towards Falkirk's town centre, the grassy bank on your left is a remnant of the Antonine Wall, the wall built across the narrow waist of Scotland between Forth and Clyde, an attempt to subdue the tribes that inhabited Scotland at that time. The wall was composed of turf with a deep ditch in front, and a military road ran behind on the southern side. A turf wall might not sound like much of a defence, but trust me, it was well-built and a tough barrier to cross. It was defended by well-trained, well-armed Roman troops, their armour and weaponry, at least, far superior to that of the local tribesmen. It had 19 forts along its 36-mile length, one or two still well worth seeing, so I'll take you there in due course!

It dates from around AD 140, but the early inhabitants of Scotland (Caledonians, the Romans called them) managed to overrun it on a regular basis, most probably to visit their relatives, cut off on the other side. The Romans finally abandoned it less than 50 years after it was built. This vast structure always humbles me, as it would any modern builders. A 36 mile long wall and ditch – running from Bowling on the River Clyde in the west to Bo'ness on the River Forth in the east, built with pure muscle power when the biggest tool and aid would probably have been an early wheelbarrow. Can you imagine the number of man-hours put into the wall? And all to last less than 50 years. There must have been old guys about who had stayed on or married in Scotland, who having worked on the wall as youths, must have thought , 'all that bloody graft – and they're abandoning it!'

So here we are driving along on the northern edge of the Roman Empire, heading towards Falkirk town centre. It is strange to put those two together. Falkirk. Roman Empire. Scotland can be a strange place.

There are a couple of roundabouts on this stretch, but just drive through them 'til you get to the roundabout with Callendar House marked off to your left. Turn in here and take the next left again, driving past some high-rise blocks of flats, the same ones you could see the tops of from Wallacestone, and then you come to Callendar House itself. It has a long frontage, looking out to parkland, and the remains of the Antonine Wall running across that parkland. There is an interesting old ice-house here too. In winter, ice and snow would be gathered and packed into this cave-like structure, and food could be stored in here – basically a giant medieval fridge-freezer!

The Livingstone family gained this estate in the fourteenth century by marrying the Callendar family heiress. The Callendar name has stuck though, not just for the house, but for the surrounding woodland too. At the core of the building is a fourteenth or fifteenth-century tower house, and over the centuries various wings have been added to give it the rambling appearance it has today. Bonnie Prince Charlie was here, as were Cromwell and Mary, Queen of Scots, and indeed many other figures from history have visited at one time or another. The house is open to the public. It is a few years since I visited, and things may have changed, but I found it quite pricey for not an awful lot to see. It is worth walking on past the house for a look at the grounds though, which are a beautiful blend of trees and water.

Back out to the main route into Falkirk. Drive on just a little and park at a metered bay or in one of the car parks here. A walk along the High Street of Falkirk will reveal a plethora of history, all in a half-mile walk. Many more famous Scottish towns would be hard pressed to offer the number of historical bits and pieces that Falkirk has to see.

As you walk the obvious rise up to the High Street and the town centre, you will notice the modern indoor shopping centre on your right, called Callendar Square. Directly opposite the entrance is a newsagent's where you will see a plaque above the door bearing the legend:

Robert Burns
Poet
Slept Here
August 25th 1787

Burns, of course, is Scotland's national poet, or as we tend to say in Scotland, *bard*, it being the old word for a poet or songwriter in Scotland. In fact, Burns is generally known here as *the* Bard, so great is his fame. Some foreigners may not be immediately familiar with his name, but they will know his work, *Auld Lang Syne* springing to mind at once, as it seems to be sung at New Year in many parts of the globe.

Just a little further on there is a tall steeple on your right, part of which was once used as a prison and therefore it is known as the Tolbooth. The High Street widens a little here, and this was the town's market place in years gone by. Marked are the sites of the town's well and of the place where the town's last public hanging took place in 1828. Behind the Tolbooth, is Tolbooth Street, the shortest street in Scotland, 46 feet in length if I remember correctly.

Opposite the Tolbooth Steeple is Dixons, the electrical retailer. This premises is on the site of the building that became Bonnie Prince Charlie's headquarters in the town after his nearby victory in the second Battle of Falkirk, fought to the south-west of the town in 1746. A little further along yet is the Howgate Shopping Centre. It was this route, originally called the Bantaskine Port, that Charlie's army used to enter the town after their victory. Walking this covered, air-conditioned route today, it is bizarre to imagine a tartan-clad army, soaked to the skin and with many wounded, entering the town in triumph.

It is worth walking to the escalators right at the rear of this mall to have a look at the stained glass that has been mounted here as a feature. This glass was brought from the now-demolished Bantaskine House, around which the 1746 battle was fought. Its theme is Charlie himself, almost life-size, flanked by two of his captains. I watch people go by here in their droves, never giving these amazing glass pieces a glance – and they really are very

fine and pleasing to the eye. They stand at the bottom of the first flight of
escalators, below the café area.

Leaving the front door of the Howgate and back into the High Street, just
a few extra yards down the street and you will see the opening into the old
churchyard on your right. It is this church which actually gives the town its
name: *Fa* meaning speckled, so the 'speckled kirk'. Its Gaelic name,
Eaglaisbreac, has the same meaning, *Eaglais* meaning church and *breac*
being the Gaelic for speckled. There has been a church on this site from the
earliest period of Christianity in Scotland, but much of the building visible
today dates from 1811, the earlier building having been burnt down in
1810. What I love are the monuments and tombs in this churchyard. Just to
the right of the entrance steps is the monument to the 'men of Bute'. Bute is
an island in the Firth of Clyde, its main town being Rothesay. Every able-
bodied man aged between 16 and 60 came from the island to fight for
Wallace and Scotland at the 1298 battle, led by Sir John Stewart, and they
all died, annihilated by the hail of English arrows. The Stewart family are
still Marquises of Bute, and they commissioned this monument, in the style
of a Celtic cross, which was unveiled in 1888.

Over a little is a tomb, surrounded by an iron railing and surmounted by
a Lion Rampant. You will notice that there are several grave slabs, each
later one lying on top of its predecessor, each bearing the inscription of the
one below:

Here lyes Sir John the Grame,
Baith wight and wise,
Ane of the chiefs who reschewit Scotland thrice
Ane better knight not to the world was lent
Nor was gude Grame of truth and hardiment'

       *   *   *   *   *

Sir John Graham, originating from Dundaff in the Carron Valley where the
remains of his castle still stand, was not only a captain in Wallace's army,
but also a trusted and apparently lifelong friend. When he fell on Falkirk's
bloody field, it is said Wallace shed tears over his friend's body. At the corner of the church adjacent to Graham's tomb is another, lying flat. This is
the last resting place of Sir John Stewart, who led the men of Bute. These
two men were fervent patriots, and heroes of Scotland. They should be better remembered. Their tombs are seldom visited, and thousands of shoppers
walk Falkirk's High Street, only yards away, completely oblivious.

There are two other interesting large stone gravestones in the churchyard.
They had been covered in spray paint when I last visited them. Scotland,
like most other societies in the world, is plagued by unthinking morons. No

sense of community. No sense of identity. We live in a country, to quote from *Braveheart*, that has 'no sense of itself'. These two large tombs are of officers in the army, defeated at the second battle of Falkirk in 1746. Although they fought for the Hanoverian regime, which was up in opposition to Bonnie Prince Charlie, they deserve better treatment than they have received. It's not as if their tombs have been defaced because of their political or religious beliefs, but simply because they are there. These men were Scots, and many of the Highland army of Prince Charlie turned out for their funeral out of respect.

I gave a little more detail about these tombs in my book, *On the Trail of Bonnie Prince Charlie*. It is strange, but this book, in which I deliberately shied away from the religious and political side of the campaign and concentrated on the places and buildings where the various events took place, has caused more controversy than anything else I have done. I received letters condemning me for glorifying either the Catholics or the 'rebels' – the Catholic criticisms coming mainly from Northern Ireland and the rebel ones from England. I can't recall receiving a single letter from another Scot decrying the book. Maybe they realised that it was only meant to be good fun!

Now make your way back to your vehicle at the other end of the High Street. The first roundabout back towards the direction of Callendar House is where we take up our route again. Take the exit marked B803, signposted for Slamannan and Falkirk Infirmary. This takes us along Arnot Street. Keep following the signs for the infirmary at the next few junctions, it's probably a lot simpler than these road directions! At the next mini roundabout, turn right onto Cochrane Avenue, then there is a staggered junction with another mini roundabout where we drive on to Westburn Avenue, and this longish straight road takes us by the infirmary, then by a large round school building. At the end of Westburn Avenue we come to a T-junction with canal locks directly opposite. Take a left here and we are now on Glenfuir Road, the canal running along on our right-hand side. A quarter of a mile on and you will see the signs for Bonnybridge and the Falkirk Wheel, pointing down Tamfourhill Road to our right. We are going to take this road shortly, but there is something a mile or so further on that I want you to see first, so carry straight on.

We pass under two large bridges, the first carrying a railway, the second carrying yet another canal. This is what the Falkirk Wheel is connected with, but we will get there shortly. Glenfuir Road becomes Greenbank Road here, but there is no deviation, the formerly wide road narrows though, to become a country lane. Take care here, as the road is very narrow, and passing oncoming vehicles is a tight squeeze.

Climbing uphill the best part of a mile on this twisty section, you will see a pencil-shaped column on your left at a tight bend. There is just about room to squeeze a car in here at the side of the road, but it is perhaps better to drive on a few yards to the next junction where the road is wider and you can park there and walk back. The monument you see here is the memorial to the second Battle of Falkirk in January 1746.

The battlefield here has remained relatively unchanged, and that is a rarity. You can walk the ground and the terrain is much like it was on the day. There is a small commemoration service at the memorial every year, and guess what? It took place on the very day I visited. It was pure coincidence that I got to this part of the book at the same time as the commemoration. There were good speeches, concentrating on the fact that an army of crofters and farmers fighting for Bonnie Prince Charlie managed to defeat an army of regular, well-equipped and trained soldiers, fighting for the Hanoverian monarch based in London. The army of the Prince was arrayed on this side of the gorge, which runs downhill from the monument, and the Hanoverian Redcoat troops faced them on the other side. There are paths down the gorge that let you really get the feel of the place. It was a day of driving sleet, and darkness began to fall when the battle was still young, and though the Prince took the day, it was an hour or two before this was actually realised as the conditions in the darkness were so bad. The dead were buried close to where they fell, so this perhaps lends an air to the place.

Sadly, the monument is in a state of decay, with much of the stonework starting to crumble. I hope that when this situation is eventually rectified, some information boards will be put in place to tell people of the major events that took place here (and if it isn't, I know a few people who will ask questions!).

I don't want to detract from the solemnity of the field of battle, but this next wee story really should be told. At the event here in January 2002, I noticed that one of my patriot friends, dressed in the garb of 1745, Kenny Borthwick, had his musket with him, loaded with black powder. Kenny was going to fire a shot at the end of the minute's silence, which is held in remembrance. He had a word in my ear beforehand. He pointed out that there were several horses within sight, the closest a couple of hundred yards away. He said 'When I let rip with the musket, you watch those horses'. So when the silence was over and I saw Kenny step forward, raising his musket to his shoulder, I raised my eyes to watch the horses, with their heads down, lazily munching grass in the surrounding fields. As the musket went off – and I can assure you it's a hell of a bang, the black powder probably ten times as loud as you would imagine – I noticed that every horse came off the ground a little. I could honestly see daylight under each hoof, as they all went straight up in the air! Then they all looked around for a few seconds before going back to munching the grass.

It made me realise how it must have been, going into battle on horseback in the days of muskets and gunpowder. I wonder if the horses got used to the noise or whether they actually went an inch or two up in the air every time there was a volley of shot? At battles like Falkirk, here in 1746, when there was a lot of musket fire, the horses must have spent more time in the air than they did on the ground!

Go back down the little road, back under the two bridges, and on 'til you again reach the junction, from this direction going off to your left, pointing towards Bonnybridge and the Falkirk Wheel. It is called Tamfourhill Road. So, on along this ordinary looking street, but if you look to your right you will notice that you are just south of the Antonine Wall, the course of it just discernible through the trees. Eventually you will come to a junction where the entrance to the Wheel is on your right. I'd love to be able to tell you much more about the engineering marvel that is the Falkirk Wheel, but unfortunately, every time I have visited it, it has been closed – repairs, building work etc. I hope you have more luck. It certainly looks impressive. It was built to connect the two great canals of central Scotland, the Forth and Clyde Canal, which, as its name suggests, links the Forth in the east and the Clyde in the west, and the Union Canal, which runs from Falkirk to Edinburgh. The canals have been cleared, cleaned and upgraded in recent years. The Falkirk Wheel was built to lift barges and boats from one canal up and onto a spur of the other, therefore making it possible to sail from Glasgow to Edinburgh, Scotland's two great cities now connected by waterway. It is, as its name suggests, a giant wheel-like mechanism, boats able to sail onto it, and that section of water, boat and all, raised to a much higher level. There are trips on boats available, and there is a visitor centre too.

This is probably the just the place to tell you about the canals themselves. The Forth and Clyde closely follows the line of the Antonine Wall right across this narrow waist of Scotland. This shows how the Romans in their day were able to chart the course, over a line of ground, which would be the most attractive to the navigators over a millennia and a half later. The canal builders in Scotland were called navigators, incidentally, which is why we call workmen 'navvies' today.

The Forth and Clyde Canal was begun on July 10, 1768. £50,000 towards its cost was given by the government, the money having come from forfeited Jacobite estates after the failure of the '45 and the slaughter of Culloden. It has about 38 miles of waterway, including the spur into the centre of Glasgow, which terminates at Port Dundas. The Union Canal was begun in 1822, and is roughly 31 miles long. Before the establishment of the railways, these canals carried much passenger transport, and their banks must have been very familiar to regular commuters.

Exiting the Falkirk Wheel site, continue on along Tamfourhill Road, following the line of the Roman Wall again for the first few yards. You swing away from the wall to cross a railway line, and the stretch of canal, leading on through a hill to the Falkirk Wheel, is on your left.

Follow Tamfourhill Road on. It's quite twisty here and there is scrubby woodland on either side. When you come out of this woodland you are on open heathy farmland. This is Bonnymuir, which takes its name from the nearby Bonny Water and the sizeable community of Bonnybridge.

Just as a couple of factory buildings start to appear before you, take a glance over into the field on your left. It was in this field that the 1820 uprising came to a sorry end, at what is known as the Battle of Bonnymuir, but a battle it was not, rather more of a skirmish, and a very one-sided one at that. After the Napoleonic Wars, many soldiers returned to what they hoped would be good jobs and decent working conditions. There was much unrest at the high-handed approach of the London-based government, and the treatment that was doled out. The French Revolution had also had an effect on the psyche of ordinary Scots.

In 1820, a group of weavers, ordinary working men, gathered in Strathaven, carrying a banner proclaiming 'Scotland Free or a Desert'. Their leader was James Wilson. The march petered out when it was realised that there were no great numbers ready to join them. Another two groups had gathered, however. One in Glasgow, led by Andrew Hardie, which followed the Forth and Clyde Canal in this direction and linked up with another group at Condorrat near Cumbernauld, led by John Baird. Baird and Hardie's group, 51 strong, decided to march on the Carron Iron Works near Falkirk, as it was at that time a munitions depot among other things. They were captured here on Bonnymuir when a body of hussars from Kilsyth caught up with them and charged. Four men were wounded and 47 taken prisoner. The group had only five muskets and two pistols between them.

The government in London decided to impose English law in Scotland on this occasion. Most of those involved were handed sentences of transportation to the colonies. Three were given the death sentence. Hardie and Baird were executed in Stirling. The axe used is an exhibit at the Stirling Smith Art Gallery and Museum. Wilson was the third. He was hanged in Glasgow, then beheaded. There is an 1820 Society active in Scotland, and I have attended one of their commemorations out here on Bonnymuir.

There is a farm gate on the left-hand side of the road about a hundred yards before the first buildings. It was in this field that the hussars rode the weavers down. The fact that English law was used to deal with these people shows the disdain with which Scotland has been treated. This was a flaunting of one of the Acts of Union. These were the acts passed to bind the two distinct nations together. Scotland could have said that such a move annulled the hated Union, but how could she? She was ruled from London and was represented from there. Most of the Acts of Union have been broken at one time or another, and she is shackled and without a voice. Oh Scotland. Have you no men of steel left? Where are your champions, your voice, your backbone?

Scotland free or a desert indeed.

Continue along Tamfourhill Road to its T-junction end at High Bonnybridge. We turn right here, downhill, under a narrow, one-vehicle-at-a-time railway bridge, and on down Broomhill Road. Continue on towards the centre of Bonnybridge. Eventually, among old factories, you will see a sign pointing off to your right, bearing the words 'Foundry Road and Chattan Industrial Estate'. There is nothing to tell you of the Roman remains up this little side road from the direction you have approached, but you will notice that on the other side, from the Bonnybridge town centre approach, the sign says 'Antonine Wall, Rough Castle, 1 1/2 miles'. So, let us deviate from our route a little up this dead-end road, as the best preserved part of the wall lies here. You drive through the industrial estate, and continue straight on, but the road starts to deteriorate. It is still driveable though, just watch your speed and take care. After a few hundred yards of this, the road swings in to a parking area. The Antonine Wall runs just alongside. Walk to the lip, and look left and right and marvel at the size of the remains disappearing into the distance. Large parts of the wall remain, but the depth of the ditch in front is particularly impressive. A few hundred yards further, across a ravine where a burn flows, is the remains of Rough Castle, a major Roman fort. There are no buildings, but there is much in the way of embankments, ditches and earthworks, all combining to give you a clear picture of the Roman occupation of southern Scotland.

Strangely, the Antonine Wall is named Grims, or Graham's, Dyke on old maps of Scotland, but I have no idea why Scots called it this. But there is something worth seeing on the opposite northern side of the wall from Rough Castle. There is a honeycomb of round pits, perhaps each a yard across, called *lillia*. These were designed to break up any frontal charge on the wall at the fort here. They have been excavated, and today are just a series of holes, but they would have had wooden, sharpened stakes at their bases when they were in working order. It's fascinating to wander around them – nearly 2,000 years old as they are.

Time to walk back uphill towards your vehicle now. But pause on the remains of the wall near the car park, as I always do, and look across to the Campsie Hills before you and, like I do, try see them as a soldier on the wall would have done all those ages ago. I wonder if those hills beyond held terrors for them. I wonder if the soldiers here were from Mediterranean lands – I suppose some must have been – and what they thought of drizzly damp Scotland in winter. It has been said, of course, that the Romans didn't build the wall to keep the Caledonians, out, but rather that there was nothing here for them, and it was to keep civilisation in. But, if that was the case, why push on from Hadrian's Wall to build this wall which was to last only a few years?

Back towards Bonnybridge then. When we reach Broomhill Road again, we turn right and continue on. We immediately cross the Forth and Clyde Canal, turn a right-hand bend and come to a roundabout in the centre of Bonnybridge.

Bonnybridge has two claims to fame. One is the 'Bonnybridge Triangle', a mickey-take of the Bermuda Triangle. More UFOs are spotted here than anywhere else in Western Europe – apparently. Whether these sightings are after the pubs have shut and it's home time, I have yet to ascertain. In the old days people always claimed to have been taken by the fairy folk. Funny how no-one claims to be taken by fairies any more, now it's abduction by aliens. Perhaps the fairies moved from their underground caverns into flying saucer production?

The other thing about Bonnybridge is that it has more National Lottery Winners than anywhere else in Scotland. People actually travel here to buy their lottery tickets!

Next we take a right turn at this roundabout in Bonnybridge, signposted Falkirk A803, and we are now driving along Bonnybridge's Main Street. Follow this road for some two miles, most of it in open countryside, and you come to a largeish roundabout called Three Bridges. The Falkirk Wheel is visible to your right. You will notice that you are on the edge of a built-up area, which goes by the name of Camelon. (It's pronounced Came-alon). This may be the Camelot of King Arthur, (a story highjacked by the English?). Arthur of the Britons, if he existed, may have been of the tribe called the Strathclyde Britons, based at Dumbarton. Camelon was an important Roman settlement at one time, and Arthur could have based himself in an abandoned Roman fortification here.

At the roundabout we take the left turning, signposted Glasgow and Denny, the A883. A little further along and you cross the Bonny Water, from which Bonnybridge takes its name. After a mile you come to a large roundabout where you turn right onto a small road, signposted B905 Larbert.

We immediately cross the River Carron on an old stone bridge, and the road turns a right angle to the right. After just a few yards you'll see the entrance to Hills of Dunipace Cemetery on your left. Drive in. There is a little one-way system in operation here and there are usually a few relatives visiting newly departed loved ones, so please respect their privacy. This has been consecrated ground and a burial place in one form or another for perhaps thousands of years. Dunipace is mentioned in Roman documents. The name is Gaelic, a corruption of *Dun-I-bas*, 'Hills of Death'. The modern town of Dunipace, which lies two miles further west, takes its name from these hills. The two remaining hills stand here within the cemetery grounds. One of the hills is circular and shaped like a miniature Mount Fuji, and I remember the first time I set eyes on it I was sure it was man-made, but it turns out that these hills are remnants of debris deposited here during the last ice-age. There was a third hill apparently, but it was dug away for its material in the early 1800s. Wonder what it looked like?

At the back of the cemetery, park and go through the entrance in the old wall leading into the oldest part of the burial ground where you will find yew trees growing all round here. I think yew trees are supposed to ward off evil or something. Anyway, according to Blind Harry, the man who wrote *The Deeds of Sir William Wallace of Elderslie* in the 1400s, the book on which the film *Braveheart* was based, Wallace was raised here by his uncle, who was the priest of Dunipace. So that would mean the very spot where you are standing, as this is the original Dunipace from Wallace's day.

There are some gravestones here dating back to the 1600s. It has a feel about it, this place, and I can sense the spirit of Wallace here. He probably got to know Sir John Graham, who died at Falkirk and is buried in Falkirk churchyard, while he was here, as Graham's family seat is further up the River Carron. There is a poignant gravestone near the entrance of this old place marking the grave of a small child who drowned in the nearby Carron. You may also notice the remains of a tower over the fence on the northern side of the cemetery. This is the last remnant of Dunipace House, which belonged to Archie Primrose, a staunch supporter of Bonnie Prince Charlie. The tartan-clad army of Charlie actually went right past this spot to ford the Carron before the 1746 Battle of Falkirk.

Back out to the road, and turn left, continuing on towards Larbert. Another mile and the edge of Larbert appears, with Old Larbert church conspicuous on its hilltop site. Just after you pass the church there is a brilliant old house on the right side of the road. It's a private house that I have always admired. Above a window facing the road there is an inscription carved on the lintel, which reads, 'Built Feb. 1635 A.N.' That would be the initials of the builder. Above a window on the right hand side of the house is carved 'Restored 1957'. Whoever was responsible for the restoration – thanks! It is great to see such an old piece of very Scottish architecture in such good condition.

Just after the house there is another roundabout. There is a plethora of roundabouts in Central Scotland, as you are probably beginning to realise! It seems the planners are throwing a roundabout into every junction these days. I find that I come across a new roundabout every time I'm out on the bike.

At this particular roundabout, turn left, taking the route signposted Stirling A9. Half a mile on, you come to a larger roundabout, which you are going to drive straight through, the route signposted Bannockburn, Stirling A9. This is the first time these historic names come into view. You immediately cross over the M876 motorway, and Glenbervie Golf Club is on your right. You will notice that the amount of tree cover is greater here as you are on the edge of what remains of the historic Tor Wood.

The Tor Wood covered a large area of this part of Scotland up until late medieval times. It stretched from the Forth to the Campsie Hills inland, and reached from Stirling to Falkirk. It was home to broken men and outlaws, but it was also a welcome haven for Scotland's freedom fighters. Wallace used it for attacks on English patrols, and King Robert I, the Bruce, amassed his army here where they trained in formation with their spears, prior to the victory at Bannockburn in 1314.

There are the remains of a broch in the Tor Wood too. A broch is a round defensive tower, built during Pictish times, and there are only a handful south of the Northern Highlands, and I remember my surprise when I discovered that there were the scant remains of one this far south. There is still a lot of woodland here though, and the Tor Wood is still very much an entity.

It is not more than a few hundred yards further to Torwood village. Just after you see the sign proclaiming this fact, there is a road off to your left, called Glen Road, and you turn in here. There are a few houses on either side of the road. Keep you eyed peeled as you drive up Glen Road for a tiny sign on your left, 100–200 yards up, which states:

Scottish Rights of Way Society
Public Right of Way
To Denovan 3km

Park and take a walk up the track this sign indicates. The thickness of the undergrowth will give you an idea of the cover the Tor Wood can offer. You could hide a hundred men in a small area on either side of this track in the summer months, and they would be invisible to passers-by. The track runs straight for the first half-mile, and Torwood Castle suddenly appears before you. It looks ruined, but it is under the care of an appreciative owner who is slowly making it habitable again. There has been a castle on this site since earliest times. As you stand at the top of the straight stretch facing the castle at the wooden gate, you are on an old Roman road that carries on to your right through the woodland.

As this road was still in use in medieval times, and was the main route through the Tor Wood, the castle would have been built to command it. When Robert the Bruce was a Guardian of Scotland, in the years before he became king, he had several meetings here with his co-guardian, the Red Comyn. The current structure you can see, although it probably contains earlier work, dates from 1566. The Foresters of Garden, whose surname comes from the fact that they were Wardens of the King's Forest here, built it. The stones of this old place must have some stories to tell. The English army came up this Roman road on their approach to Bannockburn in June 1314. Phalanxes of disciplined knights, banners flying, led by Edward II, King of England in person. Countless thousands of archers and foot soldiers, the mightiest fighting force in Christendom, all marching in perfect formation. Two days later, what remained of this force passed by here again in dribs and drabs, many wounded, as the Lion of Scotland proved her claws were still sharp.

Back to your vehicle then, and we will come back to the Roman road shortly. Drive onwards along Glen Road. You cross a wee old bridge over a burn at a tight bend, then start to climb slightly. This is a narrow stretch, so beware oncoming traffic. Eventually you come to a tight right hand bend where you turn on to a straight stretch. Pylon cables cross the road directly overhead. As you turn this bend you are on the line of the old Roman road, tarmac superseding Roman cobbles. If you look directly to your left, about a quarter of a mile away, there is a raised, scrubby patch, higher than the surrounding fields. This is the remains of an ancient fortification. You can just discern the earthworks surrounding this, a man-made ditch cut for defence. Onwards then, Stirling drawing closer.

This is a reasonably quiet stretch today, and it's hard to believe you are following the route of an army hell-bent on destroying Scotland once and for all. We do seem to be a resilient lot. We have survived from many set-backs with our Scottishness intact. As these thousands approached Stirling in 1314, they thought that Scotland was to be parcelled up between them. We sent them homeward to think again. We managed to survive the Union of the Crowns, where power moved to London. We survived the hated Union of the Parliaments in 1707. We survived the dismissal of our own royal dynasty, usurped by those of Germanic stock who still rule over us, and we have survived a London-controlled media in the technological age. I have a vision of the Third World War and the World in ruins, but a figure pulls itself from the rubble, and that figure is a Scot. We are survivors – and our time will come. Not to rule the planet – we aren't much into that sort of thing – but just to have the ability to decide our own destiny. That'll do.

You now deviate from the route of the Roman road as this road begins to twist, but it is a straightforward drive to the end where you come to a T-junction with a more major route, the A872, where we turn right towards Stirling. After just a few yards there is a large roundabout, connected to the main motorway network. From here, if it is reasonably clear, you will be able to see Stirling Castle atop its extinct volcano, so very like its sister at Edinburgh, and perhaps if the sunlight shines the right way, you will notice the National Wallace Monument atop the Abbey Craig. Both these delights have still to come. This large roundabout forms Junction 9 on the M80 Glasgow motorway, and the M9 Edinburgh motorway. Drive round it and take the third exit, signposted Stirling, a continuation of the A872 you were on.

There's lots of history in this next half-mile. On your left is the Pirnhall, a bar-restaurant type of place. Pirnhall Farm is behind this. There is a low grassy ridge that runs from Pirnhall Farm over towards the motorway. Aerial photographs that have come to light recently show the ditches that the Scots dug before Bannockburn in 1314, to protect them from charging heavy English cavalry. You can't see them with the naked eye though, so it was probably silly of me to mention it. They only show as crop marks in these pictures.

You will notice that over to your right on the A872 there is a craggy outcrop of rock, a couple of hundred yards from the road. This is Craigford. It has a few trees on the top of it, and some cottages in front. Legend states that Edward II of England stood on this viewpoint to assess the strength of the Scots positions on the far side of the Bannock Burn. The Bannock Burn, quite an insignificant little stream considering the fame that it possesses, is crossed by the road here without most people realising it. But the battle took its name from the village of Bannockburn (one word as opposed to the two of the stream) and the village took its name from the stream on which it stands. It was the proximity of the battle to the village that gave the battle its name.

You go straight through a roundabout, cross the Bannock, then take a small deviation by taking the first road off to your right by the car showroom, so I can show you an interesting site. Just in here, there is a farmhouse to your right. Park on this side-road, called Milton, and walk in towards the farmhouse. You will notice the little flow of water on your right here. This is an old lade-stream. This one deviates from the Bannock Burn, and there are several like it nearby. They were constructed many centuries ago to supply water to turn mill-wheels. The Bannock was once famous for its mills, and the area was once a great centre for tartan-weaving.

Swing down the path to your right, down towards the Bannock. There is a lovely wee refurbished mill cottage here, converted into a modern home. Down this path, at the side of the Bannock, is the site of Beaton's Mill. There is an information sign telling you the story on the right hand side of the path. It was here that James III, King of Scots, was stabbed to death after the Battle of Sauchieburn in 1488. The exact site of the battle is not known, but it was a mile or two up the course of the Bannock.

There had been civil war in Scotland, and this battle was the culmination. Disenchanted lords, with the young Prince James, later to be King James IV who died at Flodden in 1513, as part of their number, faced the forces of James III and his supporters. James III was beaten and fled the field, only to be thrown by his horse, whereupon he was carried in to Beaton's Mill. Some of the victors found him there, and he was stabbed to death. He was buried in state in Cambuskenneth Abbey, just across the Forth. Beaton's Mill survived until 1954, when it was unfortunately destroyed in a fire. Some scattered stones remain.

You can take a look at the Bannock while you are here. Just downstream the Bannock flows into what can almost be called a gorge, and it was against this natural barrier that the English were trapped at the battle in 1314. There are various walks on both sides of the stream down through this gorge, and anyone with a particular interest in this battle should walk these to give them a better grounding of the obstacles the English faced on the day.

Return to your vehicle, and just continue on along this road. This little road, Milton, goes round in a crescent back to the A872, the main route you were on, and when you reach it turn right, and continue on.

Another few hundred yards, and the entrance road to the Bannockburn Heritage Centre is on your left. This visitor centre has a tea-room, shop, displays, and an audiovisual presentation, which tells the whole story of the lead-up to the battle, and of the battle itself.

I covered the story of Bannockburn in two chapters of my book, *On the Trail of Robert the Bruce,* and Bannockburn is a topic I may write about again, as it is a constant learning process, new data coming to light, or at least to my attention, all the time. Suffice it to say that the visitor centre stands on the ground where the Scots army amassed, although there was no actual fighting here. The battle was fought on a grand scale, and over two days, but the main battle on day two was fought about half a mile east of here, on the ground north of the Bannock Burn gorge, where Bannockburn High School stands today.

Oh, and before any more nonsensical claims are made, there was not a Knight Templar in sight! These claims, which have only arisen over the last 15 years, are an insult to Scotland and the Scots. We are told we were not capable of winning Bannockburn without Templar help. For almost 700 years our history was intact. People who suddenly say that all documents, history books, eye witness accounts and chronicles are false, and that they have the truth, should be treated with suspicion. What are their motives anyway? The Templars had been annulled before Bannockburn, and I'm quite sure the English would not have been slow in complaining to the Pope if the Scots had outlawed help. No. We won Bannockburn because we had the leadership of the best king, military commander and politician we ever had, and because my ancestors' hearts were strong and true, with right on their side. To say otherwise demeans the men who fought on the day, and their descendants to this day.

Beyond the visitor centre is open grassland, where Good King Robert's own division stood, and the site is marked by a rotunda, a cairn, and the fabulous statue of Bruce on his warhorse, axe in hand, by the eminent sculptor, Pilkington-Jackson. Please don't miss this statue, with Stirling Castle beyond. It is one of the symbols of Scotland, which is burnt into our imaginations, and Pilkington-Jackson used facial reconstructions from casts of Bruce's skull to ensure he had a true representation of the hero-king.

I stand on this rise and look towards the Roman road we have already followed and I sense my countrymen standing here, silent in their thousands, long spears in hand. They are watching for the approach of the mightiest fighting machine in Christendom. Bruce himself was out on the lower boggy ground in front, checking the pits and traps that run from Pirnhall over to Foot O'Green farm before you.

The English suddenly burst out of the edges of the Tor Wood, and Bruce himself dealt the first blow of the whole battle. Such is destiny. An English knight, Henry de Bohun, charged Bruce on his mighty warhorse. Bruce neatly sidestepped him and drew his axe. He was regarded as being the greatest exponent of the battleaxe in Europe. He smashed it down on de Bohun, and cut him to the breastbone. Chain-mail and plate-armour could not withstand the mighty blow, and the Englishman toppled in gory ruin. Bruce returned to the Scots ranks to complain that he had broken his good axe! If only we had a few more today with the steel of which Bruce was made.

Back to your vehicle again, out on to the A872, and turn left. We are well into the outskirts of Stirling now and it is an increasingly built up area we are driving through. Half a mile on and we come to a busy roundabout, we take the first exit left, the B8051, Borestone Crescent. We are into the area known as St Ninian's now. The first road off to your right along here will take you into St Ninian's church, or the steeple of it, at least. This wee dead-end road is called Kirk Wynd.

The reason there remains only the steeple of the old St Ninian's church is because it was used as a munitions store by Bonnie Prince Charlie's army in 1745–6. One of the Highlanders on guard saw some of the locals trying to steal the stores kept within the church. He raised his musket to fire a warning shot to scare them off. Unfortunately sparks from his powder ignited some of the gunpowder spilt on the grass, and like a Tom and Jerry cartoon, the sparks went right into the church, detonated the munitions inside, and the church promptly disappeared in an enormous explosion. Fourteen or fifteen people died, and flying debris injured many more. There are a few stones from the original church, which was ancient indeed, it being here at the time of Bannockburn. The tower survived as it stood apart from the central building. There is a later church on the site too.

Back out and turn right again, continuing towards Stirling. This road you are on changes name several times, but it is straight and a major route, so continue on regardless. Another half-mile and you will see the large building on your left that is Randolphfield Police Headquarters, a modern building set back a little from the main road and with a grassy area to the front. If you park hereabouts and take a look on this grassy area, on the right side of the entrance road you will notice that there are two standing stones, one larger than the other at about five feet tall. These mark the spot where one of the actions of Bannockburn took place, in fact, quite a major part of the first day's action. A division of English heavy cavalry tried to outflank the Scottish position, and Bruce sent a body of spearmen under the command of his nephew, Thomas Randolph, to intercept. As they emerged from the woodland here, the English cavalry charged. Hundreds upon hundreds of knights in full armour, riding upon heavy warhorses also encased in steel. They expected to ride right over the lightly armed Scots, but Bruce had trained his men well. He had learned from Wallace, whose schiltroms of spearmen had been static. Bruce's men knew how to move in formation – a giant hedgehog of spears crossing the field of conflict.

The Scots stood firm, as charge after charge foundered on their spear points. Then the Scots began to move forward, rolling up their enemy. Ordinary peasant spearmen destroyed gentlemen cavalry in a way never seen before. It was a forerunner of what was to happen on a grander scale the following day. Bruce knew his tactics were sound.

Stand at these stones and watch the charge come in. There is a crash, horses scream as spears crack and break with sounds like gunshots under the pressure. The English shout their battle cries. The only noise from the Scots is heavy breathing, taking the strain, but they can hear Randolph urging them on. Then they push forward, over the bodies of dead and dying men and mounts.

It all happened just here.

Listen hard and you can still hear the faintest sounds as they echo down the centuries.

I remember well the first time I came across these stones. I had read an old book from the 1830s, I think it was, that mentioned the stones, but 20 years ago I did not know this area well, and did not recognise the description given of this location. I got a job as a relief driver for a few weeks, filling for a friend, and one of my deliveries was to Randolphfield Police Station. As I drove in, I spotted the two stones, and realised immediately what they were. I stopped, walked over, and it was like a flashback as I could envisage one of the actions at Bannockburn in 1314, a battle of which I had read everything I could get my hands on. I was so excited that when a police officer, much older than me, signed for the delivery I was carrying, I asked him what he knew about the stones out front. 'Ach, that's just a couple of auld stones, son', was his reply. I found it hard to believe that people can be so ignorant of things on their own doorsteps, but of course, the realisation dawned that some people just don't care about the past, or even worse, as it is the past, they don't see the point. Scotland needs to learn. Learn from her mistakes. And often in her history, she has made the same mistakes again and again.

Whilst I was in the company of Nigel Tranter, the late author of books on Scotland numbering well into three figures, we debated these stones. Nigel had a special interest in standing stones, and reckoned that they probably long predated 1314, but Bruce's nephew, Randolph, may have used the stones as a point of recognition when marshalling his men, asking them to halt and tighten their ranks there. There are many other places in Scotland where there are standing stones with connections to various battles, so it may be that as recently as medieval times, standing stones were still being raised to mark scenes of conflict.

We leave the last connection to Bannockburn on our route, and get ready to continue on, but first take a glance at the face of the little wall fronting the police offices' grassy area. On the opposite side of the entrance from where the stones stand there is a small plaque mounted at lower leg height. This commemorates the spot where in 1571, Lennox, the Regent of Scotland at that time, was murdered. Old books say there was originally a cairn on the spot, but the road has been widened considerably and the plaque has replaced the cairn.

On to Stirling town centre then. Simply continue on this road, passing through a couple of sets of traffic lights 'til you come up to the pedestrian precinct of the shopping area of the town centre, where you turn left at the t-junction onto the A811, Dumbarton Road. As you drive along this stretch, you may notice there is a large wall slanting away uphill on your right. This is the old Stirling town wall. Most Scots are surprised to find that Stirling is a walled town. Quite a lot of the walling is still complete on this, the south-western side of the old town. In fact, this stretch, apart from where comparatively modern roads push through, is complete right uphill to the castle. There is a path following the wall, known as the 'Back Walk', and it is a great way of getting to know the town a little better if you are here for a day or two, or have the time to do it.

Continuing a little along Dumbarton Road, take the first road on your right, which cuts back again at a 45-degree angle, and it is named Corn Exchange Road. As you turn up here you will notice a statue of Rob Roy MacGregor, holding his basket-hilted broadsword aloft, on your left. This sword has been replaced several times in recent years, as it seems to be a favourite target for those late-night revellers who have imbibed a 'small refreshment', to quote a Scottish phrase. Then there are council buildings on your left, with some quite interesting stonework, which contains a bust of Wallace and a statue of Bruce.

You reach a junction, where immediately in front of you is the Atheneum building which has a fabulous statue of Wallace above its front entrance, which faces downhill. Wallace is depicted with a very muscular frame, wearing a Roman toga, and his mighty double-handed sword upon his back. Scotland has many Wallace statues, and this one is among my favourites. It embodies classicism, decency and strength.

At this junction at the Atheneum, we turn left into Spittal Street, which leads steeply uphill. Stirling old town, like that of Edinburgh, is built on the residue of volcanic activity, this slope the result of ancient lava flow, with the castle at the highest point. On uphill, passing the Stirling Highland Hotel, originally Stirling's High School, then keep an eye open on your left for the Old Town Jail. It has gothic-style battlements and a tower, so it's reasonably easy to spot. It was built in 1846 to replace Stirling's notorious Tolbooth Prison, where many famous names from Scotland's past were incarcerated. The Old Town Jail is now a living history museum, which you can tour, seeing the solitary confinement cells and where hard labour punishments took place. A glass elevator goes to viewing deck on the top of the jail, giving views over the town.

A little further uphill is the entrance, again off to the left of the road, to the Church of the Holy Rude, and to the left of the church is the Guildhall. This old church dates back in its earliest form to the 1100s. It was repaired after being burnt in 1414. During trouble with King James II and the Douglas family in 1455, it was again damaged, but the King then provided funds for the building in its current form. There is a notable oak roof within the church. In 1543, Mary, Queen of Scots, was crowned in this church – she was only nine months old, and 24 years later James VI (later to be James I of England too) was crowned here when he was just a year old. The sermon was preached by John Knox, who was instrumental in introducing the Reformation to Scotland. The square 90-foot-high church tower still shows shot marks made by guns during a siege of the castle by Cromwell during 1651.

The graveyard between the church and castle has some interesting old gravestones and a good viewpoint too.

The aforementioned Guildhall, sometimes known as Cowan's Hospital, after its builder John Cowan, whose statue graces its front, was built in the early 1600s. It's a lovely wee building, and there is an interesting local legend about Cowan's statue. The kids believe that the statue, which they call 'Staney-breeks' (stone-trousers!) jumps down from his plinth at the bells on Hogmanay (midnight on the last day of the year to all you non-Scots!) and dances.

I've always had this wee scenario going on in my head, of someone dressed exactly as the statue and running across the street in the sight of some kids, and really freaking them!

Round the corner, just past the church is Mar's Wark, meaning 'work', or building project. It looks ruinous, but it was never actually completed. It was intended to be a town house of the Earl of Mar. Built in 1570, it has the Royal Arms of Scotland above its main entrance.

The stones were looted from the not-too-distant Cambuskenneth Abbey, so perhaps this building was ill-fated from the first.

Just after Mar's Wark, on the opposite side of the road, is Argyll's Lodging. Like Mar's Wark, it was a town house, built for a great lord, in this case of course, for the Argyll family. It is a fine example of its kind, and in brilliant condition. It was built in 1630, for long it was used as a military hospital, but it is now in very much its original condition and is open to the public. You can buy a ticket at the castle which gives you access to Argyll's Lodging too, so do that, behave like a true Scot and get value for money. We drive on just a few yards and we sweep up on to the Esplanade of Stirling Castle. There is a charge to enter the castle, and you may be charged to park, but it is not too excessive. I have always been given a decent corner to tuck into when I've turned up on the bike.

First thing to do after you have parked is to walk to the wall on your right when facing the castle. A favourite view. It just shouts Scotland! to me. Directly in front is a dip where jousts were held in olden days. In fact, Bruce had competitions held here between the victorious Scots and some of the English nobility that were held in Stirling, awaiting ransom, after Bannockburn. Beyond, the houses slope away, down to the coils of the River Forth below. This is why so many battles have been fought in this area. West of here the country becomes increasingly rough, and it was impassable for major armies of invasion.

East, the Forth widens, so Stirling was the first point where the river could be safely bridged, and all invaders must come this way to try to cross from southern Scotland to northern Scotland. Even Wallace's battle at Falkirk came to pass because of the strategic position of Stirling, every English army of invasion resigned to following the Forth Estuary west, due to the terrain.

You can see how the Forth meanders in its many twists and turns too, before it begins to widen on its seawards journey. Directly below you will see the old stone bridge which spans the river – the famous Stirling Bridge – site of Wallace's victory at the Battle of Stirling Bridge, in 1297. Lift your eyes a little higher, and there stands the 220-feet-high baronial tower that is the National Wallace Monument, standing atop the cliff-clad whaleback ridge that is the Abbey Craig, which overlooks the field of Wallace's victory over the 'Auld Enemy'.

Behind again rise the Ochil Hills, and I hope you get the weather to appreciate this view in all its glory.

I don't care if it is glorious sunshine, a mixture of sun and cloud, so you can watch the shadows move over that rolling vista, or with snow draped over the higher ground, as long as it is clear and you can take it in. I have stood here and looked at this view, with perfect strangers standing on either side, and I've said out loud 'Isn't it brilliant to be Scottish?', and I've heard the mumbles of 'Yeah', as there is really nothing else to be said when looking at that. I've seen this vista a hundred times over the years. I've even walked to the edge in the middle of the night and seen a full moon light it up, with the light shining in the very pinnacle of the Wallace Monument drawing my eyes like a flame draws a moth, and I want to live forever. I don't ever want there to be a time that I can't go and look at that view whenever I want. I envy the generations of Scots unborn who will one day look out over the Forth, at Stirling Bridge, the Wallace Monument, the Ochils rising abrupt as a backdrop to it all.

If you happen across this in an old bookshop in many years' time and perhaps one day end up on Stirling Castle Esplanade looking over the scene of Wallace's victory – remember that someone who had a little lease of Scotland for a while and loved her very much used to stand here and admire the view. Just as Wallace and Bruce used to stand in front of Stirling Castle and look out over it, I get to also. I'm sure Wallace loved it very much, especially after Stirling Bridge, when he could look down, put on a mock American accent, and say 'Hey, I kicked some ass down there!' And he sure did.

Before you go into the castle you might as well take a glance at the hellish statue of Robert the Bruce in front of its walls. A bearded fat man drawing his sword. I suppose it has got to be put somewhere as it is pretty old, having been erected in 1877, and it would be a shame to put it in a cupboard somewhere, but it is not how I envisage Bruce.

Onwards now through the gateway of the castle. Like Edinburgh Castle, I'll run through the things I really like, although there is more to the castle here that that. Stirling Castle was long a garrison of the British Army, and has suffered in consequence, and there is very little in it of any antiquity, and really, if I'm honest, very little to see, other than the actual fabric of the place. There is a nice wee garden just after you go in, but there is something interesting to see if you turn left and go up onto the battlements and look over the opposite side from the direction of the Wallace Monument. There is a geometric shape on the grass far below, regular in pattern, with a raised central boss. This is what is known locally as the Round Table. We will visit it shortly, but it is helpful to see it from above first to get a bird's-eye view of its layout.

Through the inner gate now, flanked by its twin round towers. A corridor off to the left here takes us into a courtyard of the castle known as the Lion's Den. As there are several mentions in our chronicles of the Kings of Scots owning lions, it is likely that they were kept in this part of the building and the name has stuck. The Royal Standard of Scotland is of course what we refer to as the Lion Rampant, a lion standing on its hind legs, with its front legs raised and clawing, picked out in red, on a yellow or gold background. The first King of Scots to use this symbol was William I, who reigned from 1165–1214. Prior to that the symbol of royalty had been the wild boar. As William owned lions, perhaps it was as he watched them here at Stirling that the idea of using one on his banner first came to mind? The Lion Rampant is a much-loved symbol in Scotland, a throwback to the days when our country was a separate sovereign nation. It is used by the Germanic stock that currently resides in London, but somehow we see it as something that represents Scotland itself, and I don't know anyone who thinks of the Windsor family when this flag is on show.

On a tour of part of Canada recently, I attended the Fergus Highland Games, and I can remember driving into the main thoroughfare of Fergus and every building was bedecked with the Lion Rampant. It was brilliant to see that, so far from Scotland, but then the people of Fergus are very much of Scottish descent, and their heritage means much to them.

Carry on to the upper square of the castle, the main open area. On your right is the very recently refurbished Great Hall. I can't make up my mind on this. It supposedly looks now as it did when it was first constructed, but I find that the brightness of the harling on the walls grates a bit, compared to the weathered stone of the rest of the buildings. Something had to be done though, as this ancient and auspicious building, dating from the time of James III, had been badly refurbished and used as a barracks since the Union, and was in a sad state of neglect. It is good to see that the interior reflects some of its former magnificence. On the south of the square are the Royal Apartments, sadly depleted of any former treasures, but at time of writing restoration works of the rooms themselves are under way.

On the north side of the square is a little passageway, just to the left of the Chapel Royal. This goes through to a little garden where the battlements give fabulous views north and west, the hills of the Highlands much closer now, rearing towards the sky beyond the Flanders Moss and the other flat-lands of the infant Forth. The cliffs fall away sheer below, and give you some idea of the impregnability of this fortress, and why it was in times past named the Key to the Kingdom, commanding as it does that vital crossing of the Forth at Stirling Bridge. If you look at the windows just above the passage you have come through to reach this garden, you will notice that there is one that contains stained glass, bearing the Douglas coat of arms of the three stars, surmounting the blood-red heart of Robert the Bruce. This is in recognition of the fact that the Good Sir James Douglas carried the heart of the late king on Crusade in 1330.

King James II had a serious falling-out with the Douglas family, and this grew so serious that the king rose and plunged a dagger into the then Earl of Douglas at dinner. Taking their lead from their monarch, other lords drew steel and stabbed the Douglas many times. His body was thrown from the window into the garden below, and this stained glass is in commemora-tion of this deed. The skeleton of an armed man was found in this garden in

1797, and is supposed to have been that of Douglas. There are other fine vantage points above the high sheer cliffs of the rock to be found within the castle, and you should seek these out, as I can guarantee that the vistas therefrom will etch into your memory.

Back out at your vehicle in the esplanade, drive back out downhill and past Argyll's Lodging. There is a one-way system in operation, so as you reach Mar's Wark again, you must turn left and into Broad Street. As is probably obvious, Broad Street was once the old town's market place and unlike the other, narrower streets, this is wider with the housing set further back. Facing you at the bottom of Broad Street is Darnley House, which contains a coffee shop, and this building is reputed to be the town house of Lord Darnley, but I doubt it is that old, although it may have James VI associations. Also in Broad Street is the Merkat Cross. The original was removed in 1792, but the unicorn atop it was preserved and a new cross was built in 1891, and the unicorn fixed on top again. It stands as near as possible to the site of the original. It was once a place of execution, and it was on this spot that Archbishop Hamilton was executed in 1571during the Reformation. Two rhymesters were hung here in 1579 for daring to write a satire on Regent Morton, and Hardie and Baird, two of the leaders captured at Bonnymuir in 1820, were beheaded here.

At the bottom of Broad Street, turn right into Bow Street, which curves downhill, continues straight on into Baker Street, then we come to a junction directly in front of the Atheneum building, with its statue of Wallace. Here we turn right, just a yard or two uphill, then left into Corn Exchange Road, so you are now retracing an earlier part of your route.

As you come down again to Dumbarton Road, the Rob Roy statue on your right this time, we turn right, and you follow Dumbarton Road onwards. A few hundred yards further on, keep your eyes peeled for the Stirling Smith Art Gallery and Museum on your right. It has pillars at the front, Italian in style. It has a car park to its right, but parking hereabouts should not be too difficult as it is further out from the town centre.

The Smith has some interesting Stirling artefacts, including the axe used to execute Hardie and Baird of 1820 fame, and they have a football that is possibly the oldest in the world! It dates from Mary, Queen of Scots' time, and may have belonged to the queen herself. There are changing exhibitions in this vibrant wee place, and there are interesting works of art, many with Scottish themes. The Mr Smith who gives his name to the place was a local man who lived from 1817–69 and left a bequest of £22,000 to build and stock this edifice. Many of the works of art were from his own collection. I was lucky enough to launch my *On the Trail of William Wallace* book here, and that day one of the Scottish national newspapers, the *Daily Record*, contained a large article about me. For some reason, they had a photo of an elderly bald man with my name underneath. I joked with the crowd about all the girls I had asked out as a teenager seeing that article, and saying to themselves 'Thank God I never went out with him, he's not worn too well', as the photo was of a man 40 years older than me!

Elspeth King is the current curator of the Smith, a woman I much admire, and whose passion for her country's history and heritage is to be applauded.

Before you start to proceed further in your vehicle, walk on just a little further down Dumbarton Road. On the same side as the Smith there is a road which cuts in, called Royal Gardens, and directly on the other side of this road there is a gate that leads into the grassy area that contains the Round Table, seen from the castle above. In fact, this is a fabulous place to view or take photos of the castle, as it stands above upon its rock. There are signs here which refer to this structure as the King's Knot. It is often referred to as that in guide books, but John Barbour, writing in 1370, when talking of Edward II of England fleeing from Bannockburn in 1314, said that he went 'Rycht by the Round Table away'. There was no doubt it was this structure that he meant. Stirling, poetically, is sometimes referred to as Snowdon or Snadoun, and Sir David Lindsay, in his *Farewell of the Papingo* (1539), also mentions it:

Adew fair Snadoun, with thy towers high
Thy Chapel Royal, Park and Table Round,
May, June and July I would dwell in thee
Were I one man, to hear the birds sound.

There have long been claims that the famous King Arthur of legend was based in Scotland, and there are many symbols in the landscape with supposed Arthurian connections, so it is surely nice to be able to tell people that you have visited his Round Table. There are ramps leading up, large enough for a mounted horseman to ride up and stand, facing the centre piece, and I can imagine a speaker in that central boss putting forward items for debate.

Back to the vehicle again, and drive on, passing the Round Table here on your right, and you reach a mini roundabout. Take a right here, driving underneath the Castle Rock. There is a lay-by here on your left for sightseeing, photographing etc. Soon another roundabout is reached where we turn right, passing the Fire Station where the road curves a little right again, and you are driving along Back O Hill Road. Follow this road for a mile or so with no deviations until you reach the roundabout at its end. Here you go straight through, following the signs for the National Wallace Monument, and directly in front is another large roundabout with a curious little clock-tower in its centre and pedestrian underpasses. You go straight through this, following the signs for A9 North and Wallace Monument. Here you cross the River Forth, and the beautiful old stone Stirling Bridge is slightly upstream to your left. At the traffic lights take the slip left onto Cornton Road, and then turn left again into Bridgehaugh Road, which leads directly onto the bridge. The bridge is very old and is for pedestrian traffic only, but you should be able to park here and walk its ancient cobbles.

This old stone bridge replaced the wooden structure which was destroyed in Wallace's battle of 1297, although that bridge may have been patched up for a while, until it was superseded. Most histories give the age of this bridge as circa 1400. As you walk up onto this structure, bear in mind that for a long time this was the only way to travel from southern to northern Scotland and vice versa – unless you fancied a good soaking. Therefore, every famous and not-so-famous Scot since this bridge was built has had to pass this way. Kings, queens, lords and ladies have walked up and over the apex of this structure, as well as many millions of ordinary Scots over the centuries.

There are two wee bits that jut out over the river in the centre, into which people would step in order to let carts pass, and the one on the right, upstream, gives a good view of the National Wallace Monument. The other thing to look at, or at least imagine from here, is the bridge that was the crux of Wallace's battle. It stood just a few yards upstream, we know this as the remains of the stone piers that supported the wooden structure still stand on the riverbed.

The English of course had to come this way to bring Wallace, aided by his co-commander Sir Andrew Murray, to battle. Wallace and Murray had been besieging the castle at Dundee when word reached them of the English army coming north. They hastened their army here, positioning them in front of the Abbey Craig, where Wallace's monument stands today, keeping a watchful eye over the scene. The English, vastly superior in numbers, began to file over the bridge. It was the morning of September 11, 1297 – an auspicious day in Scotland's history. Wallace and Murray probably stood atop the Abbey Craig, assessing numbers.

The old wooden bridge was very narrow, perhaps two horses could cross abreast, and the bridge stood at the base of a large U-shaped bend of the river. The English were regarded as being an unstoppable fighting machine, vastly superior to the Scots in men and equipment, and the danger of the trap they were marching into seemed oblivious to their commanders. They did not let it cross their minds for a moment that the Scots would offer any real resistance, and it seemed to them that they had only to 'turn up'.

As soon as enough of the English that Wallace and Murray felt they could effectively deal with, had crossed the bridge, Wallace blew hard on his horn and the noise of it echoed from the Abbey Craig to the ramparts of Stirling Castle. As its echoes died away, two pincers of Scots ran forward to capture the bridgehead and cut the English off. A causeway ran towards the Abbey Craig over the softer ground that lined the riverbanks before modern drainage. As the English relied upon heavy cavalry, they found that there was no room to manoeuvre or get themselves into formations to charge, which was what they really needed to do.

Once the bridgehead was secured, the remaining Scots could attack the heavy cavalry. They could roll underneath the heavy warhorses, out of the reach of the weaponry of the riders, and stab upwards into the horses' bellies. The frightened, wounded mounts would rear and throw their riders, and those riders would crash to the ground, encased in their armour, where at the very least they would be stunned – and other Scots would be ready to stab eye slits or shoulder joints. Even those who made it to the riverbank were bogged down with weapons and armour, and the chasing Scots would not allow them the time to divest themselves of these encumbrances in order to swim to safety.

They died in their hundreds, nay, their thousands, and their fellows, trapped on the southern shore, could only look on in abject horror, before panic gripped them and they too began to run.

There was a hundred miles of Scotland to cover before the English border was reached, and the ordinary folk rose to avenge the wrongs that had been subjected on them by the invaders.

Wallace was suddenly thrust into a position where the English garrisons evaporated and he was left as master of Scotland. Murray unfortunately was wounded, and was to die before the year was out, but at least he lived long enough to see the unbeatable beaten.

I stand on the bridge and the buildings and the traffic disappear, and I can cast myself back to the day of the battle.

In the summer of 2002 I was on a visit to Stirling Bridge with a fellow-member of the Society of William Wallace, Gary Stewart. It had been dry for many weeks, which is very rare in Scotland. We could not believe our eyes when we got to the top of the bridge and looked down on the upstream side. The water was so low we could see the piers of Wallace's bridge showing just an inch or two below the water level. I felt lucky. To see such things strips the centuries away, and I could picture it all the better.

Before you leave, go down to the water's edge on the northern bank. There is an oak tree here, small in my time, which was planted on the 700th anniversary of the battle in 1997. Polling stations were open in Scotland to decide on the nation's future – 11 September 1997. Scotland overwhelmingly voted Yes! to at least some sort of parliament in Edinburgh. The tree is surrounded by a small iron fence. The Society of William Wallace meets here on the Saturday nearest to the anniversary of the battle, for a wreath-laying ceremony, then we all have a walk along the river to Cambuskenneth Abbey. As we meet at this tree, we walk on the soil where our ancestors fought for their freedom. It is a sobering thought to look across the river, up to Stirling Castle above, and to look at the stones of the ancient bridge, and realise how the centuries interconnect.

If you look up above the southern end of the bridge, there is a grassy knoll, two cannons standing on its summit. Beside these stands the 'heading stone', where criminals were beheaded in ancient times. The Duke of Albany was beheaded here for wrongs against the Crown, but had to watch as his two sons were executed first. From here he could look out towards Doune Castle, his ancestral home, a place we will visit shortly. You can walk up this hill if you so desire, and stand at the stone where so many met their end.

Back out to the traffic lights, turn left on to the A9 again, and drive on under the railway bridge. You are on a long straight road here, Causewayhead Road. It is so called as it follows the line of the ancient causeway on which the English heavy cavalry were trapped. There is about three quarters of a mile of this road, with the National Wallace Monument drawing ever closer atop the Abbey Craig, and it is only now that the massiveness of this structure hits home. It looks much smaller from Stirling Castle because of the background of the Ochil Hills, but it comes into its own when you see it from below. But we are not going to the monument just yet, there is something else to see first that is nearby, but most tourists miss it.

When you reach the roundabout at the head of Causewayhead Road, take a right turn on to the A907 Alloa Road. There are two small housing streets off to your right, and a park on your left, then the next road on your right is the one you want to take. It cuts off right opposite the beginning of the Abbey Craig's cliff faces rising on your left. There is a small sign pointing down this road, proclaiming 'Cambuskenneth Abbey', so keep your eyes peeled for this.

This small road goes to the village of Cambuskenneth and nowhere else. It is called Ladysneuk Road. Cambuskenneth stands in one of the large loops on the north side of the Forth. The road here is alongside the river at first, at the head of another of its meandering big loops, but it soon swings away. We drive through fields, Stirling Castle now over to our right, and soon come into the little picturesque village that is Cambuskenneth.

It is connected to Stirling by a footbridge, but as this is the only road, please take care when you are parking. The abbey ruins, the tower of which is a useful landmark, stand at the road end. The abbey was founded in 1147, and it is this building which gives the Abbey Craig, where the Wallace Monument stands, its name.

The gate is generally unlocked during daylight hours, and although there is very little left of the abbey buildings, there are information boards to inform the casual visitor of their original functions. The bell tower is still complete, so take a look up at the gargoyles at the roofline, high above.

There are carven faces all round the top too, a notable curiosity. Only the outline of the various buildings remains, but you will notice the large tomb surrounded by railings, on the site of the church's High Altar. This is the last resting place of King James III and his Queen. Their bodies were uncovered in the 1800s and reburied with the new stone tomb covering them. James III was the king slain at Beaton's Mill after the Battle of Sauchieburn in 1488.

Go through the little gate over by the river too, by the private cottage in the grounds, as there are the footings of early buildings and the fragment of a tower out there too.

When Robert the Bruce died in 1329 at Cardross, a vanished manor that stood by the River Leven, just north of Dumbarton, his body was carried across Scotland to its last resting place in Dunfermline Abbey. On the first night it rested at Dunipace, already visited, and the second night it rested here. I try to envisage him lying in state in his coffin, candles burning all around, and knights kneeling part in vigil, part to honour him, through the night. It seems fitting that the site of the main action at Bannockburn is not far away across the river, and it seems right that he rested here overlooking the scene of his great victory, before he was laid to rest for eternity in Dunfermline.

There is a local legend too, that Wallace's left arm is interred here, and a stone is pointed out as the place. The English had it nailed up on the remains of Stirling Bridge to dishonour him, but the story runs that the monks here took it down secretly, and that arm at least was buried in consecrated ground. The stone is not marked, but the Society of William Wallace lay flowers on the spot during our commemoration of Stirling Bridge every year.

Back towards the Abbey Craig then, retracing your route, and again turning left to reach the roundabout at the head of Causewayhead Road. Turn right towards the monument, passing the site of the William Wallace – a pub I have been known to visit on occasion – and climb uphill. There is a tight dog's-leg bend halfway up, but carry on until you see the entrance to the car parks for the monument on your right.

The National Wallace Monument soars high above you. It is 220 feet tall, but stands atop the Abbey Craig, which is the best part of 400 feet high, so it is a notable landmark, visible for miles around.

You can park and get a minibus to the top, or more fittingly, if you are fit enough, you can walk the rather strenuous curving path to the summit. Recently I took a busload of the Tartan Army, the Scottish football supporters, on a visit to the monument. At the bottom I jokingly remarked that only Englishmen got the bus – Scots walked. It was a throwaway line, and I forgot about it right away. At the top, I saw one of the guys hobbling bravely up the gradient. He had a stooky on his leg (we Scots call the plaster cast to heal broken bones a 'stooky'). I realised that he had gone for it because of what I said. 'Ah'm no English!' he defiantly stated as he passed me.

Ah! How the spirit of Wallace thrives in Scotland!

Standing before the monument, the massiveness of the stonework is immediately apparent. There is a mighty statue of Wallace – sword held aloft, on a corner of the front, his coat of arms above the door. I like the ornamentation that runs across the building that looks like a rope, but carved into stonework itself. The little spiral bit that juts out to the right is actually the stairway to the top, but the airiness of this is an attraction in itself.

It should be pointed out that the stone was hewn from the Abbey Craig itself, as is fitting. The quarry was sited to the left of the path on the second long stretch on the way up. A little mini railway was constructed to take materials to the site. What I think is astonishing is that 80,000 people turned out to see the foundation stone being laid, in the 1860s, long before the days of motor transport! That is probably ten times the size of Wallace and Murray's army on the day. Surely this must give the lie to the fact that in the Victorian era, Scots were very much regarded as 'North Britons'.

There is a fee to pay to enter the monument, and there is a gift shop and a tearoom on the ground floor, then the slog up the stairway begins. The monument has been incredibly popular since the release of *Braveheart* in 1995, and the staircase is steep and narrow. There is constant stopping and starting as you squeeze by other visitors, but again, that too is part of the fun.

Wallace's sword is kept within a case on one of the floors, grim, huge and ancient-looking. It was left behind at Dumbarton Castle when he was taken south to his murder, but it was transferred here centuries later when the monument was constructed. If I'm brutally frank, there is not a hell of a lot else to see within, other than an audiovisual and some story boards and some busts of eminent Scots from the 1800s. But, it matters not. The sword is enough, and that coupled with the building itself makes for an interesting visit. It is what it is. It's the National Wallace Monument, and that'll do for me. Eventually you come out onto the battlements and a walk round these results in another stairway to take you onto the top, a viewing platform right up within the tower's crown. A fabulous view, the Ochils prominent, and the causeway running out to the bridge and therefore the site of the battle, laid out below. See how the Forth coils, each bend almost touching the next. Been up here in some high winds when I've had to hang on to the stonework so as not to land in Edinburgh!

There is one thing that grates though. Often there is abseiling off the monument, corporate stuff or charity raising events. I'm sorry. This is not right. This is a war memorial and a shrine to the memory of one of our great heroes. Many thousands died here, and this is a symbol of that struggle. It should not be used for such things. Show some bloody respect! I find it distasteful when I see advertising saying 'Abseil off the Wallace Monument!'. I don't see the English allowing people to use the Cenotaph in Whitehall, or Americans, even with their Disney mentality, using their memorials like the Washington Monument, for such things, so I want this to stop at once.

Before you go all the way down to the bottom of the hill, there is one thing that I feel you should see. Most visitors to the monument don't wander from the tarmac path, so walk down the road just a little and at the first bend downhill, follow the little woodland trail into the trees. There is currently a wooden sign at the beginning of this path. After a few yards you come to a few steps, and you cut between some large boulders, then rise slightly again – it's about 150 yards in total, then you come up right on the cliff edge. This is no place for kids, the drop is sheer, and of several hundred feet. In my blood I feel that this is where Wallace would have actually stood as he watched the English approach from the direction of Falkirk, visible on a clear day. He would not know then of course, of his impending victory, or that Falkirk was to prove to be such a disaster only a year later. The monument stands on the very summit of the Abbey Craig, on the site of an ancient fort, but here is by far the best viewpoint, and as I stand here I can see the Scots captains standing here watching the English approach, several centuries before. All in all, it is a magnificent viewpoint, but please be careful. Lives have been lost on the Abbey Craig. You may want to take a last glance westwards, in the direction of the bluish purple peaks that mark the southern boundary of the Highlands, and you can see how the terrain in that direction becomes wilder, more rolling, more tree clad. Walk back down to your vehicle in the car park, as it is that direction that we will head for in the very near future.

In the car park, please avert your eyes from the hideous statue of Wallace, looking like a cartoon Mel Gibson, that has 'Freedom' written across its plinth. This would be more suited to a theme park than a national shrine. I have never heard a good word said about this sculpture. It has been attacked or defaced several times, and it now has a foldaway cage built to close round it at night. It is jokingly called 'Freedom in a Cage' by friends of mine. It spoils an otherwise poignant day out.

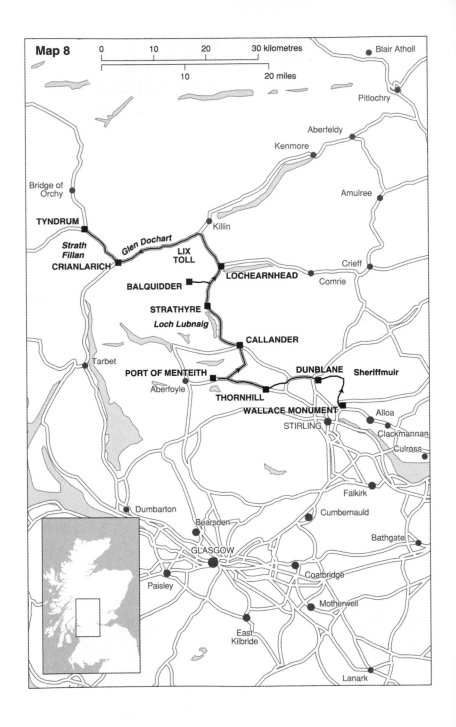

Map 8

0   10   20   30 kilometres

10   20 miles

Blair Atholl

Pitlochry

Aberfeldy

Kenmore

Amulree

Bridge of
Orchy

TYNDRUM

Killin

Strath
Fillan

Glen Dochart

LIX
TOLL

Crieff

CRIANLARICH

BALQUIDDER

LOCHEARNHEAD

Comrie

STRATHYRE

Loch Lubnaig

CALLANDER

Tarbet

PORT OF MENTEITH

DUNBLANE

Sheriffmuir

Aberfoyle

THORNHILL

Alloa

WALLACE MONUMENT

STIRLING

Clackmannan

Culross

Falkirk

Dumbarton

Cumbernauld

Bearsden

Bathgate

GLASGOW

Paisley

Coatbridge

Motherwell

East
Kilbride

Lanark

CHAPTER EIGHT

Stones and More Stones

FROM BLAIRLOGIE, THE ROUTE TAKES THE HILL ROAD TO SHERIFFMUIR AND ON TO DUN-
BLANE, DOUNE, THORNHILL, LAKE OF MENTEITH, CALLANDER, LOCH LUBNAIG AND
STRATHYRE. THERE IS A SMALL DEVIATION TO BALQUIDDER, BEFORE TRAVELLING ON TO
LOCHEARNHEAD, LIX TOLL, CRIANLARICH AND TYNDRUM.

WHEN LEAVING THE National Wallace Monument, turn right to follow the
route you were on. This is the B998 Hillfoots Road. After about a mile,
there is a small road off to your left, signposted Logie Kirk, just before the
B998 ends at a T-junction. Turn up here, and it is only a few yards to Logie
Kirk itself. This is a building dating from 1805, but its predecessor is a little
further on, with only its south front and west gable remaining. The older
church looks extremely old, due probably in part to its ruined state, but it
only dates from 1684, although a stone built-in bears the date 1598. This
stone probably comes from an even earlier version. The churchyard is fascinating, with loads of interesting old tombstones, and it is great to stroll
round it on a nice day, with the noise of running water in the background.

The Ochil Hills are close here. The terrain is very rugged – and you are
about to see just how rugged, as the road begins to narrow and starts to
twist and turn as it climbs. There is an extremely tight hairpin that also has
a severe gradient, and anything above first gear will probably have your
engine stalling. With any luck you won't meet anything coming the other
way. This is by far the most difficult piece of road encountered on this journey so far. It does straighten out a little on its climb, however, and views of
the hillsides become more apparent. You come to a T-junction meeting the
road which rises from the town of Bridge of Allan, and here you turn right,
the road still heading towards the Ochils. Just after you have taken this
right turn, have a look over to your right again. You will be able to catch
the odd glimpse down the valley of the Forth, and you will realise that you
have gained a lot of height in a short distance. This is a pleasant stretch
before you. The road is very narrow, but undulates through some beautiful
terrain. Sheep tend to roam free for the next few miles, so please take the
appropriate care, even more so during lambing season.

After half a mile you will notice there are several parking places on the
right-hand side of the road. Usually there are a few vehicles parked here, as
this is the starting point for ascending Dumyat, at 1,375 feet high, and pronounced Dum-eye-at. Although by far not the highest of the Ochils, it gives

a spectacular view as it cantilevers out from the main ridge. It is only about a mile and a half of moderate hill-walking to the summit, and you will be rewarded with a view far more spectacular than many afforded from harder to reach and much loftier viewpoints. The vista from the top reminds me of a drawing in a schoolbook, showing a river system from its rising in the hills as a mere stream, its growth to a river, then its journey to the sea as an estuary. The Forth looks a bit like that from up here. The Wallace Monument looks far below too. An hour or two will take you to the top and back, and I can thoroughly recommend it.

The name of this hill comes from the Dun of the Maeatae, an ancient tribe in Scotland, and the earthworks of their fort is on the southwest shoulder of this hill, at about the 1,000 feet contour. It dates from the early Iron Age, and it is marked on Ordnance Survey maps.

Continue onwards, and the road begins to cross countryside that is more moorland now, which is hardly surprising as you are coming onto Sheriffmuir, a famous name in the history of Scotland.

Two miles or so after the path to Dumyat, you dip to cross a burn, then the road rises to a junction, with another small road coming in from your left and the Sheriffmuir Inn just beyond. At the Inn, the road takes a hard right, then about halfway up the rise before you there is a little lay-by on your left. Park here, cross the road, cross the fence and continue straight across the heathery moor, with the Inn down on your right. About two hundred yards in you will notice a large standing stone, and with a bit of further exploration in a straight line left and right of this one, you will discover that there are five stones in all, parallel with the road where you are parked. Only one of the stones, the most noticeable, is still in what appears to be its original position, the others have fallen or are broken, but are easy enough to find. These are what are known locally as the 'Wallace Stones'.

We know that Wallace's and Murray's men were besieging the castle at Dundee when word came of the approach of an English army in 1297. To reach Stirling Bridge, the Scots would have to march to Perth, cross the River Tay there, then head south for the Stirling area. They would probably have used the road on the line of the one on which you have actually parked! The stones will long predate that era – perhaps the Maeatae on nearby Dumyat were responsible for their raising, but they would have been a handy mustering point for the army, as in 'Gather at the line of standing stones on the moorland behind the Abbey Craig', perhaps. There is water in the nearby burn you just crossed, and plenty of room for many men to gather, and to hunt, on this shoulder of the Ochils. The fact that the Scots gathered here has passed into local legend. Watch could be kept for the English approaching up the Forth, and the army could have moved forward to the Abbey Craig and the vicinity of the bridge when time was ripe.

The other interesting thing is the lack of large stones up here on Sheriffmuir, and the mind boggles as to how these examples, many tons in weight, were shifted with nothing more than muscle-power.

There was a famous battle fought here too, on the moor itself, in 1715. It was a spread-out affair, but there are relics, and I'll take you to them after you have returned to the lay-by and your vehicle.

The Sheriffmuir Inn was in existence at the time of the battle, although it was only a few years old at that time. To verify its existence, there must have been an appreciable amount of passing trade on this old road, which is quiet today. Drive back past the inn, and when you reach the road coming in just after it, on your right, turn and drive towards the town of Dunblane.

A mile along the road, you will notice the large monument on the right at a lay-by. This is the Clan Macrae stone. This clan marched all the way from Kintail in the far north to fight here, and suffered terrible losses as they fought like men possessed. The stone has inscriptions in English and Gaelic.

On the cover of my book, *A Passion for Scotland*, I am standing before this stone, having just given a speech. There are commemorations of the Battle of Sheriffmuir held here every year. Almost everyone involved turns up in the garb of the era, and the event is generally held after nightfall, the scene lit up by tartan clad and armed torchbearers, the flickering of the firelight illuminating the faces. Having been lucky enough to have stood on the stone and looked out on that scene, the thought has crossed my mind that if tourists were to happen across us here, out in the dark, all basket-hilted broadswords and belted plaids, they would probably think they had stumbled across a window that was letting them look back in time. The event in 2000 was particularly memorable, the heaviest rain imaginable coming in at an angle, accompanied by a biting cold wind. Of such things are memories made, all that sodden tartan, beards and hair dripping in the dark. It will be a talking point for years to come at least. 'Remember the bloody hellish rain that fell that year?'

The battle was fought on 13 November, 1715, between the Hanoverian forces representing their monarch in London, and led by Argyll, and the Jacobite forces, representing the now-exiled Stewart dynasty, led by the Earl of Mar. The battle should have gone Mar's way, as he had numerical superiority, but there was hesitation on his part and chances were lost. The right wing of each army overran the left wing of their opposite number, so it became a revolving wheel of a battle, with no clear victor.

A battle there was that I saw, man,
And we ran, and they ran,
And they ran, and we ran,
And we ran, and they ran awa', man!

So ran the succinct rhyme in wry humour.

Afterwards, the clans went back to their glens and the rising petered out. Scotland still hankered after the Stewarts, though, and other attempts to seat them on the throne of their ancestors were to be made. But they fought not just for the Stewarts, Scotland's ancient dynasty. The hated Union between Scotland and England had taken place in 1707, and many swords carried on that day bore such slogans as 'Prosperity to Scotland and No Union'. So many Scots had already seen several of the articles which comprised that Union being broken and ignored that they felt it should be annulled.

There is another stone with connections to this battle which you may want to visit. You follow the path that runs in behind the Macrae stone, just to its right. It may be very muddy, and not something you would wish to do unless suitably shod. Follow the drystone wall for a few hundred yards, then on the brow of the rise, another path cuts off to the left and runs for perhaps two hundred yards to a group of older Scots Pine. The Gathering Stone is here, a flattish block, protected by iron bars, where legend states that the clansmen sharpened their swords before the fight. It is a quiet spot and a nice place to sit on a summer's day, with some wee watery pools nearby. But beware the dreaded Scots midge. Like mini-mosquitoes, they gather in open areas like this *en masse*, and although small, they are voracious in their appetite for human flesh. They are not usually at their worst until the end of May, and only live during summer months, but their massed biting can cause incredible discomfort. I have often wondered how our ancestors dealt with them. You can buy sprays and the like from chemists and pharmacists here, which, I am told, do repel them, so it may be worth enquiring about some of these products if you have to deviate from the road and civilisation!

I thought that there was nothing worse than the massed biting of midgies, but I was in Canada recently during what is known as Black Fly season. How the hell did the first settlers from Scotland deal with that lot? I have been home for a few months, and I am still scratching one on my arm in particular. I asked while in Canada, and was told that it was so bad that the early settlers would dip newsprint in kerosene and wrap themselves up in it before donning their plaids! Even the midgies did not prepare me for that.

From the Macrae monument proceed on towards Dunblane. Another mile or two of moorland, then the road drops down to the start of some housing. A sharp right hand bend starts the downhill run into Dunblane. At the road end you reach a roundabout which you go straight through onto Dunblane's High Street, and down towards the Cathedral. The steeple of Dunblane Cathedral is apparent before you on the opposite side of the roundabout. Halfway down the High Street, keep your eyes peeled for a house on your right-hand side, gable wall on to the street.. It bears a little plaque. This is Balhaldie House, where Bonnie Prince Charlie resided on 11

September 1745, while on his march from the Highlands towards Edinburgh. It is still occupied as a private house, and it is a lovely old place, its name coming from the fact that it was the townhouse of Macgregor of Balhaldie.

There is another, smaller roundabout at the bottom of the hill. Due to the one-way system operating in the town, you can only turn right at this roundabout. Do so, and park hereabouts. The Leighton Library is in the old house on your left. Bishop Leighton, who lived from 1613–84, bequeathed his collection of 1,400 books to the diocese here. His nephew built this place to contain them, and other books have been added over the centuries. On your right is the little museum, in a quaint old building, the former Dean's House, dating from 1624. It contains some interesting bits and pieces.

Directly in front is Dunblane Cathedral: 'He was no common man who designed the Cathedral of Dunblane. I know not anything so perfect in its simplicity, and so beautiful, as far as it reaches, in all the Gothic with which I am acquainted ....' (Ruskin)

It is not ornate like many continental cathedrals, and has an austerity about it, but is very Scottish in demeanour and I like it very much. It was founded by St Blane – hence the name – about AD 600. The lower four storeys of the tower are a remnant of the early Celtic church, but most of the stonework visible today dates from the early to the mid-1200s, Bishop Clement being the man responsible. His effigy still stands within the church. Dunblane Cathedral has a welcome, homely feel to it, with quite a lot to see inside. There are a couple of carved Celtic stones, something I'm always delighted to come across so I can marvel at the skill and patience of those generations of the stones. How long would those carvings have taken with early tools?

There is some marvellous woodwork too, along with the stained glass, but there is one thing I always think of, and go and look at when I am in Dunblane. It is the three steely blue slabs set into the floor at the eastern end of the church, in the choir. Just stone among all the magnificence, but I am drawn back to these three stones again and again. They were actually removed in 1817, but the ensuing outcry had them replaced.

Legend states that King James IV, he of Flodden, fell in love with the beautiful Margaret, daughter of the Lord Drummond, and was secretly wed to her, knowing that his nobles would not approve of such a match. They would want him married to a princess of another European nation, in order to advance dynastic ambitions. But word of their vows slipped out, and the nobles, desirous of a marriage between James and Margaret Tudor of England, decided that Margaret Drummond should be removed. The food at Drummond Castle was poisoned, and unfortunately Margaret and her two sisters perished. They were buried here in 1502.

Before you leave Dunblane, it is worth having a walk around the outside of the Cathedral, to look down into the valley that contains the River Allan at its western end.

Back to your vehicle again, and as said, there is a one-way system in operation in Dunblane, so in our case it is best to retrace your route a little, back up through the roundabout near the Cathedral, passing Balhaldie House, this time on your left, and back to the major roundabout at the top of the hill. This time we are going right, onto the old A9, which is dual carriageway here. We only drive a short distance, crossing the bridge over the River Allan, and we reach a mini-roundabout, the right exit signposted Callander and Doune. This Callander has no connection with Callendar House at Falkirk, and as you will notice, there is a variation in the spelling.

Just down this route, there is a hard left turn, then it is a straight run out to the suburbs of Dunblane. We cross the modern A9 on a flyover, this being the main north-south route, and out into open countryside. It's rolling woodland and farmland for the next three miles until we reach Doune. Over to your right you may catch glimpses of Ben Ledi, 2,873 feet high, about a dozen miles away on the southern edge of the Highlands.

Down we go into Doune, whose badge is a pair of crossed pistols. Doune was a famous centre for gun-making at one time, Doune pistols being very sought-after items today. It is claimed that the first shot in the American War of Independence was fired from a Doune pistol.

On your left as you come into Doune are some large gates and a boundary wall. This is the periphery of Newton House, a privately owned old baronial edifice. Bonnie Prince Charlie and his army came by this property on their march south, after his night spent at Balhaldie in Dunblane. The young ladies of the family sat upon the wall, laughing and waving as the tartan-clad soldiers marched past. When the Bonnie Prince came by on his horse, the ladies asked if he would like to come in for refreshments. Charles, shrugging towards his troops, regretfully had to decline. One of the ladies then offered Charles a glass of wine, which he raised to his lips to drink a toast of health to the ladies. But one, bolder than the rest, and determined not to be outdone by her companions, ran after the Prince and asked if she could 'pree his Royal Highness's mou'. This expression in broad Scots had to be translated by one of the Prince's companions. Charles, laughing, leaned from his horse, and pulled the girl, Clementina Edmonstoun, bodily from the ground, planting kisses on her face. Her companions looked on, envious that they had not dared such a ploy.

A little further along on the left is the entrance road that takes us down to Doune Castle. It is a tight bend, and coming from this direction will probably take a shuffle back and forward to turn in. There is an old bridge before you that crosses the Ardoch Burn, but we swing right and the castle suddenly looms large before you. It is believed that there was a fortification on this site in the eleventh century, but this mass of stonework that is the renowned Doune Castle was begun by Murdoch Stewart, second Duke of Albany and Governor of Scotland, 1419–24. Murdoch was responsible for the enforced absence of the young King James I of Scots in England, and James was not too enamoured of this arrangement. When he eventually returned, he had Murdoch and his sons executed at the heading stone we have already visited, standing above the south end of Stirling Bridge.

See how all this history lark fits together like a big jigsaw?

At first glance, the castle does not look as if it stands in a particularly strong site, but a walk around it will reveal that it stands in the junction of the meeting of the Ardoch Burn and the River Teith. The River Teith is a tributary of the Forth, which is strange, as the Teith is actually longer and contains a greater quantity of water, so why the Forth takes precedence is a mystery. The Firth of Teith, or, the Teith Bridges, doesn't really have the same ring though, does it?

The main structure of the castle faces out to the landward side and you enter the castle through a gateway penetrating the main tower. Although stripped almost bare internally, the castle is windproof and watertight, and inside there is a labyrinth of rooms to explore, ante-chambers to scour, and windows to peer out of. There is a gigantic fireplace in the kitchen which has to be seen to be believed, and, always a favourite with me, you can get out onto the roof of the tower and stand on the battlements, pretending you are lord of all you survey. As you exit the castle, over to your right there is the entrance to a stone-clad tunnel. Another ice-house for keeping food fresh in the summer months, I would imagine.

There is a small lodge-house out in the car park area, with a wall immediately at its rear. I once visited Doune Castle with the late Bob McCutcheon, a man I greatly admired, and whose knowledge of history, especially of the Stirling area, was unsurpassed. He lies in the cemetery at Bannockburn, overlooking the gorge where the battle was fought, and I can think of no finer place for him. Anyway, Bob pointed at this building and said to me, 'What famous thing happened here, at that wall behind that wee lodge?' I came up with several theories, while he quietly smirked to himself. He liked to catch me out, did Bob. Eventually I had to admit defeat and bow before his superior knowledge. 'Butch Cassidy's grandfather committed suicide by hanging himself from a length of wood balanced between that wall and the roof of the lodge', came the reply. I have never been able to verify this, but knowing Bob, it is ninety-nine percent likely to be the truth!

I miss you Bob.

Driving on through Doune, you will see that it is a particularly Scottish-looking wee place, and I am glad that its Main Street looks very much as it must have done a century or two ago. You will notice the old Mercat Cross (merkat or mercat is just old Scots for market) on your left, and you turn into George Street here, which runs down on your left behind the cross itself. George Street brings us to the A84, which is the main route between Stirling and Callander. At this T-junction you turn left, following the sign pointing towards Stirling. After a few hundred yards you turn onto the large bridge over the River Teith. The story behind this bridge is an interesting one.

After the execution of Murdoch of Albany, Doune Castle became a Royal Castle, and in the time of James IV, he gifted the castle to his wife, Margaret Tudor, as a residence. She long outlived James, of course, as he died at Flodden in 1513. Her tailor was a very wealthy man by the name of Robert Spittal. He came to Doune Castle to visit her, and when he arrived at the ferry to carry him over the River Teith, he realised he had no ready money, and although he made various promises, the ferryman refused to convey him to the opposite bank. Out of spite, Spittal constructed this bridge, thereby depriving the ferryman of a living. The bridge was built in 1535, and was widened by three feet in 1866.

Not too far on the other side of this bridge there is a garage on your right, and just past this is a junction, signposted for Thornhill, B826, so turn right along this road and carry straight on. Perhaps a mile along this stretch of woodland and fields, you will notice a round tower on a hilltop over to your right. I was once told that this tower had been built as this spot was regarded as being the very centre of Scotland. But as Comrie in Perthshire is well known as the holder of that title, some doubt must be cast on this.

Another mile or two and we come to this road's end, as it comes to a T-junction with the A873, just on the edge of the village of Thornhill. We turn right into Thornhill itself, a pleasant wee place built on a ridge, and comprising of not much more than its main street, funnily enough called Main Street.

There is a pub on your right just as you come into the village, called the Lion and Unicorn, with both these beasts carved into the upper frontage of the place. I like the fact that the lion on the pub's sign has a chef's hat on. It's a minor detail, but I always find myself looking for it in passing.

The main road takes a little twist to the right as you get to the far end of the village, but just keep following the signs for the A873 to Glasgow and Aberfoyle.

A mile out of Thornhill, you will notice the flat ground over to your left. Flatlands, although with some scrubby tree cover, that still look damp and water-logged after many years of drainage. This is the Flanders Moss. It stretches away south until the ground begins to rise at the Fintry and Gargunnock Hills. It was more extensive once than it is now, but enough remains for you to get the picture. Its paths were only known to a few. Rob Roy MacGregor used it to transport and hide stolen cattle, and it was the reason that armies of invasion had to cross the Forth at Stirling. It was no place for large armies, and so proved an impassable barrier between south and north.

The road hugs the north side of Flanders Moss, running along the edge of the higher ground. Eventually you will come to a junction where the A81 cuts off north on your right to Callander. We are going to take this road shortly, but there is something special just a little over a mile further on, and we will go and look at it first before returning to this junction.

As said, just over a mile ahead, you will see signs for Inchmahome Priory and the Lake of Menteith. As you reach the lake, there is a little turn in to your left to take you into the Port of Menteith, and follow the signs for the priory. You will need to spend a little time on a boat as the priory stands on an island. There is a small car park among some trees, and it is pleasant to just walk out onto the little jetty, taking in the lake with its islets and the high barrier of the Menteith Hills on your right starting to give the landscape your first feel of the Highlands.

Why lake? It would seem this is nothing more than a slip by a cartographer, as older maps call this stretch of water the Loch of Menteith. It is often referred to as 'the only lake in Scotland', but as the referral to it as a lake is a fairly recent development, perhaps we should use the good Scottish loch as often as possible to revert it!

It is only about ten minutes in the motor boat out to Inchmahome, (*Inch* is a word often used in Scottish place names, and it basically means 'island') the island which contains the priory, but there are two other islands on this loch: Inchtalla, which means 'the Isle of the Hall', and the Dog Isle. It contains a ruined castle which was once the seat of the Earl of Menteith. The Dog Isle is merely an islet, but it once contained the dog kennels for the Earl's hunting forays.

You land on Inchmahome, just next to the ruins of the Priory. There is a little shop by the jetty. The Priory is said to have been founded by King Edgar in the 1100s, but is more likely to have been built by one of the Comyn lords in the next century. It is a jewel. Ruined, but that does not detract from its beauty. It is not a large establishment, the main body of the priory and several outbuildings is all, but it has a magic, a lot of it due to its situation.

You can walk round the island in ten minutes, but you will take longer as you are bound to stop and admire some of the old gnarled trees, and stand and watch the water lap on the shore. The views out to the hills are striking too. The landscape has changed as you have come further west, and it is surprising how the west and east coast topography differs in a country as small as mine.

There are some interesting tombs in Inchmahome. RB Cunninghame Graham lies here. He is a famous writer who spent much time in South America, where he earned the title 'Don Roberto'. He was a patriot, which was not surprising really, as he was a descendent of the Graham, Wallace's companion, whose tomb we have visited in Falkirk's churchyard.

There are some notable effigies within one of the buildings. That of Walter, First Stewart Earl of Menteith, and his wife Mary, is like no other I have ever seen. It is very weather-worn, with parts missing, but it comprises the couple side by side, holding hands, she with an arm around his neck. It is very unusual, and they must have loved each other very much in life to have left arrangements for their memorial to be constructed in such a way.

There is an effigy nearby which is of another Earl of Menteith, and which is dated to around 1330–40. With a start I realised that this is most likely to be the representation of the 'False Menteith', the man who betrayed Sir William Wallace to the English. He lies in full arms and armour, and I looked upon his effigy for quite a while, trying to analyse my feelings and emotions about this. He lies in this beautiful setting, whereas Wallace was scattered to the winds. But perhaps the way that these opposites are remembered in Scotland is enough. Wallace is loved, and he is remembered in the hearts of true Scots. Menteith is largely forgotten, or is despised by those who know the story of his betrayal of a Scot to a foreign king and power. Maybe that is enough. I am glad that his effigy stands intact. It is a monument to remembering, and realising that Scotland has had low points in its past which should never be repeated.

Inchmahome's most famous resident, however, was Mary, Queen of Scots. She was brought here as a young girl in 1547 to save her from the clutches of Henry VIII of England – he of the six wives. Henry invaded Scotland to try and force a marriage between his son and our young queen. This affair has since been known in Scotland as the Rough Wooing. Mary remained here for five months, and wandering around this little island, you can almost sense her presence. There is a little garden, still pointed out as Queen Mary's Bower, a little grassy area surrounded by trees where she used to play with her companions. If in doubt, the staff will point out its location.

Mary left here to travel to the greater safety of France, and did not return to Scotland till her late teens. It is also worth remembering that Robert the Bruce visited this place on three occasions, and I suppose apart from the ruined state of the priory, the views have not changed too much.

Back onto the motorboat now, and the journey back towards the little cluster of buildings known as the Port of Menteith.

I first visited Inchmahome when I was no more than eight or nine years old, and it has stuck with me ever since. It is a great day out, and certainly the trip on the boat and the little island with its tree covered paths made an impression on me that I have never forgotten, and I would recommend it to anyone.

It's time to retrace your route a little as we are going to take the A81 north to Callander, so we travel back a mile on the route we have already taken, till the junction is reached.

If you look over to your left at this junction you will notice that there is a farmhouse set back from the road, with the remains of a large castle tower to its immediate left. This was the seat of the Grahams of Rednock. The Grahams still live here, but the stair tower is all that remains of the large tower that was Rednock Castle.

The road climbs to cross the watershed between the River Forth and the River Teith to the north. The ridge of the Menteith Hills looks impressive to your left. Loch Rusky appears to your right, a picturesque, tree-lined little loch which always seems to freeze over in winter. This loch is said to have once had a castle on an island belonging to Menteith, the betrayer of Wallace. There is a tiny island, which appears only large enough to house a couple of bushes and no more, but perhaps the water level has risen over the centuries.

You are on the mounth (in Scotland we call high ground between two river systems a mounth) between the two river systems here (see!), and the road plunges into thick forestry, with many interesting walks branching off left and right. Then the descent towards Callander begins, and glimpses to the larger hills of the southern edge of the Highlands appear to your left through gaps in the trees.

A final fast, straight stretch takes us to the outskirts of Callander itself. There is a mini-roundabout to encounter where you turn right, and this takes us over the River Teith on an old bridge, and up to the traffic lights on the junction with Callander's Main Street. Turn left at these lights, and it is only some 200 yards till you see the sign pointing into Callander Meadows, a large car parking area, right on the north bank of the Teith, the entrance going left off the Main Street. There is a large pool in the river here, and quite a selection of ducks, swans and coots gather, always looking for titbits.

Ben Ledi, at 2,873 feet, towers over this scene to the west. It is not a big hill by Highland standards, but it is a scenic backdrop to Callander. There are high and impressive crags behind the town too, so it seems no matter where you look in Callander, there is a backdrop of rock or water. This, coupled with its Main Street, crammed with interesting wee shops, makes it a Mecca for tourists and day-trippers in the summer months.

At the eastern end of Callander Meadows you will see a symmetrical hill – a moot or mote hill, upon which a fortification once stood. It is just a smaller version of the one originally visited at Hawick in the Borders. Like the Hawick one, it has a staircase built up one side.

To get to know Callander, it is best to remain parked here, go back out to the Main Street, and turn right, eastwards. Walk the length of this road, cross it and walk back down the other side. You see, Callander is really only one street with a few additions on either side, and a half-mile walk in each direction lets you get the flavour of the place.

Not too far along is the town's war memorial on the south side, with the Rob Roy and Trossachs Visitor Centre on the opposite, northern side of the street. Notice the plaque of a Highlander bearing a fiery cross – this badge is repeated on the shield held by a Lion atop the stone column of the war memorial. The fiery cross was used as a sign of trouble and for men to muster in the days of clan society. A clansman would run from hamlet to hamlet through the glen, and each person would recognise the blazing cross as a sign that something was afoot. It is the badge of Callander – there is even a fish-and-chip shop in the town bearing that name!

Every time I visit the square where this memorial stands, my mind is cast back to the time when I owned a Harley-Davidson. There were 80 of us gathered in this square whilst on a run-out to Fort William. Most of the guys had straight-through exhaust pipes, and there were rows of Harleys in the square. They all fired up together as we got ready to move off – the noise was earth-shattering. I mean literally – the whole town shook!

I have since returned to the delights of Japanese machines – they deal with the damp weather of Scotland a lot better for a start. Harleys are good fun, though a little agricultural. In fact, you find that if you scratch away at where it says 'Harley Davidson' on the tank, it actually says Massey-Ferguson underneath. When I'm over in North America and guys roar past on them, I can understand why they chose the Harley. They suit the mentality there. Everybody rides much slower over there, and Harleys are built for cruising – but I'm afraid most of the people I know drive to arrive. Me included. I keep waiting for old age to creep up, or even just a bit of dignity to slow me down. I'm not discourteous, incidentally, I'm not interested in upsetting anyone, I'm just quick.

The Rob Roy visitor centre opposite is worth a visit. There's a bookshop with touristy things on the ground floor that you can visit gratis, or you can pay to view the exhibition on the life and times of Rob Roy MacGregor, another world-famous Scot, who was born at Loch Katrine in 1671. He was never the clan chief as many suppose, but acted as its captain. He had an extraordinary length of arm – it has been said that he could tie the garters at the top of his socks without bending! This may sound like a deformity in our day and age, but in the days of broadsword and targe, such huge reach would have given you the edge as a swordsman right away. The MacGregors, or the Children of the Mist, as they are affectionately called in Scotland, had fallen foul of the government in London due to their Jacobite tendencies, and Rob Roy decided that if they were to be treated as outlaws, he would become one *par excellence*.

Blackmail was a word that was to become synonymous with Rob. He ran a protection racket, where lairds would pay an indemnity to him, and in return, he would ensure that their sheep and cattle were not 'lifted' of an evening. The word 'blackmail originates from Scotland (we *did* invent *everything*). *Mails* were rents paid in money and kind, and it is said that the prefix black came from the black cattle that inhabited the glens. They were similar to today's Highland Cattle, only smaller, and of course, black in colour.

Rob led a charmed life, and his story has been the theme of several Hollywood films. One of my friends happened to see *Rob Roy*, starring Liam Neeson in the title role, before I did. I asked him if Liam's Scottish accent sounded good. 'Yeah', he replied, 'He sounded exactly like he did in *Schindler's List*'. Being Scottish myself, I have to say Jessica Lange as Rob's wife sounded great. Very impressive. She did it well. If Scotland ever gets an equivalent to the Oscars, the Anguses or similar, she should get one. If you want to delve into the story of Rob, the book I would recommend is WH Murray's *Rob Roy MacGregor*. I read it on a holiday in Majorca, and it had me in tears at the end. We are in Rob Roy country here, so we will return to him shortly.

Leaving the fleshpots and bright lights of Callander behind, return to your vehicle, and leaving the car park, turn left, westwards, along the Main Street. We pass several large hotel establishments, then we are out into the surrounding countryside again To our left, the Teith has split into its two head streams, the Eas Gobhain and the Garbh Uisge, but the latter is generally known as the River Leny, and it is that which the road follows.

We enter Kilmahog, a little scatter of mill shops, where the A821 branches off left, heading for the Trossachs. But we continue straight on, and the road begins to twist and turn as it enters the Pass of Leny, the tarmac hugging the bank of the river as it tumbles and bubbles down the pass. This is one of the old passes from the southeast into the Highlands, and there are fewer roads into this part of Scotland than might be imagined. The towns of Crieff and Pitlochry, like Callander, form their own gateways.

As you head through this heavily treed pass, you may notice signs for the Falls of Leny, but these are really nothing more than a stretch of rough water, and to be frank, if you are expecting a spectacular waterfall, you will be disappointed.

Two miles of twisting road, and you come up onto the shores of Loch Lubnaig, the whole countryside now Highland in character. Ben Ledi, the name meaning the Mountain of God, rises directly above the far side of the loch, and its northern spur runs out to the slightly shorter Ben Vane. Ben, or *beinn*, is the word we use for mountain, but we have a few more descriptive words, which it may be handy for you to know the meaning of. *Creag*, when used as a prefix, just means craggy. *Meall* generally means rounded. *Sron* is like a nose, *Cnoc* is a rounded lump, and *Sgurr* means jagged.

We drive the A84 as it sweeps up the length of the loch, with some parking places dotted along the shoreline should you wish to stop and take in
some of the views. Loch Lubnaig is perhaps five miles long, then at its
northern end we drive up into Strathyre. *Strath* is the word we use for a
wide glen, usually with a river meandering about the valley floor, and the
river in this case is the Balvaig. About a mile on, we come to a village that
bears the same name as the glen, Strathyre. It is a small place, one or two
shops and a hotel, and we carry on, straight through. Two miles further
north there is a junction branching off to your right, signposted for
Balquhidder. An old hotel, called the Kingshouse, stands here. I have
imbibed alcohol on several occasions within this very establishment, and
had the locals assert that Rob Roy drank there himself at one time. I'm not
sure of the age of the place, and have never been able to verify this story, but
it may well be true. I have also met locals within who have never been to
Glasgow – although it is little over an hour's drive away!

Take this Balquhidder turn, past the hotel and under the A84 you were
on. The road then heads due west up the glen, running under the Braes of
Balquhidder, made famous in song. This is a narrow road, a single lane with
passing places, so a certain courtesy is required. If you have never come
across such roads before, you will soon get the picture. You simply pull into
the marked passing places when you see oncoming cars. You should easily
be able to judge who should pull in and who should drive on, and cheery
waves are always appreciated.

You pass through the scatter of houses that is Auchtoo, and another mile
brings you to the village of Balquhidder itself. As you go through the village
you will notice a fortified looking castle-like tower on your right. It goes by
the name of the Keep. It is actually modern, built in the late 1900s, but it
really looks the business. Just after, Balquhidder Church appears on the
right, with a little road leading up to its gate where you can find room to
park. This is a place I love dearly, and never fail to enjoy visiting.

In the graveyard is Rob Roy's grave, his wife Mary on one side, son Coll
on the other. For some reason Sir Walter Scott referred to Rob's wife as
Helen, and so the cast-iron sign bears both names.

As I stand at the foot of Rob's gave, something always stirs within me.
Rob was a man and a half. A man's man, and he very much lived life by his
own rules. But he was also very much a Scot, and an independent-minded
one at that. A backbone of steel too, and we have always needed as many of
them as possible in Scotland through all its ages.

What moves me most though is the epitaph on the stone at his head.
'MacGregor despite them'.

And he was, and still is. His clan was outlawed by those who served a foreign government, hunted like animals, but the fame of the MacGregors has

survived the centuries and Rob Roy MacGregor is a name known to every Scot today. I can raise my eyes from the stone bearing this epitaph, and look out over Balquhidder, and the mountain tops and peaks all around, and see them as Rob did in his day.

I should point out that the stones that cover Rob and his family are very much older than his time. They are old carven stones, and were probably held in a reverence by the inhabitants of the glen, and so were re-used to cover his last resting place.

There is a fourth similar stone here, with a representation of a churchman with a chalice in his hands carved upon it. This stone originally stood within the church, in front of the altar, but was removed in the 1800s to destroy a superstitious desire that existed amongst the parishioners to stand or kneel on it during a marriage or baptism. Shame that, really. I suppose the minister saw it as pagan, but I just see quaint tradition. It is still called Clach Aenois, or the Stone of Angus, who, according to tradition, was a disciple of Columba and the first Christian missionary to visit this district. This stone was set upright within the church in 1917, to prevent it from deteriorating.

The main clan residing in this area was the MacLaurin clan. They are said to have acquired the land here in the reign of Kenneth MacAlpin (844–60), and were once so numerous that none were allowed to enter the church until those inside had taken their seats. This caused a lot of friction, and many brawls broke out. In one particular brawl in 1532, the vicar, Sir John MacLaurin, was slain.

There is a granite monument in the graveyard to the memory of 'the Clan Laurin, the chief of whom, in the decrepitude of old age, together with his aged and infirm adherents, their wives and children, the widows of their departed kindred – all were destroyed in the silent midnight hour by fire and sword, by the hands of a banditti of incendiarists from the Glendochart, A.D. 1558'.

These *banditti* were MacGregors, of whom Rob Roy was a descendant.

There have been four churches on this site. There was the original Celtic cell of the aforementioned St Angus. It was followed by a thirteenth-century building, slight traces of which can still be seen beside Rob's grave. There are also the ruins of the kirk of 1631, partly built on its predecessor, and the current building of 1855. This church is generally unlocked, and is a lovely place to visit. In the summer months, swallows nest in the little porch, and other than Angus's stone inside, there is a massive ancient font, shaped from a boulder. Above the altar there is a huge wooden cross suspended by wires.

My very first visit to this church was when I was quite young, and I turned up here during twilight. Finding the door was unlocked, I wandered into the church. I didn't bother looking for a light switch as there was still just enough daylight to see my way about without bumping into anything. I noticed the cross, of course, out of the corner of my eye and started with fright as I realised it seemed to be floating in mid-air. I couldn't see the wires in the half light, and there was that sensation of confusion for a few seconds, where you try to make sense of something incomprehensible.

I'm a bit older and wiser now!

There is the bell of the 1631 church on show. albeit cracked, and the bell of the even earlier church contained within an old chest. This chest was carried by Rob Roy to Loch Tay side, but was brought back here in 1930. There is an Irish Gaelic Testament known as Bishop Bedell's Bible, and a Scottish one translated from it by Robert Kirk, who was minister here, in 1685.

The little road you have driven up to the church continues for another six miles, following the north shore of Loch Voil for four miles, then passing smaller Loch Doine. The road culminates at Inverlochlarig among some large mountains, a couple rising close to 4000 feet in the shapes of Stobinian and Ben More.

I have spent quite a few days roaming these hills, just as I have roamed many places in Scotland. But one hill in particular I remember very well. I had climbed Beinn a' Chroin from Inverlochlarig, and on the summit I was enveloped in a dread, hanging on me like a blanket, as if some terrible primeval being was stalking me. Although cloud was rolling over the ridge before me, I was standing under a clear sky and could see all about me. I am not the type to worry about the supernatural, and I am not superstitious, but I felt I had to get down into the glen as soon as possible, to get away from whatever it was that was up there. For years after, I swore I would never go up that hill again, even in the company of a group of people. I have never been scared of ghosts. If they can harm me, I can harm them, if you see what I mean. And I am strong – so if there really are ephemeral wraiths that can float through me, then I have nothing to fear from them. If my broadsword were to go through them, without damage, then logic tells me they can't harm me either!

I have spent many nights out in the Highlands in some very remote places, and nothing has ever bothered me, but there was definitely a presence on that hill – one that had me asking 'Who's there?', with the hairs rising on the back of my neck. Perhaps I'll go back soon, just to see if a different time gives a different feeling.

The farm at Inverlochlarig at the road end is on the site of the house where Rob Roy died, although nothing old remains. The road from Balquhidder onwards is very twisty, with many rises and dips and bad bends, so I mention Inverlochlarig basically to inform you of where the road runs to, and unless you fancy the drive to the dead end and retracing

your route back to this spot, I suggest going back to the junction with the
A84 at Kingshouse. Another couple of miles north, and we reach the village of Lochearnhead,
standing, as its name suggests, a the head of Loch Earn, a sizeable stretch of
water. There has been a habitation here since recorded history began, as the
very scant remains of St Blane's Chapel at the southwestern corner of the
loch testifies. Lochearnhead today is a small tourist centre with hotels and
guest houses, and is known for its water sports. There is a junction here,
where the A85 comes in from the direction of Perth, and although it is a
straight through road we are on, the A84 which we have been following
now takes on the moniker of the A85. We head north, the road signposted
for Crianlarich.

We climb steeply, but it is a good road, and we begin to ascend Glen Ogle,
which has been likened to the Khyber Pass! The name Ogle is supposedly a
derivative of the Gaelic *eagal*, meaning dead. It can look daunting in bad
weather, with burns in spate and foaming, bubbling water tumbling down
its sides. The road rises 620 feet in just three miles. It is almost a box-ended
glen, but there has always been a road wending its way to the top of this
pass, and it has been a through route to the north since man first appeared
in Scotland.

The road clings to the easternmost side of the glen, and you will notice
that the line of an old railway, now sadly gone, climbs the western side. The
line of the tracks now provides an excellent walking route. I wish I could
have been on a train climbing this glen – I would have had my nose pressed
against the glass, squinting for the best view, but sadly, the railway was
defunct before my time.

I once had the end of a badly fitted exhaust on a Harley come off on this
stretch of road. It bounced away to the floor of the glen, hundreds of feet
below, and I had on the wrong boots to go chasing after it. The racket off
the unbaffled exhaust for the rest of that journey echoed off every hillside,
and it was so overwhelmingly loud that I cringed in embarrassment
although I can laugh at it now.

At the top of the pass there are parking places if you wish to admire the
view, and there is a delightful little stretch of water, with trees as a backdrop, on your left, by the name of Lochan Lairig Cheile. *Lochan* is the
word we use for a little loch – simple as that. There is a slight downhill run
for a mile on the other side of this watershed, running down to the junction
known as Lix Toll, where the A827 branches off eastwards for Killin, but
we carry onwards on the A85, now swinging west. We are in the catchment
area for the River Tay here, and for the next few miles we will be following
the River Dochart, the main head stream of the Tay. The Tay becomes a
mighty river as it goes east, becoming a wide estuary after the city of Perth,

and Dundee stands on the north shore of this estuary. The Tay is the longest river in Scotland at a tiny fraction under 120 miles in length.

It is 11 miles from Lix Toll to Crianlarich, the next habitation of any size, and this is a decent though fairly uneventful stretch. To the north, on our right, lie two hills over 3,000 feet in height, Meall a' Churain, and Beinn Cheathaich, at 3,007 and 3,074 feet respectively. Just west of the latter is a smaller hill, Beinn nan Imirean, at 2,769 feet, which I climbed one midwinter to find a combination of wind and snow had carved the most outstanding ice sculptures, weird shapes, pillars and arches, on its summit.

As we near Crianlarich, we are directly under Ben More (More being a corruption of *mor* – the Gaelic for 'big'), the biggest hill hereabouts. Its mighty flanks soar upwards above us, on our left, the south side of the road. On our right here are two lochs, the first is Loch Lubhair, the second, smaller loch is Dochart. Loch Dochart has a ruined castle on its wooded islet. This castle was built by Sir Duncan Campbell between 1585 and 1631. Before running into this loch, the Dochart, which is, as explained, really the Tay, is called the River Fillan.

We soon come into the small township of Crianlarich, which has a hotel or two, a couple of shops, and a railway station on the Glasgow to Fort William route. From here on we swing a little further north, and follow Strathfillan, the strath of the River Fillan. This is a fine broad strath, with some grand views to the hilltops, which stand well back here. The highest peak on your right is Ben Callum, with Beinn Dubhchraig over to your left. This is a fast stretch, so you have to keep your eyes peeled for the entrance road into Kirkton Farm. It stands on your right, just over two miles out of Crianlarich, at the end of the heavier woodland at the road edge. Turn in here to a stony track, which immediately swings right again because of the constriction of the River Fillan. There is room to park here. You cross the river on foot, by a wooden bridge that leads over to Kirkton Farm. This takes its name from the old ruined St Fillan's kirk here – a chapel or church is often called a 'kirk' in Scotland. In fact, the whole strath and its river takes its name from St Fillan, a Christian missionary who worked in these parts. The ruins of the chapel are just to the left of the farm as you approach, half-hidden among the trees.

This was a place of some importance in Scotland's past. King Robert Bruce was here at his lowest ebb, having suffered two crushing defeats early in his reign, and with even worse humiliation to come before his eventual success.

There are just a few low walls, with only one or two features remaining, but five relics of St Fillan were once venerated here, each in the care of a hereditary custodian. The bell of St Fillan has survived. It is a squared-off, Celtic-style bell with some decoration. It is now kept in the museum of Scotland in Edinburgh. A long-distance footpath, the West Highland Way, runs by the chapel ruins. This connects Glasgow and Fort William, almost 100 miles apart. Signboards telling the story of the chapel have been erected. There is a little burial ground nearby which has one or two interesting inscriptions, and there are other graves just up the hill, but this area has been used for burials for well over a thousand years. There are marvellous views here too, especially back to Ben More.

Back to your vehicle then, and turn out right to follow the A82 onwards. It is only a mile or two to Tyndrum, but there are a couple of things to notice in that short distance.

On the left-hand side, keep your eyes peeled for a sign for a farm named Dail Righ. There is nothing to see other than the name itself, *dail* being the Gaelic for a field, or open area, *righ* being the word for king – so, King's Field. The name comes from a battle which was fought here in 1306 between the forces of Robert the Bruce and the MacDougalls of Lorne, the latter not being too enamoured of Bruce's assumption of the crown of Scotland. During this fight, Bruce was assailed by several clansmen, and he fought back, swinging his axe in bloody strokes. One of the MacDougalls fell back, having wrenched off the King's jewelled clasp. This clasp is known as the Brooch of Lorne, a weighty Celtic-style piece of workmanship which has been a treasured possession of the Chiefs of the MacDougalls ever since. The actual site of this encounter can only be guessed at. It was likely to have been a scattered affair anyway, being mostly a running fight, but the name Dail Righ has survived.

Beyond the battle site, a few miles back from the road, an impressive mountain has come into view. This is Ben Lui, 3,708 feet high. It has two projecting ridges that protect a huge central corrie. This corrie holds snow well into early summer, and it is an epic winter ice climb. The Tay rises in this great corrie and it is known as the Cononish for the first couple of miles of its course. It is a little confusing, I know, this river being the Cononish, then the Fillan, then the Dochart, before it flows out the other side of Loch Tay, assuming that name, but this is the head stream. I like the fact that when I climbed Ben Lui a few years ago, I had to step over the stream as it issued from this great corrie. I have stood with a foot on either side of the mighty Tay! I have told people that I have straddled the Tay when we have been looking out across it. It's over a mile wide at Dundee. I can see that they think I have finally lost it completely.

Just a short hop then, and we reach Tyndrum, just inside the border of Highland Perthshire, the land beyond here being Argyll. The name is a corruption of *tigh* (house) *an droma* (of the ridge). This is obviously a reference to an original building many centuries ago. There are a few shops here today, and a selection of places where you can eat. For such a small place, it is surprising that it has two railway stations. One serves the line to Fort

William, and the other the line to Oban. Tyndrum, for the scatter of buildings it is, can be a busy wee place because there is a meeting of roads here,
and just north of the village the roads diverge. The A85 swings westwards
for the port of Oban and its connecting ferries to some of the islands, and
the A82 heads due north for Fort William.

So, it's the Fort William road we take then, heading ever further north.

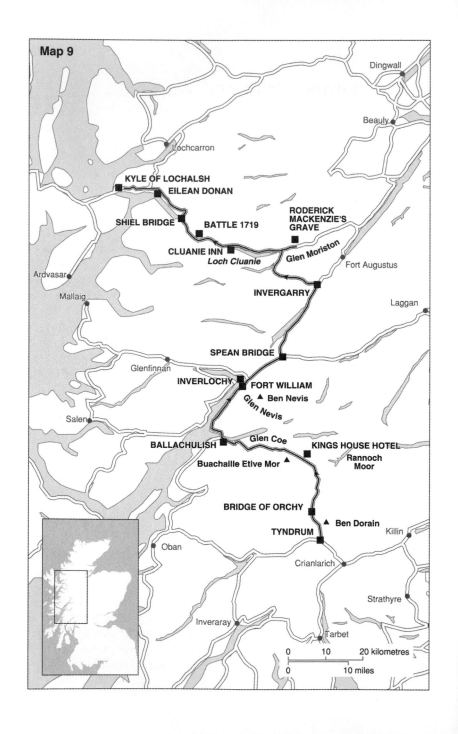

Map 9

Dingwall

Beauly

Lochcarron

KYLE OF LOCHALSH
EILEAN DONAN

SHIEL BRIDGE   BATTLE 1719

RODERICK
MACKENZIE'S
GRAVE

CLUANIE INN
Loch Cluanie   Glen Moriston

Fort Augustus

Ardvasar

INVERGARRY

Mallaig

Laggan

SPEAN BRIDGE

Glenfinnan

INVERLOCHY   FORT WILLIAM
▲ Ben Nevis
Glen Nevis

Salen

BALLACHULISH   Glen Coe

KINGS HOUSE HOTEL
Rannoch
Moor

Buachaille Etive Mor ▲

BRIDGE OF ORCHY

▲ Ben Dorain

TYNDRUM

Killin

Oban

Crianlarich

Strathyre

Inveraray

Tarbet

0   10   20 kilometres

0   10 miles

CHAPTER NINE

Glens, Lochs and Waterfalls

FROM TYNDRUM THE ROUTE GOES TO BRIDGE OF ORCHY, GLENCOE, BALLACHULISH, AND
FORT WILLIAM BEFORE TAKING A DETOUR DOWN TO GLEN NEVIS. CONTINUING ON
THROUGH SPEAN BRIDGE AND INVERGARRY, TURN EAST FOR A MILE OR TWO ALONG THE
A887 TO RODERICK MACKENZIE'S GRAVE. ON TO SHIEL BRIDGE AND KYLE OF LOCHALSH.

As you drive out of Tyndrum and start to climb on the Fort William road, you will notice there are large snow gates at the roadside. This should give you an idea of how wild the area before you can be in winter. These gates are shut to stop vehicles from venturing in when the conditions become bad. I have driven over the next stretch in some hideous conditions in winter, and been lucky enough a) not to have gotten stuck, and b) not to have been on a motorcycle at the time!

We climb here, looking back down towards Tyndrum, then the road swings to follow a narrow glen, constricted in with the railway to Fort William and the footpath of the West Highland Way. When the railway swings away to cross the Auch Gleann, opening up to your right, a massive conical hill guards its entrance to the North. Its flanks run at a steep angle all the way in an unbroken sweep to its summit. This is Beinn Dorain, famed in Gaelic poetry and loved by travelers and climbers, its familiar shape bringing back memories of many a trip north. From this angle it looks as if it is an unrelenting slog to the top, but there is a col at its northern side, accessible from Bridge of Orchy, which we will reach in another couple of miles, passing the junction where the B8074 cuts off left to run down Glen Orchy.

Bridge of Orchy is not much more than a hotel and a railway station, and there is, of course, a bridge here, which carries a little dead end road up to the mountains of the Black Mount.

This is a great stretch of road, long straights with sweeping bends, set within spectacular scenery. I have heard tourists remark that they thought Scotland would be alpine in aspect, and I think some were a little disappointed that there were not rows of mountains of the scale of the Eiger or Matterhorn. But I wouldn't change these views for anything. It may not be as spectacular as the mountains of the great ranges of the world, but when you look at these views, you really see Scotland. It cannot be mistaken for anywhere else on the planet. It has a rawness and a general feel about it, and if at any point a group of clansmen were to appear, bristling with weapons and clad in plaids, you would not even blink. It would all just blend in together. It is the whole package that appeals, I think. The history, the land, the very essential feel of Caledonia.

And I'm about to break in with a rendition of *The Hills Are Alive* ...!

A mile or two north of Bridge of Orchy on these fabulous motorcycling roads, Loch Tulla appears on your left. Follow the shore for a little, and you will see a bridge appear before you. This crosses the Water of Tulla. As this bridge comes into view, take a look over to the right where there is a farm a half mile back from the road. This is Achaladar Farm, which takes its name from Beinn Achaladar, immediately behind it. You can see a few walls of a ruined castle standing by the farm. These are the remains of Achaladar Castle. There has been a fortification here since earliest times, but these remains are of a building begun by Sir Duncan Campbell of Glenorchy, better known by his nickname, Black Duncan of the Cowl. It has a sinister ring to it, and it was well merited. He is depicted in a painting wearing a hood, which probably explains the name.

The earlier structure here belonged to the Fletcher family, and Black Duncan coveted it greatly. He used subterfuge to achieve his desire. He had three of his men take their horses into the castle's corn fields. When the Fletcher chief came out to remonstrate, a fight ensued, and the Fletcher killed one of Duncan's men. Black Duncan then made an appearance, stating that he held a royal peace-keeping warrant, but rather than take the Fletcher into custody, he cunningly told him to take to the heather. Duncan knew that Fletcher's estate would be forfeited, but he said that if the castle and lands were signed over to him, he would hold them in safe keeping till the trouble had blown over, then he would return the lands to the chief. He never did this, of course, and strengthened the castle. Black Duncan then treated the Fletchers living in this area with an attitude of tyranny.

One clansman had disobeyed Black Duncan and was sentenced to be hanged. As he was taken to the rope he began to struggle. His wife, fearful of Duncan, spurred him on by saying 'Just another step, Colin, to please the Laird'.

Black Duncan hated the MacGregors with a passion, and when Alistair MacGregor came of age, and so became chief, in 1588, he asked Black Duncan for the return of his lands in Glen Strae. They had been taken from the MacGregors by earlier Campbell subterfuge. Black Duncan, not surprisingly, refused, and the MacGregors rose in rightful anger.

Alistair MacGregor burnt Achaladar in 1603 in his rage, but was later captured and executed for this offence and many others in 1604. The castle was repaired, but was burnt again in 1689 by a party of Stewarts and MacNicols, as part of a Jacobite uprising in Scotland. The castle was never repaired after this incident.

I guess what I am trying to say here is that the place has an interesting history!

Over the bridge, and the road starts to climb in twists and turns. Nearing the top of this ascent there is a large lay-by on your left. The view is spectacular from here, looking back over the country you have just crossed. Loch Tulla is laid out below, with the mountains, in rows, disappearing into the distance. A half-mile after this lay-by, keep your eyes peeled for a tree that seems to be growing from a boulder on your left hand side. This boulder, a lone rock, stands back a few yards from the road. The deer have a habit of eating the young saplings, so none survive. But the seed of this tree had become trapped in a crevice at the very top of this rock, out of reach of hungry four-footed predators, and so has thrived. It is a symbol of my many trips north, on climbing expeditions or historical forays, and it has become an old and familiar friend. I actually say 'Hello' every time I pass!

Another short hop forward, and suddenly the vast panorama of Rannoch Moor opens up. No houses, no farms, just this road crossing the wilderness.

More water than dry land, Rannoch Moor is a labyrinth of pools, burns, islets and hummocky tufts of peat and heather – 56 square miles in area, with a backdrop of mountains. As you come into this, a large sign at the roadside announces that you are entering the *Gaeltachd*, the ancient heartland of the Gaelic people. When the sun shines it is like a window back to the time when the Earth was still young, so pure and unsullied does it look. But it can also be wild and unforgiving in bad weather.

The road you are driving was built in 1935. Prior to that there was the Old Military Road, built to pacify the Highlands, and the Highlanders themselves, for a government centred in London, England. The old road reached a height of 1,450 feet as it traversed the moor; the new one reaches only 1,143 feet, but that does not mean that snow does not still block it in the winter months. The old road is now part of the aforementioned West Highland Way, long distance footpath.

There is a railway track across Rannoch Moor too, but it lies much further to the east, and for part of its route the line is carried on floating brushwood, as the ground is so waterlogged. Other parts are roofed to protect it from blizzards.

Stop in one of the lay-bys, just to stand and take in the view. One lay-by in particular, a mile or so after Lochan na L-Achlaise (the first Loch that appears on your left) has a knoll rising opposite it on the right hand side of the road. This is a great viewpoint, and a walk to the top gives a great panorama over the moor. To the west lies the Black Mount range of hills, the two larger summits being Stob Gabhar to the southern end, and Clach Leathad to the North, pronounced 'Stob Gower' and 'Chlachlet' respectively. Between them lies the biggest corrie in Scotland, Coireach a' Ba, better known simply as Corrie Ba.

The road across the moor can be busy in the summer months. It is, after all, one of only two west-coast routes north, and this is the main one. If you can get a lull in the traffic, just to stand and take in the vistas without background noise, the serenity of the place should become apparent. Very seldom do I drive across the moor without stopping, for at least a few minutes, just to drink it all in.

Talking of drinking, I have many times drunk the water from streams running across the moor – you can actually taste the minerals in the water.

Onwards, and on over the summit of the moor where there are vast expanses of open country to be seen in every direction, and you eventually pass the access road running off left to the White Corries ski slopes. These run from the summit of Meall a' Bhuiridh (pronounced 'Mealavoory', *bh* in Gaelic is said like *v*. I'll have you fluent by the end of this book!), at 3,636 feet.

A panorama then opens up, a vista that is loved by many Scots, and I'll do my best to describe it. The entrance to Glen Etive opens up on the left. A single track road runs down the glen to reach salt water at the head of Loch Etive. It is a lovely road and a beautiful glen, but as the road is a dead end, we shall pass on. The mountains that flank the opening to this glen are spectacular. We have the very formidable wall of Sron na Creise on the left. I once scrambled down this rock face with scarcely a thought, and when I pass it now, it looks so steep and forbidding that I can hardly believe I did it.

On the right of the entrance to Glen Etive is one of Scotland's most famous mountains, loved by photographers, climbers and tourists alike. This is Buachaille Etive Mor, the Great Herdsman of Etive, which stands in the angle between Glen Etive and Glencoe.

The great rock face before you, which soars to its summit at 3,345 feet, is known as the Rannoch Wall. It is as impressive in summer, when each cleft and gully is laid bare before you, as it is in winter, wearing its snowy coat. On your right here you will notice the Kingshouse, said to be the oldest still-functioning inn in Scotland. It is not to be confused with the establishment of the same name that we passed at Balquhidder.

We drive along towards the jaws of Glencoe with the views opening on our left into the corries of the Buachaille (Boo-chall!). The next mountain on your left is Buachaille Etive Beag, and if I tell you now that *mor* means big or great, and *beag* means small or smaller, you should be able to work out the meaning for yourself.

As I write these words, I see in my mind every detail of the landscape I am describing. I can see it in all weathers. I see the wisps of cloud scudding past the summits. I can hear the water cascading down the mountain sides after heavy rain. I can even smell it! I feel so lucky. If you have never been here, and are reading this as a precursor to going, I hope that when you gaze upon it you will experience all the sensations that I do. It feels ancient, primeval, and there is that certain *je ne sais quoi,* making you feel that you, as a human, are an interloper in this scene. I have stood atop every summit in the glen, but I know the hills don't care. They were there long before man gazed upon them for the first time, and will be there long after we are gone. Again, that is what intrigues and attracts me.

After Buachaille Etive Beag, three great buttresses project out on our left. These are outliers of Bidean nam Bian, and are known widely in Scotland as the Three Sisters. Glimpses of the peak of Bidean nam Bian, lying behind, may be seen. This summit is the highest point in Argyll. The Three Sisters were seen as a backdrop several times in the film *Highlander.* 'Connor's Castle', built specially for the film, stood with them prominent in the background. The road twists with the constriction of a narrow passage through rock, and there is a scenic waterfall on your left, which looks better in the winter months as it really takes a volume of water to make it attractive. It has a lay-by immediately before it. Just after this, the view opens up, and you are into Glencoe proper. The wall of the Aonach Eagach fills the side of the glen to your right. Aonach Eagach means 'notched ridge', and this twisting turning knife-edge lives up to its name.

Anecdote time. I was at school with a guy who earned the nickname Big Boy. I had not seen Big Boy for many years. I was in Glencoe several years back, and I set off about seven o'clock one morning to traverse the Aonach Eagach, leaving the road here at the top of the glen. I had climbed several hundred feet, the hillsides silent, and wisps of early morning mist hanging on the ridges. I walked to the edge to look down to the road, now quite far below. I saw a van pull up, and the driver got out, just to look at the early morning view, as I have done on many occasions. Even at that distance, I could see that it was Big Boy. There was absolute silence at that time in the morning, and I just couldn't resist the temptation. I crawled to the edge and lay flat. In my deepest voice I cried out 'Haw! Big Boy!' I could hear it echo off the surrounding ridges. I saw his head spin round as he tried to figure out what the hell was going on. I crawled back from the edge, and carried on my way up on to the ridge, giggling. I haven't seen him since to tell him, so he is probably still wondering!

Loch Achtriochtan is visible further down the glen. Above, on the left, rises the steep cliff face of Aonach Dubh. If you look about three-quarters of the way up this wall, you will notice the large keyhole in the rock that is Ossian's Cave. Ossian is one of the old Celtic heroes of Scotland, a legendary bard of the third century, and son of Fingal, or Fionn in the Gaelic, the greatest of the Gaelic heroes.

A local shepherd, Neil Marquis, was the first to climb to this cave, in 1868.

Glencoe is of course famous for its massacre. The Massacre of Glencoe took place on 13 February 1692, and the reason for it, briefly, was as follows. After the ousting of the Stewart dynasty from the throne of both Scotland and England in 1689, there was an uprising in Scotland. The clans won a battle at Killiecrankie, sweeping the government redcoat forces aside, but the natural leader of this rising, Bonnie Dundee, was slain in the fight. William of Orange, now firmly on the throne of both countries, proclaimed that there would be a pardon, but all those who took part in the rising had to swear allegiance before 1 January 1692. The chief of the Glencoe MacDonalds has always been known as MacIain. This is in memory of the fact that Robert the Bruce granted the land hereabouts to one of his captains, Angus Og MacDonald, at the Battle of Bannockburn. Angus's bastard son inherited Glencoe. His name was Iain Og Fraoich (Young John of the Heather – Iain is John, *Og* is young and *Fraoich* is heather). The chief of the clan has used the name MacIain ever since.

MacIain was a man of honour, and he wrote to the exiled James VII, who was living at St Germain, near Paris, asking for permission to take this oath. Permission was granted, but did not reach MacIain till 31 December. That day he went to Fort William to take his oath, but was told he would have to travel 60 miles south to Inveraray to do this. He was given a letter, however, to say that he had tried to give his word within the time limit. There was snow in the glens, and MacIain was delayed by a detachment of government troops. He was not able to take the oath until 6 January. Although he presented the letter that he was given at Fort William, and it was forwarded to Edinburgh, the authorities there refused to accept it. MacIain was not informed of this refusal.

On February 1, 120 soldiers arrived in the glen. They were from Argyll, Campbell country, and their leader was Campbell of Glenlyon. The Campbells and MacDonalds had been unfriends for a long time. The Campbells gave their word of honour, swearing that they came with no ill intent, and that as the garrison of nearby Fort William was crowded, they wished to be billeted in the glen. The MacDonalds took the soldiers into their homes.

Highland hospitality was an important issue in earlier times. It could be a harsh and forbidding landscape to cross – there were no shops where you could buy a quick snack or restaurants to have a meal in, back in those days. Shelter could be sought at any small cottage, and once you had eaten at someone's table, or accepted their hospitality, it went without saying that there was a bond between householder and guest – even if that house was little more than a rickle of stones with a thatched roof.

At five o'clock in the morning of the 13th, the soldiers, who were billeted up and down the five-mile length of the glen, rose to slaughter their hosts. MacIain was shot in the back as he rose from his bed. His wife died from the ill treatment she received. Forty died, from infants to those aged over 80. At least another 40 died, half-naked and with no provisions, as they fled into the surrounding hills in blizzard conditions. A thousand horse and cattle were taken by the soldiers to be distributed among the officers at Fort William.

I think the best thing I have ever seen written about this incident is this passage taken from WH Murray's *Companion Guide to the West Highlands of Scotland*:

> The brutality of that slaughter was by no means unique in Scottish history. Numerous others with bigger death-roll had occurred in the past and been 'forgotten'. The three points that have appalled the people of our country for nearly three hundred years are the cold-blooded planning of mass-murder as a matter of public policy by men of responsible position in government, their treacherous abuse of the victims' hospitality as a deliberately chosen means, and the approval of all this by the King, even though not a man of our race.

As you could probably have foreseen, the men behind this abominable act walked away without retribution. Their names have been execrated in Scotland ever since. I can't think of anything worse than to have future generations of Scots abhor your name. Am I alone in thinking that there is nothing worse than letting down your country, or worse, to let down your fellow Scots?

A little further down the glen a side road strikes off right, to pass the Clachaig Hotel and follow the River Coe to Glencoe village. Hereabouts is the Glencoe Visitor Centre, with Signal Rock nearby. I have heard it said that the massacre was started from a signal given here, but this is untrue. This rock was where the MacDonalds would gather in times of threat or crisis.

The Clachaig Hotel sits at the bottom of a gully, the Clachaig Gully, running down a flank of Sgor nam Fiannaidh (the Peak of the Fiann). The Fiannaidh, or Fiann, were the followers of Fionn or Fingal.

I remember there was a sign on the door of the Clachaig stating 'No Hawkers or Campbells.' As you can perhaps imagine, the MacDonalds are still not too enamoured of Campbells.

Back to the main road, and continue down the glen. Here it takes a dog-leg bend right. Another mile, and keep your eyes peeled for an eaterie building on your right, and woodland on the left side of the road. This is the Rivercoe Bistro, perched above the river. If you park here, and cross over to the woodland, you will find there is a pathway running through the trees. This path runs parallel with the main road, and you need to follow it for perhaps a third of a mile back up the glen, the direction you have already driven. You will come across the ruins of a cottage with a little plaque bearing its name, 'Inverrigan'. I was told that this was the remains of MacIain's house as a boy, but this I now know to be untrue. It was in this building that Campbell of Glenlyon was billeted with some of his men. Here he seized nine of the MacDonalds, had them bound hand and foot, and then shot one by one. One was only a young boy, who held on to Glenlyon's legs and begged for mercy.

At the commemoration of the massacre in February 2003, a small party, myself included, made our way to Inverrigan to commemorate the slain. It was late in the day, the sun already sinking behind the hills. A few white roses, the little white roses of Scotland, were laid in the ruins of the cottage, and my patriot friend Brendan played a lament on the pipes, as several of us stood with our plaids and broadswords on, blue bonnets held in reverence. I looked up, and saw the sun just catch the snow on the very tops of the ridges, lighting it fiery red. There was not a cloud in the sky, and before we left, the full moon rose above the ridge between Sgor nam Fiannaidh and the Pap of Glencoe, which, as its name suggests, is a breast-shaped hill at the entrance to the glen.

Such things are memories made of, that will last till the end of my days. The last rays of the sun, the snow-covered tops, the breath issuing from my patriotic companions in the wintery air, and the pipes stirring the blood and compressing the centuries.

Back to the Rivercoe Bistro, and it is only a short drive further till we reach what is commonly called Glencoe village, although anciently it was known as Carnoch. You turn right opposite the Glencoe hotel, and the village, on either side of its single road, stretches along before you. There is a folk museum on your left hand side, which is open in the summer months. As you come up to the old bridge that spans the River Coe, there is a little road off to your right which follows the river upstream for a hundred yards or so. Here, on a knoll, stands the tallest, most slender Celtic cross I have ever seen. It is 18 feet high, atop a cairn of another seven. It is of dark red granite, and carved with Celtic knotwork. Its inscription states:'In memory of MacIain, Chief of Glencoe, who fell with his people in the massacre of Glencoe'. This cross was erected in 1884 according to the wishes of Mrs Archibald Burns-MacDonald of Glencoe, who was a direct descendent of MacIain.

At the commemoration here in 2003, I happened to be standing before the plaque on the side of the cairn, and noticed that when talking about the perpetrators of the massacre, it mentioned William III. This was William of Orange, of course, an unfriend of Scotland, and already mentioned as having a hand in the massacre. The thing is that in Scotland he is known as William II. There has only been one previous King of Scots by that name, William I, known as the Lion because he adopted the Lion Rampant as the Royal Standard of Scotland. There had been two previous King Williams of England. So, William of Orange was William II of Scotland and III of England. I was just surprised to see his English title on the monument here.

Prince Michael of Albany was present, a Stewart claimant to the throne of Scotland, and as I know Michael knows his history, I pointed this out to him. 'Perhaps they deliberately used his English title because of his behaviour', he mused. Strange, but perhaps Michael had the truth of it?

Back out to the main road again, and we turn right and continue on the A82. Just as we turn on to the main road, glance over to you right. We are at salt water here, Glencoe opening up on the shore of Loch Leven, an arm of Loch Linnhe, and both are inlets of the ocean. There is an island just off-shore, called Eilean (Gaelic for island) Munde. This is an ancient burial ground, and MacIain himself is buried here.

Centuries ago, Scotland had wolves as a native species, and people's superstitions made them use islands as burial grounds where possible. It stopped the wolves digging up bodies, apparently. It's funny how wolves are held in special regard the world over – they very rarely attack living people!

So, you can see the gravestones on the island from the shore.

You may wonder why the country you have recently traversed is so empty. Where are the MacDonalds today? The Highland Clearances took their toll, and the people being turned off the land to make way for more profitable sheep is the reason. You will see this to greater effect the further you travel up the west coast. It may look like one big unspoiled wilderness, these western glens, but these empty straths were once full of an indigenous people, and there were scatterings of crofts and little townships.

As we drive along Loch Leven side, we bypass Balluchulish village to our left. Ballachulish was once famous for its slate quarries. These, believe it or not, were opened in 1694, only two years after the massacre of Glencoe, and continued in operation into the second half of the 1900s. You can see the remains of these quarries behind the village, and you can walk around them if you have the desire. There is a house on this stretch that has an old manual railway signal and gantry in the front garden. It has been there as long as I can remember, and I can only assume that the purchaser is or was a railway enthusiast!

The Ballachulish Bridge appears ahead, spanning the narrows of Loch Leven before you. There used to be a wee ferry plying back and forth here, but huge queues would form in the summer, and the bridge was eventually built after continued public demands.

There is a roundabout just before the bridge, and we take the first exit, sign-posted 'Fort William', and continue on the A82. Do not cross the bridge though. Immediately before it there is a lay-by on your left. Pull in here. Walk towards the bridge, and you will notice there is a path climbing a few yards to the knoll above you. Here stands a strange looking monument. A square block of grey granite, bearing an inscription, is topped by a quartzite boulder. I have no idea why this was chosen as a monument, or if the quartzite boulder has a history of its own. The inscription reads 'In memory of James Stewart of Acharn, who was executed on this spot on 8th November 1752, for a crime of which he was not guilty'.

James Stewart of Acharn is better known in Scotland as 'James of the Glens'. He has also been described as 'the last clansman' – a hell of a title to bear.

This terrible crime against James Stewart was again perpetrated by Clan Campbell. After the failure of Bonnie Prince Charlie, or, to use his real name, Charles Edward Stewart, in 1745, the Stewart clan lands were forfeited. Colin Campbell of Glenure, better known by his nickname, the Red Fox, represented the Hanoverian government based in London in this area west of Glencoe, known as Appin. He started to evict Stewarts from the fertile land and replace them with Campbells.

As you can imagine, the Red Fox made many enemies. James of the Glens was one of those evicted, being turned off his family lands in Glen Duror. The Red Fox left Fort William with several mounted men, and crossed Loch Leven on the ferry where the bridge before you now stands. He turned west, and was shot twice from a holly bush on the hillside. He died instantly, and no-one got a look at the attacker. Suspicion fell upon Alan Breac Stewart, but as he could not be found, James of the Glens was arrested, even though witnesses said that he had been sowing oats on his land at the time of the murder. James was taken to the Campbell 'capital' of Inverary, where he was tried in front of a jury that contained eleven Campbells.

He was hanged at sunset on the spot where this monument stands. He must have been able to look across Loch Linnhe at the mountains of Ardgour before the rope tightened. But the Campbells were not content with his death. They strung chains round the body, and set a constant guard up, so that no-one could give James a decent burial. When the flesh eventually rotted away, they had the skeleton wired to hang here, a constant reminder of the power of the Campbells to a cowed local populace.

Robert Louis Stevenson had his own theories about the shooting of the Red Fox, and put this on paper in the form of his world-famous book, *Kidnapped*. It has also been filmed many times. He has the afore-mentioned Alan Breac Stewart as the gunman, but this may not be the case. It is said that the Stewart clan knows the true identity of the Red Fox's killer, but it is still held as a family secret.

Information boards here direct you a few miles further west to the spot where the Red Fox fell, if you desire to see it. A little cairn marks the spot, a path leading to it from the A85 Oban road. Keep your eyes peeled for a saltire carved on a post, only the cross is yellow and not white. This is the emblem of the Stewarts of Appin. The path to the cairn leads up from here.

The Campbells came to power as loyal followers of Robert the Bruce. It is a pity that this untainted backing of Scotland slipped a little over the years.

So we carry on across the Ballachulish Bridge and enter Lochaber, an area with some of the highest mountains of Scotland, but that is not apparent from this angle, that will come later. Crossing the bridge gives a lovely vista back to your right, the Pap of Glencoe looking at its best, and most shapely!

Once through North Ballachulish at the far side, the road swings left, westwards. You were too close to really appreciate it before, but behind the monument where James was hanged, rises Beinn Bheither (pronounced Vare), the Lightning Peak, with its two distinct tops. I climbed this one a few years ago, and for some reason my two companions kept telling me my hair looked like Barry Manilow's (a current American middle-of-the-road singer and pianist). Whilst descending, I had a slip and fell over a rocky ledge about twenty feet, and landed hard. One of the guys ran down, looking concerned, and said, 'Can you hold out your arms and move your fingers?' I thought he was worried that I was badly injured. Grimacing, I held out my arms from my lying flat position, and wiggled my fingers. 'Look', he shouted to the third member of the party, still standing on the rocks above, 'Barry Manilow!' The rest of the trip down to the roadside was punctuated with flurries of punching and tripping-up.

We come to the village of Onich, where the road goes inland for a short stretch. Topography dictates all routes in Scotland bar some of the ones in the central belt. Most of the roads we drive here are ancient routes, and this is no exception. After a mile or two, we reach the waterside again, on the shore of Loch Linnhe this time. On our left is the ferry across what is known as the Corran Narrows, where Loch Linnhe is almost nipped by the promontory jutting out from Ardgour on the opposite side. This ferry gives access to the sparsely populated areas of Morvern, Ardgour and to the most westerly point in Scotland, England and Wales: Ardnamurchan.

We push on up Loch Linnhe side though, and another seven miles brings us to the row of hotels and villas on our right, overlooking the loch that mark the southern extremity of Fort William. The Fort, as it is known locally, is a sizable town for the West Highlands. I know that most people who live in the heavily populated central belt of Scotland tend to think of Fort William as being quite far north. I think what would surprise them would be to look at any map, and find that Fort William actually only stands halfway between the Mull of Galloway at Scotland's southwestern corner, and Cape Wrath at its northwestern. So there is half the length of the country still to go.

Fort William is not a pretty town, but I have always enjoyed a wander up and down its one main street. There are large car parks at this southern end of the town, so it is best to park here and carry on to its High Street, now mostly pedestrianised, on foot. The main route, the A82, by-passes the town now to its west, loch-ward side, and it is a shame that although it is a waterfront town, it does not have a waterfront as such. The High Street has some nice individual wee shops lining it, and it is a half-mile walk either way to take it in. Half way down on the right is Cameron Square, which is, as its name suggests, a little haven jutting out from the High Street itself. Here is the West Highland Museum, which is packed with goodies. There are arte-facts dating from Neolithic times, many weapons of war, including a helmet worn by Montrose, and swords from Culloden, fought in 1746. There are personal effects of Bonnie Prince Charlie, and articles of everyday Highland life. Not to be missed by anyone who has a love of Scotland's history.

Fort William was originally Inverlochy. The name change came about through the London government's decision to build a fort here to house a garrison to pacify the warlike, and threatening, Highlanders. There are just a few stones to be seen at the loch front, the last remnants of the structure built in 1654. It was swept away to make way for the railway station. Bonnie Prince Charlie's men had besieged the place during the '45, but to no avail. Fort William, alas, takes its name from the same William of Orange of the Massacre of Glencoe. He was also the man responsible for the destruction of the Darien Scheme, a project where Scotland tried to set up its own colonies, the collapse of which caused bankruptcy, and opened the way for the Union with England. William, being Dutch, saw Darien as a threat to the Dutch East India company, and to England's own interests, so had Scotland's ambitions squashed. I would like to see the place resort to being Inverlochy again.

Back to your vehicle, and follow the by-pass along the loch-side. Keep following the signs for the A82 for Inverness at the roundabouts. At the top end of the town is a mini-roundabout, where the Inverness road crosses the River Nevis and swings left. Straight ahead takes us into Glen Nevis. If you want to see picturesque on a grand scale, take this seven-mile route, even though it is a dead end. Glen Nevis runs round the southwestern side of Scotland's highest mountain, Ben Nevis, although known as *the* Ben by Scots, is too bulky to be seen with any appreciation so close up. The village scenes in the film *Braveheart* were filmed in Glen Nevis, and those familiar with it will recognise the outlines of the hills as you drive up the glen, Stob Ban and Sgurr a' Mhaim in particular. They have quartzite caps and some-times, in the right light, appear to be snow-covered.

Near the Youth Hostel in the glen is a bridge over the Nevis that connects to the 'tourist path' up the Ben. It takes perhaps three to four hours to reach the top if you are fit, where for a minute or two at least you can be the high-est person in Scotland without resorting to drugs. Snow can fall on the Ben on any day of the year, and the correct clothing, supplies and footwear, must be worn. It has claimed many lives – including a friend of mine – so be warned.

The road is narrow and like a roller-coaster in parts, so care must be taken. Near its termination, there is a wee bridge which takes you over the

River Nevis, which has picturesque waterfalls on a smaller scale to what is ahead. At the end of the road is a car park. On your left here is the Allt Coire Eoghainn, a huge water slide, the water running down 1,250 feet of a shoulder of Ben Nevis. It can be quite spectacular after heavy rain. At the car park a path continues to follow the River Nevis up through the Nevis Gorge. I am told this gorge is Himalayan in character, with its boulders and tree cover. But as I haven't been to the Himalayas, I couldn't really comment. You hold to the path on the left hand side, the sides towering above, the river tumbling through rocks below, then suddenly you emerge into what looks like a meadow, with the river running placidly along. What you have come to see is directly in front, the Steall waterfall, plunging 350 feet over a shoulder of Sgurr a' Mhaim.

When there has been rain – not an uncommon occurrence in this part of Scotland – you get soaked by the spray just nearing it. I once was able to hear its roar from the summit of Ben Nevis. It is one of the three biggest waterfalls in the Highlands. The others are the Falls of Glomach in Kintail, about the same size, and the daddy of them all is the Eas a' Chual Aluinn in Sutherland, a mighty 658 feet.

There are three wire cables stretched across the river here, one for the feet, and two to hold onto. In my teenage years I told a friend I could cross by hanging onto one wire and crossing over hand over hand. I couldn't, and fell in midstream, after some valiant swinging attempts to get my legs onto the middle wire. It was rather a damp walk back.

Now it's time to follow the road back to Fort William. You will of course have paused again at the car park to take in the view. I can close my eyes and picture it now as I write.

When we get to the road end again, we are going to turn right onto the A82. A few hundred yards on, keep your eyes peeled for the signs for Old Inverlochy Castle. The turn off is on your left, just before the petrol station on your right hand side. It is only a couple of hundred yards down this road to the castle. There is an old graveyard on your left, and a sluice of fast running water on your right, the run-off from the aluminium works nearby. You cross this sluice on a little bridge, and the castle is directly before you. There is room to park.

Inverlochy Castle is like a kids' toy castle in form, a large round tower at each corner connected by curtain walls. The castle was built sometime between 1275 and 1295 by the Comyn family. It was not long finished when the Comyns fell from power, brought down by King Robert Bruce.

There was a battle fought here in 1431, when the Macdonalds overwhelmed an army led by the Earl of Mar and the Earl of Caithness, and the latter was killed. A second, more famous, battle took place in 1645, when an army comprised of MacDonalds, Camerons and Appin Stewarts, led by James Graham, the Marquis of Montrose, defeated an army led by the chief

of the Campbells. These are the two that lie on opposite sides of St Giles'
Cathedral in Edinburgh, which we have already visited. This battle took
place after Montrose's men had completed the toughest march in the long
and distinguished military history of Scotland.

His army had ravaged Argyll, the homeland of the Campbells, and
marched by here, then on up the Great Glen, heading for Aberdeen.
Campbell set out in pursuit with 3,000 men. Montrose was at the southern
tip of Loch Ness with 1,800 when news was brought that the Campbell was
on his tail, and was currently camped around Inverlochy, some 25 miles
behind him. Montrose knew that Campbell would have scouts out, and
that if he returned towards Inverlochy, he could easily be attacked. He
decided to make a detour round through the trackless mountains to the
east, and assail Campbell when he least expected it. It was 31 January, and
Montrose took his men up into the snow-covered mountains, walking
against the grain of the land. It is an amazing feat that he led his men
through the dark, sometimes in blizzard conditions, over ridge and peak,
dropping into glens to ford freezing rivers, only to climb again to cross the
next stretch of high ground. But it was not just Montrose's brilliant leadership that forced them on. It was the men's hatred of Clan Campbell that
made this march possible.

Montrose's men came down over a shoulder of Ben Nevis, and although
they had covered some 50–60 miles through hideous conditions, they
launched into a charge, the fact that they were outnumbered nearly two to
one notwithstanding.

Half the Campbell army was slaughtered, and the Campbell chief was
rowed to safety in a boat he had ready on Loch Linnhe. A famous pipe tune
came from this battle: *Come sons of dogs and I will give you flesh!*.

The flat ground to the south west of the castle was where the main action
took place.

Today, walkers, with modern equipment and attire, see the following of
Montrose's route as quite a challenge. It is quite incredible to think of an
army in brogans and belted plaids, encumbered with all their weaponry,
covering all those snowy miles, with only the supplies they had to hand to
fill their bellies. And to fight a pitched battle at the end of it! There were
some tough men in the Highlands of Scotland in those days.

The castle encloses a courtyard of about 100 feet by 90, the walls
between the four towers rising to 26 feet, though originally they would
have been 30 feet tall. There is a door at either end. The one at the opposite
side from where you are currently parked leads out to the banks of the
River Lochy, which issues from Loch Lochy and runs to Loch Linnhe.

Back out to the A82 then, and we turn left to continue on our way. A little
further on we come to a junction with traffic lights, the road off to the right
is the A830, often called the Road to the Isles. This is a reference to the fact

that this road terminates at Mallaig, a fishing port and ferry terminal, where ferries to some of the Hebrides can be caught. It is some 44 miles to Mallaig, and the scenery on this stretch is fabulous. Loch, mountain and rugged seashore, coupled with the famous white sand beaches at Morar en route, where the beach scenes of the film *Local Hero* were filmed, make it all very special. As this road would mean a return to this point, we should pass on, but let me make one suggestion first. As you will notice from the signs, it is 15 miles to Glenfinnan on the A830. It is a decent stretch of road, and the 30-mile round trip is worth it to see the monument that stands at Glenfinnan. It was here that the standard of Bonnie Prince Charlie was raised at the onset of his endeavour to regain the Stewart throne of his ancestors in 1745.

You drive through Corpach (Gaelic for 'the place of the dead' – perhaps a reference to the fact that some of the Kings of Scots rested here before being taken to Iona for burial) and then along the northern shore of Loch Eil. This is the country of Clan Cameron. You may (or may not) be interested to know that the Gaelic for nose is *sron*, so Camsron, or Cameron, means 'twisted nose'! Similarly, Campbell is 'twisted mouth', a corruption of *cam-beull*.

A couple of miles of hill country driving after Loch Eil, and Glenfinnan bursts upon you. The view is remarkable, Loch Shiel between its mountainous shore, twisting away into the distance to the south, and Glen Finnan, with its famous viaduct, to the north. This viaduct features in the train-to-Hogwarts scene in the film *Harry Potter and the Philosopher's Stone*.

There is a visitor centre here giving all the information you may need, and a tower down by the loch side surmounted by a statue of a Highlander, as memorial to the events that took place here.

For this is where the events of the historic '45, as it is called in Scotland, started to unfold. As the banner of the Stewarts was unfurled, to the cheers of the surrounding clansmen, there would be no hint of the nightmare of Culloden battlefield and its accompanying slaughter that would be the end of all the hopes of the ancient dynastic line of Scotland, And not only the end of that – it was to be the end of a whole way of life here. The destruction of the clan system.

It is a stirring place, though. To stand where the clansmen stood, where the Bonnie Prince stood, coupled with the views, make it all very memorable. Most people seem to assume that the tower on the lochside marks the spot where the banner was unfurled, but this is not the case. This tower is actually part of an old shooting lodge, and was left in remembrance of the clans. The spot where this actually took place was lost over the intervening centuries, but has now come to light.

If you cross to the other side of the River Finnan by the road bridge, you reach a few houses, with a knoll-like hill behind. On top of this there is an inscribed slab. It says, in Latin, 'Here the standard of Prince Charles was raised triumphant' and there are other inscriptions – footprints that show where Charles stood, and an 'x' to mark the site of the standard. This had been covered in foliage, but a spark from a passing steam train started a heath fire here in the 1980s and the rock was uncovered. It should not be too difficult to find – not too far behind the houses, and before the railway line, with a few trees close by to its side nearest the houses.

I have sat up here alone, and watched buses disgorging many tourists to the visitor centre: none have ventured to this side of the river.

Talking of the visitor centre, I was doing a talk there once about the Jacobites, to coincide with the release of my book *On the Trail of Bonnie Prince Charlie*. When I finished talking, I asked if there were any questions. 'What size of shoe do you take?' asked a lady in the audience. I've never yet managed to fathom out the whys and wherefores of that one!

So, back eastwards towards the Fort William area.

On this return leg, Ben Nevis, at 4,406 feet the highest mountain in Scotland, is before you. It often carries a cloud cap even on the clearest of days, so you are lucky if you see it all clearly. It is not a pretty mountain from a distance, being very bulky, but it has many attractions for the walker and climber. Facing the corrie that cuts in on its left, the Ben has impressive cliffs – the highest cliffs in Scotland in fact, and you may be able to discern them as you approach along this stretch of road. They are about 2,500 feet high and a mile in length. Huge snow cornices form in winter, cantilevering out from the cliff tops, and the unwary walking out on to these has resulted in many deaths. Snow can fall on the Ben on any day of the year – in fact, if it were a few hundred feet higher it would be capable of running its very own glacier. It looks benign in its bulkiness, but over every fifteen years or so, it claims as many as 50 lives.

Just a mile before the traffic lights on the A82, you may want to stop to have a look at Neptune's Staircase – a series of eight canal locks on the Caledonian Canal at Banavie. The Caledonian Canal runs right through Scotland in what is known as Glen Mor, the Great Glen. It was begun in 1803 by Thomas Telford, a famous engineer. It took 44 years to complete this work, which enables vessels to pass from the Atlantic to the North Sea, without the perilous trip round the north coast of Scotland. The canal utilises Loch Lochy, Loch Oich and Loch Ness on its route. Of the total length of 60 miles from sea to sea, 22 miles are canal, and the rest is passage through the aforementioned lochs.

Looking at any map of Scotland, the Great Glen jumps right out at you, dissecting the Highlands as it does. It is actually a fault line. The northern part of Scotland has 'slipped' westwards, and left this glen running coast to coast. No wonder Inverlochy Castle was built where it was, guarding the southern entrance to this major through-route.

Back to the traffic lights on the A82, where we turn left, following signs for Inverness.

You may notice after another mile or so that there are signs for another Inverlochy Castle! This is actually a baronial-style upmarket hotel, hence the original bearing the signs for 'old' Inverlochy Castle.

Another two miles and you will see the signs and entrance road for the ski lifts on Aonach Mor, sometimes called the Nevis Range ski slopes. Here you can take a ski lift most of the way up the mountain of Aonach Mor, 3,999 feet. Handy if you wish the view without the slog of the climb. There are the usual skiing facilities, cafes and such like, and it can be a nice outing on a clear summer's day.

Eight miles on from Fort William we reach the village of Spean Bridge. But keep your eyes peeled for a little road going off to your left, signposted for Highbridge. This is about a mile down the road, and it is nothing more than a few houses. But there is a little cairn at the right side of the road commemorating the Action at Highbridge – the opening action of the '45.

The name Highbridge comes from the bridge that crosses the River Spean here, part of the system of military roads built in Scotland to pacify the Highlanders. The bridge has partially collapsed, its remains standing down behind the cairn amongst trees – take care, as it is quite a long drop down to the Spean, and the banks are steep. The bridge was built in 1736, and cost £1,087-6s-8d to construct. Repairs took place in 1893, but it partially collapsed in 1913, and has been left alone since.

When Bonnie Prince Charlie landed in Scotland, two companies of redcoat troops, some 100 men, were sent to bolster the garrison at Fort William. On 16 August 1745, they were covering the final leg of their march. They were just about to cross the bridge here when they heard the sound of bagpipes. Much to the soldiers' alarm, some tartan-clad Highlanders were seen brandishing weapons on the bridge, and some others were spotted darting among the rocks at either end of it. The redcoat captain sent a sergeant and one man forward to try to ascertain the strength of this Highland horde, but two clansmen jumped on them and ran the two soldiers at sword-point over the bridge and out of sight. At that moment shouts went up from the rocks and the bagpipes started to wail again. Panic overtook the two companies of Redcoats and they began to sprint away down the road in the opposite direction from the bridge, terror clutching at their hearts.

They would have been surprised to find that the Highland horde they were fleeing from was in fact eleven men and one piper under the command of Donald MacDonald of Tirnadris.

Some more Highlanders appeared on the scene, and they all set off in pursuit of the redcoats, running up glens that ran parallel with the military road, to cut them off at the head of Loch Lochy. As the fleeing Redcoats appeared, they were met with a volley of musket fire, which killed four and wounded a dozen, whereupon they immediately surrendered. The Highlanders sent the wounded to Fort William for treatment.

Donald MacDonald of Tirnadris was a man who fought with bravery and distinction, showing great humanity too, through the '45. This action at Highbridge would seem to be typical of his daring. Unfortunately, he was captured at the Battle of Falkirk in 1746, a place we have already visited, and from there he was taken to Carlisle to be hideously executed.

On into Spean Bridge, then. The community has obviously sprung up because of the bridge over the Spean, built in 1819 by Thomas Telford to replace the earlier one at Highbridge. It is an important road junction too. The A86 cuts off here eastwards, cutting through the Highlands to meet with the main north/south route, the A9, which we last crossed at Dunblane.

We continue on the A82 though. We climb steeply for a mile or so on leaving Spean Bridge. Nearing the top of the gradient, a statue appears, just off to the left of the road. There is a road junction just beyond the monument, so turn down this road, and then left again into the car park. This statue is the Commando Memorial, erected in memory of the men who trained in this area during World War II. It comprises a group of three soldiers looking out over the surrounding countryside. It was designed by Scott Sutherland and erected in 1952. The plaque on front reads: 'United we Conquer. In memory of the officers and men of the commandos who died in the Second World War 1939–1945. This country was their training ground.'

The view is spectacular. You look back, right to left, at Ben Nevis, Carn Mor Dearg, Aonach Mor and Aonach Beag, then there is the range of hills known as the Grey Corries. It is obvious why, as the whole range is very grey in colour, compared to the other hills. Between the car park and the main road there is a little garden of remembrance, where families and comrades of commandos have left mementos. Walking round this to look at the little inscriptions is an emotional experience.

We continue on the A82. This next stretch runs mostly downhill, cutting from the higher ground down to Loch Lochy side, and so into the Great Glen. I remember once when driving this stretch, a magnificent rainbow crossed the road before me, like a giant archway directly in front. The darkness of one part of the sky, coupled with the blue behind me, has made it stick in my mind.

The trough of the Great Glen starts to appear at about ten o'clock to our left, and you can see what an obvious fault line it is.

I've always liked driving along Loch Lochy side. The road, for much of its way, hugs the loch in a long straight stretch, brilliant for driving, and allowing you to glance across the loch to the steeply sloping hills reaching to over

3,000 feet. From Spean Bridge to the head of the loch where MacDonald of Tirnadris opened fire on the redcoats, is some 15 miles. Here we drive through South Laggan, a little scatter of houses, where there are a few locks on the canal, to carry boats through this man-made stretch into the next of the lochs in the Great Glen, Loch Oich.

We cross the canal itself at the Laggan swing bridge, then we are on the Loch Oich side, travelling up the western side of the loch, as opposed to the east side of Loch Lochy that we have just negotiated. Just a few hundred yards up the lochside, keep your eyes peeled for the shop on your left. Just beyond it on your right there is room to park.

Here stands a little monument, a square block surmounted by a tapering top, and on the apex of this are carved seven heads, surmounted by a hand clasping a dagger. This is the monument to mark 'The Well of the Heads', or, as it is known in the Gaelic, *Tobar nan Ceann*. It was raised by the chief of Glengarry in 1812, to commemorate an act of vengeance.

In 1663, the young MacDonald of Keppoch and his two brothers were murdered in Glen Spean. The clan chief, Sir James MacDonald of Sleat in the Isle of Skye, sent some clansmen to hunt down the murderers. The seven responsible were duly caught, and their heads cut off, so that there was proof of vengeance. As the clansmen carried their trophies to nearby Invergarry Castle, they stopped at the well here to clean the heads. The four sides of the monument bear inscriptions in Gaelic, French, Latin and English. They read:

> The heads of the seven murderers were presented at the feet of the noble chief in Glengarry Castle after having been washed in this spring, and ever since that event which took place early in the sixteenth century it has been known by the name of Tobar-nan-Ceann, or Well of the Heads.

Obviously the road has been widened since those days, but the small stairway that goes down on the lochside side of the well takes you down to a little dark passage, burrowing under the road, and you will have to crouch down to enter it, if you can overcome any sense of claustrophobia, that is! At this passage end the water of the well still bubbles away.

The murderers were hunted down at Inverlair, and some years ago seven headless skeletons were found there.

Inverlair stands several miles west of Spean Bridge.

A mile on from the well you will see the entrance to the Glengarry Castle Hotel, cutting off to your right. If you take this long driveway into the woodland surrounding the hotel, you will come to the ruins of Invergarry Castle itself. It stands on a crag overlooking Loch Oich by the name of *Creag-an-fitheach*, which means the Rock of the Raven. This is the slogan and war cry of the MacDonells of Glengarry, a branch of the old confederacy of Clan Donald.

The castle was built some time prior to 1645, and it was burnt by the redcoat General Monck in 1654. It was restored, however, and Bonnie Prince Charlie slept here twice. The first time was on 26 August 1745, just a week after the raising of the standard at Glenfinnan. From here he took his army south over the hill passes, to take Edinburgh, Scotland's capital.

How different would his emotions have been on the second visit? That was on 17 April 1746, the day after fateful Culloden. Then he found it all but deserted, and slept on the bare floor. A few days later, the victor of that battle, the 'Butcher' Cumberland, came here, and in his spite, he put a charge of gunpowder beneath part of the building, blowing up one wing, and setting fire to the rest. The gaunt ruins stand in mute testament to the days of the clans, before those not of our blood took our land, scattering our people to the corners of the planet.

The hotel is actually the house built to replace the castle, constructed in 1868–9, but it has obviously changed its function since it was built.

Back onto the main road, the A82, – but we are only on it for another mile before coming down into the village of Invergarry itself. The term *Inver*, very common in Scotland, means a confluence or meeting of waters. It is generally found where rivers discharge into lochs or the sea, and in this case it is where the River Garry comes down into Loch Oich. We cross the Garry, then take the immediate left, the A87, signposted for Shiel Bridge and Kyle of Lochalsh. It is 60 miles to Kyle from Invergarry.

We follow the river's north bank as we take this road. The countryside here is heavily wooded in the glen floor. A couple of miles and Loch Garry is glimpsed through the trees on our left. A little side-road branches off left to follow Glen Garry towards Kinlochhourn (22 miles). Once we pass this junction, our road begins to climb. Another two miles and we reach the crest of the high ground. There is a lay-by here, where you have to pull in to see the stupendous view.

The Automobile Association has recently erected a view indicator here, which is handy for pointing out the sites of interest in this extensive vista. Far below, you can see the Kinlochhourn road snaking away up Loch Garry side, heading for the Rough Bounds of Knoydart, and sea water at Loch Hourn. Other than that road beneath your vantage point, the land looks empty, hilltop after hilltop rolling away from you as far as the eye can see. And this is not an illusion. The land here *is* empty. An austere wilderness – but once people lived in these glens.

A little further on, and the road swings north, and Loch Loyne appears to your left. The first lay-by here has a large cairn, built over the years by passing visitors just like you, who have paused here to look at that particular loch snaking away into the distant hills. This loch, with no tree cover on its shores, looks lonely indeed. The fact that it is deeper than it was originally, due to one end being dammed, means that its original banks are under water, and it gives it a barren look. A little further, and the road crosses a cattle grid, and a deer fence stretches off in either direction.

Just by here there is another lay-by, with a smaller cairn, standing above the grassy drop to the lochside. But this cairn does not commemorate the number of visitors who have paused to admire the view. This cairn marks the location of a murder mystery.

At about ten o'clock on the morning of Saturday, 6 April 1985, an Australian tourist who was walking past saw a car lying beneath this spot. He noticed that there was a badly injured man in the driver's seat. He assumed that the maroon Volvo had been involved in an accident of some sort, and so he flagged down a passing vehicle for help. One of the passengers in the passing car was a councillor, a member of the SNP (The Scottish National Party, a political party whose chief aim is to achieve independence for Scotland). Purely by chance, the councillor immediately recognised the injured man as 61-year-old lawyer and SNP activist Willie McRae. He was taken by ambulance to Raigmore Hospital in Inverness, where he was found to be in a coma, probably caused by a brain injury, so he was transferred to a specialist unit at Aberdeen. As a nurse was cleaning him there, she spotted a bullet hole just above McRae's right ear. An x-ray showed he had a bullet lodged in his brain. He never regained consciousness and died a short time later.

Though police started to treat McRae's death with suspicion, his car was taken away from the site. Later, the police could not remember the location, which led to added confusion. There was a search over the ground the following day, and 60 feet away from the crash site, a Smith and Wesson pistol was found in a stream. It had been fired twice. One of the policemen who had been there the previous day and had helped to release McRae from the vehicle, said that he had looked in the stream at the spot where the gun was found, and that there had been no sign of it. McRae's broken watch was found outside the car on some legal papers he had been carrying with him. No forensic tests were carried out to find how close the gun was when fired that caused the wound.

McRae had been working away steadily against the UK Atomic Energy Authority. He did not like their plans to dump waste in Scotland. In 1980 he successfully prevented them from dumping nuclear waste in the Ayrshire hills. He was working towards preventing them doing the same in Caithness in the far north. When he had left his office in Glasgow to drive to his home in Kintail, west of here, on Friday 5 April, he took a pile of papers with him, telling his colleagues 'I've got them!', seemingly referring to having put together a watertight legal argument. These papers were nowhere to be found at the crash site.

The official verdict to all this, shockingly, was suicide. McRae had obviously hidden the papers, shot the gun twice, fatally wounded himself, put the weapon in a stream, taken off his broken watch, walked 50 feet back to his crashed car and got into the driver's seat to die.

Who murdered Willie McRae? There have been repeated requests for an inquiry into this case, but these have all been denied by the Crown Office.

This little cairn, erected by concerned patriots, marks a site riddled with intrigue.

Onwards again, downhill, and past the dam at this end of Loch Loyne. The road twists and turns and then we come to a T-junction where we meet the road running from Inverness and Loch Ness to Kyle of Lochalsh. We are going to turn left here to continue to Kyle, but there is something important to see only a mile and three-quarters to our right, so first turn towards Inverness on the A887. You are following the River Moriston here as it flows east. Just a little after the river crosses under you to your left hand side, look for a lay-by with a small cairn at its rear end, to your right. Pull in to read the inscription on the stone set within the cairn:

At this spot in 1746 died
Roderick MacKenzie
An officer in the army of
Prince Charles Edward Stuart.
Of the same size and of similar
resemblance to his Royal Prince
When surrounded and overpowered
by the troops of the Duke of
Cumberland gallantly died in
attempting to save his fugitive
leader from further pursuit.

This road follows the track which existed here in 1745, and it was as he was on this track that Roderick was confronted by the redcoats. As he lay dying, Roderick is reported to have said 'You have slain your Prince!' Believing that they had, the redcoats cut off his head to take with them for identification, hoping no doubt to claim the £30,000 that the Hanoverian government in London had offered for Charles's person. It is to the everlasting credit of the poor ordinary Highlanders of this region, that not one of them ever made an attempt to claim the reward.

Roderick MacKenzie's selflessness bought some much-needed time, and a relaxing of redcoat patrols, for Charles to make good his escape.

This is a fast stretch of road that passes the cairn here, and most drivers fly by, no doubt oblivious to the import of the little cairn. Even less are probably aware of what lies just across the road. Just a few yards west on the opposite side, there are some steps leading down to where a little burn runs into the River Moriston. There is a grave here, containing poor Roderick's headless body, and a boulder alongside bears a plaque with these words:

> Here in consecrated ground rest the mortal remains of Roderick MacKenzie, merchant of Fisherow and son of an Edinburgh Jeweller, slain by Cumberland's Redcoat troops late in July 1746, three months after the Battle of Culloden, because he selflessly encouraged them to mistake him for Prince Charles Edward Stuart, whom he closely resembled in age, statue and colouring and whom he served faithfully to the end.

Roderick MacKenzie's head was carried to Fort Augustus, some say thence to London for identification. Local clansfolk are credited with removing his body a short distance from where he fell, now marked by the cairn across the road, secretly burying it without a headstone, here, by the Stream of the Merchant (no doubt named in Roderick's honor).

Every year in July there is a small gathering here, attended by members of the 1745 association, the Clan MacKenzie Society, in order to honour the noblest of the MacKenzies. This plaque was kindly donated by Mrs Nellie Leitch, a descendent of Roderick MacKenzie.

It feels strange to stand down here, the river tumbling over its rocky bed behind you, as you ponder the act of loyalty that took place in this vicinity. Only the odd car, travelling by at speed on the road above, jolts you back to the present from the sound of musketry in the aftermath of Culloden.

A u-turn is required now, and back we go to the junction a mile and three-quarters back, only this time we go straight on towards Kyle of Lochalsh. Although we continue on through, this stretch of road goes under the moniker of the A87, the same as that over from Invergarry.

The Clunie Dam is apparent in front of you, holding back the waters of Loch Clunie while harnessing the power for the north of Scotland hydro-electric scheme. Glen Clunie is bare of habitation, but the waters of the loch add colour to the mountain scene. At the far end of the loch we reach the Clunie Inn, an old travellers' inn. Prince Charlie crossed the glen here during his wanderings, a major undertaking, as Glen Clunie had constant redcoat patrols out looking for him. From here we follow the River Shiel down through dramatic Glen Shiel for the next ten miles to the sea loch of Loch Duich.

There is a chain of mountains to our left here, the south, all exceeding 3,000 feet. This is known as the South Clunie Ridge and is well loved by climbers. As we begin the exhilarating descent down Glen Shiel the eye-catching, pointed peak in front of you is Faochaig, meaning 'the whelk'. It hides an even more magnificent peak called the Saddle, which will eventually come into view on the left hand side of the road. Glen Shiel is constant downhill run, twisting between high mountains, the River Shiel foaming and tumbling on your left. There is one instance where the river goes through a cave in a projecting spur of rock. I remember this from my very first trip through these parts as a kid.

When we eventually cross the river to the other bank on a modern bridge, you will see the old bridge just a little downstream. It may seem unbelievable, but a battle was fought on the steep hillsides above this bridge.

It took place in 1719. Three hundred Spanish troops had landed on this coast under Scottish captains as part of a planned Jacobite uprising. A Spanish fleet was expected to land on the English west coast with 5,000 men, and weaponry enough to arm 30,000. That part of England was still loyal to King James, and would rise to depose the German usurper. The English have always had a run of luck where invasions are concerned. The weather always seems to have been to their advantage in these situations. This was no different, and the Spanish fleet was hit by storms that scattered it.

A Hanoverian force advanced through Glen Shiel from Inverness. The Jacobites had no option but to try and halt them here at the bridge over the River Shiel. The redcoats charged the positions to the left of the bridge, but were several times repulsed. Mortar shelling set the heather ablaze though, and the Highlanders had to retire. The redcoats then concentrated on the force to the right, which included the Spaniards. The Jacobite leader here was badly wounded at the onset of this action, and his men and the Spaniards set off uphill, carrying the wounded officer with them. This sad affair ended with the Spanish forces surrendering the next day.

The hill to your right here has ever since been known as Sgurr nan Spainteach, or 'the hill of the Spaniards'. This mountain forms the first peak of the famous Five Sisters of Kintail, a range of five mountains that have been the subject of many postcards and calendars, and seen to best advantage from the waterside a few miles further on.

Down into the lower reaches of the glen, and the River Shiel runs through meadows, nestling under the hillsides. On your right you may notice a little cross at the roadside. It reads: 'Erected by Glen Shiel Shinty Club and Friends, in memory of Donald Campbell, who died on February 24th, 1927. R.I.P.'

I can only assume that Donald was a hell of a shinty player then!

If you have never seen shinty, I can only describe it as a real man's game. Sticks are used, and a ball, but any resemblance to hockey finishes there. It is very physical indeed, and the ball is often smacked across the pitch at head height. It is still very popular in the Highlands, and is a fitting sport for the 'sons of the clans'.

We soon reach salt water at the head of Loch Duich, the tiny scatter of houses here known as Shiel Bridge. A road branches off left to cross the Mam Ratagan at 1,116 feet, dropping to Glenelg (try saying that backwards) where there is a ferry to the Isle of Skye in the summer months. Just by Glenelg in Glen Beag, there are two reasonably well-preserved brochs. These are ancient stone-built fortifications like the ruined one in Tor Wood (Chapter Seven), and we will come across such places again on this journey.

We now continue on the A82, with the road running along the lochside. A mile further on, a bridge cuts across a small corner of the loch. It was built to supersede the old road which ran out around this inshot of water. At the end of the bridge on your right there is a ruined church standing in its graveyard, with a memorial atop the knoll-like hill beyond. There is a lay-by on your right here, and you should pull in to have a wander around this old building and its environs. This is Clachan Duich burial ground. Clachan just means a settlement or a small village, and Duich is of course the name of the loch it overlooks. Walk up the path to the top of the knoll first. The memorial is a statue of a kilted soldier carved out of granite. The inscription reads: 'Erected by the Clan MacRae and friends in memory of the MacRaes and relatives at home and abroad who fell in the Great War 1914–18'

This monument was unveiled by Sir Colin G MacRae on 25 July 1922, and was erected by the Clan MacRae Association. These people have obviously been very active over the years. If you remember the MacRae monument on Sheriffmuir north of Stirling, then you will appreciate how far-reaching their activities have been.

The view out over the old church from the top here is delightful, the loch beyond, the scatter of houses round the fringe of the water, and the mountains standing sentinel over it all.

As you enter the graveyard below, a sign states: 'Kilduich or Clachan Duich – the ancient church and burial ground of Kintail. Dedicated to St Dubhthagh [pronounced like the loch – Duich!] circa 1050, though probably in use three centuries earlier.'

The first thing to strike you as you take a look around the graveyard is that many of the memorials bear the name MacRae. This is, of course, their ancient clanland, and this church was their holy place. Inside the ruined church itself are buried many of the clan chiefs and dignitaries. For example, one plaque is in memory of John MacRae of Conchra: 'who with most of his clan fell at the battle of Sheriffmuir on 13th November 1715, defending the cause of the Royal House of Stewart'

It would seem all the chiefs from about 1500 onwards are in the soil here, and it seems a shame that most people seem to drive by oblivious to what lies in this little church. One particular stone near the gate really moved me: 'In loving memory of Dr Christopher MacRae C.B.E. Beloved husband of Mary. Thinker and piper, who loved his family and this land, and devoted his life to them. Born 1910, Died 1990. He rests beneath his beloved hills.'

Well, can a man ask for any better than that?

The road continues along the lochside, through the village of Inverinate. Ahead, as we round a bend, the castle of Eilean Donan appears suddenly before you. As its name suggests (I've already told you what *eilean* means!) it stands on an islet offshore. It never fails to inspire me, that pile of stone and mortar. It is everything the visitor would expect a Scottish castle to be. Proud, defiant, all battlements and shot holes for defence. It has featured prominently in several films, most noticeably *Highlander*, starring Sean Connery and Christopher Lambert. But it is not all that it seems to be at first glance.

At the time of the fight in Glen Shiel with the redcoats and Spaniards in 1719, two English frigates appeared in the loch here, and bombarded the castle. It was actually restored by Lieutenant Colonel MacRae-Gilstrap between 1912 and 1932, after lying derelict for all those years. It is an ancient fortified site though. There are traces of an Iron Age fort, and records show there has been a castle here since the time of Alexander II in the early 1200s. The name itself comes from an early Christian saint named Donan. The castle commands the junction of three lochs, Duich, Long and Alsh. We cross Loch Long (*long* is Gaelic for a boat, so it basically means boat-loch, most likely because it was used as an anchorage) by a bridge, and the Isle of Skye now starts to appear over to our left, beyond the Glenelg peninsula.

We drive through the village of Dornie, then the road cuts inland for the next four miles, On this stretch, the A890 cuts off to our right, intriguingly signposted 'The North'. We will be taking that road eventually, but for the present we continue a little further west to the town of Kyle of Lochalsh, where we can take the bridge over to the Isle of Skye.

'Kyle' just means a point where a waterway narrows between two pieces of land, so the name Kyle of Lochalsh means exactly that – where there is a narrow section to Loch Alsh. The Isle of Skye is only half a mile from the mainland at this point, and when the road comes back down to the shore-line at Balmacara, it is Skye you see to your left across the loch. The Balmacara estate you are travelling through, 8,000 acres of it, belongs to the National Trust for Scotland, and so is under care.

Into the little town that is Kyle, then. With its rows of shops and small harbour, Kyle of Lochalsh has always imbued a feeling of the West Highlands and the Hebrides within me. I used to love it when you had to get the ferry across to Skye from here, but it has been superseded by the modern bridge. The ferry always gave a sense of adventure when crossing to Skye – you were using the method of transport that had always been used, a direct link to the days of the Lords of the Isles, whose territory this once was.

As you have come north, you will notice the price of fuel for your vehicle has crept up – and it will get worse the further north you go. In a sparsely populated area with few facilities, beggars cannot be choosers. Scotland has the dearest petrol prices on the planet. We are a major oil producer, but pay the highest prices anywhere on earth! What is wrong with the Scots? The revenue created from the finds in the North Sea amounts to many billions, and there are only five million of us. All that wealth grasped by London to pay off debts accrued by a nation of ten times our number.

Don't the folk here realise that if they were to use their rights to claim nationhood again, we could have had £2,000 each to spend down the pub every night? See the good grasp of politics I have? All that revenue would have made Scotland a wealthy nation. It has been squandered and wasted, and our future generations will berate this generation for it, and ask *why*? We are all Scots, both past, present and future. And we have let the future down. Scotland can be a bittersweet place for someone like myself, one of its children. We should have cherished our own, but they are scattered over the earth. We should stand as one, but sectarianism divides. If you are Protestant, in some sectors that identifies you with Union Jacks and England. If you are Catholic, that is identified with Tricolours and Ireland. I want none of it. If you don't identify yourself as a Scot, yet you live in Scotland, we can honestly do without you. If you feel your loyalties lie elsewhere – then go. How can you be born in Scotland, a thousand generations a Scot, yet put another country uppermost in your soul? It's a funny old place. And I can sit in landscape like this which stirs my soul, and I understand it not.

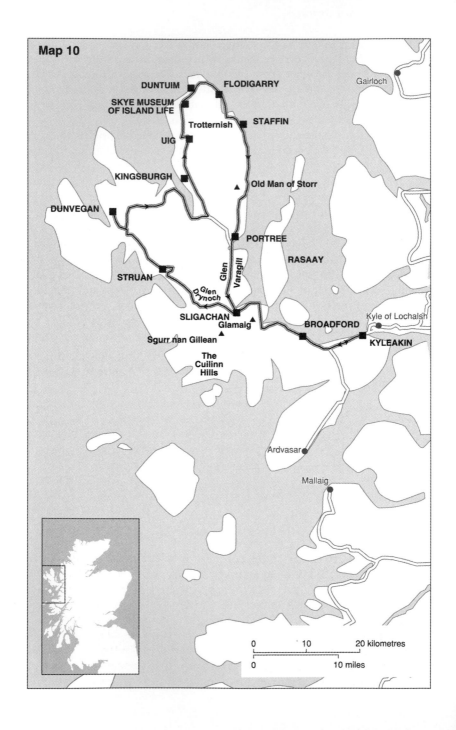

Map 10

CHAPTER TEN

Hebridean Odyssey

BEGINNING AT KYLEAKIN, THE ROUTE EXPLORES BROADFORD, SLIGACHAN, STRUAN, DUN-
VEGAN, CARBOST, UIG, DUNTUIM, STAFFIN, PORTREE, SLIGACHAN, AND THEN RE-TRACES
THE OUTWARD ROUTE BACK TO SKYE BRIDGE.

AT THE CROSSROADS in Kyle of Lochalsh, you go straight through to the toll gates of the Skye Bridge. I suppose the bridge is a logical process (or progress), but personally, I miss the old ferry.

The toll price is extortionate compared to the price charged to cross any other Scottish bridge. It is eight to ten times as dear, and the reason for this is not apparent. We pay road tax in Scotland, and that is meant to pay for such amenities. Our London masters make billions in road tax every year, and only spend a quarter of that on the roads – the rest is spent on other projects, such as defence. If I were to do that, take money for one purpose and use it for another, I would be jailed for fraud.

There is a pressure group trying to get some action taken against these charges, called Skye and Kyle Against Tolls, or Skat for short, and they do their best against the bureaucracy involved.

Even motorcycles are charged heavily – and they are free on other bridges!

Don't let that detract from what Skye is though. It is an island that has a magic, a timelessness surrounding it. And everyone who has ever visited it wants to return. It is not like the Western Highlands in character. Crossing that little strip of water takes you into a different landscape, Hebridean in aspect, and a hint of what the other islands off Scotland's western seaboard can be like. Skye does lack the fabulous beaches though, which can be found on some of the islands, especially further west on Lewis, Harris or the Uists.

The ferry used to cross to Kyleakin, and the bridge comes to land to the north of this place, but you may want to turn back for a look. From Kyle on the far shore you may have noticed the fangs of masonry that stand above Kyleakin on a knoll – these are the remnants of Caisteal Maol.

At the far end of Kyleakin a little path runs to the castle ruins. It was built by the Mackinnons between 1490 and 1500, and was originally called Dunakin. The *akin* in this case, and in the name of the village, comes from the fact that the viking fleet gathered here before an attempted invasion of Scotland, which ended disastrously for the Norsemen at the Battle of Largs in 1263. The King of Norway at this time was Haakon IV, who died shortly after the fight, and *akin* is a corruption of his name. It is a fitting place to view the strait here, from these castle ruins, imagining the many longships anchored below, their masts standing like a forest, their sails furled.

In this castle in 1513, the same year as the Battle of Flodden, various island chiefs met and agreed to support Sir Donald MacDonald in his claim to become Lord of the Isles. The place has lain abandoned since the 1700s. There is an old legend concerning the strait here. It says that a female, by the improbable name of Saucy Mary, once lived in the castle. She had a chain that stretched across to Kyle from here, and captains of passing ships had to pay a toll to her to elicit passage. Where this well-known story comes from I have no idea, but the only tolls hereabouts now are the ones on the bridge you have so recently crossed!

We drive along the A850, following the signs for Portree and Dunvegan. You will notice that the signs here are in both Gaelic and English. I will use the English spellings in this book, but reading how they are written in Gaelic should help you understand how that language is pronounced!

Ahead you may see a large rounded hill. This is Beinn na Caillich, the easternmost of the Red Cuillins. There are two large mountain ranges in Skye, the Red Cuillins and the Black Cuillins. The Reds are rounded, scree covered hills, and in certain lights they can look very red indeed. They are formed of granite, whereas the Blacks are jagged, impressive hills, constructed of gabbro and basalt.

Even from a distance you can see there is a large cairn atop Beinn na Caillich, which rises to 2,400 feet. Beinn na Caillich is Gaelic for the peak or hill of the old woman, and children will tell you that the woman in question is Saucy Mary, but it is more probable that a viking princess lies buried under the pile of stones on the summit.

We come into the village of Broadford, but it is difficult to tell where this village begins or ends! For a few miles along the coast here there is a scatter of houses and crofts, all under various names, but fairly regularly all gathered under the moniker of Broadford. The 'town centre' is quite a bustling little place, with accommodation and shops.

Just after Broadford a road cuts off to the left, running to Elgol on the coast, a place that affords a spectacular view of the Black Cuillins. It is a dead-end road, but offers many mountain views made familiar by calendars over the years.

I remember walking along this road one night in the pitch dark. When you live in a town, as I do, you tend to forget just how dark it can be when there is no light pollution. I kept falling off the side of the road, as it was so dark I couldn't see the edge. Then some animal – could have been a bird – started to make weird and wonderful noises. Quite bizarre, but I remember that night well.

On another occasion, two friends and I camped under the mountain Blaven. This road runs underneath its eastern flanks. I wrapped two cans of beer up in a jacket and used it as a pillow, only to wake in the morning with a ridiculously sore neck and no cans inside the jacket. For years afterwards laughter erupted when I was reminded of the angry line I shouted when I discovered the cans were gone: 'Which of you bastards drank my pillow?'!

But we carry on from Broadford, under the flanks of Beinn na Caillich, and after a while the road hugs the shore, the island of Scalpay off to your right. We swing in to Loch Ainort and follow this sea loch to its head. We are in the heart of the Red Cuillin here, under Glas Beinn Mor, and Beinn Dearg with its double peaks across the head of the loch. Dearg, pronounced jar-rag, is the Gaelic word for red, so it is the 'red mountain'. There is a waterfall on a stream tumbling down from the mountains at the head of the loch, and it is very picturesque.

Here the road begins to climb. On my first visit to Skye, these were all single-track roads with passing places, but are now all good driving roads, and particularly good motorcycling roads too. You have to beware of the sheep though, as they often decide that the quieter roads are a good place to have a wee sit down.

We cross the few miles over to Loch Sligachan, where again the road cuts in to the head of this sea loch. We pass the pier where the ferry sails across to the island of Raasay, seen over at two o'clock as we come down to sea water again. Especially notable on Raasay is its highest point, Dun Caan, which looks like an extinct volcano.

Raasay suffered terribly after the Battle of Culloden in 1746. Redcoat troops came here, looking for the fugitive Bonnie Prince Charlie. They burnt every house, raped all the women, removed all the cattle and sheep, and destroyed all the boats. Today the sons and daughters of Raasay are scattered over the New World. I hope they never forget the horror that oppressors can bring.

As we follow the loch up towards its head, Glamaig, the northernmost of the Red Cuillin, rises, towering above to your left. It is a shapely hill, but you will not see it to its best advantage until you reach the Sligachan Hotel. And when you reach Sligachan you are overwhelmed by one of the great mountain views, in fact, the most beloved view of Scotland by many of her mountaineers. For here the northernmost of the Black Cuillin come into view. They are often cloud covered, but I hope you are lucky enough to see them on a clear day.

I have never forgotten my first view. It was winter, and night was just beginning to fall. There was snow on the flanks of the hills, and the clouds parted and I had my first view of the shapely spired summit of Sgurr nan Gillean, the Peak of the Young Men. I can think back and remember how it struck me to my very core. How its buttresses looked black, black as the

Earl of Hell's waistcoat, and cold and remote-looking too! How its jagged pinnacles with wisps of cloud playing among them had a primeval grandeur, looking like an illustration from some sword-and-sorcery novel.

It is best to park and go and sit on the old bridge over the River Sligachan (Slig-a-han, which means the shelly place') and just look at that view, the noise of the water tumbling over the rocky bed below the perfect accompaniment.

From here Glamaig, over to your left, looks steep and impressive, its flanks rising in one long sweep to its 2,537 foot summit. I have a wee story to tell you about Glamaig, and I hope if you ever sit here on the bridge, it will make you think about this and be impressed.

In 1899, a Major Bruce came to Sligachan accompanied by a Gurkha named Herkia. Percy Caldecott, who was present and timed the following feat, later wrote: 'The land between the bridge and Glamaig is very rough going – the heather, water courses, pools etc. To this day I can see the spray thrown up by Herkia as he ran along, regardless of pools or other obstruction. The speed with which he climbed Glamaig was incredible, more like a spider than anything else. On reaching the top, he waved his arms to us, then immediately started the descent which he made at the run ... The most wonderful thing about it was that he arrived at the bridge barely out of breath.'

Herkia ascended Glamaig in 37 minutes, and was back at the bridge in under 55. You may want to have a bash and try to emulate this feat, or perhaps even beat Herkia's record! I think one view will let you know that the best thing you can do is look at the steep flanks of Glamaig in awe and wonder and applaud the superhuman efforts of Herkia!

Looking up Glen Sligachan, the impressive mountain further up the glen on the left is Marsco, but the eyes are constantly drawn back to Sgurr nan Gillian. I have stood atop its summit. In fact, I have ascended several peaks in Skye, but I have never felt the Cuillins to be friendly hills. There is an aloofness about the range known as the Black Cuillins, and many people have told me they feel the same way about them. There is an airiness and severity about their tops that other ridges and ranges in Scotland do not have. They are not soft hills. They have an exposure, a starkness about them. There is nothing feminine about these gnomish hills. The ridge runs south from Sgurr nan Gillean, so you will have to see them from a different aspect to get the bigger picture, to see the whole jagged outline like many fangs pointing to the heavens.

And the name Cuillins? Coo-lins. It seems a bit soft, too soft a word to describe these hills, but its origin probably lies in the Norse *kjollen*, meaning keel-shaped ridges. The Gaels, of course, have their own explanation, and they say that their name comes from the legendary Gaelic hero *Cu chuill fhionn*, Cuchullin, the English version of his name being 'Hero of the Fair Hair'.

Skye's name may come from the vikings too. The Cuillins are often wearing a cloud cap, so that when their longship crews saw it from out at sea, they referred to the place as *Skuyo*, pronounced Sky-a, the Cloud Island. Skye could also be from the Gaelic *Eilean a Sgiathanach*, meaning the Winged Isle, a reference to its many peninsulas. Poetically it is sometimes known as *Eilean a Cheo*, the Misty Isle, which is not too far removed from the *Skuyo* of the Norse.

Before we move on from the relative remoteness of Sligachan, the only real incursion of modernism the constant traffic here on the main road to Portree, you may be interested to know of prior times here. In October 1794 a cattle market was held here, 4,000 people attending, with 1,400 head of cattle and 200 horses and ponies changing hands. It is said the most colourful sight was the tinker camp set up nearby where music and song continued right through the night.

How I would love to be able to go back and see this sight, the Cuillins a backdrop to it all. I would have wandered the camp, examining the goods on sale. The Highland way of life was already heavily in decline, as Culloden had been lost some 50 years before of course, but I'm sure I could have purchased a good plaid, sporran or dirk, befitting a Highland gentleman!

Just before the Sligachan Hotel, the road forks and we are going to take the left fork, signposted Dunvegan. (Dun bheagan), the A863. This road follows the glen of the River Drynoch for the next four or five miles, then the salt-water of Loch Harport comes into view. We have gone east to west since Sligachan. Skye may be roughly 60 miles from end to end, but so indented is the island by its many lochs, that no point is more than five miles from salt-water.

At the head of Loch Harport a road goes off to our left, signposted Carbost and Talisker, the B8009. Talisker is the name of Skye's only distillery, and Talisker Single Malt Whisky is famous the world over. It has the taste of the sea in it, has Talisker Whisky, an almost seaweedy quality to it. Talisker, the place, is a little further over on the island's west coast, but the distillery itself is in Carbost. A little before Carbost the unclassified Glen Brittle road branches off. It is worth driving up this road to the head of the pass, two or three miles only, where a fabulous view of the Cuillins appears, the range rising like a solid wall above you. You are looking to the stretch running from Bruach na Frithe (Broo-uch na Free), the brae of the forest, 3,143 feet, south to Sgurr na Banachdich (perhaps a corruption of the Gaelic for smallpox from the speckled appearance of its rocks), 3,167 feet. Much of the range lies further south, including Sgurr Alasdair, 3,309 feet, the highest point on Skye.

From here make your way back to the junction on the A863, and continue towards Dunvegan. Another few miles following the line of Loch Harport northwest above its eastern shore, and we come down to the sea again at Loch Beag, the little loch.

We come into Struan, and when you drive beyond the village, about a third of a mile further on there are parking places on the left, for Dun Struan Beag above you on the right. *Dun* is a fortification, *beag* means small, so it is 'the little fort of Struan'. It is an easy grassy stroll of a couple of hundred yards up to this ancient place.

It dates from the Iron Age, perhaps 400–200 BC. The massive circular wall is almost five yards in thickness, and built entirely without mortar. The place was excavated between 1914–20, and iron spears and knives were found, along with personal objects of gold, bone, stone, bronze and glass, and ingots and moulds for bronze-working.

The place is only a shadow of its former self, but you can walk up the stairs that remain in the thickness of the walling that were put in place almost 2,500 years ago. Think of the feet that have walked on them since! It is reckoned that this place may have been used for some purpose or other until comparatively recent times. The view goes round from the ridge of the Cuillins, across the loch to the impressive cliffs on the far side, and on round to MacLeod's Tables, the two flat-topped hills that rise like twins to about 1,600 feet.

The eyes of the early inhabitants of this place did the same things. I wonder if the man who put these stairs in situ would believe that they have survived into this age.

I remember a visit to the Museum of Religion in Glasgow and, and a friend stood looking at the Egyptian mummy in her sarcophagus for quite a while. I asked him what he was thinking. 'She died in ancient Egypt nearly 5,000 years ago', he replied. 'She had no notion of the existence of Scotland and here she is in a display case in Glasgow. I wonder what is in store for us?' I knew where he was coming from. When she breathed her last she would never have envisaged ending up as a museum piece that people would gaze upon millennia later. Perhaps I will end up stuffed in a glass case on Mars? Never know. More likely in the foundations of a palace for a future King of Scots!

As to MacLeod's Tables, they have a good tale told about them. Their old names are Healaval Mhor and Healaval Beag, probably derived from the Norse *helgi fjall*, holy fells or hills, as their flat tops make them look like great natural altars.

Anyway, back to the story. Alasdair Crotach, the seventh chief of the MacLeods, spent some time living in Edinburgh. Some lowland nobles began to tease him, and at dinner one night, one in particular said, 'Have you ever seen a roof more impressive, a larger table, and candelabra of such quality in Skye?' MacLeod replied that he could outdo each of the criteria, and invited the nobleman to Skye. One arrival the nobleman was taken to the summit of Healaval Mhor, where tables were set out, laden with food. There was a cloudless star-filled sky, and the scene was lit with scores of MacLeod clansmen holding aloft blazing torches, standing in a circle round the scene. The nobleman was duly shamed, and no-one ever tried to embarrass Alistair Crotach again.

Onwards, the road skirting Loch Bracadale, then a short hop across the piece of dry land that connects the peninsula of Duirinish to the main body of Skye, and we come down to Loch Dunvegan itself. Continue through the village, following the signs for Dunvegan Castle, which is just a little north.

You park among mature woodland on the right side of the road. Dunvegan Castle is an ancient place, and the seat of the Clan MacLeod. It is the most famous building on Skye, and the oldest inhabited one too – in fact it claims to be the oldest inhabited building in both Scotland and England, and this may well be true. What is even more surprising is that as far as we know, it has never lain empty. Many ancient places have lain derelict and been refurbished, Eilean Donan castle being such an example, but Dunvegan has stood up to everything that has been thrown at it for well over a thousand years.

The original castle was a stone curtain wall, thick and high, with a gate (which has survived) facing the sea. The wall followed the outline of a rocky crag, and would have had timber buildings like lean-tos against the inside of the walls. Over the centuries this original castle has been added to, right up into the 1800s, so today it is a conglomerate of many different eras.

It stands in attractive and mature gardens, and as it comes into view through the trees, it is a bit of a surprise that this historic and famous place has such a drab appearance. It has been covered in harling, a type of rough-casting, to give the buildings a uniformity, and unfortunately this gives it an almost concrete box aspect. Inside, it has that musty feel that some very old buildings have, as if the island damp and rain of many centuries has somehow managed to permeate the very stones of the place. It is a wee jewel in its own way though, or of course it would not be such a famous place, and there are several artefacts inside that you will want to see.

The Fairy Flag of the MacLeods is preserved behind glass on one wall. It is very ragged now, as many previous generations have cut little squares from it to have as keepsakes, obviously hopeful that its supernatural qualities would rub off on the bearer.

The coming of the Fairy Flag, the *Bratach Sith*, into the possession of the MacLeods is of course smothered in legend. It is reported that one of the early chiefs of MacLeod took a fairy as his wife, and when, after 20 years of marriage, she had to return to fairyland, she left the flag as a parting gift.

A more reasonable story is that the flag was captured during the Crusades by a MacLeod, and brought home. There may be substance in this. When the flag was being examined before it was placed in its current frame, it was looked at by experts. They declared that the silk from which it is made was woven in Syria or Rhodes, and that the darns in it were from the Near East. It is known that Harald Hardrada, a Norse king who tried to conquer England in 1066, but who was defeated at the Battle of Stamford Bridge, carried a flag called Land-Ravager. This was shortly before the Battle of Hastings in that same year.

Harald Hardrada was known to have been in Constantinople in the early 1000s, and as Leod, first Chief of Clan MacLeod was a descendent of Harald, there is a link here that should not be overlooked.

As silk was a fabric unknown on Skye, its qualities must have made the locals think that it could only have been spun by the fairies, used to the rough homespun and woollens as they were.

The magical qualities of this flag were that if it was produced in battle, it made the enemy believe there were many more in the MacLeod force than there really were. Spread on a bed it ensured fertility, and it ensured that there would be herring in the loch so that the clan could eat!

There are tales of MacLeods carrying photographs of the *Bratach Sith* with them to ward off evil, and one man claimed that his striking success in bombing raids over Germany, and his remarkable escapes from danger during World War II, were due to the photograph of the flag which he carried in his pocket!

It is an interesting artefact to gaze upon, in its case in the castle's drawing room, and it is a flag which has seen many adventures in its history.

Rory Mor's Drinking Horn, a large horn trimmed with silver, was filled with claret and had to be drained in one go by each new chief of the clan. It holds several pints, and although there are notices to tell you the current chief achieved this task, the chances are there was an insert put inside to lessen its capacity! If you actually managed to drain this horn in one lifting, I'm quite sure the chief's next duty would be to lie down for quite a while within minutes of putting the horn down!

The Dunvegan Cup is another interesting item to look out for. It is an ancient drinking cup, encased in an ornamental body of wood and silver, and it stands upon four little legs. The casing, added in the 1400s, originated in Ireland.

There are mementos of Bonnie Prince Charlie, Flora MacDonald's corset is on show, and along with all the usual fittings and fixtures expected in such a place, there is a deep dungeon reached only by a hatch in the floor.

Have a good look around the gardens too, as there are many interesting examples of plant life on display, and the gardens are well laid-out.

Retrace your route the three-quarters of a mile back into the village of Dunvegan, then take the left turn, signposted Portree, the A850.

Not far along this road on your left is an old ruined church. There is an interesting memorial. On the church it says: 'This tablet is erected to commemorate the MacCrimmons, of whom ten generations are interred in this place. They were the hereditary pipers of MacLeod and for a period of three centuries were distinguished for their gifts, as composers, performers and instructors of the classical music of the bagpipe. 1500–1800 AD'.

This plaque is also in the Gaelic, of course. MacCrimmon is a name synonymous with great bagpiping, and known by pipers the world over.

Chiefs of the Clan MacLeod are buried in this church, and you can read over the various inscriptions. When I was a kid the chief was Flora, the 28th chief. She was very much the matriarchal figure, well-known and seemingly well-loved by her clanspeople, and her grave is here. She was born in 1878 and died in 1976.

I remember when she was an old lady, an American visitor, a female, met her, and afterwards turned to her friends, saying: 'I can't believe she looks so well, she must be some age now!' It turns out that the lady in question thought she had been speaking to Flora MacDonald, the young lady who helped Bonnie Prince Charlie escape the clutches of the redcoats in 1746, and not Flora MacLeod!

Onwards on the A850, towards Portree. When you reach Flashader above Loch Greshornish, if it is clear and you look out to sea, you may catch your first glimpse of the Outer Isles, 40 to 45 miles away. Lewis, Harris, the Uists and Benbecula, with Barra at the southern end, form a long chain out on the horizon to the west. Any clarity at all and they will be our almost constant companions until the north of the island is reached. Round Loch Snizort Beag until we reach the junction with the A87 where we turn north into the peninsula of Trotternish and head for Uig.

The road here has been greatly improved, something which was badly needed, as Uig is the ferry point for departure to the Outer Isles, and so this road takes much of the traffic destined for the western reaches of Scotland. En route to Uig, across the croft-dotted landscape, you will see the sign pointing down a dead-end road to Kingsburgh.

The celebrated Flora MacDonald married Allan MacDonald of Kingsburgh, though the original house has gone and been replaced by a more modern version. It is a private house.

We crest the brae and can look down into Uig Bay, the village of Uig a scatter of houses. When the ferry sits at the pier, it positively dwarfs the place. Uig forms an impressive harbour, the bay jutting into the land, and the water sheltered by the high sloping hillsides all around. As you descend into the place, you will notice a little round tower on your left. This martello-style edifice is actually a folly, built in the mid-1800s by a Captain

Fraser. This Captain Fraser was actually unlucky enough to have the local Free Church of Scotland minister come to him with an accusation of witch-craft, brought against a local woman and her five daughters. She had supposedly taken milk from her neighbour's cows using the dark arts – in 1880! Captain Fraser managed to talk the minister out of burning her – and her daughters.

One of my favourite signs can be seen as you come down into Uig (oo-ig – a bay!). It states:'Caution – Children and shop'

You will most likely want to drive through Uig as far as the pier, but look for the junction where the A855 cuts further north for Kilmuir, as we are going to take this route.

If you are going to visit the Outer Isles, the ferry from here docks at Tarbert on Harris or Lochmaddy on Uist. The Uists and Benbecula, con-nected by causeways, are famous for their astonishing beaches. Harris is very mountainous, as can be seen from Skye, its highest point being the mountain of Clisham. You can drive north into Lewis, as the two are con-nected. Any visitor to Lewis should not miss the standing stones at Callanish, and the broch of Dun Carloway.

Back to the A855. This road climbs in an impressive zig-zag up and over the hillsides sheltering the bay to the north. The road has narrowed too, now that the ferry terminal has been left behind. The Outer Isles are visible as a long line off to your left.

We pass the turn off for Monkstadt. The original house was built in 1732 and it was the first house in Skye to have a slated roof. It was built to replace Duntulm Castle, further north, for the MacDonald clan. We will visit Duntulm shortly. It was close to this house that the boat carrying Bonnie Prince Charlie 'over the sea to Skye' landed, where he escaped from Redcoat clutches in the Outer Isles, guided by Flora MacDonald. A Prince Charlie's Point is marked on maps, just south of the house site.

A little further and we reach Kilmuir, a scatter of crofts, and here to the right-hand side of the road you will see a collection of Black Houses, the ancient habitations in which most of the indigenous population of the isles resided until comparatively recent times. These form the Museum of Island Life, and are great fun, crammed as they are with artefacts of island life as it was, nearly all donated by the ordinary people of Skye. There is a modest fee for entry. This little collection of stone buildings with thatched roofs each have a theme. The Old Croft House, the Ceilidh House, the Barn, the Weaver's House, the Smith's House, to name but several. Fascinating. Even Flora MacDonald's egg-cup is on show! One Gaelic saying translated into English caught my eye. 'The heavier the rain, the nearer the change to dry weather'. Good advice for Scotland!

If you continue just a few hundred yards up the little right-hand slip that leads to the Museum of Island Life, you come to Kilmuir Graveyard. Not to be missed! As you go in the gate, the large rather bulky looking Celtic cross memorial marks the last resting place of Flora MacDonald, her husband, and some of her family.

Flora (1722–90) gained her fame by disguising Bonnie Prince Charlie as her maid and getting him on board a boat on the Outer Isles, right under the noses of the redcoat Hanoverian forces, and getting him over to Skye. They parted company in Portree, which we will visit shortly. She was taken by the government forces and taken to London. She was released, unharmed, in 1747, and suddenly found that she was feted as a celebrity by London society. On her return to Edinburgh she discovered that people there clamoured to see her too, and she was invited to every dinner party going. She soon returned to Skye though, and three years later married Allan MacDonald of Kingsburgh, and then moved to the east side of the Trotternish peninsula to reside at Flodigarry. She emigrated to North Carolina with her family in 1774. Her husband fought in the American War of Independence and was taken prisoner. They later returned to Skye, and this time stayed at Kingsburgh. She had five sons and two daughters. 3,000 mourners attended her funeral here, and her cross bears the inscription *Quantum cedat virtutibus aurum* – 'With virtue weighed, what worthless trash is gold!'

The memorial looks across the Minch (the name of the sea before you, an arm of the Atlantic) to her birthplace at Milton in the Uists. Interestingly, this memorial is not the original. It was raised in 1871, but was blown down and broken in a great gale in December 1873. The current cross, of Aberdeen granite, 28.5 feet high, was erected in 1880. There is a Celtic cross lying in the grass beside the current memorial, which is almost identical to the one atop the current shaft, and I can only presume that this was the one blown down in 1873. It is strange that it is just lying there, and that it has not at least been put against the wall, or similar, with a sign telling you what it is!

Two other memorials in the graveyard should not be missed. One stands almost in the centre of the place, and is a flat lying stone, raised on supports, like a table. Its inscription reads: 'Here lie the remains of Charles MacArthur, whose fame as an honest man and a remarkable piper will survive this generation. For his manners were easy and regular as his music, and the melody of his fingers will...' At this point the inscription ends and the rest of the slab is blank. It is a sad tale. Charles's son was paying for the inscription on his father's grave, and during this process he was bringing some sheep over from the island of Harris in a boat, when there was an unfortunate accident and he was drowned. The stone-carver, on hearing the news, and realising that he would not be paid for his work, merely walked away and left the inscription unfinished.

At the rear wall of the graveyard is the last resting place of Angus of the Wind. He gained his nickname from his ability to command a boat in the wildest of storms. Angus lived in the 1500s. His gravestone, which lies flat in the grass, is a long slab bearing a figure dressed in mail and armed. This stone is much older than Angus's time, and it is stated that he brought it back with him to Skye after one of his many forays. At a glance I would say that it came from Iona, where it would have been used to mark the grave of an ancient chieftain or King of Scots. Angus must have spotted it, reckoned that it was worthy even of him, and decided that it would be better used to mark his last resting place. Even more impressive is the story that Angus carried the stone up here from the shore far below on his own back!

We go back to, and continue on, the A855 to the very north of the island. Over the next couple of miles there is a really impressive, interesting stretch. The road drops again to hug the shore, and on your right are shattered cliffs, and thousands of boulders lying in heaps. Again, the land becomes primeval and raw, the power of nature apparent.

I was here with my daughter when she was 12. It was almost dark, it was winter, and I was in Skye to do some promotion for my Bonnie Prince Charlie book. The sea was crashing, and the rocks seemingly overhanging our heads looked black against the stormy sky. My daughter said: 'Dad, I really don't like this place – it is scary. Please let's go back to the car'. As I looked round, I could understand exactly what she meant. You will too, even on a summer's day, as the rocks here form their own strange architecture.

As we reach the far side of the bay, you will see some parking places on your left, and a sign pointing the way to the ruins of Duntulm Castle. It is only a few hundred yards away on a grassy path reached through the adjoining gate on your left.

There is not an awful lot left of Duntulm, but its situation makes it worthy of a visit. It stands on a 100-foot-high basalt promontory, and there has probably been a castle of sorts here since the 1200s, although there is no mention of it until 1540. In that year, James V of Scotland anchored his fleet below the castle to receive the homage of the local chiefs. The castle was held by the MacDonalds. As the castle was held by those sympathetic to the Jacobite cause, it was confiscated after the rising in 1715, of which the Battle of Sheriffmuir was a vital part. It was returned to the family in 1726, and remained occupied until the 1730s, when the family built their new house further down the coast at Monkstadt.

The view out from the castle is very fine, the sea far below, and the various headlands adding variety to the scene. Just out to sea rises a wedge-shaped rocky islet, one side sheer, the other very steep. This is Tulm Island, which probably gave the castle its name. On my last visit there was a pair of buzzards hovering above the island, obviously in hunting mode. I found this surprising, as I did not think that anything worth eating would live out there, but I must be wrong. Perhaps other birds nest there, and chicks or eggs were on the menu.

In front of Duntulm Castle a cairn has been erected; its inscription reads: 'This cairn is to commemorate the MacArthurs, hereditary pipers to the MacDonalds of the Isles during the 18th century. Their school of piping stood at nearby Peingown.'

After we leave Duntulm, we swing round the northern part of Skye, the road a little inland from the sea here.

A spine of hills runs the full length of this peninsula of Trotternish, rising to over 2,000 feet, and reaching 2,360 feet at the Storr. The character of these hills was not apparent as we drove north, but they will reveal themselves in all their immense glory on the southward drive. As we start to swing down the opposite coast, the mighty wedge at the end of this ridge hoves into view. Stark and majestic. I have often thought it strange that such a large wall of shattered cliff runs for 20 miles or so, and faces east towards the mainland. You would imagine that it should face west out to the wild Atlantic, but cataclysmic upheaval in the distant past has dictated that it look eastwards.

We come into Flodigarry, and keep your eyes peeled for the turn-off to the left that leads down to the Flodigarry Hotel. If you drive into the hotel's car park, you will see that there is an impressive view out to the mainland from this elevated spot. Flora MacDonald's cottage is round the right-hand side of the hotel's frontage. It is an attractive white building. There has been some debate over whether this is the original house, but it is certainly on the site. Flora and Allan moved here in 1751, lived here for eight years, and five of their seven children were born here.

Onwards, and we are looking forward into Staffin Bay, the hills forming an impressive wall on our right that disappears into the far distance. When we come into the village of Staffin, a road cuts off right marked 'The Quirang'. This road cuts across the peninsula back to Uig, rising to cross the wall of cliffs before you.

The Quirang (pronounced Koo-raing) comes from the Gaelic *Cuith Raing*, meaning the pillared stronghold. If you have the footwear and the breath, you can follow this road up to the cemetery called Cill a Bhealaich, where there is a car park. Following the path off to the right, steadily climbing, will take you up to the Quirang, a short last steep pull taking you up to the Needle, a 100-foot pillar of rock, and behind and to the right of this is the Prison, formed of castellated walls of rock. Above on a crag is a meadow like a football pitch, the views out to the mainland spectacular. You can also drive to the top of the pass where you can gain access to the summits of the range.

At the south end of the village of Staffin, continuing on the A855, there is
a little museum.

A little further there are signs for the Kilt Rock Viewpoint. The car park
is off to your left. There is fantastic cliff scenery down much of this side of
Trotternish, and here you will get a chance to see a little of it towering out
of the sea. When you walk to the edge, look to your left, northwards. There
is a very impressive waterfall close by, where the water emptying from Loch
Mealt tumbles vertically to the sea. The rocks are a little like tartan, vertical
basalt columns with grey Jurassic sediment laid horizontally. Certainly the
folds of the cliffs look like the pleats of a kilt. In stormy weather the water
tumbling over the cliff can be blown back upwards onto the land. There are
information boards and a railing on the cliff edge today, but before this
fence was erected, back in the 1960s, an Indian couple came here on honey-
moon. Standing on the cliff edge, a gust of wind caught the bride's sari, and
ran her over the edge. She was smashed onto the rocks at the water's edge
350 feet below.

Continue south, the island of Rona, then the northern end of Raasay our
companions out to sea, the Applecross peninsula of the mainland beyond
these.

Our road continues over moorland beneath the increasingly impressive
cliffy spine, then the Old Man of Storr comes into view, like a mighty finger
pointing skyward. The Old Man is the biggest of a dozen pinnacles on the
flank of the huge cliff called the Storr, which rises to 2,358 feet. The Old
Man itself is 160 feet high, balanced precariously on its plinth. Incredibly, it
was climbed for the first time in 1955.

On the shore below this point a hoard was discovered in 1891. It comprised brooches, bracelets and rings, 100 tenth-century Anglo Saxon coins,
and 18 coins minted in far-off Samarkand. It must have been hidden by a
viking raider, who, for some reason, was never able to return to claim it.

We drive on with Lochs Leathar and Fada on our left, then suddenly out
of the desolation we come into a scatter of houses that announces we are
entering Portree, the 'capital' of Skye.

Portree is a bustling little place, with a supermarket, an interesting collection of shops, and all the various kinds of bars and accommodation you
could wish for, within reason. You are back into civilisation with a bump,
as the traffic warden is ready to pounce on anything without a proper parking ticket.

Portree is very compact, so it does not take too long to explore the place.
The little harbour area should be visited, and when exiting the harbour,
turn left to go into Bank Street. It currently has no street sign, but it leads in
towards the Royal Bank of Scotland, and the local hospital. There is a little
hall off to the left at the beginning of this street that I played a few gigs in
when I was a teenager!

Opposite the entrance to the hospital there is a gate that leads up to the summit of the Lump, an eminence that rises above Portree Bay and the harbour. To the side of this gate there is a little plaque:

Close to this spot on June 18th 1742, Angus Buchanan was hung from the gallows with the greatest decency and without the least disturbance. His execution is noteworthy as the last public hanging to take place in the town. But no less remarkable are the circumstances which resulted in the discovery of his crime. Together with his accomplice, Duncan MacQueen, he set upon and murdered James Orr, an itinerant trader at Rigg in Trotterish. This was reputedly witnessed by a young boy whom the murderers captured and made swear upon his life that he would not tell another living soul what he had seen. The boy broke loose and fled to Rhenetra. Here he confessed to the minister he carried the burden of a terrible secret he could tell no-one. The minister directed him to tell the secret to a nearby rock. On eavesdropping, the identity of the criminals was discovered. At their trial both confessed to the crime and in passing sentence of death the judge ordered Buchanan to be taken to Portree, and there to be hanged by the neck 'by the hands of the hangman upon the gibbet until he is dead'. On the same day his accomplice met a similar fate at Gallowmuir in Inverness.'

Go through the gate and up the path onto the Lump. Its name in Gaelic is the *Meall*, which means the lump! To the right of the summit is a flat grassy area where the Highland Games are held. On the summit, overlooking the bay, is a little tower which has stairs to the top to afford an even better view. This tower was built by a Doctor Ban, who also planted the trees here. The tower is covered in graffiti and vandalised, which is a shame, as most visitors to Portree seem to amble up to it, as it is a prominent viewpoint.

The name Portree is a corruption of *Port an Righ*, port of the King. This is due to the fact that James v anchored a fleet of 12 ships here in 1540, after sailing round from Duntulm. He was here to let himself be seen by the various Hebridean chiefs and to pacify the continual unrest in these outer reaches of his realm. Many of the locals flocked to see the ships and to take part in whatever fun might unfold, and so the name stuck. You can stand in this little tower and imagine the fleet in the bay below.

As you exit Bank Street, you will see the Royal Hotel before you. This hotel stands on the site of MacNab's Inn, where Bonnie Prince Charlie and Flora MacDonald parted company. Charlie left her by saying, 'Madam, we shall meet at St James's yet', referring to St James Palace in London, but they never met again.

From Portree we take the A87 south back towards Sligachan, where we branched off towards Dunvegan. About a mile out of town you will find the Aros Centre on your right. This is a modern complex with a cinema/theatre, all beautifully done with wooden beams, a café, shop and audiovisual attraction. My favourite exhibit is a painting called *Culloden – the Aftermath*. I have many friends who have prints of this painting on their walls, but the original is much larger. It is sited high in the café, which is a shame, as it is such a complex work of art that you need to be able to look at it for several minutes, near and far, to be able to see all its intricacies.

The theme of this painting is, of course, the destruction of the Highland way of life after Culloden, and the artist, Brian Wood, has put his heart and soul into it.

From the Aros Centre, we continue south. You will see signs pointing the way to Braes. This is not so much a place as a district. Braes is famous for its 'battle' which took place in April 1882. The crofters of Braes had been denied the right to let their sheep graze on the slopes of Ben Lee. They offered, when the lease expired on the ground, to pay more than the previous tenant. But when they were refused by Lord MacDonald's Factor, they saw this as an injustice, and let the sheep graze and some withheld their rents.

Sheriff Officers turned up with notices of eviction, but were forced by infuriated Braes folk to burn the notices. The Chief Constable of Glasgow dispatched 50 policemen to Skye to arrest the ringleaders. They were met by about 100 local men, women and children, and a pitched battle took place with sticks and stones. The island became such a hotbed of discontent that warships were sent, and marines were landed at Uig! The resulting coverage at least forced the London government to take notice of the injustices which the crofters were being subjected to, and a Royal Commission was set up to make inquiries.

We head straight for the Cuillin Hills down long Glen Varragil. Bonnie Prince Charlie, during his 'days in the heather' after Culloden, walked from Portree along this glen, and all the way to Elgol at the south of the island, in one day, dressed in a plaid and barefoot! Passers-by, on seeing him unkempt and bearded, probably though he was just another Highland gentleman down on his luck after Culloden. I don't suppose there are than many people out there who when they think of Charlie, realise that he was of the direct blood-line from Kenneth MacAlpine, first King of Scots, through Canmore, Bruce and the various Jameses and Mary. The direct line of the nation of Scotland, forced to skulk in the heather of its wilds. After Culloden, many people pined for the return of the old ways:

A wind that awoke on the moorland came sighing
Like the voice of the heroes that perished in vain,
Not for Tearlach alone the red claymore was plying,
But to win back the old world that comes not again.
(A. Lang)

We are now retracing our route to the Skye Bridge and the mainland at Kyle of Lochalsh, where we will head the few miles back to the point where the A890 heads further north. Like the pining for the old ways, Skye somehow imbeds itself into our consciousness. I have had good times and bad times on Skye, but I can't escape it. I think of this island often. Its landscape is like a window back to 'old' Scotland in some ways. It comes to me in dreams, and I'm afraid that after a visit, it will appear in yours too. You might love it, you may hate it, the landscape too stark, too unyielding, too 'old'.

But you won't forget it.

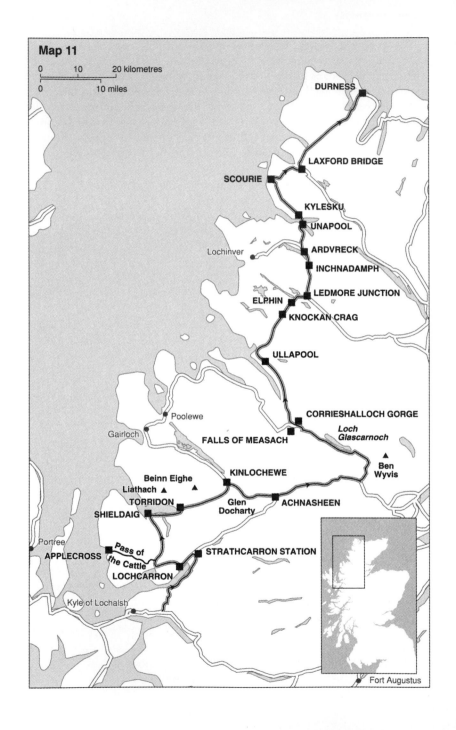

Map 11

0   10   20 kilometres
0   10 miles

DURNESS

LAXFORD BRIDGE

SCOURIE

KYLESKU

UNAPOOL

Lochinver

ARDVRECK

INCHNADAMPH

LEDMORE JUNCTION

ELPHIN

KNOCKAN CRAG

ULLAPOOL

Poolewe

CORRIESHALLOCH GORGE

Loch Glascarnoch

Gairloch

FALLS OF MEASACH

KINLOCHEWE

Ben Wyvis

Beinn Eighe

Liathach

TORRIDON

Glen Docharty

ACHNASHEEN

SHIELDAIG

Portree

APPLECROSS

Pass of the Cattle

STRATHCARRON STATION

LOCHCARRON

Kyle of Lochalsh

Fort Augustus

CHAPTER ELEVEN

The Northwest Passage

BEGINNING AT THE JUNCTION OF THE A87 AND A890 THE ROUTE EXPLORES LOCHCARRON BEFORE TAKING A DEVIATION TO APPLECROSS, AND THEN CARRIES ON TO SHIELDAIG, TORRIDON, KINLOCHEWE AND ACHNASHEEN. FOLLOWING THE A835 TO ULLAPOOL, THE ROUTE THEN TAKES THE LEDMORE JUNCTION NORTH TO DURNESS.

A FEW MILES DRIVING back eastwards takes us to the A890, branching off to our left, and we go north towards Loch Carron. The road climbs to cross the peninsula that separates Loch Alsh and Loch Carron. It has been written that Loch Carron is the boundary of the northwest Highlands, and there is certainly a change – there is a difference in the terrain, and the landscape becomes a little harder. As we climb you can see traces of the old single track road that has only recently been superseded.

We pass the turn-off for Plockton, one of the most picturesque of the many coastline villages, then Loch Carron comes into view. You will soon see the signs for Strome Ferry. There is no ferry, however. There used to be, and so the name has stuck. Believe it or not, the road you are now driving was not constructed until around 1970. You used to have to get a ferry to the north side of the loch to continue on the road there, but the tarmac at this side now continues to the head of the loch.

We are high above the water here, and the views away to the east are extensive. The road goes down to single track with many twists and turns before it drops to the loch side. Here we are right alongside the West Highland Line, the railway from Inverness to Kyle of Lochalsh. Of course, it has to follow the line of least resistance, and so takes a northern route, curving down Glen Carron before following the loch here. Road and rail are squeezed in together, the water lapping on our left on the other side of the tracks. It is so cramped for space that the cliffs come right down to the side of the road, and these cliffs often have nets covering them to protect drivers from falling rocks. At one point we even drive through a concrete tunnel to protect the road and the railway. The road widens a little as we pass the tiny railway station of Attadale, which is little more than a small platform allowing access to the train.

At the head of the loch we arrive at the little hamlet of Strathcarron with its hotel. Drive over the railway line here at a crossing, then a mile straight on over the meadows at the head of the loch until we reach a junction. The road to the right is a continuation of the A890 we have been driving, and it goes off towards Inverness. We take the left road, the A896, sign-posted Lochcarron, two miles, Shieldaig, 17 and Torridon, 24. Ah! The allure of West Highland names!

You will notice while following the north shore of the loch that there is a wee golf course squeezed in between the road and the water. Golf. A good walk ruined, I fear, but you do find golf courses in some bizarre places in Scotland.

As you see in so many places in Scotland, there is an ancient church, and nearby, its replacement, usually from the 1800s. Here we pass an austere, plain-looking church, and nearby is the ruined earlier church in its ancient burial ground. You can pull in and wander about this old graveyard, but there are signs warning about the instability of the old church walls.

Next we come to the village of Lochcarron. It is a lovely, straggly place, really just one long row of old houses, facing the loch. It has two garages and lots of signs advertising accommodation. The village was formerly known as Jeantown, but Loch Carron seems to have superseded it. There are vestiges of an ancient fortification behind the village.

It may seem incredible now, but Loch Carron district coupled with Skye, had a total of 937 fishing boats in 1893! In fact, in 1882, the fishermen here caught 77,783 barrelfulls of herring to be salted, and in 1892 they filled 89,202 barrels of cod, ling and hake! No wonder fish stocks have dwindled, as fishing has embraced modern technology since these days to increase catch sizes. I do sympathise with fishermen going out in all weathers, trying to make a living, but as they say, nothing lasts forever, and every action has an equal and opposite reaction.

When you get to the far end of Lochcarron village, you will notice a road forking off to the left, and the signs tell you that this leads to Strome Castle, three miles way. This is of course directly opposite Strome Ferry which you passed on the loch's south side.

The road is a dead end and the castle is a ruin, but just so you know, it was built before 1472. It was owned by the Camerons of Locheil, but was given to the MacDonalds of Glengarry by King James V in 1539. They had a feud going on with the MacKenzies, which ended with the latter storming the place in 1602 when part of the castle was blown up. It stands on a knoll above the pier for the defunct ferry.

After Lochcarron, the road cuts up to the next sea loch, crossing the peninsula to the north. The west coast of Scotland north of the River Clyde is just a series of lochs cutting deep into the mainland, creating all these arms of land. As the crow flies, the seaboard of Scotland from Kintyre to Durness measures only 225 miles, but is, at the very least, 2,000 by the coastal route – and that is not taking every minor indentation into account.

We travel through a little gorge on the next stretch, leading over to Loch Kishorn, known as the Pass of Kishorn, where we are hemmed in by rock on either side. Good place for an ambush, and I'm sure it has been used as such in the past!

At the end of the pass there is a little oasis of green fields with the farmhouse on our left. The waters of Loch Kishorn appear, and across the loch, the mountains of the Applecross peninsula loom large before us. From this approach, Sgurr a Chaorachain is powerful and prominent, with Beinn Bhan jutting out beyond its right side.

The road continues up to the head of Loch Kishorn, and just past here, a little road cuts off to our left, signposted Applecross.

Applecross is a tiny fishing village out on the western side of the mountainous peninsula to your left. This wee road rises to 2,053 feet to cross the *Bealach* (pass) *na Ba* (of the cattle) on its way to the coast. It is the highest-reaching road in all western Scotland, and although it is not part of our continuing route, I recommend that you drive the six miles to the top of the pass, even if you do not continue to Applecross itself. This road should not be attempted if there is snow on the hills, nor is it for the inexperienced driver. The first mile or two is narrow and twisting, but the road then swings into the corrie and begins to climb. It then goes into a series of zig-zags, with drops of hundreds of feet and gradients of one in four. It looks like the pictures I have seen of mountain roads in Switzerland. The summit is absolutely breathtaking. There is a parking place on the left, with views out to Skye, but it is the landscape here itself that attracts me. You could be on the surface of the moon. A rough, barren terrain stretching out in every direction. I sat up here for an hour one day in March, with the bike parked up, just meandering and taking it all in. I never saw a car pass, and never saw one on the way up or down either. But plenty of deer ran across the road, which can be especially scary on a motorcycle! A beautiful, desolate place, which succeeds in giving those who never wander more than a few yards from their vehicles an idea of what the high tops hereabouts can look like!

The name Applecross is derived from *aber*, the Gaelic for estuary, and the river that flows into the sea here, known locally as the Crossan. One of our early saints, St Maelrubha, arrived in this area in 673. *Mael* means tonsured, and *rubha* is red, so we can assume he had red hair. He died in Sutherland, but was brought to Applecross for burial, and stones near the church are said to mark his grave. His name is pronounced Mail-roo-ah, and Loch Maree, a little further north, is a corruption of this.

At the junction at the bottom, we turn left again to follow the A896 further north. It is a wild landscape we drive through now, with the cliffs that guard Applecross's peninsula over to our left. We come to the sea again at Loch Shieldaig, and the scatter of houses that is the village of Shieldaig itself. The road swings east to skirt the south shore of Loch Torridon. Across the loch, the large tower-like mountain is Beinn Alligan (the Jewel), and we drop into Torridon village where the bulk of Liathach (Leea-gach), meaning 'the Grey One', towers behind. We drive in a more easterly direction now, heading up Glen Torridon, where for the next three miles Liathach rises hard on our left.

This is a mountain which has always held a certain magic for me. It appears in my dreams sometimes. Its huge bands and ridges fascinate as you drive under its frowning malevolence. It is like no other mountain in Scotland, and it embedded its image into my mind when I first saw it in my early teens. If I was to be asked what my favourite mountain was, Liathach would be in the top three. It's a funny thing, but over the years I have asked many people who enjoy stravaiging Scotland, what their favourite mountain is, and they have always answered without hesitation, giving either one or two names. So it seems that there is a special mountain for every psyche!

A little further on, and at the roadside you will see a notice saying 'Beinn Eighe Nature Reserve'. When you reach Loch Clair a little further on your right, please stop and look back at Liathach. Here he looks his best. I tend to think of most Scottish hills as feminine, but not this one. From here he looks sharp and slim. Unclimbable. Insurmountable. A throwback to the dawn of creation. Almost defying anything as ephemeral as a man to stand atop his summit.

Beinn Eighe (A as in aim), Gaelic for file, is a stunning mountain too, east of Liathach and now on your left, but is completely different in character. It has quartzite rock in its peaks, which can look like a dusting of snow, and it has a certain grace in its curves swinging from summit to summit that Liathach does not have.

The next place of habitation we reach is Kinlochewe. As we approach the village, the mountain Slioch appears at about 11 o'clock. It stands above Loch Maree. As *kin* means 'at the head of a loch', you may wonder why the village Kinlochewe is at the head of Loch Maree. All will become apparent when you notice that the sea loch at the west end of Loch Maree is Loch Ewe. There is a river connecting the two, but access right up the loch must have been easier at one time, with this place being regarded as the head of the sea loch.

God! There is so much worth seeing in Scotland where scenery is concerned that I want to go down every wee road just to see where it takes me, but I'm trying to keep this as diverse as possible, so when we hit Kinlochewe, we will take a right. This road ends at the T-junction in the middle of Kinlochewe, and as stated, we turn right, onto the A832.

We immediately start to climb as the road ascends Glen Docherty. This is a spectacular glen, not because it has sheer walls like Glencoe, but because of the views it affords. Unfortunately, the views are the other way, descending to Kinlochewe, but I can't bend the route around to suit everyone, so you'll just have to stop near the top to look back and appreciate the view. The glen frames the view back to Loch Maree perfectly.

Once out of Glen Docherty, we are up into an area of softer scenery, which is the norm the further east you go in Scotland. We pass the northern shore of Loch a Chroisg, and that brings us to the hamlet of Achnasheen. There is a junction here where the road comes in from Loch Carron. Achnasheen has a railway station on the line to Kyle of Lochalsh. We turn left here, and drive up Strath Bran, a straightforward run eastwards. The road is being upgraded, so it may be greatly improved by the time you visit. We go through the village of Achanalt, then pass a series of lochs on the south side of the road, the third, Loch Luichart, being the largest. Then we hit the junction of the main north route, the A835, and we turn left, heading for Ullapool. After some of the small Highland roads we have been driving, even an ordinary single lane road like the A835 can seem extravagant!

The road follows Strath Garve, and the bulky mountains of the Wyvis range are on our right. The river that escorts us here is the Blackwater, and there is a considerable amount of woodland on the roadsides. I actually spent a night here once, with the bike pulled in and me curled up in (thank God) a good sleeping bag. It was so cold that I had to cover my face with a T-shirt as my nose was freezing, and when I woke in the morning the bike was so ice-coated that I had to roll it into the direct sunlight as the sun started to rise behind Ben Wyvis in order to thaw it out! I had some coffee, milk and sugar in a container, and I boiled some water on my wee camping stove to add to it, but everything was frozen solid. I had some sandwiches with sliced boiled egg, and when I bit into the first one, the egg had frozen solid and it was like biting glass! I had to put my breakfast inside my leather jacket, and have it later in the morning when it had thawed a bit. Don't get me wrong, it wasn't much fun, but it is at least a morning I'll remember, so it wasn't all bad.

Continuing, we suddenly rise above the trees and come onto a rough moorland. It is strewn with boulders, like thousands of standing stones, only this is not the work of man, but most likely the residue of the last ice-age. When the ice melted, these boulders came to earth, scattered as they are. This is a different landscape again from what we have seen before. After a few miles of this boulder-field, the dam at the southern end of Loch Glascarnoch comes into view. There is an inn on your left just before the dam, an old coaching inn called the Altguish – it is the only habitation in sight. The Fannich Hills are to our left. In front the view is filled with An Teallach (an-cha-lach, the anvil). An Teallach is a favourite of climbers, and has some amazing peaks and pinnacles along its main ridge. I have heard the question, 'Why is it called the anvil?' and the retort has been, 'Because climbers get a hammering on it!' Over to the right the big peak is Beinn Dearg (ja-rag, the Red Mountain).

The next junction we reach is Braemore Junction, where the A832 goes off to our left, but we continue towards Ullapool on the A835. Just past this junction you will see signs for the Corrieshalloch Gorge. This is one not to be missed, so please take the time out to see it, as it is an experience you will always remember. There is a lay-by for visitors on your right. When you park, just cross to the other side of the road and follow the signs for Corrieshalloch and the Falls of Measach.

The gorge is a Grade 1 National Nature Reserve, declared in 1967. It is the best example in Scotland of a steep-sided gorge formed by glacial melt waters during the latter stages of the great ice age between 10–13,000 years ago.

Once across the road, it is only a few yards to a viewing platform, which is like a dead-end bridge yawning over the sheerest sided abyss I have ever seen. The gorge is not wide, but it is very deep, and its plant life makes it a Centre of Special Scientific Interest. Looking back up the gorge, you will see the Falls of Measach plunging over the upper end. You will also notice a little bridge crossing the top of the gorge over the falls, looking from here like a flimsy spider's web, slung from rocky edge to rocky edge.

Walk the two hundred or so yards up to the bridge, and you will see it comprises of wooden slats, suspended from the two steel cables that span the drop. No more than six people are allowed on the bridge at one time, and as you walk out and it begins to sway, you will realise that the six person rule is not one you would like to see broken!

In the summer months, the greenery grows right up to the ends of the bridge, and as the drop is completely sheer, you walk out and suddenly you realise the drop below you. It takes a moment to adjust yourself. I can remember in my younger days, a friend and I leaned on either side in the middle to get the bridge to sway a little. There was a party of ladies coming down the path, and due to the foliage cover, all they could see was the two of us on the bridge, swinging slightly. I can still hear the shrieks as they stepped out on to the woodwork, the sudden drop revealed, and we two looking nonchalant, leaning back to make it swing!

The waterfall drops over the edge just to your left here, and the gorge runs away from you, the river coursing along its floor, to the right.

Back to your vehicle to continue north to Ullapool, another 11 miles ahead. Watch as you exit the car park, as there is a bend ahead, and cars can appear suddenly as you cross their path while turning to the right onto the main road.

You descend into the Lael Forest and the same river which plummeted over the falls now looks very placid to your left. Loch Broom appears on your left, and we follow its eastern shore. It is very picturesque, and you will soon be able to discern the white houses that comprise Ullapool in the distance.

Ullapool is an interesting wee place. It was founded in 1788 by the Fisheries Association, to further the herring industry. It has a sheltered anchorage, facing back towards the head of Loch Broom. It has quite a few shops – even a supermarket, and different levels of accommodation. It may make sense to fill up with fuel here, as going further north brings us into increasingly less populated country. There is a museum and visitor centre in West Argyll Street, housed within an 1829 Thomas Telford Church, with displays of social and natural history, along with the parish archives. There is also a curious memorial clock to Sir Arthur Fowler of Braemore, who died in 1899.

Ferries run from Ullapool to the Outer Isles, and I love to sit and watch the hive of activity as one of these boats comes in to dock. As we pull out of Ullapool, now heading for the far north, you have left behind the only sizable habitation you will see for well over 150 miles.

The A835 is signposted for Achiltibuie, Lochinver and Kylesku as we take to the road once more. The road begins to roll, every crest brings a new vista of the sea, or a glimpse up into yet another little glen. Mountains appear to your left, but not like any you have seen before in Scotland. Most of the high tops you have seen have been in groups or ranges or even long ridges with several tops. These stand alone, like primeval monsters, raising themselves from the very rock of Scotland. Stac Pollaidh (Stac Polly), Cul Beag, Cul Mor, Suilven and Canisp – all amazing mountains, very striking, and all with distinct personalities. The rock that comprises these mountains was formed millions of years ago, but ice has gouged them into these shapes, the harder masses of rock left behind, the softer eroded away.

You will notice that as we head north now, there is a series of lay-bys en route with information boards. These are really informative and point out some interesting landmarks that the untrained eye may miss.

The history of this part of the country is different from that of southern and central Scotland. It is not a history of defence against English invasions, of medieval battles and castles, of knights in armour and derring-do. This is a history of geology and the place names have mixed Gaelic and Norse roots, as centuries ago the viking influence was strong in these parts.

You pass a sign telling you that you are entering the Inverpolly National Nature Reserve, then a little further on you will see signs for Knockan Crag. This is a Mecca for geologists. There is a visitor centre which is always open, and behind stands the crag itself. It might look like an everyday cliff, but no! Many years ago it was noticed that the rock on the top of the crag was older than the rock underneath. How could this be? It is due to the movement of plates of course, with one plate moving and slipping under an older plate, and raising it over and above.

There is much of interest here, but the most fascinating is that Scotland and England were originally from opposite sides of the planet. The movement of the continents and tectonic plates took Scotland one way, England another, and they eventually met. It turns out that Scotland actually has much in common with the Appalachian Mountains of North America, in geology at least.

So, from opposite sides of the world? That explains why Scotland and England are poles apart!

There is a trail that takes you round the crag, with some great views, and it takes about an hour to do the circuit. Just after Knockan Crag, we enter Sutherland. For the furthest northwestern county of Scotland, Sutherland might seem a strange name, but the viking once raided these coasts, and to them this was the 'south-land', hence the name.

When you reach the little village of Elphin, there is a clear view of Suilven. The name is Norse, and means 'the sugar loaf'. The vikings, out in the sea to the west, thought that its shape was like a sugar-loaf, and so the name has survived the centuries.

We come to Ledmore Junction, where a road joins us from the east. We turn left here, following the A837. The sign proclaims 'North and West Highlands Tourist Route – John O'Groats 152'. John O'Groats is the northeastern tip of Scotland, so a glance at a map gives you the idea of the distance involved.

A straightforward stretch ahead brings us to Inchnadamph. A few miles east of Inchnadamph stands Sutherland's highest mountain, Ben More Assynt, 3,273 feet. I followed the River Traligill inland to climb this hill a few years ago. The river would disappear and reappear, confusing my senses to say the least. This is because it drops below its ancient bed in places, reappearing elsewhere, this again due to plates moving. Another stream a little south is the Allt nan Uamh (Oo-ah – Stream of the Caves), which also gives a clue to the attractions hereabouts for geologists and pot-holers. Caves in this area were excavated in 1917, and bones of lynx, bear, arctic fox and reindeer were found, along with two human skeletons dated to 6000 BC. This is an empty enough landscape today. It is strange to imagine humans hunting here all those millennia ago. I wonder what the world view of these people was like. Did they know of other lands and places other than the harsh landscape they inhabited here?

Incidentally, the day on Ben More Assynt was a memorable one. My companion and I scaled Conival first, a neighbour of the former. We climbed through thick cloud to appear in strong sunlight and clear skies on the summit. The cloud was like a carpet below, peaks poking through here and there, An Teallach away in the distance. The heat was so great it was a bare-chested slog. On the twisting ridge leading from Conival to Ben More Assynt, another climber approached. Owing to the narrowness, he had to pass within a few feet of us. We had not seen another human being since we left the road many hours before, and were surprised to see someone else up here. We were even more surprised when we said hello, and he very pointedly turned his face away and ignored us on his way past. I had to restrain my companion from picking up a stone and throwing it after him! Bizarre. When I meet people in remote places, they always stop to tell you what the situation is ahead, and generally a few pleasantries are exchanged.

Reaching the Traligill on the return journey, sweaty, hot and tired, I stripped off to plunge into a fairly deep rocky pool. There were still traces of snow on the summits, and as soon as my toes touched the water I realised it was so brutally cold that I had made a big mistake. My companion appeared just as I was clambering out and he asked how the water was. 'Fine', I replied, trying hard to hide the quaver in my voice and the convulsions in my body. 'Make sure you get a good jump into the deep bit so that you can get your whole body right under', I added helpfully. As he was in mid-air, having leapt from the bank, I was already running with my clothes under my arm and just my unlaced boots on. Desiring to throw a rock at a rude passer-by would have been mild compared to his reaction when he hit that freezing water. I knew that his first act on exiting that water would have been to look for a big stick. By the time he caught up with me, I was quick to point out that I was the one with the car keys – and that it was a long walk home!

We camped out that night too – and a deer ran into the tent during the night and fell on top of us. Ah! The sound of two Scotsmen, swearing graphically in raised voices, echoing off the mountains in an empty glen. The true spirit of Scotland!

At Inchnadamph (Meadow of the Stag, – aptly named), you have reached the head of Loch Assynt, a seven-mile long body of water, and the road curves to follow its northern shore. It comes as a bit of a shock in this landscape to spot two ruined buildings between the road and the lochside. The first, a rectangular stone-built edifice, is the remains of Calda House, a mansion erected about 1660 by Kenneth MacKenzie, third Earl of Seaforth, but it was destroyed by fire in the middle of the 1700s.

A little further on stand some fangs of masonry, the remains of Ardvreck Castle, on a small peninsula jutting into the loch. There is a lay-by opposite to park in, and it is only a couple of hundred yards following the little bay to the castle ruins. It is in a dangerous state, but you can still walk round and see the few features that remain, and the almost complete vaulted basements beneath.

Ardvreck was built about 1591 by the MacLeods of Assynt. It was attacked by Royalist forces in 1646 but was successfully defended by Domhall Ban MacLeod (Fair Donald). The most famous incident in Ardvreck's history was when James Graham, the Marquis of Montrose, who is buried in St Giles in Edinburgh, sought shelter here after his defeat at the Battle of Carbisdale in 1650. Monstrose and his companion, Major Sinclair, an Orkneyman, had been wandering these hills for two days with no food, and were weak from fatigue. They were captured and held at

Ardvreck, and notice of their capture was forwarded to the authorities. After several days, Montrose, suffering a high fever, was taken by horseback all the way to Edinburgh, and was hanged in the Grassmarket on 21 May 1650.

As you peer into these vaulted basements, perhaps you are looking at the spot where Montrose lay, wretched and feverish, before being taken to his execution. He was one of the greatest soldiers and commanders Scotland ever produced.

The MacKenzies, outraged at the treatment Montrose had suffered here, devastated Assynt from end to end. When the Restoration came and Charles II regained the throne of his ancestors, MacKenzie managed to secure a commission of fire and sword. Ardvreck was burnt, and the MacKenzies seized the land. This is when they built the nearby Calda House.

The estate was sold to the Sutherland family, even though the MacLeods, descendants of the betrayer of Montrose, tried to buy the land back. A party of Jacobite MacRaes burnt Calda House, and so that is why it, too, stands neglected and forlorn like its predecessor.

We know very little of the history of Sutherland and the far northwest. Records are very scant, and so for that matter are castles and fortifications. Adrvreck is the exception. The events that took place here have been saved for posterity.

A little further on there is a junction where we turn right to follow the A894, the signs proclaiming that this road leads to Kinlochbervie, Durness and Tongue. We climb here to cross over the backbone of the land to yet another fiord-like sea loch. On our left here is Quinag, a peak with seven tops, the highest rising to 2,653 feet. The name is a corruption of the Gaelic *cuinneag*, meaning 'the pail'. The north side of the mountain has impressive rock walls and buttresses. When the watershed is crossed there are a couple of hairpin bends, and the views of these are at their best here.

Loch Glencoul appears before us, stretching away south-east into the mountains. It is up by the head of this loch that the Eas a Chual Aluinn (Ess-Cool-Aulin) stands, the highest waterfall in Scotland. The vertical drop is 658 feet, and although it is narrow, it is good fun reminding North Americans that it is four times higher than Niagara!

Unfortunately the falls are not visible without a lot of leg work, but there are some sailings from Unapool, a little village before us, up to the head of the loch to view the falls. Just by the sign which states you are entering Unapool, there is a lay-by with information boards explaining the landscape laid out before you.

We then roll on to the Kylesku bridge, opened in the Autumn of 1984. When I was first here, you had to get the ferry across the loch to Kylestrome on the opposite, northern shore. You can still see the old ferry slipways below you to your right. It is a fantastic bridge. Perhaps I am being old-fashioned, but I used to love the old ferry, and the crossing to the north has lost some of its romanticism. Not fair on the locals though – I'm sure crossing on the ferry on a daily basis, especially if you were in a hurry, wasn't very romantic for them.

Just after the bridge there is a flat section you can pull into on the left. There is a cairn here that was erected to commemorate the fiftieth anniversary of the 12th Submarine Flotilla. It was unveiled on 10 April 1993:

> The security of these top secret operations was guarded by the local people of this district – who knew so much and talked so little. The silent hills remember the young men of His Majesty's x-Craft submarines and human torpedoes who were trained in these wild and beautiful waters.

As the road ascends the hill, there is a viewpoint with story boards.

The next ten miles, is, I think, the finest motorcycling road I know. Very few straight stretches, many twists and turns, and a good road surface. The landscape has grown increasingly wild, and there is very little growth, just moss and rock now, probably more reminiscent of Iceland. It is hard, primeval and volcanic. That engineers could build such a good road over this terrain, with its perfect cambers, is impressive indeed. You can keep a steady speed on this stretch, just leaning from curve to curve, but it takes total concentration too, especially with such an amazing terrain to look at.

We reach the scatter of crofts that is Scourie, with street lights and everything! The last time I drove through here, there was a Golden Eagle sitting atop of one of these street lights. Scourie has a lovely wee beach, and it is a taste of what is to come when we reach the north coast. It is a further seven miles on to the junction at Laxford Bridge. You cannot help but be staggered at the amount of water. Lochans, pools, streams – there seems to be as much water as land, and it seems amazing that a route for the road could be found through this. You might think you can picture this landscape if you have seen parts of the Highlands, but the north-west tip of Scotland is a different world entirely. You could walk 30 feet away from the road, and never know it was there unless a passing car alerted you. A conical mountain appears as you head towards Laxford. This is Arcuil, more commonly Arkle, and this hill and its neighbour to the north north east, Foinaven, have given their names to famous racehorses.

We reach Laxford Bridge – really nothing more than a junction, although it is named on most maps. The name is actually *Lax-Fjord*, the Norse for Salmon Fiord.

We continue north to Durness. The road to the east goes to Lairg, but we are now on the last 20 miles to the north coast, on the A838.

When we reach Rhiconish, a side-road branches off to Kinlochbervie, a fishing port. The road narrows, and continues out to its terminus at

Sheigra. Just before its end, a path branches off north to Sandwood Bay, a beautiful unspoiled place. It is a good few years since I visited Sandwood Bay, and the eight-mile round trip across the moorland was ridiculously boggy, almost sucking my boots off with every step. But it was worth it to see the place. At its southern tip, Am Buachaille, or the Herdsman, a rock stack like a giant finger, guards the bay. Right behind the beach itself is Sandwood Loch, a freshwater loch only separated from the sea by the sand and dunes. The beach is two miles long. A rocky rib runs out into the sea near the southern end, and a local has reported seeing a mermaid! Before you scoff, these reports were made by a reputable man, and a visit to Sandwood will reveal it is a magical place, far from the madding crowd, where anything seems possible.

Standing at Sandwood, you see the cliffs of the coast stretch away north to Cape Wrath, Scotland's northwestern tip.

Continuing north, we cross the last rise for the straight run towards Durness. Again the land changes. It is completely devoid of trees, but the rockiness suddenly stops, more green is apparent, and although still mountainous to our right, it is altogether gentler.

The road is straight, and runs in a gentle downhill slope. The impressive hills on our right are Cranstackie and its outliers, with Strath Dionard travelling eastward on Cranstackie's right.

The Kyle of Durness appears in the distance before us, an inlet of the sea, only this time it juts in south from the north coast. Here, there is a little well on the left-hand side of the road with an inscription which reads:

As a mark of gratitude and respect towards the inhabitants of Durness and Eddrachillis for their hospitality while projecting this road, this inscription is placed over this well by their humble servant, Peter Lawson, Surveyor, 1883

On my last visit I parked the bike opposite this well, used the water to brew up a cup of coffee, and sat on the bank opposite, just trying to imbed the view on my memory. I can close my eyes and see it now. I was lucky, the sun was shining in a cloudless sky, though it was mid-March. I climbed back on the bike and drove the last few miles to Durness. The road skirts the eastern shore of the Kyle of Durness, and when the tide is out, it is a place of the purest water dappled sand. It is a long, snaking inlet, very striking, and very different to the sea lochs of the western seaboard. It turns away from the road at the little spur that leads off to the Cape Wrath Hotel.

It is possible to rent a boat to take you across the Kyle of Durness, allowing access to the supply road to the lighthouse at Cape Wrath itself – Scotland's north-west tip. It is ten miles further west, and the lighthouse stands on a cliff 370 feet high. The seas crash and boil far below – and perhaps it is a good thing that it retains its remoteness and inaccessibility. Cape

Wrath is a fitting name for Scotland's end, but it is actually a corruption of Hvarf, the Norse for turning point. This is where the vikings would turn the prows of their dragon ships south to raid Scotland's western seaboard.

Where this little road branches off from the main route, a modern standing stone has been erected, tall and wafer thin, with Celtic knot-work carved upon it.

Next we go into Durness itself. The name comes from *drya-ness*, the Norse 'wolf-cape', and wolves were prevalent in this district once. In the village, there is a left turn, the road signposted to Balnakeil. Take this turn, as we drive less than a mile to its end, and there are some good things to see.

We pass a craft village on our left, and you will notice that it has been created from an old World War Two camp, the concrete flat-top buildings commandeered for more peaceful purposes. It is as it was on my first visit in my early teens, so, it is now pretty firmly established.

Half a mile along Balnakeil House comes into view on your right. It is the most northwesterly example of a fortified house in Scotland, standing on a little crag, and with the remains of other old buildings around it. These were originally churchlands, and the Bishop of Caithness had a residence here. Although the current building was erected in the 1600s, there is older stonework inside, remnants of the earlier building. It was probably built by the MacKay family, whose clan lands these were.

The castle overlooks Balnakeil Bay, a beautiful sandy sweep stretching a mile and a half, and facing west. The beaches of this part of Scotland have to be seen to be believed. They are composed of shell sand, clean and fine, and even on the finest of days if there are a handful of people on them, they seem crowded!

Park at the west side of Balnakeil House, and there is access here to the beach if the weather smiles favourably on you. I was here in a dry spell in March 2003. A girl passed me, walking some dogs, and I noticed that the girls of the far northwest of Scotland have a certain look about them – a rangy, loose-limbed look, almost Scandinavian. Most of the people here probably do have some Scandinavian blood, but their look is likely to be due more to regular exercise. No catching the bus here to go a couple of stops. People here tend to walk to the shop, or at least live a more active life than most of us city-dwellers, and there is a litheness of limb that fits the terrain.

Across the road from Balnakeil House is a little ruined church with its attendant graveyard. As stated, these were all church lands at one time. Just inside the door of the church there is an interesting old tomb on the left. The lettering is weatherworn, but reads: 'Donald Makmurchor heir lyis low. Vais (was ill) to his friend, var to his foe, true to his maister in verd and vo 1623.'

The church dates from 1619, and has an old font, and is also the burial place of Rob Donn, an illiterate poet who has been referred to as the 'Burns of the North'.

Now take the short hop back to the junction where you turned left for Balnakeil. You are now in Durness, one of my favourite places in the whole world. Not just the scatter of houses that is Durness of course, but this whole area has left its brand on my soul. I first came here when I was about 14, and I just adored it. I'm not sure if it's because it is the far northwest of Scotland, and the romantic notions that that inspires inside me, or if it is the location itself. The scenery is untamed, wild and fabulous, sea, rocks, cliffs, moor, sand and sky, all jumbled up to make this such a special place. Turning the bike towards the north has always made me feel I was setting off on some fantastic adventure, and this is as far north as you can get. There is nothing else north of the coast except the waste of the sea, all the way to the ice of the North Pole, and many is the time I have walked the cliff tops on this rugged stretch and considered it.

The beaches are spectacular, as good as the most exotic ones I have seen in holiday brochures – just a pity that for most of the year you would be more likely to get frostbite than a suntan, but sometimes the sun does shine enough to make even a swim here seem viable.

The colour of the sea is amazing too. In one or two of the inlets, especially under the Sango Sands Hotel, it is a shade of bright green that has jumped out at me on every single visit. Just by the aforementioned hotel there is a tourist information office. Just prior to my last visit to Durness, two tourists walking on the beaches discovered a viking burial, shifting sands had partially uncovered him. He still had his short sword clasped in one hand. The information office had x-rays and photographs of the body, keeping the village up to date on the story.

A little further on, and you will notice a little car park on your left and the signs pointing the way to Smoo Cave. The river on the opposite side of the road suddenly disappears down a hole in the rock, and you may want to take a look at this first. You go down a path from the car park to reach the cave. In the breeding season, many fulmars nest on the cliff faces round the entrance to the cave, every little ledge seeming to have an occupant.

You will notice that people have been collecting stones from outside the mouth of the cave to write names or messages on the grassy slopes opposite. There were many here on my first visit, and it has never changed. Some of the stones and rocks involved must have formed a part of a multitude of letters over the years! The cave has three chambers, but only the outermost one is really accessible. As you approach the entrance it is like a great cleft in the rock, 203 feet long, 130 feet broad, and 33 feet high. It has a sandy floor, with the river that has come in from above running across it. A little walkway has been built to allow you to view the second chamber, and good floodlighting has been installed recently. The second chamber is full of water from wall to wall, but the walkway allows you to see the river coming in from the cleft above, dropping in a large waterfall into the chamber. There is a third chamber to the right of the waterfall that goes back another hundred feet and is full of stalagmites. This third cave was first explored in 1833, but is for specialists only. There are old stories told of Smoo Cave (probably from the Norse *smuga*, meaning cleft) that the Devil would lurk deep in its depths, and that narrow escapes had been made from his clutches, or that dogs venturing into its chambers would reappear hairless and trembling! It is a great place to visit though, and like the Corrieshalloch Gorge, it is one not to be missed. A short stiff climb back to the car park then, and we set off again, only this time we are heading east along Scotland's northern seaboard.

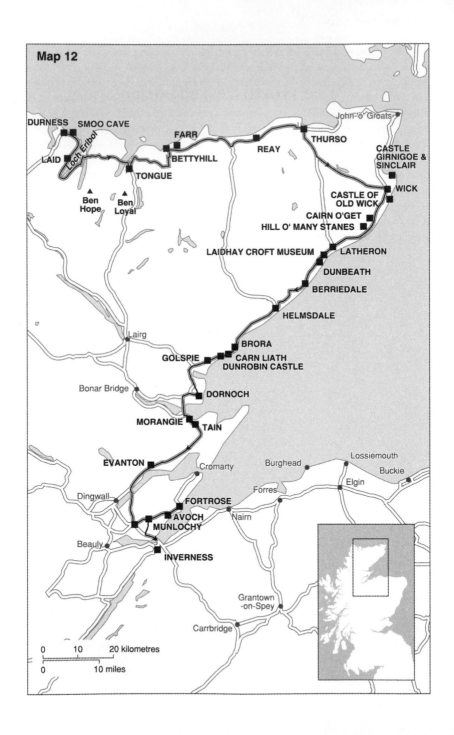

Map 12

CHAPTER TWELVE

The Northwest Frontier

ROUTE BEGINS AT DURNESS AND FOLLOWS THE NORTH COAST TO THURSO, ALONG TO
WICK, AND THEN DOWN THE A9 TO THE KESSOCK BRIDGE WITH A DEVIATION TO
FORTROSE IN THE BLACK ISLE.

FROM DURNESS, the A838 runs east for a mile or two, and you look down to
your left to glimpse some inviting little beaches that just cry out to be
walked and explored. At the small road leading off to Rispond, the main
route swings south to encircle Loch Eriboll, the biggest sea loch of this
north coast. As I look over this sheet of water, I can picture half a dozen
viking longships drawn up, sails furled, perhaps resting before negotiating
the tidal currents of Cape Wrath.

There are little houses and crofts dotted along the edge of the shore as we
drive south on this western bank, but they do little to intrude into the feeling of remoteness that this landscape can generate. Laid is the title of the
little cluster of houses that we drive through halfway down the loch, not
really big enough to be given even village status.

There have always been people ready to settle in this landscape though,
and a glance at any large-scale map of this area shows the remains of
brochs, cairns and early hut circles. The crew of HMS Hood spent some time
at Loch Eriboll prior to being sunk by the German battleship Bismark, and
the crew spelt out the word 'Hood' with stones on the hillside behind Laid.
Other crews followed suit, and several names have survived. Eriboll is a
particularly deep loch, and it saw much coming and going of shipping and
submarines during World War II. In fact, many German U-boats surrendered at Loch Eriboll.

You can walk up to the 'Hood letters' by a path beginning opposite the
little pier at Laid's Port na Con, and due west of these stands the remains of
an Iron Age wheelhouse. The name Eriboll, like many on this coast, has a
Norse origin, and basically means 'the farm on the sand'.

At the head of the loch the ground again becomes craggier, Strath Beag
(the small strath) leading away to the higher hills inland. The road curves
through the boggy terrain at the loch's head, and is then constricted under
Creag na Faoilinn as we again swing north. Already the landscape has
changed from that of Durness, and it will become noticeably softer as we
continue east.

The road follows this side of the loch for half of its length before swinging east. As the road begins to climb you will notice a little island, connected to the shore by a spit of land. This is Ard Neackie, where you would have caught the old ferry across the loch before the road was constructed in the 1890s. You will notice that there are an old house and four large stone structures built into the island itself. This is the old ferry house built in 1831 and its four attendant lime kilns. Much lime used to be produced here, and it could be loaded straight onto the ships.

We swing inland, but reach water again where the road crosses the River Hope, issuing out of Loch Hope. A little road cuts off to the south here, following the eastern shore of Loch Hope. It is a good access for an ascent of Ben Hope, Scotland's northernmost 'Munro', the name we give to a mountain over 3,000 feet. Just by the base of Ben Hope there are also the remains of a well-preserved broch right at the side of this road, called Dun Dornaigil.

We continue east on the A838, and cross the large headland between Loch Eriboll, and the next great inlet of the ocean, the Kyle of Tongue. This headland is known as A'Mhoine, which is Gaelic for 'the moss', and this is of course an apt description of this large stretch of desolate, mossy moorland. Ben Hope looks very fine, filling the views to the south, and another long-ridged mountain appears to its left. This is Ben Loyal, nothing to do with loyalty, incidentally, just a bad corruption of the Gaelic for elm tree hill. Ben Loyal is the subject of many a calendar, and its many peaks linked by its main ridge can look very impressive, belying its height and the relative ease of its ascent.

We begin the descent down to the Kyle of Tongue, similar to the Kyle of Durness in that it is shallow, sandy and very attractive, only this inlet has a bridge to take us speedily across to the village of Tongue itself.

You probably think that the unusual name Tongue is a corruption of something else in either Norse or Gaelic, but this is not the case – it actually means tongue! You will notice the eastern end of the bridge leads on to a projecting tongue-shaped spur of land. The vikings named this place Tunga as it was shaped like one, and the name has been corrupted back to English.

Tongue was a very remote community until Thomas Telford, that great engineer whose name has been mentioned several times in the last couple of chapters, built the first road coming here from the south in 1828. Before then, boat was the only way to gain access. The road east from Thurso followed in 1836, but it was not until 1894 that a road was constructed west to Durness. This road circled round the head of the Kyle of Tongue, before following the route you have just driven. Before that date you would have to have taken three separate ferries – across the Kyle here, then the River Hope, then Loch Eriboll!

The bridge across was constructed in 1971, and it is just over 200 yards long. There are parking places on the slipways leading to the bridge, which give access to the beaches below. The westernmost one has a memorial to the opening of the bridge. We come on to dry land at the village of Tongue itself. The road takes a twist as it runs through the village, first to the south, where you will see the ruins of Caisteal Bharraigh (Castle Varrich) standing on a spur of rock projecting into the Kyle. It is possible there has been a fortification of sorts on this spot since viking days, as there is mention of a castle 'Beruvik' in their sagas. The remains you see are from the 1500s, and were most likely built by the bishops of Caithness – a handy link to Balnakeil House near Durness. This would have made a great halfway house between Balnakeil and their other seat further east at Scrabster. The fact that this castle commands an important sea loch and the main north route would not be lost either.

The road swings north, and we join the A836 and continue to follow the Kyle. We turn east again at Coldbackie, a little village that has a beautiful sandy beach like so many on this coast. You turn a corner and these silvery beaches just jump right out at you, if you get my drift! The landscape can look so barren, and the contrast so great when you see these inviting little white sand havens, that they imbed themselves in your imagination. Every single one of them makes you think 'I'd love to spend an afternoon here on a warm, cloudless summer's day', but there won't be enough of those in Scotland to go round in my lifetime!

We have left the Highlands behind now, and much of what we travel through is featureless moorland for many miles to come. But it is Scotland, a different facet of her make-up, a different side to her personality.

We cross the back of the land again, and the next major north–south through-route we meet is at Strathnaver. A sign informs you of some of the attractions south of here on the Strathnaver Trail. These include chambered cairns, hut circles and standing stones, and give us an insight into the people who inhabited these glens in ancient times, but Strathnaver will always be synonymous with the Highland Clearances.

There were many villages and crofting communities in Strathnaver, over the 20 miles of it. In the early 1800s the Duke of Sutherland's factor, the execrated Patrick Sellar, appeared with his men, and burnt the houses, driving the people away to make room for more profitable sheep. This Duke of Sutherland is not to be confused with the original native line. This family came into the land, they were English and their name was Levenson-Gower. The name has become one of the most hated in the history of Scotland, and is like a black shadow standing over untold human misery. He drove some 15,000 men, women and children from Sutherland and Caithness, where his vast estates lay. These people were the children of Scotland, the seed of the Gael. They had been on this land since the last Ice Age retreated, but an incomer with money destroyed their world.

Incidentally, Levenson-Gower had the title Duke of Sutherland bestowed upon him by King William IV in London in 1833. Perhaps the memory of him as an oppressor that exists in the minds of Scots today is enough, but I hope that somehow he has had some sort of comeuppance in an afterlife for all the evil acts he committed. We make some terrible mistakes in Scotland, and the fact that we have no power to stop Englishmen holding positions of great power in our country have done us terrible injury in the past. And no doubt will in the future too. And it is made even worse by the fact that we have the ability to do something about it in a democratic manner, yet do not. We have no-one to blame but ourselves.

The road swings a little north here to reach the sea where the River Naver reaches salt water at Bettyhill. Bettyhill has a little museum, open in the summer months, that tells the story of the Strathnaver Clearances.

Bettyhill was originally a fishing and agricultural centre, but today is a little fishing and tourist resort on Torrisdale Bay. It has a good beach (no surprise there), backed by sand dunes. The name Bettyhill was coined by the Duke of Sutherland's wife Elizabeth in 1819, as some of the unfortunates cleared from Strathnaver came to the coast here to try and change their form of living from crofting to fishing.

As you drive through the village you will notice the pointed war memorial on top of a little knoll on your left, then you descend into a sheltered hollow where you will see Farr Church on your left. This church was built in 1774, and converted into the aforementioned Bettyhill Museum in the 1970s. There is also a Tourist Information Office at the roadside that is open seasonally. Park up and walk over to the old churchyard that contains Farr Church. There are some interesting old tombstones in this cemetery. Some are set into what looks like stone doorways. I've never seen this anywhere else. Don't miss the Farr Stone, a standing stone with some interesting knotwork and large Celtic cross carved upon it. It stands upright at the western end of the church. There is reckoned to have been a church on this site since 1223, and the first thing to strike you when reading the inscriptions on the gravestones is the number of MacKays buried here. This is the heartland of the old clanlands of the MacKays, and the museum deals with the clan in more depth.

We drive on, over the moory landscape. Another dozen miles and we come to Strathy, a scattered crofting community. Although small, Strathy boasts no less than four churches. Two are still used for their original function, and two have been converted. There is an unusual modern village hall, a striking building with a green roof. The Strathy Stone, probably dating from about AD 600, the work of early Christians, is housed within this hall, ensuring its survival.

The village came into being with the arrival of displaced tenants during the Clearances. Many emigrated from here to the colonies. The last manned lighthouse in Scotland is the Strathy Point Lighthouse. You can park at the car park nearby and walk the rest of the way if you so desire. It runs on electricity, was built in 1958, but was converted to automatic operation in 1996. The point on which the lighthouse stands, a little northwest of the village, has many caves, and there is even an eroded arch through the rock on the west side of the point.

A little further and we reach Melvich. Melvich has a good beach where the River Halladale enters the sea just east of the village. Botanists will be interested to know that the dunes hereabouts contain rare species of plant life such as Marshall's Eyebright and Round Leafed Eyebright.

Just outside Melvich there is a large boulder right at the side of the road that has a large split right through it. This traditionally marked the ancient boundary between the shires of Sutherland and Caithness in days gone by, although the border is further east today.

There is a local legend that the stone was split with a whip of the Devil's tail as he flew over in a fit of pique! Locals cannot pass the stone without saying 'Rabbits, rabbits, rabbits'. The reason for this is lost in antiquity!

We cross the River Halladale, where the A897 comes in from the south, but we continue on the A836 eastwards towards Thurso. We come into Reay (pronounced 'Ray'), the original seat of the chiefs of Clan MacKay, who used the name Lord Reay. Their castle was Dounreay, a little north-east of the village, and it is this castle that has given its name to the nuclear power station here. From the seat of the chiefs, this place has now become the area's biggest employer. It's most recognisable feature is the large, white, ball-shaped building, the original fast-breeder reactor, but this building is used as a store today. The place was begun in 1954, and there is a visitor centre run by the United Kingdom Atomic Energy Authority. The castle ruins stand within the perimeter fence of the modern Dounreay. It is an L-shaped building, built in the latter half of the 1500s by William Sinclair of Dunbeath. It was sold to the MacKays in 1624. Cromwell's men occupied the place in 1651, proving how well he held Scotland, as we mostly talked of his occupations and deprivations in Scotland while travelling up the coast of the southeast. The castle was inhabited in one form or another until 1861.

After we pass Dounreay, you will notice that, unusually, there are no hedges separating the fields. Flagstones are used, thin slate-like flagstones, standing thin edge to thin edge in rows. This will be a constant sight over the next part of your journey. Locals have always used what there is to hand, and there are plenty of these thin slates here and not a lot of vegetation, so thin slates of Caithness flagstone are the order of the day. It's windy on this north coast too, and a couple of wind turbines on this stretch prove the point.

Another few miles and the quite major town of Thurso appears at the head of Thurso Bay. It is the biggest habitation we have seen since Fort William, a few hundred miles ago now on our travels. The name is again Norse, meaning 'River of the God Thor', and the town does indeed sit astride the River Thurso. The ruined castle at the opposite bank of the river is visible as we descend into the town.

It is a bit strange to come into a place with so much bustle after the sparsely populated mountain-then-moor landscape we have passed through. Factories, housing estates, then into the older town centre. You will notice that the sign that welcomes you informs that Thurso is the birthplace of Sir William Smith, born in 1854, and founder of the Boys' Brigade, an organisation similar to Scouting movements in other countries.

Thurso, of course, has all the facilities of any of the other large towns of Scotland, and though we are right on Scotland's north coast, we have again entered country that has a lowland feel. It has the usual Scots town centre, the buildings constructed from the local stone, giving it a sturdy appearance. If you follow the signs for Wick through the town centre, this will eventually bring you towards the River Thurso. This will, of course, be the oldest part of the town, and was once a spot where dragon-prowed ships would be pulled up on the shingle. Take the left turn immediately before the river, and follow the road down till you eventually see the ruins of St Peter's Kirk, on your left. It was founded 1220 by Gilbert Murray, Bishop of Caithness, but most of the stonework visible today is of the 1600s. It was closed to worship in 1832.

Across the river stand the ruins of the castle. To get within a short walk of this building, drive back to the bridge, cross it, take the first left at the traffic lights, then take another left just down this road. This takes you through a few factory units then out to the riverside where you can park and walk the last stretch.

Although this building looks quite ancient, it only dates from 1872–8, its baronial style and rough stone making it look like it is of an earlier era. It is on the site of an earlier turreted fortalice erected in 1660 by George, sixth Earl of Caithness. It was in this building that Sir John Sinclair was born. He was an eminent agriculturist, and compiled the *Old Statistical Account of Scotland*.

There was a fortification of some sort on this site since earliest times though, as King William the Lion besieged the Jarl of Caithness here in 1196, and earlier vikings probably picked out this site prior to that.

If you want to continue on foot past Thurso Castle for the best part of a mile, you will come across an unusual little angular building, with several little towers. This is Harold's Tower. It is reputed to mark the grave of

Harold, Norse Jarl of Caithness, and grandson of Rognvald. He was killed in the events of 1196. The Sinclair family built this structure over the site and have since used it as a burial place.

Back to the traffic lights up at the bridge, where we turn left onto the A882, signpostesd Wick. It is about 20 miles to Wick from Thurso, following the dale of the River Thurso, then passing Loch Watten on your left, before following the Wick River into the town of that name.

On this stretch, there are many stretches of farmland, the field perimeters delineated with Caithness flagstones, standing upright in their rows like an army of soldiers. The A9 cuts off right, taking a more direct route south, but we continue in a southeasterly direction on the A882.Loch Watten appears on the left, then we come into the village of Watten itself. The sign informs you that this is the birthplace of Alexander Bain, Inventor of the Electric Clock. We cross the Wick River at the far side of the village. There is a standing stone over to the left. This area is dotted with reminders of prehistory. As it is far away from the big cities of the central belt, more have survived. A glance at an Ordnance Survey map will show a plethora of cairns, brochs, hut circles, standing stones, both singular and not only in groups, but in rows too. We will visit a few after Wick, but I recommend that if that era is your bag, get the appropriate large-scale maps of this area, and dive into a pleasure dome of artefacts!

There is a large boggy area with many reed beds to the left of the road now, but it is a straightforward run into the town of Wick itself. The name Wick is a corruption of *vik*, the Norse for a bay, and as you can imagine, the town surrounds Wick Bay, where the Wick River meets the sea. The coast north and south of the town is very rocky, and there are indentations of the sea into these cliffs that are narrow and have steep sides, and are known as 'goes', hence the reason surrounding villages have such names as Papigoe and Staxigoe. Strangely, the Ordnance Survey calls them 'geos'. I've noticed that name changes can take place in Scotland. In old books from the early 1800s, firths in Scotland are called 'friths', as in the Frith of Forth or Frith of Tay! Perhaps the 'you say *goe*, I say *geo*, let's call the whole thing off' is similar.

The first mention of Wick is around the year 1140, when Vik is mentioned in Norse sagas. Its modern history begins in 1589, when it was created a Royal Burgh by charter of James VI. The town centre consists of the route of the A99 running north to south across the river, with many side streets branching off. The town was a hugely success fishing port at one time, and incredible as it may seem, in 1862 there were 1122 boats fishing out of the harbour here! By 1893 the number of boats had dwindled to 318, but they still at that time employed 2220 fishermen and boys, and 1772 other people were directly connected with the trade.

The oldest buildings hereabouts are the three castles in the Wick vicinity. That is, apart from the remnants of prehistory with which this area is littered.

To the north of the town stand the ruins of Castle Sinclair and Castle Girnigoe. (There's that goe word again). These two lie very close together, and although they are known by separate names, Castle Sinclair is actually a later addition to the earlier Castle Girnigoe.

Girnigoe was the chief seat of the Earldom of Caithness, and the whole extent of what amounts to roughly the whole county today came under the sway of this castle. It was built by the Sinclair family, major landowners in Scotland, whose name has been synonymous with Caithness, throughout its colourful history.

William Sinclair was made Earl of Caithness by James II in 1455. He was Earl of Orkney too, but he was made to resign that earldom to James III in 1470.

The fourth Earl, George Sinclair, believed that his son, John, was trying to assassinate him, and so had him imprisoned in Girnigoe in 1571 until his death in 1578. We will come across George the fourth Earl again, in Helmsdale, a little further south.

The unfortunate John had a son called George who inherited the Earldom on his grandfather's death, and he built the newer castle on the site that it known today as Castle Sinclair. There was trouble between the Sinclairs and the Campbells in the late 1600s, which led to the castle being abandoned, and it has stood ever since as a reminder of the once-awesome powers of the Sinclair family in those days.

It is worth visiting for its situation alone, standing on a sharp spur projecting into the sea. The castle, gripping the contours of the rock, is long and thin in consequence. When I see castles such as this I have always marvelled at the abilities of the builders and masons who constructed them. I wonder how it was done. Did they use some sort of projecting scaffolding? Getting all those thousands of stones into place using ropes and muscle power and basic hoists is amazing. Did they use written plans or was there just a man in charge who said 'leave a gap for a window here'?

On the way back into Wick you will pass the Caithness Glass factory with its large showroom. They make all sorts of figurines and curios that are exported all over the world.

To the south of the town is the Castle of Old Wick. It is signposted, but I found locating it difficult and had to ask directions as I did not have a large-scale map with me to give me the route. This castle is on a similar layout to Girnigoe, standing on a projecting spur, but only the remains of a tower stands here, the rest of the ranges of buildings all but gone, only their footings remaining.

It is not sure who the builder of this castle was. It could have been Harold, Jarl of Caithness, in the 1160s, or it may have been the Cheyne family. The Cheynes were quite a famous name up to the Wars of Independence in Wallace and Bruce's time, one of them being Lord Chamberlain of Scotland in the 1260s.

In 1526 this castle was sold to the Oliphant family. They had terrible trouble with the Sinclairs, already mentioned as holding much sway in this area. The Sinclairs, with their castle to the north of the town at Girnigoe, seemed to have a problem with the Oliphants' presence. In 1569 there was a brawl between the two families in the town of Wick which ended with the Sinclairs besieging the castle here. The Oliphants had no food or water inside, obviously because they were not prepared for such an eventuality, and had to surrender the castle after eight days. The Sinclairs eventually took over the place, but why it was abandoned and allowed to fall into ruin is not recorded.

It is a short jump from the castle of Old Wick back to the A99 just a little inland, where we turn south. For the next stretch of our journey the road hugs the coast, and the sea becomes as large a part of the scenery as the land.

We pass Loch Hempriggs on our right, and a mile or two on and we hit the village of Ulbster. At the south end of the village you will see a sign pointing down a minor road on your right, marked 'Cairn O' Get'. A few hundred yards down this road, there is another sign, and you park here and cross into the field. Cairn O' Get itself is a passage grave about 25 yards long. Unfortunately, the roof has fallen in, but you still get the general idea of its function and construction. The site was excavated in 1866 and it was found to contain cremated and unburnt bone, flints and pottery. There were seven complete burials too. It dates from sometime between 3000 and 4000 BC. The Ordnance Survey Landranger Map, Sheet 12, is a handy tool for this area, as it shows a plethora of early remains all within a mile or two of Cairn O' Get.

Continuing on the A99, not long after Ulbster, the road takes a little turn inland at Bruan. There is a church on the right. Just before the road takes a tight turn left again, you will notice there is a little walled area on your left, with what looks like a grassy mound standing within it. This is the remains of a broch, an early defensive structure, but it is now completely grass covered. Unfortunately, there is nowhere close by to park, so if you want a look at these remains you will have to find somewhere to pull off road and walk back.

Another mile or two and keep your eyes peeled for the signs for the 'Hill O' Many Stanes', which has always been a favourite early site of mine. It is very unusual and easy of access, so don't miss it. On my last visit, as I turned right up the little access road, there was a field full of cows on my left. I had to double-take as I noticed in the middle of the cows all grazing there was a llama, happily grazing away too, amidst its bovine companions. Perhaps the farmer just fancied owning a llama.

A couple of hundred yards along this side road there is a parking place and a little gate lies on your left. Go through this gate, and the Hill O' Many Stanes is just on the other side. It is exactly as its name suggests – many, many standing stones covering the hillside, the largest only about a yard high. There are 22 rows, containing about 200 stones, but it is thought that there were once more than 700. It is a peculiar wee place, all those stones jutting up from the scrubby heath, and the sea off to the east only giving more mystery and colour to the whole affair. *Why?* of course, is the obvious question, and all the usual theories apply. It was perhaps a complex lunar observatory, or maybe used to chart the seasons in some way. Our early ancestors seem to have been quite a complex lot, and when one sees building projects on this scale, teamwork was obviously one of their strong points.

There is so much we take for granted today, in this age of electricity and electronics, and we tend to forget how much technology accelerated through the 1800s and 1900s. Before the industrial revolution, life had been agrarian and had not really changed drastically in millennia. The first time I visited the Isle of Coll at the age of ten, I remember that I saw men walk on the moon for the first time – grainy black and white images on a television in the ship's kitchen, yet there was no electricity in the croft I stayed in. Little gas lamps for when it got dark, and a transistor radio for entertainment. The two main names in that whole affair were of Scots descent of course. Armstrong and Nixon. Both names from the Borders of Scotland, but what I'm really trying to say is that we are of a generation that takes all this technology for granted. It is worth taking five minutes out at this spot and thinking of the people who worked together here to create this structure. I wonder if there was one guy in particular who had the whole idea of the seasons sussed out and directed where each stone should go, or was it done over many years of watching the movements of the sun and moon? Over 4,000 years have passed since these stones were erected, and it is a nice place to pause and consider – and the view out is easy on the eye too.

Back on the A9, and just a little on you will see the local war memorial in a little fenced area in the middle of a field on your right. I've sheltered in the little adjacent bus stop from the rain before.

On to Latheron, and as you approach the village you will notice a church, whitewashed and trim, down a little road on your left. It stands in an airy elevated site in the fields sloping down towards the sea. This is the Latheron Parish Church, now converted into the Clan Gunn Museum. It is open yearly from the beginning of June until the end of September. Even if the place is shut, it is worth a look at the old graveyard surrounding the place. It is crammed with old stones, many of them lying flat, and they are so numerous it is like walking on a pavement in places. Strangely, there is hardly a one with an inscription remaining. Perhaps the proximity to the sea, and the beatings these headlands can take in rough weather are partially to blame. The village of Latheron stands a little uphill and to the south. One the hill above there is an old tower, and for some reason this contained the church bells which would be rung to announce the start of services. Between this tower and the village proper are a couple of standing stones.

Carrying on through Latheron brings us straight into Latheronwheel. Keep your eyes open for the arch on the left-hand side of the road constructed from whalebones. These were taken from a whale that was unlucky enough to be washed ashore here in 1869.

Latheronwheel has a quaint little harbour. A little further and you will come across Laidhay Croft Museum. It stands gable-end on to the left-hand side of the road. It is a typical longhouse that was once a familiar sight in rural Scotland. It is called a longhouse as it contains the living quarters for the family, the byre and the stable, all in one long slim house. The animals would be brought indoors into one half of the house, merely fenced off from the family living in the other half. It would be very smelly, but it would also be very warm, the heat from the animals providing an early central heating system! This particular example of this kind of dwelling came into the ownership of a family by the name of Bethune in 1842, and it remained under their ownership until 1968. It is open from Easter till the end of October each year, and the place provides an insight into the everyday life of people in the rural areas of Scotland in the 1700s and 1800s.

One thing that I have noticed as I drive through Caithness on my travels, are the number of empty properties dotted here and there on the landscape, especially old farm buildings complete to the wallhead. You just would not see such a thing much further south, as these would have been snapped up and made into modern homes. I guess this part of the country is just a little too remote from the most heavily populated belts of Scotland for the situation to be any different.

From Laidhay we run down towards the village of Dunbeath. The road used to drop right down to cross the Dunbeath Water on the old bridge, but a modern high-rise bridge has been constructed to speed traffic through. It is a little unfortunate that it dissects the old village, as it is an interesting wee place, and well worth a look-see.

Dunbeath's most famous son was the writer Neil Miller Gunn. Neil's books like *Highland River* and *The Silver Darlings* are based in the strath of the Dunbeath Water, and capture the landscape perfectly. He was born in a house on the north side of the village in November 1891. This semidetached property is next to the grocer's shop and has a commemorative fan-light above the door.

A little downstream from the old bridge, which carried the A9 before the construction of its modern big brother, lies the Well Pool. In his book *Highland River*, Neil has the boy-hero, Kenn, battle to catch a giant salmon here. Neil M Gunn died in 1973, but on the centenary of his birth, 8 November 1991, a memorial sculpture was erected at Dunbeath harbour. Fittingly, it depicts nine-year-old Kenn carrying home the salmon caught in the Well Pool. It is an atmospheric and moving piece. 'Of all that befell Kenn afterwards, of war and horror and love and scientific triumphs, nothing ever had quite the splendour and glory of that struggle by the Well Pool' – *Highland River*.

The sculptor was Mr Alex Mann of Halkirk near Thurso, and it was cast in bronze by an Edinburgh company.

The strath of the river has many sites associated with Neil's work scattered along its length, and there is a storyboard just to the north of the old bridge. There is also a Heritage Centre in the southern half of the village, signposted from the A9.

Also just south of the village, harled white, and standing atop the cliffs, is Dunbeath Castle. There is mention of a castle here as far back as 1428, but most of what is visible are later additions. For much of its history it has been under the sway of the Sinclair family, already pointed out as having much influence in matters historical in this area. It was captured by Montrose in 1650, before his last battle, and his capture at Ardvreck Castle which we have already visited. It is a private residence.

Onwards, south on the A9. A few miles and we approach the Berriedale Braes. The road plunges to cross the Berriedale Water in a series of hairpin bends. At the foot of the hill stand the old smithy and the post office building, both decorated with stags' antlers. Near the bridge over the Berriedale Water, there are two marker stones showing the height of flood waters in 1896 and 1912. At the mouth of the river, on the south side, stand the scant ruins of Berriedale Castle, dating from the early 1300s. It was built by the Cheyne family, but was for a while in the hands of the Oliphants who owned the Castle of Old Wick.

The countryside round here is very rough, and the castle occupants probably did most of their travelling by sea. The castle stands on a defensive crag, and on the connection to the landward side, you can see a hand-carved defensive ditch that would originally have been spanned by some sort of drawbridge.

As you begin to climb the hill at the opposite side of the river, you will notice that there are sand-traps, designed to halt runaway vehicles on these steep gradients. I seem to remember there were quite a few of these apparent on the main road here when I was younger, but the road has been much improved over the years.

From Berriedale, the landscape takes on a wilder, hillier aspect, the road cutting slightly further inland to follow the contours.

I remember once driving south here in what had been fine sunny weather, and I drove straight into a haar here on the bike. A haar is a heavy sea fog, and this one was freezing! The screen of the bike froze, and I had to keep wiping my visor to rid it of its frosty coating. The cold cut right to my bones in minutes. Thank God for a bike with panniers to carry extra clothing.

As we pass the Ord of Caithness we actually re-enter Sutherland, which encircles Caithness to the west and south, and the landscape becomes a little rougher with the change of shire too. The road twists and turns, and we drop into the environs of Helmsdale, where the River Helmsdale empties out of Strath Kildonan to the sea.

I was in Helmsdale recently, as I wanted to see Helmsdale Castle. I had seen old photos of it, and old prints too, and these showed the castle standing above the river. It was built in 1488, but an incident took place here in 1567 which had intrigued me and made me want to visit the place. John, the eleventh Earl of Sutherland and his pregnant wife were poisoned by his aunt, Isobel Sinclair. She carried out this murder at the instigation of George, fourth Earl of Caithness, so that her own son would inherit the Earldom of Sutherland. This George was the same man who imprisoned his son in Girnigoe Castle, obviously a strange and devious character.

Unfortunately for Isobel, although she killed the lord and his wife, the 15-year-old heir was out hunting and so escaped to inherit the earldom. A strange twist of fate took place though, and Isobel's own son, who she intended to benefit from this secret plot, called in and partook of a glass of the poisoned wine, and he too died horribly.

Isobel Sinclair was brought to Edinburgh to be tried for this murder, but poisoned herself after the death sentence was passed, saving herself from the execution. Perhaps she did this to save the evil George from being implicated, or feared what he was capable of. George, of course, walked away from all this unscathed.

In light of all these twists and turns, I really wanted to see the place. I had travelled through Helmsdale before, but I could not remember ever spotting the castle. I parked up in Helmsdale, on the north side of the river, and walked over the road bridge to the south, looking up and downstream to try and spot it. As I reached the end of the bridge, I noticed there was a little information centre on the right hand side, and as I walked towards this for a wee look round, I noticed there was a concrete block with a plaque inserted. I paused to read it:

Helmsdale Castle was built near here in 1488. The ruins were removed in 1970 to make way for the new road and bridge.

Shocked. That's all I can say. I wondered why I could not see the castle as I crossed the bridge, and this explained it. Couldn't more of a curve have been put into the bridge construction to try and preserve what was left of the castle? I walked away very saddened. Next time I'm in Helmsdale I'll need to ask some of the locals, especially the older generation who grew up with the castle in situ, what they thought of it being bulldozed away. All that remains of it now is a broken fireplace lintel with a Latin inscription that is on show within the Timespan Centre in the village. Timespan is, as its name suggests, a museum of the history of this area, and it has had a long and not altogether trouble-free history.

The name Helmsdale means exactly that. To the vikings it was the Valley of the Rudder, or *Hjelmunsdal*, hence Helmsdale. The Strath of Kildonan which carries the River Helmsdale, suffered terribly during the Highland Clearances, and you can discover more about all this at Timespan.

There is a plan underway to erect a lasting monument to the memory of those Scots so cruelly turned off the land they had known for many genera-tion. It is hoped that a monument will be erected on a hilltop behind Helmsdale. It will not right wrongs. But it will remind Scots the world over that we are trying to learn. And, that we have not forgotten. There is a model of the intended monument inside the little information centre I men-tioned, at the south end of the bridge. It will be on a grand scale, and it depicts a Highland family, huddled against not only the cold, but the unknown, clad in the dress of the period. It will stand higher than the statue of the Duke of Sutherland that is on Ben Bhraggie, 18 miles to the south, and I will talk more of this other statue when we reach it on this tour.

The Strath of Kildonan was the scene of a gold rush in the 1860s. At its height there were some 3,000 prospectors settled on the river banks here, and even today many gold panners try their luck in the streams of this area.

It all began in 1868 when a local man, who had spent time prospecting in Australia, found a nugget, and 'gold fever' set in, with many staking claims. A shanty town set up by miners, gloried in the name of Baile-an-Or, which is Gaelic for the Village of Gold.

My disappointment at the fate of the castle here was somewhat relieved when I visited an eaterie in Helmsdale, and had local venison pan-fried in Drambuie whisky liqueur. Even now I can close my eyes and taste it, the thought getting me all slebbery – as we say in Scotland!

Sorry, all you veggies.

Over the river and onwards, and we follow the A9 down the coast towards Brora. As you enter Brora, keep an eye open for the sign to the Clynelish distillery. The distillery is off to your right, has a visitor centre, and you may want to imbibe some, purely as a matter of research. Clynelish, strangely, tastes more like an island malt. The first distillery in Brora was set up in 1819.

As you come down into the centre of town you will come to the River Brora. (You will have noticed that most of the communities you have visited in Caithness and Sutherland are all at river mouths. Partly viking influence, partly the result of the Clearances, where the people who remained moved to the coastline to fish as an alternative to the farming they knew).

A right turn just before the river will take you to the Heritage Centre. Cross the river and take the first left and it will take you down to the harbour area. There is an old ice-house down here that has been restored. The local kids have helped out with this. At one time ice was broken up and taken out of the river, and this curved, thick-walled, stone building would have been packed with the stuff. Cold keeps cold, if you get my drift, and they would use this ice throughout the summer months to pack in with the herring caught to keep it fresh. Early refrigeration. It is on the left of the road, next to the river.

At one time Brora was famous for its salt production. Salt pans were set up here as early as 1598. Big pans, which would be filled with salt water, fires lit underneath, and the water would boil off, leaving the salt. Simple as that. Salt production reached its height in 1818, when 400 tons of the stuff was produced here. Salt would be used for fishing, of course, salted herring being famous. Not a shred remains of this industry unfortunately, but it is always interesting to be in a place and know what has gone before.

On out of Brora and we continue to follow the A9. A few miles out of Brora, keep your eyes peeled for the signs for Carn Liath. Carn Liath means 'grey cairn', and this ancient broch is right on the left-hand side of the road, but there is a parking area on the immediate right. If you walk to the southern end of this parking area, a path takes you across the A9, and back to the broch itself.

It perhaps does not look like much on approach, but this is a brilliantly preserved site with much to see. The entrance door is at the opposite side, and once inside you will see that all the basic details are still apparent. Brochs were circular defensive structures, built in the last few centuries BC. They had stairways and galleries built into the thickness of the walls, and an open central area. You can still walk up the stairs, built two millennia ago, and look down from the top, over the surrounding fields. When I last walked up the stairs in the thickness of the walling, I had a heavy leather jacket on, made of horsehide, and it is like body armour. I am probably a good bit wider than the men that built these structures too, and as I squeezed my way up, I dislodged a stone from the wall. I put it back in place, of course, but I felt very guilty that they had built this 2,000 years ago, and that stone had been in place all that time, then I came along and dislodged it. Sorry, broch-builder man! Again though, it is the vast number of stones and the hours it must have taken in total to put all this together that is mind-boggling. Millions of stones involved, and all put together with no cement.

Something unusual here is the number of out-buildings, built around the original structure, still in a tolerable state of repair. Of course, there are information boards telling you the story of the place, and a visit should hammer home the abilities of our forebears. We are lucky that there is such a site to learn from, and that it has survived so well, on what has always been a major route.

Perhaps there is a certain amount of irony in the fact that, only a short hop from this memorial of the endemic people of this land, stands a building that will forever be associated with an incomer who did his best to destroy it.

Just a little further down the A9 and you will see the entrance to the driveway of Dunrobin Castle on your left. The castle, like so many attractions in Scotland, is open to the public, Easter till October. It has 189 rooms, making it the largest house in the northern Highlands. There is a large collection of furniture, pictures, china and other objets d'art. There is an old towerhouse at the core of this large building, which may date back to the 1300s, but Dunrobin has been extended greatly over the centuries.

From some angles it looks almost Disneyesque! As you approach down the driveway the work before you is due to the endeavours of Sir Charles Barry in 1835. He was responsible for the Houses of Parliament in London among his other architectural achievements. Dunrobin Castle is the seat of the Dukes of Sutherland, and it was the first Duke, who attained the title through marriage, who was the man responsible for the clearances in this part of the Highlands. His minions, Patrick Sellar and James Loch, were the men who actually carried out his orders to clear the people off the land, burning their houses as they were thrown outside, so that the land was free for the more profitable sheep. We need the control of our own destiny, of our own people in Scotland, so that this succession of people not of our blood who have decided our fate, is severed once and for all:

Once our valleys were ringing with sounds of our children singing, but now sheep bleat in the evenings, and shielings are empty and broken.

The exit road from Dunrobin brings you out on the edge of the village of Golspie. As you enter the village you cross the bridge over the Golspie Burn. Just upstream is the old bridge, so park so you can take a walk onto it. On the apex of this old bridge is a memorial to Clan Sutherland in the form of a tall stone. It bears a plaque that says:

The chief of the Sutherlands summons the victorious Clan Sutherland to the head of the little bridge.

There is also a Gaelic inscription cut into the stonework, but it is really worn and I could not make it all out.

Upstream from here, the Golspie Burn runs through the picturesque Dunrobin Glen, and it has nice walks with attractive waterfalls.

As you drive into the village, you pass the old whitewashed church on your right. It was built in 1738. I was reading recently in an old gazetteer that in 1891, Golspie had a population of 1451, of whom 713 were fluent Gaelic speakers. I wonder what the number would be today.

Golspie has a nice beach – and a swimming pool! I wonder where we last passed a town with a swimming pool?

As you pass through the town you will come to a little open area on your left, the sea behind. There are some information boards here, and an old barometer that is set into a cairn facing the sea. It is a Fitroy's Coast Barometer, made in Edinburgh. Rising above the town here is Beinn a' Bhragaidh, more popularly written on maps as Ben Bhraggie, which is more like its English pronunciation. Atop this hill is a large statue on a plinth, visible from many miles around. This is the statue of the first Duke of Sutherland, he responsible for the 15,000 men, women and children cleared from his estates. The statue and plinth are 100 feet high, and the hill itself rises to 13,00 feet. There is a footpath to the top, signposted in the town itself.

The statue was erected in 1834, a year after the Duke's death. I know you will be surprised to learn that the plaque states that the statue was raised 'by a mourning and grateful tenantry' to 'a judicious, kind and liberal landlord'. Ironic indeed.

Feelings are still strong in the north, where this statue is concerned. Many cries for its demolition have been heard over the years, and the gloomy memories of the Clearances are still strong in the mind of the modern Gael. During the Second World War, Canadians were based in this district, and they made plans to blow the statue to smithereens. After all, these Canadians were the children of those generations cleared from the land, and we Scots may make stupid mistakes, but we have long memories.

Still I hear whispers that it should be toppled, and I once saw an exhibition in Inverness where artists made images of the statues, and added their own ideas of how to make it an object of ridicule. But I want the statue to stand. A jumble of boulders scattered on a hillside means nothing. That pillar of ignominy atop Beinn Bhragaidh for all to gaze upon, is a constant reminder to us all. A reminder of the vanity of one who has wealth and power over Scots, who is not of our race. And a reminder to Scotland to learn from its past, and for its people to never let the like happen again.

Strangers will always enquire who this man is, mounted atop a plinth, looking over the landscape he decimated, and locals will retell the story and never forget.

And I hope the statue of the 'cleared' family eventually rises above Helmsdale a little north. It will stand a little higher, and the Duke here will be a target for their accusing eyes.

The A9 continues to Loch Fleet, a large tidal lagoon, famous for the amount of species of bird life that inhabits its environs. The road crosses four arches and sluices at the northern side, then continues on over a large embankment called the Mound. It is 1,000 yards long, was built in 1816, and it cost £12,500 to construct. Just as you drive onto the Mound, there is a little slip road down to a car parking area on your right. This area has information boards and good views. On the seaward side of the Mound there are huge sand-flats that serve as a stopover point for as many as 20,000 wildfowl at a time, and to the landward side there is marsh and a plantation of older trees that serves as home to many smaller species of bird life. A total of 172 different species of birds have been recorded here, so it is a must for all you ornithologists out there!

The arches and sluices where you cross on to the Mound are famous as a salmon run in season, and people gather to watch these mighty fish make their way through to their spawning grounds upstream.

I'm afraid I feel sorry for the salmon. It crosses our vast oceans, then makes its way back to the river where it was spawned, to try and regenerate its species, only to have a pause for a snack and suddenly realises it has a hook in its mouth. I can't abide fishing for sport; it just seems such a terrible waste of time that could be better spent, but perhaps that's because I'm a Pisces, and I hate to see my brothers being treated so (man).

Cross the Mound, and continue on the A9 for another couple of miles until you see the turn-off on the left, the B1068 for Dornoch. There is a junction of a minor road immediately before the B1068, so watch you don't take this in error – I have. Dornoch is only a mile or two from the A9, and we will be taking a wee circular diversion here that will bring us back onto the A9 shortly.

The B1068 comes to a junction with the A949 right on the edge of town, and it is the A949 we will be taking back to the A9.

I think Dornoch is very attractive. A lovely wee place, and loads of things to see in a town of not much more than 1,000 people. Drive into the centre of the place and park anywhere. It is best to go for a wee walk, and the first thing to visit is the cathedral. The most northerly cathedral in Scotland, no less.

It was founded by Bishop Gilbert de Moravia, 1222–45, but it has undergone many changes over the centuries. De Moravia can be translated into the surname Murray in modern English, and there was a clan feud between the Murrays of Dornoch and the MacKays of Strathnaver in 1570, which resulted in the cathedral being burnt, and its nave being destroyed. A new nave was constructed in 1835–7, on the ruins of the original, and the church was plastered internally. This plaster was removed in 1924, showing much of the original stonework, and giving the place the look it has today. Although I think there is an austere look to the place, the stained glass is very good, and brightens the place up a bit.

The cathedral was originally dedicated to the Virgin Mary, or the Madonna as she is known. It is, I suppose, fitting that the pop star Madonna was married to Guy Ritchie here in 2001, her son Rocco being christened here in the process too. It caused quite a furore in this little town, with journalists caught trying to hide in the organ assembly and such like. Shows the lassie has a bit of taste, I suppose, being married in Scotland, even if it was January, and bloody freezing!

I am told that no fewer than 16 Earls of Sutherland lie buried in the south transept, although there are no serried ranks of sarcophagi as you would perhaps hope.

In the churchyard, lying flat and embedded in a stone, is an old Scots ell, which was used during market days to measure out cloth.

Across the road from the cathedral there is a very picturesque row of traditional Scottish-looking buildings. There is Dornoch Castle, which is now a hotel, the old town jail, and some gift shops.

Dornoch Castle was built as a palace for the bishop of the cathedral. It also suffered during the feud of 1570 when the cathedral was burnt. It was remodelled in 1570, although there are some vestiges of the original work of the 1200s. The building was allowed to decay in the 1700s, then was restored in 1810–14. When the change to a hotel was made in the 1970s, a new wing was added.

Dornoch's golf courses on the links are among the most famous in the world, and it is not just modern golfers who think this. Sir Robert Gordon wrote in 1630: 'About this town, along the sea coast, there are the fairest and largest links or green feilds of any pairt of Scotland, fitt for archery, goffing, ryding, and all other exercise'.

On the way to the links from the centre of the village, keep you eyes open for the Witch's Stone. It stands in a garden of a house right on the edge of the golf course. The stone has the date 1722 carved upon it and highlighted in white, although the actual event which this stone commemorates happened in 1727. Janet Home, a local woman, was tried for witchcraft and was tried and convicted. Her sentence was that she should be burned to death in a tar barrel on this spot. She was the last woman to undergo this hellish charge in Scotland. And the charge read out? It was claimed that she had transformed her daughter into a pony, jumped on her back and ridden off on her to have her shod by the devil. And supposedly intelligent men listened to this evidence and declared her guilty. Witch-burnings are a huge stain on Scotland's history, made even worse by the fact that most of the fascination with this 'crime' was promoted by King James VI of Scotland and I of England. The King James Version of the Bible was due to this same monarch, and almost every Bible you open the world over has his name on the flyleaf. Bizarre!

He 'wrote' the modern bible, and liked to torture and burn innocent women as a wee sideline. The fact that he scuttled down to London when he inherited the English title and based himself there, largely ignoring Scotland afterwards, has never endeared him to me anyway.

But the fact remains that if I had supernatural powers of such a calibre as Janet Home, the last thing I would do is turn my daughter into a horse and have the devil shoe her. My daughter, first of all, would give me a good slap for being so stupid, and for not making a point of sussing out winning lottery numbers in advance or similar.

I could always magic up a motorcycle and ride it off to have the devil fit new tyres, I suppose. Doesn't really have much of a Satanic ring to it though.

Out of Dornoch on the A949 already mentioned, back to the A9, where we turn left, the road now signposted for Inverness.

A mile or two and we reach the Dornoch Firth, with its modern causeway cutting out a long journey inland to Bonar Bridge to cross the water. The great firths that penetrate Scotland here, the Dornoch, Cromarty and Beauly, have now all got causeways or bridge across them, and the journey times to the far northeast have been hugely shortened since I first drove them. It used to be as far by road from Glasgow to Inverness as it was from Inverness to Thurso, but a good 60–70 miles have been shorn off the northern leg of this drive by the Firths being crossed. This causeway over the Dornoch brings us onto dry land close to Morangie and here you will see signs directing you to the world-famous Glenmorangie distillery, which has its own visitor centre. Handcrafted by the 'sixteen men of Tain', Glenmorangie is the most popular single malt whisky in Scotland itself.

On crossing the Dornoch Firth, we have entered Ross-shire, so this is a little like home to me, and by some strange twist I am partial to Glenmorangie too. To be quite honest I have never come across a single Scotch whisky that I am not partial to. And I should point out that it should be pronounced mor-angy, like orangy, and not angie, as in the lassie's name!

It is then the shortest of hops to the road off for Tain. You can take a jaunt through Tain and go straight back on to the A9, as the town sits right in a bend of the main route.

As Tain overlooks the southern shore of the Dornoch Firth, its name may have a Norse root. It is probably a corruption of the word *thing*, meaning a place of council or assembly. The town stands on a bank above the low ground surrounding the firth, and it is an airy place with some fine stone buildings. As you drive in towards the town centre, look for the signs for the railway station. It is off to your left at the bottom of the slope on which the town sits. Pass the railway station, then a little bridge crosses the tracks, and the ruins of St Duthus Chapel appear on the left, surrounded by a beautifully landscaped graveyard. There are no real architectural features remaining, just four ruined walls, but I will tell you some of its interesting history, and you can walk round it and admire the views to the trees of this graveyard, and to the sand and firth beyond.

This chapel is said to be on the exact site of the birth of St Duthus, born about AD 1000, styled 'Confessor of Ireland and Scotland'. He died in Armagh in Ireland in 1065, and his body was transported to Tain for burial in 1265, and this building raised above his remains. It became famous as a sanctuary, a place where people could come to claim the protection of the church.

We now return to a much earlier part of this book, back to Strath Fillan, and the battle that took place at Dalry, where King Robert the Bruce had the Brooch of Lorne snatched from his person. At this point in his campaign, during 1307, Bruce had his womenfolk with him, but Dalry, and the near escape occasioned there, made him rethink his position. He sent the ladies, his queen, Elizabeth de Burgh and his daughter, Marjory, among them, under the care of the Earl of Atholl and his own brother Neil Bruce, north to Kildrummy Castle in Aberdeenshire and hoped-for safety there. But Kildrummy fell to the forces of the future Edward II of England, and the party of refugees again struck north, perhaps hoping to reach Orkney or even Norway where they would be safe. They reached Tain and took shelter in St Duthus Chapel, claiming sanctuary. But the then Earl of Ross, William, violated the sanctity of this place, took them all captive, and handed them over to the evil clutches of Edward Longshanks of England.

It does of course shame me that the Earl of Ross was responsible for this, but at least he had a son who would distinguish himself at the Battle of Bannockburn. It can be hellish being Scottish – all these skeletons in the family closet.

Longshanks had the Earl of Atholl hanged, then had his body decapitated and burnt. Neil Bruce was taken to Berwick where he was drawn, hanged and beheaded. But Longshanks kept his chivalric side for the ladies. The Queen of Scots was confined in the manor of Burstwick in Holderness. Bruce's sister, Christian, was confined in a nunnery. His other sister, Mary, was put in a small cage of wood and iron, and put on display at Roxburgh Castle, with no privacy in all weathers, and similarly, the Countess of Buchan was caged at Berwick. The Princess Marjory, only 12, was ordered to be similarly displayed in the Tower of London, with orders that she be allowed to speak to no-one, but at least in her case this was cancelled, and

she too was confined in a nunnery. These women remained in these bar-
baric and hideous conditions for several years. It was only after the
resounding defeat that England suffered in 1314 at Bannockburn, that
Bruce was able to gain their freedom by bargaining with the many high-
ranking English captives he had taken. The ignominy that Scotland has
suffered over the centuries, and still there are those who cannot see the correct way forward.

As I sit at these remains, I can see the original doors being forced, the
menfolk doing their best to protect the ladies against overwhelming odds,
their ideals of chivalry steeling them, in a way in which the mighty
Plantaganet, self-styled Hammer of the Scots, could never understand.

The idea of sanctuary eventually led to the chapel's demise. In 1427,
McNeill of Creish in Sutherland pursued Mowat of Freswick in Caithness,
south. Mowat took shelter in the chapel, claiming refuge. McNeill set fire
to the place and burnt Mowat and his followers within – and also managed
to burn all the ancient town records which were kept here too. There must
have been some real animosity between these two!

Back up to the centre of town. The large Gothic tower is the old
Tolbooth, or town prison. The original date of construction is unknown,
but it was repaired in 1706 by monies collected locally by the General
Assembly of the Church of Scotland. It has been incorporated into later
public buildings. The old Mercat Cross stands in an angle formed by the
buildings here, moved in here from its original site.

Just before the Tolbooth, a gate takes you into the old churchyard, and a
visitor attraction is based in several of the buildings here, called 'Tain
through Time'. The old church here was built in 1360, as a collegiate establishment, and confusingly it too is called St Duthus.

There are also low walls of an early establishment of Culdee origin, the old
Celtic church, beside this 1360 building, that dates from even earlier times.

When St Duthus' Chapel was burnt by McNeill in 1427, the saint's
remains were transferred into this 1360 building for safe-keeping, and con-
sequently this church became a centre of pilgrimage. Its shrine status meant
that Scottish kings visited this place, but it will forever be associated with
King James IV, of Flodden fame. James visited St Duthus' remains in this
1360 building for 20 years in succession, from 1493 to 1513. In fact, he
was here in August 1513, probably with little realisation that his end was
soon to come. Flodden took place on 9 September 9.

James IV did seem to be a man of religious convictions, but he did have a
mistress in the shape of flame-haired Janet Kennedy, who lived not too far
from here, so there may have been matters both spiritual and worldly that
James attended to.

His son, King James V, also made a pilgrimage to St Duthus' Church in
1527, walking barefoot. A rough footpath across the moors in the uplands

of this parish is traditionally pointed out as the route he took, and is still called the King's Causeway.

This church suffered badly at the Reformation in the 1560s and the remains of St Duthus himself disappeared at that time. I have already made my feelings known about the acts of vandalism that occurred during this period. The Church needed to be reconstructed, but did all this destruction have to accompany it?

This church was allowed to decay, and it was neglected for many years, but it was happily restored by local benefactors between 1849 and 1882 at a cost of £1,110. Today, it is a nice place to visit, and I feel the history of it. One of the buildings of the Tain through Time attraction houses the Clan Ross centre, and as Tain is the 'capital' of the Ross clan lands, this is only right and fitting.

There is some nice architecture in Tain, and a wee wander is essential to take it all in.

Next, follow the signs through the town, back to the A9 southbound for Inverness. A couple of miles and we reach Nigg roundabout, where we continue right, on the A9.

Shortly afterwards we cross a river, signposted Balnagown River. A little upstream stands Balnagown Castle, the seat of the Ross Clan. It was purchased round about 1980 by Mohammed Al Fayed, owner of Harrods in London. I have been lucky enough to have been allowed to wander this place, having been granted permission to do so, and visited it in the company of my friend from the Society of William Wallace, Muriel, who lives in Kirriemuir. The item that I most wanted to see was 'Wallace's Chair', a huge, thick-legged piece of furniture, reputed to have once belonged to the hero of Scotland himself. This chair came from Lamington Tower, which stands beside the Clyde near the little village of the same name. According to legend, Wallace's wife was Marion Bradefute, the heiress of Lamington, and this very impressive and mighty chair came from there to Balnagown through intermarriage many years ago. It was in storage within the castle when the change of ownership took place.

When Mr Al Fayed bought the Balnagowan estate, it was neglected, and the castle, though roofed, was in urgent need of care and attention. Much money has been spent on the place, and now many locals are employed in the day to day running of the estate. What I found a little disconcerting though, was that the place was decked out in both the insignia and tartan of the Ross family, and the arms of the chief were displayed at the main gates. Money does not give one a right to the chieftainship of a clan, or automatic inclusion to that bloodline of course! But the improvements to a rundown property, its fate safeguarded for the foreseeable future, have to be balanced against that.

If there is not too much leaf cover on the trees, it may be possible to catch a glimpse of the towers of Balnagowan, but please remember it is a private house.

Lands here were given by William, Earl of Ross, to his half-brother, Hugh, around 1350. A castle on the site is first mentioned in 1490, and the oldest parts of the current building date from that time. In 1569 the Privy Council of Scotland received reports that the eighth laird, Alexander, was terrifying the neighbourhood, and had so destroyed some of the local crown properties that they were unable to pay their rents. We all have a few black sheep in the family!

We follow the north shore of the Cromarty Firth southwestwards, the water full of oil rig platforms at time of writing. We pass Alness, then as Evanton appears over on our right, you will notice what looks like a sculpture on the hilltop beyond. It consists of pillars and a central arch, and this is Fyrnish Hill. It commemorates the victory of Sir Hector Munro at the battle of Seringapatam in 1781, and it was erected by the local tenants. The seat of the Munro family is at Foulis Castle, which is near Evanton, so this explains this strange sculpture.

Just as the bridge across the Cromarty Firth comes into view, you will see the Storehouse of Foulis on the lochside. It is, as its name suggests, an old storehouse, yellow-harled, quaint, small-windowed, with outside stairs giving access. It is now a visitor centre.

We take the left turn at the roundabout onto the bridge, following the A9. The land on the far shore is the Black Isle. The name is deceiving, as the Black Isle is not an island at all, as the western end of this peninsula, between the Cromarty and Moray Firths, is very firmly attached to the mainland shire of Ross and Cromarty.

There have been many theories as to the origin of the name Black Isle. One of my favourites is the fact that snow seldom lies on the low lying land here, and certainly approaching up the A9 from the south, this peninsula looks very black when compared against the snow covered landscape which surrounds it.

Continue across the Black Isle until you reach the roundabout at Tore. Here you take the first left exit for Munlochy and Fortrose. Munlochy comes up after a couple of miles, a nice wee village with the interesting Munlochy Bay beyond. This cuts deep into the southern side of the Black Isle from the Moray Firth (pronounced Murray). It has steep cliffy sides, and the tide recedes to expose huge sand flats, a haven for bird life. A fast straight stretch takes us round a last bend and into Avoch (pronounced Och!).

As Sinatra would sing 'My kind of town Avoch is …' and it *is* my kind of town. The sign welcoming you into the village shows some kilted Scots raising a Saltire. Not many places in Scotland show that sort of patriotism. The reason for this is because legend tells us that it was here that the 'north rising' began in 1297. While William Wallace was clearing the English invaders from southern Scotland, a young knight named Andrew Murray began a similar campaign in the north. He raised the Saltire of Scotland at his castle on Ormonde Hill, and then set about clearing the English from all the castles of the north. Andrew had been captured by the English whilst trying to defend his country at the Battle of Dunbar in 1296, and he was imprisoned at Chester. He managed to escape, and came north to his family lands here to start the fight back.

If you would like to see the spot where the standard of freedom was raised, you need to go down to the road that runs right along the waterfront in front of the houses. This is Henrietta Street. If you drive to the far end, a small country road cuts uphill and inland. A track then cuts off left at the top of this hill, leading towards Ormonde Hill, a symmetrical bowl-like hill. Cars have to be left behind on the road. The track circles round the hill, where a stile is crossed, and there is a short stiff pull up the last 100 feet or so onto the hilltop. There are only a few fragments of stonework and the well remaining from the once-mighty castle that stood here.

What is interesting is the view, from Ben Wyvis inland, to the Moray Firth stretching away eastwards, and the cairn which graces the summit. This cairn with its large flagpole, usually flying a Saltire in a ragged state due to the winds that blow up the Firth, was erected for the 700th anniversary of the flag raised here by Murray in 1297. Charlie Beattie, who lives in the village below, was the man responsible for this cairn, and a look at it will make it all the more impressive when I tell you that Charlie carried all these stones up here to create this memorial. When I picture Charlie I see him in his plaid and bushy beard, looking every inch a throwback to the more martial days of the Highlands. The authorities that are in place for promoting Scotland's history and heritage did not like this cairn being raised, and made advances to try to have it demolished, but it is now a feature that I associate with Avoch, and has become part of what this place *is*.

An event is held here every year now, with a walk out from the centre of the village, the local kids kitted out in traditional Scottish garb, even one or two on horses! The walkers arrive on this hill top where a speech is made, and the old Saltire lowered, and a fresh one raised. If you know just where to look, you can just discern the cairn, flagpole and Saltire in the distance from the road through the village.

There is a great wee pub and eaterie in Avoch, and there is always a healthy size of portion served. I couldn't finish mine on a previous visit, and a lucky herring gull who happened to be just outside the window was thrown my chips, and they were big fat chips, one by one! Some companions had not finished theirs either, and the gull was duly given these too. It was a determined gull, and it snatched at every morsel as if it had not seen food for days. It was a big sleek craitur (a Scots word for a creature, and I think the American term 'critter' comes from the same source!) so that was certainly not the case. Anyway, the best bit of this was that when the gull finally realised that it had had the very last scrap it was going to get, it tried several times to take off, and couldn't manage it. It was so full of chips and other assorted bits and pieces that its wings would not lift it! Eventually it managed to get up on a garden table, where it settled down for a wait of a few hours to let nature take its course. I just remember being in hysterics watching this thing trying to get off the ground. Bet if I asked the gull though, he would have no regrets, and would do it all again if given the chance.

From Avoch, the B832 continues for a mile, hugging the edge of the water, till it reaches Fortrose. Fortrose is another lovely wee place, all old bungalows and villas, clustered around the ruins of Fortrose Cathedral. There are many wee towns in Scotland that are clustered round the ruins of an ancient place of worship, and every one of them is given an air of antiquity, of distinction, by this happy coupling. Fortrose is no exception to this rule. In times past, the cathedral has been the point of focus of the town, in fact, is probably the reason the town is here at all. That is why it still seems to keep a watchful eye over proceedings. It sits in a grassy area in the centre of a cluster of buildings. All that really remains of a much grander building is the south aisle, built by Euphemia, Countess of Ross, and a grand niece of King Robert the Bruce. The countess was buried within the finished work, and the easternmost of the three canopied tombs is thought to be hers. The cathedral was founded here in 1227, replacing an earlier church in Rosemarkie. Cromwell stole much of the stonework from this site to build a fort in Inverness, and that explains why there is so little today.

After Andrew Murray cleared the English garrisons from the north, he marched his army south to Dundee, where he made contact with Wallace. These two young patriots seemed to have hit it off right away, joined forces, and began to besiege the English-held castle of Dundee. Word came that an English army had assembled and was heading north to deal with their 'insurrection'.

Wallace and Murray smashed this army at Stirling Bridge in 1297, a place we have already visited on our journey. Unfortunately, Murray suffered wounds in the fight from which he would not recover, and what little evidence we have would seem to point to the fact that he was buried here at Fortrose on his family lands. Although there is no actual tomb, it is interesting to think that one of Scotland's greatest patriot sons may be resting for eternity within the church precincts. It certainly makes it special for me.

Fortrose is almost a twin town, so closely linked is it with Rosemarkie, just a little further on. Rosemarkie is an old-worldy sort of place with a nice main street, and a beach for frontage. At the far side of the houses is the

Fairy Glen, an idyllic place where the burn trickles through woodland to reach the sea. There is some good rock scenery here too. In the churchyard there is an ancient symbol stone, bearing a cross on one side and Pictish symbols on the other.

Between Fortrose and Rosemarkie, there is a long finger-like peninsula that juts right out into the Moray Firth. It is signposted Chanonry Point, and a road runs right to the lighthouse at its tip. This is another must-see. The road runs out to the point through the local golf course, and there is car-parking out on the water's edge. A memorial stands here, the plaque on it erected by the pupils of Fortrose Academy, the local secondary school, founded in 1791. This boulder marks the spot where the Brahan Seer was burnt in a tar barrel.

The Brahan Seer, whose real name was Kenneth MacKenzie, or in the Gaelic, Coinneach Odhar, was noted for his gifts of second sight and prophesy. Some of these prophesies have strikingly come to pass. For example, he predicted that one day ships would sail behind Tomnahurich Hill in Inverness, and although many scoffed at this prophecy at the time, it came to pass in the building of the Caledonian Canal some two centuries after the fact.

Another of his predictions claimed that one day the people of Ross-shire would be driven from the land by sheep. Although this seemed impossible, the Highland Clearances created that situation.

His end came when he offended the Countess of Seaforth by saying that he saw more in the playing of the children of the common folk, than he saw in the games of the children of nobility. She accused him of witchcraft in her spite, had him seized and brought to Chanonry Point to suffer burning in a tar barrel, a common punishment for sorcery.

The upper Moray Firth is almost landlocked here, due to Chanonry Point on this side, and the peninsula containing Fort George projecting from the southern side. Fort George was built by a London government to subjugate the Highlands, and the less said about it, the better.

There are dolphins in the Moray Firth, and I have watched them here. The best time is at the turn of the tide, when the dolphins feed on the fish running through the narrows. Like many of these things, it just comes down to luck. It is a sight worth seeing though, dolphins only a few yards from the edge, leaping from the water, and for a while it is possible to think that all is well with the world.

We return to the A9 from here, and if you wish to vary the drive back, you can turn left when you reach Munlochy and follow the A9161 back to the main route.

Only a little further on the A9 and you will see the signs for North Kessock, the road down into the village going off to your right. The ferry across to Inverness used to ply from here, but it has been superseded by the mighty Kessock Bridge. The bridge soars high above the southern edge of the village, which is really only houses on one side of the road, facing across the water to Inverness. Dolphins used to be spotted regularly here too, but sightings are now becoming rarer.

Halfway along the village street, keep your eyes peeled for little signs proclaiming 'Targemaker'. This is the home and workshop of Joe Lindsay, and Joe makes reproductions of outstanding targes from history. Just in case you are not familiar with the term, a targe is a round highland shield, two or three disks of wood covered in deerskin and leather, studded and covered in ornamental Celtic knotwork. Some have removable spikes that can be fitted into their central bosses, which make them weapons for not only defence but attack too. Joe has such an array of styles on show, that when I first purchased one, I was like a kid in a sweetshop, unable to decide what I actually wanted, holding one while looking at others. Joe is part of a breed that seems to be springing up over Scotland, rediscovering the old ways, and taking pride in craftsmanship. I know so many of his kind that it gives me hope. People who are proud of Scotland and its history and heritage. They seem to have reappeared over the last couple of decades, and whether it is building memorials or crafting things with a peculiarly Scottish flavour, I realise that there are people out there that care as much about Scotland as I do.

Back up to the A9, and enjoy the fun waiting for a space in the traffic to make it over to the southbound lane. We drive straight on to the Kessock Bridge, and we cross the Firth and soar over to the Inverness side, the town already laid out below.

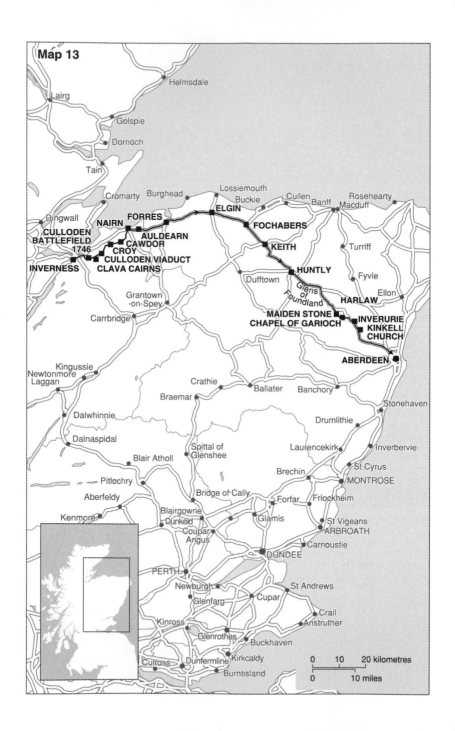

Map 13

CHAPTER THIRTEEN

Pastureland

BEGINNING AT INVERNESS, THE ROUTE TAKES IN CULLODEN BATTLEFIELD BEFORE MOVING ONTO NAIRN VIA CAWDOR. FOLLOWING THE A96 IT TAKES A SMALL DIVERSION VIA CHAPEL OF GARIOCH, INVERURIE, AND THEN MOVES ON TO ABERDEEN.

AFTER WE CROSS the Kessock Bridge, we come to a roundabout, where a right turn will take you into Inverness, the 'Capital of the Highlands'. Following the signs will take you into the town centre. Although Inverness is not surrounded by mountains, a radius of roads branches out from here in every direction, and for many remote Highland communities, Inverness is the nearest large town with various amenities.

Sitting at the head of Loch Ness, itself part of the Great Glen, Inverness straddles the River Ness as it reaches salt water. It has always been an important through-route from eastern to western Scotland, the other end of the Great Glen having already been visited as we came through Fort William.

There are quite a few things for the tourist to see in Inverness, but I will keep it concise by listing just a few of my favourites. Strangely, for such a venerable place, there is nothing really ancient to see in Inverness itself.

There is a sham castle on a hillock above the River Ness, built in 1835, and it houses the Sheriff Court, but it is on the site of an old castle that may date back to the time of David I, who was born in 1084, and reigned from 1124–1153. A walk around the outside gives an elevated view over part of the town and the river. On the opposite side of the castle from the town centre there is a statue of Flora MacDonald, the helper of Bonnie Prince Charlie, who aided him to escape the clutches of the Hanoverian redcoats.

The original castle that stood on this site was taken by the English during the Wars of Independence, but Inverness had a stout Provost, one Alexander Pilche. He, together with Andrew Murray, soon drove the invaders from the town. The English captured it again, but they were soon dispelled by the followers of King Robert the Bruce. James I was here in 1427 when on a progress through the north to punish troublemakers. In 1464 James III lived in the castle for a while, and his son, James IV, was also here. Mary, Queen of Scots was refused entry to the castle as it was occupied by enemies to the Scottish Crown, and she was forced to take up residence in a townhouse. The Highlands and Islands Development Board offices are on the site of this town house. Montrose's men besieged the place too. The Hanoverian Government garrisoned the place, of course, when the

Royal House of Stewart was ejected from London, and Bonnie Prince Charlie was instrumental in finishing off the castle by having the place dynamited, much to the joy of the local populace. He had among his troops a French sergeant named L'Epine, who had some knowledge of explosives. L'Epine blew up the towers of the place in succession, but the last charge failed to detonate. He ran forward to try and ascertain the problem, and as he leaned over the charge, it went off. He was blown into the air, and his body was later found and recovered from the river. Poor L'Epine. You may want to pause a moment to consider this poor man's fate as you look out over the river. I suppose he would have been buried locally, but there seems to be no record where.

As you descend from the castle down to the town's Bridge Street and High Street, there is a large tourist information centre, and between this and the castle is the town's museum. This is a great wee place, and I always make a point of having a wander round when I'm in town. Felicity is in one of the display cases, and I always like a look at her. Felicity is a puma, and she was captured at Cannich, near Loch Ness, in 1980. She must have been released fully grown, obviously by someone rich enough to have a menagerie in the first place. She was caught by a farmer who had spotted her on several occasions. I can imagine the man in the local pub, telling his companions that there was a puma wandering the locality, and the derision he must have had to endure. I suppose if that is the situation, you would really have to go out and capture the beast to have the last laugh! She was kept at a wildlife park, and when she eventually died, the taxidermist took over, and she now graces the museum.

There are some Jacobite artefacts and some items personally connected with Bonnie Prince Charlie on show too.

There are some nice individual shops in Inverness, instead of the usual chain-store stuff, and I particularly like the architecture of the Victorian Market, a covered marketplace from the 1890s. I love these old places, and Inverness has one of the best. It is slap-bang in the middle of town, has several entrances, so I'm sure you won't miss it. There is one of these modern mall-type shopping centres in Inverness too, the Eastgate Centre. On the upper floor there is a large ornamental clock, shaped like a boat and full of animals, and all sorts of things happen when it strikes the hour. I know it is meant to be for the kids, but I have found myself lingering when I realise that it is five to!

There are many bits and pieces to see in Inverness, and the Tourist Information will give you all the information you require.

We take the route out of Inverness signposted for the A96 Aberdeen road. There is a roundabout beneath the A9, where we continue on, or if you have crossed the Kessock Bridge without turning into Inverness, you take the turn off to the roundabout, where the road off to your left is the one you want, signposted A96, Nairn and Aberdeen. We pass Inverness Retail and Business Park, then you will see the sign, pointing off to your right, for Culloden Battlefield, 4 miles. You follow this road into Culloden village. Just as you hit the village, you see another sign for the battlefield, where again you turn right, and continue on towards the site itself.

You are on higher ground now, and over to your left the Moray Firth is visible, the Black Isle comprising the opposite bank. Ben Wyvis rises like a giant whaleback to the north, where snow patches linger deep into the summer months.

The battlefield of Culloden Moor appears, hard on the right of the road. When I was a kid it was covered with trees, but it has been taken back to the scrubby, heathery moor that it was in April 1746. You will notice the red flags with a white rose first, and these mark the line of the Jacobite army under Charles at the onset of the battle. A few hundred yards on and you will see that there are another two flagpoles bearing flags. These are yellow though, and they bear the black rose that symbolises the Hanoverian dynasty. Just after, the access road to the visitor centre opens up to your right. The centre has a well stocked bookshop, a café, an audiovisual presentation telling the story behind the events that took place here, and it has a little museum-type room with artefacts from the battle. There is some great stuff in there, swords, dirks, sporrans, targes and muskets. It would take me a long time to get bored of looking at these.

Right outside the visitor centre is old Leanach cottage. In the aftermath of the battle 30 or 40 wounded Highlanders crawled into this building seeking shelter and sanctuary. The victorious Hanoverians found them there and killed them all.

You walk from here over towards the great central cairn, which was the original visitor centre. Here you start to discover the graves of the Highlanders that 'fought for Scotland and Prince Charlie', and it would be a hard-hearted person indeed who did not feel the sorrow of this place, and the enormity of what the Hanoverian victory meant to the destruction of the way of life in the Highlands of Scotland.

I can't really put into words how much this place affects me. I love to visit it, but I hate it too. Culloden was the end of everything. The end of the Royal Line of Scotland, the end of clanship, and for a long time afterwards, Scotland became North Britain. There are many who see Culloden as a delivery. There are many in Scotland who are glad that a Hanoverian army of the Protestant persuasion decimated a people who they think of as predominantly Catholic, under a Prince of French/ Italianate stock.

Most of Charles's army was actually Episcopalian, Charles himself was a Protestant for most of his life, and he was a direct descendant of King Robert the Bruce. But history tends to be written by the winners, and I cannot help but feel for my fellow Scots who died here, and the fact that Scots did die in their droves is more important to me than anything else. I am tired of foreign interference in my country, historical or current, and I wish it never to happen again. It is within the power of the people of Scotland to make that change. They need to stop listening to politicians who say to them 'You are Scottish, you are not capable of controlling your own destiny'. And it is Scots who say this to Scots. 'Don't forget you are Scottish,' as if it is some kind of stigma. 'We are such a small nation we have not the wherewithal or ability to go it alone'.

Like the downtrodden in any relationship, if they are told they are rubbish often enough, it seems that they begin to believe this is the case.

But Culloden Moor has the ability to bring all this dissent about Scottishness home to me. Hard. And the words of Lang ring in my head:

A wind that awoke on the moorland came sighing,
Like the voice of the heroes that perished in vain.
'Not for Tearlach alone the red claymore was plying
But to win back the old world that comes not again'.

The outcome of Culloden, in retrospect, seems to have been an inevitability. Charles had landed in Scotland the previous year. His standard was unfurled at Glenfinnan, and a small army gathered. Edinburgh once again became home to the Stewart dynasty. Prestonpans was won and the march into England began. They were only three days' march from London at Derby when the ill-advised retreat began. Back in Scotland, the second battle of Falkirk (the first being Wallace's in 1298) was won, but retreat continued. On the eve of the battle, the Duke of Cumberland, leading the Hanoverians, celebrated his birthday at his billet in Nairn. The Jacobites, realising that there would be drunkenness in the enemy camp, made a night march on Nairn to elicit a surprise attack. This night attack came to naught, mostly due to hunger and fatigue, but it was a move of daring and genius, and it is one of those 'if only' moments of history. The next day, the 5,000 men of Charles's army were decimated by the 8,000 under Cumberland's command. But it was not the battle itself that ended the ties of clanship so much as the slaughter that visited all the Highlands in the aftermath.

Most Scots I speak to who have visited Culloden Moor have spoken of the emotions the place stirs within them. It is as if the blood that has soaked into the peaty soil speaks to them. It speaks to me. And I walk the paths between the various burial sites, and back and forward between the lines of the Jacobite and Hanoverian positions, and I look out to Ben Wyvis, to the Moray Firth, and to the moors rising inland. I sense the useless slaughter, and the end of the old world that comes not again. I sigh, and return to the bike waiting in the car park, and for the first few miles there is always a thoughtfulness, a calm that comes again to the picture of that stretch of moor, and I analyse the details again and again as I ride. But I eventually

have to put it to one side as the past is the past, and we cannot change it –
we can only learn, and the throttle is opened up once more.

For the visitor on this journey though, when exiting the car park at the
visitor centre, you should turn to your right, following the B9006 east
again. You reach a junction after just a few yards, where a minor road
branches off to your right, signposted Clava Cairns 1.5 miles. Turn down
this road, going straight through the wee crossroads ahead. Culloden
Viaduct appears on your left. It is an immense structure, a marvel of engineering, carrying the main railway line to the north over the River Nairn.
It is comprised of thousands upon thousands of dressed, reddish sandstone
blocks. It was built between 1893 and 1898, spans the river on twenty-
nine arches, and soars to 124 feet in height. Even the approach
embankments carrying the lines must have taken an immense amount of
manpower to construct. If a train happens to cross as you are in the vicinity, it gives more of an idea of scale, as the train looks so tiny compared to
that mass of masonry.

A sign appears, telling you it is only a half-mile further to Clava Cairns,
down a little road to the right. A large standing stone in a field on your
right, followed by a few more, gives an indication that you are about to see
something special. A little car park appears on your right, and the first of
the famous cairns is just on the other side of a small gate.

There are three huge cairns in all, surrounded by standing stones. They
date from 1800–1500 BC so are attributable to our Bronze Age ancestors.
Some of the stones are very large indeed, and there must have been tales
told of Herculean proportions regarding their construction!

At the time of the cairns' raising, the people venerated the elderly, and so
who better to venerate than their dead ancestors! The cairns would originally have contained the remains of the dead, and the narrow entrance
tunnels allowed access to these worshipped remains, deep inside their
stone structures. One thing that has remained constant among human
beings is the grief at the loss of a loved one. This was obviously a way in
which our ancestors dealt with this trauma. Thought went into their siting
too, as the midsummer sun shines directly down the passages into the centre
of the cairns.

It is a leafy spot today, trees having sprung up all around this site, but
that only helps to create an air of mystery, and adds a sense of nature and
pleasantness to the site. On my last visit a bus full of American tourists
drew up just as I did. They obviously had their stipulated 15 minutes or so,
and they meandered around the site, chattering loudly, snapping away
with cameras, and one or two contriving to create kilts out of tartan rugs to
give their photo images a Scottish feel. When they left I had the place to
myself, and the peacefulness of time and truly ancient structures again fell
over the place.

Perhaps a little of the blood in my veins is of a builder of Clava. I wish that knowledge was passed down through the generations, instead of being swallowed up by time. It is funny how, two or three generations on, our children seem dismissive of the experiences of our own time. That seems to be the way that nature has it ordained.

Back to the junction just after the Culloden Visitor Centre. Turn right to continue on the B9006 again, but only for a few yards. There is a lay-by on the right here, so pull in to it. Immediately beside you stands a huge boulder, some eight feet high, and perhaps twenty by ten across its surface. Iron staples have been inserted into one side to allow the visitor to climb upon the top of this boulder and read the inscriptions carved on it.

It has carved on one side 'Cumberland's Stone', and the words on top tell how the Duke of Cumberland surveyed the field of battle from this position. Sorry. He may have stood near the stone, but I find it is too much of a stretch of the imagination to believe he stood atop it. Unless there was a crane handy, of course. Cumberland was grossly overweight, and it would have taken an almighty show of muscle by his staff to have pushed him up there. There is a story of him eating in the shelter of the stone, and frankly, that sounds more like the truth. Interesting spot to visit though, and it seems most visitors to the battlefield miss it, as it is a little further on. The wording was carved into the stone in 1881 by Duncan Forbes of Culloden.

Onwards on the B9006. We follow the valley of the River Nairn through woodland and pleasant rolling fields. We pass Croy, and when Clephanton is reached, we turn right, following the signs for Cawdor, and Cawdor Castle.

We cross the River Nairn by means of an old humpbacked bridge.

As we come into the village of Cawdor, there is an old church on our right. It has an unusual tower and a Norman doorway. Cawdor is a picturesque wee place, and it is nice to stroll round the village to take it all in. Cawdor Castle has widespread fame, due to Shakespeare's *Macbeth*, and the well-known fact that he was at one time Thane of Cawdor. Cawdor Castle is also reputed to be the place where the murder of Duncan took place, but the oldest part of the building dates from 1454. Don't let that detract from the fact that this is one of Scotland's most picturesque castles though. It was founded by the descendant of a brother of the famous Macbeth, and the events that led up to this castle being built are quite extraordinary.

John, the eighth Thane of Cawdor had a dream. In this dream he was directed to load a donkey with gold, and let the donkey loose. It was told to him that wherever the donkey rested, there he should begin to build his new castle. So he put a weight of gold on a donkey's back and let it loose. The donkey wandered from one interesting thistle to another, but eventually, fatigued by the weight it was carrying, it lay down to rest under a hawthorn tree. Here John decided to build his castle.

This might sound like your archetypal fairy story, like some legend spoken of round the fire in olden days. But there is a twist to this tale. Underneath the principal tower of the castle, in a vaulted basement, stands a gnarled old hawthorn tree, its branches reaching into the stonework. The tree was obviously in situ before the tower was erected. Very curious.

The family for long have drunk toasts to 'the success of the hawthorn!'. In 1498 the succession of the family came down to a young heiress named Muriella Cawdor, the name sometimes spelt 'Calder'. In 1499 she was walking near the castle with her nurse, when a party of 60 Campbells appeared, obviously with the intent of seizing the young heiress. Her nurse, seeing them approach and realising what was afoot, bit off a joint of the girl's little finger so that her identity would be known. When the Campbells disappeared with their prize, she ran to the tower to alert the family. Her relatives and men at arms pursued the little girl. Campbell of Innerliver saw them approach, and turned a large cooking pot upside down, as if it was concealing her. He then instructed his seven sons to defend it to the death. As the Cawdors came up and saw the seven swordsmen surrounding the pot, they immediately assailed them, assuming the girl was underneath. The other Campbells, meanwhile, hastened off with their prize. By the time the seven had been slain, and the pot turned to reveal that it had all been a ploy, further pursuit was useless.

In 1510 she was married to Sir John Campbell, her severed pinky, as we Scots call the little finger, proved that she was who she said she was, and she returned with her husband to claim her heritage. From this union the current family, the Campbells of Cawdor, are descended.

The castle is open to the public, June till October.

Continue onward on the B9090, through Brackla, which has a large Dewars Whisky distillery. Keep your eyes peeled for a sign pointing towards a road that branches off to your left. It proclaims 'Nairn, 2.5 miles', and is numbered B9090, the same as the road you are on. This road designation number actually goes round through this junction with you.

You re-cross the River Nairn, and pass the railway station as you come down into the town centre. Nairn is held to be the division between the Highlands and Lowlands. At one time it was claimed that Gaelic was spoken in its western half, and English in the Eastern!

It has been mentioned already that the Duke of Cumberland had his headquarters in Nairn before the Battle of Culloden, and as we come into the town centre, it is best to park and continue on foot along the High Street to locate this property. It is number 36, and although it looks to be of comparatively recent construction, this is actually a later facade, encasing older work. There is a Latin inscription on this frontage, the translation of which is:

All earthly things by turn we see,
Become another's property.
Mine now must be another's soon,
I know not whose, when I am gone,
An earthly house is bound to none.

A little plaque states: 'This building was in former times the townhouse of the Roses of Kilravock'.

Strangely, as Cumberland was lodged here in the Rose's townhouse on the eve of Culloden, Bonnie Prince Charlie dined with the Rose family at Kilravock Castle, their main residence.

Just a little further up the street, a red sandstone pillar stands before the County Buildings. This was the old town cross, constructed in 1757 to replace an earlier example. It was moved to this site during various road-widening operations. An old sundial, the Horloge Stone, originally stood in the town, and the sundial placed on the market cross is probably this old Horloge Stone.

The main route between Inverness and Aberdeen, the A96, runs parallel with Nairn's High Street, a little to the north, so follow the A96 eastwards towards Forres and ultimately, Aberdeen,

Just a mile or so outside Nairn, look out for the junction of the B9111 to Auldearn branching off to the right. This is a wee circular route that branches off to run through Auldearn, and then it rejoins the A96, so divert yourself a little to take Auldearn in.

As you drive into Auldearn, you will notice the old doocot on a knolly hill to your left. It is unusual in the fact that it is circular: most doocots in Scotland are square. It is painted a creamy-beige and it is very prominent. There is a sign pointing the way up a short gravel road to the car park. It states that the doocot and 'battle viewpoint' are under the care of the National Trust for Scotland.

Park the car, cross the stile, and it is a short haul up to the doocot itself. This is a fascinating site, with plenty of history. Auldearn Castle formerly graced this spot, and it was in this castle that King William I of Scotland, better known as William the Lion, signed the second charter of the Burgh of Inverness in 1179. The reason this spot is known as 'battle viewpoint' is because James Graham, the famous Montrose, fought a battle here in 1645. So where this Boath Doocot now stands, is the spot where Montrose's gunners looked out over the surrounding farmland, watching the movements of their enemies over the muzzles of their waiting artillery. The Battle of Auldearn was one of Montrose's many victories, and there are information boards on the hilltop, although they were defaced when I last visited. It is a good vantage point, and it makes it easy to understand the ebb and flow that took place between the two forces.

Drive through the little village of Auldearn, and the road takes you back round to the A96, and we continue eastwards. A couple of miles further and you will notice the sign welcoming you to Moray. This great northern shire has always been one of the bases of nationalism in Scotland, its men following Andrew Murray to Stirling Bridge to fight alongside Wallace in 1297, and this area was one of the first to firmly support King Robert the Bruce on his campaigns.

Another couple of miles and you reach the tiny village of Brodie. In the village you will see the signposts directing you to Brodie Castle. The access road goes off to the left, then swings hard right and runs straight for half a mile to the castle's entrance. As you turn left into the grounds there is a little lay-by on your left, where the Rodney Stone stands. It is a ninth-century Pictish symbol stone, which was rediscovered in 1782 in the churchyard at Dyke, while the foundations were being laid for a new parish church. It is a 'class 2' cross slab with Pictish symbols and Ogham inscriptions on one side and a cross on the other. The carvings on the stone include the Celtic Beast. This strange animal is found on many carved stones. It is a quadruped, sort of horse-shaped, but with a long snout like a crocodile. I have heard it referred to as the 'elephant', but the trunk-like appendage comes from the top of its head, and always hangs backwards over the spine of the creature. It has always intrigued me, especially as it is found on stones all over Scotland. I often wonder what our ancestors were trying to tell us with their carvings of this fabulous beast. It is very clear on the Rodney Stone, and if you visit, please take a good long look at it.

Why is it called the Rodney Stone? When it was found in the churchyard, an admiral named Lord Rodney had won a victory over the French and Spanish fleets, and it was named in his honour. Or so one version runs. Local tradition states that the gravedigger who uncovered the stone was Rotteney, so perhaps it is he who the stone was named after. It does seem a Scottish trait to refer to things after their finder, and 'Rotteney's Stone' seems feasible to me. The stone is roughly six and a half feet high and three feet wide. A little wooden roof has been erected over it to protect it from the worst of the weather.

On we go up the driveway to Brodie Castle itself.

There have been Brodies here for some 800 years. It is believed that they may have been granted the land by Malcolm IV in 1160. They would have had some sort of early fortification here, but the nucleus of the current building is a 'z-plan' tower house – a central rectangular keep with a tower at opposite corners, which gave defenders a good covering field of fire. This construction dates from 1567, and its builder was the twelfth Brodie of

Brodie. A western extension was added in the 1600s, then in the 1800s the architect William Burn added the eastern wing.

Once you have driven through the extensive grounds and come up to the parking areas before the castle, you will find it is a very impressive building indeed. It is open to visitors from April to October, there is fine furniture, plasterwork and works of art to be seen, and although the castle and grounds are under the care of the National Trust of Scotland, the current Brodie still lives within the castle.

It has a chequered history, this place, having been partially burnt twice by the Lords Gordon and Huntly, due to the then Brodie signing the National Covenant. This opened the door for aggression from his neighbours during the religious strife that wracked Scotland in the 1600s.

On a different note, many of the varieties of daffodil that we have today were due to the twenty-fourth Brodie of Brodie, a keen horticulturist who dabbled with various hybrids.

As you exit the castle grounds, look for the signs pointing the way to 'Macbeth's hillock', one and a quarter miles distant. It stands 161 feet high, and is reputed to be the spot where Macbeth met the three witches who foretold his destiny.

Continue on the A96. We cross the River Findhorn, a river that rises in the Highlands, but flows into the Moray Firth a little north-east of here, via Findhorn Bay. This is a funny wee, almost landlocked, basin.

Shortly after, we come to the outskirts of Forres. We take a right turn into the town, signposted B9011. You will notice the Dallas Dhu distillery is down to your right. We go straight on, crossing the Castle Bridge, erected 1823, into the town centre. Just after we cross the bridge, you will notice an obelisk, standing some 50 feet high, on your right. This was erected in memory of James Thomson, a surgeon who saved many lives during the Crimean War. Strangly, Thomson was born in Cromarty, but lived in Forres for a while, and the granite obelisk was raised here. It stands on the site of Forres Castle, hence the reason the nearby bridge is called Castle Bridge.

Two charters signed at Forres Castle by William the Lion are dated 1189 and 1198, and one by Alexander II is dated 1238. King David II was here in 1367, and Robert II was here in 1371. But the history of the castle here goes right back into the Dark Ages and the time of the legends. It is claimed in some sources that King Duffus or Dubh was murdered here in 967, and there may be mentions of the place attributable to a date as early as 535.

As you drive along the High Street you will see the Tolbooth on your right. All these little towns you have been driving through have their tolbooths. Imposing buildings, they are the centre of town life, or have been through its history, being used as prison, council chambers, courtrooms and archive storage. This particular example was built in 1838, but there will have been earlier versions here dating back to the 1200s.

Forres is famous for its parks and gardens, and consistently wins competitions. If it is during the summer months that you are visiting, please explore the place and take a good look. Some of the animal flower-sculptures are great, and Forres is obviously very lucky in its council gardeners, who are very skilled indeed.

As you drive through the town you will note Grant Park on your right, with the Nelson Memorial, a tower built in 1806 to commemorate Lord Nelson's victory at Trafalgar. It is atop Cluny Hill at this eastern end of the town, is open 2–4 pm from May to September, and there are extensive views from its top.

Just after the park, look for the police station on your right. Park and look for the Witch's Stone at the roadside, directly in front of the police station. During the evil times of the witch burnings in Scotland, these unfortunates were taken to the top of the aforementioned Cluny Hill, where they were put into barrels with spikes driven in through their sides. The tops were nailed on, then the barrels were rolled down the very steep hill to bounce and jolt down to the levels below. The occupant would, of course, be impaled and eventually mangled on this journey, and where the barrels came to a halt, tar or pitch would be added, and the barrel burnt to ashes. This stone marks the spot where one of these incidents took place.

Someone, a couple of hundred years ago, tried to break up this stone for building purposes, but the town authorities got wind of this, and had iron staples inserted to hold the stone together, and this is how it stands today. Certainly an interesting spot to visit, and it is at least a memorial of sorts to the poor soul who was martyred due to ignorance and superstition in the name of the Church.

Just a little further on, there is a sign pointing down Findhorn Road, stating 'Sueno's Stone 200 yards'. Findhorn Road is now a dead end, superseded by new roads, but whatever you do, don't miss this one. The stone is massive. Certainly the biggest standing stone I have seen in Scotland by far, and first sighting of it takes the breath away. It is covered in carvings. To protect the stone from erosion and damage, it has been encased in an armoured glass box. I have heard comments decrying this, but I think that it is well done, and actually adds to the aura of the stone in its own way. It is lit at night too, and this adds to the mystique of it all.

The stone stands 23 feet high, but there is another 12 feet below ground. How did they manage to erect such an astonishing monument? I wonder if the carvings were done before or after it was raised? The name Sueno's Stone was invented in the eighteenth century when the stone was discovered buried in the ground. The name has no bearing on the origin of the monument. Only the stone itself and its location can give any hint of why and when it was created, and on whose orders. One possibility is that the stone marks the vanquishing of the Picts by the Scots, under Kenneth Macalpin in the mid-800s. Or the stone may refer to a battle fought at Forres in 966, during which King Dubh was slain. In my book, *A Passion for Scotland*, I said of King Dubh, 'Apparently his body was put in a shallow grave under "a certain bridge" near Kinloss, and from that moment on darkness shrouded the whole kingdom. The sun only began to shine again when his body was found. Perhaps there was an eclipse at this time, and this is how it was perceived by the chroniclers, as in medieval times eclipses were often thought to be harbingers of some major event.'

There is an object carved near the bottom of this stone which looks like an arched bridge. Could it be that the specially framed head of one of the decapitated bodies on this carving is that of King Dubh? The stone may be a memento of the battle fought at Forres then, and Kinloss, where Dubh's body was hidden, is only a mile or two distant. Surely the carvings of armed men upon the stone commemorate a battle of some sort.

Out from Sueno's Stone to the road we were on, where we turn left to continue. A few hundred yards and we reach a roundabout where we rejoin the A96, the main route, and we turn right to continue eastwards. The water visible beyond the roundabout is Findhorn Bay.

We drive on for another ten miles or so until we reach the outskirts of Elgin. This is a fascinating town, the medieval plan still in use, with the castle on its hill at the western end, and the main thoroughfare with its marketplace leading to the cathedral at its eastern end.

To get to know the centre of Elgin, you are best to park and walk the town's High Street. The hill, where only scant remains exist of the castle dating from the time of King David I, is known as the Lady Hill. This name comes from the fact that the chapel that once stood within the castle was dedicated to the Virgin Mary, and the name has stuck. The main structure on the hilltop today is a large Tuscan column, erected by subscription by the inhabitants in 1839 to the memory of the last Duke of Gordon.

It is a short steep pull up onto the top of the Lady Hill, and it gives a good vista over the town. On the right-hand side of the street stands Thunderton House, now a hotel. Bonnie Prince Charlie resided within at one time. There are two old crosses within the High Street. One, the Muckle Cross, stands near St Giles' Church in the centre of the street, and the other, the Little Cross, a little further on. From this cross, College Street carries off left towards the ruins of Elgin Cathedral.

This once-mighty edifice was known as the Lantern of the North, and only St Andrews Cathedral was said to be its equal in magnificence. Like so many of the great Christian establishments of this country, only its gaunt ruins stand in mute testament of its former glory. It had suffered a serious fire in its early days, and the damage had only just been repaired when the notorious Wolf of Badenoch descended upon the place in 1390 and burnt the cathedral and part of the town.

The Wolf of Badenoch was the moniker bestowed upon Alexander Stewart, son of King Robert II. The Wolf wished the Bishop of Elgin to annul his marriage, as he desired to wed another. The Bishop refused to be threatened, and the Wolf seized some of the church lands, an act for which he was excommunicated. He took his terrible revenge by burning the place.

There was repair work, and the place was worked on for the next two centuries, but its end came in the shape of the Reformation of 1560. The cathedral was abandoned, the bells were taken, the ornate interior wood-work was broken up, and the lead roofs taken away. The great central tower had been so weakened that it eventually collapsed in 1711, pulling down much of the nave with it when it fell. In 1807, a local cobbler, John Shanks, took on the responsibility of clearing the place, and he did the job so efficiently that the Office of Works stepped in and tidied the site up to the extent that we see today. It is now under the care of Historic Scotland. John Shanks is buried in the cathedral churchyard, where his inscription refers to him as a 'drouthy cobbler'. Another interesting gravestone dated 1687 bears this inscription:

This world is a city,
Full of streets,
And death is the mercat
That all men meets,
If lyfe were a thing
That monie could buy,
The poor could not live
And the rich would not die

Behind the cathedral there is a biblical garden, beautifully laid out, which you may want to wander around. It says on the gate:

The kiss of the sun for pardon,
The song of the birds for mirth,
One is nearest God's heart in a garden
Than anywhere else on Earth

At the end of King Street, past the entrance to the cathedral, is the Bishop's House. It bears the date 1557 and the arms of Bishop Patrick Hepburn.

Back to the A96. It is well-signposted, heading eastwards towards Aberdeen. We pass the Baxters' factory. Baxters' soups are famous the world over. It is still a family business, and the works here even have a visitor centre. Immediately beyond Baxters', we cross the River Spey, Scotland's second-longest river, and the source of so much of the world's supply of Scotch whisky.

The A96 runs right through the centre of the village green of the little village of Fochabers. There is a folk museum in the village. At the far end of the village the road forks, the A98 running to Fraserburgh, and the A96 to Aberdeen. We continue to follow the A96.

After we leave Fochabers, the road starts to climb, and we enter a hillier countryside, with many new plantations of pine. The road twists and turns, then we come down into the town of Keith, which straddles the River Isla. Chivas Regal own the large Strathisla distillery here. After you have crossed the River Isla, and started to climb the hill on the opposite side, you will see Seafield Avenue, just beyond a church on your left.

If you drive downhill to the bottom of Seafield Avenue, then turn left again, after a short distance you will come across the last remaining tower of Milton Castle, standing on the left of the road among trees. The River Isla is directly on the other side of the road, and has at one time formed part of the castle's defence. This tower is the surviving portion of the ancient castle of Milton, built in 1480. It was the home of the royalist Ogilvy family, who fought with Montrose; in fact John Ogilvy of Milton was slain fighting with Montrose at the Battle of Alford in 1645. The Blessed John Ogilvy, a Jesuit Priest who was martyred at the Cross of Glasgow in 1615, was also a member of this family. The castle passed by marriage to the Oliphants, a noted family of Jacobite supporters, in 1707, but fell into ruin after the failed Jacobite rising of 1715. You can still walk into the vaulted basement of this tower, and a floor or two survives above. It is not signposted, but it is well worth the short deviation from the main A96 route to see this little historic place.

There are one or two other incidents in Keith's history that are worth mentioning.

A battle almost took place here in June 1645, when the Covenanting forces under General Baillie offered to fight Montrose, but he considered their positioning too strong. Montrose was here under very different circumstances in 1650, on his way south after his capture at the earlier-visited Ardvreck Castle in Sutherland. It was a Sunday, and he, chained, ragged and unkempt, was taken to church to listen to a sermon directed at him. Montrose, perceiving the drift of the orator, said 'Rail on!' and stood through it in silence.

There once operated in this area a well-known brigand named Peter Roy MacGregor, who does not seem to have been any relation to the famous Rob Roy. In 1667, he and his band made a descent on Keith, and the inhabitants of the town, tired of his deprivations, fell upon them in a bloody encounter. This took place in the town's old churchyard. Peter Roy was taken prisoner and was eventually executed at Edinburgh. In 1745, a Major Glasgow, fighting with the forces of Bonnie Prince Charlie, surprised a detachment of redcoat Hanoverian troops in Keith, and carried off 80 prisoners.

After Keith, the A96 runs through a little glen, then twists and turns through more hilly country. We then cross the River Deveron, this name another corruption of the Gaelic for river, Abhain, the *bh* pronounced as a 'v', and reach Huntly

Just after the river, we take a left turn and drive into the town centre of Huntly. It is a solid-looking wee town. The local stone which is used extensively gives the place a very Scottish feel. When you reach the town centre, turn left, passing the elegant, slender war memorial. We go through the archway formed by the buildings of Gordon School, and this takes us into the castle grounds.

North of the town here, the River Deveron is joined by the River Bogie, so the castle is contained within a defensive and strategic site.

Huntly Castle, though an imposing ruin, is only the latest of various castles that have stood on or near this site. The original castle was called Strathbogie, and was a little west of the present structure. It was a motte-and-bailey affair, mostly constructed of timber with defensive earthworks, and was built by the Earls of Fife. This earlier structure was burned down in 1452 by the Douglas Earl of Moray. The aforementioned Earls of Moray initially backed King Robert the Bruce in the early part of the Scottish Wars of Independence, but unluckily for them, they made their peace with the English just before Bruce and Scotland's mighty victory at Bannockburn in 1314.

Bruce confiscated their lands here, and gifted them to Sir Adam Gordon, of Huntly in Berwickshire in the Scottish Borders. There is a town of the name of Gordon in Berwickshire too, but the family name is now associated with the northeast.

Anyway, after the burning of 1452, a new stone castle was constructed, and some of this is incorporated in the building visible today. The basement therefore, dates from 1452, the main part above from 1553, and the top storey, with its elaborate stonework, and the adjoining round tower, is circa 1594.

Huntly Castle is famous for the inscription carved in large letters into the exterior stonework, there is nothing like it anywhere else in Scotland. It reads: 'George Gordon – First Marquis of Huntlie',

and this is set above 'Hentriette Stewart, Marquess of Huntlie'. The date 1602 is added to this. It is a unique ornate touch.

An interesting marriage may have taken place in this castle in 1496, although other sources state that this union took place in Edinburgh. Perkin Warbeck, called Duke of York, was a pretender to the English throne. He claimed to be the younger son of Edward IV of England, and rightful heir to the English crown over the then occupant, Henry VII, who had usurped the throne.

Obviously, it suited James IV of Scotland to believe this fanciful tale, as it brought pressure to bear on the English, the presence of Warbeck in Scotland a threat Henry VII took seriously. King James gave Warbeck the hand of Lady Catherine Gordon, daughter of the second Earl of Huntly, in marriage. It was a lavish affair, and jousting followed in which the King of Scots himself took part.

Eventually Warbeck left Scotland for Ireland, the Lady Catherine with him, and from Ireland he attempted an invasion of England, landing in Cornwall. He was soon captured, and was a prisoner of Henry VII for two years before he was hung. The Lady Catherine's fate, whether left in Ireland or accompanying her husband to England, is not recorded.

Drive back through Huntly, directly through the town this time, to reach the A96 again. This will give you a chance to get a look at the place, the elegant main square etc. You pass the old Stewarts' Hall with its steeple, reminiscent of the tolbooth steeples we have seen in many Scottish towns.

You turn left onto the A96. As you leave Huntly, look to your left and you will see there is some higher ground, tree covered, on the edge of the town. King Robert the Bruce was here on Christmas Day 1307. He had had a seizure of some sort, most likely brought on by the endless stress of sleeping rough and living on a knife edge. He had been fighting the English as well as trying to quash his enemies inside Scotland itself. His womenfolk were in cages, his friends and brothers murdered. A man can only take so much, and although he is remembered as a hero-king, he was still flesh and blood like the rest of us. His men formed a human cordon about him. The Earl of Buchan approached with his army; Buchan was a sworn enemy of Bruce. He obviously thought the time was ripe to attack Bruce due to the illness he was suffering, but was intimidated by the ferocious demeanour of Bruce's army.

A few spears were thrown, and a few flights of arrows were exchanged, then Buchan backed off. This skirmish is mentioned as having taken place at Slioch, marked just east of Huntly on some maps, as of course the name Huntly did not exist at the time of Bruce.

A time of reckoning between Bruce and Buchan was to come though, and we will talk of that shortly.

After leaving the environs of Huntly, we drive through hillier country again, the road traversing what are called the Glens of Foudland. Wishach Hill at 1,375 feet, rises first to our right, the south side, followed by the Hill of Foudland at 1,529 feet. It is a straightforward stretch here, and for several miles we continue on. Once we have passed the Oyne area, keep watching for a minor road that goes off to the right, signposted The Maiden Stone, ½ mile and Chapel of Garrioch. We can follow this road round in a semi-circle and return to the A96 in a few miles. Follow the road uphill, through woodland, for the afore-stated distance, and you will see the Maiden Stone by the right side of the road. There are parking places immediately beyond it.

I really like this sculptured stone; it is a favourite of mine, in an area rich in fine examples. It is a pinkish granite, and has very interesting carving on it. We do not know the meaning of many of the inscriptions on these stones, but as this stone has a mirror and comb prominently displayed, it is reckoned that this stone was raised to commemorate an important lady – hence the name, the Maiden Stone. You will notice that it too has the Celtic Beast carved upon it. If only we knew the significance of this fabulous animal.

I have a friend, Ronald Henderson, who resides in Bridge of Earn. Ron carves stones, in the same way as our early ancestors, and his works are a thing of great beauty. He has spent a lifetime studying the carving work of the ancients, and reckons that the Celtic Beast is a representation of a kelpie. Kelpies were beasts of legend in Scotland. They lived in lochs, but could emerge onto dry land and assume the guise of a horse. The unwary would happen across one of these 'water horses' and climb onto its back, whereupon it would gallop back into the water with its victim, who would never be seen again. Even though this may be the case, why were they carved onto these stones? What did these symbols mean to our ancestors?

The back of the stone has knotwork carved upon it. There is a chip into the side of the stone, a gouge, but it is not the result of damage, as the carved work goes into this area too. The Maiden Stone is not covered in any way, but I feel that such an enigmatic example of the works of our ancestors should perhaps be protected, even if it detracts a little from the stone sitting out as some sort of sign in the open, as it was originally intended to do.

About 100 yards back in the woodland on the opposite side of the road from the Maiden Stone, there is a modern statue of the Maiden herself. It actually stands just inside some private ground, so show some consideration. She stands about 12 feet high, is Amazonian in aspect, and is holding the same mirror that is depicted on the stone itself. Very impressive. I don't know who sculpted this representation of the legendary maiden, but it is quite overwhelming. She looks out over the countryside from her stony eyes, but she has that certain something that some statues have, where you half expect her to suddenly start to move. Hmmm. Anyway, if you start to walk back to your vehicle, take a quick glance over your shoulder in case she has started to follow you.

Continue on to the tiny village of Chapel of Garioch. The very prominent hill to your right is Bennachie, with its highest top nearest you, named Mither Tap, at 1,698 feet. Bennachie is a much-loved hill in these parts, as it somehow symbolises the people themselves, similar to the way the Scots

Borderers feel about the Eildons. Ageless. Timeless. The first settlers here looked upon it very much as we see it today, and that still means something. It basically shouts 'home' to all who live within view of it, and has done for a hundred generations.

The name Chapel of Garioch is old, and obviously takes this moniker from an early church that stood on this site. The current church in the village was built in 1813.

Through the village, and continue on this minor road. A ruined castle appears on your left on the lowest part of the ground, near a stream. There is really only one wall standing: the rest is rubble. It has been one of your standard four-square tower houses, so prevalent in Scotland, but is a sad ruin now. This is Balquhain Castle. Following the road uphill after Balqhuain, after a few hundred yards you drive beneath some power cables, running from pylon to pylon. As you go under these cables, look over into the fields on your left. About halfway up the rise opposite, there is a stone circle in one of the fields. Although this is a field used for crops, the farmer ploughs round, leaving these ancient artefacts alone, so you should be able to spot them easily enough.

As you broach the top of this rise, coming back down towards the main road again after this little meander, you will see a tower in the distance at about ten o'clock to your position. This memorial was raised to commemorate the battle of Harlaw, and we are going to drive over towards it.

When we again reach the A96, it is only a slight stagger, and we take the road off to our left, almost opposite where we have just joined this main route. This wee road is signposted Brandsbutt. This road takes us down towards the quite major town of Inverurie. We do not go into the centre of town yet, though. When you reach a roundabout, take a left turn signposted Rothienorman, B9001. Follow this road a little until you reach a road branching off on your left signposted Balhalgardy and Harlaw. Along here, just by a bend, is the battle site.

Harlaw was a bloody affair, so much so that the battle is often referred to as 'Red Harlaw'. It was fought on 24 July 1411. The actual site of the main encounter is the area of heathland stretching northwest of this monument. Donald, the then Lord of the Isles, raised an army to try and force through his claim to the vast Earldom of Ross. The King of Scots, James I, was not intimidated by these threats. Donald said that he would burn the city of Aberdeen, and he advanced through Moray, Strathbogie and Garioch with fire and sword. The inhabitants of Aberdeen were in great alarm at this dreadful threat growing ever closer. The Earl of Mar, who owned land in this area, started to raise an army to counter the threat, the army of Donald now numbering some 10,000 men. Many joined the Earl of Mar from the surrounding area, many gentlemen coming from Angus and the Mearns, and many burgesses of Aberdeen came forward under the command of their provost Sir Robert Davidson. They advanced to Inverurie, and saw that Donald's host was camped at Harlaw. Although greatly outnumbered, Mar decided to give immediate battle, trusting that his armoured and better-equipped force would make up for lack of numbers. He placed the well-armed knights at the front and drove forward.

Donald's Highland army, nothing loth, with a terrific shout, came to meet their foe. They met with a tremendous impact, but it was held by Mar, his lance and axe-wielding knights cutting down the lightly armed Islemen. Sir James Scrymgeour, Constable of Dundee, cut his way forward with his column, carrying death, but for every Isleman slain, there were ten ready to take his place. Scrymgeour's men were soon surrounded, and fought to the last man, each life costing their enemy dear. Somewhere in this carnage the Constable of Dundee fell, his horse stabbed, and then he too was dispatched by the dagger. One by one they fell.

The Earl of Mar then penetrated deep into the enemy with his main array, and the clash continued on till nightfall, when both sides fell back in a stalemate. The result of the battle was indecisive, but the impetus of Donald's Islemen was lost and the threat to Aberdeen lifted. In Aberdeen Harlaw is still remembered as a great deliverance, but deliverance at a heavy cost. Many of the families of the Aberdeen area lost not only the head of the house, but many of the males of the family. Leslie of Balquhain, the ruined castle we passed so recently, fell along with six of his sons, in view of their own land. Among the death roll were Sir James Scrymgeour, Sir Alexander Ogilvy, Sheriff of Angus, his eldest son George Ogilvy, Sir Thomas Murray, Sir Robert Maule of Panmure, Sir Alexander Irving of Drum, Sir William Abernethy of Salton, Sir Alexander Straiton of Lauriston, James Lovel, Alexander Stirling and Robert Davidson, the brave Aberdeen provost. All fell, never to rise, surrounded by 500 of their men at arms. Donald's army left 900 dead on the field, including the chiefs of Clan Maclean and Mackintosh.

The monument was designed by the scholar-architect William Kelly 1861–1944, and was erected by the Burgh of Aberdeen in 1911, the 500th anniversary of the battle. There is an inscription round the top of the monument: 'To the memory of provost Robert Davidson and the burgesses of Aberdeen who fell here, 1411'.

Looking out from the monument today, over fields populated by nothing more war-like than the odd cow or sheep, all is quiet other than the sighing of the wind, or the carrying sound of car and van engines on the A96. But, once men fought here, locked in a struggle to the death. Their blood has fertilised the flora here, and centuries on I think of them, and again wonder if I could ask them if they felt their lives were lost needlessly, how would they reply? One side fought to further a claim for land, and the other fought to protect their homes and womenfolk, and the battle had to be fought. Much as I don't like Scot fighting Scot, we all have decisions in life to confront, but I hope the time does not come again when Scotland is badly led or divided enough for the like to happen again.

Retrace your route back to the roundabout you were at on the edge of Inverurie, and when you reach it take the first left towards the town centre. The name is self-explanatory. *Inver* is the Gaelic for a river mouth, like Inverness or Inverlochy, on the Rivers Ness and Lochy. Here the River Urie flows in to the larger River Don, hence the name.

There is a museum in the town, at the top end of its main street, and here, at a roundabout, you will see signs pointing to Old Meldrum. It is about four miles or so from Inverurie to Old Meldrum, and it was on the line of this road that the crunch came between King Robert the Bruce and the Earl of Buchan, that was referred to when we were at Huntly. Bruce had a force of 700 or so, Buchan had about 1,000. During May 1308 Bruce advanced from Inverurie, following the line of the modern road, the B9170 towards Old Meldrum where Buchan was based.

Buchan's men were surprised by the forcefulness of Bruce's attack, and their forward movement was halted, then became a retreat, but panic took hold and it became a rout. It was a running fight, so was spread over quite a large area, but the main action probably took place under Barra Hill, a prominent grassy height to the east of the road.

The Earl of Buchan's power was broken by this action, referred to as the Battle of Old Meldrum, but Bruce took a terrible retribution on the Buchan area to destroy his enemy's support there once and for all. Men were put to the sword, farms were burned and cattle were slaughtered. John Barbour, Archdeacon of Aberdeen, who wrote an epic biography of Bruce in the 1370s, mentions that 50 years on, men still mourned the 'Hership [harrying] of Bouchane'. There is no memorial to this battle, unlike nearby Harlaw, but Bruce's fight is worth the mention, these two battlefields being in such close proximity. In fact, there was a third major action which took place in the town itself. On 23 December, 1745, Lord Lewis Gordon, with 1200 Jacobites, surprised and defeated 700 Hanoverian loyalists under the command of the Laird of Macleod in Inverurie.

Continue on through Inverurie, and when you are on the far edge of the town centre, look for a road going off left, signposted Keith Hall and Whiterashes, the B993. Take this road, cross the River Urie, then you come to a cemetery. This cemetery is built around the Bass of Inverurie, a perfect specimen of a motte-and-bailey construction, the earthworks of an early medieval castle. Park so you can take a look. It is said that the basic structure of the Bass is natural, though it looks man-made. If this is the case, it will be have been created by deposits from the last ice-age, either the River Don or Urie carrying detritus down, and the swirling waters creating this conical shape. Perfect place for a fortification, and obviously some work of human endeavour has gone in to making it ideal for that purpose. It is about 50 feet high, and very steep sided, a bit of leg-muscle work needing to be used to get you to the top. Mary, Queen of Scots visited the Bass in 1562.

Drive on from the Bass, and follow the signs directing you to Kinkell Church. We will be retracing our route here, but it is worth driving on a little to see this church. As the road goes on round a tight left hand bend, you continue straight on, the sign telling you Kinkell Church ½ mile. Again the road swings left, but you continue straight on. The River Don is on your right here, the Urie having flowed into it just a little nearer the town.

Round a last bend there are a row of cottages, and the church is directly behind them. It is well-signposted. Kinkell is a corruption of the Gaelic for 'head church'. When it was originally built is not recorded, but it was rebuilt in 1524 by Alexander Galloway, the rector of the place. It was unroofed in 1771 to furnish materials for Keithhall Church, and was allowed to deteriorate from that time. What exists today is a rectangular block, three of the walls rising to about 12 feet in height, and low remnants of the fourth wall. The church was dedicated to St Michael, and in its north wall is an interesting sacrament house. This ornate little inshot was for storing the consecrated host for services, and it is dated 1524. There is also a bronze replica of a cavalry, the original is now lost, but it was dated 1525. Both of these bear the initials of the aforementioned Alexander Galloway.

Something most interesting is the graveslab of a knight slain at the Battle of Harlaw. Only two-thirds of the original survive, but luckily it is the top two-thirds, so there is much detail to see. It is the grave of Gilbert de Greenlaw, and Gilbert has his hands clasped in prayer and is dressed in full armour. He wears a dirk at his waist, with a large claymore-style sword to his left, and his coats of arms is carved on either side of his head, clad in helmet and mail coif. I suppose many of the knights who died at Harlaw had such graves, but this is the only one I know of that exists today.

Back to Inverurie, and when we reach the main road again, turn left. We cross the River Don into the suburb of Port Elphinstone. Continue on, and if you take the last left just before the roundabout on the very edge of the houses, you will see there is a henge and standing stones in the grassy area on your left. Seems people have lived in Inverurie for a long, long time.

Quick u-turn and back to the last roundabout, and again it is the A96 and onwards to Aberdeen. Dual carriageway all the way. It comes as a bit of a culture shock, dual carriageway, after standing stones and empty battlefields. Almost like being thrown into the present, changing time dimension to do so. Sometimes when I have been out on the bike, lost in what I am doing and lost in my own perspectives of time, driving little back roads, stopping to look at ruins or interesting old church yards, noticing the birds, and the changing seasons on the trees, it is a real shock to drive into a city with a huge amount of traffic and bustle.

Aberdeen always gets me like that. It is as if there is a boundary that 90% of the traffic does not cross, and I suddenly drive into it. You sit quite high on a motorcycle, higher than in most cars, and I look over the rows of car roofs at the traffic lights. It's the stop start of city traffic after having had the unbridled joy of tootling along at my own speed that jars. I do sometimes drive too fast, but that is reserved for routes I have driven hundreds of times. I tend to drive very slowly on roads I don't know. Not just because I could be caught out by a too-tight bend and end up as a decoration on the front of an artic. I just enjoy roads I don't know well, and I want to absorb every detail. My eyes constantly scan the surroundings, looking for something, anything, that smacks of Scotland's history. And I look down at every stream on every bridge crossing them, and at every height and eminence in the landscape.

I love being Scottish. It's just the right size.

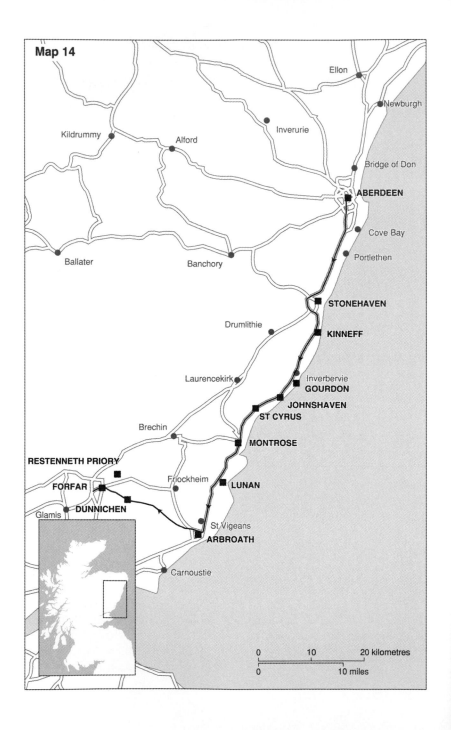

Map 14

CHAPTER FOURTEEN

Following the Grey North Sea

FROM ABERDEEN THE A92 IS FOLLOWED DOWN TO ARBROATH WITH A SMALL DEVIATION AT KINNEFF BEFORE REACHING FORFAR. THE ROUTE ENDS WHEN THE ROAD GOES UNDER THE A90.

AS YOU DRIVE into Aberdeen, Scotland's third largest city after Glasgow and Edinburgh, keep your eyes peeled for signs pointing the way to 'Old Aberdeen'. 'Why *Old* Aberdeen?', I hear you ask. King Edward III of England was good enough to burn the place in 1337, and the city was rebuilt. After that date there were two entities, Aberdeen, and the original Old Aberdeen. Although they ran into each other, they were actually regarded as separate entities right up until 1891.

As Old Aberdeen is the northern part of the city, it is there we will head for first, and our first port of call is St Machar's Cathedral. You follow the Great Northern Road, coming into the city from Inverurie, till you come to the junction where St Machar's Drive goes down to your left. The cathedral stands in Chanonry Street, a little leafy street, and it is signposted, but it is easy to miss. If in doubt, just ask. Scots are generally a helpful lot, and trust me, I ask constantly – there is nothing to beat local knowledge.

St Machar's is a powerful, squat-looking building. Endearing, although it does not have the airy lines of many English or European cathedrals. Most striking are its twin towers, giving it an immediately recognisable aspect, and separating it from any other cathedral I have seen. It was founded around 1136, although the earliest part still to be seen dates from the mid-1300s. Legend does say that there was a place of worship on this site from the year 580. Machar, of course, was its founder. He was a companion of St Columba of Iona.

You approach the entrance through its very busy graveyard. There must be quite a bit of jostling going on underground, so many generations of Aberdonians having been buried here. There really isn't a lot of room for any more gravestones!

As you enter St Machar's, the first thing to jump out at you is the roof. For a start it's flat, like a ceiling. It's wooden, and there must be a feat of engineering involved in some way, as it is just wood, with no visible support. It was built in the time of Bishop Gavin Dunbar, between 1518 and 1532. The heraldic panels set upon it give colour to the place. They are the coats of arms of some European royalty, and of some of the noble and ecclesiastical arms of Scotland, 48 in all.

There is a lot to see in St Machar's, but look out for the recently restored Sanctuary Cross. The original head has been mounted on a modern pillar. There is a stone Pictish incised cross too. My favourite, though, is the carved oak triptych, raised as a memorial to John Barbour, who was an archdeacon in the cathedral, and who died in 1395. Barbour is often regarded as the father of Scots verse, and I am a fan of his work. He wrote an epic poem about the life and deeds of King Robert the Bruce, using eye-witness accounts and speaking to men who had actually fought in Bruce's campaigns to give a clarity to his work. *The Brus*, finished around 1370, is the earliest major work of Scottish literature, and still one of the finest. If you can get hold of a modern copy, do so and see what a readable patriotic work it is. It does not seem dated in any way, and it gives an insight into the days of some of our great heroes, like Douglas, Moray and Bruce himself, coupled with stirring tales of the battles they fought. I have avidly read Barbour's work and can identify with the feelings he had for his native soil, and all of his underlying emotions. He very much feels the same way as I do, though over 600 years separate us. So I find it humbling, as a writer, to visit the site of the place where he worked. He is buried beneath the floor of the aisle where his monument stands.

The first panel of the triptych shows Bruce addressing his men before the Battle of Bannockburn. The second shows the Auld Brig O' Don, also known as the Brig O' Balgonie, a single-arch bridge built in the early 1300s, which stands a little to the north of the cathedral. The third panel shows Barbour himself working away at his desk in the cathedral. The panel beneath states:

> To the glory of God and in memory of John Barbour, father of Scots verse, Archdeacon here for forty years, died 1395, buried in this aisle. He wrote *The Brus*.

There is also a quote from the poem:

> A! Freedom is a noble thing!
> Freedom gives man security and comfort.
> Freedom allows a man to be admired.
> He who lives freely lives at ease!

The plaques were carved by Roland Fraser from Stonehaven. I like the fact that half the cost of the commission was met from Aberdeen's Common Good Fund, which was established in Aberdeen by Robert the Bruce for the benefit of the citizens of Aberdeen. A direct link down the centuries, then.

I think of Barbour working away, and I suppose he just wanted to record the story for fellow Scots. I wonder if he could ever have guessed that all these years on, someone like me who admires his work would be happy to visit his burial place. He has shown us that ordinary Scots have their role to play in the fight for Scotland's freedom, and his poem is part of the enduring legacy, just as it has come down from Wallace and Bruce themselves.

If you walk round the back of the cathedral, you will find that there are ruined walls and tombs of pre-Reformation date, and it is also worth walking to the little gate at the back right hand corner of the graveyard to take a look at a wee feature there.

As you go through the gate into the street beyond, turn and look at the wall on your left, just at the side of the gate you have walked through. There is an inscription of a star on the stonework, and local legend states that an arm of William Wallace is buried here. The legend is untrue, as the trial accounts of Wallace's murder in London state that the quarters of his body were sent to Newcastle, Stirling, Berwick and Perth.

My friend Brendan, who I met up with at St Machar's, had the idea that perhaps part of Montrose's body had been sent here, as he occupied Aberdeen on three separate occasions. Montrose's body was cut to bits and displayed in various parts of Scotland, so this is a possibility. One of the attendants, though, had the idea that it was the amputated arm of a minor nobleman who had been caught stealing that was buried at the spot. Nonetheless, whatever the story, you can at least have a look at the star!

When walking back through the graveyard you may want to look for the Glover family burial ground. A member of the Glovers was Thomas, not widely known in Scotland, but a big name in Japan. He was one of the founders of modern industrial Japan. He introduced the first steam locomotive, opened the first coal mine, had its first real dock built, which was constructed in Aberdeen, and founded the Japanese Navy with three Aberdeen-built ships. He had an affair with a Japanese lady called Maki Kaga, and this romance was the prototype for the opera *Madame Butterfly*. He founded the Mitsubishi Corporation too. By a strange twist, the bombing of Nagasaki during World War II was due to the amount of industry built in that area under Glover's influence. He died in 1911, aged 73, and was buried in Nagasaki's Sakamoto-machi cemetery, but his ancestors are in the tomb here.

As we leave St Machar's, we head for the city centre. You will have noticed by now that Aberdeen is almost entirely constructed from grey granite. In fact, many Scots refer to Aberdeen simply as the Granite City. It is a pleasant light grey though, with many sparkly bits embedded within, and it does not give the place the dour aspect you might expect.

I have a fondness for Aberdeen. I spent a couple of childhood holidays there, and I like the people. They do not have the inherent bigotry of

Glasgow, and it doesn't have the cosmopolitan feel of Edinburgh. It seems more purely *Scottish*, somehow. Takes me an hour or two to adjust to the accent though! But I like to hear the folk talk in their 'mither' tongue.

The main thoroughfare in Aberdeen is Union Street, which dissects the city from east to west. It is a pity that the street bears this name, a throwback to the Union that was foisted on Scotland. King Robert the Bruce had associations with Aberdeen, left a legacy of money to the city, but does not have fitting monument to his memory. Perhaps Union Street should be renamed 'King Robert the Bruce Street'! Head for Union Street, and park as near to its eastern, seaward end as you can, and I'll take you on a wee tour from there.

At its eastern end Union Street comes to an abrupt end at a large gothic building with a soaring castelated tower. This is the Salvation Army Citadel. Before this is Castle Street, with its pedestrianised area where street markets are still sometimes held. The name Castle Street is of course a clue to the site of the old Castle of Aberdeen, long gone, and of which not a stone remains.

In the centre of this pedestrianised area stands the Mercat Cross, a large canopied affair, with a pillar atop it. A unicorn holding a shield bearing the Lion Rampant sits upon this pillar. Unusual here are the portraits of the Stewart monarchs of Scotland, carved in stone around the Mercat Cross. Running in order, they are James I, James II, James III, James IV, James V, Mary, Queen of Scots, James VI, Charles I, Charles II and James VII, who was king when this edifice was built in 1686. It cost £100, which was paid out of the guild wine funds.

Cross towards the right-hand side of Union Street. You will notice that just a few yards down there is a square of cobbles on the road, about a yard square, just beside the pavement. This is the site of the old gallows of Aberdeen where executions took place.

Directly opposite, there is an old bank building on the corner of Castle Street and Marischal Street, which bears a plaque facing you, stating:

John Barbour, Poet 1316–1395, Author of the Bruis, lived nearby

So, Barbour's own home must have been in this vicinity, but why they have changed the spelling of Brus to Bruis, I have no idea.

If you actually glance down Marischal Street, you can see ships at berth in the harbour just a few yards down at the bottom of the hill. There can't be many cities where you are in their main shopping street, and you can see sea-going ships just a few yards away, as you can here in Aberdeen.

On along Union Street a few yards, and Broad Street goes off to your right. On the right of Broad Street is a stunning granite building in a gothic style. This is the Marischal College, part of the university. The original buildings were part of the Franciscan Monastery, suppressed at the

Reformation. And what was left of the monastery was incorporated into an earlier version of the college. These old buildings were swept away and replaced by this imposing one between 1837 and 1841. It was designed by Archibald Simpson, and it cost £30,000 to build.

The reason it bears the name Marischal College is because the original buildings were founded in 1593 by George Keith the Earl Marischal.

If you walk through the arch at the far end into the internal square, you will find that the doors at the opposite side of this square take you up an imposing staircase to a great wee museum. This museum is free to enter, and that is guaranteed to warm the heart of any Scot, and Aberdonians especially!

When you reach the top of the stairs, take a look through the doors ahead of you, before you turn left into the museum itself. You can see The Great Window of the Mitchell Hall before you. It is a kaleidoscope of colour. It contains, in stained glass, 68 coats of arms, ten full length portraits of distinguished individuals, and ten medallion portraits, all of which are connected with the college in some capacity.

So, into the museum. I met up with Jim 'The Bull' and Bruce, Aberdonian patriots, just before I entered, and so with Brendan there were four of us. We walked into the museum, and had the place to ourselves! There was not another soul inside, and it was summer, the start of July no less, though it was mid-week. For a little historically-minded group like us, a museum with a collection like this is like putting a bunch of kids in Santa's Grotto. There are claymores, basket-hilted broadswords, – one in fabulous condition, inscribed 'Saint Andreas, prosperity to Scotland and No Union! God save King James VIII' That was obviously around in 1715 when that James was proclaimed king. There is a targe, a highland shield complete with spike, which was used at the Battle of Clifton in 1745. There were coins struck at the old Aberdeen mint, a large wooden plaque with the arms of King James VI that once adorned that self-same mint. Communion plates, Pictish stones – one with the Celtic beast. The list goes on. All set in old cases, all with a dusty, fusty feel (fusty, pronounced foosty, is a peculiarly Scottish word, meaning a bit old and dusty) but I loved it, and could have spend a day in that part alone.

The right turn off from the top of the entrance stairs takes you into the vast collection gathered by Robert Wilson. Wilson was born in Banff in 1787, and graduated in medicine from Marischal College in 1805. He joined the East India Company as a ship's surgeon. For six years he travelled through the provinces of the crumbling Ottoman Empire, the present countries of Egypt, Syria, Turkey, Iraq and Iran, and beyond to India. He retired to Moray, and when he died in 1871, he donated the collection he had gathered to his old college to form the basis for a museum. Wilson was sometimes underhand in his quest for artefacts, but you cannot help but be impressed by this collection. I don't know how I would feel if I was from, say, Iran, and saw this lot. Probably the same way I'd feel if I travelled thousands of miles and saw a collection of Scottish artefacts. You get the gist.

When you exit Marischal College, your next port of call is only a few yards away across Broad Street, but it is hidden from view. There is a large, fairly modern office block called St Nicholas House opposite, and if you walk through between the concrete legs it is raised on, you will see there is an old stone building to your right. This is Provost Skene's House, built in the 1600s, and open today as a museum. Free. Hooray! Again, we had the place to ourselves, extraordinary when there is so much squeezed into this great old place.

It was formerly the town residence of Sir George Skene, Provost of Aberdeen 1676–85. It was restored by the Corporation of the City of Aberdeen. It was opened as a museum on 30 September 1953, by a wee woman of Germanic stock who lives in a palace in London.

There is some of the old painted plasterwork intact. It was found under later work when renovations were taking place in 1951. It is unusual in Scotland, as the pictures contain scenes from Jesus' life; most of these types of work were destroyed at the Reformation here, and so are rare indeed. Nice place, but it has a skeleton rattling in its closet. The Duke of Cumberland stayed in this house on his way north to destroy the clans at the Battle of Culloden in 1746. There is a portrait of this dietarily challenged young man on the stairway.

I don't care where your loyalties lie. I have a problem with foreigners killing Scots on Scottish soil. I'm glad to say I'm not the only one. A grateful London government named a flower in his honour – Sweet William. In Scotland, we call it Stinking Billy.

If you go back along to Union Street and continue on, on your right will soon appear the Grecian facade that leads into the graveyard of the Kirk of St Nicholas. This impressive facade was constructed in 1830 at a cost of £1,460. There are twelve ionic columns, 32.5 feet in height, and each is carved from a single block. They must be immensely heavy, and I can only marvel at how they were transported here from the sculptor's yard, and how they were put in place.

There are many interesting memorials in this graveyard, especially along the wall on the eastern side. St Nicholas's is interesting in the fact that there is building work in the fabric of the building that is as early as the 1100s, and as recent as 1935. There is some good woodwork and stained glass within the church, but many visitors come to see the four large needlework panels, sewn around 1665 by Mary Jamesone, daughter of George Jamesone, Scotland's earliest known portrait painter. Her work *The Finding of Moses* is interesting, as she has the bridge over Aberdeen's River Dee in the background!

What I like about St Nicholas's personally are the effigies within the church. They are not in their original places, but the fact that they have survived is enough. One effigy is believed to be that of brave Provost Davidson, who fought at the Battle of Harlaw in 1411. There are also some fragments of early carven stones.

Onwards on Union Street, and we cross the Union Bridge, another of Thomas Telford's creations. It is 70 feet wide and was constructed between 1800 and 1803 at a cost of £13,342. It was built to cross the Den Burn originally, and before its building, folk used to have to scramble down one side of this valley and up the other!

Once across this bridge turn right into Union Terrace. A couple of hundred yards on at the end of this street stands the massive statue of Sir William Wallace, 'returning defiant answer to the English ambassadors before the battle of Stirling Bridge'. It has been cast in bronze, and stands mightily upon its tall granite plinth. There are many statues of Wallace in Scotland, but this, along with the one on the Athenium Building in Stirling, is a particular favourite of mine. It was designed by WG Stevenson RSA, and was unveiled by the Marquis of Lorne in 1888. It is the gift of Mr John Steel of Edinburgh, who left £4,000 for the purpose. Thanks, John! There is a surrounding fence with inserts of the Wallace coat of arms.

I have given a speech by torchlight at this statue, and the spot has good memories for me. Wallace stands, hand outstretched, long-haired and bearded, with his sword in his opposite hand. It is a worthy memorial to the man, and any visitor should not miss it. Its only drawback is that the street has the word 'Union' in its title. Everything that Wallace abhorred.

There was an earlier Wallace statue in Aberdeen, now sadly gone. I came across this reference in a book from the late 1800s:

A building, called the Wallace Tower, having in its niche a rude and very ancient effigy of Wallace, and said to have been occupied as a hostelry, stands in Nether Kirkgate: and another old tenement, known as Mar's Castle, with a diminutive crow stepped and corbelled gable, circular staircase, and small square openings for windows, stands in Gallowgate, and bears the date 1494. The two have strong generic likeness to one another, and challenge more attention from antiquaries than many old buildings of higher note.

This old, rude statue of Wallace intrigues me. It must have been the very first statue erected to Wallace's memory, as the earliest we have still standing is the one visited very early in this book above the River Tweed at Dryburgh, erected in 1814. Sadly, both the above-mentioned houses are long gone, the Nether Kirkgate too, although it stood near St Nicholas's Kirk.

After the Wallace statue, if you turn right into Denburn Viaduct, it is only a few yards to the Art Gallery, which stands opposite Belmont Street. It has

collections of paintings, sculptures, crafts, silver, ceramics and much more –
admission free!

As you return towards the east end of Union Street where you first began
this wee tour, look for a little curving street called Ship Row going off to the
right. It is before the block containing the building with the Barbour plaque.

Down here, overlooking the harbour, is Aberdeen's Maritime Museum.
It is excellently placed. It is a modern building, with large glass windows
overlooking the docks. This is an interesting place in itself, but adjacent
to the modern part is the oldest surviving house in Aberdeen, Provost
Ross's House.

Provost Ross's House was built in 1594, but ended up in a derelict state
and so was acquired by the National Trust for Scotland, and was opened as
a museum by the Secretary of State for Scotland in 1954. The Maritime
Museum was later built next door, and Provost Ross's House has been
amalgamated into part of it. It is a great looking old place from the exterior,
but it is a bit of a disappointment in the inside. Not the stuff on show – that
is really good, but the job that has been done to the interior. It just looks
like a 1950s house! Panelled doors and dull plasterwork everywhere. It
couldn't be more different from the outside aspect, in fact, it's hard to
believe it is the same building. I guess the fact that it was 'renovated' in the
early 50s has been responsible for this, and I'm glad the National Trust for
Scotland has learned a few things since!

So this has been a wee quick 'jouk' about the Granite City, and there is
much to see, but we are going to push on with our tour.

From anywhere in the city centre, follow the signs pointing the way to the
A90 and the south. On the outskirts of the town you will cross the River
Dee, which gives this city its name, Aber (the mouth of) Deen (an amalga-
mation of the two rivers, Dee and Don). It has in the course of its history
been written as Aberdoen, Aberdon, Aberdin, Aberdene etc.

We drive south from Aberdeen on the A90; the coast to our left is cliff-
girt, and for much of the way we are looking out over the North Sea, dotted
with the odd ship or fishing boat. I remember much of this stretch just
being dotted with the odd hamlet, but most of the little villages have
expanded hugely over the tail end of the 1900s, from Aberdeen's boom
years of oil, and from overspill from the city itself. Some of these original
villages hug the clifftops in attractive settings.

Fifteen miles south of Aberdeen you will see the turnoff for Stonehaven
on your left. Taking this road down to the town takes you through a
wooded defile where once Montrose's men skirmished with the
Covenanting forces. As we come down to Stonehaven Bay we go under an
old stone railway bridge. Immediately after this bridge there is a very sharp
left turn that takes you up towards the local golf club. A few yards up this
road a little path goes down towards the sea, where there is a little ruined

church. There is just enough room to park a car on this road if you are considerate, and plenty of room if you have a motorbike. It wouldn't have been lucky to have been on a bike on my last visit though. I was here with my friend Brendan McCabe, a good patriot who stays in this vicinity. This was the same Brendan who played the pipes at the ruins in Glencoe, and accompanied me through Aberdeen. The rain came in sideways off the sea, and we were soaked to the skin in seconds. Didn't stop me rummelling around the ruins and clifftops though, always eager to explore.

This little church is Cowie Church. An early chapel once stood here, dedicated to St Nathalan, whoever he may be, and was replaced by this church in 1276. It was built by Bishop William Wishart of St Andrews, and it gained the appellation St Mary of the Storms. That was certainly a fitting title up here on the clifftops on our visit! Although much ruined and with much of its side walls missing, the east end of the building still has three very interesting lancet windows. The western end is an extension built in the 1400s. On the outside of this end of the church there is an old turf-covered, stone-built mort-safe, a place where bodies could be placed before burial, or to let them decay for a while so that they would be useless for 'resurrectionists' to try and sell onto anatomy students.

Some interesting old gravestones in the churchyard too.

If you walk to the bottom of the graveyard, at the right-hand corner there is a gap through the wall where a path runs to a makeshift bridge over the Kirk Burn, a little stream that runs down to the sea. There is an abiding old legend of gold having been buried on the banks of the burn here, so as you cross remember to have a look down into the water, just in case a few coins have been dislodged and are glittering in a pool below!

Just a few yards further on stands the site of Cowie Castle. The place is just discernible, a few dips in the ground, and a few stones on the clifftop are all that remain, but it was quite a strong place once. It is traditionally said to have been founded by Malcolm Canmore, King of Scots, who reigned between 1057 and 1093, and it would have stood guard over this stretch of coast. As we walked over to peer over the edge, Brendan pointed to the strange northeast-running strata on the stony waterfront below the cliffs. The Highland Fault Line. The fault that separates the Highlands and Lowlands in Scotland runs from Arran in the Firth of Clyde, northeast to reach the coast at Stonehaven here, and it would appear that you could see it.

Down into Stonehaven below. The road here is the old north–south road, and was until recent years, but now Stonehaven has been bypassed. On this edge of town there is a now rare open-air swimming pool. Every year a march leaves from here at the end of August, patriots marching the few miles south to Dunnottar Castle to commemorate Sir William Wallace. We will come to Dunnottar shortly. Follow the road on through the town. Stonehaven has a nice open square at its heart, to the right of the main route.

There is a bridge over the Carron Water, then the town's High Street goes off to your left, leading to the original older part of the town, round its harbour. Taking this route, look on your right for Number 30 High Street. The door has a portico of wrought iron with a lamp in the middle, surmounted by a crown. There is a plaque here which reads:

> Christians House, built in 1712. Around 1746 this house was used for Episcopalian services by the Reverend Alexander Gregg, when, because of the support for the Jacobite cause, government legislation forbade congregations larger than 5. In the 1850s it was the family home of Peter Christian, solicitor and sheriff clerk of Kincardineshire, and this plaque was erected by Stonehaven Heritage Society in 1991.

The old Mercat Cross is on this street, as is the Steeple, where King James VIII, known to the Hanoverian government as the Old Pretender was proclaimed King of Scots in 1715. He was the father of Bonnie Prince Charlie, and the direct heir of the throne of the Stewart Kings of Scotland.

There is a fire festival that takes place every Hogmanay in Stonehaven. Hogmanay is the old Scots word for New Year's Eve, and is the name that every Scot today uses.

The young men of Stonehaven converge on the High Street with fireballs, paraffin-soaked rags in cages of wire netting at the end of long wire ropes. At the stroke of midnight the fireballs are set alight and the lads move off along the street whirling the balls around their heads. Traditionally, this puts evil spirits to flight and ensures the town's prosperity through the coming year.

Hogmanay still invokes many traditions in Scotland. When I was a kid, as the church bells were heard at the stroke of midnight, the doors had to be opened to let the old year out. Most people I know do this, and my daughter, currently 15, always automatically does it when the church bells near our house begin to ring.

At the end of the High Street you reach the town's harbour. Some lovely old buildings overlook this. Stonehaven was always referred to as Stanehive, and this name was common right up until the early 1900s. The 'stane' in question actually existed, and was right in front of the harbour, giving the town its name. The original stone was blown up when the modern harbour was laid out after 1826. On the left-hand side of the harbour is the town's museum, housed in a historic old building.

Back to the main through route now. At the base of the High Street, turn left, a short drive takes you out of town, then the road starts to climb, twisting and turning through woodland. At the top of this road you come to the A92, the road that runs down the east coast of Scotland. Turn left, but shortly you will see signs pointing the way to Dunnottar Castle, and you take this small diversion off left to look at this fabulous fortress.

After a few hundred yards you will reach the little car park at a lodge house. The road before you continues onwards to Stonehaven, but it is a one-way system, which accounts for our short detour onto the A92. It is up this route that the Wallace March wends its way each August.

From the car park you can see some of the castle buildings projecting over the lip where the land meets the sea, but it is only when you walk down the approach path that the dramatic situation of the castle becomes apparent. The name is Gaelic: *dun-oitir*, the fort of the low promontory. It stands on a stupendous rock, rising from the sea to a height of 160 feet, and severed from the mainland by a chasm, down which many steps descend to give access to the gateway defences, whereby you rise again to the plateau on the summit on which the castle stands.

Dunnottar figures early in history, as we hear of a siege here by Brude, King of the Picts, in AD 681. In 900 Donald, King of Scots, was slain here by Danish vikings.

If you stand on the clifftop and survey this place, you will immediately realise that prior to the era of artillery, this place was well-nigh impregnable, unless of course it was full of Englishmen and William Wallace was determined to take the place.

The old parish church of Dunnottar actually stood within the walls of the early fortification here, and even today it stands complete to the wallhead, surrounded by later castle buildings. It is said Wallace came here before Stirling Bridge, and managing to break through the defences, started to slay the many southern invaders within. The English, realising that there was no escape other than plunging over the precipitous sides of the rock and into the sea, packed themselves into the old church and claimed sanctuary. Wallace barred the doors and burnt them all within. We tend to see Wallace through rose-tinted spectacles, but his job was to destroy the invader whenever and wherever he came across them, and he was determined to free Scotland from occupation.

There is a short memorial service here after the march each year, and a wreath is laid in memory. Only a few lines are said: 'You know who he was, and you know why you are here.' We do too.

There are some interesting tales surrounding Dunnottar, and I'll tell a few of them here. William Keith, Great Marishal of Scotland, did a deal for some lands with Lord Lindsay of the Byres. Lord Lindsay received some lands in Fife and Stirling, and Keith received lands here, including the castle. He did a lot of building work to further strengthen the place, but decided he would build a church in a more convenient place for the parish, rather than have them use the one within the castle precincts, which of course involved the steep climb down and up into the castle. This was done, but the Bishop of St Andrews excommunicated him for violation of sacred ground. Keith was forced to write to Pope Benedict XIII, telling him of the necessity to strengthen the fortress, and that he had built another church to avoid any offence, that was more accessible etc. His Holiness issued a Bull, dated 18 July 1394, directing the annulment of the excommunication. The Keith family continued at Dunnottar until the forfeiture of the last Earl in 1716, due to his adherence to Scotland's Royal House of Stewart.

Edward III of England managed to take Dunnottar in 1336, but it was retaken by the Regent of Scotland in the minority of Robert the Bruce's son, David II, Sir Andrew Murray. This Murray was the son of the Murray who died of wounds received at Stirling Bridge in 1297, fighting alongside Wallace. He was born after his father's death, but obviously inherited his father's patriotism, and is remembered as a great freedom fighter, and a good regent.

Montrose came here and offered terms to the then Earl Marischal to capitulate peacefully. When he refused, Montrose burnt his surrounding property. Watching this, the Earl regretted his decision, but Andrew Cant, a minister who was part of the party within the castle, assured him that 'the smoke-reek would be a sweet-smelling incense in the nostrils of the Lord, rising, as it did, from property that had been sacrificed to the Holy Cause of the Covenant'.

Sorry, I've never been able to understand that sort of fundamentalism!

Charles II visited the place in 1650,where he was entertained by the seventh Earl.

When Cromwell invaded Scotland, it was decided that Dunnottar was the safest place in the Kingdom to house the Honours – the Crown Jewels of Scotland. Cromwell, being a parliamentarian and anti-royalty, would of course try to destroy these ancient symbols of the Kingdom of Scots, and he brought an English army north under the command of Lambert, to capture them. As often happens, it was the ordinary men and women of Scotland who came to her rescue. Some miles south of Dunnottar stands Kinneff Church, and the minister and his wife, the Reverend and Mrs Granger, hatched a plan. Mrs Granger made a visit to Dunnottar, ostensibly to visit Mrs Ogilvy, the wife of George Ogilvy of Barras, who commanded the castle for the Earl Marischal. Mrs Granger received a pass for the castle. On admission, she packed up the Crown in a bundle of clothes and wrapped the Sword and Sceptre in a length of lint, as though they were a distaff, or spindle in the middle.

On leaving the castle, the English general actually assisted her on to her horse in a gallant manner. It seems extraordinary that Mrs Granger actually pulled off this deception, and we can only guess at the strain she strove to cover carrying her treasure from the castle itself. As she rode away she must have been pinching herself in disbelief that she had achieved her aims.

Failure would have meant incarceration in a dank dungeon somewhere, but Mrs Granger realised that Scotland had a need, and she must answer it.

When she reached home and her nervous husband, incredulous at her success, they decided to bury the Honours under the flagstones inside their church. I can imagine how that must have felt, unwrapping these semi-mythical artefacts, and how the breath must have been caught in their throats at these symbols of Scotland's ancient nationhood laid before them, the gold of the Crown containing the circlet worn on Bruce's brow at Bannockburn – just one small part of the historical tapestry involved.

We will visit the little church of Kinneff shortly.

The garrison at Dunnottar was eventually starved into submission, and the castle fell. The Honours had gone, and no-one was able to, or would, say where they had gone. Two and two were never put together regarding Mrs Granger's visit, and Scotland's dignity remained intact.

Dunnottar was used in the year 1685 as a state prison for 167 Covenanters, men and women, who had been seized in the west of Scotland during their persecution under Charles II, after the Restoration of the Crown following Cromwell's death. The term 'Covenanter' had changed over the last generation, had taken on a different slant and perspective since Montrose's time, and these people were imprisoned for their beliefs. In the vault where they were kept, nine of them died in the horrible conditions. About 25, in a state of desperation, crept out of a window and tried to escape, but two perished, falling to their deaths from the precipice. The rest were captured, and suffered the most hideous tortures. You can visit the building in which these poor wretches were kept, and you may notice how smooth the walls are within, up to about head height from the floor. This is due to the fact that the prisoners would lick the walls to try to gain some moisture, as they were deprived of food and water. This smoothness is a chilling reminder of evil times, times that we must ensure never happen again in Scotland.

In 1720, the dilapidated estate of the last Earl was sold to the York Building Company of England, and the castle's fixtures and fittings were stripped out, leaving it very much as you see it today. It has gone through several owners, and is still privately owned, though happily open to the public. The current owner has been amenable to such activities as the Wallace march, and is sympathetic. It hurts me to say that a member of staff has done all he can do to discredit this good work, and make things as unfriendly and uncomfortable as possible for those wishing to remember their past with pride, even going as far as to throw a wreath over the cliffs just after it was laid. He is a Scot, one of those who puts another nation first, and is a worthy successor to the false Menteith – the Scot who betrayed Wallace. I can think of no better insult, as we are men of honour, and will not rise to the bait, or sink to his level. He will not understand this, as honour he has none.

Back to the A92, where we turn left and head further south. Beautiful rolling farmland this, the road rising and dipping, the sea our constant companion. I love it when it is that mixture of sun and cloud, when the wind blows, and the cloud shadows, interspersed with light, scud and flit over the landscape. And me, on a motorbike, answerable to no-one, and with a euphoria, pure happiness running through my veins.

We come to a little village called Kinneff. There was once a castle in this little hamlet. An old gazetteer I read says:

> Kinneff Castle was garrisoned by the English when they overran Scotland during David Bruce's (David II) minority. It went gradually to ruin till only one high, strongly cemented wall remained standing in the early part of the 18th century, and now is represented by nothing but a fragment of its foundations.

That was written about 1890. An urn was discovered by the castle ruins many years ago which contained a number of bronze rings, and an earthen pot containing a number of silver coins, said to have been hidden by the English garrison, was found in the church yard in 1837.

In the village, you will notice a sign pointing off left to Kinneff School. Take this road. Just after the school the road forks, and you take the left-hand fork. When you get to the junction at the very bottom the sign to the left says Catterline, but we turn right. A little further along you will see a little road going steeply downhill towards the sea. It has a 'dead end' sign, but there is also a smaller sign to look for on your left that says 'The Old Church of Kinneff'. This is the place we have come to see. There is ample room to park just outside the gate of this austere old place. It is generally unlocked and visitors are welcome, so walk through the graveyard and through its front door and take a journey back through history.

The church here was first consecrated in 1242. There is much early work, but there were additions in 1738, and the north aisle was added in 1876. It is a very Scottish-looking church inside, with its little balcony, and there are several interesting monuments. There is one to Graham of Largie (1597), one to Governor Sir George Ogilvy of Barras, the keeper of Dunnottar, one to the Honeymans, for four generations ministers of Kinneff, 1668 to 1781. And of course, there is a memorial to the Grangers, who are buried here, where once they buried Scotland's Honours. There is a touching memorial to them on the wall, with the Sword, Crown and Sceptre of Scotland depicted upon it. It is in Latin, but there is a translation which reads:

> Behold the spot where Grangers' ashes lie, who from besieged Dunnottar safe conveyed the insignia of Scotland's Royalty, and in this

hallowed ground in secret laid. Where now he rests himself heaven shall bestow meet recompense in such desert as his. He, who his country's Honours saved below now wields a sceptre in the realms of bliss'.

Translation, January 1876 from the original stone on the wall above.

It is a bit strange that the epitaph concentrates on the Reverend Granger, and is a bit lax in mentioning his wife, who took the risk in rescuing the Honours in the first place. The inscription came from a more chauvinistic age of course. But what I do need to point out is how well the Grangers looked after their charge. Every three months, in strictest secrecy, the Grangers would dig up the Honours and air them in front of a fire, to try and preserve them from any damage. At the Restoration of Charles II in 1660, the Honours were handed back, and have been kept in Edinburgh Castle ever since.

Charles II, not a wise man in his judgement, made the brother of the Earl Marischal, Earl of Kintore. Ogilvy of Barras was made a Baronet and given a new coat of arms. But the honest Grangers were given no honour or reward. Scotland remembers them though, and that is worth more than a title conferred.

Take a last look round the little church before you close the door and walk the few yards back to your vehicle. At the top of the hill turn left, and continue on your way. You will again reach the A92, and continue south.

We soon come into Inverbervie by way of the Bervie Jubilee Bridge, opened in 1935 by the Right Honourable The Viscount of Arbuthnot, the Lord Lieutenant and Convenor of Kincardinshire. It rises quite high above the Bervie Water, but that is not really apparent as it arcs its way over. Inverbervie, again, is a name that means what it says – the mouth of the Bervie.

Park in the street to the right, at the immediate end of the bridge. Here stands a monument to the memory of Hercules Linton, which is a good name! He was the designer of the famous clipper *Cutty Sark*, and was born in Inverbervie in 1837. He died in the house where he was born, and he is buried in Inverbervie churchyard. His memorial is a copy of the figurehead that originally adorned the ship he created. It is a likeness of a girl in a scanty shirt, grasping a grey horse's tail. She, like the name of the ship, comes from Robert Burns' famous poem *Tam O'Shanter*. In this epic poem, Tam, the worse for drink, comes across a coven of witches dancing at Alloway Kirk in Ayrshire. One young, buxom witch in a flimsy shirt catches Tam's eye. Such a garment was called a cutty sark in Scotland, and so Tam shouts 'Weel done Cutty Sark!'. He is chased by the whole coven for his trouble. He makes his getaway on his grey mare Meg, galloping for the nearby River Doon, as he knows witches cannot cross running water. Just as Meg reaches the bridge, Cutty Sark grabs her tail, and the horse's tail is all she is left holding as Tam has managed to cross the bridge.

So, the statuette here is Cutty Sark, holding the horse's tail, and she represents the ship that bore her name. She is about life size, and painted in full colour. This memorial was dedicated by the people of Inverbervie on 11 July 1997, replacing a memorial unveiled by Sir Francis Chichester, the famous round-the-world yachtsman, in 1969.

You will notice an information plaque on the wall here, that informs you that the Hercules Linton memorial stands on the site of a Carmelite Friary. It was erected in 1443, and dissolved at the Reformation of the church in 1560.

If you walk down the street just a little, you will see there is an earlier bridge over the Bervie, and below that the remains of an even earlier bridge! If you peer over the wall you can see part of the central part of a two-arched bridge built in 1696. The later bridge over that dates from 1799. The Jubilee Bridge, taking a different route over the Bervie Water is the most recent of the three.

Continuing through Inverbervie, the town square is just a little further on your left. The old Mercat Cross stands in the square, and it bears the date 1737.

John Coutts was born in Inverbervie in 1699. He was the father of Thomas Coutts, who was the founder of the famous Coutts Bank.

David II and his queen visited Inverbervie, but apparently by accident. His ship was blown off course, and eventually made land here on 4 May 1341. Unfortunately the land he 'made' was Bervie Brow, a headland rising to 451 feet at the north end of Bervie Bay. Tradition says he was shipwrecked at its base, where there is a place called the 'King's Step' and a nearby farm is Kinghornie Farm. The headland itself is called Craig David on old maps. He seemed to have no hardship with this though, as he gave the town a charter, making the place a Royal Burgh, and the various privileges that went with it. This status was renewed by James VI in 1595.

Inverbervie, or just plain 'Bervie' to most of the locals, has a stony beach, with Hallgreen Castle near its southern end. It is said the first castle on this site was built by the Dunnet family in 1376, then the land passed to the Raits in the 1400s. The building is an attractive private house today.

Follow the A92 on. Just after Inverbervie is left behind, you will see signs and the road going off left to Gourdon. This is an attractive little fishing village, its houses huddled along the seashore, down below the main road you are on. There is one road in and out, and if you are not in a hurry, it is worth going for a wander round this little place. Gourdon faces the sea in more ways than one. It has been the living of the place for centuries.

There is an old lifeboat preserved in the village, called the 'Maggie Law'. She is housed in a wee museum staffed by volunteers. She is a shallow draught surfboat, launched in 1890, and was in operation until the 1930s. Thirty-six lives were saved by this boat.

Keep an eye open for the barometer on the front, dedicated to Lt. William Farquar of the Royal Navy, who was lost with 98 others in the wreck of HMS Racehorse. This wreck was not off Gourdon I hasten to add, as the Maggie Law would have made a difference there!

Gourdon (pronounced Gurden by the locals) has been settled for a long time. Gourdon Hill behind the village has a cairn on top, with burials dating back 5,000 years. The first reference to the current village was in 1315 – the year after the victory of Bannockburn.

The harbour, built by Telford, as so many in Scotland were, is still a hive of activity, and you can sit outside the Harbour Bar and watch the comings and goings.

Back to the main road above Gourdon. A few miles on look for a sign that points the way to the Mill of Benholm. I have driven this way many times, and the last time I actually drove past the sign, when I decided to turn back and take a look. It was a good thing to do. The mill is just off to the right, and it was a find and a half. I parked, and walked down the gradient to the cluster of old buildings, with the mill lade-pond at the far side. A bearded gentleman, every bit looking like an oldie-worldie miller, introduced himself. Pete then showed me round. 'Would you like to see the wheel working?', he asked. I hastily agreed that I would, eyeing the large wheel at the side of the old mill. He opened the sluice gate, and water began to run from the lade-pond, tumbling over the wheel. When the third slat began to fill, the weight was there, and the wheel began to turn slowly. It quickly built up speed. Pete took me inside to see all the workings of an old mill in full swing. All the different pieces of machinery working off that water power. The most astonishing thing about my visit was that no-one else was there! Not another soul came to visit during my look around, and it was a really, really good look round. One of those places you find by chance, stop at, and drive away very pleased with yourself that you have seen something so excellent. Go. Simple as that. Go and learn, and marvel at this old place.

This mill is first mentioned in the 1100s. A charter tells us that William the Lion, King of Scots, granted the lands of Benne, including its pastures, moors, woods and mills, to Hugo, who then was known as Hugo de Benne, that is, Hugo of Benne. A charter of 1492 tells us John and Isabel Lundy granted the lands and barony of Benhame with the mill, to their son, Robert.

We actually know all the names of the millers from 1696 onwards. And this was still a working mill right up to 1982, when the last miller, Lindsay C Watson, died. Benholm Mill slowly started to deteriorate as it lay silent and deserted by its stream. In 1986 it was purchased by Kincardine and

Deeside District Council, and the process of putting this mill in working order again began.

All those years of the clack-clack of water-driven machinery. Wouldn't it have been tragic if that sound, which resounded in this little hollow for over a century before the time of Sir William Wallace, had been silenced forever?

There were many mills like this in Scotland once, and the huge part they once played should be saved for posterity. There is more to see than you think. A scatter of buildings with their particular functions, the mill-pond and its sluices, and don't forget to walk up the stream a little to the weir that siphons off the water to power all this.

The best bit of my visit? I sat inside the mill with Pete, the mechanism all turning away, and we discussed spring and how some years the house martins turn up first, how some years it is the swallows, who both nest in the buildings, and how the summer could be judged by which species turns up first. In the middle of this, Pete said 'I want you to hear my favourite thing of the day,' and he pulled the lever to stop the water running to the wheel. We sat for the best part of a minute. The click-clack eventually began to slow. Seconds began to separate the noises. Then everything fell silent. We two sat in this silence. A loud silence after the incessant noise. After about 30 seconds of this I turned to Pete and I said that I understood what he meant. That silence meant that the working day was over. For nigh on a thousand years, millers here had shut down their wheel and silence had enveloped the mill. I can imagine them taking a last look round, then closing the door for the night, leaving the place to the family of mice who would scavage for the odd dropped grain during the night.

All the history of the ordinary people of my nation is wound up in the stonework of Benholm Mill.

Writing this, months after my visit, there is still a feeling of satisfaction in the time that I spent there. And it is as much a part of Scotland as the frowning crags of Liathach, or the Wallace Monument on the Abbey Craig, standing watch over the valley of the Forth. I had the place to myself. I really can't believe it, and I hope when you finally go, the mill is ringing to the footsteps and laughter of children, and interested dads watching the cogs and sprockets do what they do. If they are there, I have done my stuff and spread the word, and let all those generations of millers at Benholm know that their mill is in safe hands.

The mill is open daily from Easter to the end of October, from 11 o'clock in the morning till 5 in the evening.

Onwards again.

Only a mile or so after the mill, while driving through some woods, you will see the sign pointing off left to Johnshaven. I think this little fishing village is the twin of Gourdon, but whatever you do never mention that in Johnshaven itself. Gourdon and Johnshaven are like two dogs eyeing the same bone, and neither village has much good to say about the other. They were once connected by the railway that ran up this coast. It is gone, but it now forms part of an excellent cycling and walking path. Johnshaven is obviously named after John somebody-or-other, but who he was is lost to history. It is still a haven to boats though, and there are usually several sitting on the quayside, some painting or refitting going on, and adding to the picturesque aspect of the place.

Heading on from Johnshaven, we crest the rise and if it is clear you will be able to see the blunt cliff of the promontory of Red Head jutting into the sea some 20 miles to the south. The defunct line of the railway runs to our left now, and ahead you will see the steeple of the church of St Cyrus rising above its village. Like Johnshaven, there is a bit of a mystery about how St Cyrus got its name. There are two Cyruses mentioned in world history, but one was martyred in Antioch, and the other hailed from Alexandria, so how this place got the name is open to conjecture. May have been a local saint of that name of course, who has quietly disappeared from our record books.

The village used to stand down by the shore, but it has moved uphill. All that remains of the earlier site is a ruined chapel by the old burial ground at the bottom of the cliff. The seafront in the St Cyrus area is a vast nature reserve and many rare species of flora and fauna exist here. The beach itself is a beautiful clean sweep of sand. About a mile northeast a little structure stands on a cliff top. This is the ruined Kaim of Mathers, a refuge built by a Barclay in 1421, after he had slain a sheriff of the Mearns, as this area is called. It stands near Milton Ness, a prominent cliff at the north end of the bay.

We push on towards Montrose, quite a major town, but first we have to cross the North Esk, one of the major rivers of this seaboard. We cross it on an old bridge, the Lower Northwater Bridge, which is only really wide enough for one vehicle at a time, so as you come round that last bend onto the bridge, don't attempt to cross of there is a lorry coming the other way! It is quite a remarkable structure, not least as it has stood the test of time, with modern traffic thundering over it. At the far end of the bridge there is a large stone, almost like an overgrown gravestone, on your left. If you are not on a motorcycle like I was, and able to park on the pavement for a minute to run back and have a look at the inscription (there is nowhere to park a car) it begins:

> Travellers pass safe and free along this bridge, built by subscription to which the town of Montrose and the two adjacent counties contributed a large share. The work was first projected and a liberal sum directed to be given by Thomas Christie, provost of Montrose. He died before the subscription was opened, but the design was ably taken up and success-

fully followed out, by his eldest son Alexander Christie, the succeeding provost. The foundation was laid October the 18 One Thousand Seven Hundred and Seventy Five.

So it took five years to construct, and very impressive it is too. It is a massive bridge for that time, built only 30 years after the Battle of Culloden. I often wonder how they dealt with the flow of the river to lay the foundations for the piers of the bridge. They have done a fantastic job though, and the bridge looks as if it will be in situ for generations to come.

Just a little downstream is the railway bridge, only half as old as the road bridge, and here we are less than a mile from where the North Esk runs into the sea. It seems a shame that there is nowhere to park to examine this old road bridge, or to photograph it, as I suppose many would like. I can only suggest that you take the little road that goes off to the beach on your left, just before you drive onto the bridge, and see if you can tuck in there.

The North Esk is the ancient boundary between those historic areas of Scotland, Angus and the Mearns. South of the North Esk is Angus, one of the old Earldoms of Scotland, and a name synonymous with the Douglas family. From the bridge it is only a short run into Montrose.

Continue through the suburbs of Montrose, through various sets of traffic lights, until you reach a roundabout on the edge of the town centre. The road branching off to the right takes you onto the bypass that encircles the town centre, and the left fork takes you into the town, which is where we want to go. This takes us into the High Street, a broad thoroughfare formerly used as the market place. You might be able to park in this vicinity with a little patience.

One thing you may notice about Montrose is that for a town of 12 or 13 thousand people, it has a great number of statues. In the High Street alone there is one of Joseph Hume MP (1777–1855) that was erected in 1859. Hume was born in Ferry Street, Montrose. A little further down is *Bill the Smith* by William Lamb, who was a prolific local sculptor. Lamb died in 1951, and his studio on Market Street, just east of the High Street, is open to the public from July until mid-September, 2–5pm, and admission is free. There are several of his pieces on display in the town, and a leaflet listing the many statues and sculptures to be seen in Montrose is available from the museum or tourist information.

The Guild Hall is the imposing building which projects out into the High Street, effectively narrowing it at its southern end. There is a passageway leading through this building, and if you walk through you will discover that there are tombs in a space beneath it on your right. A strange arrangement.

A plaque reads:

Montrose Guildhall. The original Guild Hall was completed in 1763. In 1819/20 considerable extensions were made including the building above designed and constructed to avoid disturbing these family vaults, which already existed as part of the graveyard covering this area.

Immediately through this passageway is Montrose's large eighteenth-century church. A lane goes off here, signposted 'Museum'. You can drive round to the museum, but if you would rather walk down, this is the way to go.

Continue south, passing the statue to Sir Robert Peel (1788–1850), sculpted by Handyside Ritchie. Ritchie's statues grace many Scottish towns, his statue of Sir William Wallace on Stirling's Athenium building a particularly fine example. Sir Robert Peel was founder of the modern police force.

Here the High Street becomes Castle Street and swings away right. On the right side of the road is the impressive library building, and opposite you will see a three-quarters life-size statue of Montrose, a man whose name we have come across many times as we have travelled around Scotland. James Graham, first Marquess of Montrose, may have been born just behind the site of the statue here, but more of that shortly. This statue was unveiled by the current Duke of Montrose on 4 August, 2000, to mark the 350th anniversary of the original Montrose's execution at the Mercat Cross in Edinburgh. Montrose was a fair poet, and either side of his plinth is inscribed by words that he penned. One side reads:

He either fears his fate too much,
or his deserts are small
That puts it not unto the touch,
to win or lose it all.

The other reads:

But if thou wilt be constant then
and faithful of the word,
I'll make thee glorious by my pen
and famous by my sword.

The building directly behind this statue is known as the Castlested. It is currently the town's Job Centre. It has baronial-style battlements atop it, and was the site of the old medieval castle of Montrose. It is possible that there are some traces of early work within the more recent structure. Edward Longshanks of England was here during his invasion of Scotland in 1296. After John Balliol, King of Scots, had been captured and brought before Longshanks at Stracathro Church near Brechin, he was stripped of his royal insignia and humiliated, Longshanks throwing the Crown of Scotland to his footsoldiers in derision. Balliol was then stripped of his Lion

Rampant surcoat, whereby he earned his nickname Toom Tabard, Scots for 'empty coat'. Longshanks declared that the Kingdom of Scotland then ceased to exist. Balliol was brought here to the castle of Montrose before being sent south to London, then exiled to France, where he died around the time of the Battle of Bannockburn.

Scotland has gained a little more respect and identity in recent years. One last push for freedom and we can wipe out the stains of these years and cancel Longshanks' memory once and for all. It may do Scots visitors good to picture the events that happened here in 1296, and steel their resolve. Wallace came here during his campaign in the following year. Montrose himself may have been born in the castle.

There are a few other events worth noting from Montrose's long history. When Sir James Douglas, variably known as the Black Douglas or the Good Sir James, sailed on Crusade with the heart of King Robert the Bruce in 1330, he may have sailed from Montrose, but Berwick upon Tweed seems more probable. James VIII, father of Bonnie Prince Charlie, and known derisively as the Old Pretender to the Hanoverian regime, did sail from here at the close of the 1715 rising, the 1715 being an attempt to return the Stewarts to their ancestral throne.

To drive to the town's museum, take the left directly before Montrose's statue, George Street, then take the second left into Panmure Place. The museum is on the left. There is another statue by William Lamb in front of the museum, this one entitled *Le Paresseux* (lazy person). There are some good things to see in this museum. The prize exhibits must be the sculptured stones of Pictish origin. These were discovered in the burial ground to the south of the town by gravediggers in 1849. I'll take you to the site of this find as we exit Montrose.

The museum has Jacobite artefacts, a sword reputed to have belonged to Montrose, and even a death-mask of Napolean, and a bicorne hat said to have been worn by him!

Drive out by passing Montrose's statue at the Castlestead, and continue on. We soon reach the town by-pass, but keep south down Bridge Street, which takes us towards the bridge over the River South Esk. You may catch glimpses of Montrose Basin to your right. This is a large stretch of water, almost islanding the peninsula on which Montrose stands. It is full of water at high tide, but low tide reveals many sandflats. It is a haven for bird life, many rare migratory species can be seen here. It is a strange, land-locked expanse, quite similar to Loch Fleet which we visited in Sutherland.

We cross the concrete bridge over the South Esk, the lagoon of the basin on our right, glimpses of large ships in Montrose's harbour to our left, and we are onto what was formerly Rossie Island, an island no longer, due to the large oil terminal constructed here.

You come to a large roundabout, and here you take the turnoff to the left, signposted 'Oil Base', then take the minor road immediately left again into Braoch Road, which leads to Old Rossie Island Cemetery. Here there is a square stone tomb, built upon a grassy mound, rising a little higher than the gravestones round about. This is the site of an ancient church, and it was here that the sculptured stones in the museum were found. It is now the sepulchre of the Duncan and Scott families. I was so lucky with the weather on my visit, and just got my horsehide jacket off and sat on the grass verge at the road, the bike beside me, as I munched into that bikers' favourite – a pint of milk and a couple of sandwiches.

Incidentally, I know it isn't a pint any more, it's a half-litre or similar, but habit still makes me ask for a pint, and shop staff always know what I mean without asking. The wee birds hereabouts liked the crumbs they got anyway. I'm always a sucker for a sparrow watching me eat, little head cocked to one side (the sparrow that is – I'm just cramming it in as fast as I can get it down!)

Back to the roundabout, and we follow the A92 signposted for Arbroath. We climb above the south side of the Montrose Basin, and you can see how extensive it is from this viewpoint. Follow the main road here for a couple of miles, then look out for the turn off to Lunan, once the wide expanse of Lunan Bay comes into sight. Lunan Bay beach is a wide expanse of inviting, beautiful sand, with a raised crag halfway down its length that has the ruins of Red Castle atop it.

As you come down into Lunan you pass a tall obelisk in memory of Lt. Col. James Blair, who perished at sea on August 12 1847. Most of the ground in view was once the domain of the Blair family, hence the monument. We pass through Lunan village, its little church boarded up, and cross the Lunan Water on its picturesque little bridge. A quarter of a mile after the bridge, the castle is on our left on its crag. As you hit the edge of some woodland, there are some indentations on your right where you can squeeze a car in, and there is a gate with a path on your left leading uphill to the castle.

A short stiff pull takes you up to the neck of land that connects you to the peninsula on which the castle stands. The Lunan Water is down to your left. You will see there are many concrete structures on the sand and river mouth below, tank traps and the like, left over from the Second World War.

There is not really an awful lot left of Red Castle, bar half the original keep, and part of a curtain wall which may have contained a hall-house of sorts. You can see right away why it is called Red Castle at least, as it is constructed of fiery red stone.

The older curtain wall was probably built by the Balliol family around 1200. Prior that the lands here were granted to the Berkeley family by King William the Lion. They may have had an even earlier wooden fort on this site. The stone keep would have been added around 1400 by the Stewart family.

There are great views out from here, the beach below and the lapping waves particularly inviting on a summer's day. The people of Angus are particularly blessed with good beaches.

When you descend to your vehicle, carry on along this minor road. You can see how red the soil is in these parts. There is a redness to the stone too, hence the castle, and when the sun shines the cliffs here glow with a reddishness too. This also accounts for the cliff at the southern end of Lunan Bay being named Red Head.

Following on, there is a large estate wall on your right. This will give you warning of a junction that lies not too far ahead. When you reach it, take the left turn, signposted Arbroath. There is another junction just ahead, but keep straight on. Some nice farmland we are driving through, and this allows you to see the terrain of Angus at its best.

Another mile and you will pass an old Blacksmith's house with the intriguing name of Drunkendub. A dub is a pond or a puddle in Scotland, but I would like to hear the tale behind the name! The old smithy is on the right of the road, a private house now, but it has an interesting castle-like coat of arms on its side wall, carved into the stone, and bearing the initials WH and EM and the date 1848. Not far ahead at the edge of woodland, the road forks again, and a right turn will take you back to the main road, the A92. The woodland here is known as the West Woods of Ethie. It is only a mile or two south to the outskirts of Arbroath.

Arbroath was a town that was special to me before I had ever visited it. This was because of a document written in Arbroath in 1320, a document that meant a lot to me, even when I first heard of it at a tender age. This document was drawn up in the town's abbey, and as we come down into Arbroath you will see signposts pointing the way. The abbey is off to our left, and there are a couple of wee car parks in close proximity to the ancient ruins, where you can park and walk the last few yards.

There is a new visitor centre, a recently opened addition to the abbey, and this adds to the attraction of the place. Like so many of Scotland's great religious houses, the abbey of Arbroath lies in ruins, but one can still discern what a magnificent building this must have been in its heyday. Big too. So much has taken place in this building that is a vital part of the fabric of Scotland that a visit is almost like taking part in an old-time pilgrimage.

The building was founded in 1178 by King William the Lion, and dedicated to Thomas à Becket, an English archbishop who had been murdered in 1170, the King of England, Henry II at least partially responsible for this sacrilegious act.

William the Lion is, of course, the man who adopted the Lion Rampant as the Royal Standard of Scotland, and the flag he coined is a potent symbol of Scotland today, unchanged since its inception. When King William died on 4 December 1214, his son, the future Alexander II, helped carry his coffin to its place of burial in front of the High Altar of the abbey. Building work was still taking place, and the abbey was not completed until 1233.

There was some work taking place in Arbroath Abbey in 1816, a general tidying of the ruins, when William the Lion's tomb was rediscovered. The little crypt was lined with hewn freestone.

A later gravestone now marks the spot, and William is only one of a handful of our monarchs whose last resting place is known and marked in some way.

It pains me to tell you about an incident that took place in 2003, when some members of the Society of William Wallace posed at William's tomb with a Saltire and a Lion Rampant. The staff asked them to put the flags away. They replied that they were just taking a photo and that the man buried below was the originator of the Lion Rampant in the first place. They were then informed that an election was due, and that the flags could not be flown.

What is going on in Scotland?

The national flags of Scotland are apolitical. There is something seriously wrong when your country's flag is seen as offensive. Your politics should result from the love of your country, and politics can never be more important than the entity that is Scotland itself. I demand reasons for such acts. I am tired of Scottishness being something that has to be kept under wraps. The flag of Scotland should be flown by Scots in any part of Scotland that they wish to fly it, and it goes without saying that this is a statement beyond reproach. Our forefathers died for that flag. In their tens of thousands. Let's never forget it.

There is an effigy on show at the abbey which may be that of King William, but it is possible that it may be from the tomb of a leading churchman.

The Reformation was, of course, the main reason for the ruined state of the abbey today, when the buildings became a handy quarry for the townsfolk, and many of the houses of the town have stones which can be clearly identified as having once been part of the fabric of the abbey.

But the abbey's main claim to fame is in the shape of the aforementioned document, dating from 1320, and world-famous as the Declaration of Arbroath. War with England had dragged on for another six years after Bannockburn in 1314, and King Robert the Bruce turned his attention to the Pope, requesting him to intercede on Scotland's behalf where England was concerned. The famous Declaration was the outcome, asking that little Scotland be recognised as the nation state that she is.

The Declaration in full is a major document, but I wish to quote some of it here:

We pay to you to admonish this King of England ... that he should leave us in peace in our little Scotland, since we desire no more than is our own, and have no dwelling place beyond our own borders.

Scotland is Scotland. We are content with it, and are not covetous as are other peoples. And I, as a Scot, do not desire more than is my own.

No document of this time talked of their monarch the way the Declaration talked of Bruce. Many since have adopted its stance, and it laid in stone what we Scots know, that all men (and women!) are created equal. As our poet Burns stated, 'we are all Jock Tampson's bairns', that is, we all are 'everyman':

Yet Robert himself, should he turn aside from the task he has begun, and yield Scotland or us to the English King and people, we should cast out as the enemy of us all, as subverter of our rights and of his own, and we should choose another king to defend our freedom.

This was centuries ahead of its time. The sovereignty of Scotland lies within its people, always has done. Bruce recognised this too, when he referred to the Community of the Realm when speaking of the Scots themselves.

There are lines in the Declaration that most Scots know. They were meant with steady hearts and hands when our ancestors wrote them, and there is a debt that we owe our forebears, that we have been lax in repaying:

As long as a hundred of us are left alive, we will yield in no least way to English domination. We fight not for glory nor for wealth nor for honours, but only and alone we fight for freedom, which no good man surrenders but with his life.

Oh Scotland! You have done yourself a disservice over the centuries. What other country has given away the freedom its ancestors fought for so dearly, for such a cheap price? We owe the Scots of prior centuries much more than that. We are only the current keepers of our land, and we owe our future generations too.

In 2001 I travelled to Chicago, to take part in some Tartan Day events. By chance I ended up at a dinner where a Scots Labour politician was speaking. I am not a political animal. I do not have an axe to grind, except where my country is being maligned. The speaker, one Wendy Alexander, then stood and told her audience, mostly the business community of Chicago, how the Declaration of Arbroath was the first real document of 'Unionism', without quoting from the document itself. I should perhaps explain that Tartan Day in North America is celebrated on the anniversary of the Declaration, 6 April, 1320 being the date of issue. The American Declaration of Independence owes a huge debt to the Scottish one, something like half the signatories of the American document being of Scots descent.

I sat listening to this, growing more incredulous with every second. I could stand this no more, and stood to tell Ms Alexander that I would recite the original to her, and to the whole room, so they could make up their own minds. When I quoted the passage, 'as long as one hundred of us remain alive ...' and finished, there was a mixture of applause and laughter. This woman denied her birth, denied her people, and put another country before her own. Auntie Tom, no less. The recalling of it still shocks me. Bought and sold for English gold, as Burns so succinctly put it. As I said, I have no axe to grind with the English, – they are the English. But I cannot stomach a Scot in denial. My problem is with the Scots, not the English.

Please don't let that last tale detract from Arbroath Abbey, and what it means to the hearts of true Scots. There has been debate about who actually penned the finished document in 1320. Most sources place it firmly at the door of Bernard de Linton, Abbot of Arbroath, Chancellor of Scotland, and close personal friend of King Robert. Thank you, Bernard. Your passion, the passion that I see in so many from our history, far outweighs the detractors of our heritage, and has imbued the spirit, that same spirit within Wallace himself, that will bolster us in time of need.

When the Stone of Destiny was liberated from Westminster Abbey in 1950 and brought back to Scotland, there was a huge police hunt for it. The Stone was left one night at Arbroath Abbey, most Scots probably hoping that the authorities would realise the passion that this ancient talisman evokes, and that perhaps it would be left in its home country. But no, it was hurriedly taken back to London, where it would remain for another 35 years.

If you continue further on the A92 through Arbroath, you will see a building on your left, on the waterfront at the southern edge of town. It is white-painted, and like a watch-tower in aspect. This is the Signal Tower Museum. It was built in 1813 as the shore station for the Bell Rock Lighthouse, built by Robert Stevenson, grandfather of Robert Louis Stevenson, author of *Kidnapped* and *Treasure Island*. The Bell Rock is a notorious place for mariners, many ships having sunk there over the years. The lighthouse stands 115 feet high, and it was the first lighthouse ever built whose base is submerged at high tide. The Signal Tower Museum is an interesting wee museum, and just to gladden the hearts of Scots everywhere, there is no charge for admission.

Continue on the A92, past Arbroath Football Club's stadium, then pass under a railway bridge. Right before you stands a statue commemorating the 1320 Declaration of Arbroath. I was very impressed the first time I happened across this. It is good to see the town of Arbroath commemorate this epic event in our nation's history in this way.

The statue is by artist David Annand, and was dedicated on Friday 19 October 2001. There are the figures of Bernard de Linton on the left and

Robert the Bruce on the right, holding aloft a very good copy of the Declaration. The figures are in bronze, standing atop a sandstone plinth. There are plans to have the statue floodlit at night, which would be a welcome addition. It is one of the first things that visitors coming from the south see as they enter the town, and as the Declaration is becoming rightly more famous, especially with Americans, it is only fitting that Arbroath utilises its history.

The stretch of grassland here is known locally as the Cricket Common. To take a good look at the statue it is best to take the route to the right of it, Viewfield Road, where you should find a place to park, and walk across the grass to the statue itself.

Continue up to the top of Viewfield Road, and when you reach the T-junction at its terminus, turn left onto Arbirlot Road. At the end of this road, turn right onto Westway. At the top of Westway, turn left, and you will soon see the Forfar road, where we follow the signs for that town, turning left. This main route is the A933.

Follow the A933 for a mile or two. There is a large fence on your right. This is the perimeter of the Royal Marines Condor Establishment. As you see the signs for the main gate, keep your eyes open for a little road branching off at ten o'clock on your left, signposted Letham. Ignore any signs you may see for Letham Grange, as this is a different entity. This one is a little farm route, but it is well surfaced, and if clear, the views are spectacular. The road rises a little, and there is quite a panoramic view forward to Strathmore – the lower ground before you which runs right across the country here north-east towards Stonehaven. The edge of the Grampian hills rises beyond.

Eventually you come to a junction, where the B961 crosses your path. You go straight over – it is almost a crossroads, just a few feet of a stagger. The sign reads Letham 3 miles. You might wonder where all this is leading, but you will just have to trust me! Good views though.

Just over a mile on you pass Dumbarrow Farm, and just on the other side of a wee bit of woodland there is an old tower over on your right. It is stone-built and round, and it is the remains of an old windmill. There aren't a hell of a lot of them in Scotland.

You will then come across signs pointing to Letham itself, but ignore them and carry straight ahead on the road you have been following. You come into a tiny village called Bowriefauld, and here you will see a sign pointing right to Dunnichen, ¾ mile. It is Dunnichen we have been heading for, so drive towards the place. The village of Dunnichen is a tiny place. Behind rises the ridge of Dunnichen Hill, all very pastoral in aspect, but a huge part of what Scotland is today was shaped in this vicinity. As you drive into the village, the first thing you will see is a squared off cairn of stone blocks, about seven feet high. Turn in right just beyond this cairn, into the road signposted Friockheim (which is pronounced something like Freak-'em!) There is a little church here, and there is plenty of room to park. Walk the few yards back to the cairn. It reads:

> To commemorate the 1,300th anniversary of the Battle of
> Nechtansmere 20th May 685AD,
> when the Picts under King Brude decisively defeated the
> Northumbrians under King Ecgfrith.

It was this battle that created the separate entity that we know today as Scotland. It severed the influence that was emanating from the southern tribes, and made my people very much what they are today. This battle took place almost as far in time before Bannockburn, as we are away from the time of that great victory under King Robert the Bruce. This struggle was as important in creating freedom as Bannockburn. In fact, if Nechtansmere was never fought, there would have been no Scotland to fight Bannockburn over.

There has always been that divide. When the Romans came, they sensed it, and built their wall. Scotland has a Celtic background, the English Anglo-Saxon. As I explained earlier, the two countries even originated in different parts of the globe. I advocate home rule for England. They deserve that. They are a nation state and they have the right.

If you walk just a few steps to the right of the cairn and look beyond the area of the church into the low lying terrain, you are looking to the field of conflict. There is a small lochan there today, surrounded by fields.

If you go back towards your vehicle, you will notice there is a standing stone right in front of the gate to the churchyard. There is a little sign here saying of the battle:

> On the 20th May, 685AD the Picts led by Brudei routed invading
> Northumbrians under the King Ecgfrith who was killed in the fighting.
> The Picts ambushed their enemy between Dunnichen [The fort of
> Nechtan – *Dun* means fort in Scotland, *nichen* is a corruption of
> Nechtan] and the moss which lies behind the church. The
> Northumbrians withdrew south of the Forth and North Britain became
> the independent realm of Scotland. Erected by Letham and District
> Community Council 1997.

This standing stone is not the original. It was deteriorating, time and the weather having taken their toll. As it dates from the time of the battle, I believe we can safely say that it is a monument of some sort connected to the conflict in some way. The little sign reads:

> The Dunnichen Stone is an example of the earliest type of Pictish stone,
> dating from the 7th Century AD. The original, which was found at East

Mains of Dunnichen in 1811, may be seen in the Meffan Museum in Forfar.

East Mains of Dunnichen is just a little further along the road running down the side of the church, so it was close to the original field of battle, and to the fort which originally stood here.

An old book I have at home (c. 1890) says of Dunnichen:

A Caledonian or Pictish fort, on a low southern shoulder of Dunnichen Hill, had left some vestiges, which were partly removed for building dykes, and partly obliterated by a quarry. In a sanguinary battle, fought on the East Mains of Dunnichen, the Picts defeated and slew Ecgfrid, the Northumbrian King, recovering thus their independence, 20 May 685. Their victory has left its vestiges in stone covered graves, with urns and human bones, both on the East Mains of Dunnichen , and in a round gravel knoll near the Den of Letham.

It is easy to turn in the circle around the standing stone, and we continue to follow the road we were originally following. It is only a little over three miles from Dunnichen to Forfar. After a mile you reach the B9128, and you turn right, the signs stating 'Forfar 2'. Straight road all the way down into the town, through the line of houses called Kingsmuir en route.

We come to a roundabout. Go straight through. There is a set of traffic lights directly in front. At these lights you should turn right. This will take us away from Forfar, but it is just to visit a site and we will return shortly.

After the lights, ignore the first road signposted Aberlemno, but just after this on the left is a road signposted Montrose B9113. Take this road through the outskirts, then there is a straight stretch of about two thirds of a mile. Just before the trees at the end of this straight – watch your speed: I overshot it first time I visited – there is a little road that runs off at a right angle on your left, signposted Restenneth Priory. 100 yards in there is a little place to park. You walk by the white house here, and if the dogs are there they will have a good bark at you. Don't worry – they are locked up! The owners also keep exotic chicken-like creatures, and they are usually pecking about. In fact, there was one adult chicken walking about with a little fluffy duckling in tow. Obviously adopted, although my daughter, who was with me last time I was there, wanted to kidnap the duckling and take it home! It might have been wee, but it wasn't stupid and it could run too!

Through a gate and there is a path between two fields that takes you down to the priory. It is an unusual place this, and very ancient indeed. The stone spire is the most obvious feature as you approach. The base of this steeple has been the cause of some disagreement between historians, some authorities stating that the stonework may date from as early as AD 700. Most of the work you can see dates from the 1100s, which is still very early, although the pointed stone spire is from the 1400s. There are not too many features to see, other than a few graveslabs, but I do like to stand right in the centre of the base of the steeple, and look all the way right up the stonework to the very top of the spire from the inside. Still the big metal hinges of the long varnished doors to be seen in place here too. It has not been used as a church since 1591, although burials still occasionally took place. It may seem strange looking out from the priory now, but this was once a narrow peninsula jutting out into a loch, Restenneth Loch, which was drained at great expense in the late 1700s. I'm told it was for the sake of obtaining a rich supply of shell-marl that was in its bed. So the scene has certainly changed here over the centuries, and the church must have been picturesque on its peninsula.

Back to Forfar then. Driving back into town takes you straight into the town centre, and into East High Street. Forfar is not a big place, so it is best to park here and go for a walk to absorb the place. There are some old buildings about, mostly houses with shop fronts, and these are dotted here and there on the High Streets, East and West.

You reach the town hall at the top of Castle Street, where East High Street becomes West High Street. This sturdy building was erected in 1788 to a design by James Playfair.

Continue on, and just before you, you will spot the sign on the right-hand side of the street for the town's Meffan Institute. It is a gallery, museum and exhibition centre. The name Meffan comes from a local family who provided two provosts of Forfar. There are some carven Pictish stones within, including the original Dunnichen Stone, the replica of which we have already seen at the Battle of Nechtansmere site. The 'witches' branks' are also kept here. This device was fastened around the neck, with a strip of metal going over the top of the head. There is a projecting spur that goes into the mouth, thereby gagging the wearer. It was fitted to women destined to be burnt as witches. The victims were led by chain to the stake at Witches' Howe, a hollow to the north of the town. The branks would stifle their agonised screams as they were burnt to death, and could be retrieved from the ashes to be used again. Nine women were burnt at Forfar between 1650 and 1662. The crimes that have been perpetrated in the name of religion are many.

One thing you should go and see in Forfar is the site of the original castle. It is hidden away behind later buildings, and you would never know it was there unless you had been steered in the right direction. Go back to the town hall, and turn into Castle Street. Walk down to where the street narrows, and look for a stationery shop called Adamson's on your left. This shop is where the key is kept for the castle site. Just across the road from the shop, a little down on your right, is Canmore Street. On the right of this street you will see a steel gate that slides open like a lift or elevator door.

Unlock it, and climb the steps that disappear upwards beyond it. Eventually you will arrive at a little grassy area where the castle once stood. In the centre of this stands a little stone tower, octagonal and battlemented. An iron staircase spirals round the outside of this tower to the top, where there are views over the town. When you are up here you can see how this elevated site is hidden, and how it would originally have been a good site for a fortification.

The stone castle was built by King William the Lion around 1180, but had been the site of a fortification prior to that.

When Edward Longshanks of England invaded Scotland, the castle here, commanded by Gilbert de Umfraville, held out against him. When it later fell, Longshanks stayed within its walls from the third until the sixth of July 1296. It was assailed by Robert the Bruce in 1308, when he was ably assisted by a local, Philip, the Forester of Plater. The castle was described as being 'stuffit all with Inglismen'. The attack took place at night, the garrison was slaughtered, and Bruce broke down parts of the wall so that the English could not re-garrison the place, a practice he often used. You may want to consider some of this history when standing up here.

The castle lay derelict after this time, and it was used to furnish building material for the old steeple and west entrance of the later church, and for many houses of the town. There were still traces discernible around 1800, showing that it had been quite extensive in size.

The tower here today is actually the town's old Mercat Cross, built in 1684, which formerly stood at the east side of the Sheriff Courthouse at the top of Castle Street, behind the Town Hall. It restricted the movement of traffic, even back in 1799, and so was moved and rebuilt on the castle hill in that year!

Drive on along the West High Street, then straight on at the traffic lights, following the signs for Coupar Angus. You go through various roundabouts, and under the A90, the main road between Dundee and Aberdeen. Keep following signs for Coupar Angus and Glamis Castle, our next port of call, now heading west again into the heartland of Scotland.

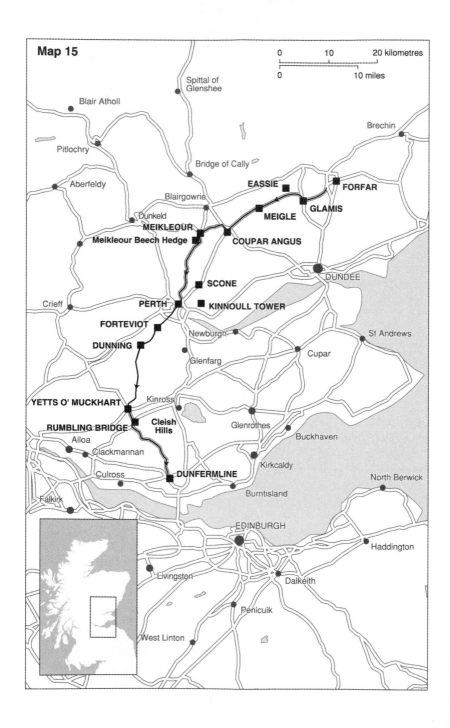

Map 15

| 0 | 10 | 20 kilometres |
| 0 | | 10 miles |

Spittal of Glenshee

Blair Atholl

Brechin

Pitlochry

Bridge of Cally

Aberfeldy

Blairgowrie

EASSIE

FORFAR

GLAMIS

Dunkeld

MEIGLE

MEIKLEOUR

Meikleour Beech Hedge

COUPAR ANGUS

SCONE

DUNDEE

Crieff

PERTH

KINNOULL TOWER

FORTEVIOT

Newburgh

St Andrews

DUNNING

Glenfarg

Cupar

YETTS O' MUCKHART

Kinross

RUMBLING BRIDGE

Cleish Hills

Glenrothes

Alloa

Buckhaven

Clackmannan

Culross

Kirkcaldy

DUNFERMLINE

North Berwick

Falkirk

Burntisland

EDINBURGH

Haddington

Livingston

Dalkeith

Penicuik

West Linton

CHAPTER FIFTEEN

Through Old Pictavia

STARTING AT GLAMIS, THE ROUTE EXPLORES MEIGLE, COUPAR ANGUS, MEIKLEOUR, SCONE, PERTH, FORTEVIOT, RUMBLING BRIDGE, AND ENDS AT CLEISH.

IT IS ONLY A few miles on to Glamis, but en route look for the sign pointing the way to Jericho, an oddly named place for central Scotland. Glamis is pronounced as if the *i* is silent, by the way.

The village nestles to the right of the road, among many mature trees. Just follow the signs for the castle, the entrance is just beyond the village itself. There is an archway that leads to a driveway which is lined here with some impressive mature woodland. You come round a bend, and you can see the castle about a mile ahead, its little pepper-pot turrets rising above the reddish stonework.

Halfway down the drive you will see the doocot on your left. You can park just beyond the castle itself. I was saddened to see a Union Flag flying from the topmost tower. Even the local primary school flies the Saltire. Parts of the castle are open to the public, and there is an admission charge. If you like a guided tour round a richly decorated house, Glamis is for you. There is much in the way of fine china and paintings. Some nice weaponry too. The house is owned by the Bowes-Lyon family, who are Earls of Strathmore and Kinghorn. The best bit during my last visit was the American lady who asked the tour guide 'Does the Earl work, and what does he do for a living?' Brilliant, especially considering the money she had just spent on admission! The castle is a working castle, centred on huge estates too.

There are various ghost stories and legends centred around Glamis Castle, especially as there are more windows on the outside of the place than there are on the inside, and the walls are incredibly thick in places. This has led to stories of secret rooms hidden in the thickness of the walls, where a 'monster', born into the family is kept hidden. Or there is a tale in which the devil discovered some men playing cards in the early hours of the Sabbath, so he had them bricked up in their little room to play cards for eternity. To be honest I'd have thought that Auld Nick would have been happy with a bit of card playing on the Lord's Day, but there you go. I did listen at a few of the thicker pieces of walling to see if I could hear any cries of 'Snap!' reverberating through the stones, but to no avail.

The greater part of the castle dates from 1675–87, but there is an old tower with 15-foot-thick walls at its core. The chapel is particularly interesting with some Dutch painter who painted the portraits of the various King of Scots at Holyrood Palace responsible for the artworks here. Being Dutch, he has painted spectacles on one of the angels, because specs were invented in the Netherlands! What next? The Resurrection of Lazarus bearing an Edam cheese?

As you drive out of the castle policies, the one-way system takes you into the village of Glamis. The village church is immediately on your left, with car-parking space just beyond. If the church is unlocked, don't be fooled by the austere appearance of the place, take a look inside. This church was built in 1792, but if you walk through the building to the back right corner, you will find that a doorway leads through to the Strathmore Aisle, built between 1459 and 1484, in memory of Patrick Lyon, the first Lord Glamis. He died in 1459, and his wife Isabella Ogilvy began work on the place. Her tomb is on the left as you enter. It has a vaulted roof, and the place is in the 'second pointed style of Gothic'.

Right opposite the front of the church is the manse. In the front garden of this manse is a massive standing stone, with a Celtic cross on one side, and a serpent, fish and mirror on the other. Local legend calls this King Malcolm's Gravestone, due to the fact that Malcolm II of Scots died in the Glamis vicinity. One of the old chronicles mentions that he was injured in battle in 1034 at the age of 80, and he died of his wounds at Glamis three days later. No matter what, the physical size of this stone is quite extraordinary. Although it sits within the manse garden, the minister seems happy with the fact that visitors will want to enter and take a look at the stone, so just go through the gate and try to be unobtrusive.

Follow the road further on – it is called Kirk Wynd, and you will see the low row of cottages on your left that form the Angus Folk Museum. It is open Friday to Tuesday, Easter to September. Here you then turn right into the main street of the village. There is a nice thatched cottage on your right. This takes you back out to the approach to the castle, so you turn left, and this will take you back to the main route you were on, driving towards Couper Angus, the A94.

Continue on for just under two miles, look for a little lodge house with a turret with a pointed roof on your left. Just immediately beyond it on the right there is a little road going in to Eassie, a tiny farming hamlet. This road goes round in a semi-circle to rejoin the A94. It is easy to overshoot this little road, so stay alert. As you drive in, you will see the ruins of an old church on your right, atop a grassy mound. The little church is of uncertain date, has some interesting old grave slabs in the graveyard, but is well worth visiting to see the Eassie sculptured stone. The stone stands within the east end of the church, and it has been encased in glass to protect it from the elements. It originally stood near the church, but has been moved inside the ruins, again to afford it some protection:

> The Eassie Cross Slab. This is the work of Pictish craftsmen and was carved in the 8th or 9th century. On the front is displayed a cross with interlaced patterns characteristic of Christian art of this period. Above the cross is an angel and below a hunting scene, showing a Pictish warrior armed with a spear and various animals. The back of the slab is also carved with figures, animals and symbols.

One of the creatures depicted upon the stone is our friend the Celtic Beast, and we will see a lot more of him (or her!) shortly.

Another few miles and we come into Meigle. Just after you enter the village you will se the sign pointing left to 'Pictish Stones'. Up to the end of this short street, a right turn, and the museum is on your right. It is just a little hall, but it has an amazing collection of sculptured stones, brought here to protect and preserve them. There is a fee for admission.

A diligent look around will reveal that there are three Celtic beasts among the carvings on the stones. What is quite interesting is that the largest stone, standing in the centre of the place, is often referred to as Vanora's gravestone. Vanora is one and the same as Guinevere, legendary wife of King Arthur. There are various inscriptions on the stone that people associate with her story. Just a story though, as the inscriptions could also represent Daniel in the lion's den! Good fun for arguing about yet another link with King Arthur being Scottish!

Meigle museum is as good a place as any to learn about the various symbols found on carved stones, and it is nice to see a collection like this where you can compare one with the other.

Continue on from the museum, again to rejoin the A94, and again turning left. On your left, on the edge of the village, is a strange red-stoned building with an old stone-slated roof. It is a strange place, like something out of a fairy story, a goblin's hall or such like. It lies empty and boarded up. This intriguing place is a bit of an enigma. Who its builder was, what its function was, and just how old it is, I have been unable to ascertain. Certainly, it is very old, and I have never seen anything like it anywhere else in Scotland.

Onwards to Couper Angus. As we come down to the centre of the place there is a mini-roundabout. Take the road to the right, the A923, towards Blairgowrie. As we drive out of Couper Angus you will see a large river on your right. This is the River Isla which rises high in the eastern Grampian mountains, flows down Glenisla, eventually to reach the River Tay. We cross the Isla on a stone bridge. We then take a left turn, signposted Dunkeld 14, the A984. This road follows the course of the Isla for a couple of miles. Although it has an A-road designation, it is very narrow in places, as narrow as some of the single-track Highland roads we have visited. This road crosses the major route, the A93, at Meikleour *(Meekle-our)*, and we turn left to follow this road south towards Perth.

On your right stands the Meikleour Hedge. You can't miss it! It follows the right side of the road for more than 600 yards. It's a beech hedge, the best part of 100 feet high. I don't know if that sounds big, but it's certainly impressive in reality, like a wall towering high above the road, oncoming vehicles tiny in comparison to the hedge as a backdrop. It was planted in 1746, the year that the Battle of Culloden was fought. The old way of life in the Highlands dwindled as this hedge grew. It is kept flat-walled and trim, and I have no idea how it is cut, but I take my helmet off to the men who accomplish it!

After the hedge, there is a junction with a road going off to the right marked Kinclaven 1. This road immediately crosses the River Tay on an old bridge. At the far end of the bridge, in the woodland over to your left, stands the ruins of the medieval Kinclaven Castle. It stands on the opposite bank of the junction of Isla and Tay. It consists of a once-mighty curtain wall with corner towers, like a toy castle. Wallace stormed this place to liberate it from the English invader. It is seldom visited, its stones are now overgrown and trees sprout from its defences. The river slides silvery below its now breached battlements, but the Wallace himself looked out at the Tay here once, and these old stones have seen daring deeds in their time.

We continue on the A93, crossing the Isla by bridge, just before it meets the Tay, Kinclaven hidden to our right by the woodland. I suppose it is a bit funny to meet the Tay again. We last passed it on our way north, at its source in Strath Fillan, many miles west of here.

Eventually you will see signs for 'Scone Palace – 200 yards'. What was once the most hallowed site in Scotland stands within the grounds of the palace, and it is a place that anyone with an interest in the history of Scotland will want to visit. For it was at Scone that the Kings of Scots were crowned. Perusing a map will show that there is a village called Scone, or New Scone, a mile to the east, but we will go into that shortly. They are all pronounced *Scoon* by the way. Except for the cakes – they are *skons*!

You pay a fee to go into the grounds and the palace – the palace being the home of the Earl of Mansfield. It is a strange building. Battlemented, but not defensive, and it doesn't really look like anything else in Scotland. A bit too bulky and square in aspect.

A house was built on this spot by the Earl of Gowrie, but there was a major falling-out between that family and King James VI. James VI then bestowed the property on David Murray of the House of Tullibardine, ancestor of the Earls of Mansfield, and he completed the building work around 1605. Major rebuilding took place between 1803 and 1808 costing £70,000, incorporating the earlier building, and the result of that is the house we see today.

Touring the house reveals some fine furniture, portraits, china etc. The thing that captured me most was a blue carpet. It had an astonishing pile to it, and I can say it is the best I have ever walked on!

In front of the palace stands the Mote-Hill, today crowned by a small chapel. Its top measures 100 yards by 60 yards. It is not overwhelmingly impressive, rising as it does just a few yards above the surrounding landscape, but its history is interwoven with that of Scotland.

Scone occupied a position between the northern Picts and southern Picts. The chronicles mention that it was here in AD 710, that Naitan, King of the Picts, publicly stated the correct date to celebrate Easter. In 844, King Kenneth MacAlpin united the Picts and Scots, and it is he who is credited with bringing the Stone of Destiny here, and making it his capital. Remember the old legends state that wherever the Scots go, the Stone will go too, and wherever the Stone stands is where the Scots shall be ruled from.

The chronicler Bellenden stated:

The Scottis sall bruke that realme
as native ground
(Geif weirdis fayll nocht) quhar evir this
Chair is found

When Celtic Scotland eventually mutated into feudal Scotland, neither the importance of the place or its mystic stone diminished. John of Fordun, chronicler, wrote:

No king was ever wont to reign in Scotland unless he had sat upon this stone at Scone.

From the time of Kenneth MacAlpin till the coronation of James IV, all Kings of Scotland were crowned at Scone in an unbroken line. After that time the only king who received this accolade was Charles II, King of both Scotland and England, in 1651. The last to be crowned seated on the Stone was John Balliol, as Edward Longshanks stole it in 1296 and took it to London.

On top of the Mote-Hill today, a rough copy of the Stone stands in mute testimony to the once magnificent ceremonies that took place here. Most visitors can't resist having a wee sit down on it.

Behind this copy stone stands a little chapel. When David Murray received the estate from King James VI in 1624, he built a new parish church atop the Moot Hill. Of this only an aisle now remains, used as a family mausoleum. I'm not quite sure that I like this arrangement. This mound, where the Stone stood, was the most hallowed spot in all Scotland, and it has become a family burial place. I am aware that this vault, as stated, is the remains of a church, but there should never have been buildings allowed on the spot in the first place. It should have been left as it originally was. Here, generations of Scotland's dynasty were seated upon the fateful Stone. Perhaps it was the legendary Jacob's Pillow, where Jacob had the dream of the angels ascending and descending from Heaven, as mentioned in the Bible. The circlet of gold was lowered onto the brow of Robert the Bruce here, the gathered assembly looking on with awe.

When I first visited many years ago, I expected there to be some tangible link with those days, and for it to be commemorated in some way too. I was disappointed to find only tombs of a family in the chapel on the site. This, I suppose, is the problem with being ruled from somewhere else. There seemed to be no authority to say yea or nay to Scotland's sacred places. There should at least be lists of the events that took place here and of the dates these events happened, all the crownings here put into perspective.

An abbey stood near here once too. It is believed that it stood before the house, and to the right of the Moot Hill. It was founded by Alexander I in 1114. During the Wars of Independence, the monks here did their best to defy the claims of England, and the abbey was burnt by the English in 1298. Abbot Thomas took part in Bruce's coronation, and suffered in an English prison in consequence. The Abbey possessed the precious relic of the head of St Fergus, who died around AD 700. King James IV provided money for a silver case for this relic.

The Abbey was utterly destroyed by a mob from Perth in 1559, fired up by ministers at the time of religious reformation. A great loss to the fabric of my nation's history.

Beyond the abbey site there is an old gateway, and just on the right through this gateway is the ancient town cross of old Scone. You see, the village was moved to its current site many years ago, and its cross is all that remains. There are many instances of towns losing their market crosses, but this is the only cross which has lost its town! A little to the right of this cross is the old burial ground, perhaps on the site of the old cemetery connected to the abbey, but although there are some old stones within, there is nothing of the antiquity of the old abbey that once stood here.

There was a royal burial here too. Robert II, grandson of Bruce, and first of the line of Stewart kings, was interred at Scone, probably before the High Altar of the vanished abbey. It is a shame there is no reference to him, some sort of marker or memorial in the vicinity to tell the story would be appropriate.

There is some nice woodland in the vicinity of the palace, and I nearly always spot red squirrels scampering among the trees on a walk round. Where I live in central Scotland, our native red squirrels have been ousted by the bigger greys, imported for some reason I cannot fathom, from North America. So I hope that our little Scottish reds continue to thrive here for many generations to come, unmolested by aggressive invaders.

Oh! And there is a good maze at Scone Palace too, and like all red-blooded males I thought 'I'll dae this nae bother!' But it was difficult, even keeping one hand on a hedge, which is meant to take you to the exit eventually.

When you leave Scone, and turn right onto the main route again, it is only a hop, skip and jump into Perth. But a little detour will give you a fantastic view, although a little walking is involved. As you come down into the start of the houses, look out for a stretch where the road is walled on either side. There are garages let into the wall on your right. As traffic lights appear in the distance, King Street appears on your left. If you don't have the energy to do this next bit, going straight on through the traffic lights ahead will take you shortly to the bridge over the River Tay on the right where we enter Perth proper.

So, up Keir Street, some 150 yards to the junction. Cross the main road here onto Dupplin Road, passing various stone villas. You reach Gannochy Road, where you see the signs pointing the way to Kinnoull Hill Woodland Walks. Follow this sign again at Muirhall Road, the entrance to the hospital on the corner. You begin to climb uphill here, and a view unfolds back to the eastern edge of the Highlands. You will see the sign again at Corsiehill Road, where this takes you into a parking area. Don't go right into the car park in the old quarry if there is room in the inshots just before, because the path cuts uphill from here. There is a map board, and the path is well defined. I want to take you to the top of Kinnoull Hill. It involves an uphill walk of about half a mile. The gradient is reasonably gentle – nothing too severe – and it is through nice woodland the whole way. There is a viewfinder just a few yards up for the view back, pointing out the prominent hills on the edge of the Highlands. Push on. There is a panoramic view from the top that far outweighs the effort involved in getting there.

So go straight uphill, without following any of the side paths that may meander off here and there. There is a last steeper pull of about 20 feet onto the top, where there is a concrete trig point, and a direction indicator. Perth is down below. Walk on past the trig point, and you will find that there is an old stone slab where visitors have carved their names, some of the dates a couple of hundred years old. A little further on is the edge. You are on the lip of a basaltic cliff, the drop to the Tay far below is over 720 feet. It is quite spectacular, and I surely don't need to expound on the dangers of such a spot. The Lomond Hills twin summits are south of you over in Fife. The Ochils stretch away south-west. Below, looking almost as if you could jump from here and land in it, the Tay begins to widen into an estuary. It is a vista that you will not forget.

You will notice that there is what appears to be a ruined castle with a round tower, along on the next piece of projecting crag to your left. You can follow the path along, crossing the top of the Windy Gowl, a steep descent, once famous for its echo, but now too overgrown with trees for that to happen, on to this little castle. It is actually a folly. Below here there is a cave called the Dragon Hole, where Wallace is once said to have lain in concealment, but I would ask you not to search for it! The drops around here are too severe. There is a large castle down below to your left here. This is Kinfauns Castle, now a hotel.

Make your way back to the trig point, and then back downhill to your vehicle.

We then make our way down towards Perth. Follow Gannochy Road right to the bottom of the hill, where you come up to a set of traffic lights. Directly opposite is the old bridge over the River Tay. Cross the bridge – unfortunately the parapets are a bit too high to give you a view up and down the river, but we will remedy that shortly.

At the far side of the bridge, take a sharp left into Tay Street. Follow the course of the river along this street. Go through the traffic lights, where you will see a railway bridge before you. Go under this bridge, and ahead is a mini-roundabout. Go straight through this, but take the immediate right into the car park. We are going to do a little circular walking tour around Perth, and this is the place to park. You have to pay to use this car park, but it is reasonably priced.

This car park sits on the edge of the town's South Inch. Perth has two large open grassy areas on either edge of the town. The North and South Inches. Inch is old Scots for an island, so the Tay probably meandered out and round these grassy areas at one time. We tend to look at our rivers with a different eye in this day and age, where modern drainage has tamed them, but the Tay is a Highland river, and given to spates after heavy rain. At times the water would have spread right over the flood plains on either side. The Tay still very much has a mind of its own – as you will notice by the parapets surrounding it, and you will notice that gates along its length can be sealed shut to contain it in times of heavy rain.

I wish you to walk back down along Tay Street, the street you have just driven. At the corner at the mini-roundabout you have just driven through is an unusual little building. This was originally the Perth Water Works, constructed in 1832. It is in the form of a rotunda, its walls up to five feet thick. They support a cast iron dome which acted as a reservoir until 1862, holding up to 146,000 gallons of water! The chimney of the old pump has been disguised to look like a classical column. This great wee place is now a gallery dedicated to the works of JD Fergusson (1874–1961), a celebrated Scottish artist who is recognised as one of the leading figures in the development of twentieth-century Scottish painting.

Born in Leith of Highland parents, he spent much of his life in France. Contact with French Impressionist and Post-Impressionist art and artists is reflected in many of his bold, colourful paintings. Well worth a walk round.

Continue on down Tay Street, under the railway bridge. Look for an entrance on your left that leads to Greyfriars Burial Ground. It is the site of the Franciscan Friary that was founded in 1496.

As you go down the little lane and into the cemetery, you will find that the place is mostly hidden away behind later buildings. Over to your left a shelter has been built to help preserve some of the older, more interesting stones. You will find the oldest stone in the graveyard here, stapled up against the wall, the Buchan stone, dated 1580. The other stones hereabouts are intricately carved, one, the Neasmith stone, has what looks like a party carved upon it, with people kissing, and some holding aloft glasses of wine. There is a gravestone that commemorates a man who was a glove maker, and his has a pair of gloves carved upon it. Quite a brilliant collection of unusual memorials.

I'm not of a macabre disposition, but I always find myself drawn to old graveyards like this. All human life is there!

Onwards, and cross Canal Street. You are now passing the Perth Sheriff Court. One of the window frames facing the Tay contains a large bronze plaque, with a depiction of Gowrie House in relief upon it. the plaque below reads:

Within gardens bounded by the Tay, near this spot, stood Gowrie House, noted for the historical event called the Gowrie Conspiracy of 5 August 1600. Built in 1520, taken down in 1807.

There are also the coats of arms of the King of Scots, and of the Gowrie family.

The Gowrie Conspiracy is a strange and intriguing affair, one that will never be satisfactorily explained, and so is one of those historical mysteries that have caused much debate.

In August 1600, King James VI and many of his courtiers were hunting near Falkland, off to the south of Perth. What happened next comes from the account of the king himself, and cannot be substantiated by alternative evidence. Here he was approached by the Master of Ruthven, brother of the Earl of Gowrie. The Master told him a wondrous tale of a 'mannie with a pot of gold' that he had discovered, and King James agreed to accompany the Master to his family home at Gowrie House to see this man and his gold.

He dined with the brothers, then was taken upstairs to see the subject of this tale. According to the king, all there was in the turret room was a stranger in armour, whereupon the Master informed the king he was about to die. Even though this was the case, King James managed to reach a window, which he opened, and called to his startled followers below, 'Treason!'. They immediately ran into the house and the Gowrie Brothers were stabbed to death.

Many did not believe the king at the time, and many have not since. Theories abound. One is that King James, noted for his homosexual behaviour, may have approached one or other of the Gowries, been repulsed, and the rest is history. James did have much to gain with these two out of the way.

What intrigues even more is that the people of Perth, on hearing the news of this incident, appeared mob-handed at the house. There were cries of 'Come out son of Signeur Davie!', showing that the townsfolk believed that James was not the son of his father, so to speak, but the son of David Rizzio, secretary to his mother, Mary, Queen of Scots. The same Rizzio that was stabbed to death at Holyrood Palace which we visited earlier in Edinburgh.

King James escaped the clutches of the mob by being secretly conveyed to a boat and rowed away up the Tay.

You then pass the main frontage of Perth Sheriff Court, with its twelve magnificent fluted columns. Cross South Street, one of Perth's main thoroughfares. Just after you will see a little lane called Water Vennel. It is so called as this is where the old ferry boats crossed the Tay, before the advent of the bridges. This lane also formed the edge of the grounds of Gowrie House. Perth had welcomed Bonnie Prince Charlie's army in 1745, so perhaps that is why they presented Gowrie House to the Duke of Cumberland after Culloden in 1746. Obviously trying to retain 'royal' favour. Cumberland immediately gave the house over to the British Army, who used it as an artillery barracks until its demolition in 1807. There is a little plaque just within Water Vennel giving this information, but I smiled when I saw that someone had scored through the 'His Royal Highness' before Cumberland's name, and had written in the word 'Butcher' instead. He slaughtered Scots, and butcher he was.

On the front of Number 44 Tay Street you will see a plaque saying that this was the birthplace of General Accident, the worldwide insurance company.

You may want to take a look into St Matthew's Church in passing, it is generally open to the public. It was built between 1870 and 1871, and has a spire that rises to 212 feet. As you reach the point where High Street reaches Tay Street, the building on the corner opposite is the Municipal Building and City chambers. If you go in through the door just up High Street and into the reception office, you can inquire if it is possible to view the stained glass in the old Council Chambers upstairs. There may of course be a meeting on, but if it is vacant they are generally receptive to allowing visitors to see it.

The Chambers are impressive, the roof very eye-catching with its thistle-painted woodwork. The room measures 41 feet by 25. The large stained glass overlooking Tay Street is most striking, depicting King Robert the

Bruce's capture of Perth in 1311. Bruce is in full armour, clasping a spear, and he and his fellow Scots are fighting to gain a foothold on the parapet of the city wall. I particularly like the faces on the defending English soldiers, all staring-eyed and aggressive, fighting to repel the Scots.

Going round the room to the side overlooking High Street, all the characters depicted in stained glass are from Sir Walter Scott's famous novel *The Fair Maid of Perth*. They are, in order, King Robert III, Lord Provost Charteris with sword in hand, Simon Glover, the Fair Maid of Perth herself, Hal O' the Wynd, with a sword taller than himself! The Duke of Rothesay, then the Glee Maiden form the last two. The Glee Maiden plays a lute.

I hope you get to see these works. They made my day, and I can still picture them clearly in my mind's eye. There are other pieces of stained glass on the stairway, but Robert the Bruce does it for me.

The building was opened in 1879, and has a plaque to the Polish army on its frontage. I have a great deal of admiration for the Poles and all they have been through in their history. They are resilient, and have suffered many aggressive inroads in their time. They lost 20% of their population during World War II. One in five killed: it seems unbelievable.

Continue on Tay Street, passing a church that has been converted into flats, but it retains some of its gargoyles. You are now nearing the old bridge of Perth, with its nine arches. Cross the road to take the lane that goes down under the bridge. There is a plaque on the wall that tells its story. There was a bridge here in 1209, but it was swept away by floods. The chroniclers tell us that it was at the bridge of Perth that King Alexander II met the funeral cortege of his father, William the Lion, and accompanied it on to Arbroath Abbey.

The present bridge was built by the architect Smeaton in 1771, its nine arches 880 feet long. To give you an idea of the Tay in spate, the floods of 1773–4 almost reached the parapet! It seems unbelievable on a visit on a summer's day. The only real change to this bridge over all those years and withstanding all those floods has been the addition of the walkways for pedestrians, projecting from either side.

If you look over the edge where the information board stands, you will see that there is water flowing out beneath you into the Tay. This is the exit sluice for the town lades, and I will come to them shortly.

Standing here was a 'gentleman of the road', pushing his belongings in a shopping trolley. He began to speak to me, using the odd snatch of Gaelic, and we spoke of the bridge, then the conversation went round to the Battle of Culloden. He knew his stuff, this old guy, and I felt bad when I had to cut off the conversation and push on. He had the answer to every question I put to him. Never take a Scotsman at face value!

If you go under the bridge, this takes you onto the edge of the North Inch. You will see the defences to try and stop the Tay from inundating the town.

Under the bridge and over to your left there is an interesting memorial to the 51st Highland Division. It is in the form of a statue depicting a kilted soldier, and a young girl offering him flowers. It is called Tunes *and Flowers*, and the plaque tells you it is 'One metre and twelve years' – the gap between the soldier and the girl. It was unveiled on 26 October 2002 to mark the sixtieth anniversary of the battle of El Alamein. This statue really moves me. I have stood and looked at it and it turns emotions within me. It is not that it overly large or impressive. It is the subject matter itself. The Scottish soldier, the bagpipes under his arm, and the innocence of the girl. Its genius is that you are using your imagination to decipher what is happening. Has her town been liberated, and she is thanking the soldier with the little posy? I can only recommend that you look at it yourself, and see how it makes you feel. I can only congratulate the sculptor for choosing such an emotional scene, and one so different from any other war memorial I have ever seen.

Just by this memorial there is an obelisk to the Perthshire Volunteers, who were raised in May 1794.

Back to the end of the bridge where you crossed the Tay as you drove into the town. Directly before the bridge is George Street. On the right-hand side is a large, cream coloured building with a green dome, the town's museum.

Perth Museum and Art Gallery is great. It is not large, but it is crammed with goodies. It has many medieval artefacts that have been discovered in Perth itself, which is quite unusual. There are weapons, everyday articles, historical data, and a good collection of Pictish stones. Over and above things with a purely Scottish flavour, there is art, furniture, glass and ceramics. All in all an Aladdin's Cave, and some time should be put aside for a good perusal.

The building work on the museum was commenced in 1932, and it was opened in 1935.

When you exit the museum, turn left back towards the bridge, but this time go round the corner and into Charlotte Street, passing North Port after the end of the first block. We will be returning to North Port shortly. Continue on down Charlotte Street. On the corner ahead with Blackfriars Street there is a plaque about eight feet from the ground. This plaque commemorates some epic moments in Scotland's story, but it is crumbling, most of the wording missing, and if anybody from Perth's council is reading this, I suggest you get a replacement erected as soon as possible.

The name Blackfriars Street is an obvious clue. The plaque commemorates the site of the Blackfriars Monastery, founded in 1231 by King Alexander II. What is left of the wording says:

King Robert viewed the Battle of the Clans that fought on the North Inch in … James I of Scotland was murdered here …

The rest of the wording has crumbled away, but, of course, I will tell you the story.

On 23 October 1396, lists were staked off, as if in readiness for a great tournament, and benches and stands were erected for spectators. A great crowd gathered to see the forthcoming spectacle: a judicial combat between opposing clans, thirty of their champions on either side. They were to fight with bows, swords, axes, spears – to the death. This was arranged to settle some now long-forgotten dispute.

The two were Clans Chattan – MacIntoshes and MacPhersons, and Clan 'Quhele', thought to be the MacKays. There are various slight differences in the old accounts of what happened next. Apparently one of the combatants took fright and ran to the Tay, where he swam to the far shore and made off. A blacksmith of Perth said that he was willing to make up the numbers for a fee, and for a pension of sorts if he survived. This was accepted.

King Robert III apparently watched the proceedings close to the spot where you are now standing, on a flower bedecked stand like a little bower, built on the Blackfriars Monastery.

When battle commenced, it was as violent and bloody as you could possibly imagine, huge splashes of blood, limbs flying off, agonised screams of men, coupled with screams and fainting in the crowd. It was a no-holds-barred vicious carnage, and at its conclusion there were ten men left on one side, a single survivor on the other, all sporting wounds of one sort or another. But the outcome was clear, and by the law of the day, justice had been done.

You stand looking out at the North Inch from here, traffic passing on the main route between you and the edge of the grass, and you can try to put your mind back to the Autumn of 1396 and see the signal given when the two lines of men facing each other suddenly sprang forward, screaming their war cries.

It's a strange old world.

It seems that the North Inch was no stranger to judicial combat. A fight is reported as having taken place here in the time of King Robert the Bruce. This was one on one, though, the opponents on that occasion being Hugh Harding and William de Saintlowe.

As reported on the crumbling plaque, King James I of Scotland was murdered here. Most Scots know this story, or at least a little of it, somewhere in the recesses of their memory.

King James, when in Perth, liked to reside within the Blackfriars Monastery. There were probably apartments there that were more comfortable than staying within a draughty castle, and James was with his Queen, Joan Beaufort, and her ladies-in-waiting.

There was a tennis court within the precincts of the monastery, and James liked to play. He was a robust, athletic individual, good at sports. He had been losing tennis balls down a hole at the side of the court, so he had his workmen fill this hole in. Tennis was a popular game with the higher echelons of society in Scotland, and a medieval tennis court still exists at Falkland Palace in Fife.

One evening, James was relaxing with the queen and her ladies, when the noise of armoured men was heard, approaching up the stairs. As the occupants of the room turned to look at the door, it was noticed that the bar that acted as a lock was missing. Doors at that time either had iron staples at either side where a wooden bar could be placed in order to stop access, or there would be holes in the stonework of the door frame where a drawbar could be inserted.

One of the ladies, Kate Douglas, ran to the door and placed her arms in the staples. It was remembered that there was access into an underground chamber, or perhaps a sewer of sorts, beneath the floorboards. James quickly pulled up the boards and dropped into the space below. The boards were replaced and a carpet rolled over the top. The attackers broke the door down, smashing the bones of Kate's arms in the process. They hunted for the King within the apartment before realising he had escaped through the gap in the floor.

The King had had a few moments in which he should have successfully made his escape, but fate had intervened. The exit from this vault had been the very hole, at the side of the tennis court that James had ordered to be filled in only days before. His assailants cornered him there, and unarmed James did his best to defend himself, using his athletic prowess to hold them off. But eventually a dagger plunged into the King's breast, and 16 more times daggers rose and fell. So died the King of Scots, in a hole in the ground. The Queen's vengeance was terrible. The murderers were rounded up and caught, and suffered terrible tortures until the axe eventually gave them blessed release.

The brave Kate Douglas was from that time called Kate Bar-lass in Scotland, and families with the second name Barlas claim descent from her.

Strangely, James was to be buried at another monastery in Perth, the Carthusian. Perhaps his wife did not want him incarcerated in the establishment where he met his untimely end. She was to join him there in due course, and I will take you to the spot shortly.

A little crumbling plaque on a wall, and people walk by never glancing at it.

Now retrace your steps a little, back to the North Port, and turn up this little street.

At the end of the row of older buildings on your left, there is a restaurant, in a particularly attractive old townhouse. If you look at the left hand gable wall of this place, there is a small plaque about a foot square, and perhaps eight feet from the ground. It reads: 'In this vicinity stood the castle of Perth, destroyed by a flood in 1210 AD.' – told you the Tay could be a bit unruly!

North Port leads into Curfew Row, and on your right is a plaque to Lord John Murray, MP for Perthshire 1734–61. There is then a picturesque little building, long pointed out as being the residence of Catherine Glover, the Fair Maid of Perth, heroine of Sir Walter Scott's book of the same name. The Fair Maid married one of the survivors of the Clan Battle on the North Inch. The building is old, of that there is no doubt, but I do not think for a moment that the date inscribed on the front, 1393, is authentic. There is a fairly modern inscribed stone on show too, which says, 'Grace and Peace'. The house is a two-storeyed affair, with a circular stair tower. There is a niche at first floor level that looks as if it may have held a statue at some time.

Continue on up Curfew Row, cobbled here, where it cuts off opposite the Fair Maid's House, into Mill Street. When you reach Mill Street, turn right and continue on. Perth Theatre is on your left. Cross Kinnoull Street, and on to cross South Methven Street. Before you stand some of the old mill buildings of Perth. What I want you to look at here are the town lades. After you have crossed South Methven Street, look over the low wall on your left. You will see that there is water flowing rapidly in one of the old lades. It appears from under the old mill before you. These lades were old even in the days of Wallace and Bruce.

Perhaps I should explain what a lade is? It is a man-made channel with running water, diverted to run mill wheels. In Perth, the lades come from the River Almond a little west, run through the city, then empty into the Tay. The mill before you, which is now home to a tourist information office, had a wheel that was powered by water running over its base. Hence the reason the lade passes right under this particular example.

But the lades have had other uses over the centuries. Here, they once formed part of the moat that surrounded Perth, acting as a defence along with the city walls. Remember the stained glass window of Bruce assailing the place in 1311? Well, the story runs like this.

The Scots under Bruce had besieged the walled town of Perth for six weeks. Perth was a difficult place to prise out of English hands. It was well defended by its walls, and its deep moat fuelled by the lades. The English could be provisioned by boats sailing up the Tay. Bruce, with his usual genius for these things, realised that a ruse of sorts would save time, effort, and spare much Scots blood from being shed. Under cover of night he had close inspections made of the walls, ditches and moat, then ordered his men to pack up all their gear and depart. The defenders of Perth, of course, took this opportunity to shout abuse and make various rude gestures at Bruce's departing force. Bruce took his men westwards towards Methven, where there was much woodland cover.

They lay there for a week, letting the garrison in Perth be lulled into a false sense of security. Then, one dark night, Bruce put his plan into action. They came back to Perth under cover of darkness, and Bruce informed his men he had discovered a section of the moat that was no more than neck-deep. He explained that they would quietly wade across, then use their scaling ladders to clear the walls. The Scots had invented the rope ladder for such a purpose, which they would unroll, lift with a spear, and a hook at the top would catch securely on the stonework.

There was a French knight of great renown in Bruce's company. He was there as an ambassador for the King of France. He later reported his aston-ishment as Bruce himself began to strip off and make ready to drop into the icy water. He could not believe that a king would behave so, and stood amazed as Bruce was the first to wade in, a dirk between his teeth. This was the root of Bruce's genius. He knew that Scots fought best when led by example, and he would not have his men do any task that he would not attempt himself.

The scaling ladders were hooked in place, and silently, the Scots clam-bered up and spread out over the walls. Our French friend reported that Bruce was the second man over the top.

While Bruce kept a band of men with him, ready to give numerical aid to wherever it was needed most, the rest of the Scots spread out through the town. All opposition was dealt with, and by sunrise Perth was back with its rightful owners.

I can gaze down to the flowing water here and it gives me a little window back to that night where my forebears took back their own from the hands of the invaders.

A plaque on the side of the mill here informs that mills here were gifted to King Malcolm III.

If you walk round the mill here, you will see there are other old mills beyond, one of which has been converted into a hotel. As stated, this build-ing now contains the tourist information office. If you walk round to its entrance, you will see opposite, part of an old building with a close leading through it (a close in Scotland is an entry or alleyway through a building) which states on its front 'Hal O' the Wynd House'. Hal, already mentioned, is a character from the novel *The Fair Maid of Perth*.

You can walk through this close back to the main route of South Methven Street, where you turn right. Continue along this street, by various shops, and cross High Street, Perth's main shopping street. You then reach South Street, where there are traffic lights. You will notice at the corner opposite there is a reddish-coloured pillar, some ten feet high. Glance to your right on South Street, there is a pub here called the Robert Burns lounge, that has a statue of Burns at first-floor level.

Cross over for a look at this pillar. It marks the site of the old Carthusian Monastery of Perth. The pillar bears an inscription upon it:

Within these grounds stood the Carthusian Monastery founded by King James I of Scotland in 1429. It was the only house belonging to this order in Scotland. In the precincts of the monastery were buried The Royal Founder, his Queen Joan Beaufort, and Margaret Tudor, Queen of King James IV.

So this is where James I was buried after his murder at Blackfriars. James IV was the king slain at Flodden, and his English-born wife was later buried here.

The pillar sits within flower beds, and behind you will notice an interesting large building. If you walk up just a few steps you will see that it has a large inscription on its wall, above the entrance, which states, 'Founded by King James VI in 1587'.

This building, on the site of the Carthusian Monastery, was originally constructed as a hospital, and served that purpose for many years. It was converted into dwelling houses in the nineteenth century. Most of the work you can see today dates from around 1750.

Go back to the lights, and turn down South Street. Continue on down this busy street until you see King Edward Street going off to your left. Turn up here, and you will see St John's Place branching off right. Over to your left as you turn you will see the Mercat Cross and the entrance to St John's shopping centre, Perth's large covered shopping mall. Down St John's Place you will arrive at Perth's St John's Kirk. This place has figured hugely in Perth's history. In fact, it is probably the main reason that the town sprung into such a metropolis, and it gave the place its original name, St John's town of Perth. This title survives in the name of the local football team, St Johnstone.

Although I have a deep-rooted love for Scotland's history and the places where momentous events took place, I have to be honest and say that I find St John's Kirk a bit of a disappointment. I can walk round it and appreciate it, but it does not grab me. It has been unsympathetically restored, and you do not feel the age of the place as you should. And it is old. It is believed there has been a church on this site since Pictish days. In the twelfth and thirteenth centuries, it was both magnificent and extensive, but for some reason it fell into disrepair. It was more or less restructured in the 1400s, the choir dating from 1450, the nave 1490, and the central tower has a fifteenth-century steeple. But it is hard to discern age within the building. There has been much re-pointing work which makes the masonry look fairly modern.

Fordun, one of Scotland's great chroniclers, states that King Edward III of England stabbed his brother, John, Earl of Cornwall before the High Altar, although English sources merely state that John died at Perth. There is a memorial to the Mercer family, who have a large burial vault under the church, and they were interred here from 1380 to 1925. The Mercer family are said to have exchanged the North and South Inches to the city for the right to have their vault here. Perth undoubtedly won in this deal, but there is an old couplet that was once cried aloud by the folk of Perth:

> Folks say the Mercers tried the town to cheat,
> When for twa Inches they did win six feet!

An old gazetteer states that in the east end of the church stands a blue marble tombstone with figures upon it, and this was said to have been the memorial of James I and his Queen. It had obviously been removed to St John's when the Carthusian was destroyed. I visited St John's several years ago to make enquiries about this stone, as there was no sign of it within the church, but nobody knew anything about it. It must have been removed during one of the many restoring 'improvements'.

St John's at least has a redeeming feature in its bells. One of the bells of which there are very many, is the Boudon Bell, which weighs 28cwt 14lbs (a ton and a half!) which makes it more than twice the weight of any other pre-Reformation bell in Scotland. It was cast in the early 1500s. One rare bell is the Ave Maria Bell, which weighs 7cwt, is strangely shaped, and bears an inscription in Latin, stating: '*Hail* Mary, full of grace, the Lord is with thee'. It was cast around the time of the Battle of Bannockburn in 1314.

In 1559 the whole interior of the church, ornaments, statues, images, tombs, hangings and altars were destroyed by the mob. The preacher John Knox, espousing Protestant doctrines, incited the congregation of Perth to root out and destroy all images of idolatry. The destruction spread out to all the monkish establishments of the city, and by the time they had slated their godly duty, all that remained was the ruined walls of these places.

I have stated several times before that the Church in Scotland may have been in need of change, but I don't think if there is a God up above, that he would condone wanton destruction. I wish I could have seen all these establishments with their memorials of history.

As you exit the kirk, walk to the rear of the building, where you reach St John's Street, and turn right. Facing you at the end of this street is the Salutation Hotel, standing on South Street. It has two large kilted figures, statues set at first floor level on the front of the building. Here Bonnie Prince Charlie stayed during his army's march south in 1745. There is a plaque on the front just above the ground floor windows that states that it is the oldest established hotel in Scotland, dating from 1699. The room that Prince Charles occupied is still used, and is room number 20.

During the trial of a certain Colonel Bower at York after the failure of the Jacobite rising of 1745, it was stated that he had worn a white cockade in his bonnet, and that he had been seen 'shaking hands with Prince Charles at the Salutation Hotel in Perth'. An interesting old place indeed!

Just a few seconds' walk will take you back to Tay Street, where you can turn right and return to your vehicle. No doubt you will want to spend a little time gazing over the wall to the river. I did on my last visit, and watched a bunch of teenage boys jumping from the South Street bridge parapet into the river. It wasn't that warm a day – they just obviously fancied it. Boys after my own heart. Many a time I have done such pointless jumps just for the hell of it. At least I know where the water is deep enough now to get away with such a jump.

When you reach the car park on the edge of the South Inch, you may be interested to hear that Cromwell built a great fortification here to cow the people of Perth in 1652. It was a solid work, 266 feet square. Many buildings were demolished so that the Englishman could build this work. These included the hospital, the school, parts of the bridge and many of the gravestones were looted from Greyfriars cemetery, already visited, for the same purpose. After the restoration of the monarchy, it was used as a public quarry and removed piecemeal. Even the ditches surrounding it were eventually filled in, and no trace of it now remains.

Edinburgh Road across the South Inch now crosses the spot where it stood.

As you come out of the car park, turn left towards the mini roundabout, then left again at the mini roundabout, following the edge of the South Inch. The road swings right when you reach the railway station, but keep following the signs for the inner ring road. This is Leonard Street. Following the signs takes you onto St Andrew's Street, then Caledonian Road, and here you will see the signs for Glasgow A9, which you follow out of Perth. Follow the Glasgow Road to the outskirts of Perth, gently climbing uphill all the way.

Keep your eyes peeled for signs for Cherrybank Gardens, and the turn-off for Forteviot and Dunning. This road goes off at an angle to your left. You drive uphill, and you will eventually see the entrance to the car park for Cherrybank Gardens. Bells Scotch Whisky are the sponsors of this place. There is a visitor centre with a shop and café, with various types of Bells Whisky on sale too. These are free (not the whisky, but the visitor attractions!) but there is a fee to visit the gardens themselves.

The gardens cover a seven-acre site, containing some 50,000 plants, but it is particularly famous for its collection of different types of heather – an incredible 900 varieties in all! It is a very attractive place, immaculately kept, with beautiful paths and streams of running water. The visitor centre has information on the history of Perth.

As you come out of the gardens, turn right, following the B9112. You go under the M90 motorway, and climb out of the valley that Perth nestles in. You are crossing a mixture of moor and planted forest. We come over the lip of Strathearn, the valley of the River Earn, where there are some great panoramas, and drop toward the tiny hamlet of Milltown of Aberdalgie. The River Earn runs below to our left.

On a little, and we pass the gates of Dupplin Castle. This is a private residence, not open to the public. There was an ancient pile on the site, destroyed by a fire in 1827,and the current mansion was built to replace it between 1828 and 1832.

Dupplin is a name from Scottish history though, as a battle was fought in this vicinity on the night of 12 August, 1332. There is no memorial to this fight that you can visit, and even the site of the conflict is open to much conjecture, but as you are in the area it should be mentioned.

After King Robert the Bruce died in 1329, covetous English eyes turned northwards once more. His two great captains, Douglas and Randolph, did not long outlive him, Douglas dying in Spain on a crusade with Bruce's heart, and Randolph expiring of sickness in Musselburgh. The regency of Scotland for Bruce's young son, David II, lay in the hands of Donald, Earl of Mar, Bruce's nephew.

King Edward III of England became desirous of setting up the son of the long-dead John Balliol on the throne of Scotland. So 88 ships full of English soldiers sailed from England's River Humber north, with Edward Balliol in their midst.

They landed on the Fife coast, and marched north for Perth. Mar waited for them on Dupplin Moor. Balliol and the English forded the River Earn near your current position, and battle was joined. The Scots held the repeated charges, but as had happened so many times before, and would happen again shortly at Halidon Hill, the English longbowmen broke Scottish hearts with their deadly massed fire. The cloth-yard shafts tore gaps in the Scottish ranks, and the dead included the regent Mar, a bastard son of Bruce, and Randolph's heir.

Edward Balliol pushed on to Scone, where he was crowned on the moot-hill. But he was not long to hold his position as a second King of Scots against David II. The Scots gathered an army, led by yet another Randolph and another Douglas, and defeated him at Annan in the south, after which Edward Balliol made his escape over the Border, half-naked on an unsaddled horse.

A mile after Dupplin, the road swings left to cross the River Earn on an old bridge. Another two-thirds of a mile and you cross a railway level crossing, and the road swings right towards Dunning. You may want to divert a little though to take the road off to the left, the B935, which crosses the Water of May into Forteviot.

Forteviot is a tiny place today, a few houses, and its old church, but a thousand years ago it was regarded as a veritable metropolis! According to legend, Angus MacFergus, King of the Picts (731–61) built a church here. No doubt the church today, built in 1778, is on the site of its predecessor.

There was a royal palace here, and I have been informed that it stood at the west end of the village (the end at the church!) overlooking the Water of May, on an eminence called the Halyhill, a little north of the church.

Walking the path down the side of the church south does lead to some interesting flat areas of land with banks sloping down towards the river too. Kenneth MacAlpin spent much time at this place. He was the first king of the Scotland we know today, being the first to rule over the united Picts and Scots. He died here in AD 860. He is buried on Iona.

The chronicler Wynton records a curious story that Malcolm Canmore, King of Scots who reigned 1057–93, was an illegitimate son of King Duncan, his mother being the daughter Forteviot's daughter. Certainly, Malcolm spent a lot of time at the palace here. The mill stood a little further down the Water of May towards the River Earn, the name surviving in the name of the farmhouse, Milton of Forteviot. It is also recorded that Edward Balliol's army was encamped on the Miller's Acre of Forteviot before the aforementioned Battle of Dupplin.

In the village itself, there is a group of white houses on the left-hand side of the road. There is an arched entry in the centre of this row, and it has a stone plaque inserted above it. It states: 'This village was rebuilt by John Alexander, 1st Baron Forteviot of Dupplin, in the years 1925–26 and occupies part of the site of the Pictish capital Fothuir-Tabaicht, a royal residence from the VII to the XII centuries. Here Kenneth I (MacAlpin) died AD 860.'

Retrace your route the short hop to the junction, turn left, and continue towards Dunning. It is only a little over two miles on the B934 into Dunning itself.

Dunning is not a big place, but it has a lot of history in its few streets. If you park in the centre of the village, it is just a few yards' walk in each direction to see some interesting sites and artefacts. The name Dunning is a corruption of *Dun-an*, Gaelic for the 'little fort'. The name may come from a native fort, as several hereabouts can be identified from aeriel photographs, or it may refer to a marching camp that the Romans built, the site of which is marked on Ordnance Survey maps, a little northwest of the village.

St Serf brought Christianity to this district around AD 500, and it is St Serf's Church that dominates the village today, no doubt constructed on the site of his original chapel. There is an abiding legend that on reaching this place, St Serf slew a dragon that had been terrorising the district:

Armed only with the breast plate of faith, he entered its lair and slew it by a blow of his pastoral staff.

Today part of the village is known locally as Dragon, pronounced Dray-gon, in commemoration of this deed.

There is a standing stone in a field just north of the village, east of the B9141, that is said to be where the Abbot of Dunkeld was slain in the Battle of Duncrub, fought in AD 964. If you drive or walk down the B9141, sign-posted Dalreoch 2, you come to the town's little cemetery on your right. If you walk to the back of the cemetery you can see the standing stone in the field before you.

St Serf's Church's most prominent feature is its tower, built in the 1100s. It looks its age, but it is in really good condition. It is large and imposing. An ancient stone stands within its base bearing the design of a Celtic cross, and this could be a throwback to the days of St Serf himself. (Author's Note – this stone has been removed to Edinburgh for testing. It is hoped that it will be returned to the church shortly). Incidentally, it was at Dunning that he died, although he is buried at Culross in Fife. The rest of the church is of a later date, and the body of the building was remodelled in 1811.

Inside, the main attraction is the Dupplin Cross. This cross originally stood in the open in a field to the south-west of Dupplin Castle, but has been brought into the church to preserve it from further deterioration. It has been brilliantly sited, standing framed by an old archway in the base of the ancient tower, and lit in a sympathetic fashion. It actually catches your breath as you enter the church and look at it, ancient and carven. It was raised on the hillside at Dupplin, overlooking Forteviot, and it would be of some significance to the Celtic peoples visiting. It has an inscription upon it saying that it was dedicated to Constantine, King of Scots.

The Dunning Burn runs through the village at the far side of the church, and it has several wee bridges over it – even a ford at one place!

If you walk down Kirk Wynd to the left of the church, where the road turns round the back of the graveyard, there is a little old house facing you. It has recently been restored and is lived in once more. This house has quite a story. After the Battle of Sheriffmuir in 1715, the site of which we visited earlier, the Jacobite army retreated through Dunning. For some reason they burnt the town, leaving the inhabitants homeless. I have no idea why this burning took place, or why this horror was inflicted on the villagers. Only one house survived, this one before you, a reminder of stark times indeed.

There is another memento of 1715 in the village. After the burning the villagers planted a thorn tree to remind them always of this event. The orig-inal tree survived until 1936, but has been replaced twice since. The present tree stands within a little walled area in front of the Thorn Tree Inn, with a little metal sign explaining what it is. It is to the left of Muckhart Road. I have had good times in the Dunning Hotel too, I hasten to add, sometimes wee things happen that endears a place to you, and I have that good feeling where Dunning is concerned.

We are going to take the Muckhart Road over the Ochil Hills, but there is something just outside the village that I would like you to see first.

Continue straight on along the road past the church. It is signposted the 'Auchterarder Road' from the centre of the village. About a mile out look for a memorial of sorts on the right-hand side of the road. There isn't really anywhere to park, but you are on a straight stretch, so you will be okay to tuck a bike in. Put your hazard warning lights on in a car. There is a little gap in the wall that runs alongside the road that will give you access.

There is a cairn of stone blocks, perhaps six or seven feet high, with a long slim stone projecting above, looking like a standing stone, smooth and rectangular. On top of this is a stone cross. In white paint on the front is written: Maggie Wall. Burnt here 1657 as a witch. This is a curious memorial. There are several recorded witch burnings in this area, but none of them concerning the Maggie Wall mentioned on this monument. It is possible that it was done by local vigilantes, who were no different from a Wild West lynch mob, and the memorial raised afterwards in penance and regret. The monument is looked after, and the inscription thereon is kept freshly painted, but no-one locally seems to know who tends it, or at least they do not want to say so! I really like this memorial. It is different from anything else I have seen in Scotland. The nearby farm flies a Saltire too, which is always guaranteed to make me happy. I love to pass houses in Scotland where the Saltire flies. The sight of it makes me feel I have a bond, something in common, with the people who live there, even though we have never met. We do have something in common of course, a shared heritage and history. Their ancestors fought and suffered in the same campaigns as mine. Scots together.

Back into the centre of Dunning, and we take the Muckhart Road off to our right, just before we reach the church again. It is also signposted 'Yetts of Muckhart 9'. Yett is the old Scots for a gate or doorway, and as it is at the southern entrance of this pass through the Ochil Hills, its name is self-explanatory.

As you drive out of the village the road immediately begins to climb the main ridge of the Ochils directly before you. You may notice a large baronial edifice before you, its large tower framed by the hills behind. It looks very much like an ancient castle at a distance, but is actually a mock-baronial mansion from the 1800s. It is currently a nursing home. So there will be a lot of kipping at Kippen House (sorry – that was dreadful!)

The road really begins to twist and turn, gaining height, and it is quite narrow, so care is needed. You pass the entrance to a farm called Quilts on your right, then the following farm called Knowes has a rough-track private-access road. Several hundred yards up this road, and over to your right on the edge of a field and by some trees, is a large monolith called the Gray Stone. This marks where the Maormor of Atholl died of wounds received in

battle. Unless you are a motorcyclist, it is difficult to park to gain access to the farm track, so show consideration.

The road continues upwards, circling round the corrie created by the Thorter Burn, and the views out, back towards the edge of the Highlands, are quite extensive. You come into forestry plantations, not native species, this stuff is planted purely for commercial gain. But there are walks and paths through all this growth, most of them signposted. There are pleasant views out here and there though. This is quite an uninhabited landscape, though you are very close to the industrial heart of Scotland. It is my aim of course to take you from place to place here and there, by little known by-ways like this.

Once the watershed is crossed (you will notice the burns now flow south), you drop to follow some narrow and interesting wee glens. These routes will have been used since the last Ice Age retreated 10,000 years ago. I'm quite sure our ancestors used the direct routes that streams have carved through the hills; they are after all the lines of least resistance.

A mile or so north of Yetts O' Muckhart we cross the River Devon just after it has flowed out of Castlehill Reservoir. You catch a glimpse of the large dam up its glen to your right. I have seen quite a few cars parked along the roadside here when there has been a really warm summer's day in Scotland, and people have been sunbathing and going for a swim in the several pools in the river on this stretch. The road follows the right bank of the river for a little here, then we come to a junction with the A823. We turn left. Following the signs for Dunfermline. It is quite a blind junction looking back up the A823, so take a little care in pulling out. (I'm talking from experience – I cut a guy off quite badly here once, and completely unintentionally.)

Just in front you will see the sign welcoming you to the Yetts O'Muckhart. Then you hit a complicated wee junction. A strange configuration this, they way it is set up, I haven't seen another junction like this. You take a right, following the sign for Stirling and Dunfermline. Another 100 yards on there is another junction and here you turn left, continuing to follow the signs for Dunfermline.

I'm really looking forward to this next bit. I have always liked to take people somewhere special and little-known. You will see Muckhart Golf Course on your right, then keep your eyes peeled for a sign pointing to your left, saying 'Rumbling Bridge Gorge'. There is parking space available at the rear of the building here, the local nursing home. But please do this the way I recommend, as I like to achieve maximum impact. Walk a little further down the main road, past the nursing home. There are nice gardens in front, so you can walk through these, but stick to the wall and hedge at the roadside on your right. You reach a gate on your right after about another 100 yards, go through this gate, and the bridge is immediately before you.

Please beware of traffic on this narrow old bridge. There is a little projection out on either side halfway across. Go to the one on your left and get ready to lean over. I've never seen anyone do it yet without an expletive! The drop is quite incredible, and this, coupled with the narrowness of the chasm, less than a score of feet wide, is totally unexpected. You can just glimpse the River Devon far far below. It actually disappears here and there as the gorge is a little crooked, the way it has eroded, and the overhangs hide the water. I know we have been to the Corrieshalloch Gorge near Ullapool, and it is impressive, but this one is in the Lowlands where you don't expect to see geology on such a majestic scale.

I have steered several motorcycling friends to Rumbling Bridge when they have enquired what a good destination for a run would be. I don't think anyone has ever felt let down!

Have a look over the other side of the bridge too, downstream, before we move on. You look directly down a gap here to a pool, a dizzyingly far way below. To give you an idea of how nutty I am, I have wondered how deep this pool is, and whether you could drop straight from the parapet here into the pool. I really shouldn't have written that – you'll look over and say 'He really is off his head!'

From the bridge, go back through the gate, and you will see there is a path down to a viewing platform, just below the bridge. As you come down to this platform you will realise there is an older bridge still intact below the one you have just looked over. The older bridge was built by William Grey, a local, in 1713. It spans a gap of 22 feet, with an arch 12 feet wide. It has no parapets – never did have! The gradients down to it must have been very steep, and going over it on a horse and cart must have been an experience. Bonnie Dundee, who was later killed at the Battle of Killiecrankie heading the Jacobite army in 1689, used to march his men over this old bridge during his patrols of this district.

The upper bridge carrying the modern road was built in 1816, to remove the steep gradients involved for the old bridge. It stands 120 feet above the water, but it looks and feels much more due to the topography.

Back up to the edge of the gorge and continue upstream. There are some information boards – a little faded, but still legible. They tell how the gorge was formed during the last Ice Age. Below these boards there is another walkway viewpoint, but it stops short of the far side. As you reach the bottom of the steps down, there is a little plaque on the rock face stating: 'Constructed by 202 Field Squadron Royal Engineers (v) 1997'.

Obviously the impact can be different here in different weather conditions. After snow-melt in the Ochils, the gorge, incredibly narrow in places, is a madness of frothing, foaming, tumbling white water.

Back up, and a little further upstream there is another viewpoint, this standing just above the Devil's Mill. And it does sound like a mill! The

sound of the rocks being churned beneath the water is exactly like the sound of the grinding stones at work in an old mill. The reason the locals gave it the name Devil's Mill is because mills did not operate on a Sunday, the Lord's Day. So, this constant milling was attributable to Satan!

Above the Devil's Mill, only a few yards further, there is a bridge that crosses the gorge, much lower in height now. There are various walks that continue from here that you may wish to follow. The river below this bridge is constricted to something like 18 inches wide, being squeezed through the rock walls in boiling foam. All in all very impressive, and the power of Nature very apparent.

Rumbling Bridge Gorge is a magical place, like something from *The Lord of the Rings*. I'm sure you will be impressed, especially with that first view from the bridge. I visited it just the day before I wrote this. It was mid-July, it was the middle of a heatwave, about six in the evening, and I never saw another living soul. It was not always like this though, and in the late 1800s these woodland paths were crammed with people. You see, there was once a railway station at Rumbling Bridge, and it became a great tourist attraction, trainloads of people turning up to see it. It is a quiet place now.

Return to the information boards you have already passed, and here a path strikes back to the nursing home where you parked. As you exit the car park, continue left to drive over the bridge itself. You will realise that you have no indication of the drop below you, and I have realised that many people must drive over this strand of stonework with no idea of the sights to be seen just a few yards away.

Through the little village here, then you reach a junction on quite a major route, the A977. Turn right, following the signs for Dunfermline. Only a mile, and you will see a junction going off to your left, the A823, again signposted for Dunfermline. You will also see signs for Knockhill Racing Circuit, 5.

On the A823, conical Cult Hill rises before you. It has the remains of an ancient fort upon its summit. The glen of the Pow Burn opens off to your left, with the Lomond Hills visible in the distance. You may spot the top of a white-harled building projecting from the trees about a mile away, on the left side of Pow Burn glen. These are the battlements of Aldie Castle, built in the early 1500s by the Mercer family. It is a private residence.

The road then rises to quite a height, and again there are extensive views in every direction. Knock Hill comes into view. It is the large hill with the communication masts on its summit. It is 1189 feet high. Knockhill Racing Circuit stands on the eastern shoulder of this hill. It is used for every kind of motor sport imaginable. I have watched motorcycles fly round this track, and its height, coupled with its cambers, sometimes make it look that if riders came off, they would tumble away down the hillside. They even have truck racing here, which I can't even image!

There are panoramas here away to the south. Edinburgh on the other side of the Firth of Forth, the towers of the Forth Road and Railway bridges discernible. As we passed these on our way north, you can now see that we have done a vast circuit of the northern part of Scotland.

Another mile and we come to the junction with the B914. It is just really a crossroads, and we go straight over towards Dunfermline. The sign pro claims, Dunfermline 3 3/4, so we are not too far away.

As you come over the last rise you can see the Forth Road Bridge at about 11 o'clock, about eight miles away.

We hit Wellwood, really a northern extension of Dunfermline, but continue straight ahead. As you near the town centre, you come through older villas, all in grey stone, the local stone of Dunfermline. It is quite amazing how the colour of the houses can vary in Scotland, village to village, town to town. Reds, greys, browns, yellowy colours of stone. Modern houses are just modern houses of course, but I like how the colour of the older stone houses in Scotland varies from area to area, as they used local sources then.

We pass the Carnegie Centre on our left. Andrew Carnegie was born in Dunfermline and was responsible for Carnegie Halls all over the world, so his is a well-kent name, and we will speak of him further. When you reach the traffic lights just after the Carnegie Centre, a stately grey stone edifice, turn right onto the major route through Dunfermline, Carnegie Drive. It is a broad street, partially dual carriageway, so hopefully you won't miss it. Continue on, over the Glen Bridge. Once you have crossed the bridge, take a left at the lights. This takes you into a street with little shops, Chalmers Street, then you turn left again into a large car park. Chalmers Street becomes one way, so you have to turn into the car park. You have to pay to park here, but it is not excessive, and it is central for many of the attractions in the town, most of which are only a few minutes walk away.

Anyone who has a love of Scotland and its history will adore Dunfermline. So we must do a quick little walking tour around the place so you too can benefit from its attractions, and hopefully get to know it a little better.

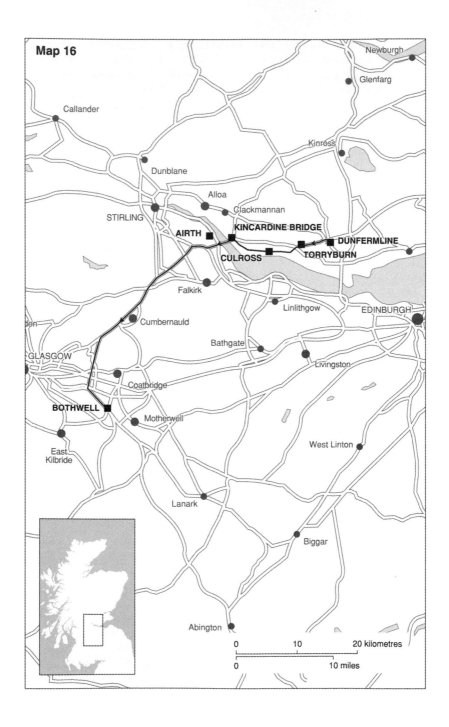

Map 16

Newburgh

Glenfarg

Callander

Kinross

Dunblane

Alloa

Clackmannan

STIRLING

AIRTH

KINCARDINE·BRIDGE

DUNFERMLINE

CULROSS

TORRYBURN

Falkirk

Linlithgow

EDINBURGH

den

Cumbernauld

Bathgate

GLASGOW

Livingston

Coatbridge

BOTHWELL

Motherwell

East
Kilbride

West Linton

Lanark

Biggar

Abington

0   10   20 kilometres

0   10 miles

CHAPTER SIXTEEN

Dunfermline and the
Crossing of the Scotwater

FROM DUNFERMLINE, THE ROUTE TRAVELS THROUGH CAIRNEYHILL, KINCARDINE BRIDGE, AND THEN TACKLES THE MAJOR ROAD NETWORK TO BOTHWELL.

IN THE NORTHWEST corner of this car park, looking to the right of the Glen Bridge you so recently crossed, there is a little stone building. It has one door, one window, and says simply 'St Margaret's Cave' on its frontage. This little building is the entry to the eighty steps that lead down to the cave, where Margaret, Queen of Scotland, was wont to pray.

Of course, the cave was not always buried underground as it is today. It was once perched above the right bank of the Tower Burn, surrounded by woodland. Margaret was an extremely pious woman – in fact, she is credited with introducing Roman Catholicism into Scotland. Not sure if that was a good thing or not, as it spelt the end for the Columban Church in Scotland, a home-grown version of Christianity. It at least was a church of compassion with very little ornamentation.

Everything evolves and changes, I suppose. I'm not a particularly religious person, but that does not detract from the fact that I have an interest in my country's history, and religion is a very large part of that. I would have liked to have seen what the now-ruined abbeys to Scotland were like before the Reformation destroyed their splendour.

Anyway, Margaret used to walk upstream from the Royal Castle to this cave, where she could pray in peace. When this car park was at the planning stage, it meant that the cave was going to be covered in concrete, gone forever. There was an outcry, and this tunnel that contains the steps was built to preserve access. So you go through the little building, and down the tunnel that resembles something that goes down to the platforms of an underground station. There are information boards all the way down, telling the story of the cave, the story of Margaret, Queen of Malcolm Canmore, who reigned from 1057–93, and how Margaret was eventually canonised.

Eventually you reach the little cave. It is only 12 feet by 9 feet, and 7 feet high, and there is a statue of Margaret in a position of prayer in the middle. It is strange to stand here today, far underground, and to realise that Margaret used to actually pray here the best part of 1,000 years ago.

It is still a place of pilgrimage for many people. The story of Margaret and Dunfermline are very much intertwined. Margaret is credited with bringing the Holy Rood to Scotland. If you remember, it was from this piece of the True Cross that Holyrood Abbey in Edinburgh got its name. Along with the Stone of Destiny, it was regarded as the great talisman of the Scottish people. It was stolen by English Longshanks, returned, and captured once again at the battle of Neville's Cross. The English presented it to Durham Cathedral, where it was displayed for many years, only to disappear at the Reformation.

Entrance to the cave is free.

Back up to the car park, and walk over to the entrance on Chalmer's Street and turn left. At the bottom of the street there are large gates on your right that lead into Pittencrief Glen, which we will visit, but we will enter by a different route. You turn left here into Bridge Street, a main shopping street. On the left-hand side of Bridge Street, on its corner with Kirkgate stands Dunfermline's large town house. It replaced an earlier version, and was constructed between 1875-9. It is a mixture of Scottish Baronial and French Gothic in style, and on the corner it has a huge clock tower 150 feet high and 23 feet square. The principal entrance is round arched, having massive buttresses and granite columns supporting a balcony over which are carved the Royal Arms of Scotland. The frontage to Bridge Street has busts of Malcolm Canmore, St Margaret, Robert the Bruce, and his queen, Elizabeth. I once did an illustrated talk on Wallace in the old court room within this building, and I recall it having some interesting paintings and impressive wooden ceiling works.

Go down Kirkgate, and you will see the abbey just before you, but turn left up into the Maygate and walk on a little until a pink-harled old building appears on your right. This is the Abbot's House, the oldest house that is still occupied in Dunfermline. It was built, as its name suggests, as a house for the daily business of the nearby abbey. It has been lovingly restored, has a café on its ground floor, where the tables are arranged in the old vaulted stores in the basement of the place. Upstairs is a museum, which has some medieval-style painted roofs, and loads of interesting artefacts, some connected with Robert the Bruce, who is buried in the abbey itself. There is a little garden out the back of the house, tastefully done. On the west wall of this garden there is a plaque in memory of Wallace's mother, Margaret Craufurd of Corsbie. This plaque shows Margaret in the vicinity of the Abbot's House, sitting against a tree, holding William's little brother John. William sitting opposite and only a boy, is making himself a wooden sword. Between them stands a thorn tree on a small mound.

If you then walk to the gate that leads into the abbey grounds, and look slightly over to your right, you will see the thorn tree on its little mound as depicted on the wall plaque. This is the reputed site of the last resting place of Wallace's mother. It's not the original tree of course, but the womenfolk of Dunfermline have replaced the tree with another every time its predecessor's life has gone.

Blind Harry, Wallace's biographer, who wrote in the 1400s, tells us how Margaret died here in Dunfermline.

Standing here, if you look up towards the tower at the east end of the abbey before you, you will notice that there are larger letters incorporated into the masonry at its top. These read 'King Robert the Bruce'. This eastern end of the church was reconstructed in the early 1800s and during the course of the building works, Bruce's tomb was rediscovered. The architect then changed his plans to incorporate this feature.

Dunfermline has been special to me since my mum brought me to the abbey as a little boy. I remember, young though I was, how standing near the last resting place of the mighty Bruce awakened patriot feelings in my heart. It was never drummed into me. I just knew. It's still such a special place to me. So many of Scotland's royals are here. Bruce. Wallace's mother. A veritable hot-bed of patriotism.

The church is open to the public at peak times. You go through the door facing you here, into the rebuilt half of the building. There is a little shop just inside the door, and as you walk through this shop you may be surprised to know that some of Scotland's royalty lie beneath its floor. You see, the tombs of the kings were destroyed by the mob at the time of the Reformation, when the Catholic Church was ousted in favour of the Protestant. Ornate tombs were thought to be a sign of Popery or idolatry. Then a steeple fell in 1753, and a tower followed in 1807. Everything was left in a shambles. The shop stands where many of the tombs in the original building stood.

Work was begun in 1817 to try to clear the debris prior to new building work. On 17 February 1818, the tomb of King Robert the Bruce, the hero-king of Scots, was discovered. He was wrapped in cloth of gold, and his breast bone had been sawn asunder, so that his heart could be removed for the Good Sir James Douglas to carry on crusade. I gave as much detail on the finding of his body as I could in my book *On the Trail of Robert the Bruce*.

If you walk forward to the pulpit, underneath is the brass memorial plaque that marks where his re-interred body lies. Many is the time I have stood or knelt here, thinking, dreaming, contemplating. Here is the man who fought so hard and lost so many loved ones in the pursuit of the freedom of his country and her people.

And the descendants of those who fought so hard against tyranny gave it away. But as I look down upon his grave I will him to know that there are many like me who will never let the hope and the dream go. So many times I have stood here with a group of others, and I can't ever remember any conversation taking place. We just stand, and we look, and we then walk away, and it is always when we are outside before any talk resumes. It's because we all know. We were in the presence of greatness, his story one of the greatest in the whole history of everyone who ever lived on this planet.

Do yourself a favour. Go and buy a copy of the *Bruce Trilogy* by Nigel Tranter. I know it is a novel, but the historical data is all spot-on, and it is an easy way to educate yourself about what this man's life's work was all about.

Also within this building were buried Malcolm Canmore and his queen, St Margaret, their sons, Edward, Edmund and Ethelred, King Donald Ban, King Edgar, Alexander I and his queen Sibylla, David I and his two queens, Malcolm IV, Alexander III and his queen Margaret, their sons, David and Alexander, Bruce's queen Elizabeth, and their daughter Matilda, Annabella Drummond, queen of Robert III and mother of James I, and Thomas Randolph, Bruce's companion, who was one of the captains at Bannockburn, and Regent of Scotland during the minority of David II.

The saddest thing of all is that there is no tomb or marker for any of them (Malcolm Canmore and St Margaret are no longer here, but more of that in a minute). The names of the royalty interred here are carved upon wood-work within the church, but I had visited the place many times and had never even noticed it before it was pointed out to me. A modern memorial would be entirely appropriate, just to say something along the lines of 'In this vicinity are buried …'.

We need to bolster our individualism, and cementing our history helps us understand what we are. Any erosion of our history also erodes a little bit of what it means to be Scottish.

Like all old churches, Dunfermline lies facing east towards the cradle of Christianity. This should help give you your bearings when I tell you that the grave of Bruce's queen, Elizabeth de Burgh, was discovered about three yards away from that of Bruce himself, lying out from the northeast corner of the more modern pulpit under which he lies.

There are several more modern memorials in the abbey, and one or two artefacts on show – a cast of Bruce's skull in a glass case being one of these. But it is quite an austere place other than that.

Exit the door directly opposite the one you entered at the little shop. This brings you out on the south side of the building, the view out to the Forth Bridges and Lothian beyond, the lines of the hills just as they would have been to Bruce himself.

Turn left, and walk the few yards round to the end of the building. There are the low remains of the walls of a shrine here, and even the central plinth which contained the shrine itself has survived. Here were transferred the remains of Malcolm Canmore and Margaret after she had been canonised. Pilgrims flocked here to visit her tomb. This continued right up until the Reformation. Strangely, what few bones of Malcolm and Margaret that have survived the centuries are now at the Escorial in Madrid, a palace built for Philip II of Spain. He was a great collector of relics, and he had two urns in his possession, one with the bones of Malcolm, the other containing Margaret.

From here, cut across the graveyard towards the remains of the palace block before you. The stonework that is left will leave you in no doubt as to the size and splendour of this building when it was in use. On the way over you may notice the stone that marks the last resting place of the poor souls that lost their lives during a cholera epidemic in Dunfermline.

There is a little shop and ticket office tucked away in the ruins of the palace, and here you can purchase a ticket for the palace, and this will gain you admission to the older, eastern half of the abbey.

Let's deal with the abbey first. It was founded in 1072 by Malcolm Canmore, obviously influenced by Margaret The idea of it being used as a royal sephulcre was apparent from its planning. It was completed and further endowed in 1115, under the reign of Alexander I. It was then remodelled as a Benedictine Abbey in 1124 by David I, who brought monks from Canterbury for that purpose.

At its height it was a magnificent establishment, much more to it than can be seen today. The English chronicler, Matthew of Westminster, stated:

> Its boundaries were so ample ... and having so many princely buildings, that three potent sovereigns, with their retinues, might have been accommodated with lodgings here at the same time without incommoding one another.

Edward Longshanks occupied the place several times during his invasion of Scotland. He wintered here between 6 November 1303 and 10 February 1304, and he set fire to the abbey and its palace on his departure, causing much damage to the place. The fact that his sister, Alexander III's queen, was buried here seemed to make no difference. Bruce spent much money restoring the place, although it probably was not as fine as before, but the real damage was caused by the Scots themselves on 18 March 1560, when the Reformation-fired mob wrecked the abbey.

The old nave still stands complete, with its old towers at its western end. When you walk in, the first things to strike you are the mighty pillars. The stained glass panels in the great West Window are a touch of class. These were paid for by Andrew Carnegie in 1884, and cost £3,000. The artist was Sir Noel Paton, a patriot who was responsible for many Scottish works of art. The four figures depicted in this window are William Wallace, standing with his mighty sword in hand, a blond girl crouched down between his legs. She is Scotia, the spirit of Scotland, and Wallace stands guard over her – a nice touch. Next, on Wallace's right, is Malcolm

Canmore, then St Margaret, then Robert the Bruce. Their respective coats
of arms are inset below them.

In the northwest corner of the nave stands the tomb of William Schaw of
Sauchie, Sauchie being the name of an estate with an old tower, just north
of Alloa. The Friends of Sauchie Tower have done much good work
recently on the preservation of this old fortified house, and I am indebted to
David and Carol Roscoe for the selfless work they have done in promoting
Scotland and its history, over and above their sterling work for Sauchie.

Schaw is credited with the founding of modern freemasonry. He was the
Master of Works for James VI of Scotland, appointed to the post in
December 1583. As with the unsubstantiated legends that surround Roslyn
Chapel, there is much nonsense spoken about Schaw, but the lodge system
of the freemasons was originated by this man.

Exit the abbey to walk the few yards to the palace remains. This building,
which became the home of kings, grew up from the guest quarters that
most large church buildings had. The original version may have been in situ
as early as 1100, but it is more likely that work was begun during Bruce's
time – and after the departure of Edward Longshanks. The place was partially burnt by Richard II of England in 1385 (no shock there – it actually
gets monotonous having to report the number of stately buildings in
Scotland that were burnt by English invaders). It was restored and enlarged
about 1540 during the reign of James V. It seems incredible to report, but
the building became neglected after the time of Charles II. I suppose the fact
that royalty was from that time based very much in London, it was
inevitable. It became roofless in 1708, and fell into total ruin. Looking
around the gaunt masonry today, it is hard to see it all decorated and full of
splendour, but David II, Bruce's son, was born here in 1323, James I was
born here in 1394, Charles I in 1600 – as was his elder sister Elizabeth in
1596, the 'Winter Queen' of Bohemia.

When one thinks of the historic figures who once walked through these
rooms! Bruce, the Stewart Kings, especially James IV who liked this place,
James V and Mary, Queen of Scots too.

At the opposite side of the Palace from the Abbey, runs the deep defile of
the Pittencrieff Glen, and down in the glen, where we are going to go next,
there are imposing views of this building and much hidden stonework more
in evidence. There is a gate at the western end of the Abbey, with a gate
directly across leading into Pittencrieff Park. Walk over into this delightful
place, the path running downhill, with views down to the Tower Burn over
to your right. As you descend the slope surrounded by many species of trees
and shrubs, there is a little path with steps branching uphill to your right. A
few yards up this side path and you reach the remains of the 'original'
Dunfermline, the tower house of King Malcolm Canmore. The name, as
stated, comes from this ancient edifice, which is first mentioned in our his-

tory books at the marriage of Malcolm and Margaret in 1069. *Dun*, you will remember, generally means a fortified hill or rock, *ferm*, the middle syllable, comes from the Gaelic *fiaram*, which means bent or crooked, and *linn*, which is a waterfall or stream. Hence Dunfermline, the fort on the crooked stream.

All that remains of Malcolm's tower here is one wall, still bulky, though stripped of its facing stone. It has been landscaped and surrounded by a circular modern wall. Once you have had a good look at these remains, carry on, along the little path you were on. It passes the castle site and goes down steeply by way of stone steps to the original path you were following. It is only as you descend you will suddenly realise what a defensive site this is. It has steep drops all round, and the stream curves right round the base, making this the fort on the crooked stream. Dunfermline.

I like this site – a fortification that far predates the time of Wallace and Bruce.

Once back on the main path, only a few steps on takes you to a high stone bridge over the Tower Burn, and here you will get to see just how ornate and beautiful Pittencrieff Glen really is. There are some exotic examples of trees and shrubs, and it is at times like this I wish I knew more about them. I would like to be able to identify species of trees at a glance. Need to get myself a book! There are quite a few peacocks wandering about too, and Pittencrieff Glen was the first place I ever saw a peacock right on the top of a tree. I mean, I knew they could fly, but I only ever seemed to see them walking about, and it looks pretty bizarre to see a big one sitting on top of a pine tree.

Looking down to the curve of the stream from the bridge, the little summer house sitting above it, just completes the scene perfectly. The stream itself looks as if it could be a bit cleaner, but that is my only complaint. Have a wee peer over the side of the bridge. It actually is a fair wee drop below. Not on a Rumbling Bridge scale though!

If you walk on, take a left at the other side, and this will take you along to Pittencrieff House, standing on the edge of the ravine of the burn, on the opposite side from the Royal Palace. This is a good example of a semi-fortified laird's dwelling, and Pittencrieff Park once formed the policies of this house. It was built in 1651 by Sir Alexander Clerk, comprises one long block and a stair tower, and it stands three storeys high. It is today a little museum with some regular exhibits, and it has visiting exhibitions too. It is free to enter, and this gives you access not only to see what there is on show, but allows you to get the *feel* of this old place.

It states in the stonework above the door: 'Praised be God for al his giftis'.

At the other side of the house there are greenhouses with some exotic plants, cacti and the like. I'm sure you will want a wee walk around

Pittencrieff Park, that is, if the rain is not coming in sideyways! There are some nice walks. You may want to walk down the side of the stream to look at the palace walls up above. You may even stumble across 'Wallace's Well'. It is on the side of the stream nearest the palace, nothing more than a little upright grate covering a hole in the ground, but has long been called by Wallace's name, the reason why lost in antiquity.

Back up towards the Abbey. When you come to the park gates turn right, and walk down to the pend, the old archway through the abbey buildings. I can remember when you could drive through this archway, narrow as it is. On my first visit to Dunfermline, although I was very young, I can remember this happening. Boyishly intrigued that you could drive right through the old stonework. Didn't think then I'd be writing about it either. The road leading down to the archway is called St Catherine's Wynd, and as you come out the other side you are in Monastery Street.

The Palace buildings now soar above you on your left, Pittencrieff Glen falls away to your right. I look up at these walls, with the towers of the Abbey peeping over the top of the ruined masonry, and I think how magnificent this must have been in the days when all this was at its height. The Abbey, with its many ornate tombs of those that have gone before. And the Palace, with the King in residence, the bustle, the coming and going of courtiers. I can imagine riding up to the gates here, glancing up at the pennons flying from the towers, proud to be Scottish, proud of the opulence on show.

Today it is crumbling stone walls. Windows merely holes in the stone, unglazed. Perhaps the scene is not too far removed from Scotland itself. A warrior, sleeping. But one day it will come out of its slumber, one day it will shake off the last vestiges of sleep, shake its shoulders, and make its children proud once again.

A little further, and the town's war memorial is on your right, with some nice flower beds here adding colour to the scene. At the end of the street, turn right, downhill, this being St Margaret Street. Only a few yards, and a little cluster of buildings appear at the corner in front of you. This is the birthplace, and museum dedicated to Andrew Carnegie. But on your right, just before you cross to this museum, look at the old fragment of masonry that stands here, and the little plaque above the sign that says 'St Margaret Street' which says:

> The Abbey Lower Gate. The monks were protected by a high wall around their grounds. You can still see a small part of it in Canmore Street. There were three gates in the wall and this is all that remains of the lower one – the Netheryett. The others no longer exist.

We cross to Carnegie's birthplace. Andrew Carnegie's story is one of inspiration. And I find a walk around this place inspirational. Andrew's family lived in a part of the little cottage tacked on at the side of the later museum. He was born in an upstairs room on 25 November 1835, in a box bed set in the wall. His dad was a weaver. The family struggled to make ends meet. As a child, Andrew used to look over the railings into Pittencrieff Glen, and like all small boys, he wanted to go into that forbidden territory to play. But the children of Dunfermline were not allowed to go into the private policies of Pittencrieff.

His family set out in search of a better life, sailing for America on 19 May 1848. As you walk round the museum, the story of Carnegie's life unfolds in chronological order. How he got a job, how he purchased stocks and shares. At this time the railways were starting to spread out over America. He invested in sleeper cars, and he started to make money. He began to invest in steel, railroads and oil, but he sold his oil interests, saying 'Put all your eggs in one basket – and then watch that basket!' He realised that steel was what was needed, for the construction of the vast spreading network of rail, and to build the frames for the mighty skyscrapers that were beginning to spring up in American cities. In 1875, he opened a steel plant. In its first year of operation it turned out more steel than all the other mills of the US combined. He opened up iron ore mines on Lake Superior, and this ore was shipped in a fleet of Great Lakes steamers. From the port on Lake Erie where it came ashore, Carnegie built a railway to carry the ore to the steelworks he had built, the largest and most modern in the land.

The profits were astronomical. Carnegie eventually sold out in the 1890s, a banking conglomerate raising the cash to take over his shares in his business, for $400,000,000! At 1890s prices! He was the richest man on the planet. He came back to Scotland, and purchased an old castle in the north, dating back to 1275, Skibo Castle, and he rebuilt it into a palatial mansion.

Over 20 universities awarded honorary degrees to Andrew Carnegie. When his three-year term in office ended in 1905 at St Andrews in Scotland, the students re-elected him without a contest. One student said, 'Previous rectors talked to us, or at us, from the platform, but Mr Carnegie sat down in our circle and talked with us.'

From his 'retirement' in Scotland, Carnegie donated some $60,000,000 to open almost 3,000 public libraries over the English-speaking world. I have done talks on Scottish history in libraries abroad that were paid for by Carnegie, so even I, another Scot, have been touched by his work – a century on.

He was given the freedom of his birthplace, Dunfermline, in 1877. He had a passion for organs, and thousands of halls and churches the world over have an organ paid for by Carnegie. And Carnegie Halls are famous in many cities too.

But what meant most to Carnegie himself? As a boy I was told this story, and I understood its implications, and it still pleases me greatly today. We have taken a walk around Pittencrieff Park and Glen, the place from where Malcolm Canmore once ruled Scotland, and which was a private estate that Carnegie peered at through its railings when he too was a boy. Carnegie bought Pittencrieff, and later declared:

> I'm Laird of Pittencrieff – the biggest of all titles to me. It means more to me than being King Edward [the king in London at the time]. He is not in it. The abbey and palace ruins, the glen, King Malcolm's tower, St Margaret's shrine – all mine!

He then turned it into a park and presented it to Dunfermline, so that the children could wander it – and it became theirs.

Carnegie is buried in Sleepy Hollow cemetery, Tarrytown, New York. A Celtic cross stands above his grave, carved from the stone that surrounds Skibo Castle in the north.

We make our way back to the car park at St Margaret's Cave, to continue on our way. Turn right back up Chambers Street to the lights, and this time turn left. Continue straight on, right out of town. You follow the signs for Kincardine Bridge, the A994. You come to a wee long village that lines the road. This is Crossford. There is another Crossford in Scotland, in Clydesdale, that we will visit eventually, but this is the Fife one. On your left as you go through the village, you will see a large gateway with signs proclaiming that this is Dunfermline Golf Club, Pitfirrane. If you turn in and follow the road up to the clubhouse, through the greens (I hope you don't get whacked by a stray ball!), the clubhouse may come as quite a surprise.

It is a large fortified house, very Scottish, and yellow-harled. It was built in 1500 by the Halket family, whose coat of arms is over the entrance, along with those of James VI. There are later additions to the building, but particularly attractive are the little pepper-pot turrets. You can drive up to the car park to have a look at the exterior of the place at the very least.

Back out to the A994, and continue on to your left, westwards. We drive through the next village, Cairneyhill. On the other side of Cairneyhill we reach a major roundabout. We are taking the second exit, signposted Torryburn, and Culross.

Culross is a National Trust for Scotland property. We drop downhill into Torryburn, and find we are on the edge of the Firth of Forth. We follow the Firth for the next two or three miles. We pass through Newmills, then as the road starts to climb uphill, there is a branch off to the left, signposted Culross and Fife Coastal Tourist Route. Through Low Valleyfield, and we drive into Culross (pronounced coo-rus) itself. Continue right through the village. There are a couple of tight twists and turns, and you will catch the odd glimpse of the delight that Culross is. It is one of the best-preserved old villages in Scotland, many of its little houses dating from the 1500s on. You will espy the tollbooth with its steeple and beyond it a yellow-harled building called the Palace. It is grassier here, the buildings pulling back a bit, then the car park at this end of the village is on your left. Pull in here, right on the waterfront. There are information boards with details of some of the attractions in Culross. Looking out towards the water of the Forth, there are mud flats in the foreground, not altogether attractive. They are nevertheless, a haven for wildlife, seabirds and shellfish.

There is quite a contract in aspects here too. We look across the wide estuary of the Forth to the oil-refinery of Grangemouth to the south, and we are about to visit the well preserved old world village behind us. Two very different faces of Scotland looking at each other across the water. I am often asked why there are not more Culross-type places existing in Scotland. Why has this ancient village survived intact on the north shore of the coast, and not elsewhere? I suppose one explanation is that it is off the route of invasion from down south, which does help. Continued English inroads led to destruction and burning. Culross was tucked out the road.

At the edge of the car park there is a curved stone structure, like a little aircraft hanger. I'm not sure about this, but it does look like an ice-house or similar, where ice would be packed in the winter to preserve things in hotter weather. No doubt I'll be appraised of its purpose in the near future!

Now walk the few yards back towards the edge of the village. You come to the mustard-yellow Palace. It was built between 1597 and 1611, for Sir George Bruce of Carnock, and though it was really only his impressive house, everybody seems to refer to it as the Palace. And I suppose a palace it seemed to ordinary passers-by. It was paid for by the wealth George amassed from local coal mines he had opened, along with the salt-pans he had along the shorefront here. These large pans were filled with salt-water, the water was then boiled off, leaving the valuable salt behind.

King James VI came to visit Culross in 1617. He expressed a desire to be shown round George's coal mines. George at that time had constructed what was regarded as the greatest wonder in Scotland. One of his mines led almost a mile under the Forth, whereupon a shaft, insulated, and constructed of stone, led up through the water to a little wharf, where the coal could be loaded directly onto ships to sail for continental Europe. King James was brought up to the top of this little wharf, saw that he was completely surrounded by water, and panicked, shouting 'Treason! Treason!' George had one of his boats take the horrified first king of Great Britain back to shore.

George had many of his boats return with such goods as Dutch glass, floor tiles and Baltic pine from their forays abroad. These were all incorporated in the house. I particularly like the little wooden-shuttered windows. There is a really interesting garden behind the palace too, rising in steps up the steep hillside on which Culross is built.

Just a little further along from the palace is the old town-house dating from 1626, though the steeple was added in 1783. The National Trust for Scotland has its visitor centre within this building, and you can purchase a ticket here allowing admission into several of the Culross sites.

But the real delight of Culross for me is just to walk up into the village and wander around the cobbled streets, just looking at, admiring and absorbing the architecture. A little cluster of tiny houses, all those little rooms containing the stories of generations of Scots. Some of them bear inscriptions on their fronts, or above their doors, a particular favourite on the snuff-maker's house, dated 1673, is 'Who would have thocht it, noses would have bocht it!'

You reach the Mercat Cross in the little square, overlooked by the Study, a tall, almost tower-like house. It was a sometime residence of Bishop Leighton of Dunblane, who used it on his diocesan visits to Culross. It has an outlook tower with views over the Forth.

The red pan-tiled roofs of the houses are a special attraction here, offsetting their white-harled fronts. This is a feature you only see in the east of Scotland. Houses in the west have the traditional grey slates. This is because ships based in the east parts, after unloading their cargoes, would purchase these red tiles from the Dutch ports as they made useful ballast for the return journey. They would then sell them to the locals on their return, and so many old houses on the east coast of Scotland have these red Dutch tiles on their roofs.

You will also notice how the narrow lanes have a raised causeway in their centres. This raised part is said to have been for the wealthier pedestrians, the lower classes being forced to walk in the edges where rubbish would gather. This tale may well be true, but I'm quite sure the lower echelons of society made a point of walking in the middle when the streets were quiet!

From the little square with the Mercat Cross, one branch goes steeply uphill, little houses lining the sides. It is a steep pull, but it is worth walking up to the ruined abbey at the top.

The first church on this site was founded by St Serf in the 500s, the same St Serf we spoke of at Dunning, so it is an ancient Christian site. The Abbey itself was founded by Malcolm, Earl of Fife, in 1217, and was a Cistercian establishment. It was abandoned around 1500, and although what remains is very ruinous, it is still an interesting place to wander about. There are some good views to be had from some of the ruins, on their elevated site, and you can look out over the Forth. By the ruins is the parish church, actually constructed on the choir of the old abbey and containing some old work. It was altered in 1824, and restored in 1905. Within this church is the Bruce vault, which has a magnificent alabaster funeral monument of Sir George Bruce, his wife and eight children, the same Sir George that was responsible for the palace below. There are gravestones in the surrounding churchyard which are well worth perusing too.

As you return to your vehicle, you will realise that you have seen something special in Culross, a window back to an earlier time. There is one nice touch you may want to see. When you get back down to the Mercat Cross, if you take the left fork, as you come back down to the main through route, take a look at the last building on your right. It looks very much like the other houses in Culross, but this house is actually the electrical sub-station supplying the village with power, sympathetically built inside this old property to keep the feel of the place intact.

As we continue on westwards, there is a huge chimney before you, dominating the skyline. This belongs to the coal powered generating station of Longannet. It used to burn local Scottish coal, a direct link to the mines of George Bruce at Culross, but the mines are gone now. I am assured by workers at Longannet that the imported Eastern European coal does not have the same superior qualities as our good Scottish coal!

At the road end you come to a junction with the access road to Longannet. Just opposite, almost a crossroads, is a minor road that runs into Kincardine on Forth. There is work now beginning on adding a second bridge to alleviate the traffic snarl-ups that can build up on the approaches to the bridge here at peak times, so you may have to turn right and circle round to Kincardine by a different route. You will see the Kincardine Bridge in front of you from the junction and that will allow you to get your bearings. In the interim, cross over the Longannet approach road, and drive down this minor road the last half-mile into Kincardine.

Most drivers simply drive straight through Kincardine, it being simply the cluster of houses at the north end of the bridge to them. But the western half of the town, at the other side of the approach to the bridge, has some very interesting old houses, many bearing dates and inscriptions. It is not too far removed from Culross in many ways. Narrow little lanes, and houses at angles, with some nice traditional Scottish architecture, many properties with red pantiled roofs.

One old house in the village is now the Unicorn Inn. In a prior life it was the birthplace of the physicist and chemist Sir James Dewar (1842–1923) who was the inventor of the vacuum flask, and who among us has never used one of them? He also was the first man to liquefy hydrogen gas and co-invented the explosive cordite.

A ferry once plied across the Forth here, but it was superseded by the bridge built in 1936. It is a good idea to walk or drive down to the old stone jetty just to the east of the bridge, just for a look out across the river. When the tide is right out, you will notice that the skeletons of several old wooden boats lie embedded in the mud at the bottom of the river. If it is clear and you look upstream between the pillars of the bridge, you can see the

Wallace Monument projecting like a finger from the top of the Abbey Craig several miles upstream. I have seen large groups of seals gather here, and just a few years before writing a minky whale swam right through the bridge and got stranded on the mud upstream, where unfortunately it died, although there were attempts to re-float it.

We now cross the bridge – a milestone this as we cross from the northern half of Scotland to the southern, the barrier formed by the Forth and Clyde having always been a psychological barrier. In the old days the English used to refer to this as the Scotwater – the barrier between north and south. The bridge was built with the central section able to turn, as there used to be quite a bit of river traffic. You will notice the little control room is still in situ, high above the water. From here a section of the bridge the size of a football pitch,could be rotated to allow passage. It was last opened in 1994, and has sadly been dormant since. There is a much greater volume of traffic using this bridge than was intended, so plans are now under way to build a second bridge, each carrying one direction of traffic.

There is a straight run of a mile south of the bridge, over the old flood plain of the Forth, and then we reach Bowtrees Roundabout. At the round-about we are taking the right exit, signposted Airth. As you go along this road, you will see Airth Castle on its whaleback ridge, at about ten o'clock. As stated, this was all marshland at one time, spates causing the Forth to flood all this ground, so the castle up on its ridge must have been a defensive spot indeed.

The oldest part of the castle is the tower furthest away from you, dating from the 1400s, but there were earlier fortifications on this site. The rest of the building work stretching out in the direction of the road was carried out a century later. The building is now a hotel, and half a mile after the round-about the entrance gates are on your left. Up the driveway, and you swing left into the hotel car park. You might think you have pulled up in front of the wrong building, so different does the frontage look from the rest of the castle. This part was added in the early 1800s, and you actually have to walk round to the right of this building to see the side of the original tower, and the old stonework thereon.

Blind Harry, Wallace's biographer, tells how Wallace's uncle, the priest of Dunipace, was captured by the English, brought to Airth, and kept captive in a cave beneath the fortifications. The structure here in Wallace's time would probably have looked very similar to the wooden palisade type of building that was shown in *Braveheart*. Wallace had local guides take his party over the surrounding marshland, and the castle was stormed. According to Blind Harry, one hundred Englishmen were slain.

A couple of years ago, I was speaking at a *Braveheart* convention, run by John and Linda Anderson from Edinburgh, that was being held at the Airth Castle Hotel. One of the girls working in the place took me down into the basement to get some tables to set up. I noticed there was a glass panel in the floor. 'What's that?', I enquired. 'Oh, there's a sort of cave thing under the floor here', she replied. Knowing Blind Harry's work passing well, I was taken aback. I realised that this was the cave where Wallace's uncle was held captive, as mentioned in his work. Academically, we cannot take Harry's work literally, as there is no other data to back up some of his sto ries of Wallace's life, but sometimes wee things fall into place, and at least the cave exists! I had been to Airth before, but until this chance encounter, I had not known of its existence.

If you walk round to the right of the later facade as previously mentioned, the original old square tower of Airth can be examined closely. You can see how the window sizes have been altered as its use as a defensive structure diminished. There are blocked-up small windows, that would have been the source of light originally, and larger windows have been created.

This tower is commonly called the Wallace Tower, although as it was built in the 1400s, and Wallace was murdered in 1305, you can easily see the time scale is out. It most likely stands on the site of the structure from Wallace's time, though. There is a bar in this tower that you may be able to get access to, and you will see that walking into it from the adjacent extensions shows the vast thickness of its walls. It is nice to sit and enjoy a good whisky on the site of one of Wallace's victories over the invaders, and I have had a drink here on a few occasions. Being Scottish though, I grudge paying hotel prices for a drink!

Airth has had a chequered history. It was burnt at the time of the Battle of Sauchieburn, a conflict of civil war in Scotland in 1488. When King James IV came to the throne after his struggle, he gave £100 towards the rebuilding of the place.

There is something in the trees though, to the left of the castle, that lies shamefully neglected, and I fear for its future safety. From the castle frontage you will be able to catch a glimpse of a ruined church among the greenery. This is Airth Church, fenced off and unloved, and deserving of far better. It stands on ground owned by the Radisson group that own the hotel, but it should be cleaned up and transformed into the visitor attraction that it is capable of being. It has an arched arcade that dates back to the 1100s, and was founded by churchmen from Holyrood Abbey in Edinburgh. There is later work that has been added through the ages, right up until the 1600s. It is the bits and pieces that exist within, however, that should be cleaned up and investigated. There is an old bell tower, now becoming ruinous, and there are little coats of arms carved into the stonework, with several examples of the red and yellow saltire of the Bruce family.

One aisle has a row of knights' tombs mostly grown over by weeds, but the odd date, from the 1500s, can be discerned. One beautiful work is the wall niche, with a girl in effigy, hands clasped in prayer and with a little dog at her feet. This tomb has been dated to 1330, so perhaps this girl saw Robert the Bruce himself. On my last visit, children had gone through the odd gap in the surrounding fence and had laid a posy of picked flowers on her breast. At least they understand the sanctity of some things, even if the authorities don't seem to.

The graveyard is packed with the tombstones of almost a thousand years of burials. There must be hundreds hidden under the thick foliage that now covers it, but the odd example projects through, showing just enough carving to entice. There are two old mort-safes lying around the church too – coffin shaped but made of heavy iron. These were to allow bodies to decay, so that they were useless to the 'resurrectionists' who stole bodies to sell to medical students.

Without going into too much detail, as the church stands on a raised site and is neglected, parts of the banking are giving way and exposing human remains. They are packed in here, after all these years of burials, and I have seen a skull projecting from the soil, surrounded by leg bones, fingers etc. There is something far wrong in Scotland when we have so little respect for our ancestors that they are forgotten so. After all, these are the forebears of those walking the roads around here today. All the owners have done is fence the place off, and the relevant historical bodies in Scotland are either walking around with tied hands or blinkered eyes. Airth church should be restored and landscaped, and the knights' tombs themselves would be something worth seeing, never mind the other finds that may come to light. I can't imagine a similar church in England being left to rot like this. Perhaps when freedom comes we can make more of an impact on preserving our heritage. There are modern houses being built within a few hundred yards of this church. Do we really want the kids roaming around this place – as they will – I would have at the age of ten! And we certainly don't want them finding human remains.

Back down the driveway now to the main route, and turn left to go through Airth itself. In the centre of the village, to the left of the main road, stands the village's old Mercat Cross. There are a few of the old houses still existing in Airth, and still lived in. They retain their old features, and I have always been a sucker for crow-stepped gables! In case you are not familiar with the term, we use it in Scotland to describe the edges of the roofs at the gables. Instead of 45 degrees, they go up in a series of steps due to them having been created by a succession of stone blocks. We call them crow-stepped gables, a familiar term, due I suppose to the fact that crows could step up them!

On through Airth, and when you reach the far end of the village, keep your eyes peeled for a sign pointing down a road to your left, stating 'The Pineapple'. You enter this road, then take a right fork by a little lodge house, and follow this narrow road across a field into the trees opposite. There is a parking area here by a large walled garden. It is only as you walk into this walled garden that you will realise that there is an extraordinary building before you – a giant stone pineapple. This has been called the most bizarre building in Scotland, and on top of that, it is great fun too.

It was originally the focal point of the walled garden of the Dunmore estate, and was built in 1761. Sadly, the architect is unknown, but you cannot help but admire his work. The segments, all individually carved, with spiky leaves, are a work of genius. The Earls of Dunmore had an extensive estate here once, the remains of their original tower house, and some parts of the house which superseded that, still exist further west. The estate went to dereliction, and the pineapple lay unloved for many years. Happily, it has been restored, and it is now available to let as holiday accommodation. You can go and admire it from the outside at any time, and the little recess at its base has information boards giving its story, including a photo of it in its earlier ruined condition. Just a look at this place is guaranteed to bring a smile to your face, and it is quite an unlikely place to stumble across in Scotland.

We now return to Bowtrees Roundabout, the one we went through before we came into Airth. Breaking a little with the roads we have traditionally covered in this book, we will be driving on motorway for half an hour. We have already crossed Scotland a little south of here, and so I wish to take you further south in one fell swoop into pastures new.

So when we reach Bowtrees Roundabout, go right round, and take the exit onto the M876, which leads to the M9 motorway. Ignore the turn off to Falkirk, and carry on round the very tight bend as the M876 meets the M9. Keep to your left, as we are only on the M9 for about a mile, and we take the first exit left, this stretch of motorway also under the name M876, signposted Glasgow.

Driving along this stretch takes us through the vestiges of the old Tor Wood, already visited. As we cross the River Carron, Dunipace, with its cemetery and strange-shaped Hills of Death, where Wallace was raised by his uncle, is on the left. Uphill after the Carron, and we meet the Stirling/Glasgow motorway, the M80 where the two roads merge, and we continue to follow it towards Glasgow. Two miles on we drive under an old railway viaduct just before a right hand bend. This bridge stands on the line of the Roman Antonine Wall. Thousands of commuters drive under it every day, never giving it a thought that they are driving in and out of the northern borders of the Roman Empire! The Romans didn't manage to hold their sway in Southern Scotland for very long though!

We pass Cumbernauld, continuing on through the large roundabout at Auchenkiln, and another mile or two on keep your eyes peeled for the slip road off to the left, the M73, signposted Carlisle. Several miles of this and we reach the M74, the main north/south route between Scotland and England. We turn southbound, the two roads merge, and again it is just a case of following the signs for Carlisle. I know this sounds very complicated, but it's pretty straightforward, and if I knew a better way of describing this, I would do it that way!

A few miles south on the M74, and we pass Bothwell Services. Just after the services is junction 5, the turnoff signposted Bellshill, Coatbridge, East Kilbride, A725. At this junction, we drop to a roundabout. Go right round, passing under the M74, and take the A725 towards East Kilbride. Stay in the outside lane though, as we come to another roundabout and we are taking the exit marked Bothwell and Uddingston. There is a junction here, where we go right towards Bothwell, the signs saying 'Welcome to Bothwell' immediately before you.

Now that we have covered some 25 miles of modern road network, it is time we got back to examining some of the sites pertaining to Scotland's history.

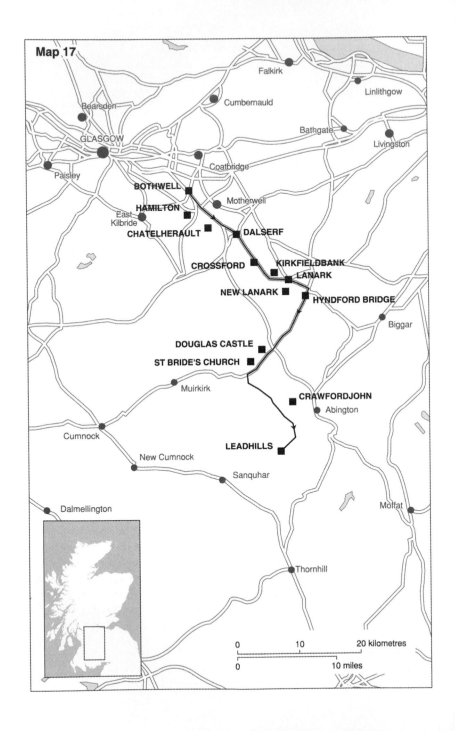

Map 17

Falkirk

Cumbernauld

Linlithgow

Bearsden

Bathgate

GLASGOW

Livingston

Paisley

Coatbridge

BOTHWELL

Motherwell

HAMILTON

East Kilbride

CHATELHERAULT

DALSERF

CROSSFORD

KIRKFIELDBANK

LANARK

NEW LANARK

HYNDFORD BRIDGE

Biggar

DOUGLAS CASTLE

ST BRIDE'S CHURCH

Muirkirk

CRAWFORDJOHN

Abington

Cumnock

LEADHILLS

New Cumnock

Sanquhar

Dalmellington

Moffat

Thornhill

0   10   20 kilometres

0   10 miles

CHAPTER SEVENTEEN

Environs of the Clyde

BEGINNING AT BOTHWELL CASTLE, THE ROUTE TAKES IN HAMILTON AND CHATELHERAULT AND THEN AT LARKHALL FOLLOWS THE A72 ALONG THE CLYDE VALLEY TO LANARK. FROM HERE IT TAKES THE A70 TO DOUGLAS, CRAWFORDJOHN AND LEADHILLS.

THIS ROAD IS actually Bothwell's main street, and a half mile on we reach the rows of shops that mark the town centre. You will see that many of the buildings here are a warm red sandstone, the colour of the rock hereabouts – and you will see a few interesting structures created from it in the near future!

There is a pedestrian crossing with traffic lights ahead, and I want you to park in this locality, as 100 yards past these lights there is a large church tucked away on your right. The pub immediately before the church is called The Douglas Arms, and this is a clue to much of the history on Bothwell's doorstep.

The first thing that strikes you about Bothwell Parish Church is its massive square tower, which rises to 120 feet. It is a landmark that can be seen at a fair distance. The flagpole on top flies the Saltire of Scotland, something for which I have always wanted to congratulate the minister. I have seen churches in England fly the St George's cross, and I wish more of the Scottish churches flew their national flag. Cathcart Parish Church in Glasgow is another that always flies the flag, and I would just like to say to the gentlemen concerned that there are those of us who notice and appreciate such a gesture.

The church, of the warm red local stone, was built in 1833, and from the front may look like a good example of architecture of that period, but there is a little more to this building than meets the eye. If you walk round the church, you will see that the hidden back part is a much older structure. This is the choir of an old collegiate church, with the newer front tacked on. The church was founded in 1398 by the then Earl of Douglas, Archie the Grim. He was so called because of 'his terrible countenance in warfare against the English'. He had obviously inherited his martial ability from his father, as he was a bastard son of the Good Sir James, the Black Douglas, Bruce's companion. I'm sure he would be delighted to see the flag of Scotland flap valiantly from that tall tower!

The old church is buttressed, and has stone flags forming its roof. The church is occasionally open for visitors, or you may just be lucky. On my first visit within, I had by chance turned up as a member of staff opened the place to ready it for a funeral service. He let me have a quick look around. Lucky for me, not so lucky for the person whose funeral it was.

There is evidence inside of an even older establishment than the church of 1398. Round the walls are inset many inscribed stones that have been found beneath the floor or similar during building works. There is one with a carving of the Tree of Life, several with crucifixes and swords, and one striking one with a large axe carved upon it. Quite a collection. One of the stones is believed to be the tombstone of William the Rich, the founder of nearby Bothwell Castle, and uncle of Wallace's companion, Andrew Murray.

You can walk through into the older church and see some of its ancient features, and monuments to two later Archie Douglases, Earls of Forfar, one of whom was mortally wounded at the Battle of Sheriffmuir in 1715.

As said, I have seen the church open to visitors at certain times, and I hope you can be lucky. There must have been some sort of place of worship on this very spot since earliest times, as many of the stones on show far pre-date the 1398 church.

Before you leave, take a look at the memorial to Joanna Baillie which stands before the building. Joanna (1762–1851) was born at the now-gone Bothwell Manse, daughter of the Reverend James Baillie of this church. She was an eminent and very famous poetess in her day. The monument is cleverly done, the faces on it created from mosaic, and containing lines from Joanna's work. There is a portrait of her, and a depiction of Bothwell Castle too. The memorial tells us:

> Nearly 70 years of her life were spent in London, but she retained a Scottish heart to the end, and spoke often and fondly of the scenes and companions of her early years.

Continue on from the church, through a set of traffic lights, then look for a sign saying 'Bothwell Castle', and pointing down Blantyre Road to your left. Halfway down this road another sign points to your right, stating 'Bothwell Castle 1'. Follow this road, the first part of it over speed bumps, until the entrance road to the castle appears on your left. It is flanked by two carvings, one bearing the arms of Murray, three stars, and the other the heart of Bruce, which comprises the arms of Douglas.

Go through the trees and the castle appears before you. I first visited Bothwell as a teenager, and I don't really know what I expected, but it was much larger than I had anticipated, all towers and high curtain walls. There is parking space available, and once you have parked up, just take the place in. It is of the same warm red sandstone as many of the houses in Bothwell, only a little more weather-worn, but the colour is especially striking against the background of trees. Before you do anything else, take a walk round the castle in a clockwise direction.

Once round the first corner, you will see that it is a much more defensive structure than you would imagine at a first impression. It stands on a large projecting slab of bedrock, again, the local red stone. The walls follow the contour of this rock, thus ensuring that mines could not be dug under the walls. Attackers had to deal with getting to the base of the walls on top of this rock, which made them vulnerable to defenders on the ramparts high above. And you will realise that here the sluggish and deep River Clyde runs below to your left. In fact, it curves round the perimeter of the castle site, ensuring a defence to the south. A little further round and we come to the great tower of Bothwell that stands above the Clyde. This is just an absolutely fabulous piece of history, architecture, defence, Scottishness – all rolled into one. The Great Donjon, as this type of tower is called, is in a ruined state, but that only serves to help you understand its construction. It is huge, its mighty walls soar away high above you, and you have to lean back to take in its physical presence and size. As parts of the wall of this great circular keep have been destroyed, you can see its make-up. The outer and inner walls have been constructed of dressed stone, the centre is tightly packed rubble and mortar – 20 feet in thickness! You can see how this great breach has been repaired by a straight wall at a later date.

You then walk round to the modern entrance of the castle, but notice that there are footings of other buildings on the flat stretch of grass opposite.

Bothwell is one of the earliest stone castles in Scotland. The Murray family dated a charter here in 1278 and this is the first mention of it. Tradition says that it was built by William Murray, thought to be buried in Bothwell Church, and in our history books he is known as William le Riche. When you look at the amount of money it must have cost to build Bothwell Castle, in poor medieval Scotland, he was obviously well named 'the rich'.

We are not really sure if the defences were completed when the War of Independence broke out. The English captured it, then the Scots recaptured it in 1299 after a blockade of 14 months. The chances are that Wallace visited the place. He was, after all, born in Clydesdale, and it was the family of his companion at Stirling Bridge who owned the place.

Edward Longshanks came north in person and recaptured the place in 1301. He had a wooden siege engine built in Glasgow and rolled the several miles to Bothwell, a mammoth task in itself, and proof of his determination to subdue Scotland. It was put against the castle walls and allowed the enemy to gain access, probably at great cost where lives were concerned. The English held on to the place until the aftermath of Bannockburn in 1314. Many of the higher ranking fugitives of Bannockburn made their way to Bothwell on their way south, trying to get back to English soil. The governor promptly handed over the castle and those within to the victorious Scots.

These captives included the Earl of Hereford. Bruce was able to exchange Hereford alone for his Queen, his daughter the Princess Marjorie, his sister Mary, and his staunch supporter, Bishop Wishart of Glasgow. Poor Wishart may have got his freedom, but he would not see his beloved Scotland again, as he had gone blind during his years in English captivity. He is buried in an unmarked tomb at the back of the crypt in Glasgow Cathedral, where Union Jacks hang above him. A great insult to a man who gave all for Scotland.

The prisoners captured at Bothwell alone brought great wealth to Scotland, but don't get the behaviour of King Robert the Bruce wrong. The English prisoners said that they were treated so courteously that Bruce 'completely won their hearts'. And this from a man whose brothers were butchered horribly by them and his womenfolk kept in cages for many years.

Edward Bruce, King Robert's brother, damaged the castle so that the English could not re-take and hold the place. Edward III of England, emulating his grandfather Longshanks, took the place in 1336, and stayed in the castle for a month. Murray, the son of Wallace's companion, and the rightful owner, recaptured it, and it was he who destroyed part of the Great Donjon, the damage of which we look at outside.

David II granted the castle remains to the Douglas family, and it was the same Archie the Grim who built the flat wall inside the tower, who also built the old church. James IV, who died at Flodden, visited Bothwell Castle in 1503 and 1504.

In the 1690s, some of the castle was demolished to provide materials for a new mansion which stood just to the east of the castle. I have seen old photos and prints of the castle where you can see this house in the background. That is why there is modern walling at the entrance to the castle, as the old gatehouse was part of the fabric removed for the building work. The later mansion was demolished in 1926, and so the castle has long outlived its offspring.

Bothwell has been under state care since 1935. There is a charge for entry, and although the courtyard contains empty and ruinous buildings, there is access to the battlements, and rooms and staircases to explore. There is a large moat-like ditch between the Great Donjon and the rest of the castle, and you can see how defensible it must have been – no wonder part of the walling was destroyed. So much effort was used to capture it back from English control, that they must have been trying to ensure they did not have to go through all that again.

Look out for graffiti carved on the walls by many centuries of visitors too.

After your exploration, return to the car and retrace your route to Blantyre Road, the first T-junction you reach, right after the speed bumps. If you turn right and continue downhill, you will eventually come to a turning point directly above the Clyde, where a footbridge continues over to

Blantyre on the opposite bank. At the opposite end is the birthplace of David Livingstone, the famous explorer of Africa.

As you approach this bridge, the wall on your right is the boundary of the Bothwell Castle estate. It runs for many miles, encircling the policies of the castle, but is breached here and there by more modern housing projects. The bridge rises high above the river, and you will see there is a large weir just a little upstream. This supplied water power for the mills that used to line the river banks. At the Blantyre end a fish ladder has been built. The River Clyde has been cleaned so much recently that salmon have returned to spawn after an absence of many years, and the ladder has been built to facilitate ease of access to the spawning beds upstream.

At the right side of the end of the bridge is a tall house with a circular stair tower projecting from it. I always admired this house when I was young – and it lay derelict. I'm glad someone saw the possibilities and restored it. I'd love to stay somewhere that had the constant sound of water close at hand.

Up from the bridge end is the entrance to the David Livingstone Centre. It is housed in a large tenement building called Shuttle Row, and Livingstone's family had a single apartment home within this tenement. Livingstone was born here on 19 March, 1813. As a child he worked 14-hour days at the local mill. He was raised as a devout Christian, and as soon as he was old enough he trained to become a missionary. He also gained a medical degree at Anderson's College in Glasgow. In 1840, Livingstone boarded a ship for Africa. It was the start of a life of adventure for him. He made treks of thousands of miles across what was then the Dark Continent. On the course of his travels he became the first white man to see Victoria Falls, and he plotted the course of African rivers, writing about his experiences. He did much to introduce Christianity to Africa, and worked tirelessly to abolish the then-prevalent slave-trade.

He disappeared from the ken of the western world for a while, and the New York Times commissioned reporter HM Stanley to try and make contact with him. Stanley eventually encountered Livingstone, and greeted him with the words 'Dr. Livingstone, I presume?', now one of the most famous phrases from history.

Livingstone's constant hard work, covering vast areas over swampy terrain, often in torrential rain, took its toll on his health. On 1 May 1873, his followers found him dead, kneeling at his bedside in prayer. His heart was removed by the natives and buried under a tree near to where he died. His body was carried to the coast on an epic trek, and his body was taken to England, where it was buried in Westminster Abbey.

The David Livingstone Centre has many of his personal effects on display. The story of his life is told in great detail. On one of his travels, Livingstone was badly mauled by a lion, and never fully recovered the use of one of his arms. The bone was removed, and it sits in a display case, distorted and misshapen, a little piece of the man himself on display like an ancient relic.

Follow the road straight back up from the Clyde to Bothwell's Main Street. You emerge just a few yards past the church. Retrace your route back through Bothwell to the mini-roundabout where you came up from the main road network, but this time go straight through this roundabout towards Hamilton. You immediately drive onto Bothwell Bridge, crossing over the River Clyde. You will notice that there is a tall pillar immediately before the left side of the bridge, the monument to the battle that was fought here in 1679. There is not really anywhere to park to take a look at the monument and the bridge itself, although a little road that goes off to your right opposite the monument may give you a place to park and examine these structures.

Although widened over the centuries, the bridge carries the original structure from the 1400s at its core. The Clyde is wide and swift as it flows beneath. There are a couple of paths leading away from the bridge that follow a little along the river's course, and although it is ensconced among the motorway network, I have seen some interesting examples of wildlife on the riverbank.

The battle itself came about through religious differences. The Covenanters had taken to having outdoor prayer meetings, as their religious practices were not in line with those that the King in far off London considered correct. On 1 June 1679, at one of these open-air 'coventicles' at Drumclog, a party of Dragoons under John Graham, Viscount Dundee ('Bonnie Dundee' to his followers) attacked them, but the Covenanters were armed and defeated their assailants.

Many joined the Covenanters and they soon had 5,000 in their ranks. They marched on Glasgow, but found it well defended, and withdrew here to Bothwell Bridge. A government army under the Duke of Monmouth appeared at the other end of the bridge, from the direction of Hamilton, numbering 15,000 men. Stupid religious differences became the order of the day among the Covenanters, arguing about who was the worthiest in the sight of God. Although the bridge should have been held, the ranks broke, and those who thought they were worthier in the sight of God ran with the rest. There were some singular acts of bravery on the part of the Covenanters, but there was, at least, very little killing by Monmouth's troops in the aftermath. Many prisoners were taken, though, and these became the poor wretches imprisoned in Greyfriars Churchyard that we visited in Edinburgh.

The monument, in the form of a tall obelisk, has as its inscription: 'In honour of the Covenanters who fought and fell in the Battle of Bothwell Bridge, 22nd June 1679, in defence of civil and religious liberty. Erected by

Public Subscription in 1903'. There is a little gate you can go through to read the inscriptions on the other faces of the monument.

We cross Bothwell Bridge and continue on along the straight road by the racecourse, making for the centre of Hamilton. Pass through a mini-round-about, but continue straight along this road when it swings left, downhill. At the bottom of the hill there is a roundabout, and a left turn takes you to the car park of the Low Parks Museum, an interesting wee place, one of the buildings once part of the complex surrounding the now gone Hamilton Palace, home of the Dukes of Hamilton. There are artefacts and photographs inside from this once magnificent structure. Its downfall was caused by subsidence caused by coal mining operations. It seems incredible that the vast fortunes that were spent constructing this once imposing structure, are all turned to dust. The museum also contains the regimental museum of the Cameronians, a now defunct regiment, and a sword or two from Bothwell Bridge.

If you continue on just a little, past the museum, there is a junction, and a right turn here will take you to Hamilton Mausoleum, a very phallic-looking structure! It bears a Latin inscription on the higher stonework, attributing its construction to Alexander, the tenth Duke of Hamilton. You can park in front, and walk the last few yards up to it. Details of access can be gleaned at the nearby museum.

A walk round will reveal that the M74 motorway runs just beyond it, and you may be interested to know that the clump of trees between the mausoleum and the motorway hide the remains of the earliest settlement here. This was a moot hill of sorts once, a defensive structure, and when the motorway was being constructed an old sword was discovered. It is very early medieval, and is on show at the Kelvingrove Museum and Art Gallery in the west end of Glasgow. There are also a pair of stone lions reposing at this side of the mausoleum, one sleeping, one awake, and companions have never failed to comment that these lions both have 'a magnificent pair o' stane baws!' Which comment I have left in Scots to spare the more sensitive among you.

The mausoleum was finished in 1852, and cost £130,000 to build, an imitation of the Castle of St Angelo in Rome. The dome stands 120 feet high. It was originally intended that the mausoleum building could be used for church services, but there is an extraordinary echo within the building which made this impossible. A door being shut is like a rolling peal of thunder, but this echo itself has made the place a magnet for visitors, eager to hear it.

As you return towards your vehicle, the mausoleum behind you, if you look over to your left, almost on the horizon and just before the tree-line, you will notice a reddish castellated structure. This is Chatelherault (pronounced Chateau-le-rowe) part of the once broad acres of the Hamilton estate, and it is this structure we head for next.

Go back to the roundabout at the museum, turn left, and continue on. Here you are actually driving across the ground where Hamilton Palace stood. Now there is a large supermarket and retail park on its site. It was crammed with works of art and fine furniture. In fact, there was a sale of its treasures on 20 July 1882, in 2213 lots. Ruben's *Daniel in the Lion's Den* was sold for £5,154, two secretaires, little writing desks which belonged to Marie Antionette, were sold for £9,450 each – just an example of the money realised at this sale.

Through some roundabouts in quick succession, but keep following the signs for Larkhall B7078. We come out of Hamilton town centre, pass the Avonbridge Hotel on our right, and cross the bridge over the River Avon from which the hotel takes its name. The parapets are a little high to afford any view though. We then drive through the scatter of buildings that is Ferniegair, and then you will see the entrance to Chatelherault on your right. Drive in – there is a parking area further on, on your left. As you continue towards Chatelherault, you will notice that there is an adventure playground for children (of all ages?) here. It has a large slide, or as we call it in Scotland, *chute,* at one end. A few years back I slid down this. It has a hump halfway down. It was in good condition, and all you aficionados of such playground equipment know, you get fast chutes and slow chutes, and they can vary day to day. Anyway, I went down this like a rocket, shot up in the air on the hump, hit the edge, cracked my coccyx (that wee bone at the base of your spine), and fell to the ground. I just lay immobile. The pain was exquisite, and I lay still for a good 15 minutes before I got up and made my way to hospital. It hurt badly for weeks, but I can laugh at it now. My mate Jock from Lanark has broken his too, only his now protrudes at a strange angle. He was on a Triumph motorcycle as a youth, and to impress two young ladies, he drove past them standing on the saddle. As he went round the corner and out of sight, he fell off and actually snapped his coccyx off! I can only grimace at how sore that must have been!

Up to the buildings, and I should perhaps inform you that the name Chatelherault comes from a French title that the Duke of Hamilton held. I should also inform you that these magnificent examples of architecture were actually the Duke's dog kennels! Built in 1734 by the architect William Adam, it was also designed to be a folly, to be viewed up a wide avenue from the palace below. Plaques facing down to Hamilton in front of the buildings explain this.

The place lay ruinous until the 1970s, when the structures were taken over by Historic Scotland and restored. The right hand buildings have some magnificent plaster work within them. Something you should try, is just taking a walk on the stone path immediately in front of this building. You can actually sense the mine workings underground here, your idea of balance going awry. Walking across the floor of the interior actually makes me almost stumble, so far out of kilter is the structure.

At the rear there is an exhibition building with a tea-room. The big attractions for me though are the things to be seen in the near vicinity. If you walk down the paths to the right when facing the front of the house, down by the circular car park at that end, we shall see what we shall see. Keep an eye open for some of the famous white cattle, some of which may be in the fields below the house's frontage. They have fawn noses, and are the original wild cattle of Scotland. These were the beasts that roamed the woods of Caledonia when men first came. There are, as you can imagine, few examples left, and the small Chatelherault herd are highly prized. They are not to be approached though, gentle bovine creatures they may appear, but they can have a wild temperament, feral beasts as they are.

Follow the paths down into the woodland, heading for the River Avon below in its gorge. The size of this gorge is quite surprising, not expected in central Scotland. We crossed the Avon as we came out of Hamilton, but it had come out of this gorge at that point – it has an entirely different character here. There is an old stone bridge over the river running far below, steep wooded banks plunging to the waterside. It is a sylvan scene, very picturesque. And if you raise your eyes from the spectacular drop to the clifftop immediately downstream from the far end of the bridge, you will see that a castle perches there – Cadzow Castle, the old seat of the Hamilton family, built long ago as the predecessor of Hamilton Palace.

Local legend attributes its original building to one Caw, prior to the era of the Scottish monarchy. It was a royal residence in the time of Alexander II and III. It passed to the Hamilton family in the time of Robert the Bruce, and has often been rebuilt over the centuries. Due to the Hamilton influence the name came to represent the nearby town too. The ruins are fenced off due to their ruinous state, but you can walk round, and on reaching their upper perimeter, with a bit of care you can peer over the edge to the river far below. As the stonework of the castle is to your immediate right, you can only wonder at the skill of its builders. How did they manoeuvre those blocks into place and mortar them, with that drop into the abyss under them?

If you walk down to the bottom end of the castle to the bridge end, take the path that continues on from the bridge, through a gate. You are on a wide path that follows the edge of the drop to the river, walking upstream. A quarter of a mile on, the path cuts round a little burn flowing down to the Avon, that has cut its own little gorge. There is a tiny stone bridge. As you come round the other side, cut up to your right, and look at the most amazing forest stretching away in the grass before you. These are the famous Cadzow Oaks, planted by King David I, who reigned 1124–53. They can look radically different with the seasons. In winter, their leaves gone, they look primeval, gnarled, stark, something from a Grimms' fairy tale. In summer, they are a mass of green, reminiscent of rebirth, softness belying their antiquity. On top of all that, it is just nice to see them!

As you look out to the oaks, turn and look directly behind, and you will se that you are standing on the edge of a grassy, circular area, with the remains of a ditch encircling it. This is an old Iron Age fort, its outline still discernible. In the space of a half mile, we have seen the opulence of Chatelherault, crossed the gorge to a medieval castle, and walked on a little to these ancient oaks, attended by this fort from the earliest history of Scotland. Yet, many times I have walked these paths and seen not a soul, and they must have been busy at one time. You can follow the paths on upstream for a mile or two, as there are two bridges crossing the river, and you can walk back on the opposite bank through attractive woodland.

Otherwise, head back to Chatelherault. Skirting round the back of the house will reveal some giant Redwood trees and other exotic species, brought to Hamilton on Dukely orders in the days when the estate was at its height.

At the entrance, turn and drive right towards Larkhall, and the old estate wall of the Hamiltons' policies is on your right. Scotland is peppered with examples of these walls – we have seen a few on our journey. The cost of all those shaped stones to build these miles of walls must have been a small fortune. A mile after Chatelherault, we take the A72 to Lanark, which branches off to our left. There are large brown signs which announce the 'Clyde Valley Tourist Route', and it is this route we will be following for the foreseeable future. We cross the M74 on a flyover. A short run downhill and we are on the side of the River Clyde, and we will be following it upstream to Lanark.

The Clyde is picturesque and lined with pretty villages as you go upstream. A very different image from the one in most people's minds of industry, and its past glories of shipbuilding. It was the late great Glaswegian writer Jack House who pointed out that during World War II, there was three times the tonnage of shipping launched on the Clyde than there was in all the USA – a jaw-dropping fact. In fact, Jack once told this to an American audience and was booed for his trouble!

It's hard to equate that with this rural stretch ahead. As we follow the Clyde at first, you may notice a large ruined building over on the left, a field's distance away on the opposite bank. This is the derelict Cambusnethen House, still complete to the wallhead. It would make a good restoration project for a lottery winner!

We climb away from the water, just for a moment, to go through a roundabout, but we just keep on up the valley for Lanark. It is strange that the name Clyde Valley should be the title that everyone uses for this stretch. It

should, of course, be Clydesdale, the world-famous horses originating from
this vicinity. Why the traditional dale has been superseded by valley is a
mystery to me. We still use dale in most other cases, Tweeddale, Teviotdale,
Liddesdale, etc.

We drop again to the Garrion Bridge, an old bridge over the Clyde, built
in 1817. It is now a 'double' bridge, its new partner alongside having been
opened in 2002. You treat these two bridges almost like a roundabout,
crossing the river on the old bridge, as they are each one way, and returning
on the new one to continue towards Lanark. Less than a mile on, look for a
little turn-in on your left, leading to the tiny hamlet of Dalserf. You go
between two rows of cottages, past the church, and there is room to park at
the church's far side.

One thing that makes me smile here is that one of the cottages on the left,
with a particularly low door, has a wooden sign upon it, stating 'Duck or
Grouse'. I hope that your mental capabilities don't take you too long to
work that one out!

We have come to see the little church though, dating from 1655. It has an
unusual metal steeple, and it stands on an ancient Christian site. Once a
ferry plied across the Clyde just north of here, and it seems strange now, but
there were once five alehouses in the village. The building of the Garrion
Bridge changed all that though, the passing trade having passed to use a different route.

Below the spire you will notice a strange long hogsback tombstone, a little like an upturned boat. This dates from the eleventh century, and was
found in the graveyard in 1897. This at least shows the antiquity of this
site. Many of these hogback stones I have come across were originally
Viking in origin, and covered some Norseman's last resting place. Makes
me wonder if they were able to navigate their longships up the Clyde a
thousand years ago.

As we leave Dalserf and continue, the road begins to really twist and
turn, as it will for stretches, all the way to Lanark. I can recall a few years
back, being on a group motorcycle run along this road, all of the group riding on Harley Davidson motorcycles. A few bolts were lost, and I can
remember sparks flying here and there, as the riders tried to negotiate these
corners with the low ground clearance of those particular machines. I've
owned a few Harleys in my time, and they are old-fashioned and almost
agricultural beasts. In fact, it is rumoured that if you scratch away at the
Harley-Davidson badge, it actually says Massey-Fergusson underneath!

We pass a couple of old lodge-houses with attendant bridges on this
stretch, the entrances to past lordly estates. The next village we come to is
Rosebank with a large hotel called the Popinjay. This is the old Scots word
for a parrot, and as parrots were often used for either targets or prizes for
archery contests, the name is self-explanatory. Wapinshaws were held on

this flat stretch by the riverside once, the word just a Scots corruption of medieval training exercises called 'weapon shows'. It wasn't real parrots that were used of course, but artificial ones, created with dyed feathers.

Three miles further and we reach the village of Crossford (there was another Crossford just after Dunfermline) and we cross the River Nethan as it makes its way down to the Clyde. Just as you come past the 30 mph sign on the edge of the village, look for the road that cuts up at a steep angle to your right, signposted Craignethan Castle. It is about two miles of a diversion to Craignethan, and we will be returning to our current location, but it is an interesting old place, and unusual in construction.

We climb uphill, then the gorge of the Nethan goes off on our right. As we emerge above the trees, you have a great view, the village of Crossford laid out below and the valley stretching out in either direction, holding its river. At the top of the hill, follow the signs pointing the way to the castle, along the road off to your right. We drop to a little oasis by some steep twists and turns, a little hidden patch of greenery, where the River Nethan runs in its coils. You may notice Craignethan above you to your right. We climb by a few even steeper twists out of this hidden haughland, the sign at the hilltop welcoming you to Tillietudlem. This scatter of houses has taken its name from a Sir Walter Scott novel, where Craignethan Castle was called by that name. Strangely, there was a railway station here once (the remains of the station are among the bushes just past the castle access) and many visitors once came to see the place where this tale was set, and the name has actually transferred itself to this area.

The access road to the castle is on your right. You meander along for the best part of a mile, to a car park. When you walk to the edge of this car park, the castle suddenly looms into view, laid out before you. The oldest part is the tower and its surroundings further away from you. The buildings in the foreground within the curtain wall are of later construction. What is not immediately recognisable is the fact that the whole lot is built above the beginnings of the Nethan Gorge. There are impressive drops at the other side of the castle, and the side you are at is the only means of approach. Obviously, artillery could be sited on the higher ground at this side to pound the stonework, but there was at one time a defence against that option.

The building in the left foreground, currently the home of the castle's custodian, was built in 1665, by a famous Covenanter, Andrew Hay. The outer court in which it stands was there before 1579. The original tower at the rear was begun in 1531, built by the Hamilton family. The Hamiltons were often at odds with the ruling house of Scotland, from the time of James v, through the reign of Mary, Queen of Scots, to that of James vi. The castle changed hands several times between the Hamiltons and the Crown, but usually without a full-scale siege.

The castle has a feature that I have never seen anywhere else in Scotland, and I believe it is the only one in existence outside continental Europe – a *caponier*. To have a look round the castle entails paying a small fee, so if you enter, I will explain. As you walk towards the deep ditch that separates the outer courtyard from the inner, you will realise there is a strong, stone-built, curved building in the bottom of this ditch. It cannot be seen from outside the castle, and it was one of its secrets of defence. Defenders could go down into the caponier, and were safe from attack. But any assailants, having to cross this ditch, were exposed to raking gunfire from this edifice. Hidden in the ditch bottom, it was safe from cannon fire, and its existence would only become apparent as an assault on the main block began.

On the edge of the opposite side of the ditch stood a high and very strong wall, as high as the tower beyond, that protected the main structure from cannon fire. In 1579 the Hamiltons once again had a fall-out with the Crown, and levies were raised whereupon this high wall was tumbled into the ditch to make the castle more vulnerable.

It was only in 1962, when this rubble was being cleared, that the caponier was discovered! A stairway at the far side of the ditch goes down through stonework to give access. The large original tower is worth investigation, and you will discover that there are various stone rooms and cellars hidden beyond it. An interesting place, it was gifted to state ownership in 1949. There are abiding legends that Mary, Queen of Scots, stayed within the castle before the Battle of Langside, which occurred near Glasgow in 1568, but these legends also surround Cadzow Castle, which we have already visited.

Retrace your route down to Crossford, turn right and on towards Lanark. I like this next section, particularly on a motorcycle, where sweep after bending sweep makes for an interesting journey. We drive through Hazelbank after another mile.

You will have noticed quite a few greenhouses on this section. Clydesdale was once famous for fruit growing. It still goes on of course, but on a much reduced scale, and many of these greenhouses now lie empty. There are still fruit trees scattered around the vicinity, and on some of the side roads I have seen apples and pears hanging from trees, throwbacks to the days when this was orchard country.

On into Kirkfieldbank, the last settlement before the road rises steeply up to Lanark. You may catch glimpses of the spires of Lanark ahead on these stretches. Blind Harry mentions this area in his account of Wallace's life, calling it Kilbank or Gilbank in his narrative. In fact there is still a farm called Kilbank in the area. There was once a tree hereabouts that people associated with Wallace, but it has been gone for a couple of centuries.

We pass a green bridge that carries a pipe over the river. This is where Jock fell off the bike and broke his coccyx! We cross the Clyde on a fairly modern bridge, but just upstream and hidden from view is the old bridge, dating from the 1600s. If you wish you can park in one of the side streets and take a look at it. From here the road rises very steeply up towards Lanark. You will pass a large sign telling you that Lanark was created a Royal Burgh in the time of David I, away back in 1140.

Although Lanark is an ancient place, the name a corruption of the Cymric *llanerch*, meaning a forest glade, there is not a lot of real antiquity in the town. I like the place though. The Wars of Independence are my personal favourite of all the intricacies of the mosaic of Scotland's history. Lanark was where many of the seminal moments of that struggle took place, where sparks were ignited. I can't help but be attracted. It is as if the years mean nothing, as if some shade of past events has been left behind, and an attraction is created within me.

We climb to the top of the hill in zig-zags, and reach the junction with the A73, where we turn right into the town centre. After a half-mile the street narrows, obviously following the lines of long-gone medieval buildings, then you emerge, with St Nicholas' Church on your right, into the High Street. I want you to park in this vicinity. Your best bet is to turn hard right as soon as you emerge into the High Street, into the town's Castle Gate, and park as soon as possible.

Facing St Nicholas' Church at this side, in a gap between the houses, is a little wall, with a plaque set into it. It is an old stone plaque that bears a few words upon it, and those few words are part of the fabric that has shaped the Scotland we know today. It says: 'Here stood the house of William Wallace, who in Lanark in 1297 first drew sword to free his native land.'

And William Wallace himself would probably be surprised at how the events of that night have embedded themselves into the psyche of a nation.

The story runs something like this. The house was actually the town house of the family of Wallace's sweetheart, Marion Bradefute. Her father was the Laird of Lamington, a dozen miles upstream on the Clyde. There are still the remains of a tower house of a later date between Lamington Village and the Clyde that was the family home. Being landowners of a little wealth, they had a town residence too, which stood on this spot. One day in spring 1297, Wallace walked down the town's High Street, making his way to the house to see Marion. (She was 'Murron' in the film *Braveheart*, but that is just the Scots way of saying Marion). His physical size attracted various unpleasant comments from the English garrison in the town. Wallace shrugged off this abuse. Then one individual got a bit too close for comfort and spat at Wallace, 'I hear the local priest has been dropping in for a fuck at your wife during your absences'. This is the line that has come down to us through local legend. Wallace exploded, and his hands reached behind his head for his mighty two-handed sword, and in one swift movement it came hurtling round in a murderous figure-of-eight. The Englishman jumped back, but the slash severed one of his hands at the wrist. He fell back screaming, in a welter of blood.

Every Englishman within earshot came running, drawing cold steel. I am used to wielding two-handed swords, and you should never underestimate the killing power of one of these weapons. The average weight is about five and a half pounds, they are gyroscopic when in a swinging motion, and are razor sharp. When in a full figure-of-eight motion, the tip moves at 70–80mph. Anything that gets in the road, comes off. Trust me.

William ran down the hill of the High Street. Marion had seen the events unfold from a window of the house, and went to open the front door. William ran in, Marion bolted the door behind him, and he made his way out of the back door, through the garden, over the wall, and away down towards the Clyde. There is a cave in the Cartland Crags near the town, still pointed out as Wallace's Cave, and it is reckoned he made for here to lie low. He never for a minute thought that retribution would be carried out on Marion, a local girl of some standing, but Heselrig, the English Sheriff, saw things differently.

Marion was dragged from the house, and an example was made of her in the street before where St Nicholas' Church stands today. Wallace had many friends in the town, and Marion was a well-known and liked girl. I don't envy the man who made his way to William's hide-out to appraise him of Marion's fate. Wallace would have blamed himself, but the deed was done, and he quickly came to a decision. Heselrig must die. Offers of assistance came from the men of Lanark, tired of the depredations of the invader.

From this spot, continue on down the Castlegate, either on foot or by vehicle. At the bottom of this road, just where the houses end at Castlebank Park, there is a car park, with the slope up to the entrance of the local lawn bowling club to its left. As you walk up here, you will see there is a stone with a plaque on it, telling you this is the site of Lanark Castle, and that parliaments of Scotland were once held here.

It is difficult to imagine, looking out over the bowling green, that this was where Wallace exacted revenge, plunging Scotland into renewed assault against its old enemy, the spark ignited to rouse the people. Heselrig was in residence here when Wallace and his patriotic band stormed the place. I can imagine the grim face on Wallace as he fulfilled his goal, and had Heselrig before him. 'I am Wallace. Die, Englishman!', as he plunged steel deep within him. There was no going back now, and as the news spread, young men all over Scotland flocked to Wallace's banner.

I have sat here and listened to the click-clack of the bowls on a summer's evening, and heard the echo of Wallace's cry of revenge. It is a private club today, so try not to be intrusive, but a walk to the hedges at the back and a look over will reveal that there are still the ridges of the earthworks of this place discernible on the slopes. The original entrance was obviously on the same site as the modern way in, with the other sides sloping away steeply.

Back up to the High Street, and you will notice that there is a large statue of Wallace at first-floor level on the frontage of St Nicholas'. The church was built in 1777. The statue of Wallace was added in 1817 by a young self -taught sculptor named Robert Forrest. I am always intrigued at the way Wallace is often portrayed as a late middle-aged individual in older statues. Perhaps their creators wished to portray Wallace as a man of some experience, but in reality he was only in his early twenties.

We know that Heselrig's slaying is a fact, as it was read out at as an indictment at Wallace's sham trial in London in 1305. The story of Marion's murder has come down to us as the reason, through local folklore. What is interesting though, is that 60 years after the fact, a Northumbrian knight (Heselrig himself was from the Valley of the Till in Northumbria), Sir Thomas Grey, was captured and imprisoned in Edinburgh Castle. He began to write a book there, and in this book, the *Scalachronica*, he told how his father was one of the garrison in Lanark in May 1297. He tells how Wallace fell upon the place at night, killed Heselrig, and set fire to the place. His father had good reason to remember all this, for he was wounded in the castle assault and left for dead. Had he not been left lying between two burning buildings he might have perished in the night, but he was found the next day by a comrade, William de Lundy, and was tended by him until he recovered. This account gives us a little window back in time to the Lanark of 1297.

St Nicholas' Church contains what is claimed to be the oldest church bell in the world, cast in 1110. It was originally hung in the old St Kentigern's Church of Lanark that we will visit next, but was moved here when this church was built. Perhaps Wallace was familiar with the toll of this bell – another throwback to the days of this great Scottish hero. It has an inscription upon it, that it has 'three times, Phenix-like, past thro' fiery furnace' – in 1110, 1659 and 1740.

Continue on up Lanark's High Street. I'm told in ancient times a stream ran down the middle of its wide road, but it has long ago been tunnelled underground. At the top the road forks, and we are taking the right fork, still marked Clyde Valley Tourist Route, along with Carlisle A73. The fact that we started off in the Carlisle area shows that we have almost gone full circle, but there is still much to see in south-west Scotland.

We pass Lanark Station, and the tourist information office is also on our left, then we come to a junction, Carlisle to the left, Carluke to the right. I actually want you to go almost directly across, where a small access road takes you up to a lodge house and the gates of the local cemetery. Park in to your left before the lodge, and walk the last few yards into this old graveyard. It is packed with hundreds of years of burials, and many more centuries' worth before the time when graves were even marked.

In front of you is an ancient ruined church, or at least a wall and an arched arcade of an ancient place of worship. This is St Kentigern's, not to be confused by a later, more modern church of the same name in the town. It is first mentioned as early as 1150, when David I granted it to the monks of Dryburgh Abbey. It continued to be used for some time after the Reformation, but seems to have been ruinous by 1657, and was eventually superseded by St Nicholas' Church in 1777. Blind Harry tells us that it was in this very church that Wallace first laid eyes upon Marion while attending a service, and that it was in this church they were wed. Possible and probable, as this was the only church in Lanark at that time. If you walk straight through the building and out to the back, if you look to your left there is a gravestone with a very pronounced skull carved upon it. The inscription on the other side reads:

> Heir lyes William Hervie, who suffered at the cross of Lanark, 2nd of March 1682 aged 38, for his adherence to the word of God and Scotland's covenanted work of reformation.

William Harvie was part of a party that denounced 'Popish' statutes of which they disapproved, then took hammers to the cross at Lanark. For taking part in this act Harvie was 'Laid by the heels and hanged'.

There are some interesting old carved gravestones in the churchyard, and it is worth a wander. Some of the buildings connected to the old ruins of the church have some old stones with skulls and similar, set into their walls. Nice view out too, towards Tinto Hill. It has a large ancient cairn on its summit which you can discern even at this distance. Tinto is 2,335 feet high, and seems all the more impressive because it stands alone. From its summit on a clear day, you can see from the Highlands to Ireland. It was once a place where the ancients lit Beltane fires, is said to have been a place of heathen worship, hence the large cairn, and it has been used as a beacon hill to warn of invasion. The name Tinto actually means Hill of Fire, and a path runs to its summit from the A73 south of here.

As we leave St Kentigerns, we will turn left at the junction on the main road, to take a look at 'New Lanark'. Just a little down this road, you will see signs pointing the way, and we take a sharp turn to the left. Follow the signs until you reach New Lanark itself. It stands on the banks of the Clyde. It is a big place, and to do it justice it needs a bit of time spent exploring it. New Lanark was a successful experiment, set up by David Dale in 1783. David Dale was born at Stewarton in Ayrshire in 1739. He trained as a weaver, then covered the countryside buying the linen spun in houses at that time. By 1763 he had a business importing yarn from the Low Countries, and he had prospered so much that in 1784 he decided to open his own mill at what was to become known as New Lanark.

The first mill opened in 1785, the second, after a setback with a fire during construction, in 1789, and a third and fourth were later added. Each mill was 160 feet long, 40 feet wide, and seven storeys high. A tunnel was constructed to carry water from the Clyde to power these mills. It is 300 feet long, cut through solid rock, and it has a fall of 28 feet.

In 1799, Dale's daughter married a man by the name of Robert Owen. Owen was a Welshman, and eventually bought the business at New Lanark from Dale. Dale himself died in 1806 and is buried in the Ramshorn Kirkyard in Glasgow city centre. Owen had radical ideas regarding the running of his new business, not just interested in making as much money as possible, but wishing to ensure that his workforce was well-educated and well-treated. Two thousand people lived and worked at New Lanark, many of them young children who worked long hours. Kids as young as five worked thirteen-hour days. Owen changed all that. At New Lanark you did not start work till you were ten, and ten-hour days became mandatory. He opened schools for his workers, supplied them with proper outlets to improve themselves, providing a good library etc. He was the first real industrial humanitarian, and working practices the world over have taken their cue from the work of Owen. He was the first real socialist, and was also responsible for funding the co-operative movement.

New Lanark today is a visitor attraction, all the original mill buildings having been converted for other uses. Some are houses, there is a hotel, visitor centre, even an audiovisual theatre show. The place is picturesquely sited in a hollow of the Clyde, the river running by, and it is a popular destination for a day out in Scotland. The buildings themselves are worth seeing, a throwback to the early days of manufacturing, and there must be something to see for everyone, young and old.

Back up to Lanark, and turn back to your right to pass the entrance to St Kentigern's and carry straight on, on the A73. We pass Lanark Loch in its Country Park, and another mile takes us downhill to cross the River Clyde on the old Hyndford Bridge. This narrow old five-arch bridge was built in the 1700s. It is still as it was, and traffic lights control the traffic flow as it is only wide enough to let one direction cross at a time. It has its original inshots into the sides, so that pedestrians could stand in when carts passed. It is a tribute to the original builders that articulated lorries cross with no problems, on a bridge built in the age of horse traffic.

When we cross the bridge we turn right, taking the A70 towards Douglas. The Clyde is on our right for the first mile or so, then it swings away for Lanark and the Clyde Valley, where we have already been. The Douglas Water flows into the Clyde here, and it is the shallow valley of the Douglas that we are now following. This river is the source of the surname

Douglas, found all over the English-speaking world, and there are no fewer than 56 towns and villages scattered over the planet called Douglas. They all come from the name of this stream, from the Gaelic *dubh glas* (doo-glas), the Black Water. Incidentally, the locals call it the Doo-glas, the correct Gaelic pronunciation. The name of the Douglas family is synonymous with the medieval history of Scotland, and this country is their birthplace and heritage, and we will discover more in the village of that name.

Tinto rises away to our left, and the road before us runs straight over the scatter of green fields. One or two bad bends where you have to be wary of oncoming traffic though, but they do make things interesting. We skirt Rigside, and another mile or two and we come to a roundabout just before the M74 motorway, the main north/south route. We go straight through and under the motorway, continuing on the A70 for Douglas. The old estate wall, like so many others we have seen, skirts the road on your right.

We come down into Douglas itself. When you reach the Douglas Arms Hotel, you take a sharp right into the town's Main Street. The line of this street has obviously not changed since medieval times, and although most of the buildings are of a later date, the lay-out has not changed. As you drive down, keep an eye open for a gap in the housing on your right, where a little memorial stands. It is dedicated to James Gavin, who was a tailor in Douglas. Gavin was a Cameronian, a follower of Richard Cameron, a noted Covenanter. His house and premises stood on this spot, and he was unlucky enough to receive a visit from a party of dragoons hunting out Covenanters on 4 August 1685. His ears were cut off with his own tailoring scissors, and he was then banished to Barbados in the Caribbean. In later life he returned to Douglas, and the lintel stone from his house, showing a carven ear and scissors, is inset in his memorial. Lintel stones are a common feature in older buildings in Scotland, usually bearing the initials of the builders, the date, and perhaps a feature or two pertaining to the family concerned.

You will notice there are some interesting old houses in Douglas, but I can't say that it is a pretty place. It has an austerity about it, but it is very Scottish in feel. A little further on and the old Church of St Bride appears on your left. Park hereabouts, and we will explore further on foot. The gate leading into the churchyard has a sign upon it informing you who the key holder is, and you can go and get the key to allow you access into St Bride's itself. The church was much larger once of course, only a fragment survives of its former glory, but it matters not. This is a place that has the very heart and soul of Scotland imbued in its fabric. Before you go inside, take a look out to the Douglas Water, and the hills beyond, as many a patriot soul of Scotland has done in the past.

St Bride's was founded in the 1200s and is now represented by only its choir and a small spire, although there are a few walls left of other parts. As

you enter there is a strangely life-like marble and alabaster monument of
the Countess of Home. So eerie is it, that I don't like to turn my back on it
for too long!

To your left as you walk in, there is a wall recess, containing the tomb of
one of the greatest soldiers, nay, greatest sons, that Scotland has ever produced. Because here is the effigy of the Good Sir James of Douglas, the
Black Douglas to some, freedom fighter, captain at Bannockburn, friend of
the mighty Bruce, and the man who carried the heart of the hero-king
on crusade.

I have travelled to Andalusia and stood on Douglas's last battlefield. I
have learned as much as I can about the life of this remarkable man, and the
fact that I can look upon his tomb is a humbling experience, which fills me
with various emotions. I give a lot of detail about Douglas in my book *On
the Trail of Robert the Bruce* – his career, his death and his subsequent burial here. His effigy, of dark stone, is cross legged, his feet resting upon a
lion, but it is unfortunately much worn and defaced. Cromwell is partly to
blame, as he used this church as a stable for his horses during his sojourn in
Scotland, but the church lay open for many years, and anyone could come
and go as they wished – a shocking state of affairs. The local school once
stood in the churchyard, so you can imagine the scenarios that would have
developed from that.

Various other members of the Douglas family are interred here, all
famous names from the history of Scotland. You will notice that there are
two hearts set within cases that are on display behind glass, set into the
floor of the church. One is reputed to be that of the Good Sir James, the
other that of Bell-the-Cat, a Douglas Earl who tamed James III of Scotland.
The oldest tomb is that of a girl from the 1200s.

This should be a place of great pilgrimage to most Scots, but in all my
many visits I think there has only been one occasion when there were others
present within the building. You will notice that there are two heavy marble
doors set into the floor, leading to the burial vaults below the floor. I believe
these may only have been opened twice in the last century. The last time
was about a year before I began this book, and I was lucky enough to be
allowed access. The vault was completely 'restored' between 1879 and
1881, and old accounts state that 'the old coffins were removed'. I can only
assume they were reburied in the churchyard outside. The vault is separated
into a lot of individual lairs, several in length, and three high down one side.
About two-thirds are full, with their openings sealed up. It is completely
watertight and dry down there, and I can't recall seeing even a spider's web!
The Douglases that lie there are all from Victorian times, and I hoped that
there might be some tombs of early members of the family among them, but
I was to be disappointed.

The Church of St Bride was the scene of a famous event in Scotland's history – the 'Douglas Larder'. Douglas Castle had been taken by the English, and the Good Sir James asked leave of Robert the Bruce to go and effect the liberation of his family lands. There is a romantic old tale tied up in all this. A beautiful English maiden, the Lady Augusta de Berkley, had said to her many suitors that she would give her hand in marriage to the man who could hold the perilous castle of Douglas for a year and a day. Sir John De Walton asked leave to try and fulfil this task, and so was granted wardenship of the castle. For several months he discharged his duty.

But Douglas had returned and made contact with the people in the village. Thomas Dickson, a loyal Scot, informed Sir James that the English would go to the Church of St Bride to celebrate Palm Sunday, and that may be their chance to strike a blow at the invader. So, on Palm Sunday 1307, Douglas and many of his followers mingled with the English garrison, weapons hidden under their clothes as they entered the church. At a given signal they rose and attacked the garrison. The English, taken completely by surprise, were slaughtered, no escape available in the tight constrictions of the church, and Douglas had made sure the door would be held fast. He led by example, and it is said that 26 were slain in St Bride's, and another 12 were taken prisoner. He intended to use these captives as part of a ruse to gain entry to Douglas Castle, but they were not needed.

The Scots ran the half-mile to the castle, and found that only the cook and porter were in attendance. The Good Sir James knew that the English would come back in greater force and re-garrison the place, so drastic steps were taken. He had everything usable taken out of the castle, then had all the food stocks and barrels of wine, the grain and the corn thrown into one big heap in the centre of the place. The dead were brought from the church and thrown into this mess, and the prisoners were butchered and added too, making everything unusable to the enemy. Finally, Sir James set the castle's woodwork on fire. The Scots, wryly, called this incident the Douglas Larder. It is told how the letter to John de Walton from his lady-love was found on his body, and Douglas, being a man of chivalry, was much moved. This may seem strange when prisoners had been slaughtered, but this was a total war, and the English were the aggressors. Bruce's supporters, when taken, were butchered horribly, as in the case of his brothers at Carlisle. Sir James was determined to make any Englishman think twice about trying to hold his castle again.

Before we leave the church, take a look up at the little clock on the tower dated 1565. This clock was a gift to the Douglas family from Mary, Queen of Scots, and is said to be the oldest working clock in Scotland. The motto of the Douglas family is *Jamais Arriere* – Never Late, so the clock is always set a couple of minutes fast. Isn't that brilliant?

The only drawback to that last story is that I was once 'doing' the story of Bruce in an illustrated talk. I was well into it, and had a slide of St Bride's Church up on the screen. I told the story of the Douglas motto, *Jamais Arriere* – how the Douglases were never late, and how they were the first to charge in any fight. At that exact moment, Willie Douglas, one of my compatriots from the Society of William Wallace, entered the hall, saying 'Sorry I'm late, I couldn't find the place', much to the hilarity of the audience, and it somehow blew my Douglas story out of the water!

So, we will need to visit the little that remains of Douglas Castle. This place is also sometimes called Castle Dangerous, partly because it was so difficult to hold the place, partly because Sir Walter Scott referred to it as such in his final book. Although wracked by ill-health, Scott was determined to visit Douglas when he was writing this book. It is reported that tears welled up in his eyes on seeing the place, so enmeshed as it is in Scotland's story.

Continue on up Douglas's Main Street, until you come to the gate that leads into the old estate. You are allowed pedestrian access into the policies. It is a little under a half-mile to the castle itself. You pass a monument to Polish airmen who were based at Douglas in World War II, then on by a loch, where there are usually some swans in attendance. You pass another memorial, this one to the now disbanded Cameronian Regiment, both raised and disbanded in Douglas, and the single remaining tower of the old place is now in view. You can see what a defensive site this is, the Douglas Water meandering on the little waterlogged plain below, the castle on a little craggy height above.

Why just this fragment of a once-proud fortress?

The castle was sacked by King James II in 1455 during his suppression of the Douglas family. They were the most powerful family in Scotland after Bruce's time, and the monarchs of Scotland saw this as a threat, and action was taken. You may remember the Douglas window incident at Stirling Castle, and these two episodes were very much linked. A later version of the castle was destroyed by fire in 1755, and I believe this tower was a survivor of that incident. That version was replaced by a four-storey baronial mansion in 1757. Mining subsidence caused that building to be demolished in the 1940s.

In the St Bride's Centre in the centre of the village, the focal point and community centre, there are a few photos on the wall showing the last version of the castle, with the tower standing today nearby. So it is of an earlier version.

Once you have had your fill of the castle site – something I have never had, and I go with never-monotonous regularity – make your way back to the village. If you have a look at the far side of the churchyard, there is an old building, now the village museum. It is staffed by local volunteers, and

if you visit at the weekend you may be lucky enough to catch it open. They
have some interesting bits and pieces, nothing alas from medieval times, but
they are helpful as can be. I even bought a mini-version of St Bride's Church
here once, that is sitting on my mantelpiece as we speak. Actually turned to
have a look at it there!

Just by the museum there is a statue which commemorates the raising of
the Cameronian Regiment in 1689. It is a very good statue, the Earl
of Angus, founder of the regiment, depicted looking out over the Douglas
Water.

Back to your vehicle, drive back up the Main Street, where we turn right
to continue along the A70. We follow the course of the Douglas Water for
two miles, then a little side road strikes off left to cross the hills to
Crawfordjohn. Take this road, but as you go on to it, take a look at the
large house over on the other side of the A70 we have just left, several hundred yards on. This is Hazelside, a private house, but it is on the site of the
house of Thomas Dickson, aide of Sir James in the Douglas Larder. Robert
the Bruce in fact granted him the lands of Symington in Lanarkshire, as well
as ratifying the deeds to his lands of Hazelside here, for his loyalty to
Scotland. His descendants lived here until the seventeenth century.

We now continue on this little unclassified road, which strikes through
the hilly moorland here. Although this is empty country today, there are,
here and there, vestiges of industry. There is one mine still in use, on your
left just as you cross the bridge over the Glespin Burn. Over the next couple
of miles, the road begins to rise, until we reach the watershed at a cattle grid
on a shoulder of Mosscastle Hill, its summit up a rise to your right. There
used to be a fabulous view from here, rolling hills and dales stretching out
in every direction, with Tinto prominent to the east, and Cairntable, a large
hill by Muirkirk, to the west. But forestry planting has hidden this view,
and as the trees grow larger, there is less to see.

I used to always put the bike on its stand here, and just look out over the
vast panorama of landscape, able to name the hills one after another. There
is still a view south though, looking towards the wall of the Lowther Hills,
the highest of this range, Green Lowther, bearing prominent radar masts.

Over the top then, and the road descends for a mile or two until it reaches
the junction with the B740, which follows the valley of the Duneaton
Water. We then turn left, and less than two miles brings us 'Out of the world
and into Crawfordjohn'. This saying comes from the fact that Crawfordjohn
is an isolated farming community, seemingly far from anywhere, although it
is only a few miles west of the M74 motorway. It is quite a distance from any
sizeable habitation, certainly by Scottish standards anyroad. There is a heritage museum in the old church behind the school, which is a helpful place
for tracing family connections in this area, having access to documents and

title deeds other than the artefacts that you would expect in such a place. It is open from 2–5pm at weekends, April to September.

Other than that there is a pub and a scatter of houses, but there is quite a history of Covenanting stories in this area, Crawfordjohn once being a hotbed of religious upheaval.

The road we are going to take is on your right as you first drive into the village, signposted for Leadhills. This little unclassified road drops to cross the Duneaton Water, and there is a nice picnic area at the far side. The road then climbs up a little side glen, through woodland, with a fair drop to the little burn on your right. We are now well into the outliers of the Lowther Hills, a rolling country of grassy heights. Our little road swings right and drops to connect with the B797 climbing up from the side of the River Clyde four miles or so to the east. We turn right towards Leadhills, some three miles further west. This is a wild bit of countryside, one of the wildest in Scotland south of the Highland line. I have always found it a little strange that visitors coming by car up the M74, hurry north to find solitude and make directly for the Highlands. The Highlands can be crowded with tourists in parts, and walking off the beaten track can sometimes be the only way to get away from the madding crowd. What they miss is the hill country in southern Scotland. Some of it is wild, untamed, and you can find quiet lay-bys everywhere, streams tumbling down their own little glens, and the only other life you will come across on a regular basis is the sheep who haunt these heights.

From Clydesdale right down to Galloway there is some lovely wild hill scenery, and the same applies to many other areas south of the Forth and Clyde, all missed by those rushing to the hills of the Highlands.

We follow the course of the Glengonnar Water up towards Leadhills, the road and stream together running up the valley floor between steep flanks of the surrounding hills. You will notice that these hillsides are scarred, and that there are mounds standing here and there on the valley floor. These are the detritus of 2,000 years of mining in this area, and when I explain a little more you will discover that Leadhills is a fitting name for the village that we are approaching. It is said that the Romans mined here at one time. There are records of the Romans finding lead while they were in Scotland, and Leadhills is the number one suspect! Gold too – there have been findings of gold in this vicinity since records began. The gold in the Crown of Scotland, as seen with the other Crown Jewels in Edinburgh Castle, originated in the Leadhills area. There are regular gold-panning championships held on the Glengonnar Water, and it still gives a steady yield. Our ancestors wore gold jewellery, armlets and ornamental chains, as seen in the Museum of Scotland, and that gold had to come from somewhere. This area has obviously seen mining operations on various scales, for many millennia. The 1600s saw the beginning of mining on a systematic scale. In 1810, Leadhills mines produced 1,400 tons of lead. In 1892, it was 2,019 tons, with 1 ounce of silver on average per ton of lead. The industry is gone now, but the remnants of its glory days are still evident on the landscape.

We climb steadily into Leadhills village itself, situated at a height of 1,350 feet. There is only one village in Scotland that sits at a higher altitude, and we will be visiting that at the beginning of the next chapter. Although we are at quite an altitude, Leadhills is still an area dominated by the Clyde. The Glengonnar Water empties into that river, and the whole water system here is connected to the Clyde. 1,350 feet might not sound much if you came from the centre of the United States, for example, but there is nowhere in Scotland more than 60 miles or so from salt water, and that, in comparison, is an impressive height for a village.

Leadhills is a random scatter of small terraces and single cottages, always a surprise to first time visitors, very attractive, almost pretty, but not in a chocolate boxy way. It has a hard edge too, due to the landscape, and the fact that these houses were built by men who knew the extremes of labour of the hardest sort. But these men of labour knew the benefits of education, and in 1741, 23 of the miners clubbed together to start a subscription library, the very first in either Scotland or England. The library exists to this day, has many intriguing old books, and is open Saturday, Sunday and Wednesday, May to September. There is a very small fee for admission. The library building is on your left just beyond the village school. One thing to look out for is the walking stick hanging on the wall of the library, reputed to have belonged to John Taylor, and we will talk of John a little more shortly.

The town's graveyard is over to your right at the 'bottom' end of the village, that is, when you first drive in. If you park in its vicinity, you will see there is a monument on the rise before the graveyard. This is to commemorate William Symington, pioneer of steam navigation. He was born in Leadhills in 1763. Noted Scottish poet Allan Ramsay (1686–1758), whose work includes *The Gentle Shepherd*, was born in Leadhills, a son of a superintendent of the mines here.

On the opposite side of the wall from the monument to Symington, there is the grave of the aforementioned John Taylor. It is a flat gravestone, standing by a Celtic cross. It tells how John was born in 1633, moved to Leadhills to work as a miner, retired in 1751 at the age of 117, and he died at the grand old age of 137 in 1770. It is easy to scoff at this information, or to put it down as a mason's error, but there is documentation surrounding John that seems to verify this great lifespan. He was quizzed of course, during his lifetime, and he could recall being called up from the mine he worked in 1652, to see 'day being turned into night'. He recalled birds falling from the sky in their confusion, and the event he described was the total eclipse that took place that year. He would have had to have been over 15, as that was the minimum age for an underground worker at that time.

No way of proving any of this for definite, of course, but I'm sure you will be interested to stand at the grave of this man!

Leadhills also has a nine-hole golf course, famous for being the highest in Scotland, and another attraction is the little railway that runs from Leadhills up towards nearby Wanlockhead. Its track has a two-foot gauge, there are several quaint railway engines, and it is run by enthusiastic volunteers. It is good that this relic of the old mining industry has remained as a tourist attraction. It operates weekends from May to September. We often hear reports on the radio in Scotland of trains down south not running because of snow on the line. It is just as well this rail service does not run during the winter months, as I have seen blizzard conditions in these hills – and it can be brutal!

We continue on uphill through Leadhills and out onto still-rising moorland, the highest hills of these parts before us to the left of the road. I have a couple of friends in Leadhills, and once went for a walk out here with them and their dogs. We came to an iron grating, perhaps five feet square, covering the top of a shaft that plunged down into the ground, the relic of an old mining enterprise no doubt. I stepped onto it and peered down to see if I could see the bottom, but the shaft disappeared into darkness. My friend said I should get a rock, something just large enough to fit between the iron criss-cross that I was standing on, and drop it. I duly collected something that was about four or five inches across, and dropped it through. Silence. He casually rolled a cigarette, then a bang echoed up the shaft. 'Jeez!', I said, 'How bloody deep is that?' 'Goes all the way down to sea level, 1500 feet below,' my friend replied. Standing on the grating suddenly took on a different aspect!

We climb up to the watershed, which marks the border between Lanarkshire and Dumfriesshire, and as we cross this we leave the head-streams of the Clyde behind.

The other side of this watershed is the catchment area of the River Nith, one of the great rivers of southwest Scotland, and we go over and into pastures new.

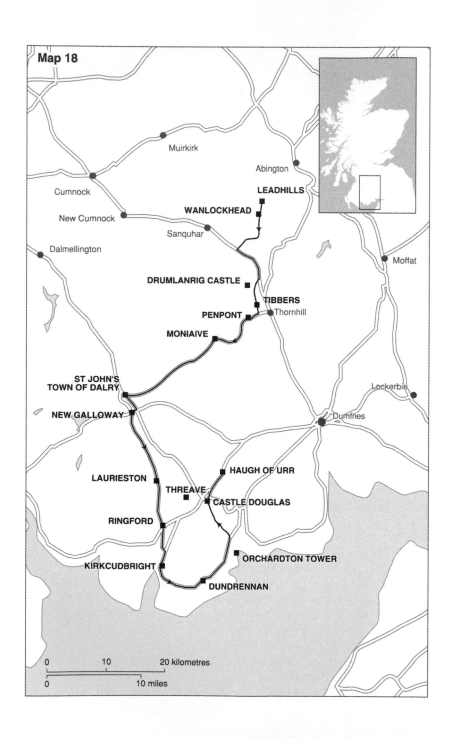

Map 18

CHAPTER EIGHTEEN

Into the Southwest

TAKING THE A76 SOUTH FROM WANLOCKHEAD THE ROUTE EXPLORES DRUMLANRIG CAS-
TLE, PENPONT, NEW GALLOWAY, KIRKCUDBRIGHT, ORCHARDTON TOWER, AND THEN
TRAVELS NORTH TO CASTLE DOUGLAS ALONG THE A75.

JUST AFTER WE CROSS the crest, we drop to find there is another scattered
village before us – Wanlockhead, the highest in Scotland. I suppose this
must be a surprise to many folk who would assume that such a place would
be in the Highlands, but it is the mining that has caused a settlement to exist
in such an airy place.

Just before the village, a little road cuts off to our left, the access to the
weather stations on top of Lowther Hill, 2,377 feet, and Green Lowther,
2,403 feet. It is a private road, but you are allowed to walk it to the summits if you so desire. From the top you can see England, Ireland and, I am
told, the Isle of Man on a clear day. Been up to the tops a few times, but one
trip in particular sticks in my memory. These hills take the brunt of any
storms coming in off the Atlantic, and I once decided to go to the tops with
a few friends in wild weather, which was snow by the time we reached
Wanlockhead. The power of the wind was just astonishing. We could
barely keep upright, bent over as we were.

I found a large bolt, the type used to hold railway lines onto the sleepers
that sit below them. It must have been several pounds in weight. We sheltered between a couple of the buildings on the summit, which were covered
in carvings of ice and snow shaped by the wind. We could at least get a
breather from the punishment the cold wind was meting out to us. The
wind was whipping past the gap at the end of the buildings we were huddled between. I launched the bolt down the space, and as soon as it hit the
wind it shot sideways to the left, like a bullet, and disappeared out of sight,
as if hit by a giant baseball bat in mid air!

Exhausted is the only word to describe how we were when we returned to
the roadside. I have been caught in some brutal weather conditions on the
tops in the Highlands, but I think that day in the Lowther Hills shows that
even the grassy hills of the south can have a hidden side.

If you do venture up to these tops, it is worth remembering that East
Mount Lowther, although a lower cousin about a mile southwest of
Lowther Hill, has great views too.(it is East Mount Lowther, although it sits
to the west!)

Wanlockhead, being the highest village, is able to boast many 'highest' signs on its buildings. The highest pub, the highest shop, even the highest bowling green in both Scotland and England. There is a long distance walk right across the Southern Uplands of Scotland, over 200 miles long, funnily enough called the Southern Upland Way. It passes through Wanlockhead, and it will have brought many travellers through this once lonely place. I'd like to *do* the Southern Upland Way one day. Various things keep my life too busy just now, but I hope when I am a little older I can spend my days doing such things, and getting to know Scotland a little better.

The main attraction for the visitor to Wanlockhead is its mining museum. It shows visitors how life was in the old days, as well as giving access to part of one of the old mines.

We continue on the B797, and as we leave Wanlockhead, we literally plunge into the Mennock Pass. The road drops rapidly, high hills rising on either side. There is just room for the road and the infant Mennock Water, dropping rockily from pool to pool. It is Alpine in aspect (I've never been to the Alps, so allow me a bit of artistic licence here!) in fact, it would be the perfect spot for one of those film scenes where the car goes over the edge, bursting through the safety barriers, and plunging down the gradient, exploding at the bottom. I should really be using my limited knowledge of Scotland to find locations for film producers (for a small fee).

When the road and the Mennock Water eventually level out a bit, the hills stand back just a little, and there is delightful greensward by the water's edge, used often by picnickers in the summer months. Little side glens branch off, each containing a tumbling stream, and looking worthy of exploration. The last mile or two of the pass is spent driving through woodland, and then we reach the A76, a major route which runs between Kilmarnock and Dumfries. We turn left to follow the valley of the River Nith on its course towards Dumfries and the open sea at the Solway Firth.

It is a pleasant, picturesque river, the Nith, rocky in places, the road hugging its eastern bank. It runs through sections that are almost gorge-like, and it is generally too far below the road to catch more than a glimpse of the water, but there are lay-bys and parking areas where you can stop and see more. Attractive countryside this, the odd green field, deciduous woodland, and no part where you could say the land was flat. We follow Nithsdale for about seven miles, then a side-road goes off through woodland on our right, signposted Drumlanrig Castle. Drumlanrig is an ancient Douglas stronghold, and the Dumfriesshire home of the Duke of Buccleuch (pronounced Buck-loo) and Queensberry. .

Go down the road, and you will meet another after just a few yards at a junction. Continue right, and you will come to a pretty lodge house, where there is an old stone bridge over the Nith. At the far end of the bridge, a sign pointing to the right proclaims 'Drumlanrig Castle, 1 mile'. We follow this red coloured drive through the attractive parks of the castle, dotted with sheep and cows. Drumlanrig is a long hill (*drum*) at the end of a long (*lang*) ridge (*rig*), hence the name. There have been Douglases here since the time of the Battle of Otterburn in 1388, when William, son of the Douglas who died at that fight, inherited the lands here as first Laird of Drumlanrig. We visited Otterburn at the very start of this book.

One last sweeping left-hand bend, and the castle appears before you, half a mile distant. You cannot help but be impressed, the building perfectly situated to impose Ducal splendour upon you on this magnificent approach. It is a stately edifice, the double-curving staircase to the front door, with its clock tower rising high above most noticeable. The clock bears the date 1686, is surmounted by a large stone crown, and the Douglas arms are carved on the stonework below.

There was an old tower house on this site, built around 1513, and some of it is incorporated into the palatial building before you, built between 1675–89. You can park just a little to the right at the front of the house, where the stable blocks here have various attractions inside. You may purchase a ticket here to tour the house, which has many works of art and fine furnishings collected over many centuries. Everywhere within you will notice the Douglas arms, containing the heart of Robert the Bruce, emblazoned in stone, lead, iron, wood, leather and carpeting.

There have been many distinguished visitors to Drumlanrig, from James vi to Neil Armstrong, the first man on the moon, and himself the descendent of a Scots Border family. Bonnie Prince Charlie stayed here on the retreat from Derby, a few months before fateful Culloden, in December 1745, and the bedroom he occupied is very much as it was. There are personal relics of his on display, including rings worn by him, and a money box. The Highlanders with Charles did not think much of a painting of King William iii of England and damaged it by throwing 'a certain liquid' over it. The repaired painting still hangs in the staircase hall. I have been lucky enough to have made the acquaintance of Andrew Fisher who is the Duke's archivist and resides at Drumlanrig. Andrew is an author, and his book on William Wallace is a good academic work. In fact, Andrew's book was probably the first modern work to look at William's life in any great depth.

You will notice before you drive away from Drumlanrig, continuing on to the left of the castle's frontage, that there is a sign giving details regarding the large sycamore tree before you. It stands 112 feet tall and covers a sixth of an acre. It is estimated that its annual water consumption is 134,000 gallons!

Follow this road downhill, past some of Drumlanrig's walled gardens on your right. We come to a junction, where the red road we are on merges with a grey surfaced road, and we turn right. The River Nith is now over on our left. Just a couple of hundred yards on there is a gate into a field on our left, a path disappearing across this field, and there is a little wooden signpost pointing down this path, proclaiming 'Tibbers Castle'. You can park at the gate, taking care not to block it, and follow the path down for a half mile or so. A little burn on your right gurgles and trickles along as your companion as it makes its way to the River Nith.

Tibbers is an interesting place, and I find it especially so because it has lain abandoned since the time of Bannockburn in 1314. It is very ruined, and was very overgrown a few years ago, but enough of the undergrowth has been stripped back for you to discern its outline, traces of all its walls and towers still visible. Even the name contains a strange story. It is said that the Romans built a fortification on this spot, naming it after the then-emperor Tiberius Caesar, and Tibbers is a supposed corruption of that.

You cross the little burn, and the castle remains are atop the large mound on your right. A path climbs and goes through the original gateway towers. It is a defensive spot, with the River Nith on one side, and the once high curtain walls atop the steep sides of the mound must have made it formidable indeed. There was an old timber castle here, then in 1298 this castle was built by Sir Richard Siward, a traitor Scot, who sided with England's Edward Longshanks.

Edward himself was here after his defeat of William Wallace at Falkirk in 1298. The battle took place in July, and he was here in the following September. Shortly after Robert the Bruce's coronation in 1306, the Scots captured this place, but the English quickly rallied reinforcements and retook it, hanging John de Seton, Bruce's captain. We will talk further of the Seton family when we visit Dumfries. When the might of England lay crushed after Bannockburn, the Scots recaptured Tibbers and dismantled parts of the defences so that the English could not re-garrison it. It has lain derelict ever since.

Local people would not have been backward in helping themselves to the stone, of course, and it would have been purloined in the seven intervening centuries. A large stone in the middle of the castle covers the old well. I can remember that this was not closed off during an early visit, and it went down to the water level of the Nith, opening up a little near the bottom, like a bottle dungeon. I always wanted to abseil down and explore it. I have since discovered that it was examined in the mid-1800s by archaeologists, but the report did not mention if anything interesting was found.

Back through the entrance there is another rise to the south, and there are traces of a ditch surrounding this. It would have been used as a bailey, a place where horses and cattle were kept, along with ancillary buildings. Perhaps there was a drawbridge of sorts that ran from this to the castle across the intervening dip.

I wanted to take you to Tibbers partly because of its close proximity to Drumlanrig. It is interesting to compare these structures, not only for the few hundred years (and yards!) that separate them, but also because of the fact that Drumlanrig is still in use as a residence and has survived the ages.

Back to the gate, and we continue south, the Nith mostly unseen to our left, but only a field or two's length away. We continue past various estate buildings, the odd lodge and farm for almost two miles, until we come to the junction with the A702. We are going to head further west here, striking over towards Galloway, the most south-westerly region of Scotland, but we shall take a detour just a little east first. So, turn left onto the A702, and just a couple of hundred yards on there is a single lane stone bridge that crosses the Nith, taking you into the town of Thornhill. (There is another Thornhill near Stirling, which we have already driven through).

Directly before the bridge, there is a lay-by on your right, and if you park here you will notice that there is an ancient cross in the field on your right, just a little behind you. Closer inspection will reveal that it was once a Celtic cross, with a circle around the shafts of the top, but the top has eroded to a stump. The shaft is covered in exotic carvings though, double beasts intertwined and some interlaced knotwork. I wish I could tell you more about this old relic, but even old parish records have nothing to say about its history, or why it was placed here. It's a nice spot though, over-looking the Nith, and the cross is about nine feet high and surrounded by a little iron railing. Many people probably drive by it on a daily basis and don't even give it a glance, but it will have stood on this rise above the river for well over a thousand years, its inscriptions meaning something to our earlier generations.

Next, retrace your route a little by turning back west on the A702. We pass a red-painted church, then on our right a strange cairn is visible, stand-ing on a rise above the road. There is a lay-by just after it on our right, where a little gate allows access into the field if you wish to have a look at it. It is about 10 or 12 feet high, is made up of blocks of the local very red stone, and it is shaped like a giant egg! It has only recently been constructed – very cleverly too – all the blocks perfectly put in place with no mortar or cement used. I don't know its purpose, or if a plaque or an inscription is to be added, but it offers a nice view further west to the increasingly hillier ter-rain we are driving towards.

Just after this we drive through the village of Penpont. Its church is con-structed from the local stone, and so is the same shade of red as our recently visited eggy cairn. Penpont is from the Cymric *pen-y-pont,* meaning the head of the bridge. This is probably a reference to a bridge that once crossed the Scar Water which circles round the south of the village. This old bridge was ascribed to Roman times, had one large semicircular arch, was covered in ivy, and was demolished in 1801 to make way for a new bridge. I always think it's a shame when such things are long gone, and there is not even a photograph to see what it once looked like.

You may be interested to know that the inventor of the bicycle, Kirkpatrick Macmillan, was born at the blacksmith's cottage at Keir, just south of here. It has a plaque on its wall announcing the fact.

Onwards another few miles, until the road turns round the base of a prominent hill by the attractive name of Shancastle Doon, rising above us on our right. We then arrive at the tiny hamlet of Kirkland, its name coming from Glencairn Kirk which stands on the right of the road. Pull in and have a walk round this interesting old graveyard.

She has no tomb, but legend states that Annie Laurie, the subject of the famous love song, is buried here. It is a ballad known the world over, at least in its more modern, tidier form. The original runs something like this:

Maxwelton Banks are bonnie where early fa's the dew,
Where me and Annie Laurie made up the promise true,
Made up the promise true, and ne'er forget will I,
And for Bonnie Annie Laurie I'll lay down my head and die.

She's backit like a peacock, she's breastit like a swan
She's jimp about the middle, her waist ye may well span
Her waist ye may well span and she has a rolling eye
And for bonnie Annie Laurie I'll lay down my head and die.

The words were written by William Douglas, a soldier and fabulous swordsman who resided in this area, but fought in continental wars in Europe, selling his sword to the highest bidder. He returned here in 1694, and was known as a staunch Jacobite and a supporter of the exiled James VII. He fought several duels, once wounding and disarming a noted professional swordsman. He obviously fell head over heels in love with Annie, who was the daughter of the Baronet of Maxwelton, and penned the song. But the romance was ill fated. Perhaps it was his loyalty to the ousted Royal House of Scotland that upset Annie's father, but both William and Annie ended up marrying others. The words of the song have survived though. Annie lived to the ripe old age of 83, and as stated, it is believed that she was interred here.

The most interesting part of the graveyard for me is to the right of the church, where two old gable walls stand, surrounded by a veritable phalanx of old gravestones in the local red stone. They all face the east, the direction of the Holy Land, where all the occupants wait in readiness to rise and face the Risen Lord on Judgement Day.

You can see by the gap between the gable ends of the early church that it was once a building that was a fair size. Each gable has tombs built into it dating from the 1600s. The eastern one has quite an ornate memorial with skull and crossbones, the hourglass etc. to remind us of our own mortality. There has been a place of worship on this site since St Cuthbert visited in the seventh century. St Cuthbert was obviously quite a figure in his day, as there are places associated with him all over this region. The gables in the churchyard date back to the 1100s. The church today dates from 1836.

As I wander around rural churchyards I always think that there must be a comfort in being born in an area where you look at your local church, and know that one day you will lie there for eternity, alongside those you know, and all those who have lived in these hills before you. Even if you roam the planet, you have that pull, that essential feeling of 'home' in some rural community in Scotland, where a scatter of houses huddle round their church. I probably envy it because I am not part of it. Born on the edge of a city, having moved house several times, and my ancestors scattered here and there, I don't have that corner of a graveyard where I will be laid to rest with the dust of my own. I suppose leaving that sort of legacy for your own future generations is as good a thing as any to leave behind. Unfortunately, break-ups have destroyed my hopes and chances of doing something like that myself. But I can still wander around such places and see how generations are here together, and wish them well.

From Kirkland, it is a straight run of two miles on to Moniaive. This is a beautiful place, a rural idyll, even better in summer when many of the houses have flower baskets hanging from them, embellishing the village in a riot of colour. Its old cottages, its pubs and coaching inn, coupled with its narrow streets, give an old-world feel with an aura of tranquility to Moniaive. As you come into the centre of the place, you will notice the pillar of the old village cross, bearing its date of 1638. We are going to turn left at this cross to follow the A702 to New Galloway, but it is worth looking at a few things in Moniaive itself. Just by the cross there is a house with a large clock tower. Always a feature handy for impressing the neighbours! No excuse for being late though, living in a house with a large clock face on its frontage.

The B729 leads out of the town at this end, heading for Carsphairn, and a little down this road, just outside the village, is a monument to James Renwick. It stands on the right of the road at the top of an incline. It was erected in 1828. James was born in Moniaive, or Minnyhive, as it was written phonetically in the old days, and the monument reads:

In memory of the late Reverend James Renwick, the last who suffered to death for attachment to the Covenanted Cause of Christ in Scotland. Born near this spot 15 Feb 1662 and executed at the Grassmarket Edinburgh 17 Feb 1688. 'The righteous shall be in Everlasting Remembrance.'

We take the New Galloway road from the old cross. Galloway can be a wild region, and this lovely hill road from Moniaive is a good introduction. It is a twisting, turning section through mostly bleak moorland, punctuated by pine forestry plantings. I'm not a fan of these regimented forests of trees not native to Scotland, but I also realise that they give work to the two-legged natives that reside here. That is, if they are not plantations created as a tax dodge by some rich businessman in London.

There are glimpses of fine views here and there, as Galloway is a hilly region, not as mountainous as the Highlands, but it certainly has its moments! This road takes a fair bit of concentration over the next dozen miles or so. There always seems to be a pair of attendant buzzards on this stretch, their mighty wings making flying look effortless. There is about 12 miles of this empty country, heathy moor and plantation. Plenty of life in the form of black cattle and sheep though!

We come downhill at Borgue, where there is a farm, and then there is junction off on our left, the B7075, signposted for New Galloway. Follow this road a mile or two until it meets the more major A712 by Balmaclennan. Turn right. It is only a short hop to a staggered junction at the Ken Bridge Hotel, the sign telling you it is only a mile into the town of New Galloway. We cross the River Ken by its old large, five-arched bridge, built in 1822. We soon come into the northern portion of New Galloway, a few villas and the parish church, then we come into the village proper. It consists of one long main street, running north to south. The place really only sprang up after it was given Royal Burgh status by King Charles I in 1629. New Galloway very much has a Borders feel to it.

Now we are in Galloway proper, I feel I should perhaps explain the name. In Gaelic, a Gall-Gael means 'foreigner Gael', and it seems that the people settled in this area had much in common with the people who inhabited the old Lordship of the Isles in Scotland, stretching from Harris, Lewis and Skye, right down to Northern Ireland.

Galloway comes from a corruption of the Gaelic/Celtic name for the people of this region, and it seems Gaelic was spoken here until a comparatively late date compared to the rest of Scotland south of the Highland Line. They were aggressive, ruthless warriors too, these Galwegians, much feared in battle, and regarded as being particularly bloodthirsty.

Drive straight through the village, following the A762, signposted Kirkcudbright, and whatever you do, don't pronounce it as it looks, as we actually say it Kirk-coo-brie!

As you come out of New Galloway at the top of the rising main street, and into woodland, after half a mile keep a lookout for a house on the left by the name of Kenmure Steading. Just after it, on the same side of the road, there is a gate, set back about a dozen feet from the road, with a grass covered driveway leading down through the trees beyond. Park in here, go over the stile at the left of the gate, and walk down the drive. There are mature trees lining your route, and after a couple of hundred yards you will see there is a large mound before you, with a ruined castle on top. The path swings to the left and climbs the mound in a circular motion. I should tell you that sheep often graze this site, and the ground can be covered in sheep shite (had to wash the bloody mats after the last time I visited it in the car!). The place is complete to the wall head, but the roof has gone, and the windows stare out, unglazed and featureless. It doesn't really look that old at first glance, just an empty old mansion, but a bit of closer inspection shows that behind the facade of the main block there are vaulted basements, and to the left there is an old staircase. The thick rubble walls inside give the game away too, that this is an ancient place with later additions.

The mound too, may look man-made at first glance, but there is a bit of rock protruding here and there, showing it is a natural feature. You can catch a glimpse of Loch Ken through the trees too, showing that the bogginess surrounding this castle to the east would help make it reasonably unassailable. I should point out that exploring this semi-ruined building is inadvisable, and me telling you about it, and then bits falling on you, does not give you the right to sue!

I have an interest in the place as legend states that John Balliol, King of Scots 1292–6 was born here. Certainly there are records of him spending much time at Kenmure. Wallace of course fought in the name of Balliol, as it gave his cause legitimacy. Balliol was deposed by England's Edward Longshanks, and no king of another nation has the right to interfere in the affairs of Scotland. Balliol was the son of Devorgilla, the Lady of Galloway, and she seems to have been quite a woman. We will meet her again before this work is done. Kenmure was one of her major strongholds.

I recall Nigel Tranter, that late great Scottish author, saying that he visited Kenmure in the late 1930s and it was very much a thriving mansion. There is a forlorn television aerial still projecting from the northern tower, which shows that it was inhabited in fairly recent times. I'd love to use the firm that erected that aerial, as I have had several come down in stormy weather, and this one has had everything thrown at it and has managed to survive!

After the fall of the Balliol family, and the rise of Robert the Bruce, Bruce granted Kenmure to the Gordon family – the same who owned the castle of Huntly northwest of Aberdeen, already visited. In the 1630s, King Charles I created Sir John Gordon the first Viscount Kenmure. The Gordons were very loyal to the Stewarts, and Kenmure was partially burnt by the enemies of Mary, Queen of Scots, because of their support. It was again attacked by Cromwell, due to the aforementioned John Gordon's adherence to King Charles. William Gordon, the sixth Viscount Kenmure, took an active part in the rising to support the exiled King James VII in 1715. He was captured and imprisoned in the Tower of London, where he was executed by the axe on Tower Hill in 1716. So this forlorn old place has seen much action, and it has been visited by many of the names from our history books.

The arms displayed on the front of the house are those of the Gordon family. In 1817, the house was remodelled, the addition of the driveway causing all the surrounding ancient remains to be swept away, and the roughcasting, or harling, was added, giving the place a sort of mock gothic look. On my last visit, it was dusk, and I set up the colony of bats that have taken over the premises. It was great to watch them, little mouses (!) with wings, fluttering about with the dark blue sky as a backdrop, completely silent to my limited human ears. I would like to have lain back in the grass to watch them flit, but I remembered the sheep shit and decided against it!

I'm told it was a fire that caused the evil times that this house has fallen on. The family abandoned the place afterwards. There has been a residence here for a thousand years though, and perhaps it is the birthplace of a king, so I have an affection for it.

We continue onwards on the A762, running towards Kirkcudbright (Kirk-coo-brie, remember?) The road hugs the west shore of Loch Ken for the first stage of our journey. It is a nice contrast, the silvery surface of the loch with the darkness of the trees. Loch Ken is a big loch for this far south of the Highlands. It is narrow, but it is many miles in length.

I don't think I have ever driven this road without seeing a few fishermen sitting on the narrow strip between road and loch, and little yachts tacking across its surface. Just as the road leaves the lochside, there are signs for Upper Benane Viewpoint, and a little road cuts off right for a few hundred yards to a parking place, where there are a choice of routes to the top. The steep route is 800 yards, the easier route is 1 1/2 miles. There is a good view over Loch Ken and the surrounding area from the top.

A little further down the A762 you will see signs for a forest road, open at certain times, named the Raiders' Road. This name comes from the work of Samuel Rutherford Crockett, who wrote about this area. One of his stories talked of the Raider's Road, and so it is now signposted.

We go through the tiny hamlet of Mossdale, which has a shop and post office. That isn't two different entities incidentally, that would be an extravagance in this sparsely populated area – it's a shop *and* post office in one.

There are some picturesque lochans on the right of the road next, with lay-bys so you can stop and take in the scene. Woodhall Loch is the largest of these.

You then come into the village of Laurieston. It comes upon you suddenly – you just drive out of the trees and into the village, so keep your eyes open for the 30mph signs. As you come to these signs, pull in on the left where there is a lay-by, and you will see there is a monument here to the abovementioned Samuel Rutherford Crockett. The monument's inscription says he was 'author of the Raiders and other tales of Galloway. A native of this parish 24 September 1860 – 16 April 1914. A faithful son, and constant lover of that grey Galloway land where about the graves of the martyrs, the

whaups are crying, his heart remembers how.' The memorial is a giant
squared off cairn, about 20 feet high and constructed out of the grey stone
of Galloway which you will become increasingly familiar with as you travel
through this area. It is well looked after, and the people of Laurieston seem
proud of their writer son. Wonder if I'll ever be good enough to warrant a
memorial? Don't answer that!

Onwards. You will notice a large pyramid shaped edifice on a hill over to
your left. This is an early ordnance survey post, and not a memorial as you
may think. We soon reach Ringford, and as we come through keep following the signs for Kirkcudbright. The village has a Celtic cross war memorial
on your right. We reach the A75, following the signs for Stranraer and
Kirkcudbright, then the A762, where we turn left.

On this last short run into the town, we follow the River Dee on our
right, with its large reed beds and water meadows. Very picturesque. We
then cross the Tongland Bridge, built in 1805 by Thomas Telford. We have
passed or crossed many of Telford's edifices on this journey, many of them
in the Highlands. Telford has changed the face of Scotland, and in his day
he changed the lives of so many of its inhabitants. We take his bridges for
granted nowadays, but 200 years ago people were still fording our many
rivers and streams, until the man bridged them. He was actually born in this
Dumfries and Galloway region, at Westerkirk, on 9 August 1757, and he
died on 2 September 1834 in London.

On into attractive Kirkcudbright, bright being the operative word, with
its many gaily painted old houses.

Now, there is one thing about this part of Scotland that I wish to mention. You might think that there is a different version of the Scots tongue
spoken right along the Solway coast, but it is an English accent you are
hearing. On summer days while covering these roads, stopping once in a
while to examine an interesting site, I am always taken aback by the fact
that every voice I hear is unmistakably English in origin. The other side of
the Solway Firth is England of course, but the opposite case does not seem
to apply. There is a huge influx of 'white settlers' right across this region,
for better or worse, and it *is* worse in certain aspects. Scotland is chained to
the concept of 'Britain' and people can settle where they wish. But when
there was a referendum to reinstate Scotland's parliament in 1997, this
region was the only one that voted against. I would imagine that the influx
of foreigners played a large part in that outcome, and I have at least to
question the rights and wrongs of that. This influx means that people can
make a decision that has an effect on the future of Scotland, yet these voters
are voting for their own standards, upbringing and beliefs, not necessarily
those that natives of Scotland share. It is a tricky subject, but it has to be
said, hard fact as it is. Why should they be allowed to decide what is best

for the people of Scotland? Because they have the money to buy property here?

As you drive into Kirkcudbright and reach the town centre, you will notice there is a Celtic cross on your right on the roadside, at the grassy area. If you can, park in this vicinity. Take a look at this cross, and you will see it bears the inscription that it was erected by:

> Cecely Louisa, Countess of Selkirk, in loving memory of her husband Dunbar James, Earl of Selkirk. Born 22 April 1809, died 11 April 1885. A man greatly beloved.

Unusual, as at first glance I think most people would assume it was the town's war memorial. The cross stands on an area of greenery, almost like a town square, and beyond this rises the parish church, built 1836–8 at a cost of £7,000. From the cross stroll over to the harbour area, where there is a tourist information centre, in front of which is an unusual wooden statue of a mother clutching a daughter, called *In memory of loved ones lost at Sea*.

The River Dee looks almost like a little landlocked loch here, due to the meanders of the river. The not exactly attractive iron bridge you can see upstream looks reasonably modern, but it was built from 1865–8 at a cost of £10,000. It is 500 feet long.

On a knoll to your left is the town's principal feature, known as Maclennan's Castle, built in 1582 by Sir Thomas Maclennan of Bombie. There was an earlier fortress, which stood a little nearer the harbour, which would seem to have been a strong place of some importance. In the 1800s some mounds of this former castle still survived, surrounded by a ditch that used to flood at high tide. It was originally owned by the Balliols, and Edward Longshanks stayed in it for ten days in 1300, along with his Queen and court. It then belonged to the Douglases, and they held it until 1455, when they fell out of favour with James II of Scotland. King James visited it on his march to crush the Douglas power. England's Henry VI resided here while his queen, Margaret, visited the Queen of Scots in Edinburgh in 1461. When the town came into the power of the Maclennans, the old place was abandoned and the new, now empty, castle was built. This castle is under state guardianship – has been since 1912 – and you can purchase a ticket to wander its remains.

The town's striking war memorial stands immediately before the castle, a crouching armed warrior atop its stone.

Go round behind the castle into the High Street, probably the oldest part of the town. The houses are painted a variety of colours, making Kirkcudbright a very attractive and happy looking place. None of the dourness that is reminiscent of many Scottish towns is apparent here. Kirkcudbright is known as the 'Artists' Town', and many artists have flocked to the place over the years to be inspired and just to paint. It is said

there is a quality to the light here which lends itself to the painting fraternity. Certainly the town has plenty of little galleries, and there is usually an
exhibition of some sort on.

On the right of the High Street is Broughton House and garden, owned by
the National Trust for Scotland. The house is being restored, but the garden
is open. It is a secretive little place, with narrow paths between the flowers
and shrubs. There are many interesting stone features to seek out, a twelfth-
century cross, a child's coffin, curling stones, a bust and old sundials.

You will notice that the High Street takes a left-hand bend at its end, and
in the junction before you stands the old tolbooth and town house. The
town house was built in the 1500s using stones from Dundrennan Abbey, a
place we will visit shortly. It is a very attractive old place with a forestair,
and the ancient and weatherworn town cross has been mounted on top of
these stairs.

There is a plaque on the front of the building:

Royal Burgh of Kirkcudbright
Quincentennary
1455–1955'

There is also a plaque to a woman of Germanic origin who lives in
London, who calls herself Queen of my people, and who opened the refurbished building in 1993. The building is now used as an arts centre and has
a gallery on the top floor, an audiovisual theatre in the centre, with other
bits and pieces to see, and a cafe on the ground floor. It very much features
work by Jessie M King, one of a group called the Glasgow Girls, who had a
great effect on the development of art in Scotland in the late 1800s and
early 1900s.

There is a bell in the tower, made by Michael Burgerhuis in Holland in
1646. This bell used to be rung to announce that the market was open for
business in the street in front, or as an alarm bell to warn of danger.

A great wee feature on the front of the forestair are the old town taps.
You pull the iron levers, and water surges out of the faucets below. Try
them and see!

The plaque reads:

This fount, not riches, life supplies.
Art gives what nature here denies,
Posterity must surely bliss
St Cuthbert's sons who purchased this
'Water introduced 23 March 1763
This tablet renewed in 1985

St Cuthbert is the patron saint of Kirkcudbright, and the name of the town
may be some sort of corruption of the kirk of St Cuthbert. It is possible that

the derivation is *Caer-cuabrit*, the Cymric for 'the fort on the bend of the river'. As you continue up the High Street, there are some interesting little alleyways arching through the buildings. Closes, we call them in Scotland.

Continue, and then you will reach St Mary's Street, where a left turn will take you back to the vicinity of your vehicle. Just around the corner though is a mock Gothic castellated structure, the town's museum, which was opened in 1881. It is actually called the Stewartry Museum, as that is the title the locals use to describe this area of Scotland. It is a great wee place, dated and a bit dusty-looking, old display cases absolutely crammed with goodies, and none of that modern interactive nonsense. There are many artefacts that have been found locally – Stone Age axes, a Bronze Age rapier, a viking sword, medieval swords, a good collection of early pistols, and very many examples of everyday articles from various eras. Well worth a wander.

So, when you return to your vehicle, drive back past the museum, and continue on down St Mary's Street out of town, and we are following the A711 towards Dundrennan. The road skirts Kirkcudbright Bay – very pleasant – then cuts inland at Mutehill, where the road rises, all the land between here and the Solway used by the Ministry of Defence as a firing range. Another four miles and we drop down towards Dundrennan. Just before Dundrennan there is a sign pointing down a little road to your right, announcing Port Mary 1 1/2 miles.

You can drive down this road to the edge of the Solway, ignoring farm turn-offs and Ministry of Defence gates, until you get to a grassy area right beside the shingle of the shore. The name Port Mary is a bit misleading, as there is no port, just a rocky shore, but it was from somewhere here that Mary, Queen of Scots, stepped from Scottish soil for the last time to climb aboard the boat that would take her to England. She expected help from her cousin, Elizabeth I of England, but all she got was a long imprisonment, and ultimately she was murdered, beheaded by a drunken axeman. She lies in Westminster Abbey in London today, where the sign states that she was executed for treason. Another insult. How can the monarch of Scotland be guilty of treason to England?

I'm told that there is a rock that is traditionally the place where Mary actually stepped on board, but to be honest the actual one has never been pointed out to me, so until then I will be guessing!

Back to the main road, and we come down to Dundrennan. There is a row of houses on our left, and the once magnificent Dundrennan Abbey stands ruined on our right. We turn into the parking area, and we will take a look at this venerable pile. It is constructed of the now familiar grey Galloway Stone, and it stands on the Abbey Burn which runs down to Port Mary.

Enough stonework remains to give you an idea of how grand a place this was in its heyday. It was founded for Cistercian monks in 1142, either by King David 1 or by Fergus, Lord of Galloway. The men who built such structures had amazing vision. These places were built to last forever, a lasting showpiece of devotion and magnificence, and it is sad that the old adage, nothing lasts forever, is so true.

The name Dundrennan is the Gaelic *Dun-nan-droigheann*, fort of the thorn bushes, which shows that there was probably a fort in this vicinity long before the abbey was built. The Chapter House remains are interesting, and the remaining transepts of the church still stand proud. There are some carven graveslabs, and the Cellarer's Monument, dated 1480. Just to the left of the entrance in an inshot is a thirteenth-century monument to an abbot, whose feet stand on the figure of a man. The story goes that this abbot was murdered, and the effigy was carved like this with the abbot standing upright, and the murderer depicted lying under his feet, to demean the man and the shameful act committed.

Mary, Queen of Scots resided within the abbey during her last night in Scotland, before making her morning sail at Port Mary on 16 May 1568. The building was taken under royal control in 1587, then annexed in 1621 to the Royal Chapel at Stirling. It then fell into neglect, and the locals were not long in seeing the opportunity to purloin the dressed stone. Many of the buildings and walls in the Dundrennan vicinity contain stones that were once the fabric of the abbey, and as stated, even the tolbooth at Kirkcudbright was constructed from its stones.

In 1842, happily, the Commissioners of Woods and Forests put the building in a state of conservation, and cleared out any debris. To the left of the abbey's entrance, over at the corner of the outside wall, stands a tree. Its little plaque reads:

Planted 16 May 1998 by the Marie Stuart Society, to mark the 430th anniversary of Mary, Queen of Scots' departure from the shores of Scotland.

As we drive on through Dundrennan, at the left end of this little village is the church, built in 1865. It's a strange shaped wee place, a large rose window on its front, but high-roofed and stumpy in aspect, with its unusual little steeple. The War Memorial for the village sits in front.

As we drive on the road twists and climbs through some woodland. Halfway up the hill on your left is a small quarry, and I wonder if some of the stone for the building of the abbey was dug out here. At the top of the hill there is a standing stone in a field to your left. There are views up into the eastern Solway Firth on this stretch. Then we come down to Auchencairn, with Bengairn and Screel Hill acting as backdrop to the left.

Through Auchencairn, still following the A711, and an arm of the Solway, Auchencairn Bay, is just over to our right. There is a straight stretch ahead, with some knoll-like wooded hills forward and to our left. Look out for the little road that cuts off right telling you it is the route to Orchardton Tower, three-quarters of a mile away.

Orchardton Tower. I actually have trouble saying that. Orchardton Tower. I usually fall over one of the syllables.

Anyway, head up this little roller-coaster of a road, and the tower is over a dip and on your left. You can park right beside it, and although it is under state care, there is no fee charged to have a wander around. It is an unusual place, being a standard Scottish fortified tower house with all the usual features that apply to every one of them. But this one differs in the respect that it is round. It is the only tower house in Scotland that is not oblong in plan. Why? No one knows – they obviously just wanted to build it that way, and very nice it looks too. Reddish stone this time, unlike the greyish Galloway stone we have got used to. It was probably built by Alexander de Carnys – Cairns in modern speak – Provost of Lincluden, a place we will later visit. As a churchman, he was chosen to be one of three ambassadors to visit France in 1412, and £200, a huge sum then, was provided from the Scottish exchequer. Storms meant that the voyage to France never took place, the £200 was never returned, and although there were many accusations and much finger-pointing, Cairns seems to have got away with it. .It may have been these funds that paid for this tower!

After a few generations of Cairns ownership, the tower became the property of the Maxwell family. One of these Maxwells fought for Bonnie Prince Charlie at Culloden, where he was unfortunately wounded and captured. He was taken all the way south from the battlefield to Carlisle, where he expected to suffer the hideous English death of hanging, drawing and quartering. Many of the prisoners of the '45 were disembowelled as they did not recognise the claims of the German/English Hanoverian dynasty. This Maxwell tried to destroy all his documentation, was discovered and stopped, but the magistrate found Maxwell's commission making him an officer of the King of France. This meant that he could be seen as a prisoner of war, and not a 'rebel'. He was deported to France, obviously diplomatic niceties being observed, from where he was able, eventually, to return to Scotland. He turned up at Orchardton, claimed it as heir of his grandfather, Sir Robert Maxwell, and he himself became Sir Robert Maxwell, seventh of Orchardton.

The tower stands beside the remains of some external cellars, which originally had a hall above. You can go into the stone vaulted basement of the tower, and see that the walls are at least eight feet thick here. A little stair gives access on the outside to the floor above. Inside there is an ornate aumbry set into the wall on the first floor. This is a type of cupboard, and it probably came from Dundrennan Abbey when that building was fair game to anyone who was seeking building material. I can imagine the laird at Orchardton noticing it at Dundrennan, and thinking 'that's a fair piece of carved stonework – it would look great on my living room wall!'.

Although the rest of the internal floors have gone, you can climb the stair that rises within the thickness of the walls, to emerge out of the little cap-house onto the parapet defences. Orchardton stands on the side of an attractive little dale, dotted with cattle and sleep, and you can look out over this, as no doubt the proud lairds did here in days gone by.

Return to the A711, but this time we cross directly over it, and follow the signs for Castle Douglas, one or two junctions further on route, but it is well signposted. On the first leg of the five-mile drive to the town, you will see that there are some impressive pine trees lining the route, some of the biggest I have seen in Scotland. There are one or two well-signposted junctions for Castle Douglas, then we come up beside Carlingwark, the local loch, and it is this stretch of water that caused Castle Douglas to come into being. There was only a tiny hamlet here, by the name of Causwayend, but drainage began on the loch as it had marl beds. Marl is a mixture of mud and lime in a rocky form, which can be broken up to be used as a fertiliser. So the town began to thrive and took the name of Carlingwark from the loch. In 1792, these marl pits became the property of Sir William Douglas, and was renamed by him, Castle Douglas. It is a bustling little place in the summer months, with a long main street with many shops.

When you reach this main street, coming to it at a right angle, a turn left will take you to the local attractions. After a mile you reach the Threave Estate, which is under the care of the National Trust for Scotland, and contains a mansion built in the 1800s. It has fine gardens, especially noted for its daffodils and rhododendrons. A little further on and you reach a round-about on a newer stretch of the A75 where it by-passes the town. You drive straight through this roundabout on to a minor road that goes to, and is signposted, Threave Castle.

There is a little car park, from where there is a walk of three-quarters of a mile to the castle itself. It is a pleasant walk on a dry day, the well defined path running between fields where you will get a chance to say hello to the local cows. It is a level walk, and this brings you to the edge of the River Dee, where the castle stands proud on an island in the centre of the river. It is a tall, square, battlemented tower, massive but roofless, and surrounded by remains of a strong outer wall, with circular towers at the four angles. It has a long and complex history, this place, and I will touch on some of it here. There was most likely timber fortifications on the island before the days of the current castle. King Robert the Bruce's brother, Edward, is on record as having burnt an island during his campaign in order to suppress revolt in Galloway, and it is likely that this was the place. Bruce's son,

David II, granted Threave to the Douglases in 1369, and it was Archie the Grim, a man we have already come across in this book, who built the castle before you.

In 1455, James II marched on Threave to quash Douglas power, and in the bombardment, mighty Mons Meg, the enormous cannon kept today at Edinburgh Castle, was deployed. From that time on Threave became a Royal fortress, but had a succession of keepers, including another Douglas. Its keeper in 1513, Sir John Dunbar, was slain alongside King James IV at Flodden.

In 1640 the castle was besieged for 13 weeks by a force of Covenanters. It was in use right up to the time of the Napoleonic Wars, when the castle was used to house prisoners. It then fell into ruin, but was handed over to the state for preservation in 1913.

The island on which the castle stands is 20 acres in extent, and so had ample room for cattle or sheep to graze, for a small community to reside, and to make the fortress self sufficient. The river in which it stands, issues from Loch Ken, already visited. There is a ferry service that carries visitors over to explore the castle and island, and although it is only a short hop over the river, it gives an extra edge to an interesting visit.

Make your way back to the roundabout on the A75, where we turn left, eastwards, towards Dumfries, only one leg of our journey left before we leave Scottish soil.

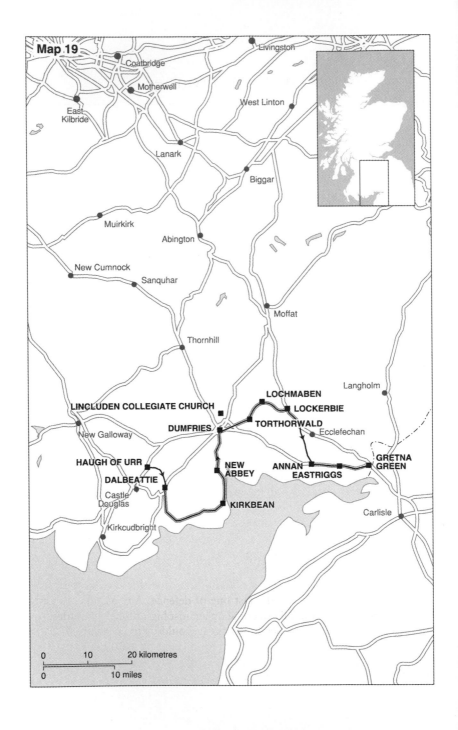

Map 19

Livingston

Coatbridge

Motherwell

West Linton

East
Kilbride

Lanark

Biggar

Muirkirk

Abington

New Cumnock

Sanquhar

Moffat

Thornhill

Langholm

LOCHMABEN

LINCLUDEN COLLEGIATE CHURCH

LOCKERBIE

DUMFRIES

TORTHORWALD

Ecclefechan

New Galloway

GRETNA
GREEN

HAUGH OF URR

NEW
ABBEY

ANNAN
EASTRIGGS

DALBEATTIE

Castle
Douglas

KIRKBEAN

Carlisle

Kirkcudbright

0   10   20 kilometres

0   10 miles

CHAPTER NINETEEN

The Final Frontier

THIS CHAPTER BEGINS AT THE TURN OFF FOR HAUGH OF URR AND EXPLORES DALBEATTIE, NEW ABBEY, DUMFRIES, LOCHMABEN, LOCKERBIE, HODDAM, ANNAN AND GRETNA GREEN, AND FOLLOWS THE A74 SOUTH TO THE BORDER.

CONTINUE TO FOLLOW the A75, and a few miles on you will see the sign pointing the way off to your right to the Haugh of Urr, the B794. We drive down past the village, and after half a mile, the Motte of Urr can be seen a few hundred yards away on our right. It is a large man-made earthwork, the centre of which rises high and circular over the surrounding fields, so you should be able to spot it easily enough.

Just after you have driven past it, Netheryett Farm is on your right. It should be possible to park at the farm if you show a little consideration. Netheryett basically means the back or lower gate.

The access to the farm leads down to a ford on the River Urr, but the water is deep and not to be attempted. Once you have parked, you will notice that a path runs along the river for a hundred yards to a little metal bridge, where you can cross, and come back on the other bank to the opposite side of the ford. Here a gate with its little sign saying 'Motte of Urr' lets you gain access to the field in which the motte stands. Don't look at it from a distance and think you can't be bothered. A walk to the top is an absolute must, as you get a completely different aspect of this place from the top, and it is nothing like the view from the road. From the top you can understand the defensive nature of its construction.

The path up takes you through a breach in the outer ditch. From here you walk toward the central mound within the inner ditch. If you walk round to the other side of this, there is a path running up the central mound at an angle of 45° which is the easiest way to the top. Once on the summit, walk to the far edge and look down upon the ditches. The outer ditch actually runs round a pretty big area, forming a fortified and defensible 'bailey', where there would have been outbuildings and room for cattle and horses. This higher central area was the last line of defence. Any attackers would have to cross the ditches, only to come up against high timber palisades.

Standing up here lets you see how easy it would be to spear an assailant down in that ditch, never mind standing atop defences to do the same. This place is the best part of a thousand years old, and it must have been an incredible sight when it was at its height of power.

But it is not really that which really knocks me out about the Motte of Urr, it is the work that has gone in to the building of the place, the actual man-hours involved. It is all man-made of course, and that huge outer ditch was dug with nothing more than muscle power and rudimentary spades. I wonder if they had wheelbarrows?

And more than this is the organisation to do it all. I know the Egyptians managed the pyramids, but they had a whole empire to work on them. Here, the lord has got the locals together, and they have built this impressive relic of lordly power.

The ditches must have been quite a size originally if there is that much on show today, vegetation growing over them, and animals walking over them. You should take a stroll around the inside of the outer ditch and marvel at the work involved. Urr is probably the biggest example of this type of fort in Scotland.

And who built it?

It may be that the area within the outer ditch is ancient, and probably around 1000, the Lord of Galloway created the motte in the middle, with a timber-built pitch or mud-coated tower on its summit.

We stroll back down across the bridge over the River Urr, where you get the odd splash on the river's surface from a fish trying to catch a tasty midgie, and there is usually an angler in sight somewhere trying to catch those self-same fish. Never been tempted by fishing; maybe it's because I'm a Pisces, maybe it's because I don't see the glamour in hooking some poor beast through the mouth.

Follow the road on, and it is only a few miles to the little town of Dalbeattie. Just before you enter the town, you may catch a glimpse of a tower house over to your right. This is Buittle Place, built in the 1500s and still in use as a farmhouse. To its east are the scant remains of the earlier Buittle Castle, which was the home of Devorgilla of Galloway, mother of King John Balliol. Many of the stones of the earlier structure are probably incorporated in the later tower.

Dalbeattie was founded as a little village in 1780, and it grew and prospered because of the granite quarries that opened in its vicinity. Hundreds were once employed here as quarriers, hewers and polishers. It was granite from Dalbeattie that built the docks at both Chatham and Liverpool in England, and the famous Thames embankment in London is constructed from Dalbeattie granite.

If you wish a look at the place, simply follow the signs for the town centre, and then continuing right through the centre, the road will lead you to the A710, signposted for the Solway Coast. This pleasant road runs through some little hamlets like Barnbarroch and Colvend. We then come into Sandyhills, which as its name implies, has an enormous beach, very much a tidal place, and there are some vast reaches of sand exposed when the tide is out. England is now clearly visible to the south. The hills of England's Lake District are very prominent.

The road hugs the coast for the next few miles, but unfortunately there are few good views south, as there are bushes growing profusely between the road and the beaches below which stop you seeing the panorama, unless, of course, it is winter.

Inland, on your left, there are some quite big hills, this peninsula that juts into the Solway containing high Criffell and its outliers.

Through Mainsriddle, and then a fragment of a castle appears, standing beside a farm a few hundred yards away on your right. You can, if you wish, drive down the little side-road for a look. This is Wreath's. There is only a corner fragment, perhaps 25 feet high. It was built in the 1500s, and it belonged to the Regent Morton. He became regent of Scotland after Mary, Queen of Scots' flight to England, but when James VI came to the throne, Morton's downfall was plotted. He was executed by the axe in Edinburgh in 1581, and he is buried in Edinburgh's Greyfriars Churchyard, but his grave is not marked. The Maxwell family then inherited this tower, but it fell into disuse centuries ago, and its stones were purloined for other purposes.

A little further on and we drive into the pretty village of Kirkbean, Criffell rising to your left. You will see the sign pointing off to your right, marked 'John Paul Jones' Cottage 1¼', There are one or two junctions on the minor roads, but they are well signposted.

The cottage where he was born is open April to September, 10–5, Tuesday to Sunday. As you approach the place, there are the gates to a large house and estate, but John Paul Jones was not born anywhere as grand as that, his birthplace is a tiny cottage just a little further on the right.

John Paul was born here (he added the Jones later) on July 6, 1747, the year after Culloden. Obviously, the proximity of the cottage to water shaped John's train of thought. At 13 he signed on as an apprentice seaman, and by 21 was a captain. He seems to have had a violent temperament, and his is a life punctuated by many exploits, good and bad.

At the outbreak of the American Revolution, he was in command of a ship of the then tiny American Navy. He made a daring raid on Whitehaven, across the Solway in England, and it was this exploit that made him famous. He fought a naval battle off Flamborough Head, and during this engagement, when asked if he wished to surrender, Jones replied, 'I have not yet begun to fight'. Another of his famous lines was, 'I wish to have no connection with any ship that does not sail fast, for I intend to go in harm's way'.

Jones died of pneumonia in Paris on July 18, 1792. He was only 45.

In 1905 his body was exhumed from its unmarked grave in Paris, and returned with great honour to the United States. Today he lies in a magnificent marble tomb, modelled on that of Napoleon, in the chapel crypt of Annapolis Naval Academy. From birth in this humble cottage, at the end of his life he was regarded as the founding father of the American Navy.

The cottage has artefacts of Jones' life and has an audiovisual attraction too.

Back to Kirkbean, and onwards on the A710. Criffell dominates on your left, and when the tide is out, the Solway on your right can look like a huge expanse of sand. We are heading for New Abbey, the village taking its name from the abbey that still dominates the place. It is *New* Abbey because the building here was new in comparison to Dundrennan, although this one dates back to the 1200s.

As you drive into the village, you will see the tower of the abbey, and you drive in to the car park on your right.

Sweetheart, as this is the abbey's name, is red, warm bright red, and very different to the grey stone of Galloway. Makes a bit more sense though when you find that the stone of Sweetheart Abbey was brought across the River Nith from Dumfriesshire, where this red stone is more prevalent.

If you look beyond the car park, you will see that much of the old precinct wall of the abbey is intact – an unusual thing to see. And you will notice that it is constructed of the local grey stone. There are some large boulders in the fabric of this wall, and again, it must have involved some Herculean effort to build it. Scotland must have been very rocky at one time. Over the centuries all the stone lying about has been used to build walls like this, to construct houses, and fields have been cleared and the stones used to build drystone dykes to enclose them. Must have been stones lying everywhere at one time. Now you know why cairns of stones are the traditional way of marking something in Scotland. Handy. And cheap too.

At this side of Sweetheart Abbey lies its graveyard. Nothing too ancient in the way of gravestones, but it must have been used as a place of burial for many centuries. We will have a look at this first before we go into the abbey.

As you enter, you will see a stone facing you, with the inscription: 'Near this spot is the unmarked grave of William Paterson who died in 1719. Founder of the Bank of England, 1694. Originator of the Darien Scheme, 1698. Paterson was born in 1658 at Skipmyre Farm, Tinwald, Lochmaben.'

I remember being quite taken aback and excited the first time I discovered this stone. Paterson was born into a humble origin, but had a good head for finance, and among his other achievements he, as you can see, founded the Bank of England. His ideas for Darien were reasonably sound too. It was the planning for the expedition that was wrong. Darien was the Scots' stab at starting a colony of their own. William of Orange was on the throne of England, and did not want the Scots to form trading bases abroad. He saw it as a rival outfit to the Dutch East India Company, and he was, after all, a

Dutchman. The Scots took the idea of Darien, modern Panama, to heart, and something like half the monetary wealth of Scotland was sunk into the project. Everyone who had money to invest, from the landed gentry to your ordinary Scot in the street who had a little money in savings, invested in the scheme.

The three ships that set out from Leith, the port of Edinburgh, had patriotic Scots names: the *Caledonia*, the *St Andrew* and the *Unicorn*. England made it clear that they would not impede any attacks made on the Scots settlers by other seafaring nations.

The place chosen in Panama was given the name New Caledonia. The Scots were unaware of the humidity and the sickness that they would encounter, and carried a bizarre cargo of combs, parasols and Bibles – things that they thought they would be able to trade with the natives. The scheme eventually collapsed, most of the settlers dying, including Paterson's wife, and all the money invested was lost. The only bright spot in all of this was that when attacked by a force of Spaniards numbering some 1,600, 200 of the Scots routed them with much slaughter. When word of this fight reached Edinburgh, the mob took to the streets, fired up at this display of 'the auld Scots spirit'. They demanded that every house in the city should have a light in the window in recognition of this feat, and then marched about the streets smashing any window unlit. They managed to cause £5,000 of damage at 1700 prices! The loss of money at Darien had bankrupted Scotland, and promise of reimbursement to the gentry, who of course were the only ones entitled to vote, pushed through the Act of Union with England in 1707.The ordinary people rioted on the streets of Scotland's cities in protest. No wonder that Robert Burns penned the lines: 'We are bought and sold for English gold – such a parcel of rogues in a nation!'

The modern Panama Canal is the reality of the dream that the Scots had of creating a colony on the narrow isthmus here. The canal has proved that it was not just a fanciful idea, and the colony, if successful, would have reaped the rewards of ships not having to navigate the 10,000 extra miles on any voyage to round Cape Horn.

We could have been contenders! We blew it. So you may want a stroll around the graveyard, admiring the abbey with the backdrop of Criffell, then as you leave you can glance again at this stone to Paterson and think about what might have been.

Sweetheart Abbey has a tale of romance behind its foundation. I have already mentioned Devorgilla, the mother of King John Balliol, and it is her we should thank for this beautiful edifice, ruined as it is. Devorgilla's husband was John de Balliol, a nobleman who died at Barnard Castle in England in 1269, and was there buried. All of him, that is, but his heart. Devorguilla loved him deeply, and she had his heart embalmed and placed in an ivory casket. She took this casket everywhere with her. She caused work to be started on the abbey here in 1275, naming it Dulce Cor, or sweetheart. It was a Cistercian establishment. She died in 1290 at the age of 80, and she was buried here, her husband's heart clasped to her breast.

You can pay a fee and wander the ruins of Sweetheart Abbey, and most visitors want to see Devorgilla's tomb. She is carved in effigy as she was laid to rest, recumbent, holding her husband's heart. Alas, the tomb is badly damaged, centuries of neglect have taken their toll, but modern sections have been inserted to show you how it once was. Quite a woman, was Devorgilla. She founded Balliol College at Oxford in England, and built the bridge over the River Nith at Dumfries, which we will visit shortly. She obviously had the money though, which matters considerably. We can all fall deeply in love, but we don't all have the wherewithal to express it by building Sweetheart Abbey or the Taj Mahal! Acting Devil's Advocate against my own writing now! Beautiful place, Sweetheart Abbey, and one visit will make it imbed itself into your soul.

There are other attractions at New Abbey. The old corn mill is open to visitors and is on your left as you drive through the village. It was built in the 1700s, is water-powered, and demonstrations are given to visitors. You can purchase a ticket for this place and the abbey together.

Just beyond, among the trees, stands Shambellie House, which contains a Museum of Costume. The house was built for the Stewart family in 1856, and the great-grandson of the original owner, Charles Stewart, donated the house and private clothing collection to the National Museums of Scotland in 1977.

Shambellie is one of those almost funny Scottish names that we all take for granted, and tourists find fascinating. Like Crossmyloof. Or Gowkthrapple. Or the destination boards seen on the frontage of Scottish buses, like Auchenshoogle.

My mum actually got on a bus to Auchenshoogle once, just so she could see where it was, and what it was like. When she returned home she was laden with weird trinkets and talismen that she had bought from the locals. Only kidding about that last bit, but she did get on the bus.

The woodland surrounding Shambellie is regarded as having the finest Scots pines in Scotland, although I'm not sure who does the marking for that one.

As we follow the road towards Dumfries, the River Nith is over to our right. Although it is not visible from the road, we are following its shallow valley. We last encountered the Nith at Drumlanrig Castle, but here it is on the last course of its journey down to the Solway.

We come to the outskirts of Dumfries, known as the 'Queen of the South' and this is also the title of the town's football team. At our road's end we turn right towards the town centre on the other bank of the Nith. As we come down to the bridge over the Nith though, there is a little detour I would like you to take. You will notice that the road that branches off left at the traffic lights is the A76 leading to Kilmarnock. There is an old place I would like you to see a mile or two up this road, so turn left on this small deviation. On the first stretch there is a modern church on your right that has a bizarre steeple where the sloping roof almost reaches the ground. Straight on, through a few roundabouts, still following the signs for Kilmarnock. We pass a strange statue of a rhino and its baby, then look for the sign that points off to your right: 'Lincluden Collegiate Church 1mile'. Just follow the signs through the housing, then you come to the Abbey Inn, at the head of Abbey Lane, and you are best to park here and walk the last few yards.

Lincluden is an interesting place, standing within its grassy park, and not often visited. Most times I have been here, there has been perhaps just one or two others, if there are any other visitors at all. There is no charge for entry. If the gate is unlocked you can stroll round. It may look very ruined at first glance, but in many ways Lincluden is a gem, and it has much to commend it.

Nearest you as you enter the gate is the collegiate (call-e-gee-ate) church. This was founded by our old friend Archie the Grim in 1400, shortly before he died. Enter and you will see that there is still much ornamentation visible in the stonework. There is enough tracery to show us how rich, beautiful and varied this place must have been in its heyday, all those roundels and bosses once painted in bright colours.

The most striking feature though must be the ornate tomb, a little decayed and weatherworn, at the other, left-hand end. This is the last resting place of the Princess Margaret, daughter of King Robert III of Scotland. She married Archie, the fourth Earl of Douglas and first Duke of Touraine in France. He was slain in battle at Verneuil in France in 1424, and is buried at St Brides in Douglas. Margaret retired to Lincluden and made it her home.

The range extending out from the church has six vaulted cellars, and here resided the Provost and 12 canons who ran the place. In 1560 when Provost Stewart took over, he added the fortified tower, and adapted the range of cellared buildings, turning them into a fortified house. You will see by the footings in the grass in front of the church that there were once much more extensive religious buildings, but these may have been used to build the tower.

A walk round to the other side will reveal that there are the remains of an ornamental garden, and here was once a bowling green, flower garden and parterres.

One thing you must do is walk to the top of the mound beyond the church. It is thought that this may be a motte-hill, man-made, and the site of an early fortification. There do appear to be the remains of ditches etc.

around the perimeter. From here you suddenly realise what an impressive site this is. The River Nith is suddenly apparent at the other side, and you will notice that the Cluden Water runs round the other side of the church grounds to run into the Nith, making this quite a defensive site. The view of the church and ancillary buildings is very impressive.

There was a nunnery on this site before the current buildings, founded by the Lord of Galloway in the 1100s, but Archie the Grim had them expelled for 'insolence' and other irregularities. I would like to have known just what these nuns were up to!

So, we have the motte-hill, the grave of a princess, the ruins, the gardens and the now-vanished nunnery. Quite a lot in what looks like a fairly uninteresting ruin at first glance.

From here, follow the A76 back towards the centre of Dumfries. When the traffic lights are reached, you turn left to cross the River Nith. A glance to your right, downstream, will reveal Devorgilla's bridge. If at all possible, try and park in this area. Obviously Devorgilla's Bridge will be our first objective. It was built in the 1200s and originally had nine arches. The river has been contained over the centuries, and three arches have disappeared. That is why there is a flight of steps to give access now at one end.

If you look a little downstream, there is a weir-like thing, usually a few seagulls standing atop it, legs in the current, which the locals call the Caul. There is an arty memorial to Devorgilla at either end, facing each other across the river.

At the far end of the bridge the old Bridge House is open as a little museum. It is quite a tiny place, but its few rooms are crammed with old and interesting artefacts. Robert Burns, Scotland's national poet used to visit this place at one time, and it is regarded as being the oldest house in Dumfries, as it was built in 1660 by James Birkmyre, a barrel-maker.

From here if we turn left at the bridge end and walk downstream a little, we come to an old mill, now used as a visitor centre which has a museum dedicated to Robert Burns. Entry is free to most of the building, but you can pay a small fee to gain access to other parts. The Caul was constructed to supply the water for this mill, and although it is now disused, its stones, stretching across the Nith, form a large part of the mental picture that Dumfries conjures up.

A walk uphill from this Burns Centre (you can ask for directions inside) will take you up to the town's museum, a fascinating place, with many historical artefacts found in Dumfriesshire, and there is a camera obscura there too. Don't know what a camera obscura is? Only one way to find out!

We really want to take a walk through Dumfries town centre to have a look at some of its attractions, and it is best to walk onwards from the bridge where we drove over the river. That was the Buccleuch Street Bridge

(Buck-loo, remember?) and we walk along Buccleuch Street leading from it. At the end of this street, we turn right into Castle Street.

Castle Street, of course, holds a clue in its name. The large church on the other side of the road, Greyfriars Church, is on the site of the original castle of Dumfries. Greyfriars was built in 1866–7, and has a spire 164 feet high. It succeeded a previous church on the same site, built in 1727, using some of the materials from the ancient castle. It was most likely this site that gave the town its name *dun*, meaning fort, and *phreas*, among shrubs. On his way to the siege of Caerlaverock Castle, south of here, Edward Longshanks seized and garrisoned Dumfries Castle. He built a high square keep, part of which remained standing until 1719.

Dumfries suffered over the years, due to its proximity to the English border. It was burnt several times by raiders from down south. But the town had at least a little taste of revenge, when after another burning by the English in 1536, local nobleman Lord Maxwell, raised a body of men and raided south, burning to ashes the English town of Penrith.

Castle Street leads into Burns Square, with its white statue of Robert Burns, Scotland's national poet, in its centre. It was unveiled on 6 April 1882, and was the work of a Mrs DO Hill. The monument has the poet's dog, Luath, lying at his feet. As my publisher is Luath, you now know where the name came from. Luath, the Gaelic for swift, is actually pronounced loo-ah, but all the non-Gaelic speakers in Scotland tend to just say Loo-ath!

You must look for the plaque that graces the wall between two shops in the square, with the Lion Rampant of Scotland at its head. Its inscription reads:

> Here stood the monastery of the Grey Friars, where on Thursday 10th February 1306, Robert the Bruce aided by Sir Roger Kirkpatrick slew the Red Comyn and opened the final stage of the war for Scottish Independence which ended on the Field of Bannockburn 1314. I mak siccar.

It was erected by the citizens of Dumfries and the Saltire Society. This plaque marks a crucial incident that shapes the Scotland we know today.

Sir William Wallace had been murdered in London on 23 August 1305. Scotland was a rudderless ship. There were two men capable of leading Scotland in renewed resistance to Longshanks, and these were Robert the Bruce, and John, commonly called the Red Comyn. These two were like dogs eyeing the same bone. Legend says that Comyn had betrayed Bruce to Longshanks, and Bruce confronted him with this in the monastery that once stood here. Hot words were spat out, tempers flared, then Bruce drew his dagger and plunged it deep into Comyn's chest. As Bruce had stabbed Comyn in front of the church altar, he was well aware that this would be seen as an act of sacrilege, and he knew that when word of this got as far as the Pope in Rome, that he would be excommunicated – so he had to act fast.

As he stumbled outside, his followers asked what was wrong. He replied that he 'feared he may have slain Comyn'. One of his captains, Kirkpatrick of Closeburn, when he heard that Comyn may only be wounded, replied, 'I mak siccar!' (I'll make sure). It has ever since been his family's motto.

Kirkpatrick then ran inside and dispatched Comyn, while Sir Christopher Seton, Bruce's brother-in-law, slew Comyn's uncle.

So, Bruce immediately took Dumfries Castle, just across the road in 1306, and it was the first castle to fall to him. From here he went north to be crowned on the Moot Hill at Scone.

Anyway, the reason I go into this is because when the row of shops at the plaque was being built in the 1800s, the remains of the Greyfriars Monastery were uncovered – with the bodies of Comyn and his uncle at one side of the altar. After a bit of an archaeological investigation, the building work went ahead. The remains of the monastery still lie underneath. The shops at the plaque do not have basements, whereas the others in the row do. There was a gap left underneath the shops at the plaque, with a roof-like structure over the remains. It is strange to stand here knowing that the Red Comyn still lies below. We've all got to end up somewhere, I suppose.

From the plaque, continue on into the High Street, now completely pedestrianised. On your left you will see the close that leads into the Hole i' the Wa' Inn. That, of course, is local speak for the Hole in the Wall. This pub has graced the town since 1620, and as Robert Burns (1759–96) used to have the odd drink in this establishment, his portrait hangs above the entrance, with a stone lion on either side. A little further and you will see there is a column on your left, raised to the memory of the Duke of Queensberry, and it bears the date 22 October 1778. Here stands one of those edifices that every town has, something that the locals identify with as *theirs*. It does not have to be the biggest or most magnificent structure in the place, just something that they collectively have real affection for. Even in Chicago, a city with mighty skyscrapers such as the Sears Tower, all the locals tend to recognise the old water tower, an early stone construction which stands dwarfed in Michigan Avenue by the grandeur round about, as their talisman.

In Dumfries, it is the Mid-steeple, which stands in the centre of the High Street. It was built in 1707 on the site of the Mercat Cross, and it became the heart of the place. It was the town hall, town guardhouse, and weigh-house. At the far side it has a staircase, and here you will notice a strip of iron attached to the wall. This is the Scots ell, and it was used for measuring cloth by the locals to make sure they were getting their money's worth! We last saw one in the churchyard of Dornoch Cathedral. There is also a plate showing the distances to various towns on the side of the building. One of these place mentioned is Huntingdon, deep in England, and this may seem a strange addition, but the Earldom of Huntingdon was a fief held by the earlier kings of Scotland, and so has been mentioned here.

A little further, and the cobbled street widens, and here stands an iron ornamental fountain that is gaily painted and dates from 1882. The building directly right of this fountain, currently a bookshop, was the Commercial Hotel in the 1700s, and it was here that Bonnie Prince Charlie lodged on his return from England during the '45. The Jacobite army demanded 1,000 pairs of shoes from the town, which is not surprising, as they had marched all the way from Glenfinnan in the Highlands, to Derby, deep in England, then back to Dumfries. Many of Charlie's army, of course, merely took the footwear off the nearest townsfolk, seeing their own need as the greater.

It seems that Dumfries folk have long memories too. About a year back, I was giving an illustrated talk on the Jacobites to a party of children in a school at Linwood, near Glasgow. As I was showing slides in the school hall, a teacher, just passing through, looked at the screen and said: 'Jacobites! – took our shoes!' Speaking to her in the staff room later, it did indeed turn out that she was from Dumfries!

A little further, there is the entrance to a little shopping mall, called the Loreburne Centre. This name is a throwback to the days of English invasions and burnings of the town. When the alarm was raised, the cry went out 'A' loreburn! A' loreburn!' At the side of the town, facing the English border, there was a stream that ran to the Nith called the lower burn. For the townsfolk to try to defend their town, they would gather at this natural barrier, the cry being a corruption of 'All to the lower burn!'

Other than this titbit of history, Dumfries people call themselves *Doonhamers*, a Scots version of 'down-homers'.

See Scotland? See the colour?

On the left of the street opposite the Loreburne Centre, stands the close leading to the Globe Inn. The Globe has a strong association with Robert Burns, and is a must for anyone with an interest in the man. It was built in 1610, and as you walk through to get a look at it, you will see the walls are actually out of line, the building having settled over the centuries.

Burns actually stayed here on occasion, even the chair he used whilst having a drink is still on show. If you ask nicely, and they are not run off their feet, the staff may be good enough to let you see some of their Burns memorabilia. A barmaid took a friend and I through to a side-room crammed with Burns artefacts, where sits his chair, then upstairs to the bedroom, exactly as it was when Burns last slept there with his wife. The barmaid informed me that sometimes huge Burns lovers (good descriptive word) come to hire this room and spend the night here. I asked her if she was 'going steady', and when she said yes, I asked her if she was never tempted to spend the night here with her boyfriend. 'No way', she said, 'This room gives me the creeps!', and I actually saw her shiver. I can understand that. You can actually sense his presence here more than in any other place I have visited that is connected with the man. He has scratched some lines on the window with a diamond ring too, and you can still see him crouched here, working away, in your mind's eye.

The Globe is not a posh establishment, and on one visit when there was a Rangers/Celtic football match on television, the place was crammed, and the language was choice. It was probably not far removed from the Globe that Burns knew on a weekend evening. But that was his strength. He read the passions, mind and emotions of the ordinary Scot, of the ordinary man, and he put them down in words in a way that had never been done before.

When I see Burns in paintings, I think I see a softer, even slightly effeminate version of the real Burns. He was a man that liked his drink, and his women, and good company. He was a ploughman, and knew the real meaning of a long day of hard labour. I think the real Burns would have been quite 'hard'. The sort of sinewy, fit man you would not really like to have taken a punch from. But he had it all. He had a fabulous ability, coupled with good looks. The ladies liked him, and men admired him. He died young, only in his 30s, but that has only served to increase the legend. And to top all that, he was a Scot.

He had to be really.

We have a few more things connected with Burns to see, so we continue on to the end of the street. Keep your eyes peeled for direction signs for Burns' house.

Almost opposite High Street, just slightly right, is St Michael's Street, and we follow this. There is a little street off to the left called Burns Street, and Burns' house is down this a little on your right. It's free to get in (hurray!) and the house, as you can imagine, has Burns relics, and he has carved his signature onto one of the windows upstairs. He wrote some of his most memorable work while in Dumfries, including *A man's a man for a' that*, and *My love is like a red, red rose*. He penned the words to *Scots wha hae wi' Wallace bled*, using an old marching song from the time of Wallace and Bruce as his melody, and it has since become the unrecognised National Anthem of Scotland. Here too was written *Auld Lang Syne*, which is sung all over the planet. These were either written in this house or in a house he occupied in the town's Bank Street. He died in this house though, on 21 July 1796. His wife, Jean Armour, lived here until her death in 1834.

Back to the end of the road, where the imposing steeple of St Michael's Church is just across the junction.

Never have I seen a graveyard as crowded as this; there must be some jostling for position going on underground here. It is packed with obelisks, columns, urns, and many large gravestones – 3,300 in the original graveyard in all! It has since been extended at its far side. There will be many more Scots buried here than there are markers, though, as there has been a church on this site for more than eight centuries. The present church was built in 1744–5, finished just in time to see Bonnie Prince Charlie march into Dumfries.

If you walk through the graveyard you will notice that the graves of Robert Burns' personal friends are marked. There is a pedestal to the right of the church listing them and where their graves lie – 45 of them in total.

If you go to the back right-hand corner of the graveyard you will find the little white-painted mausoleum where lies the body of Scotland's national poet, his wife Jean, and their children. You can look through the door and see where he lies.

At the back left-hand corner of the graveyard, the site of his original burial place is marked. Burns was buried in a single grave, but he was later moved to the mausoleum, and when his wife died, she joined him here. A report has survived regarding the opening of his original grave, on 19 September 1815. It was written by John MacDairmid, later editor of the *Dumfries Courier*, the local newspaper:

> The remains of the great poet, to all experience nearly entire ... The scalp still covered in hair, the teeth perfect and white. ... Some of the workmen stood bare and uncovered, and at the same time felt their frames thrilling with some indefinable emotion as they gazed on the ashes of him whose fame is as wide as the world itself. But the effect was momentary for when they proceeded to insert a shell case below the coffin, the head separated from the trunk, and the whole body with the exception of the bones, crumbled into dust.

When Jean Armour was interred beside Robert, a cast was taken of his skull, and I have seen several examples on my travels. One belongs to my friend, Colin Hunter McQueen, who seems to know more about Burns than any man I have ever met, and has an astonishing collection of Burns memorabilia. On top of that he is a fabulous artist and handyman and seems to be able to make things like replica swords as if he were born to it. Yes, I am jealous!

From St Michael's, you may want to walk down to the River Nith and return to your car, but if you can be bothered with a slight extension to your walk, go for this one. Turn right as you exit the church, up Brooms Road. A few hundred yards further at the roundabout, turn left into Leafield Road. Follow this until you reach York Place, but en route you should be able to spot the facade on the top of St Mary's Church showing just ahead of you. The church is on the opposite side of York Place, standing atop a small mound-like hill. This slight eminence has a name – the Crystal Mount, a strange name, and a fascinating story behind it. I was really pleased with myself when I put it all together. I did make a point of asking people when I was last in Dumfries if they could direct me to the Crystal Mount, but the name seems to have died out of common usage. But they were all able to direct me to St Mary's, which stands atop it. St Mary's was built between 1837 and 1839 and cost £2,400. It stands on the site of a chantry built in the early 1300s, and this is the story of that earlier religious establishment.

After Bruce's slaying of the Red Comyn, where his brother-in-law, Sir Christopher Seton killed Comyn's uncle, Edward Longshanks came seeking vengeance. Bruce had made Seton captain of Loch Doon Castle, and, when that castle fell, Seton was brought back to Dumfries to be horribly executed, an example to be made of him to try and dishearten those who fought for Scotland's freedom. He was executed on an eminence on the outskirts of Dumfries, the spot where St Mary's stands today. Robert the Bruce's sister, Christian or Christina, depending on the source used, loved Seton dearly, and was so distraught at his death that she founded a little chapel on the spot, dedicated to the Holy Rood.

It was while reading through the work of John Barbour, his epic poem written about the life of Bruce in the 1370s, that I noticed he referred to Seton as 'Sir Christoll'. It has been said that the common people of Scotland, with whom he was a particular favourite, coined the nickname. That would explain why this spot was called locally the Crystal Mount.

There is still a little relic of the original chapel built by Christian Bruce in memory of her brave husband. In front of the church, at the top of the stairs leading up, there is an old sundial to the left, but an interesting stone structure to the right. It looks like an aumbry, similar to the one seen inside Orchardton Tower, taken from Dundrennan Abbey. It has an inscribed stone set into it which, unfortunately, is becoming very weather-worn, but a little plaque has been added giving the original inscription:

These stones, relics of the ancient chapel, dedicated to the Holy Rood, endowed by King Robert the Bruce, in memory of Sir Christopher, or Chrystal Seatoun, are here placed by Major James Adair 1840.

Well done, Major James, a little something saved for posterity. It means someone like me can come along, over 160 years after the fact, and appreciate your efforts.

If you walk to the back of the church, you can see the tall spine of Greyfriars church over at about ten o'clock from your position, and this will give you your bearings to return to your original location.

There are road signs all over town directing you towards Lockerbie on the A709, and it is this road we take next. We cross the A75 on the outskirts of town at a roundabout, but just keep following the signs for Lockerbie. You cross the northern part of the flat expanse of Lochar Moss, a once waterlogged morass that served to partially defend Dumfries' eastern approaches.

The ground starts to rise as we drive up into the little village of Torthorwald, a pleasant wee place, with a panoramic view back towards Dumfries and Criffell. Torthorwald Castle remains are on your right as you enter the village. Torthorwald Castle is quite difficult to approach. The castle was built in the latter half of the 1300s by the Carlyle family, but it stands on earlier earthworks, the remains of a prior fortification. This was built in the 1200s by the de Torthorwalds, who have given their name to the village. The ditches are still quite waterlogged, and you have to pick your approach carefully. You can see that there is a rougher grey stone used on the outer walls, whilst there has been red dressed stone used on the inside.

In 1609 the Carlyle heiress married a Douglas and brought the castle under that family's control. Why the place fell into decay, I have no idea, but it has obviously lain derelict for many, many years.

On through Torthorwald, admiring the view to your left as the road swings to climb the escarpment. A few miles and we drop into the little town of Lochmaben, the Kirk Loch on our right, as we hit the town. As we swing into the town's broad main street, there is a statue of Robert the Bruce to your left. It stands on the site of the town's mercat cross. It stands on a pedestal ten feet high, of Dalbeattie granite. The statue itself, crafted by John Hutchison RSA is eight feet high, has Bruce clasping his sword in his left hand, and was unveiled on 13 September 1879. It is fitting that such a statue stands here, as the Bruces were Lords of Annandale, and Lochmaben is one of its main settlements.

Drive down the main street, and you will see the church in front of you. If you take the road into the right directly before this church, called Mounseys Wynd, facing you over the wall at the end of this street is the old mote-hill that once held the castle of the Bruces. It is first mentioned in 1173, when it was held by King William the Lion. After the collapse of their main seat at Annan further south, which we will soon visit, this became their main power base. It is about 20 feet in height, is about 200 feet across, and it now stands on the edge of the town's golf course.

It was superseded by the later Lochmaben Castle, which we will visit next. Back out to the church, and a road runs off down the other side of it, the B7020 signposted Dalton. Follow this for a mile along the wooded western edge of Castle Loch, until you see the sign pointing into a little side road to your left, marked Lochmaben Castle. There is a few hundred yards of this road, the last part a little rough, but drivable with a bit of care.

There are places to park by the castle ruins, and the banks of the Castle Loch are just over to your right. You are on a promontory that juts out into the loch here, and it was once a very defensible site. All the facing stone from the castle has been stripped away, leaving only the rubble constructed cores of the walls, but you can still see what a power this castle once was. There was once a canal cut across the tongue of land jutting into the loch on which the castle stands, adding to its defences, and making it easy to get supplies to the garrison. The remains of this canal, still full of water, run right into the core of the castle.

Although thought by many visitors to be the castle of the Bruces, this castle was actually founded by England's Edward Longshanks to try and consolidate his hold on Scotland after his victory over Wallace at the Battle of Falkirk in 1298. This place, built during the Wars of Independence, has, as you can imagine, seen much action. Robert the Bruce attacked it in 1299, and again in 1301 with an army numbering some 7,000. He captured it in 1306, the English recovered it, but it fell to the Scots again around the time of Bannockburn. As the Bruce family then abandoned the mote hill on the golf course to move here, it has since been linked to their name.

Edward III, with that tiresome English trait of wanting to annexe Scotland, again took Lochmaben in the 1300s. He added some more building work, but good old Archie the Grim captured the place in 1384, bringing it under Douglas control. It remained in Scottish hands from then on, coming under royal control in 1455, and from then on it was much visited by the various King Jameses. By the 1700s the castle lay empty, and like so many other strengths, it was robbed of its stones by enterprising locals.

Although few features remain, it is worth walking around the ruins as it is such an atmospheric place. I always cast my mind back to the days of great armies and siege engines, and I strip away the surrounding trees and the call of the rooks and replace them with flying pennants and the clink of armour. I look at the remains of the rubble inners of the walls and marvel at their builders, who packed the dressed outers with stones and mortar. One or two facing stones remain here and there to give you an idea of what the finished work of its masons once looked like.

From Lochmaben Castle, we retrace our route back to Lochmaben town, and when we come to the church again, we follow the main road right, the A709, for Lockerbie. We follow the opposite shore of Castle Loch for a while, looking across to the trees which hide the castle, then after a straight stretch of a mile we come to the narrow bridge that crosses the River Annan. Over this old bridge, and another straight mile then sees the road swing left and climb out of the dale of the Annan.

Up on the edge of the escarpment, you will see the sign pointing in to a little car park on your left, stating Dryfesdale Cemetery and Garden of Remembrance. You can park and walk straight through the gate into the cemetery. I have always found this graveyard to be a little unusual in the fact that the inscriptions generally give you the address of the house in which the person died. It must be strange if you live locally and notice here that you have passed the grave of someone who died in your house 80 or 100 years ago. In fact, you could probably spot a few with your own address on them.

At the rear, and to the right of the cemetery is the Garden of Remembrance, built in memory of those who lost their lives in the terrorist bombing of Flight 103. That Boeing 747 was blasted out of the skies here on 21 December, 1988, killing the 259 people on board, and 11 residents on the ground. Their ages ranged from two months to 82 years.

A little garden has been created, with a view out to Annandale and Dryfesdale, and the memorial stands facing this scene, the names of the 270 listed upon it. I have been here several times with different people, and although they know what to expect, I have never seen a face yet without the trace of a tear on it.

What really gets everyone are the plaques and stones all around, placed here by the families of the victims. Such inscriptions as 'Dad, we know you are still trying to get back to us', are guaranteed to tug the heart strings.

I remember that time, the time of the Lockerbie Disaster well. I was sitting at home with a few friends when my mate Derek came in. 'I just heard something on the radio about a Jumbo Jet landing on the M74', he said. We were all a bit nonplussed at this information and turned on the television. Bit by bit the news came in. Then there were the photographs over the press during the next few days. All of Scotland was stunned, and I can remember the anger of ordinary Scots that such a thing could happen over their airspace.

I was actually meant to be in Lockerbie the next day. I was working as a relief driver, and I had a series of calls to make in that area, one at the Lockerbie Butter creamery. That day's work was cancelled, and in fact it was weeks before a call was made there again. I remember trips down the M74, and the huge tear in the landscape through the edge of the town, the traffic diverted down the opposite carriageways while emergency repair work was carried out.

It was strange how the bombardment of information in the media affected you. I can remember people glancing up with a flicker of fear every time a particularly low-flying plane went over, or when the sound of aero engines suddenly jumped out of the sky at you.

Lockerbie is just not the sort of place you associate with terrorism, although the place itself has had a turbulent past with the constant feuding of the Maxwells and Johnstones that went on in this area. But, like it has been since the days of clan feuds, a new generation has grown up in

Lockerbie since 1988, which does not remember the disaster, and the horror that it involved.

Standing at the memorial, you can hear the constant rumble of traffic on the M74, only half a mile away. We return to our vehicle and continue on towards Lockerbie and we cross the motorway as we come into the centre of town. Just to the right of the bridge we cross is where the main body of the plane came down, and the large gash that once cut into the town.

At the junction with the main thoroughfare through Lockerbie, we are going to turn right, southbound for Annan, but you may want to turn left first into the centre of town, just to have a look at the place.

Lockerbie's most striking feature is its town hall, with its imposing baronial appearance. It was built in 1891 and cost £8,000. On its first floor there is a memorial window to the disaster, which contains the flags of the 21 nations from which the victims came.

In the area where the Dryfe Water flows into the Annan about a mile west of the town, there was once a huge battle between the Johnstones and the Maxwells, in an area known as Dryfe Sands. The Johnstones, although outnumbered, charged the Maxwells and forced them back towards the town. It was from this fight in 1593 that the famous expression 'a Lockerbie lick' comes, a sword slash to the head, especially a back-handed one delivered from horseback.

There were at least two tower houses in Lockerbie at one time belonging to the Johnstones, as these are mentioned in documents of 1585. One remained until recent times, by the main street, but it has now disappeared.

We head south, where we come to a roundabout, and we follow the B723 for Annan, and once again cross the M74 on a flyover. This is a nice quiet road, with a contrast of woodland and green fields. We pass through a little village called Kettleholm, and a mile or two on you may spot a little tower house on a hilltop before you. This is Repentance Tower, and we will visit it shortly. We come down to the stone bridge over the River Annan, the river now wide, deep, sluggish in places, but wood-lined and attractive.

If you can, pull in to your left and park without being an obstruction just before the bridge, and look over to your left. A field length or so away on the side of the river, you may notice that here is a cluster of gravestones. You can walk along the side of the river to reach them. This cemetery, the old burying ground of Hoddam, is on the site of a chapel founded by St Mungo in AD 573. St Mungo founded the city of Glasgow and is buried in Glasgow Cathedral.

We cross the bridge, and the entrance to Hoddam Castle Caravan Park is immediately on your right. This is the old estate that once surrounded Hoddam Castle, and you can drive in, on through its old woodland on a little one-way system. The castle stands right in the middle of the camp site, derelict but impressive. It is a complex building, with various wings and towers, although not as large as it once was, as one wing has been demolished.

It was built in its current form in the mid-1500s, although earlier work has probably been incorporated. It belonged to Lord Herries, a leading light of the Maxwell Clan, and it probably saw quite a bit of action due to their constant feuds with the Johnstones of Annandale, and because of its proximity to the border with England.

Part of the castle structure was built by stones from a chapel that was pulled down by Lord Herries, and this incurred the wrath of the Archbishop of Glasgow. With its Glasgow connection, this chapel was probably the one that stood at Hoddam burial ground, down at Annan bridge. To try and appease the irate Archbishop, Lord Herries agreed to construct a watchtower that would be of benefit to this neighbourhood, able to warn the folk of English invasions, and it is this tower we will visit next.

Drive on through the caravan park, and you eventually emerge onto a leafy country road, where we turn left. A little further on you will see a signpost, with its path climbing uphill, leading to Repentance Tower. It is a short pull of a few hundred yards up to this little building, looking just like a standard Scottish tower house, but it has a square projection like a big chimney on its roof. This is actually the stance for a brazier which would contain a beacon fire. There is a view from the hilltop over much of the countryside that comprises Scotland's West March of the Border. This fire would be seen from other beacons, and these too would be lit to spread a warning of English invasion.

The tower itself was never used as a residence, but it contains three floors inside. The roof is made of stone slabs to make the building fireproof, and it also once contained a bell to be rung to warn of alarms too. It was built in 1550 or thereabouts, and there was obviously good reason for its construction up here on Trailtrow Hill. A letter was written to the King of Scots in 1570, which stated 'The wache towre upoun Trailtrow callit Repentance mon be mendit of the litill diffacing the Englische army maid of it'. On the lintel of the door, the word REPENTANCE has been carved, and the tower today is surrounded by some old gravestones. The name comes from the fact that it was built to appease the wrath of the bishop of Glasgow.

Back down to your vehicle and a short hop further along takes us to a junction with the road we were on before we diverted through the caravan park. Turn right back onto the B723, and we drive the last few miles on to the little town of Annan.

As you approach the town, most prominent is the tower of its town house. We cross the River Annan to enter the town, on a handsome three-arched bridge built in 1824, at a cost of £8,000. As soon as you have crossed the bridge, take the first left into Battery Street. You can either park here and walk up, or continue round to where you see Moat Road, and the gateway on your left just past here takes you straight into the old mote-hill. As you got through the gate, the bailey of the fortification runs off to your left, its summit some 250 feet across. On your right is the mote-hill, still very tall and with steep sides, but a walk to the top of it will reveal the disaster that overtook it.

It was built by the Bruce Lords of Annandale, from whom came Robert the Bruce, the hero-king. It probably dates from the 1100s, but it only served as their power base for a generation or two when it was swept away by a massive flood of the River Annan. From the top you will see it is only half a mote, the other half-gone like a cake half-eaten.

After this the Bruces moved up Annandale to the mote we visited at Lochmaben.

A later castle was built at Annan to defend the place from the repeated deprivations of the English invaders. It is said that the future King Robert Bruce founded it in 1300. The puppet king, Edward Balliol, whom we last spoke of in connection with the Battle of Dupplin, was here demanding homage from the locals in December 1332. He was surprised by the Lord Douglas at the head of 1,000 horsemen. Henry, Balliol's brother, was slain, and Edward Balliol narrowly escaped over the border to Carlisle on a saddle-less steed in his underwear.

We could do with some more of the Douglas's calibre in this day and age in Scotland.

In 1547, the English invaded under Lord Wharton and sacked and burned the town. Again in 1570, the invaders came, led by the Earl of Sussex, and he grievously damaged the castle. So, in 1609, the townsfolk either used its stones, or converted it into a church, as the repeated deprivations had left them without enough money to build their own. Now no trace of this stone castle survives, as the church it was converted into was swept away in 1875. The old churchyard in the town was the site of the place, obviously its surroundings were used as a cemetery when it was a building used for religious purposes.

Back up to the main street, and the town hall with its impressive steeple dominates this end of the town. It replaced an earlier building, and this one was constructed in 1876 and 1877 at a cost of £4,000.

Along the main street a little, just past the traffic lights, there is a building with a pub at ground-floor level, called the Auberge. This building was Bonnie Prince Charlie's headquarters on his army's retreat back into Scotland on 20 December 1745. It may not look as if the architecture is old enough to date back to that time, but the facade of the building was replaced. You will notice it bears the dates 1700 and 1903 on the front. 1700 was the date of the original building and 1903 was when the reconstruction work was done. There is a sundial on the frontage, and two heads

in profile. It is possible that one of these at least is a likeness of Charlie himself, but don't quote me on that!

On my first visit I recall entering the pub – just after it opened one week-
day morning. There were a few worthies already in place, with half-pints or
whiskies. I had an old photo of Annan, about a century old, in my hand. I
was in the process of following Charles's route for my *On the Trail of
Bonnie Prince Charlie* book. I was sure this building was the one in my old
black and white photo, and I wanted to ask to be sure. In the pub I asked if
this was the Prince's HQ? It was as if I had walked into a western saloon and
said 'Draw!' I could see the regulars were thinking of phoning Lockerbie to
see if they had one missing! As usually happens in these circumstances,
somebody eventually said they knew what I was on about, and spoke a little of the local legends about 1745. They said, among other things, that the
Highland army had camped on the north side of town.

Before we move on from Annan there is one wee thing I noticed before,
which is worth putting in print for future reference. A little further back on
the same side as the Auberge, there is a lane cutting back to some houses,
called Fairfield Place. It has a gate on it that is usually locked to retain residents' privacy, but from the gate you can just see that there is a bust on the
front of the house at the rear of the lane on the right hand side. On inspection I saw that this bust was a common likeness I have seen to represent Sir
William Wallace, helmeted, with a dragon atop his helm, and bearded. I
was just pleased to come across a wee Wallace artefact I previously did not
know existed.

As I was looking at this, a lady came by and asked what I was looking at.
'The relief of Wallace on the wall at first floor level', I replied. 'Oh', she
said, 'Is that meant to be Wallace? I always thought it was Burke and Hare',
and she walked on. For a moment my head was full of dominoes that were
all 'chapping'. As Burke and Hare were a pair of famous Edinburgh murderers during the time of the trade for bodies for medical examinations, I
couldn't understand why she thought this bust of a martial figure could
possibly represent two people. I'll never know the answer, I suppose, and
I'll have to put it down as one of life's mysteries.

We follow the B721, taking the signs for Gretna at the roundabout on the
edge of town. We are only a few miles from the English Border now, and we
continue through the villages of Dornock and Eastriggs. The landscape is
fairly uninteresting, and I hate to say it, uninspiring, and the hills of
England's Lake District to the south at least give the vista a bit of a
panoramic backdrop.

But there is a little bit more to this area than meets the eye. Every time an
English army invaded Scotland by the western route, they would actually
march to the southern shore of the Solway here, and wait for the tide to go
out and reveal the huge expanses of watery sand. They would cross and

come onto Scottish soil in this area, where they could swing a little west and march up Annandale. The area around Gretna, further east, was too boggy for heavy cavalry, and the Solway was the obvious course.

When we reach the little hamlet of Rigg we are directly opposite Burgh by Sands on the English side of the Solway, and it was there that Edward Longshanks breathed his last. He had gathered a huge army to crush Scotland once and for all, the continued successes of Robert the Bruce having stoked his temper into a white hot rage. This army marched out onto the grasslands bordering the southern edge of the Solway, preparing to cross, when Longshanks suffered his final stroke.

He was able to look at the hills of Scotland across the water and curse Scotland. It was the last thing he would see, this murderer of Wallace, before he went to hell. Legend tells how he ordered his son, the future Edward II of England, to boil his body after he had died in order to separate the flesh from the bones. The flesh could be discarded, the skeleton was to be carried before his invading army until the last Scot was crushed underfoot.

His son, homosexual and more suited to the pleasures of court in London than the battlefields of expansionism, had other ideas. Longshanks was disembowelled and had his brain removed to be buried in the abbey of Holm Cultram in Cumbria, and the rest of him was sent south to London's Westminster Abbey, where he still lies.

I go and visit him on occasion, just so I can whisper through the cold stone that we are still here. Final and total independence for Scotland would eradicate his memory for ever. I hope that day will come. And I hope he is rotting in hell. No foreigner has the right to dictate terms to my land and its people. We might make mistakes, and the odd really stupid decision. But it's our decision, and that does not give anyone else the right to sort it out for us.

We roll on into Gretna, the brick buildings giving it an almost English aspect. We come to the Crossways Roundabout, where you can turn left to visit the Gretna Green visitor centre, your last chance to buy a plastic 'kilty', or a cuddly Nessie monster. Gretna is of course famous for its runaway marriages. Scotland, happily, has retained its separate laws, and for a period during the late 1700s and early 1800s, runaway English couples would come north to get married in Scotland because the laws of matrimony were different. Gretna was brought to the forefront in this trade, simply because of its proximity to the border, but so many elopements and runaway lovers have tied the knot here, that Gretna will forever be imbedded on the psyche as a place of romance. Couples still come from all over the world to take their vows here.

If we take a right at Crossways Roundabout, we come down towards the Sark, the little stream that forms the border between the two nations. On the north bank stands the Sark Toll House, bearing on one side a sign declaring 'Last house in Scotland', and on the other 'First house in Scotland'. In one six-year period over 1,300 marriages were performed at this toll house. As we pass it and cross the little bridge we are in England. The road swings left and there is a flyover above the M74, where you can then turn right to follow this road into England's heartland

One interesting thing is the fact that there are a row of cameras slung under this bridge to monitor all the traffic coming south from Scotland – the Border is only a few yards to the north. There are 14 of these surveillance cameras. What are they looking for? Does Auld Caledonia still form a threat? Are they silent witnesses to the fact that one day the North may rise again? And down below, the signs proclaim 'Welcome to England'. Often, written in spray paint above is written 'You're'.

And it is now 1.36 am, and I've got to get up early tomorrow to travel up north to Aberdeen and Stonehaven to take part in the northeast Wallace weekend. It is 29 August, 2003, and all I have left to say is:

Caledonia. We are your sons and daughters. And we will again be free.

Some other books published by **LUATH** PRESS

On the Trail of William Wallace
David R. Ross
ISBN 0 946487 47 2 PBK £7.99

How close to reality was *Braveheart*?

Where was Wallace actually born?

What was the relationship between Wallace and Bruce?

Are there any surviving eye-witness accounts of Wallace?

How does Wallace influence the psyche of today's Scots?

On the Trail of William Wallace offers a refreshing insight into the life and heritage of the great Scots hero whose proud story is at the very heart of what it means to be Scottish. Not concentrating simply on the hard historical facts of Wallace's life, the book also takes into account the real significance of Wallace and his effect on the ordinary Scot through the ages, manifested in the many sites where his memory is marked.

On the Trail of Robert the Bruce
David R. Ross
ISBN 0 946487 52 9 PBK £7.99

On the Trail of Robert the Bruce charts the story of Scotland's hero-king from his boyhood, through his days of indecision as Scotland suffered under the English yoke, to his assumption of the crown exactly six months after the death of William Wallace. Here is the astonishing blow by blow account of how, against fearful odds, Bruce led the Scots to win their greatest ever victory. Bannockburn was not the end of the story. The war against English oppression lasted another fourteen years. Bruce lived just long enough to see his dreams of an independent Scotland come to fruition in 1328 with the signing of the Treaty of Edinburgh. The trail takes us to Bruce sites in Scotland, many of the little known and forgotten battle sites in northern England, and as far afield as the Bruce monuments in Andalusia and Jerusalem.

A Passion for Scotland
David R. Ross
ISBN 1 84282 019 2 PBK £5.99

David R. Ross is passionate about Scotland's past. And its future. In this heartfelt journey through Scotland's story, he shares his passion for what it means to be a Scot.

Eschewing xenophobia, his deep understanding of how Scotland's history touches her people shines through. All over Scotland, into England and Europe, over to Canada, Chicago and Washington – the people and the places that bring Scotland's story to life, and death.

The Early Scots
Wallace and Bruce
The Union
Montrose
The Jacobites
John MacLean
Tartan Day USA

and, revealed for the first time, the burial places of all Scotland's monarchs.

On the Trail of Bonnie Prince Charlie
David R. Ross
ISBN 0 946487 68 5 PBK £7.99

On the Trail of Bonnie Prince Charlie is the story of the Young Pretender. Born in Italy, grandson of James VII, at a time when the German house of Hanover was on the throne, his father was regarded by many as the rightful king.

Bonnie Prince Charlie's campaign to retake the throne in his father's name changed the fate of Scotland. The Jacobite movement was responsible for the '45 Uprising, one of the most decisive times in Scottish history. The suffering following the battle of Culloden in 1746 still evokes emotion. Charles' own journey immediately after Culloden is well known: hiding in the heather, escaping to Skye with Flora MacDonald. Little known of is his return to London in 1750 incognito, where he converted to Protestantism (he re-converted to Catholicism before he died and is buried in the Vatican). He was often unwelcome in Europe after the failure of the uprising and came to hate any mention of Scotland and his lost chance.

FICTION

Six Black Candles
Des Dillon
ISBN 1 84282 053 2 PB £6.99

Me and Ma Gal
Des Dillon
ISBN 1 84282 054 0 PB £5.99

Driftnet
Lin Anderson
ISBN 1 84282 034 6 PB £9.99

The Fundamentals of New Caledonia
David Nicol
ISBN 1 84282 93 6 HB £16.99

Milk Treading
Nick Smith
ISBN 1 84282 037 0 PB £6.99

The Road Dance
John MacKay
ISBN 1 84282 040 0 PB £6.99

The Strange Case of RL Stevenson
Richard Woodhead
ISBN 0 946487 86 3 HB £16.99

But n Ben A-Go-Go
Matthew Fitt
ISBN 0 946487 82 0 HB £10.99
ISBN 1 84282 014 1 PB £6.99

The Bannockburn Years
William Scott
ISBN 0 946487 34 0 PB £7.95

Outlandish Affairs: An Anthology of Amorous Encounters
Edited and introduced by Evan Rosenthal and Amanda Robinson
ISBN 1 84282 055 9 PB £9.99

The Tar Factory
Alan Kelly
ISBN 1 84282 050 8 PB £9.99

Grave Robbers
Robin Mitchell
ISBN 0 946487 72 3 PB £7.99

The Great Melnikov
Hugh MacLachlan
ISBN 0 946487 42 1 PB £7.95

POETRY

Tartan & Turban
Bashabi Fraser
ISBN 1 84282 044 3 PB £8.99

Drink the Green Fairy
Brian Whittingham
ISBN 1 84282 045 1 PB £8.99

Talking with Tongues
Brian D. Finch
ISBN 1 84282 006 0 PB £8.99

Kate o Shanter's Tale and other poems [book]
Matthew Fitt
ISBN 1 84282 028 1 PB £6.99

Kate o Shanter's Tale and other poems [audio CD]
Matthew Fitt
ISBN 1 84282 043 5 CD £9.99

Bad Ass Raindrop
Kokumo Rocks
ISBN 1 84282 018 4 PB £6.99

Madame Fifi's Farewell and other poems
Gerry Cambridge
ISBN 1 84282 005 2 PB £8.99

Poems to be Read Aloud
introduced by Tom Atkinson
ISBN 0 946487 00 6 PB £5.00

Scots Poems to be Read Aloud
introduced by Stuart McHardy
ISBN 0 946487 81 2 PB £5.00

Picking Brambles
Des Dillon
ISBN 1 84282 021 4 PB £6.99

Sex, Death & Football
Alistair Findlay
ISBN 1 84282 022 2 PB £6.99

The Luath Burns Companion
John Cairney
ISBN 1 84282 000 1 PB £10.00

Immortal Memories: A Compilation of Toasts to the Memory of Burns as delivered at Burns Suppers, 1801-2001
John Cairney
ISBN 1 84282 009 5 HB £20.00

The Whisky Muse: Scotch whisky in poem & song
Robin Laing
ISBN 1 84282 041 9 PB £7.99

The Ruba'iyat of Omar Khayyam, in Scots
Rab Wilson
ISBN 1 84282 046 X PB £8.99

Men and Beasts: Wild Men and Tame Animals
Valerie Gillies and Rebecca Marr
ISBN 0 946487 928 PB £15.00

FOLKLORE

Scotland: Myth, Legend & Folklore
Stuart McHardy
ISBN 0 946487 69 3 PB £7.99

Luath Storyteller: Highland Myths & Legends
George W Macpherson
ISBN 1 84282 003 6 PB £5.00

Tales of the North Coast
Alan Temperley
ISBN 0 946487 18 9 PB £8.99

Tall Tales from an Island
Peter Macnab
ISBN 0 946487 07 3 PB £8.99

The Supernatural Highlands
Francis Thompson
ISBN 0 946487 31 6 PB £8.99

THE QUEST FOR

The Quest for Robert Louis Stevenson
John Cairney
ISBN 0 946487 87 1 HB £16.99

The Quest for the Nine Maidens
Stuart McHardy
ISBN 0 946487 66 9 HB £16.99

The Quest for the Original Horse Whisperers
Russell Lyon
ISBN 1 842820 020 6 HB £16.99

The Quest for the Celtic Key
Karen Ralls-MacLeod and
Ian Robertson
ISBN 1 842820 031 1 PB £8.99

The Quest for Arthur
Stuart McHardy
ISBN 1 842820 12 5 HB £16.99

ON THE TRAIL OF

On the Trail of Mary Queen of Scots
J Keith Cheetham
ISBN 0 946487 50 2 PB £7.99

On the Trail of Robert Burns
John Cairney
ISBN 0 946487 51 0 PB £7.99

On the Trail of John Muir
Cherry Good
ISBN 0 946487 62 6 PB £7.99

On the Trail of Queen Victoria in the Highlands
Ian R Mitchell
ISBN 0 946487 79 0 PB £7.99

On the Trail of Robert Service
G Wallace Lockhart
ISBN 0 946487 24 3 PB £7.99

On the Trail of the Pilgrim Fathers
J Keith Cheetham
ISBN 0 946487 83 9 PB £7.99

LUATH GUIDES TO SCOTLAND

The North West Highlands: Roads to the Isles
Tom Atkinson
ISBN 0 946487 54 5 PB £4.95

Mull and Iona: Highways and Byways
Peter Macnab
ISBN 0 946487 58 8 PB £4.95

The Northern Highlands: The Empty Lands
Tom Atkinson
ISBN 0 946487 55 3 PB £4.95

The West Highlands: The Lonely Lands
Tom Atkinson
ISBN 0 946487 56 1 PB £4.95

HISTORY

Scots in Canada
Jenni Calder
ISBN 1 84282 038 9 PB £7.99

Civil Warrior
Robin Bell
ISBN 1 84282 013 3 HB £10.99

Reportage Scotland
Louise Yeoman
ISBN 0 946487 61 8 PB £9.99

Plaids & Bandanas: Highland Drover to Wild West Cowboy
Rob Gibson
ISBN 0 946487 88 X PB £7.99

POLITICS & CURRENT ISSUES

Scotlands of the Mind
Angus Calder
ISBN 1 84282 008 7 PB £9.99

Trident on Trial: the case for people's disarmament
Angie Zelter
ISBN 1 84282 004 4 PB £9.99

Uncomfortably Numb: A Prison Requiem
Maureen Maguire
ISBN 1 84282 001 X PB £8.99

Scotland: Land & Power – Agenda for Land Reform
Andy Wightman
ISBN 0 946487 70 7 PB £5.00

Old Scotland New Scotland
Jeff Fallow
ISBN 0 946487 40 5 PB £6.99

Some Assembly Required: behind the scenes at the rebirth of the Scottish Parliament
David Shepherd
ISBN 0 946487 84 7 PB £7.99

Notes from the North
Emma Wood
ISBN 0 946487 46 4 PB £8.99

NATURAL WORLD

The Hydro Boys: pioneers of renewable energy
Emma Wood
ISBN 1 84282 016 8 HB £16.99

Wild Scotland
James McCarthy
ISBN 0 946487 37 5 PB £8.99

Wild Lives: Otters – On the Swirl of the Tide
Bridget MacCaskill
ISBN 0 946487 67 7 PB £9.99

Wild Lives: Foxes – The Blood is Wild
Bridget MacCaskill
ISBN 0 946487 71 5 PB £9.99

Scotland – Land & People: An Inhabited Solitude
James McCarthy
ISBN 0 946487 57 X PB £7.99

The Highland Geology Trail
John L Roberts
ISBN 0 946487 36 7 PB £4.99

Red Sky at Night
John Barrington
ISBN 0 946487 60 X PB £8.99

Listen to the Trees
Don MacCaskill
ISBN 0 946487 65 0 PB £9.99

SOCIAL HISTORY

Pumpherston: the story of a shale oil village
Sybil Cavanagh
ISBN 1 84282 011 7 HB £17.99
ISBN 1 84282 015 X PB £10.99

Shale Voices
Alistair Findlay
ISBN 0 946487 78 2 HB £17.99
ISBN 0 946487 48 0 PB £10.99

A Word for Scotland
Jack Campbell
ISBN 0 946487 48 0 PB £12.99

BIOGRAPHY

The Last Lighthouse
Sharma Krauskopf
ISBN 0 946487 96 0 PB £7.99

Tobermory Teuchter
Peter Macnab
ISBN 0 946487 41 3 PB £7.99

Bare Feet and Tackety Boots
Archie Cameron
ISBN 0 946487 17 0 PB £7.95

Come Dungeons Dark
John Taylor Caldwell
ISBN 0 946487 19 7 PB £6.95

Luath Press Limited
committed to publishing well written books worth reading

LUATH PRESS takes its name from Robert Burns, whose little collie Luath (*Gael.*, swift or nimble) tripped up Jean Armour at a wedding and gave him the chance to speak to the woman who was to be his wife and the abiding love of his life. Burns called one of *The Twa Dogs* Luath after Cuchullin's hunting dog in *Ossian's Fingal*. Luath Press was established in 1981 in the heart of Burns country, and is now based a few steps up the road from Burns' first lodgings on Edinburgh's Royal Mile.

Luath offers you distinctive writing with a hint of unexpected pleasures.

Most bookshops in the UK, the US, Canada, Australia, New Zealand and parts of Europe either carry our books in stock or can order them for you. To order direct from us, please send a £sterling cheque, postal order, international money order or your credit card details (number, address of cardholder and expiry date) to us at the address below. Please add post and packing as follows: UK – £1.00 per delivery address; overseas surface mail – £2.50 per delivery address; overseas airmail – £3.50 for the first book to each delivery address, plus £1.00 for each additional book by airmail to the same address. If your order is a gift, we will happily enclose your card or message at no extra charge.

Luath Press Limited
543/2 Castlehill
The Royal Mile
Edinburgh EH1 2ND
Scotland
Telephone: 0131 225 4326 (24 hours)
Fax: 0131 225 4324
email: gavin.macdougall@luath.co.uk
Website: www.luath.co.uk